Righteous PROPAGATION

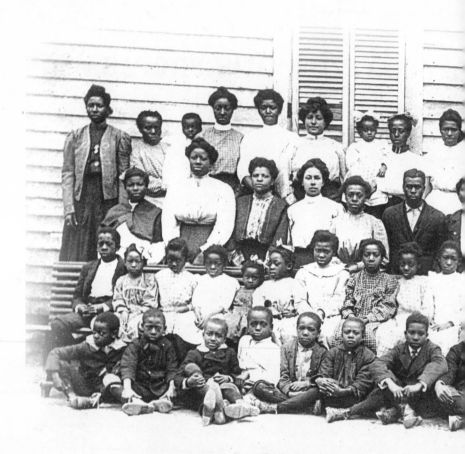

Righteous

Propagation

AFRICAN AMERICANS AND THE POLITICS OF RACIAL DESTINY AFTER RECONSTRUCTION

BY MICHELE MITCHELL

The University *of* North Carolina Press

Chapel Hill & London

© 2004 The University of North Carolina Press
All rights reserved
Set in Monotype Bulmer, Didot, and Rosewood types
by Tseng Information Systems
Manufactured in the United States of America
The paper in this book meets the guidelines for permanence
and durability of the Committee on Production Guidelines for
Book Longevity of the Council on Library Resources.

Library of Congress Cataloging-in-Publication Data
Mitchell, Michele, 1965–
Righteous propagation : African Americans and the politics of
racial destiny after Reconstruction / by Michele Mitchell.
p. cm.
Includes bibliographical references and index.
ISBN 0-8078-2902-1 (alk. paper) —
ISBN 0-8078-5567-7 (pbk. : alk. paper)
1. African Americans—History—1877–1964. 2. African
Americans—Politics and government. 3. African Americans—
Race identity. 4. African Americans—Sexual behavior. 5. Sex
role—United States—History. 6. Sex—Political aspects—United
States—History. 7. Human reproduction—Political aspects—
United States—History. 8. African American intellectuals—
History. 9. African American political activists—History.
10. United States—Race relations. I. Title.
E185.61.M674   2004
973'.0496073—dc22
2004007403

A portion of this work appeared earlier, in somewhat different form,
as "'The Black Man's Burden': African Americans, Imperialism,
and Notions of Racial Manhood, 1890–1910," *International Review
of Social History* 44, no. 4 (1999; supplement 7): 77–99, published
simultaneously in *Complicating Categories: Gender, Class, Race and
Ethnicity*, ed. Eileen Boris and Angelique Janssens (Cambridge:
Cambridge University Press, 1999), 77–99, both © Cambridge
University Press, and is reproduced here with permission.

cloth   08 07 06 05 04   5 4 3 2 1
paper   08 07 06 05 04   5 4 3 2 1

For my
grandparents,
Wilma Wilson Jones,
John Wesley Jones Sr.,
Annie Lee Daniels Mitchell,
and
C. J. Mitchell Sr.,
a man I only wish I could
have known, and for my
entire family, blood kin
and beyond

CONTENTS

ILLUSTRATIONS

ACKNOWLEDGMENTS

Completing this book has been one long, arduous haul. There have been more moments than I can now remember when I have been tyrannized by a blank screen, when I have doubted my own ability to bring the project to fruition, when I wanted to consign my drafts to the rubbish bin, when I could not stand to revise a sentence for the umpteenth time, when chapters morphed into unrecognizable entities. But for every discouraging moment that I weathered, there was a rejuvenating epiphany, an unexpected discovery, an encouraging word, or an edifying recognition. Indeed, I have enjoyed an unusual level of support from numerous individuals and institutions. If the act of writing itself is a solitary and often lonely endeavor, producing a book is a unique collective process, at once indirect and direct, in which relationships are forged and debts incurred.

For me, some of these debts and relationships extend back almost twenty years ago when I was an undergraduate at Mount Holyoke College. Daniel Czitrom, Jonathan Lipman, Eugenia Herbert, William McFeely, John Faragher, Dolores Janiewski, George Lipsitz, Bruce Laurie, and Peter Viereck helped me realize that history was a viable, exciting field of inquiry that I could pursue on a formal and sustained basis; Joan Cocks, Douglas Amy, and Vincent Ferraro opened my eyes to the myriad ways in which scholarship is political. Before I left Albuquerque for South Hadley, it had never occurred to me that I could attend graduate school or become a working intellectual, thus it is hardly an overstatement to say that these scholars changed the trajectory of my life.

At Northwestern University, I was both inspired and challenged by a range of scholars: Jonathon Glassman, John Hunwick, Ivor Wilks, David W. Cohen, Henry Binford, Tessie Liu, and the late Leon Forrest. Harold Perkin's faith in me still brings tears to my eyes. James T. Campbell's willingness to engage in lengthy, energetic conversations about late-nineteenth-century African American history introduced me to many of the themes that have engaged me over the past thirteen years. In critical regards, this project originated in an independent reading that I did with James Oakes. Not only did he provide me with the intellectual tools to understand dynamics that fascinated me, Jim also gave me some of the best advice that I ever received in graduate school: "no chips, no game." Micaela di Leonardo and Nancy Fraser were both instrumental in my development as a feminist scholar, while Charles Payne was an indispensable mentor who knew when to listen and when to guide. Adolph L. Reed Jr.'s generosity and profound knowledge of Afro-American intellectual history pushed me in directions that ultimately enabled me to formulate this project; his wit made the process immensely enjoyable. Nancy K. MacLean was an exacting advisor whose high standards made me a far better historian than I would have been had I not worked with her. She told me when my writing was far too vague and urged me to get inside my sources as opposed to relying upon jargon. To this day, I remain grateful that she tolerated the somewhat haphazard way in which I went about conceptualizing and writing the dissertation that provided the foundation for this book. I also benefited greatly from knowing Africana studies librarian Kathleen Bethel. Her mastery of Africana studies was nothing less than indispensable as I began working on this project; her counsel and friendship kept me going.

I am also grateful for support that I received from my peers in graduate school. From Nancy MacLean's dissertator's group, I received invaluable feedback—not to mention primary source material—from Steven Reich, Leslie Dunlap, Wallace Best, and Marissa Chappell. Naoko Shibusawa not only read chapter drafts, but her insights on gender, race, and historical analysis enabled me to produce far more nuanced work. Michelle Marresse, Lane Fenrich, David Johnson, Brad Schrager, David Gellman, and Michelle Boyd were all supportive friends. Micaela di Leonardo's interdisciplinary feminist reading group, with Cathy Flynn, Jacalyn Harden, Leslie Dunlap, Gina Perez, Diane Gross, and Shannon Jackson, helped me reconceptualize how I think about the production of history. So did interaction with a vibrant Africanist community of graduate students, including Catherine Burns, Keith Breckinridge, Keith Shear, Lynn Thomas, Doug Anthony, and Catherine Cole. I felt an instant kinship with Stephan Miescher the first day that I met him; he is, in several regards, responsible for my decision to engage both masculinity and sexuality in my work. I cherish Lane Clark's friendship and humor. Eric Silla did far more than house me during my several research trips to Washington, D.C.—he and Stacey Suyat enabled me to arrive at the archives refreshed and relaxed.

I received critical support from beyond the confines of Northwestern as well. At Stanford University's Martin Luther King, Jr., Papers Project, Clayborne Carson provided vital encouragement and mentoring. At Duke University's Center for Documentary Studies, Raymond Gavins, Robert Korstad, and William Chafe gave me the opportunity of a lifetime. By selecting me as a field researcher for the Behind the Veil Project, they introduced me to wonderful colleagues—Anne Valk, Leslie Brown, Paul Ortiz, Tywanna Whorley, Tunga White, Sally Graham, Charles Houston, Mausiki Matsimela, Greg Hunter, Kate Ellis, and Felix Armfield—and vivified the production of history for me in ways that deeply informed the way in which I went about writing this book.

The Carter G. Woodson Institute at the University of Virginia provided critical financial and temporal support as it created a community of scholars engaged in pathbreaking work on African American, United States, Latin American, and African Diaspora history. Emilye Crosby, Jenny Walker Ward, Brian Ward, Cornelia Sears, Mieko Nishida, Scot French, Rebecca Popenoe, and Harry West were all wonderful colleagues from whom I learned much. Indeed, one of the best things about being in Charlottesville was meeting Emilye Crosby; she and Kathy Connelly have my undying gratitude. I also had the good fortune of exchanging ideas with Cynthia Blair, Kenda Mutongi, Lisa Lindquist Dorr, and Gregory Michael Dorr. Others made my time in Charlottesville immensely rewarding, especially Edward Ayers, Eileen Boris, Reginald Butler, Deborah McDowell, Tejumola Olaniyan, Eric Lott, Elizabeth Thompson, Ann Lane, Cindy Aron, Nelson Lichtenstein, Peter Onuf, and Julian Bond. Mary Rose and Gail Shirley Warren provided invaluable assistance and support, while William Jackson's compassionate leadership was a beacon of light on a regular basis and in times of crisis. I shall always be grateful to the late Armstead Robinson for his instrumental role in bringing me to the Woodson.

As a fellow at the Rutgers Center for Historical Analysis during the first year of its Black Atlantic project in 1997–98, I was privileged beyond belief to engage in intellectual exchange with Anne Bailey, Rudy Bell, Jennifer Morgan, Herman Bennett, Carolyn Brown, David Brown, Tolonda Tolbert di Franco, Matthew Guterl, Belinda Emondson, Faith Lois Smith, Christopher Vaughan, Amrita Myers, Gregory Mixon, Al Howard, Renee Larrier,

Peter Levine, Christopher Brown, Brent Edwards, and Wanda Mills. Extra special thanks are indeed due to Deborah Gray White, Mia Elisabeth Bay, John W. Chambers, and Lynn Shanko Strawbridge for giving me the intellectual space to begin conceptualizing what are now Chapters 4, 6, and 7.

If being at the RCHA helped transform this project, the University of Michigan's willingness to give me a year off up front enabled me to go the RCHA in the first place. Moreover, the University of Michigan has been an incredibly active, stimulating, and rigorous intellectual environment. Indeed, over the past five and a half years, both the Department of History and the Center for Afroamerican and African Studies—not to mention the Program in American Culture, the Program in the Comparative Study of Social Transformations, and the Rackham Summer Interdisciplinary Institute—have hosted more talks, panels, brown bags, and conferences than I could possibly attend. Such activity has enriched me immeasurably.

I am, moreover, grateful for my colleagues—present and former—in both the Department of History and the Center for Afroamerican and African Studies. Sandra Gunning, Frieda Ekotto, Maria Montoya, Julius Scott, Elisha Renne, and Susan Juster were supportive, reliable mentors and friends. A number of colleagues either read or commented upon portions of the manuscript: Martin Pernick, Gina Morantz-Sanchez, Sandra Gunning, Maria Montoya, Sue Juster, Mamadou Diouf, Augustin Holl, Sueann Caulfield, Kali Israel, Nancy Rose Hunt, Kevin Gaines, Dena Goodman, Geoff Eley, Frederick Cooper, Jane Burbank, Earl Lewis, Rebecca Scott, and the Executive Committees in both History and the Center for Afroamerican and African Studies. As I worked my way through the publication process, Kali Israel, Scott Spector, Sue Juster, Leslie Pincus, Helmut Puff, Valerie Kivelson, Gabrielle Hecht, Laura Lee Downs, Richard Turits, and Hannah Rosen lent supportive ears, provided advice, and shared their own experiences with their first books; by doing so, they buoyed my confidence and thus enabled me to persevere. Mary Kelley, Martin Pernick, Rebecca Scott, Richard Cándida Smith, and Earl Lewis were amazingly generous and encouraging at times when I was beyond discouraged. Kathleen Canning took me seriously as a historian of gender and sexuality, had faith in my abilities, and stood behind me when things looked bleak. In similar yet distinct ways, Sonya Rose, Carroll Smith-Rosenberg, and James Jackson played decisive roles in enabling me to finish the manuscript during the summer of 2003. I can not begin to list all of the amazing graduate and undergraduate students whose insights have helped me clarify my thinking about the writing and analysis of history as I completed this book—please know that I am indebted to you all. Furthermore, I could not have completed this book without help from the staffs of the Department of History and Center for Afroamerican and African Studies; I also thank Kidada Williams for alerting me to an advertisement for *Floyd's Flowers*, which appears herein, and Nicole Stanton for transcribing ACS letters.

A number of people outside of Michigan have read or commented upon portions of the manuscript, including Elsa Barkley Brown, Robin D. G. Kelley, Steven Hahn, Ellen Carol Du Bois, Judith Stein, Louise Newman, Ada Ferrer, Laura Edwards, and Gail Bederman. I am particularly grateful to Elsa, who has been an amazingly incisive critic and unfailing champion. I am also indebted to Tera W. Hunter. Whereas Tera did not read drafts or provide specific suggestions, her willingness to coedit a special issue of *Gender & History* with Sandra Gunning and me quite literally enabled me to finish this book. Tera and Sandra may not know it, but working with them made me a better writer. The encouragement—not to mention occasional questions about when I would finish the book—that I received over the years from both Nancy Hewitt and Darlene Clark Hine helped me to realize that this project was worth completing. Members of the Berkshire Conference of Women Historians—especially Annelise Orleck, Mary Beth Norton, Claire Potter, Kathi Kern, Barbara Baillet, Susan Yohn, Isabel Hull, Vicki L. Ruiz, and Margaret Hunt—provided words of wisdom and comfort when I doubted that this book would ever see the light of day.

Being a scholar-in-residence at the Schomburg Center for Research on Black Culture during my fourth year at Michigan was simply a phenomenal experience. Scholars' seminars gave me access to the fascinating work and minds of all of my colleagues. It was during such a seminar that I received timely, critical feedback on what is now Chapter 7 of this book from Rhonda Frederick, Jeffrey Sammons, Lisa Gail Collins, Miriam Jiménez-Roman, Colin Palmer, and Barbara Katz-Rothman. I benefited greatly from informal interaction as well: Samuel Roberts generously shared a number of important citations with me; Barbara Savage's insight, encouragement, and friendship kept me going; Rhonda Frederick unfailingly offered vital feedback during the many hours that we both labored in the scholars' office; Miriam Jiménez-Roman's engaged interest in my work and her many suggestions helped me clear several conceptual and evidentiary obstacles.

I would be truly remiss if I failed to acknowledge assistance that I received from Schomburg Center staff. Not only did Diana Lachatenere find me a place to live, the time that she took to orient me to the Schomburg was integral to my ability to begin significant work so soon after my arrival. I extensively used books from General Research and Reference and found that division's staff incredibly helpful. Sharon Howard, Betty Odabashian, and Michael Roudette patiently fielded questions about books and periodicals; furthermore, Betty Odabashian promptly secured items through interlibrary loan. Genette McLaurin, Cynthia Rollins, Troy Belle, and Ernest Blackwell assisted me at many junctures; the pages endured my frequent requests with good humor. The entire staff of Photographs and Prints provided critical assistance as I chose illustrations for my book, and curator Mary Yearwood's amazing knowledge about the Schomburg's holdings greatly facilitated my search through cartes-de-visite, cabinet card, daguerreotype, and stereograph collections. Linden Anderson, Jim Huffman, Andrea Jones, Michael Mery, and Antony Toussaint made the hours that I spent in Photographs and Prints thoroughly enjoyable; I sincerely thank Thomas Lisanti of the New York Public Library's Photographic Services and Permissions department as well. In Manuscripts, Archives, and Rare Books, Aisha Al-Adawiya and Steven Fullwood enabled me to make efficient use of their division; Nurah-Rosalie Jeter thoughtfully brought in a doll that was sold to Garveyite children during the 1920s. Last—but hardly least—Peter Hobbs tirelessly and carefully combed through numerous Afro-American periodicals and the Schomburg clipping file for discourse about miscegenation and information regarding legislation against interracial sex. His labors undoubtedly made this book a far richer piece of scholarship.

In terms of additional research support, the interlibrary loan staff at the University of Virginia's Alderman Library was truly amazing. I also wish to express my gratitude to the staffs at the Library of Congress, Howard University's Moorland-Spingarn Collection, and Special Collections at Northwestern University, the University of Virginia, the University of Chicago, Duke University, and the University of Michigan. Completion of this project would have been impossible without financial support from the Committee on Institutional Cooperation, Northwestern University, the Carter G. Woodson Institute, the Organization of American Historians, the Ford Foundation, the Rutgers Center for Historical Analysis, the University of Michigan, the Schomburg Center for Research in Black Culture, and the National Endowment for the Humanities.

I am quite fortunate to be publishing this book with the University of North Carolina Press. Kate Douglass Torrey expressed interest in this project before it was a completed dissertation, and she provided incredibly insightful readings of several chapters. Sian Hunter is a phenomenal editor:

she knows when to encourage, when to listen, when to push, how to enable an author to let go of clunky passages that resist every attempt at revision. I also thank David Hines, Ron Maner, Liz Gray, Stephanie Wenzel, and other members of the UNC Press Staff for putting up with me as I made my way through the final stages of preparing the manuscript. This book is all the stronger for having undergone the scrutiny of two exacting readers. Keith Wailoo's meticulously rendered critiques forced me to refine my overall argument as well as clarify specific points within each chapter. Deborah Gray White not only understood the more subtle interventions that I am trying to make herein, her exceptional skills as a historian showed me ways to make my overarching argument considerably sharper and more textured. No words can truly express what her support has meant to me—I can only hope that she is pleased by the final product.

Whereas all of the aforementioned people and institutions have helped bring this project to fruition, I am a historian because of my family: my aunts, uncles, cousins, and distant relatives. My mother, Barbara, gave me a most precious gift when she taught me that the written word was a passage to worlds unknown; my father, Richard, impressed upon me that learning was a privilege that was never to be taken for granted and that I could, with hard work, realize my dreams. Furthermore, my parents constantly told us—me, my sister, Lynette, my brother, Richard, and eventually my niece, Chandi— stories about our ancestors and about segregation that fueled my desire to "do" history. My stepmother, Ruth Randall, has been an inspiration and blessing as well. Her passion for history made her a fast comrade; her generous heart and willing ear kept me going when my energy flagged. My stepsisters, Celia Benitez and Makea McDonald, have enriched my life. I shall always be grateful to Makea, Cathy Lange, and the late Marion Lange for opening their home to me as I finished this book during the summer of 2002. My grandparents—Wilma Wilson Jones, Annie Lee Daniels Mitchell, John Wesley Jones Sr., and C. J. Mitchell—shall always inspire me. As African Americans born during the opening years of the twentieth century, they experienced hardships that I can not fathom. These women and men sweated through the type of hard labor that I, by the accident of birth, was spared. Whereas they would not know quite what to make of a granddaughter who reads, talks, and writes for a living, they are present in every single line that I produce.

NOTE ON USAGE & TERMINOLOGY

Herein I use several different terms to refer to people of African descent in the United States. This shifting on my part is not for the sake of variety nor is it entirely random: quite appropriately, historical context has influenced my decision to use one term as opposed to another in any given circumstance. In several cases I have opted to follow the lead of my sources. "Negro," "Afro-American," "mulatto," and "colored" appear in primary documents from the late nineteenth and early twentieth centuries as do a host of other terms less familiar to contemporary readers; these terms appear throughout this work as well. I make no pretensions of replicating language from a bygone era. Still, I think it fitting to recall words people used when referring to themselves—both in terms of understanding the past and providing a textured account of that past.

One particular phrasing that appears within these pages deserves special comment. "Race woman" and "race man" could, at times, be generic euphemisms that some people found dismissive, reductive, or offensive. More often than not, however (and especially prior to the 1920s), Afro-American publications, reformers, activists, and public speakers invoked "race" as a means of connoting status and aspiration. For example, a "race woman" or "race man" was usually a self-made or high-achieving person who contributed to a local community and labored on behalf of the larger collective; a "race paper," "race organization," or "race worker" typically displayed marked commitment to the advancement of African American people.

My usage of "race" as an adjective, then, is meant to invoke a certain sensibility and pride that existed among postemancipation women, children, and men. Over the last fifteen years "race"—and, of course, "gender"—has been amply theorized as a social construct, and my thinking has been profoundly influenced by a number of scholars across disciplines. All the same, as a historian, I have endeavored to write about race in ways that take into account the viewpoints of people who experienced the aftermath of Reconstruction.

I use "aspiring class" throughout this book for at least two reasons. For one, applying standard class labels—"working class," "middle class," "owning class"—to African Americans who lived during the late nineteenth and early twentieth centuries obscures the specific circumstances of a people that were, for the most part, barely liberated from chattel slavery. The post-Reconstruction years were indeed an industrial era. Yet, over 70 percent of African Americans still resided in the rural South by 1900, and approximately 90 percent were workers. I therefore believe that slightly different terminology enables us to better understand class dynamics among people of African descent during the late nineteenth and early twentieth centuries. Herein, "working poor" refers to people who struggled to survive—sharecroppers, domestics, underemployed seasonal workers. "Elite" indicates the relatively wealthy descendants of free people of color as well as college-educated professionals, many of whom were prominent in national organizations, owned well-appointed homes, or had successful businesses. Since "elite" connotes community standing as well as access to the burgeoning postemancipation world of African American letters, most reformers and activists defy easy categorization. I use "aspiring class," then, as a means of differentiating African American strivers from contemporaneous middle-class white Americans and to acknowledge the quickening of class stratification within African American communities.

"African American" and "black" appear throughout this work, too. The choices made here regarding the written representation of each have been partially informed by discourses on the social construction of race and partially by ongoing conversations regarding African diasporas. As much as I find the political impetus behind capitalizing "black" compelling, it is rarely capitalized in these pages. There is also the matter of whether "African American" should always be hyphenated. Many forms of popular writing hyphenate it as standard procedure to underscore both the literal and symbolic connection of black people in the United States to Africa. Herein, I have decided against hyphenation.

Of course, the very use of "African American"—or "black American," for that matter—is complicated by the fact that the United States is only part of the Americas. For immigrants to the United States from the Caribbean and for people from regions of the Black Atlantic, I attempt to identify people by referring to land of origin. I also invoke the terms that people used when speaking about themselves. In the final chapter's discussion of the Universal Negro Improvement Association I try to reserve "African American" for those women, men, and children who were born in the United States or claimed U.S. citizenship.

Finally, the word "miscegenation" appears throughout this work—an entire chapter is even devoted to the subject—despite the fact that I find it highly problematic. When one considers the word's Latin components and etymology it quickly becomes apparent that "miscegenation" is freighted with mid-nineteenth century notions about breeding and "race," purity and pollution. Whereas "misc" means "mixed" as opposed to "wrong," "miscegenation" nonetheless implies that people from different "racial" backgrounds should not engage in heterosexual intercourse—let alone cohabit or marry—since any potential offspring would be products of *misbreeding*. Given that it was coined during the Civil War, "miscegenation" specifically suggests that sexual contact between blacks and whites is an abomination that sullies ostensibly pure gene pools and endangers the body politic.

Although my feelings about using, analyzing, and perpetuating this word are quite strong indeed, I resort to discussing "miscegenation" for two reasons. For one, the history of "miscegenation" as a concept—not to mention as a word—is germane to the subject of this work. And, sadly, for all of the scholarly engagement with discourse and social construction, frightfully resilient notions about so-called race mixing persist to such a degree that U.S. English currently contains no real alternative.

Righteous PROPAGATION

We thought that with the abolishment of slavery the black man's destiny would be accomplished. . . . [Yet today] a condition of affairs confronts us that [abolitionists] never foresaw: the systematic destruction of the Negro by every device which the fury of enlightened malevolence can invent. . . . This new birth of the black race is a mighty agony. God help us in our struggle for liberty and manhood!
—Pauline Hopkins,
  Contending Forces

Most of the writers and public speakers of the day talk of the destiny of the Negro as though the getting of money, a smattering of education, and houses and lands were the principal thing in . . . national or racial development. These are, all of them, necessary and important, but what are they worth to a race that accepts a state of servility as its fixed destiny? . . . What are houses, land and money to men who are *women*?
—John Wesley Grant,
  Out of the Darkness

Is this a race doomed to destruction? or is it one possessed of those qualities, and so morally disciplined by trial, as to augur a vital destiny, and high moral uses, in the future?
—Alexander Crummell,
  "The Destined Superiority of
  the Negro"

Would it not be well for us women to introduce into all our literary circles . . . topics on th[e] subject of heredity and the influence of good and bad conditions upon the home life of the race, and study this subject in the light of science for our own and the benefit of others?
—Frances Ellen Watkins Harper,
  "Enlightened Motherhood"

Self-respect, self-reliance, and the ambition to be and to do. . . . the Negro is realizing the importance of self-help. Good books, among other agencies, will deepen this impression. . . . "Destiny is not about thee, but within; Thyself must make thyself."
—Daniel Culp,
  *Twentieth Century Negro
  Literature*

We too have come to learn that the purity of the woman means the purity of the family and the purity of the family the purity of race and nation, and whosoever insults that purity is an enemy to society, and in league with hell. . . . We are struggling to make our race a race of purity, sobriety, and christian power.

—John Wesley Bowen,
An Appeal to the King

What a privilege to carve the destiny of a race! . . . A colored mother lives not only for herself and for her own children, but she must live for the race. . . . The colored mother beautiful must . . . study more about the laws of heredity and child culture to prepare the child for its race battle, unhampered by inherited mental or physical tendencies.

—Emma Azalia Hackley,
The Colored Girl Beautiful

This race has increased . . . and is still on the increase. . . . Kindness, sobriety, manfulness, courage, morality, intelligence, religion, and duty marks her destiny.
—George H. Burks, *Future* (1890)

The Negro race . . . has survived all the punishment and unjustness to which a race could be subjected, and in its short birth of freedom points . . . to a record unequalled by any other race . . . under like conditions. Our destiny is now in our own hands.
—Arthur G. Shaw, *Age* (1915)

PROLOGUE: TO BETTER OUR CONDITION ONE WAY OR ANOTHER
AFRICAN AMERICANS AND THE CONCEPT OF RACIAL DESTINY

An epidemic hit Afro-American communities during the twilight of Reconstruction. It was an affliction with peculiar, distinctive symptoms: those affected generally reported feeling agitated, and a few began acting in a single-minded or even furtive manner. Some women and men started speaking about leaving their spouses; others became determined to part with earthly belongings; still others began to embrace risky behavior. Desperation was often a palpable manifestation among the infected, especially if they were poor. In time, race leaders feared that the phenomenon was symptomatic of a creeping insanity that led individuals and families to sell the very implements with which they eked out their livings. "Liberia fever" did cause people to act in seemingly rash or bizarre ways—but not because the "fever" was a literal disease. Rather, the term was a colloquial reference to an emigration craze pervading the Deep South, Arkansas, and Oklahoma Territory during the late nineteenth century. A phenomenon similar to the "Kansas fever" that resulted in waves of southern Exodusters headed for a midwestern promised land, "Liberia fever" spread as far north as Massachusetts and as far west as Colorado, producing women and men convinced that they could best work out their destinies by returning to Africa's west coast.

Nineteen-year-old Annie Williams was among the afflicted living above the Mason-Dixon line. In March 1878, the young cook from Baltimore, Maryland, sent a letter to American Colonization Society (ACS) secretary William Coppinger indicating that she was rather "[a]nxious" to become "one In the Number that you Will Select To go to affrica." Whether by word of mouth or from reading broadsides, Williams discovered that the American Colonization Society sent only those prospective emigrants to Liberia that it deemed worthy. Williams quickly composed another missive in which she took pains to convey that she was a hardworking, upright, churchgoing Methodist who could help teach school once in Liberia. Still, securing a place on an ACS ship required more than intense desire, moral rectitude, and an admirable work ethic. Annie Williams also needed money.[1]

Whereas she could manage to pay her own way to the docks of New York City in order to meet the society's ship, Williams's paltry wages prevented her from contributing toward passage or provisions. The fact that Williams was paid less than five dollars a month contributed to her desire to emigrate, as did other personal realities that were subtly, though urgently, articulated: "I . . . have no one to look to for Anny help as I am alone with the exception of my father and he drinks. . . . If you can please sir let me go. . . . I have benn supporting my self entirely ever since I was 15 years of age and kept my self decent and respectable Which you as a gentleman no doubt having Had experience In the World know that it is No eassy thing to do having . . . no one really interested in my Well faire dont you think I am cappable . . . that I can get Along[?]" Williams presented her intemperate father and sexual vulnerability as compelling reasons for the society to deliver a friendless, industrious young woman from a living purgatory. Moreover, the plaintive tone of Williams's entreaty for Coppinger to "please please please . . . annser" her letters underscored that she "want[ed] to go so bad" despite "know[ing] Nothing of the country."[2] Somehow, Annie Williams had heard that scores of other African Americans were trying to get to Liberia in order to improve their lot, feel secure, and find freedom—all that she desperately wanted for herself.

Approximately 1,500 miles away in Louisiana, Henry Adams also believed that Liberia provided a better life for African Americans. The former slave and ex-Union soldier was sufficiently vocal about black civil rights as to become a moving target for local whites who resented his ideas that "'spoil[ed] the other negroes.'"[3] Knowing that white men wanted to take his life hardly quelled Henry Adams's activism. Adams headed a "National Colored Colonization Council" and, in the midst of "mania for Kansas," his grassroots networking made him a leading advocate of Liberian emigration throughout Louisiana and parts of Texas.[4]

During the late 1870s, Adams sent President Rutherford Hayes and Congress at least two petitions enumerating why removal to Liberia was necessary for the race's political and physical well-being. The January 5, 1878, draft of Adams's petition was as much jeremiad as it was supplication: "We find our race in a worse State of *Slavery* than *before*. Being denied those rights that Belong to us . . . we Cry out with a *full heart* that . . . unless some protection is guaranteed to our race that we will cease to be a race. . . . We feel that our only hope and preservation of our race is the Exodus of Our People to Some Country where they can make themsselves a name and nation." Peaceful coexistence in the U.S. South between blacks and whites seemed increasingly impossible to Adams, a man who maintained that disfranchisement, "buldozing," and "murderous . . . whites" generated "thousands and thousands" of prospective emigrants with each mounting act of discrimination and terrorism. Adams further contended that if black southerners' civil rights could not be protected, African Americans deserved either a territory of their own within U.S. borders or federal assistance to emigrate. Adams might have had little luck in getting a response from Washington, let alone securing a land grant or federal aid, but he refused to be deterred. When he wrote ACS secretary William Coppinger in November 1878, the tireless organizer declared that he was "more determined for Liberia than ever."[5]

Whereas neither Annie Williams nor Henry Adams appears to have ever sailed for Liberia,[6] Amanda Berry Devine Smith made it to Africa and eventually published her views on emigration. Smith was a twice-widowed, clearheaded laundress possessed of a "mighty faith" who became a missionary in 1878, twenty-two years after an initial conversion experience marked by vivid premonitions and nagging periods of doubt.[7] In 1882, Smith began proselytizing in Liberia, where she attempted to convert indigenous Africans to Christianity and temperance. Smith poured her energy into "our country" until 1890 when the itinerant evangelist returned to the United States.[8]

If Williams's and Adams's words dramatically indicate the desires of African Americans to make a better way for themselves after Reconstruction, Smith's observations powerfully underscore just how elusive African Americans' attempts to secure a promising future in Liberia could be. Part travelogue, part sociopolitical analysis, *An Autobiography: The Story of the Lord's Dealings with Mrs. Amanda Smith* bristled with opinionated commentary. Smith assessed the strengths and weaknesses of Liberia as a colonial enterprise and remarked upon emigration to the coastal republic. Much of what she wrote was less than flattering.[9]

One episode involving freshly arrived emigrants to Maryland County, Liberia, particularly irked Smith. Sometime during late 1886 or early 1887, a group of Americo-Liberians held a mass meeting to welcome approximately one hundred women, men, and children from South Carolina to their settlement, Cape Palmas. Sister Smith took considerable umbrage that women were barred from attending: she literally carried her own chair into the proceedings, ignored reproachful glances, and seated herself in a conspicuous spot.[10] The interloper and self-described "privileged character" then witnessed a parade of men spouting lofty, charged rhetoric:

> Mr. Jacob Tuning was the speaker of the evening. He had a very lengthy paper about Jacob receiving his brethren. . . . I knew that more than half . . . [of it] was only worth the paper it was on. . . . All the prominent men of the place were present. . . . When they were all through expressing themselves, [they] heartily welcom[ed] the emigrants to their country, this free country where they were not oppressed by white men; the country where they could be *men*; where they had the rights of law and were independent, and all the other big things we can say.

If Smith chose not to analyze women's absence from the meeting in terms of its larger implications for African Americans, Americo-Liberians, or Liberia itself, she did not hesitate to critique the manly hubris that suffused the Cape Palmas meeting.[11] Indeed, as far as Smith was concerned, men prone to "big talk" did not necessarily have the wherewithal to succeed in the frontier republic, let alone lead the race.[12]

Although Smith bridled at particular assertions of manhood, the preaching woman nonetheless understood why black men who "fought and bled, and died" for the United States craved a space where they, too, would finally be considered full-fledged men.[13] Smith additionally appreciated why a fledgling, all-black nation in Africa offered appealing prospects for African Americans wanting land to sustain their spirits and bodies. Smith thus supported emigration—as long as it was carried out by the "right kind of emigrants." From her vantage point, however, only the poorest of the southern poor crossed the ocean, and she despaired that too many of these hardscrabble "greenhorns" were illiterate, ill prepared, and ignorant of what it meant to start anew in a "strange country among strangers."[14]

Whether readers found her characterizations empathetic and moving or harsh and condescending, Amanda Smith's expositions on Liberia were certainly timely. The 1893 publication of *An Autobiography: The Story of the Lord's Dealings with Mrs. Amanda Smith* occurred when emigrationist movements were controversial, widely discussed, and, for working-poor black Americans, compelling.[15] Smith's memoirs were released following a groundswell in emigrationist sentiment, but what does that rush of sentiment among black Americans such as Annie Williams reveal about a particular moment in African American history, in U.S. history? How was that rush of sentiment connected to a sense that African Americans formed a collective whose destiny would be either exalted or debased, depending on the actions of its members? If activists such as Henry Adams were bound and determined to "better [their] condition one way or another," what issues other than emigration grabbed African Americans' hearts and minds?[16] Did other attempts by African Americans to improve the race's lot after Reconstruction have gendered dynamics similar to — or different from — those described by Amanda Smith?

The era following emancipation was an era of cautious optimism for most African American women, children, and men. No longer divided into categories of "free" or "slave," people of African descent acted upon assumptions that the race was unified, that institution building was possible, that progress was imminent. Organizing freedom was arduous work that entailed individual initiative as well as collective endeavor, but for all of its challenges Reconstruction presented novel opportunities for black mobilization. With the Compromise of 1877 and the subsequent, steady erosion of civil rights, however, the fortunes of black women, children, and men became decidedly less certain. Between 1877 and 1930 — an era of heated debates about immigration, class struggle, industrial capitalism, women's suffrage, imperial activity, and "the Negro Problem" — the status of African Americans was in constant flux, and black Americans did not always agree upon how to bolster their collective prospects. Yet, as the United States emerged as a world power and national destiny became a signal topic, Afro-American thought was dominated by debates about racial destiny.[17]

Notions of "racial destiny" in the United States dated back to the expansionist years between 1830 and 1850 when the American school of ethnology classified racial types and "the concept of a distinct, superior Anglo-Saxon race with innate endowments" began to "permeat[e] discussions of American progress."[18] "Racial destiny" thus connoted a hierarchical scale of humanity typically crested by "Saxons"—as opposed to "Teutonics," "Celts," "Gauls," or "Aryans"—before the Civil War.[19] Prior to 1865, African American intellectuals countered racialist hierarchies that invariably placed people of African descent at the bottom rungs of humanity by producing vindicationist ethnologies, including Frederick Douglass's *The Claims of the Negro, Ethnologically Considered* (1854) and William Wells Brown's *The Black Man: His Antecedents, His Genius, and His Achievements* (1863). Black activists, many of whom debated the controversial issues of colonization and emigration—among them Henry Highland Garnet, Mary Ann Shadd, Martin Delany, and James Holly—also deployed ideas about race and collective fate throughout the antebellum period.[20] Abolitionists such as Maria Stewart did so as well.[21] Still, it was after the Civil War that African Americans began applying "racial destiny" to an even broader range of issues.

It was with emancipation that freed people faced formidable pressures to make a way for themselves, and it was with emancipation that race activists devised an array of strategies built around and upon notions of collective destiny. "Racial destiny" therefore became a notably more inclusive and flexible concept during the late nineteenth century as African Americans increasingly invoked the concept when speaking of themselves. For post-emancipation women and men, the wide-ranging yet singular notion that black people shared a common fate enabled activists to propose a number of strategies—political, social, cultural, moral, physical, religious—to ensure the collective's basic human rights, progress, prosperity, health, and reproduction. Messianic visions of the race's fate inspired emigration to Liberia; ecclesiastic visions of destiny suffused "civilizing missions" undertaken by Afro-American missionaries. Other African American concepts of collective destiny promoted full inclusion in the American body politic or situated the weal of black people within the United States by stressing the need for separate race culture, institutions, and even territories. The desire to secure a productive, progressive future for the race further motivated reformers bent on improving habits and habitats as it enabled activists to connect material culture to collective weal. Individuals who embraced nationalist ideologies also tended to believe that people of African descent would recapture past greatness once the race was truly unified.[22]

8

In these pages "racial destiny" is not limited to the ecclesiastic or the nationalistic. Rather, the crusading idealism of activists drives the narrative. Herein I use the concept of racial destiny to explore how African Americans, like sundry other collectivities—racial, social, political, imagined, and otherwise—"construct[ed] themselves as members of . . . [a] collectivity not just because they, and their forebears shared a past, but also because they believe[d] their futures to be interdependent."[23] This book therefore examines critical moments when African Americans contended that the race shared particular interests as a sociopolitical body and that the collective's future depended upon concerted efforts to police intraracial activity.[24] Since concepts of racial destiny helped create collective consciousness among African Americans, this book is a story of identity formation as much as it is an exploration of key issues around which black activists mobilized during the late nineteenth and twentieth centuries.

As utterly disparate as ideas about racial destiny could be throughout the post-Reconstruction era, those ideas increasingly focused on intraracial reform by the early twentieth century. Between 1890 and 1900 when Progressivism generated a widespread reform ethic throughout the United States, African American ideas about racial destiny turned inward as black activists focused upon changing individual and collective habits. The motivations of people who decided to engage in various forms of reform work were varied and complex. Black reformers lived in a postemancipation society where many ex-slaves and their descendants still lived in conditions that were little better than they had been during slavery. Available housing stock was often derelict and living spaces overburdened. Nutritious foodstuffs were frequently scarce, and disease an ever-present reality. As a result, reformers took it upon themselves to attack what they believed to be the root problems plaguing black households.

Reform activists certainly came from the ranks of the Afro-American elite—Mary Church Terrell, Margaret Murray Washington, and W. E. B. Du Bois among them—yet a number of black reformers hailed from the aspiring class as well. From seamstresses to small proprietors to teachers to skilled tradesmen, the black aspiring class was comprised of workers able to save a little money as well as those who worked multiple jobs to attain class mobility; significantly, it included self-educated women and men as well as those who had attended normal school or college. The socioeconomic status of aspiring African Americans tended to be particularly tenuous in that economic downturn or personal calamity was more likely to move aspiring African Americans into poverty due to limited opportunity. Some aspiring-class women and men fought to work in professions for which they had trained, others became relatively prominent yet still struggled to make ends meet. The characteristic common to the overwhelming majority of the black aspiring class during the late nineteenth and early twentieth centuries was an abiding concern with propriety—not to mention a belief that morality, thrift, and hard work were essential to black progress. Thus, in many regards, this book is as much about class stratification among black people in postemancipation U.S. society as it is about a particular cohort of ambitious activists.[25]

The majority of activists discussed within the following chapters were, for want a better term, "self-made" individuals—including Nannie Helen Burroughs, Josie Briggs Hall, Victoria Earle Matthews, Lucius Holsey, Reuben Pettiford, and A. Wilberforce Williams—and virtually all experienced privation or loss at some point in their lives. These race women and men believed that they knew how to improve the surroundings of families trapped in poverty; they felt that it was up to them to inspire people who had yet to gain access to education, which was critical in affording black Americans a modicum of upward mobility. Reformers who had lost children, spouses, siblings, parents, or friends to premature death even took it upon themselves to address sensitive subjects. Imbued with the spirit of reform, aspiring-class activists came from backgrounds that made them feel uniquely qualified to change the lives and ways of their brothers and sisters. But a welter of racialist theories pertaining to sexuality and reproduction also produced a reform impetus among African Americans. Between 1880 and 1920, fluctuating black birthrate statistics, black morbidity levels, and comparatively high occurrences of infant death fed speculation that black people were particularly "degenerate." So-called scientific theories generated additional pronouncements along these lines. Mainstream medical discourse charged that poor health, disregard of hygienic child culture, and venereal disease among African Americans primed the race for extinction. Social Darwinist theories implied people of African descent simply lacked the intelligence, discipline, and virility to make it in a competitive industrialized world. Popular eugenics suggested black women and men, due to sexual practices which were allegedly impure and haphazard, were scarcely capable of reproducing themselves, let alone creating "well born" babies.

For African Americans and other Americans alike, sexuality entailed a range of issues, exchanges, and actions: promiscuity, monogamy, fornication, flirting, proposition, erotic desire, same sex intercourse, masturbation, courtship, marital sex, adultery, rape, prostitution, molestation, incest. Still, for African Americans alive during the late nineteenth and early twentieth centuries, certain sexual issues, exchanges, and actions were particularly racialized, including rape, concubinage, and "miscegenation." By 1900, rhetorics of lynching demonized black men as rapists, and black women experienced rape as a result of mob violence both during and after Reconstruction.[26] Retributive interracial sex, along with other coerced or consensual relationships between black women and white men, resulted in a number of postemancipation black activists being concerned that concubinage and miscegenation were among the legacies of slavery that compromised the race's moral progress.

Illicit propositions had a similarly racialized association for African Americans given that slavery's dynamics resulted in a postemancipation atmosphere in which black women were considered sexually available to any man. Black men were usually unable to intervene whenever their partners and relatives were approached or assaulted by white men. To compound matters, mainstream discourse generally portrayed black women as indiscriminate and insatiable, black men as oversexed and bestial, and black children as so sexually precocious as to preclude innocence.[27] As contemporary commentary typically portrayed the race as immoral and African Americans were considered a syphilitic race by the beginning of the twentieth century, promiscuity assumed additional meanings for black women and men. Moreover, gender roles and performances deeply informed Afro-Americans' sexuality after emancipation. Since slavery had purportedly engendered wanton sexual behavior and warped how black women and men interacted with each other, striving race members of the postemancipation period considered it critical that women radiate inviolable modesty, that men embody controlled manliness, that couples marry and establish patriarchal households. Indeed, sexuality—in the richness of its expression, the complexity of its dynamics, the pervasiveness of its racial stereotypes—was particularly fraught for African Americans.

Rampant allegations that the race was inherently lascivious and degenerate were anything but benign: such allegations rationalized lynching and ritualized rape, legitimated segregation, and restricted employment opportunities. Such allegations circulated when the black birthrate appeared to be experiencing a precipitous drop. If claims regarding a sharp decrease in African Americans' fecundity were overheated, those claims nevertheless raised questions about high black infant mortality and, for race women and men concerned with collective progress, generated concern over mating, domestic spaces, and behavior. The impetus to secure a positive, hopeful, robust destiny for the race therefore became all but synonymous with reform activism.

Reform activists who labored on behalf of the race were imbued with a politicized mission to change the habits, environments, morals, and lives of African Americans. Two of their most effective and sweeping attempts to do so occurred within the realm of sexuality and domesticity. Activists, many of whom were ambitious strivers, took it upon themselves to convince their sisters and brothers that progressive individuals behaved in certain ways, that proper homes had strong patriarchs, pure mothers, and children schooled in race pride. Moreover, specific anxieties — over everything from masturbation to incest, promiscuity to venereal disease — generated a dynamic intraracial discourse that brooked propriety by approaching sexuality with a fair degree of openness. As much reformist discourse emerged out of specific concerns, it also reflected increased class stratification and intraracial tensions.

Attacks on African Americans' collective character and individual bodies further heightened an already palpable reform ethic among black women and men. Oppression generated and even sustained intraracial reform work as the crusading spirit of Progressivism expanded the cohort of black activists into a fairly sizable and diverse one. This cohort reached the conclusion that racial survival was especially contingent upon eliminating poverty, alleviating morbidity, promoting mainstream gender conventions, eradicating vice, reducing illegitimacy, and ensuring robust production of morally upright, race-conscious children. Such reform would reach its zenith after the turn of the century.

The concept of racial destiny, then, politicized the most private aspects of black life and spurred race activists to evaluate intraracial sexual practices rigorously and advocate moral purity. Politics and religion certainly informed African American activists' ideas about racial fates and fortunes, but these same activists also realized that the continued existence of black Americans literally relied upon biological reproduction. Reformers thus concentrated on more than the deleterious effects of racism — they sought to alter black self-perceptions, habits, and lives. Moreover, race activists wanted to reinforce black manhood, encourage women to be attentive mothers, and change both intraracial and interracial sexual conduct. Gender, sexuality, and morality were therefore constitutive elements of late-nineteenth- and early-twentieth-century African American discourse.[28] If the very definition of black protest is transformed through analysis of gender and sexuality, analyzing Afro-American discourse on racial reproduction and destiny furthers our understanding of how and why subordinated peoples appropriate mainstream discourses to their own ends.

As prevalent as racial uplift ideology was after Reconstruction, and as much as that ideology involved dissemblance, respectability, and moralizing,[29] African American considerations of sex were often just that: black women and men discussed intimate relationships, venereal disease, so-called perversions, reproduction, sexual behavior and comportment. Since public considerations of their own sexuality emerged when African Americans' very survival was both questioned and scrutinized, one way to further our understanding of the period after Reconstruction is to consider demographic reasons why sexuality, health, morals, and reform were so prominent in analyses of the race. It is critical, furthermore, to analyze how sex, social phenomena, political conditions, and the broader culture informed black people's thoughts about their own future. It is also necessary to investigate discourses behind reform efforts and mass black sociopolitical mobilization.

Such an approach to African American history benefits from both social history and intellectual history methodologies; thus, it is difficult to label this book either a "social history" or an "intellectual history." Indeed, this is a history of ideas, but it is one concerned with the impact that sociopolitical and material realities had upon African Americans' attempts to ensure their own collective survival. I therefore consider *Righteous Propagation: African Americans and the Politics of Racial Destiny after Reconstruction* a social history of thought, one that utilizes diverse primary sources ranging from correspondence and speeches to early sociology, from conduct manuals and fiction to newspaper columns. Gender and sexuality appear in dynamic, germane ways throughout these sources. In certain documents — especially those pertaining to emigrationism, imperialism, and nationalism — black manhood is rendered as simultaneously vanquished and virile. Sex becomes both blight and blessing in various domestic and conduct manuals; in the same texts, motherhood is typically idealized as fertile yet chaste. I use these sources to underscore three main points: concepts of racial destiny shifted over the years; despite such shifting, attendant usages of gender and sexuality remained relatively constant; the implications behind racial destiny were ultimately different for women than they were for men. The fourth, overarching point of this book is that between 1877 and 1930, mounting factors led people of African descent to turn increasingly inward in their efforts to preserve themselves.

I analyze and then situate the ideas of working-poor, working-class, aspiring-class, and elite black Americans within the context of material conditions that confronted the race during the late nineteenth and early twentieth centuries. Whereas I am fascinated by discourse, I am not necessarily inclined to engage the work of theorists to drive my argument. I prefer instead to juxtapose arguments in order to recreate debates that emerged from specific historical exigencies. I have tried to "listen" to my sources—to their internal contradictions, silences, inconsistencies—in order to capture nuances within intraracial discussions about sexuality. I have further tried to make sense of the complex ways in which African Americans assessed gender tensions and increased class stratification within their communities during the years between 1877 and 1930 by ordering the chapters in thematic fashion. I have done so largely because specific overarching themes emerged from the sources themselves and to underscore overlapping ways that racial destiny arguments focused on women's ostensible role as reproducers of the race.

In the broadest sense, this book is about how race activists fought for the continued existence of Afro-America once embattled federal attempts to ensure black civil rights and reconstruct a war-torn nation sputtered to an ignominious end after Rutherford B. Hayes became the nineteenth president of the United States. My study does not focus upon how white Americans subverted the quest for black civil rights after Reconstruction, nor does it consider white activists, writers, or intellectuals at length. I also do not discuss black towns, electoral politics, economic strategies for self-determination, religion, or Ethiopianism in any depth.[30] I instead scrutinize various strategies that people of African descent launched in the name of their own collective well-being. I attempt to understand those strategies by invoking the zeitgeist in which post-Reconstruction African Americans found themselves: as such, I analyze social Darwinism, imperialism, popular eugenics, and nationalism; I assess ways in which race women and men situated themselves within Progressive Era reform as I seek to uncover how Americans of African descent dealt rhetorically with massive demographic shifts. As a work on a postemancipation society, this book attempts to make sense of a time when no one knew for certain what was to become of the descendants of slaves.

Overall, *Righteous Propagation* offers sustained analysis of why arguments concerning racial destiny were built around assumptions about gender, sexuality, and class at the same time that it connects gendered, sexualized notions about racial destiny to material realities and changing circum-

14 [PROLOGUE]

stances. The narrative considers the impact that racialist theories such as popular eugenics had on black analyses of intragroup vitality and draws connections between those analyses and contemporaneous phenomena. This study also reveals myriad ways in which African Americans reproduced themselves after emancipation—by seeking a better future for themselves and offspring, by producing diverse texts about and for the race, by advocating sex reform, by promoting specific forms of material culture, by making pointed arguments about racial purity.

The story that unfolds herein abounds in discomfiting interactions. Emigrationists tended to ignore ways in which Liberia was a colonizing enterprise for indigenous Africans; black men swept up in the rhetoric of empire overlooked how their own desires for dominion had the potential to oppress other people of color. The concept of racial destiny stressed collectivity, yet it enabled African American women and men to judge—often harshly—what they perceived as weaknesses, failings, and pathologies on the part of other black people. Impulses to change sexual practices within the race spurred reformist women and men to speak of the "masses" in ways that echoed mainstream, racialist notions of black degeneracy as anxieties over racial reproduction resulted in women and men making less than flattering observations about one another. Pronouncements regarding racial purity not only uncloaked uncomfortable matters such as intraracial prejudice but also resulted in confrontations both rhetorical and corporeal.

What follows is an account of communion and conflict, one in which various voices—especially those of aspiring women and men—engage, agree, dissent. From Ollie Edwards, who took in laundry as she dreamt about going to Liberia, to Black Cross Nurse Kate Fenner, whose candor angered men in the Universal Negro Improvement Association, fairly obscure people populate these pages. These women and men have intrigued, shocked, confused, and even amused me on occasion. They have also taught me that the past is filled with surprises, that the historian is as much conduit as writer, that their acts of "calling out" contemporaries deserve as much careful attention as do their determined efforts to maintain themselves as a people.

God is just and with his own hand,
He will shape our destiny;
If our future be in this land,
Or in that beyond the sea.
—*A History of the Club Movement*
  Among the Colored Women of the
  United States of America (1902)

1

A GREAT, GRAND, &
ALL IMPORTANT QUESTION
AFRICAN AMERICAN
EMIGRATION TO LIBERIA

Emigrationism became increasingly popular as a strategy for collective advancement once the demise of Reconstruction signaled a certain death of federal efforts to protect black civil rights. Diminution of interventionist tactics to integrate African Americans into the national polity facilitated reconciliation between North and South, which was further enabled by the relatively new discourse of social Darwinism. Social Darwinism suggested that a "natural" biological hierarchy made it difficult, if not impossible, for different races to inhabit the same territory as equal beings since the manly, competitive Anglo-Saxon was bound, in theory, to dominate weaker colored races. The supposed failure of Reconstruction substantiated social Darwinist claims that, by fiat of biology, black people were incapable of reaching the same heights of civilization as "Anglo-Saxon," "Alpine," and "Nordic" peoples.[1]

The United States endured severe, recurring economic depressions and successive labor strikes throughout this era of political backlash and racialist theory. As the chasm between rich and poor widened, as tensions between working and owning classes erupted into outright warfare on occasion, most black Americans remained in impoverished surroundings little better than those of their enslaved ancestors. African American women, men, and children simply refused to accept their immiseration, however. In addition to building an array of "uplift" institutions between 1877 and 1900, black people used various forms of migration to seek opportunity and avoid, if only temporarily, what appeared to be unrelenting persecution. From "Exodusters" who tramped toward Kansas during the late 1870s to people who left rural backwaters for towns, from workers who ventured north for better jobs to sharecroppers who pushed westward in search of land they could call their own, African American people associated freedom with territory. Even when black women and men merely fantasized that New Mexico, Texas, and Oklahoma would one day become all-black states, the seductive connection between territory and freedom fostered hope that there was a place, somewhere, where the race would face less hostility, exploitation, and turmoil.

Whether their destination was Pennsylvania, Arkansas, or California, many late-nineteenth-century African Americans shared the opinion of James Dubose of Orchard Knob, Tennessee—they simply could not remain below the Mason-Dixon line. "How much lonnger are we to be left hear to suffer and dy[?]," Dubose wondered with dolorous yet righteous overtones. "I wish to God that there was a Law passed in the United States to day that would compell Every collord man to leave the Southern States as it would bee all for the better for boath Whyte and Black. We never can live in peace . . . with the whytes." Black people, Dubose contended, needed to squeeze from under the heels of whites and "go to them Selves" by crossing the ocean to Liberia.[2] In 1891, two years after Dubose uttered his desire for collective liberation, Thomas Cox expressed his own belief that Liberia presented the greatest freedom for black Americans. "We the Anglo-African race . . . are constantl[y] wandering from one territory to another to breath a few breaths of liberity," Cox wrote. "The Negroes of the South wan[t] to emigrate to a land of liberity and peace. . . . I myself have heard Thousands say if they knew How to get to Liberia they would go immediately."[3]

The "thousands" of black Americans willing to contemplate leaving the United States were, in a sense, part of a massive, international demographic shift that began during the late nineteenth century. Economic downturns, religious persecution, and ethnic strife induced a variety of Europeans to leave their native countries, while the availability of jobs abroad encouraged Chinese, Japanese, Korean, and Filipino workers to sail for Hawaii and the western coast of the United States. Immigrants from Asia and Europe alike were propelled by powerful, interconnected forces active during the 1870s, 1880s, and 1890s: "the movement of workers, capital, and technology across national borders." Score upon score of dislocated workers, many of whom worked the land, left their native countries with hopes of obtaining property or finding work that paid a living wage. By the early twentieth century, an "enormous intercontinental population movement" resulted in "settler" societies throughout the Americas, Australia, and Africa.[4]

The willingness of certain black Americans to uproot themselves and begin anew on another continent corresponded with broader global patterns in that African American emigrants' hunger for autonomy was similar to the thirst for opportunity felt by Asian and European immigrants to the United States. Still, given that African Americans were making the transition from chattel slavery to free labor during the late nineteenth century, emigration to Liberia was a relatively unique phenomenon, if not a delayed reverse migration of a people rented by the Atlantic slave trade generations earlier. Even the mere desire to emigrate on the part of people unable to leave the United States due to poverty, misfortune, or timing called matters of race and citizenship into question.

Working-poor people — tenant farmers, domestics, washerwomen, day laborers — viewed Liberia as a place where they could improve their prospects and feel the self-possessed satisfaction of uncontested citizenship. Men and women with education or training craved upward mobility as they harbored hopes that their hard-won skills would blaze the path of progress. Teachers, doctors, preachers, and missionaries were similarly motivated by longings for personal and collective development; many of these race men and women believed Liberia a propitious site for civilizing missions. Whatever their occupation or educational attainment, the emigration-minded were frequently influenced by ongoing racial antipathy and conflict; as early as 1878, lynching, election violence, harsh conditions, and rank discrimination generated prospective emigrants in state after state.[5] Emigrationists wanted to inhabit land where the integrity of their manhood and womanhood would no longer be assailed on a daily basis; they wanted their children to flourish in an environment free from racial and sexual terrorism.[6] These desires hardly disappeared by the end of the century. As James Harris of St. Louis, Missouri, confessed in 1894, "we are starving . . . lynched worse than cattle and we have not any protection of the law whatever. . . . We would do better if we were all in Africa."[7]

Prospective emigrants embraced politicized concepts as well. When

Thomas Fields wrote to the American Colonization Society from Texas in 1883, he simultaneously expressed his "zeal . . . for Africa" and noted his appreciation for lectures by a prominent ACS associate, the Afro-Caribbean intellectual Edward Wilmot Blyden. W. H. Holloway of Cleveland County, Arkansas, harbored nationalist sentiments similar to those expressed by African Methodist Episcopal (AME) bishop Henry McNeal Turner. As Holloway divulged in 1891, "I appreciate the land of my Mother and Father and [am] a Race lover of the deepest strain. . . . [I] want to inhabit a free and independent country where Ethiopia can stretch forth her hands unto God and be a mighty nation. . . . My people here . . . are tired and cannot stand the oppression . . . of the high-handed Southern white man." Seven years later, a man from Oklahoma Territory named James McHenry believed that "America negroes" lagged behind other people because the race had no nation to declare, embrace, defend. For McHenry, peoplehood was synonymous with nationhood; "becom[ing] a people" required concerted, collective effort to build up "our own . . . Little Republic of Liberia." Black nationalism might not have informed everyone interested in emigration, yet as the sentiments of Cox, Holloway, and McHenry attest, it could wield considerable influence.[8] Put another way, if yearnings for peoplehood on the part of emigration-minded African Americans emerged out of longings to secure a positive destiny for the race, some individuals expressed those longings in race-based, nationalistic terms.

In rhetoric as well as strategy, incipient forms of black nationalist thought informed sizable grassroots movements such as South Carolina's Liberian Exodus Association. Even small independent clubs where like-minded individuals primarily exchanged ideas and shared dreams were founded out of impulses to preserve African Americans as a people. Individual women and men not belonging to clubs often invoked race pride in order to plead their case to the American Colonization Society. Those women and men that wrote to the society were likely, and perhaps acutely, aware of its problematic legacy as far as African Americans were concerned; they requested information, passage, and support from ACS agents nonetheless.

If black Americans' decisions regarding emigration involved a variety of factors, emigrationist sentiment contained gendered and sexualized aspects. Some African Americans and Americo-Liberians even viewed Africa as a haven where black men could at long last express, flaunt, and flex their manhood. Emigrationist thought offered somewhat less overt pronouncements about womanhood, yet it still incorporated apprehensions regarding women's sexuality. Emigrationism did not challenge gender norms and sexual behaviors promoted by the aspiring class and elite, but convictions—some of which were gendered—about African Americans' right to claim U.S. citizenship generally left leading race women and men chilly toward emigration during the 1880s and 1890s.[9]

Elite and "representative colored men" tended—as a group—to be firm antiemigrationists while those most likely to contemplate emigration were aspiring-class, working-class, and working-poor black Americans.[10] Emigration was hardly a last-ditch strategy of the downtrodden, however. As part of a complicated nexus of migratory impulses and contemporary anxieties, emigration suggestively connected two paramount issues—collective survival and national identity. As Alabama minister J. P. Barton put it, "the better class of the colored people" wanted to see their "fatherland" in order to make an informed choice between a new life in a frontier settlement and continued existence in a contentiously heterogeneous, postemancipation society. For an emigrationist such as Barton, the very act of investigating possibilities in Liberia made a woman or man particularly enterprising.[11]

In certain communities where emigrationist fervor took root, emigrationists could proclaim that the "better class" consisted of those individuals wanting to build a black nation on the northwest coast of Africa. Going to Liberia both entailed risk and demonstrated considerable pluck—an independent spirit that drove women and men to persevere in the face of illness, heartbreak, frustration, and misgivings. For those longing to go to Liberia, emigration was a means of resolving a deep-seated question about where African Americans could best work out their own destiny. Emigrationists' desire to "settle this great, gran[d] and all important question" likely seemed a noble quest to end the misery of a people still in bondage decades after the official abolition of chattel slavery.[12] By century's end, however, emigrationist women, men, and children would find out what many pioneering members of the Liberia Exodus Association discovered during the late 1870s: emigration involved its share of peril as well as promise.

By the late nineteenth century when black women and men searched for possibilities and acted upon convictions, African Americans' interest in—and debate over—settling outside the United States had existed for over three-quarters of a century. Paul Cuffe financed his own exploratory mission to West Africa from Boston in 1811 and then accompanied thirty-eight other African Americans to Sierra Leone in late 1815.[13] Cuffe's latter expedition would prove somewhat of an isolated effort: no other early-nineteenth-century independent black-conceived schemes sent emigrants to Sierra Leone, let alone Liberia. After Cuffe's singular effort, however, emigration schemes began to encounter considerable resistance within free black communities. This was particularly the case during the 1830s when abolitionist fervor led many northern black women and men—including prominent race men such as James Forten, Absalom Jones, and Richard Allen—to equate emigration with racists' desire to fortify slavery by colonizing free blacks outside of the United States.[14] Moreover, as emigration and colonization were collapsed together by black abolitionists eager to make the point that free blacks should not estrange themselves from those who remained in bondage, Liberia seemed especially tainted by its association with the American Colonization Society.

Established in 1817, the American Colonization Society began as a benevolent cause that, whether its founders intended or not, at times functioned as a front for the interests of southern slaveholders. The ACS was opposed to slavery but was nonetheless at cross-purposes with mainstream abolition: the ACS considered free people of color a threat to national stability, and many of the "free" people the society sent to Liberia were manumitted with the expressed understanding that they would leave the United States. Founding members were imbued with a belief that colonization would spread Christianity among Africans, and some even hoped to establish an American empire in Africa. As a whole, colonizationists did not adhere to "crude negrophobia," yet one of their major aims was to rid the nation of Negroes. If the ACS fell far short of this goal, the society did remove approximately 11,200 people of African descent from the United States between 1817 and 1866. And, whereas the society functioned in a reduced capacity after the Civil War, it still managed to provide free passage and rations to over 4,000 additional emigrants.[15]

Certain constants informed the guiding philosophy of the ACS over the course of the nineteenth century. To begin, the society never championed African American civil rights, and it retained a basic assumption about blacks' capacity to become productive citizens. Some white colonizationists argued that African Americans were indeed U.S. citizens, and many contended racial prejudice was the largest stumbling block in the path of black collective progress.[16] Colonizationists generally recognized that racism was "historical and cultural in its origins"—something created rather than innate—still the society envisioned a decidedly bleak future for people of African descent in the United States: citizenship was something that "God meant [negroes] should have, but which [they] cannot have here."[17] White colonizationists routinely expressed discomfort over the presence of black people in the United States, and that discomfort, in turn, infused the society with a palpable white nationalist sensibility. The ACS also constructed colonization as a resolutely "masculine endeavor," one that would ostensibly enable black men to achieve manhood in Liberia as pioneers, heads of household, and political actors. Not only was colonization gendered male by the ACS, men dominated the very debate among African Americans over the legitimacy of colonization and Liberia—a debate that remained lively until the Civil War.[18]

Between 1820 and 1840, free blacks generally rejected both the American Colonization Society and emigration to Liberia, as emigrationists typically advocated black removal to Canada, Haiti, the North American West, Mexico, and the British West Indies.[19] Liberia was more than controversial among black emigrationists—it was all but universally loathed. In 1832, for instance, an anonymous race woman from Philadelphia who advocated black emigration to Mexico was repulsed by the idea of supporting anything associated with the American Colonization Society. Whereas this Philadelphian did not share Maria Stewart's sentiment that being impaled by a bayonet was preferable to either emigration or affiliation with the ACS, she did proclaim that "no one detests [their cause of colonization] more than I do. I would not be taken to Africa, were the Society to make me queen of the country."[20] In many respects, each woman represented two prevalent free black attitudes toward colonization before 1850: complete rejection of emigration altogether or conditional support of emigration to any location but Africa.

At midcentury a watershed occurred that considerably influenced the reception of emigrationism among free blacks: in 1850, the Fugitive Slave Act made it legal for interested parties to capture fugitive slaves who would then be returned to slave masters or placed on the auction blocks of the slave South. Given that freeborn blacks had little recourse if they were identified and seized as escapees, the law swiftly "precipitated an exodus [to Canada] from every northern city with a sizable black population" as it markedly increased the willingness of northern blacks to contemplate emigration.[21] During the 1850s, free blacks held National Emigration Conventions in which men such as Martin Delany, James T. Holly, and Henry Bibb dominated the proceedings while women such as Mary Miles Bibb and Mary Ann Shadd garnered the occasional leadership position. Despite the relative paucity of women in leadership, women established a presence for themselves at these conventions: in 1854, for example, women managed to comprise approximately a third of all delegates.[22]

Such activism hardly meant black women and men warmed toward the idea of exodus to Liberia.[23] Indeed, emigration-minded women and men of the 1850s "walk[ed] a fine line between unflinching hostility toward white colonization societies and an openness toward proposals for black independence and national autonomy."[24] Black emigration conventions of the 1850s, for example, banned any and all consideration of "[e]migration to the Eastern Hemisphere." Three of the decade's prominent emigrationists distanced themselves from Liberian settlement as well: Mary Ann Shadd's *A Plea for Emigration: Notes of Canada West* extolled the virtues of the country to which she had moved shortly after passage of the Fugitive Slave Act; Martin Delany and James Holly both advocated black removal to the Caribbean and Central America. Whatever their individual feelings about Africa itself, Shadd, Delany, and Holly eliminated Liberia from consideration for the primary reason that the colony cum nation was, quite literally, an outgrowth of the American Colonization Society.[25] Delany took pains to distinguish between colonization, which he viewed as the racist removal of blacks from the United States, and emigration, which he considered independent initiatives by blacks to leave the United States. Indeed, when Delany eventually embraced Africa as a possible destination for black emigrationists during the late 1850s, he felt compelled to revise—and in print, at that—his own earlier assertions.[26] Whereas Shadd would also reconsider her views about emigration to Africa by the early 1860s, in 1852 Shadd offered the trenchant observation that supporting Afro-American colonization of Liberia was tantamount to "moral and physical death, under a voluntary escort of [our] most bitter enemies at home."[27]

If Liberia remained unpopular among emigration-minded free blacks in the North, William Nesbit's scathing 1855 pamphlet undoubtedly discouraged those free women and men who did find African emigration appealing. His *Four Months in Liberia: or, African Colonization Exposed* dismissed Monrovia as "ancient and dilapidated," claimed Afro-American mortality in Liberia was exceedingly high, and condemned the Liberian government as corrupt and "pusillanimous." A thorough rebuttal published by Reverend Samuel Williams in 1857 attempted to convince Afro-Americans that the black republic had its share of positive and negative realities as did any other country. "Although Mr. Nesbit prophesies the speedy downfall of our little republic . . . I hope . . . the people may see right," Williams confessed, "and move to Liberia . . . to build up a great nation." By making his hopes, opinions, and experiences public, the reverend—who, incidentally, sailed to Liberia with Nesbit as part of the same company and then chose to make the young republic his home — might have managed to rehabilitate Liberia's reputation among some people inclined to relocate there. Still, most African American women and men continued to distance themselves from both the colony and African colonization.[28]

Once the American Colonization Society granted Liberia its independence in 1847, Liberia not only began to lose its stigmatic connections in the eyes of free blacks, some African Americans began celebrating the former colony's nationhood during annual galas. Moreover, after emancipation, the young republic seemed more of a proving ground for black self-government than a questionable exile. Liberia Day celebrations in the United States subsequently became more elaborate — and, in the South, more open. For example, in Savannah, Georgia, the "first public celebration" occurred in 1865. One resident tellingly observed that Liberian independence had been privately "celebrated [in Savannah] for fifteen years by a few hearts that have ever burned with . . . liberty." Some fourteen years later the city's American Union Ethiopian Association sponsored a massive commemoration that attracted celebrants from Atlanta, Macon, Charleston, and Beaufort. After a parade and music regaled an estimated crowd of 3,000, Reverend J. C. Haines delivered the keynote address. Although Haines advised his audience against impetuous mass emigration, one witness believed Haines "'completely entranc[ed] hundreds of his hearers and stir[red] up considerable enthusiasm on the subject of colonization in Liberia.'"[29] On at least three occasions during the 1880s Americans of African descent in New Orleans unfurled "the fabric of race pride" on the anniversary of Liberian independence. Replete with singing children, readings of Liberia's Declaration of Independence, and fireworks, these celebrations fortified people's identification with Africa as they stoked interest in emigration. Henry Adams was even among the eager participants at the 1883 celebration.[30]

If African Americans in New Orleans regularly feted Liberia's independence and a thousands-strong Colonization Council emerged in Louisiana under the leadership of Henry Adams, South Carolina was another state where emigrationism took firm hold. The state's black citizens had certainly witnessed their share of racial terrorism during Reconstruction. In 1871, Republican activist Willis Johnson encountered a mob bent on using violence to prevent him from "vot[ing] the radical ticket" in Newberry County; that same year, a Spartanburgh resident named Charlotte Fowler lived through the ordeal of having a gun held to her head immediately after a bullet blasted a gaping hole through her husband's skull. Not only did it take Wallace

Fowler some time to die, "brains and blood came out over his eyes" with each ebbing breath that he drew.[31]

African Americans' encounters with politically and racially motivated violence forged the race into a more cohesive population as it stoked emigrationist desires. In early 1875, a Mrs. Martin of Columbia, South Carolina, published an evocative song that encouraged emigration-minded women and men to think of themselves as pioneers imbued with a race pride capable of sustaining a nation:

We are going! We are going!
To the Golden Guinea-land,
Where the sky and earth are glowing,
And the sparkling waves are flowing,
To the sunny sea-kissed strand.
Yes! We're going, gladly going,
Oh, come join us heart and hand!

She is pleading to us, pleading,
Our country, far away.
Oh, can we be unheeding,
When our help she's so much needing?
While she calls on us to-day,
Oh, can we resist her pleading,
And here longer from her stay?

As she implored people to develop race pride and to demonstrate that pride by devoting their lives to an African nation, Martin's idealized Liberia presented a stark contrast to the daily experience of many blacks in the southern United States. Her song appeared at a particularly fortuitous moment as well. Whereas it is difficult to know how many people actually heard Martin's song or read its lyrics and whether Martin herself was of African descent, a veritable outbreak of emigrationism spread through the state soon thereafter.[32]

Any number of factors prodded black South Carolinians to consider emigration. Charleston *News and Courier* correspondent A. B. Williams—a white man who covered the state's growing exodus movement—noted that black women and men frequently cited low wages and tenancy as primary motivations to leave the South. Politics and mob violence exerted considerable influence as well: Williams heard emigrationist blacks recount tale after tale of "'political persecutions'" carried out by "'Ku Klux'" and "'Night

Hawks.'" At one point in 1876 the skeptical reporter came across "an honest looking colored man in Columbia [who told] a knot of listeners that he had *seen* . . . five colored women tied to trees and disembowelled with bowie knives by Democrats."[33] A series of politically inspired race riots erupted in and around Charleston that same year. Although the region's black majority was able to fend off successive acts of racial violence during Reconstruction, some black South Carolinians apparently decided that bidding farewell to the United States was preferable to the noxious blend of depressed wages, tenancy, and the seemingly unending wave of terrorism they endured. "Red-hot emigrationist" Henry McNeal Turner characterized the situation thusly: both "the meanness of the country . . . [and] the crimson blood of 46,000 men and women, who have been slaughtered like brutes . . . persuaded so many to leave."[34]

Following proemigration Fourth of July and Liberian Independence rallies in 1877, black South Carolinians joined forces with their neighbors in nearby states, organized the Liberia Exodus Association (LEA), and set out to recruit "one hundred and fifty males . . . and a like number of females."[35] The LEA soon made $10 shares for its Joint Stock Steamship Company available to interested parties, while its leaders—including Reverend B. F. Porter, one-time probate judge Harrison Bouey, former state senator Samuel Gaillard, and none other than Martin Delany—trumped up additional interest through speeches and canvassing. Mass celebrations were yet another critical means of mobilization; in particular, the public consecration of the association's ship, the *Azor*, drew an especially large crowd and proved decisive in winning converts to the cause. On Thursday, March 21, 1878, a throng witnessed Anna Thompson, daughter of the LEA's treasurer, deliver a short address and present a Liberian flag to Delany, after which emigrants struggled through a rush of bodies to inspect the ship. If the sight of a vessel purchased independently with the race's money was not emotional enough, Henry Turner closed the day with an oration during which he claimed that the name "Azor" was Hebrew for "to aid." For a beleaguered folk eager to leave the South, Bishop Turner's fleeting, indirect reference to the Israelites was a poignant suggestion that their exodus movement might, in time, reach biblical proportions of its own.[36]

Not only did the Liberia Exodus Association tap into a local groundswell, existing demand actually outstripped the organization's resources. While members had managed to raise an impressive $6,000 through stock sales, by the time they procured the bark *Azor*, there was not enough money left in LEA coffers to purchase adequate provisions for the over 200 emigrants the association hastily dispatched to Liberia in late April 1878. Unfortunately, in their haste, organizers made several unfortunate miscalculations. One misjudgment was immediately apparent: as the packed *Azor* pulled out of Charleston Harbor, some of the women, men, and children watching the ship fade into the horizon were disappointed would-be emigrants led to believe that there was ample room in steerage. Shaky start and all, the Liberia Exodus Association was the first independent, black-run emigration effort to send blacks to Africa since Paul Cuffe sailed to Sierra Leone some sixty years before. And, although the emigrants left behind would likely have been hard pressed to grant as much, the fact that organizers produced more emigrants than the *Azor* could possibly carry demonstrated that the LEA was a rousing success, at least in terms of grassroots mobilization.[37]

Once the *Azor* left, surplus emigrants and other interested parties could follow the first voyage's progress merely by picking up a newspaper, since the *News and Courier*'s A. B. Williams continued to cover the exodus by embarking on the *Azor* himself. His dispatches would be less than glowing. Williams was appalled that the ship had no competent doctor—the reporter derisively referred to the man on board providing medical services as "'Pills'"—especially once measles, respiratory infections, and "ship fever" started claiming passenger after passenger. In the process of interviewing a newly widowed woman, Williams discovered her deceased husband had invested in tools and provisions that were nowhere to be found. He spoke to other passengers who possessed little more than clothes and a few personal effects due to donating their very last dollar to the association before leaving Charleston. The disgusted correspondent concluded: "The 'Steamship Company' seems to have remorselessly drained these people, having actually started some of them off in a penniless condition. This, with the criminal neglect which allowed the emigrants to come over at the beginning of rainy season . . . without physician or shelter . . . savors strongly of criminal misappropriation of funds and breach of trust . . . regarding the lives and welfare of a band of helpless people." Despite constant death, an absence of ready cash, and a shortage of both food and water, the overwhelming majority of "exodists" made it to their destination. If they had been dispirited aboard the *Azor*, women, children, and men cheered upon seeing the shoreline of their new home; the passengers were soon greeted by an orator who praised them for possessing the initiative to return to "their fatherland."[38]

The success of the Liberia Exodus Association was ultimately mixed: considerably more of its emigrants died en route than did emigrants on ACS expeditions; organizers made inadequate plans regarding the Azorites ar-

Ashmun Street, Monrovia, Liberia, 1893. ACS emigrants typically disembarked in Monrovia. Some emigrants were overcome with emotion upon setting foot in Africa, while others were delirious from ship fever, and still others were stunned by the city's appearance. Courtesy of the Library of Congress, Prints and Photographs Division, LC-USZ62-129866.

rival in Monrovia; despite ongoing sale of shares, the LEA eventually lost the *Azor* due to outstanding debt.[39] To compound matters, returnees began drifting back to the United States in 1879 with sundry tales of horror. Eighteen returnees who had stayed in Liberia a little over a year had their story publicized in a damning New York *Herald* exposé claiming, among other things, that only five dozen *Azor* emigrants were still alive and that every last one would head back to Charleston given the opportunity. As the *Herald* would have it, the "pilgrims" had tremendous difficulty finding gainful employ once in Liberia, and their store of a half-year's provisions lasted a mere three weeks after debarkation. This catastrophic shortage of food and work reportedly cast the Azorites upon the mercy and benevolence of people in Monrovia. The paper further portrayed returnees as a part of a dejected lot of "poor wretches" that "found many more graves than homes in the young colored Republic." Echoing the Charleston *News and Courier*, the *Herald*'s final assessment was more indictment than insinuation—the LEA had indeed swindled a band of unsuspecting victims.[40]

One particularly prominent Americo-Liberian, Daniel Bashiel Warner, was among the former emigrants who publicly challenged the veracity of sensational news items. After leaving the United States as a boy in 1823, Warner went on to become Liberia's president during the 1860s. Warner additionally served terms as secretary of state and vice president, and he became an agent of the American Colonization Society in 1877. In 1880 the eager booster for the fledgling nation used the pages of the *African Repository* to rebut sensational stories that "one-half of [the emigrants] die and the larger portion of the other half . . . return to the United States." Most Azorites had actually begun to prosper in Liberia, according to Warner. He further asserted that whereas a frontier existence had its share of travails, those hardships were nonetheless preferable to life in an American South ruled by Democratic Redeemer governments.[41] Ironically, immediately following the Azorites' arrival in Liberia, Warner sent letters to ACS secretary William Coppinger in which he detailed their woes, missteps, and presumptions. Warner even privately dismissed the struggling enterprise as "this Azor blunder."[42] Warner's published opinions in the *Repository* were, then, a furtive attempt on his part to disabuse the reading public of lingering notions that emigration itself was folly.

As suggested by Warner's public, more positive assessment of the Azorites, some of the emigrants sent by the Liberia Exodus Association indeed prospered. Harrison Bouey reported from Royesville that "to the astonishment of all Liberia," emigrants had established their own "Azor settlement . . . in the forest where no settlement at all existed." Bouey was quick to challenge charges issued by U.S. papers about excessive mortality among *Azor* emigrants as well. According to him, the emigrants-turned-settlers had easy access to abundant food, regular Christian fellowship, and a school that operated five days a week. Both G. S. Daniels and Jackson Clark were busily engaged on separate coffee farms in what Clark referred to as "the only home for the people of color." Even Nancy Irons, a woman who left Charleston only because her husband decided to emigrate, conceded that Liberia was "a good enough place to live in." By 1888, Clement Irons—who had been a well-respected, prosperous inventor and machinist back in South Carolina—made a success of his steamboat operation on a river just northwest of Monrovia, thereby enabling the entire family to enjoy a life of relative comfort. Nancy Irons returned to the United States for over a year during the mid-1880s, but only to visit: this one-time reluctant emigrant was more than willing to return to her farm in Millsburg, Liberia, where the family raised an impressive array of produce and occasionally employed "native" labor.[43]

Coffee plantation, Clay-Ashland, Liberia, 1893. The prospect of owning a coffee farm appealed to many prospective and actual emigrants despite the fact that purchasing large parcels of land was generally beyond the means of African Americans and Americo-Liberians alike. Race activists opposed to emigration were quick to charge Americo-Liberian planters with exploiting indigenous laborers. Courtesy of the Library of Congress, Prints and Photographs Division, LC-USZ62-129864.

The experiences of those connected with the *Azor*—whether disappointed prospective emigrant never able to reach Africa, unhappy returnee, or eventual success story—foreshadowed the mixed track record of black emigration over the remaining years of the nineteenth century. Whatever the triumphs or failures of the Liberia Exodus Association, its organizers demonstrated that the race could make it to Liberia without assistance from the American Colonization Society or the federal government. The association's greatest accomplishment, perhaps, was that it fomented similar efforts in Arkansas, Louisiana, Florida, North Carolina, Georgia, and Mississippi. These independent clubs emerged out of sheer demand, a demand so large that neither the proliferation of small clubs nor the American Colonization Society had the capacity or finances to settle all those prepared to relocate in Liberia.[44] If a significant sector of the race considered emigration sheer folly, with each passing week, more and more black folk were "up in arms for that Great Republic [Liberia]."[45]

Emigrationists contemplated various means of assistance and relief throughout the late nineteenth century, one of which was to petition the federal government. Around the same time that South Carolinians were preparing for the *Azor*'s inaugural voyage, the North Carolina Freedmen's Emigration Aid Society drafted a petition requesting $100 per willing emigrant. Members of the Emigration Aid Society believed that competition with white laborers placed black workers at a decisive disadvantage. They craved "freedom from competition with any but our own race" and relished the notion of ample land in an all-black country.[46] The petitioners from North Carolina were unsuccessful in obtaining financial aid, but their corresponding secretary, teacher and Shaw University graduate Sherwood Capps, applied for and received passage from the American Colonization Society in late 1877. Once in Liberia, Capps mailed an effusive letter to a friend: "I have already cut my farm myself and am now building me a house upon it. I am satisfied here . . . [and] I tell you . . . this is no country to be idle in. . . . It is a country for industrious people, who are willing to take hold and labor. With such emigrants we can and will soon show the world that we intend to be a people — a strong nation." Although Capps himself emigrated through the ACS, he remained committed to the idea of race folks taking part in an "independent movement." Capps subsequently told others what to bring to Liberia if they wanted to be successful and advised emigrants to be prudent in handling funds and provisions. He even purchased his two-hundred-acre farm near Brewerville with the hope that other enterprising black Americans would come join him and establish a new town. Capps's enthusiasm paid off: within three years he established a family, built three houses, and was a small-scale coffee planter in addition to being a teacher.[47]

Sherwood Capps's good fortune hardly reflected the efficacy of petitioning Congress. The Freedmen's Emigration Aid apparently failed to secure federal funding, thus some of its members might have followed Capps's contingency plan. There was, after all, some probability of receiving passage from the ACS: not only had the society sent thousands of free blacks and ex-slaves to Liberia between 1816 and 1866, almost 250 ACS emigrants left the United States in the wake of Reconstruction. During the late 1870s until the early 1890s, single men and families had the best chances of being sent by the society, whereas the few single women selected by the ACS tended to be women who could serve as teachers, missionaries, or — in rare cases — doctors. The likelihood of any Afro-American group obtaining financial assistance to emigrate from the government was, in contrast, relatively slim in 1877.[48]

Submitting petitions was not a terribly effective measure, yet the "memorial" nonetheless gained a measure of popularity among emigrationists as the century wore on. This popularity can be explained, in part, by economic factors. The price of cotton dropped with an unrelenting steadiness throughout this period and many sharecropping black families found themselves plunging further into debt with each passing year.[49] To exacerbate matters, a national recession that began in 1884 soon degenerated into full-scale depression. Most African Americans were likely to find themselves in a compromised financial state whether they cultivated cotton or not. For those who wanted to emigrate, asking the government for assistance was, if nothing else, an attempt to better one's situation. In 1886 and 1887 alone, black women and men from a reported fourteen states and territories petitioned Congress for funds: a group of Texans argued that "low wages and high rents" were two intractable problems facing themselves and other black people in the United States; the African Emigration Association of Topeka cited a desire to ensure "the pe[r]petuity of our race, which is here losing its identity by intermixture with the white races" among the reasons its members wanted to move to Africa.[50]

The act of petitioning reflected a certain belief among working Afro-Americans that the U.S. government would aid those able to present a compelling or well-argued case. "Memorials" additionally reveal how people— many of whom considered themselves destitute—mobilized on their own behalf. The history of the African Emigration Association is rather suggestive in this regard since its petition was submitted almost five years after the association's founding. During this intermediary period, organizers most likely canvassed their communities, held meetings, and assessed dues while members exchanged ideas, recruited friends, and elected officers. Even if the association only existed on paper between 1881 and 1886, its organizers were eventually able to convert "a large number" of their neighbors into fellow petitioners; persistent activism, the depression of the middle 1880s, or a combination of both galvanized locals around the cause of emigration by 1886. By the late 1880s organizers probably even persuaded a few former Exodusters that their Canaan was located in Liberia, not Kansas. And, if "millenarian" Exodusters once believed that they would receive federal assistance to migrate to Kansas, emigrationists also hoped that the government might underwrite their passage to Africa.[51]

Furthermore, the very language of the petition from Kansas underscores that intimate matters were at the heart of emigrationism for some people. The women and men of Topeka not only singled out miscegenation as a reason to emigrate, they believed that their cherished cause of black nationality depended upon racial purity. The petitioners also made a cryptic reference to "other troubles" that might well have emerged from economic and political traumas—"troubles" such as the rape of black women and the sexualized lynchings of black men. Sexuality was not always explicitly discussed within emigrationist petitions; consensual interracial sex and sexual terrorism likely crossed the minds of some petitioners all the same.

As specific concerns and local exigencies compelled black people to send petitions to Congress, activities on Capitol Hill itself encouraged some emigrationists to hope that the government would aid their cause. In January 1890, Southern Democrats John Morgan, R. L. Gibson, and Matthew Butler introduced separate pieces of legislation that would fund black removal from the South. The Butler Bill, for example, called for $5 million in federal aid to assist African Americans that "desire[d] to emigrate from any of the Southern States." Butler did not specify any particular country to which African Americans should emigrate and only Morgan referred specifically to Africa, but most emigrationists assumed that these bills—Butler's was the best known—would send black Americans to Liberia.[52]

Antiemigrationists unhappily reached the same conclusion. The African American press, by and large, balked at the suggestion that federal dollars be used to deport black people from the country, and the controversial bills were even ridiculed at a major meeting of race activists. During the 1890 convention of the Afro-American League in Chicago, H. C. C. Astwood offered a tongue-in-cheek proposition that the "Honorable Congress" provide "free transportation and lunch" to any put-upon white person desperate to escape a community where blacks outnumbered whites. The only form of black emigration that leaguers were willing to entertain was to the western and northern regions of the United States; the one congressional bill they were willing to back was the Blair Educational Bill that supported universal education.[53] The overwhelming majority of "best men" belonging to the league—including editors T. Thomas Fortune, Edward E. Cooper, John Mitchell, W. Calvin Chase, attorney Ferdinand Barnett, AME bishop Alexander Walters, and politico John Dancy—opposed emigration bills outright.[54] With the possible exception of proemigrationist leaguer William Heard,[55] most leaguers believed that black people had a duty to fight for full inclusion in the American body politic.

More humble men and women had trepidations of their own about proposed legislation concerning emigration. In Valdosta, Georgia, B. J. Kirkland and Monroe Rice found their attempts to establish an emigration club hindered by white opposition, black fears, and "bad stories" about how members of Congress wanted to "send the Nigeroe to Affraca." Organizers elsewhere promoted their own club by reproducing the Butler Bill on handbills; Kirkland chose to dismiss discussion in Washington about proposed bills as "grumbling." A few states away in Arkansas, J. S. Daniels and his wife found "the great talk . . . [that] the Congrass will Colanize & send us home" so hard to believe that they decided not to wait for senators and congressmen to debate the matter. Soon after the bills were introduced, the Daniels family wrote to the American Colonization Society requesting "full infermation as to our getting over there."[56]

These Arkansans and Georgians were struggling folk seeking assistance to emigrate. Unlike the relatively privileged conventioneers in Chicago, they could not necessarily afford to joke about Congress providing Negrophobes with lunch and a train ticket. Finally, the prospective emigrants may have been worried that anyone emigrating to Liberia with federal funds would be sold into slavery, whereas the leaguers were more likely to suspect that proposed bills were ploys to diminish the number of black Republicans in the South.[57] Whatever their respective positions and perspectives, the issue soon became moot for both contingents: none of the bills passed.

The failure of these bills did little to squelch interest in Liberia as emigrationists kept canvassing. As they organized "independent orders" and "colonization clubs" across the Deep South, Middle South, West, and Northeast, organizers generally adopted one of three structures. A society could function primarily as an intellectual space for people who applied for passage through the American Colonization Society; a club was a loose configuration often formed by prospective emigrants who resided on adjacent plantations or in the same county; an order was typically an elaborate organization with by-laws, an executive council, and a treasury. In Rich, Mississippi, an "auxiliary colonization society" met on a regular basis, assessed dues, and was prepared to send a delegate to Washington, D.C., as a representative to the American Colonization Society, whereas members of the Cedar Grove Colonization Association of Arkansas were willing to sail on ACS vessels.[58] Just as organizational structure varied among black-run clubs between 1878 and the early 1890s, local groups had different approaches to grassroots mobilization as well: clubs held open mass meetings or sent delegates to general race conventions. Other activists operated on an underground basis because interested individuals feared retributive mob violence. Cornelius Smith was certain he could "organize an Association . . . of not less than 100 or 200" in 1883. Smith was just as certain that he would soon be dead if he did so out in the open.[59]

Regardless of structure or mode of operation, a club was more likely than not to have both female and male members—at times in sex-specific auxiliaries[60]—since prospective emigrant groups tended to include both nuclear and extended family units. Officers were typically men, but that hardly means women did not take on active leadership roles. Men dominated some organizations, such as the one in Rich, Mississippi, while in others, women were leaders that recruited friends, raised money, held meetings, and mobilized peers.

A women's organization in New Orleans had five hundred reported members that saved "one dollar at a time . . . for the purpose of emigrating" in 1878. Over a dozen years later, Mary Jackson was a leader among five hundred and fifty members belonging to an Atlanta society that was pooling resources in order to secure their own ship. Jackson was chosen by her club to correspond with the ACS; she wrote to ACS secretary William Coppinger on behalf of her own family as well. In the emigrationist hotbed of Morrilton, Arkansas, Ines Dargan kept her father's example of leadership alive by filling out or supplying ACS applications to those who sought her out after the Reverend James Dargan sailed to Liberia. At times, emigrationists even suggested that women's efforts surpassed those of their male counterparts. A proemigration letter to the *Voice of Missions* implied that men were laggards and goaded them by claiming, "if you are not going to do anything, say so, and we sisters will do it." In 1897, after emigration had weathered its share of trials, Samuel Chapman declared that he wanted "colored women to take a part" in his Liberian Emigration clubs "because the men have made a poor out at it ever since the emancipation down South."[61] In terms of gender and civic politics, women were able to exercise a fair amount of authority within emigrationist associations and operate on a level of parity that was slowly disappearing in other late-nineteenth-century black organizations containing male and female members. Post–Reconstruction era emigrationist organizations provided one arena in Afro-American public life that had potential for black women to be active as well as valued. Indeed, emigrationism may have been more open to women's active participation after Reconstruction than it had been during the antebellum era.[62]

For both women and men who took leading roles in black-run clubs, something as deceptively simple as deciding whether to publicize affiliation with the American Colonization Society was, in reality, a matter of strategy in grassroots organizing. In 1889, J. N. Walker of Denver decided it was best for his organization to downplay any connection whatsoever to colonization or, for that matter, emigration. "Owing to the very unpopular feeling . . . among my people I have changed the name of our concern from the African emigration society to that of the independent order of African sailors." Walker further admitted that he had "made it a secret order with strict laws in order to keep out the thoughtless and worthless element." A few years later, S. A. Billingslea believed the best way to establish legitimacy for a smallish club among local blacks in Providence, Rhode Island, was to announce that the ACS handled the club's finances. An official business relationship with the society would, Billingslea reasoned, show "[our] friends . . . that we mean what we are talking about." Whereas J. N. Walker felt the need to underplay contact with the society as early as 1889, Billingslea was willing to maintain a public relationship with the society *after* the ACS weathered numerous scandals and dwindling resources during the early 1890s. By the time Billingslea was organizing in 1894, shifty characters who did not represent the ACS were routinely swindling potential emigrants, and the society might well have looked comparatively trustworthy. Billingslea's and Walker's different approaches suggest that timing, local conditions, and community attitudes all influenced organizers' decisions about whether to invoke the ACS as a recruitment strategy, then.[63]

Whether publicly or not, local leaders were willing to correspond with the ACS in order to serve their constituencies more effectively: they inquired about organizational structure and financial matters, asked for information on procuring supplies and chartering ships, and requested up-to-date intelligence about Liberia. The society's "Information About Going to Liberia" was likely a cherished document. The slender pamphlet covered health concerns, described the country's flora and fauna in lush detail, and told emigrants what to take and how much land they would receive upon arrival. Not incidentally, it promoted the benefits of self-government as well. Once an organizer perused "Information," she or he probably felt considerably more competent when fielding a range of questions from emigration-minded women and men.[64]

Inquiries from local organizers were part of a much larger body of Afro-American correspondence to the American Colonization Society—missives claiming "thousands" wanted to emigrate poured into the society during the late 1880s and mid-1890s. Afro-Caribbean intellectual Edward Blyden toured the United States on behalf of the ACS in order to capitalize upon such emigrationist furor and help generate additional black interest in Liberia. The native of the Danish West Indies had lived in Liberia since the 1850s from where he produced *Liberia's Offering* (1862), in which he argued that any progress made by blacks in the United States had come "at the expense of . . . manhood." Blyden wrote passionately about Africa by invoking a rhetoric of Negro nationality; he "exhorted Afro-Americans to volunteer for service" in their ancestral continent. When he wended his way through the South in 1889, Blyden made no secret of his belief that antiemigrationists were likely to be "mulatto" as he implored African Americans — especially darker-skinned members of the race — to view themselves as " 'independent and distinct . . . [with] a mission to perform.' "[65] Indeed, Blyden was such an effective spokesperson for emigration to Liberia that an impostor in Arkansas was able to defraud emigration-minded men and women in Poplar Grove, Holly Grove, and other locales throughout the state.[66]

During this period a range of activity — fraudulent and otherwise — indicated the depth of Afro-American interest in emigration and migration; the United States and Congo National Emigration Company announced it would ferry people to Liberia; W. H. Ellis tried to promote colonization of Mexico; the settlement of Mound Bayou in Mississippi began a black-town movement that extended into the next century; a small but persistent minority of the race even called for the establishment of an all-black state in the West.[67] The concept of self-determination was sufficiently popular at the end of the century that it inspired emigrationism as well as other movements. While the push for Mexican colonization and the black-town movement clearly resulted from desires for black autonomy, emigration arguably attracted more people interested in self-determination. The idea of living in Africa was especially appealing because it offered an independent existence removed from the memories of American slavery and the realities of American racism. Liberia was a distinct black nation, not a vulnerable piece of land within the United States or a neighboring country. For those black women and men who cherished the concept known as "nationalization" Liberia offered Americans of African descent the surest, most honorable destiny.

Rock-bottom cotton prices fueled interest in Liberia as well. Most African Americans resided in rural areas at the end of the nineteenth century, and the majority engaged in agricultural work. When cotton prices hit unprecedented lows between the late 1880s and 1900, a number of small-scale farmers and sharecroppers were thrown into a state of turmoil which, in turn, fostered emigrationism. In 1889, William Fairly wrote to the ACS on behalf of people seeking relief from hardship brought on by economic downturn: "We have consulted often to ourselves and we know no other chance But to apply to you. We are in a condition By the Oppressors that we cant help one another. We do not appreciate going West[,] we rather go North.

times . . . here got so hard that we cant feed and clothes our people Rent are so high. . . . the way we are oppressed By our land owners. . . . we are not as well to do now as we were 20 years ago. . . . we ask you for assistance that we may get out from under our task master and Be a people."[68] Some people were simply sick of life as they knew it. One man in Arkansas was tired of being "Driven from one State to the other"; another Arkansan "really [did] not wish to be cornered up into the United States"; a few states away in Illinois, yet another Afro-American wanted to live where it was possible to have "eakwil rights and . . . [for our] children [to] stand as a free nation."[69]

Ollie Edwards of Columbus, Georgia, no longer wanted to depend upon capricious white employers who paid her whenever they saw fit. A laundress in her late thirties married to a day laborer ten years her senior, Edwards had five children, belonged to the Shady Grove Baptist Church, and was eager to join her sister in Liberia. The working mother applied for passage through the American Colonization Society in the summer of 1889 on behalf of her family. She then waited and hoped, scrimped and saved, prayed and planned, knowing she would "never . . . give the struggle [up] while life is in the body." Edwards wanted to touch African soil so badly, in fact, it pained her just to think about it.[70]

A woman who craved information about emigration, Edwards received copies of the *African Repository*, read the journals "through and through," and then shared them with at least three other families. Her generosity and fervor converted these families into prospective emigrants. In time, though, Edwards became anxious that her efforts would come to naught, since Coppinger still failed to send word of whether her family would be given passage after she had arranged for her sister and nephew in Liberia to contribute toward rations that the Edwards family would receive. Three months after telling Coppinger she was "tired of waiting," however, Ollie Edwards and her family were at last bound for Liberia; once underway, the washerwoman must have relished the fact that her initiative and persistence had finally paid off.[71]

Edwards was much like other black ACS correspondents in several respects. A woman who lived in an urban community, Edwards received emigration intelligence in much the same way that her rural counterparts did: through word of mouth, "Information About Going to Liberia," and the *African Repository* and other periodicals. The frequency of her letters is also representative: she sent several letters—written on everything from a writing tablet to blank ACS application forms—instead of a single inquiry.

And like other emigrants, Ollie Edwards sent intimate letters filled with her dreams as well as details from her daily life. Edwards's multiple letters also placed her in a class with people such as Emma Jones and James Dubose, who wrote to the society over a period of months, if not years.[72]

Something else about Edwards's letters is particularly revealing: she authored all of them, yet a few were produced by a different hand. Like many prospective emigrants with limited literacy skills, the mother of five may have written some of the letters herself and dictated others to her children or neighbors. As a woman born around 1852, Edwards probably gained literacy as an adult: Edwards could read some and write a little, yet at one point she had to "wal[k] all day" trying to find someone who could help her decipher the order for passage sent her by Coppinger; she had to seek out another person to assist her emigration process. If less than half of all African Americans were literate by 1890, it was not uncommon for women and men to rely upon neighbors, pastors, and relatives to read a document or write a letter. For prospective emigrants such as Ollie Edwards—or someone such as Carter Payne, whose wife Sophie wrote their letters to the ACS— the decision to emigrate often involved a network of relatives and neighbors, even for those who did not belong to a local club.[73]

The Edwardses were neither small-scale farmers nor sharecroppers like so many other emigrants, but they were among the ranks of the black working poor. Ollie and Jerry Edwards were, furthermore, people who no longer wanted to struggle for mere subsistence. Ollie was especially concerned about Jerry's getting older; her letters further suggest that she wanted better opportunities for her two daughters and three sons as they reveal that Ollie wanted to stop slaving over a washtub for other people. What is more difficult to say is whether the wife and husband wanted to emulate the patriarchal ideal promoted by the ACS; the society stressed that going to Liberia made one "a *man*" as it privileged groups of emigrants lead by men; lists of emigrants published by the ACS only noted men's occupations.[74] If Jerry found the society's patriarchal vision of African American families both enticing and appealing, Ollie took the lead in seeking information about emigration for the Edwards family.

Above and beyond the society's attempt to project a public image that a sole breadwinner—and a male breadwinner at that—led emigrant households, the ACS actively discouraged single women from emigrating. This policy was connected to the society's preference to allot land to families and single men, which emerged from anxiety concerning lone women and social dissolution. More specifically, officials apparently believed that lone women were likely to fall into a vicious cycle of dependency and vice once in Liberia.[75]

Even with the society's attempts to control who emigrated and how the public perceived those emigrants, a few single women were selected to be settlers. And, although the ACS did not publicly acknowledge as much, coupled female emigrants such as Ollie Edwards were laboring women who worked as farmers, cooks, domestics, seamstresses, milliners, and day laborers to earn indispensable income for their families. Emigration-minded women — single and married — were not only wage earners but some sought better employment and creative opportunities. Boston's Nellie Richardson, for example, decided to leave the United States during the early 1880s because she could not follow her chosen profession. Richardson was "an artist in Wax Work" forced to make a living by taking whatever work came her way.[76] Just as male emigrants sought a larger arena for their talents, female emigrants did as well.

Emigrants typically wanted to build strikingly different lives for their children. For example, over four years after the Edwards family bade farewell to Columbus, Georgia, David Green and J. W. Sessions left their homes in Washington County, Georgia, and traveled to Washington, D.C., seeking an appointment with the man who succeeded William Coppinger as ACS secretary, J. Ormond Wilson. When Wilson was unable to see the two men, Green and Sessions drafted a moving account of why the "250 or 300 familys" they represented wanted assistance to "get to our Fathersland":

> We should be able to build our houses, clair up our farms, & to do what is need to be done to make a settlement. The anxiety of our people shows that they are willing to undergo whatever trouble may confront them, in order to lay . . . the foundation of the future prosperity of their children. We as their parents feel it our duty to look to the future for our children. If there is any future in America for our children we cannot see it. . . . Our condition is but little better than it was when we were emancipated. . . . If you will carry us to Africa we will risk living after we get there.

If uncertainty was preferable to what these Georgians already knew, Liberia represented a chance to freely engage in agriculture, trade, mission work, and the professions.[77] Granted, their vision of Africa was idealized, yet such idealization coexisted with acute awareness that the price of emigrating might be life itself — perhaps the life of a cherished daughter or son.

A variety of other reasons beyond desires for their offspring induced women and men to consider emigration. Dr. Georgia Patton opted for short-term emigration because she wanted to "relieve . . . suffering and help build up Africa." S. W. McLean was imbued with a similar "missernary . . . spirit"; the time was ripe to go to Africa for McLean, who believed that too many whites were exploiting the continent's people, land, and resources.[78] Mob violence was a decisive factor as well. In one of many letters to the ACS, H. C. Cade relayed the story of white men who invaded his township in Arkansas, where they pistol-whipped and shot a man after setting the house where he sought refuge ablaze during the winter months of 1891. Approximately four months earlier, Cade's neighbor C. W. Wofford reported that white gangs reveled in the weekly activity of mobbing blacks on their way to church. Perhaps such mob violence also influenced other emigration-minded African Americans who felt that there was simply no place for them in the United States. Mary Evans and her husband James left Mississippi in 1891 for greener pastures in Oklahoma, but after only five months in Muldrow, Evans was ready to quit the United States for good. "If we ever . . . get passage we want it for 1892 for god sake dont put us off till 1893," Evans wearily relayed to Coppinger, "we have no home in Mississippi and we aint got no home in Indian T[erritory]."[79]

As the palpable sense of desperation in Evans's letter suggests, the people most likely to contemplate emigration had experienced hardships that primed them to believe that peonage, privation, and terrorism were the only things in store for African Americans as long as they remained stateside. Emigrationists were no hopeless lot of people, but they were less optimistic about their chances for mobility and equality in the United States than were the majority of aspiring race women and men. Not only had many prospective emigrants not benefited from the normal schools and colleges attended by their more fortunate sisters and brothers, prospective emigrants tended to be neither interracial intermediaries nor members of an intraracial elite. In fact, the women and men who wanted to set sail for Liberia often likened their daily existence to slavery. Emancipation had brought little lasting change to these people's lives: it failed to provide them greater educational, economic, social, political, and creative opportunities.

Some women and men who had enjoyed the fruits of freedom went to Liberia on either a permanent or temporary basis. Both Sherwood Capps and Georgia Patton were graduates of prestigious black colleges; Patton's peers considered her a leading race woman. Still, most elite people did not feel compelled to emigrate. Privileged Afro-Americans faced the threat of lynching and rape as racial discrimination loomed over their daily lives.

Nonetheless, these race women and men generally believed that civil rights would one day be extended to all Americans. Many were deeply invested in race institutions as well.

There were a few professional or prosperous African Americans besides Georgia Patton who were attracted to emigration. For example, Dr. Gemel Rutherford considered leaving behind his steady Memphis practice, and machinist Clement Irons not only left the United States, he also managed to parlay his prosperity in Charleston into success in Liberia. The majority of prosperous blacks — especially those that came up from nothing to acquire homes and build comfortable lives — were not about to gamble with their hard-won fortunes in like manner.[80] Indeed, for black women and men who had struggled long and hard to become "respectable" within their communities, the very idea of abandoning all they had attained seemed ill advised at best.

A person's situation and outlook, then, determined whether they responded favorably to emigration. Sexual matters motivated some tenant farmers and workers as well.[81] George Giles of Pittsburgh planned to lead others to Africa; he was also part of an interracial marriage, had faced his share of "dificulty," and wanted to reside in a land where a black man and white woman could live, unharrassed, "a[s] man and wife." When Giles inquired about his chances of leaving in November 1884, he received a terse reply from Coppinger that the ACS aided "colored people only." The secretary did not bother to tell Giles that there was a precedent regarding emigration and interracial couples: during the antebellum period at least two women with white husbands went to Liberia. As willing as the ACS was to assist the cause of black nationality, it was not inclined to help a black man and white woman escape an environment where their sexual relationship might very well result in death.[82]

Interracial sex presented decidedly different concerns for other emigrationists. In a plaintive petition entitled "A Colored Application to Git out of Egypt," residents of Pastoria, Arkansas, observed that the only land local whites were willing to allot a black person was "6 feet by 4 wide 4 ft. Deep[,] an[d] not that untel . . . Dead." Petitioners then described how widows of men killed for daring to vote were being forced at gunpoint to submit to white men. One frequent correspondent to the American Colonization Society, James Dubose, cut to the quick when he outlined why many men — and women — wanted to live in an all-black nation. Writing to ACS secretary William Coppinger in 1891, Dubose complained that black families could do little to prevent illicit sex between black girls and white men. Arguing that black men could not be real men as long as they remained in the South, Dubose was both direct and discreet when he bemoaned the fact that throughout the region far too many "whyte mans childern" were attending "collord school[s]." Why, he asked, should "the collord people . . . stay in the South[?] . . . Can we Raise our Doughters hear with no law to pretec them[?]"[83]

If James Dubose believed that miscegenation sullied black womanhood and insulted black manhood, the *Voice of Missions* assessed sexuality, gender, and racial reproduction in even more sensational fashion. In an 1894 article, an anonymous author maintained the "menace, danger, and degradation" endured by American blacks had such a negative "effect upon fecundity" that racial degeneration was already underway and would continue "until absolute dwarfishness [is] the result." Oddly entitled "A Nut for the Negro Philosophers to Crack," the article stopped short of claiming that emigration was the surest way to improve the quality of the Afro-American collective. However, the nameless author — probably founder and editor Bishop Henry McNeal Turner — implied that antiemigrationists hindered development of racial manhood. If the race wanted black women to bear offspring of "manly stamina," then it had better give serious consideration to how ongoing racial conflict prevented healthy reproduction of the black collective. If, moreover, women's fecundity was ever going to increase, an increase was most likely to occur in an all-black nation.[84]

The editorial decision to link emigration, sexuality, and extermination was shrewd: the notion that black Americans were not reproducing at an adequate rate was sufficiently popular during the late nineteenth century that its pointed analysis of fecundity reinforced the idea that black people needed to seize control of their own sexuality, that concubinage and rape resulted in racial degeneracy, that women needed to be monitored because their reproductive labor built the collective. Moreover, in the process of insinuating that emigration could rehabilitate Afro-American sexuality, the article underscored that black male sexuality was compromised as long as white men had access to black women's bodies.

In 1894, the year-old *Voice of Missions* reached members of the venerable African Methodist Episcopal Church and was edited by an AME luminary that happened to be the leading emigrationist of his day. The *Voice* was not nearly as established as its coreligionist rival, the *Christian Recorder*, but it was more than Turner's "personal propaganda sheet" — the *Voice* included antiemigrationist editorials, church intelligence, updates on missionary work, general race news, and articles on topical subjects like heredity and well-born children. The *Voice* vigorously connected emigration to racial destiny in a far more forceful fashion than did the *African Repository*. Turner's impassioned advocacy of black self-determination and willingness to upbraid opponents in print ensured a healthy circulation of thousands who either read the *Voice* or had someone read it to them.[85] In fact, the paper's staunch emigrationism generated so much excitement that the *Voice* office was flooded with requests from people who believed the paper could help them get to Liberia; for almost a year, an uncharacteristically flustered Turner cried, "let us alone" to these particular enthusiasts.[86]

The *Voice of Missions* incited its readers to action as Turner routinely contended that life in the United States offered only emasculation and eventual "extermination" to black people—subjugated people were effeminate, and effeminate people lacked the strength to survive. Even emigrationists with divergent viewpoints deployed arguments similar to Turner's. T. McCants Stewart, for one, was convinced that self-government in Liberia would grant respectable, hard-working "colored Americans . . . the full stature of manhood." Stewart used hereditarian concepts to assert that "fusion with the natives" was the best way for emigrants to create a progressive race in Liberia; he further believed emigrants that intermarried or married Americo-Liberians would no longer be able to produce within three generations. Stewart was more concerned with class than Turner—Stewart's support for emigration was conditional because he believed that only "educated brains" should go—yet both men concurred that manliness and sexual potency would take the race to new heights.[87]

Prospective emigrants harbored concerns related to their own sexuality, especially whenever mates would not or could not leave the country. F. Marion's wife was so determined not to emigrate that she was prepared to divorce him if he left Mississippi for Liberia. Peter Lawrence of Boston, Massachusetts, was unwilling to part with his wife when work prevented her from sailing in the spring of 1884. In contrast, when Carter Payne's wife, Sophie, unexpectedly refused to emigrate, Payne decided that he could emigrate without her since they had no children. Wisconsin resident and house painter John Carter was willing to separate from his wife, but only temporarily. The entire family was about to embark when prominent locals persuaded Carter that any man worth his salt would precede his household, establish himself in the new country, and then send for family members. When Coppinger sent Carter a telegram in November 1883 informing him that the society did not send men ahead of their families, Carter was appalled—he demanded the return of his passage money and declared he would find a way to Liberia himself. As it turns out, between Marion, Lawrence, Payne, and Carter, the only one to make it across the Atlantic on an ACS ship was John Carter, who departed the United States in late 1890 on the same ship with Ollie Edwards and her family.[88] The remaining members of the Carter household remained in Wisconsin, perhaps never to leave.[89]

Plans to emigrate were often scrapped altogether when husbands, wives, and children refused to depart from home—or when resources simply were not available for emigration. When in-laws, cousins, aunts, uncles, and friends decided not to go, they withheld financial contributions and strained the resources of a party before it even embarked. Among the leading reasons that people changed their minds were reports from regretful emigrants. Unhappy emigrants who could not negotiate a return to the United States were likely to have relatives stateside—relatives who could provide compelling counternarratives to proemigrationist arguments.[90] Returnees, moreover, frequently claimed that nothing but horrific maladies and fantastic privation awaited anyone going to Liberia.

The story of Anna Logan provides a compelling case in point. The seamstress was ready to set sail for Liberia in 1891 with her teenaged daughters Julia and Louella. Letters that Logan sent to Coppinger from Atlanta conveyed considerable excitement about beginning anew in "the land of [the] forefathers." Unlike many prospective emigrants, Logan was able to contribute at least fifty dollars toward her family's passage, and she could even pay their way to New York. The Logans were hardly wealthy, but they were "respectable," churchgoing people: Anna made a good living with her own sewing machine; Julia earned a regular salary teaching and aspired to become a missionary in Africa; Louella attended school. Anna Logan was driven by zeal for Africa rather than poverty—she was so caught up in emigrationism that she encouraged acquaintance W. W. Watkins to request passage through the ACS and then influenced two single men, two single women, and two couples to do the same.[91]

As she was selling off household items in order to pay for her family's passage, however, Logan began to hear a variety of disturbing rumors. One of the most troublesome things she heard was that white crew members on ACS ships accosted "unprotected" black women—the very possibility of being sexually assaulted en route to Liberia was incredibly distressing for a single mother with two girls. Above and beyond the uncertainties of emigration, this particular rumor severely shook Logan's resolve to leave Georgia. Coppinger tried to assure Logan that such tales were "base and wicked untruth[s]"; still, the Logans were further vexed by claims made by former emigrant Green B. Parks, who went to Liberia in May 1891 with his wife Nancy and their eight children. He returned to Atlanta within five months and started giving lectures in which he maintained that Americo-Liberians enslaved indigenous people, fresh food was a rare commodity, and starving emigrants were desperate to return to the States. These tales of starvation, enslavement, regret, and randy ACS personnel were ultimately too much for the Logans to bear. Despite her strong conviction that blacks and whites could not coexist in the same nation, Anna decided against emigration because her daughters had "heard so much they [were] dissatisfied to leave America." Anna Logan nevertheless held onto her faith that the race would one day thrive in Liberia; as far as she was concerned, it was a crying shame Parks had expended so much energy only to give Africa "a black eye." [92]

Parks's return in late 1891 was only part of a tumultuous year for emigrationism in Atlanta. A grassroots organizer affiliated with the United States and Congo National Emigration Company named Thomas Peak had canvassed Georgia the year before and created a frenzy over emigration. The Congo Company was an independent, profit-seeking enterprise that had stockholders and sold tickets to those interested in emigration. Georgia was particularly fertile ground for emigrationism—the state had contributed a large share of emigrants to the historic *Azor* expedition, and Bishop Turner's philosophies were enormously popular there—when Reverend Peak set about his business in the state, proselytizing and spinning speeches about the glories of Africa. Peak's zeal led him, it seems, to inform his followers that they would be able to emigrate by the end of the year. [93]

There would be no ship for the eager followers. Peak stalled people until January when they then started to pour into Atlanta by road and by rail. Within a week, over a thousand would-be emigrants had arrived in the city; this "African Band" waited and waited as Congo Company officials tried without success to procure a ship. Peak and others went to Washington to meet with representatives of shipping firms; approximately fifteen hundred dollars exchanged hands several times, Peak and another man were indicted, and the company realized that it would have to issue refunds. Both the mainstream and race press portrayed the whole affair as little more than a scam, and the company soon dissolved. As for hopeful members of the African Band stranded in Atlanta, they would have to find their own way to Liberia—or back home. [94]

Anna Logan began corresponding with the ACS a mere two months after the "African Band" debacle. Whereas she did not mention the Congo Company in her letters, Logan likely knew about Peak, his activities, and his followers' unproductive layover in Atlanta. What this suggests is that Logan was not easily dissuaded from emigrating and believed that she could trust the ACS in the midst of scandal. And, throughout Georgia, interest in emigration remained sufficiently high in the wake of the Congo Company debacle that one-time emigrant and former Congo Company agent Benjamin Gaston was able to resurrect the defunct organization as the Liberian Emigration Company. The new organization was somewhat shady and the ever-vocal Green Parks proclaimed Gaston a charlatan. Benjamin Gaston somehow managed, however, to dispatch two small companies by 1894.[95]

By the mid-1890s, a number of women and men besides the Logan family were becoming "dissatisfied" with emigration. In fact, the very fervor that encouraged emigration resulted in a proliferation of swindles that exacted a toll on emigrationism as a popular movement. "Liberia fever" was so widespread that scam artists and impostors reaped sizable profits by collecting and then absconding with fare money scraped together by hope-filled women and men. At least six major scandals—involving everything from disgruntled returnees, impostors, confidence rings, stranded bands of starving emigrants, and murder—occurred between 1878 and 1900.[96] In 1894, for example, a reported one thousand women, men, and children in Laurens County, Georgia, longed to emigrate, but activist Reverend D. E. Brown hesitated to organize them. Brown bemoaned, "[we have] been Deceived so much by our own color that we some what Dread to start"; for Brown, the stakes were particularly high as there had been "a man shot to Death" locally who claimed to be an emigration agent working with Bishop Turner. Three years later, AME bishop Wesley Gaines claimed that there were at least two factors behind dwindling interest in emigration: the relative lack of successful missions once the ACS ceased sending emigrants and the proliferation of swindles. "[Our people] have been fleeced time and again by so-called emigration agents, tramps, and frauds," Gaines ruefully noted, "[and have therefore] made up their minds to work out . . . their destiny in the South and Southwest."[97]

In short, scandals and the sheer lack of capital effectively ended plans for large-scale emigration by the late 1890s. All the same, emigrationist sentiment did not completely wither and die: after 1900, people such as Georgia Anderson continued to submit petitions to Congress; George W. Washington and Alfred Sam both attempted, in 1907 and 1913 respectively, to trump up interest in emigrating to Liberia among Afro-Oklahomans.[98] The working-poor and aspiring people who believed that it was necessary for African Americans to take some form of action in order to secure the collective destiny of the race began looking for solutions other than emigrationism after the late 1890s. And, as these women and men began to shift their focus, some would begin to share certain preoccupations of the race's elite.

When Henry McNeal Turner staged a major convention on the "'future of the race in America'" during late November 1893, the Indianapolis *Freeman* asked over three dozen elites for their views on emigration and published the results as its "Thanksgiving Symposium." Many of the *Freeman*'s respondents were clergy, the overwhelming majority were men, and most were less than enthusiastic about the idea. J. W. Carr opposed emigration because Afro-Americans were nothing less than "legitimate citizens" of the United States. J. W. Hood thought it made more sense for Africans to traverse the Atlantic. T. McCants Stewart wanted Turner's conventioneers to initiate trade with Africa, while Booker Washington dismissed the very prospect of emigration as "nonsense." Other respondents spoke explicitly to the matter of class, including Reverend T. W. Henderson, who favored only the best of the race emigrating to Africa as opposed to "the poor or ignorant." The lone woman in the symposium, Ida Wells, suggested that the convention consider "judicious emigration from lynch-infested districts." In so doing, Wells stood out among prominent African Americans in her willingness to link oppression, terrorism, and the desire to leave the United States.[99]

Indeed, Wells and those leading activists who supported emigration stood out among their peers, since the majority of prominent race thinkers had staunchly opposed emigration since the 1870s. For example, in 1878, Wilberforce University professor W. S. Scarborough believed that leaving the United States was nothing less than "suicidal." Another academic, W. H. Crogman, wrote to the ACS in 1883 and requested literature on Liberia; a year later, he concluded in his *Talks for the Times* that emigration "hindered" both the home life and education of the masses.[100] One exasperated rank-and-file race man wondered, "How long will the leaders of our race discourage race movement? . . . It is better to die in the dark continent of Africa than to [remain] in the South."[101]

Some *Freeman* readers were probably interested in the idea of an all-black nation, and many probably abhorred the rapid European partitioning of Africa. All the same, an appreciable number of club women and professional men were not likely to consider living in Africa themselves; these representative race women and men often thought of Africa primarily in terms of Christianizing the continent. Black Democrats—a minority within a minority—tended to eschew emigration as well. In contrast, emigration-minded folk were so weary of the exploitation and oppression of their daily lives that the idea of living in Liberia was attractive indeed.

In addition to class, economic hardship was a major informant of emigrationism in more ways than one. Prospective emigrants were aspiring women and men in search of better fortunes for themselves and their children; before contemplating emigration to Liberia, many had already moved from state to state attempting to forge a better life. Furthermore, emigration fever was highest in areas struck especially hard by economic downturns: when cotton prices dropped, when rental prices increased dramatically, when tenant farmers were evicted, the American Colonization Society received an especially voluminous amount of mail. Democratic overthrow of Republican Reconstruction governments in the South, moreover, had no small impact on emigrationism; terrorism—especially mob violence, rape, and lynching—created more than its share of prospective emigrants. Yet, the influence of successive depressions during the 1870s, 1880s, and 1890s cannot be underestimated given the overall influence of economic factors in global migration patterns.[102]

Finally, economic considerations also help explain why so many black people turned to the American Colonization Society in the first place. In letter after letter, black women and men informed the society that their primary reason for initiating contact was a deep desire to go to Liberia—these were people who scraped and stretched to make a living, people who simply could not raise money for passage on their own. Letters to the ACS from Afro-Americans frequently expressed gratitude, and many reveal a certain sense of fraternity as well. Still, these same women and men made it clear that what they really wanted from the ACS was financial support. In other words, the individuals and independent societies who corresponded with the ACS did so in order to fulfill their own needs; they did so in order to effect real change in their lives. As people who lived under what was often unrelenting persecution, exploitation, and terrorism, dealing with an institution such as the American Colonization Society was a minor concession for the black women, men, and children who desperately wanted to "inhabit a free and independent country" across the Atlantic.[103]

Whether they dreamt about emigrating or actually embarked on a ship, many prospective emigrants might not have interrogated the ways in which Liberia was a colonizing, imperialist venture itself. In the years leading up to and following the turn of the century, however, imperialism became a far more prominent issue for them as well as for other Afro-Americans. The matter of empire placed the question of racial destiny—specifically the matter of where race could work out its future as a collective—in new light. The European partitioning of Africa certainly affected how African Americans discussed race and place, yet it would be U.S. participation in wars for empire that had a pronounced impact on Afro-American assessments of their collective destiny. Imperial wars and expansionist visions, moreover, cast racial destiny in resolutely gendered terms—terms that would shift and transform as the nineteenth century closed and the twentieth opened.

Take up the White Man's Burden —
Send forth the best ye breed —
Go bind your sons to exile
To serve your captives' need. . . .
Comes now, to search your manhood
Through all the thankless years,
Cold-edged with dear-brought wisdom,
The judgment of your peers!
—Rudyard Kipling, "The White
Man's Burden" (1899)

Take up the Black Man's burden —
"Send forth the best ye breed,"
To judge with righteous judgment
The Black Man's work and need. . . .
Let the glory of your people
Be the making of great men,
The lifting of the lowly
To noble thought and aim . . .
—J. Dallas Bowser, "Take Up the
Black Man's Burden" (1899)

2

THE BLACK MAN'S BURDEN
IMPERIALISM AND RACIAL
MANHOOD

In addition to the migratory impulses of
black Americans who sought relief from conditions in
the U.S. South, another contemporary phenomenon
proved just as powerful in exposing the relationship
between race, territory, and oppression: the push for
empire. Imperialism loomed large for African Americans during the last twenty years of the nineteenth century for at least two reasons. American expansionism,
to begin, both indirectly and directly involved black
women and men in efforts that exacerbated or resulted
in the subjugation of Native Americans, Hawaiians,
Cubans, and Filipinos. Even further, European encroachment in Africa threatened the fragile stability
of Liberia and challenged the sense that Africans and
descendants of Africans could always lay claim to a
sovereign haven all their own. Gambits for empire,
then, contributed to a sense that people of color —
whether in Africa, the United States, or elsewhere —
were at risk of losing literal contests where only the
"fittest" would survive. Not only did imperialism fuel
discussions on the relative status of races and nations,

European colonization of Africa fed African American anxieties about the future of that continent in particular.

In 1899, about fifteen years after the Conference of Berlin accelerated the partitioning of Africa, forty-year-old black American Henry Blanton Parks fervently believed that the fate of Africa would be determined during the twentieth century. Parks struggled long and hard as a young man to secure an education in Georgia and rise in the ranks of the AME Church; he earned a reputation for having an expansive outlook in the process. By the time that he became secretary of home and foreign missions, Reverend Parks not only located Christian redemption of Africa within the promise of a new century, he authored a book to convince other African Americans that it was their duty to conquer the continent for God, for Africans, and for themselves. In *Africa: The Problem of the New Century*, Parks contended that if the AME Church failed to secure a righteous "destiny . . . [for] the junior races of the world [and] . . . historic Africa," the scramble for Africa would blight the continent with liquor, vice, and genocide. Africa's destiny was a signal issue for Parks, but so was the question of imperialism.[1]

Parks was hardly alone when he worried about the "native simplicity" of Africans being corrupted by Europeans — other African American women and men pondered the ramifications of imperialism in Africa before Parks was even elected secretary of missions.[2] Some shared racist assumptions about "darkest Africa" commonly found in popular travelogues; others felt that European forays into Africa would enlighten the continent.[3] Prominent newspaper editor T. Thomas Fortune, for one, railed against British, French, German, and Belgian encroachment during the 1880s. By the 1895 Congress on Africa, however, he projected that European imperialism would, in time, have a beneficial outcome. Fortune conceded that while "laying the foundation of empires" occurred at the expense of "savage tribes," the "intermingling of so many race elements must work for national and spiritual and material strength in Africa."[4] In 1892, Fortune's one-time colleague Ida Wells expressed tempered optimism as she uneasily acknowledged the European foothold in Africa. Wells nevertheless held fast to a belief that black Americans could prosper there since the continent had not been completely overrun by "the rapacious and ubiquitous Anglo-Saxon." S. H. Johnson was more pessimistic than either Fortune or Wells. The same year Wells published her opinions in the *A.M.E. Church Review*, Johnson used the columns of a prominent race paper to maintain that European ascendancy in Africa ominously signaled that whites would soon subjugate blacks across the continent. Whether these journalists or other black Ameri-

Pressroom of the Richmond Planet, *ca. 1899. Race periodicals not only facilitated and circulated debates about imperialism among African Americans; prominent newspapers such as the* Planet *also attempted to forge a collective sensibility on a range of international and domestic issues. Courtesy of the Library of Congress, Prints and Photographs Division, LC-USZ62-99055.*

cans believed Europeans would eventually succeed in wrenching all rights and land from Africans, Reverend Parks had a job to do. He needed to convince African Americans that Africa was theirs to save.[5]

Henry Parks was able to do so by skillfully manipulating the language of empire. He proudly informed his black American readers that "the A.M.E. Church [is] confronted with responsibilities as . . . broad as the new American policy of empire. . . . [It] stands on the threshold of a policy of expansion. . . . Africa—the second largest continent in the world—is the new colonial possession of the Missionary Department of the A.M.E. Church." Enlightening Africans with Christianity and progress was not "the white man's burden," Parks continued. Rather, race pride alone should convince blacks in the United States that if spreading civilization involved bearing burdens, people of color should make sure that imperialism was benevolent.[6]

Christian zeal clearly blinded Parks to the possibility that religious imperialism might be anything but benevolent in the eyes of prospective converts, but why was he so eager for black Americans to build their own empire in Africa? Why were the pages of *Africa: The Problem of the New Century* peppered with militaristic images of "warlike conquerors" and a "marching army" of civilization? And why, when soliciting donations, did Parks liken the financial needs of his "missionary campaign" to funding a war? Parks did so because he was a man of his era: he accepted contemporary notions that empire building required militaristic demonstrations of prowess. Thus, when Parks wrote that the "conquest of the cross" was far more potent than "conquest by war," he could actively suggest that the real men in Africa were not European soldiers or colonists, but black missionaries who would save the day for Africans and the race as a whole.[7]

Like many African American texts written between 1890 and 1910, *Africa: The Problem of the New Century* made both subtle and blatant claims about imperialism, race, and manhood. Placed within its historical context, Parks's plea for Africa assumes significance for other reasons as well. First of all, it was produced during an era when racial oppression in the United States was at once extreme and common. Negotiating their lives around the realities of disfranchisement and low status, existing in a country where mob violence was a palpable threat, few black American men fully exercised the prerogatives of manhood at the turn of the century. Parks could therefore appeal to black men by arguing that going to Africa was a decisive opportunity for them to create and belong to "a better manhood."[8] Such an appeal was most likely to resonate with men like Parks—ambitious strugglers within a cohort of aspiring-class African Americans whose status was anything but secure.

Secondly, Parks's book appeared when social Darwinism was tremendously popular in the United States.[9] Social Darwinism complimented gendered notions of conquest implicit in imperialism as it provided a rationale for subjugating people of color. By ranking racial "types" on a hierarchical scale according to fitness, character, and culture, social Darwinism promoted notions that each race had its own domain or place. Notions about race were varied, imprecise, overlapping, and even antonymous, yet darker peoples were generally deemed backward, irrational, inept.[10] "Colored" races were less fit for civilization because they were less manly; they were less manly because they were not white.[11] And, since science, technological innovation, and industry were largely considered the provenance of white men in Western Europe and North America, people of African descent— along with Native Americans, Pacific Islanders, and a host of tawny peoples —were often considered incapable of progress and self-determination. If, by logic of mainstream Western thought, science, technology, industry, and

[THE BLACK MAN'S BURDEN]

empire were all arenas in which "male attainments and male potential . . . [could be] measured," then men of African descent were found wanting.[12]

The fact that social Darwinism, science, and technology were at the core of imperialism was anything but lost on Henry Parks; thus, *Africa: The Problem of a New Century* contained its share of social Darwinist and technological assumptions about progress and prowess. Parks praised rail construction that enabled Africa to be "penetrated" and he proudly noted the AME's establishment of an "Industrial College" on the continent.[13] More significantly, Parks categorized Africans and American blacks as two *distinct* races: blacks in the United States were supposedly more evolved due to constant contact with Anglo-Americans and the acquisition of modern tools of progress. In the process of outlining how the trappings of civilization enabled blacks in the United States to inch further up the evolutionary ladder, the minister also subverted a critical tenet of social Darwinism by presenting Africans as inherently manly. Parks did not go as far as AME bishop Henry McNeal Turner, a fiery orator and leading advocate of emigration to Liberia, who claimed that West Africans were *manlier* than their counterparts across the Atlantic. For his part, Parks insinuated that by working in tandem with Africans to "civilize" the continent, black Americans would bolster their own racial manhood.[14] Henry Parks was influenced by social Darwinism and attendant racialized theories about acquisition of technology, then, but he warped them just enough to suit his own concepts of race, civilization, and manliness.

Finally, when *Africa: The Problem of the New Century* appeared in 1899, there was an ongoing, heated debate among African Americans over the implications of the Spanish-American and Philippine-American Wars. Whereas some African Americans were staunch anti-imperialists who believed any form of imperialism had dire consequences for people of color, many others welcomed U.S. wars for empire. They did so, in part, because imperialism involved attributes closely associated with masculinity: if black men bravely served in American war efforts, for example, they might succeed in refuting long-standing charges that manliness was forever beyond their grasp. While Henry Parks was trying to enlist soldiers for God with the promise that the AME's work was akin to "the new American policy of empire," U.S. expansion presented its own opportunities.

If fin de siècle Afro-American discourse was strategically gendered, that gendering frequently involved interconnected concepts of race and manhood. The connection between U.S. imperialism and imperialism in Africa within this discourse is particularly important. U.S. imperialism initially seemed to afford black men a rare chance to prove themselves better men than their white contemporaries. After these hopes proved illusory, Africa appeared to be one of the few fields where black Americans felt they could flex muscle, build nations, and demonstrate virility by fending off white-skinned intruders. In other words, whereas U.S. imperialism potentially bolstered masculinity within the race, the prospect of a black American reclamation of Africa proved just as, if not more, promising.

Significantly, ambitious men within the aspiring and elite classes produced the majority of extant Afro-American commentary on race and empire. These men were most likely to view imperialism as an opportunity to improve their station and fortify black manhood: like Henry Parks, many aspiring and elite men overcame formidable obstacles to achieve and acquire. Given steady disfranchisement, escalating racial violence, and the unstable economy at the century's end, aspiring and elite men were likely to feel that their hard-won gains were slipping away; ironically, such men usually offered little explicit commentary about class when commenting on imperialism. Even aspiring and elite men hostile to expansionism relied upon a trope of manhood constructed around race, as did men who believed class mobility could be best achieved outside U.S. borders. Class informed rather than defined Afro-American discourse on imperialism in that anxieties over class were articulated through racialized language about manhood. If there was relative silence concerning class, there were other important silences as well. Since the push for empire was primarily gendered as a struggle over manhood, it is not surprising that aspiring and elite black women, while not altogether silent on imperialism, focused their energies on moral rehabilitation, the sexual politics of respectability, club work, and antilynching activism during this period.[15] Race women carved out prominent roles in reform work as black men dominated Afro-American discourses on empire.[16]

At no time between 1890 and 1910 were all U.S. blacks of one mind about imperialism, but by 1910 greater numbers of African Americans were against both U.S. imperialism and European imperialism in Africa. However, at times even anti-imperialist blacks all but suggested that some form of civilizing conquest was necessary if Africa ever hoped to keep apace with Europe, North America, and Asia in the march of progress. Existing literature has certainly accounted for the complex relationship between African Americans and imperialism; indeed, historians have even commented on the ambivalence of black soldiers who participated in wars for empire.[17] Still, interpreting how African Americans responded to imperialism and understanding what came to be known as the "black man's burden" during the

56

late nineteenth and early twentieth centuries requires scrutiny and analysis of racialized ideas about manhood and sexuality.

In the rapidly industrializing and newly reconstructed United States, gender informed how black Americans organized households, established institutions, and negotiated work arrangements. After Reconstruction, gender assumed special significance for African Americans due to persistent arguments that blacks were "feminine" compared to "masculine" Anglo-Saxons, that slavery left black men emasculated and made black women into viragos.[18] The abolition of slavery hardly meant that concerns surrounding the ways in which African Americans embodied womanhood and manhood ceased to be relevant. After emancipation, black women were frequently derided in popular discourse as aggressive, immoral, and slovenly, while black men were either demonized as oversexed brutes that ravished white women or satirized as servile—and impotent—"uncles." Most black Americans resisted such racist characterizations: they responded to attacks on their collective character by emphasizing respectable femininity in women and uncompromised manliness in men and the race as a whole.

As much as African Americans were concerned about the impact stereotypes and racial oppression had on black women, the possibility that the race was losing its "manhood stamina" within the confines of the United States was a specific anxiety.[19] Exclusionary practices left many black men chronically underemployed during the 1890s while black civil rights were tenuous and under attack. Moreover, attempts by black men to seize prerogatives of manhood—particularly the franchise—often resulted in retributive mob violence at the hands of white men; conflagrations in Wilmington, North Carolina (1898), and Atlanta, Georgia (1906), were both sparked by conflicts between black and white men over political rights. White vigilantism exacted certain and brutal tolls on black women and children, and black women were indeed lynched, but lynching and mob violence were perceived as having the greatest impact on black masculinity and black male bodies.[20] As an angry Henry Turner put it, such oppression was "so repugnant to the instincts of respected manhood" that black Americans were at risk of either "transmit[ting] . . . servility to their posterity" or, even worse, "*unracing* themselves."[21]

To further compound matters, black men's sexuality was relatively circumscribed in comparison to white men, who routinely enjoyed both consensual and coerced sexual intercourse with women of color. As much as it is somewhat of an anemic historiographical truism that black men bitterly resented not being able to protect "their women," black men were certainly incensed by the racialized, sexual double standard that prevailed in most regions of the United States. AME bishop Wesley Gaines gave voice to collective frustrations when he commented that "the white man who does not hesitate to use violence toward a colored man for illicit intercourse with a white women, even with consent, does not scruple to live in adultery with a colored woman."[22] For Afro-American men in the late nineteenth century, then, asserting a claim to "manliness" was a potent means of countering restrictions in their daily lives.

A range of African American discourse was therefore gendered and sexualized during the period of American expansionism; an overwhelming amount of it emphasized the "manhood" of the race. Of course, "manliness" and "manhood" were frequently used by black and white Americans as generic terms that could include women.[23] But again, due to the particularly low status of black American men, Afro-American emphasis on manhood and masculinity was often a strategy to confer dignity and power upon men who were, in reality, accorded little respect or dominion.[24] Black commentary on racial oppression in the U.S. South reflects this strategy: in 1890, for example, an article by an obscure author named Lucy Norman insisted that mob violence could never diminish black manhood. In contrast, the much better known Bishop Turner was so outraged over conditions in the South, he observed with no small amount of disgust that *there is no manhood future in the United States for the Negro. . . .* He can never be a *man*— full, symmetrical and undwarfed." Black men could not be masculine men, Turner contended, until they went to a country where their manhood was respected.[25]

For many black men and women that country was Liberia. Whereas emancipated slaves and free blacks emigrated to Liberia throughout the nineteenth century, it was not until the 1890s that scores of working-poor and aspiring-class black Americans viewed removal to Liberia as a means of gaining access to opportunities and alleviating their immiseration.[26] As one Arkansan noted in 1891, "The people in my community are up in arms for that Great Republic. I think by this spring . . . I will be able to Get 50 or 60 familys ready. . . . I am using my energy to delive[r] my people from under the [pressure] in . . . Ark[ansas]. We are tyard of Race Problem[s] and Mob Rule and we believe that there are peace . . . and pros[p]erity in another section of the world."[27] Black women and men across the United States formed their own "exodus associations" and "independent orders," while many others turned to the American Colonization Society, an agency with strong—if problematic—ties to Liberia. Letters claiming "thousands" wanted to emigrate poured into the society. Some people chose to maximize their chances of leaving the United States by participating in local movements *and* requesting aid from the American Colonization Society. Mary Jackson of Atlanta, Georgia, was struggling to make ends meet when she joined a local emigration club and pooled her resources with others. Jackson wrote to ACS secretary William Coppinger to request assistance and to tell him about her diligence in saving whatever money she could in order to book passage and head for Liberia, "the place for the best advantage of the Negro."[28]

Liberia was especially attractive to aspiring-class men as an "open door" to opportunity. Lewis Lee looked forward to building a "Negro nation" where he, as a thirty-four-year-old farmer, could freely "exercise . . . privilege." John Lewis—a molder forced to work as a waiter due to discriminatory practices in the skilled trades—felt that since whites would "not let the Negroe advance beyond a prescribed limit," he had nothing to lose by emigrating. Twenty-six-year-old R. A. Wright was also unable to follow his chosen profession. A lawyer by training, Wright taught in a school and longed to live where both his ambition and manhood would go unrestrained. "There are several reasons why I desire to go," Wright confessed, "chiefly among them [is] I desire to go where a man of color can, if he will, be a man in the true sense of the word . . . where [I] may rise to the same degree of . . . perfect manhood as our white brethren have . . . in this country and elsewhere." Lee, Lewis, and Wright associated masculine prerogative with prosperity, integrity, and black uplift; each man was frustrated in his separate quest for mobility, yet none expressed his frustration in terms of class. Letters sent to the ACS did, however, express anxieties over the sexual proclivities of white men who had a taste for black women. A group of prospective emigrants in Arkansas wrote that two factors shaped their desire to leave the United States: their inability to vote and the frequent murders of black men whose wives were then seized, terrorized, and assaulted by white mobs. Along similar lines, James Dubose of Orchard Knob, Tennessee, ruefully observed that it was impossible "to be a man" in any Southern state.[29]

Emigration was rather controversial nonetheless. In contrast to working-poor and aspiring folk who found emigration appealing, elite or otherwise privileged black Americans were more likely to warn against viewing Africa —and especially Liberia—as a refuge or proving ground. Charles Taylor, a vocal black Democrat who served as the U.S. consul-general to Liberia during the Cleveland Administration, acidly referred to Liberia as "an independent farce" where Americo-Liberians "convert[ed] nobody . . . and g[o]t rich off of the natives." Taylor even went so far as to imply that in Liberia masculine power was routinely outstripped by feminine force. Taylor stopped short of claiming men became eunuchs in Liberia, but he nonetheless suggested that women were the manly ones within the Americo-Liberian populace.[30] Like Charles Taylor, Amanda Berry Devine Smith also spent time in Liberia, but she was involved in mission as opposed to diplomatic work. Initially, the skeptical evangelist believed that Afro-American emigration to Liberia could be successful only as long as the educated and the propertied crossed the Atlantic. After witnessing successive waves of the southern poor arrive in Liberia, however, Smith wound up dismissing emigration as "an enterprise . . . detrimental in every possible way to our people."[31]

Levi Coppin, the prominent editor of the *A.M.E. Church Review* who later served as a bishop in South Africa, attacked emigration on a different level: "Those who favor the scheme of emigration . . . ask significantly if we would rather stay here and be menials than go back to Africa and be men. Well . . . the argument is misleading. . . . When the American Negro . . . goes to Africa in search of an asylum, it will be well for him to remember that the man from whom he flees has gone on before . . . and planted himself." According to Coppin, leaving the United States was futile given the possibility that Europeans in Africa would assume onerous, oppressive roles. If black men really wanted to showcase their manly resolve and virile constitutions, they should remain in the United States to "secure . . . the manhood and independence that we seek."[32] Negative press was effective in deterring emigration, and news about Europeans in Africa shook the resolve of a few hopeful emigrants, including one man who informed the American Colonization Society that the presence of Europeans in Africa might well turn him against emigration.[33] Prospective emigrants might have been disinclined to compete with Europeans, yet Americo-Liberians contended that anyone could succeed in Liberia as long as they possessed "self-dependence and . . . manhood." In 1894, one recent transplant, *Christian Recorder* correspondent A. L. Ridgel, proudly reported that the "*master* continent" of Africa held wonderful "prospect[s], especially for the Afro-American."[34]

Ironically, European activity on the continent led Afro-Americans to underscore ways in which imperialism allowed men of African descent to demonstrate masculine prowess. AME bishop and former Ohio legislator Benjamin Arnett, for one, believed African Americans and Africans could join forces in redeeming Africa by defending the continent in a manly fashion.[35] John H. Smyth, a Howard University–trained lawyer who completed a long, tumultuous stint in Liberia as consul general during the 1870s and 1880s, contended that black manhood would always prove more formidable than European power. Smyth's speech at the Congress on Africa in 1895 expressed unwavering faith: "[Whereas] European contact has brought . . . political disintegration, social anarchy, moral and physical debasement . . . Africans cannot be influenced by aliens, who, however Christian, seek to subvert their manhood. With the African at home, service to God . . . will not be yielded if manhood be the sacrifice."[36] Similarly, following the defeat of Italian forces in Ethiopia in 1896,[37] Sarah Dudley Pettey—who served as general secretary of the AME Zion's Woman's Home and Foreign Missionary Society—declared the Ethiopians' victory as nothing less than "the uprising of an oppressed race daring to assert manhood." Although Pettey's tone was clearly celebratory when she rhapsodized that such masculine prowess would restore the race's "ancient glory," neither she, Arnett, nor Smyth argued at length that African or African American men were superior to white men.[38] Rather, during the mid-1890s, the majority of African American observations about race, manhood, and imperialism in Africa were often basic affirmations that Africans and African Americans possessed manliness.

That would change by the end of the decade as the United States became involved in far-flung political crises in Hawaii, Venezuela, Puerto Rico, Wake Island, Guam, and Samoa between 1893 and 1900. It was the 1898 entry of the United States in the War for Cuban Independence—commonly referred to as the Spanish-American War—that forged salient connections between race, manhood, and empire for African Americans. Just as the feats of black Union soldiers made the Civil War a "watershed for black manhood," black men's exploits in Cuba transformed 1898 into a similarly definitive moment.[39] As one race paper put it, if black men heartily joined the American show of force in Cuba, they would, at last, be "treated as men among men." The Washington *Colored American* even declared the Spanish-American War an arena where "the Negro's manhood [would be] placed directly in evidence" alongside white soldiers. Black participation was controversial among African Americans, and black journalists were no exception: one editor argued that any black man who served a racist nation in a racially segregated army sorely needed "a few grains of self-respect."[40]

With the realities of segregation and terrorism on the home front, U.S. imperialism was an uneasy vehicle for black manhood. A speech delivered by club woman Nannie Helen Burroughs in mid-1898 cogently expressed the predicament facing black men—whether they should fight for a country that routinely denied their humanity. Although black manliness was systematically trampled upon by lynching and disfranchisement in the United States, Burroughs argued that no African American man should shrink from duty only to "sulk in his tent" at home. To "sulk," she implied, was to make the race vulnerable to further assault.[41] African Americans were acutely aware of their liminal status in the United States, then, but the war with Spain still became a tremendous source of race pride. Black soldiers even found their experiences in Cuba so exhilarating they wrote home that Spanish combatants found them to be more ferocious than white enlistees. In late July 1898, for example, Sergeant M. W. Saddler of the Twenty-Fifth Infantry sent a dramatic dispatch from Santiago:

> Our men began to fall, many of them never to rise again, but so steady was the advance and so effective was our fire that the Spaniards became unnerved and began over-shooting us. When they saw we were "colored soldiers" they knew their doom was sealed. . . . Thus our people can now see that the coolness and bravery that characterized our fathers in the 60's have been handed down to their sons of the 90's. If any one doubts the fitness of a colored soldier . . . [the] Spaniards call us "Negretter Sol[d]ados" and say there is no use shooting at us, for steel and powder will not stop us.[42]

The manly derring-do of "Negretter Sol[d]ados" stirred up commentary earlier that month when black soldiers reportedly rescued Teddy Roosevelt's heralded Rough Riders at San Juan Hill. The Rough Riders were hardly damsels in distress, but in the eyes of many Afro-Americans, they would have perished had it not been for gallant black rescuers.

After he initially praised the efforts of black cavalrymen, Theodore Roosevelt vehemently refuted notions that the black men of the Tenth Cavalry "saved the Rough Riders from annihilation." Some white soldiers, however, willingly conceded that during the charge up San Juan Hill—an iconic event that "showcas[ed] American masculinity"—black men proved themselves superior fighters.[43] Kenneth Robinson, a wounded Rough Rider, not only claimed that black men saved his unit, he quipped, "'without any disregard to my own regiment . . . the whitest men in this fight have been the black ones.'"[44] If a white soldier could go on public record lauding black heroism, then the widely reported bravery of black soldiers in Cuba did not pass unnoticed among African Americans on the home front. Women in Brooklyn

*"Some of our brave colored Boys who helped to free Cuba," ca. 1899. Diverse media—
including stereographs intended for mainstream audiences—helped sell the enterprise
of war and expansion to African Americans. Courtesy of Photographs and Prints
Division, Schomburg Center for Research in Black Culture, New York Public Library,
Astor, Lenox and Tilden Foundations.*

distributed materials regaling black troops; Stella Brazley's "The Colored
Boys in Blue" praised "scions of a warlike race" whose feats "renew[ed]
the prestige" of African American people. Katherine Davis Chapman Tillman rewrote the last stanza of one of her previously published poems to
memorialize those who "charged with such good will [a]nd saved the Rough
Riders at San Juan Hill."[45] Other black Americans argued that man for man,
black soldiers were literally superior specimens of physical manhood who
were immune to tropical diseases as well as bullets.[46] Booker T. Washington
even presented the manly heroism of black soldiers as part and parcel of
what would create "a new Negro for a new century."[47] During the Spanish-
American War, then, the mixture of race, manhood, and imperialism became
powerfully suggestive as a number of black and white commentators other
than Kenneth Robinson dubbed black soldiers "the whitest men" in the war.

The Philippine-American War was a slightly different matter. Black
Americans, for the most part, felt a racial affinity with both Cuban rebels and
Philippine insurrectionists. The major difference, of course, was that black
Americans and Cubans were allied in the struggle against Spain whereas in
the Philippines, Afro-American soldiers would be fighting against Filipinos.
The *Colored American* concluded that whereas Afro-Americans were bound

to side with Filipinos due to "racial sympathies," they could not afford to forsake the United States. The Kansas City *American Citizen* unequivocally disagreed: black American soldiers should not fight other "negroes," the paper flatly stated, only to "fall the prey to southern hell hounds and civilized American cannibals." Other African American newspapers concurred with the *American Citizen* and summarily condemned imperialism as a coercive means to "blight the manhood of the darker races."[48] Even Sergeant Saddler, who once brimmed with enthusiasm over his exploits in Cuba, conceded that it was difficult to relish a fight against "men of our own hue and color" in the Philippines.[49] In other words, when it came to the Philippine-American War, the question of allegiance — and imperialism — was a rather tricky matter for African Americans.

Both torn loyalties and domestic factors fueled black anti-imperialism by 1899. Whereas participation in the Spanish-American War filled African Americans with the hope that their display of patriotism at home and courage abroad would reduce racial oppression within U.S. borders, the war "in fact accelerated the decline, the loss of civility, the increase in bloodshed, the white arrogance [as it] . . . enlist[ed] the North as an even more active partner in the subjugation of black Americans."[50] Not only did the Spanish-American War mend regional fissures caused by the American Civil War, black veterans returning from Cuban battlefields often faced intense resentment and violence. For example, black veterans of Cuban campaigns who were stationed in Huntsville, Alabama, during late 1898 proudly possessed "enough manhood to resent any insult cast upon them" by local whites. As a result, two black soldiers were gunned down in the street — reportedly by another African American — after a local white resident "put out a reward for every black tenth Cavalrym[a]n" assassinated.[51] Thus, by the time black soldiers were deployed for the Philippine-American War in 1899, an appreciable number of black veterans chose to reenlist rather than remain in the South.[52] An undeniable tide of racial violence — such as the infamous Wilmington massacre which claimed eleven black lives and effected countless others — certainly influenced many black men to enlist or reenlist; that same racial violence piqued black anti-imperialism during the short span between the two wars.[53]

But if black anti-imperialism was both perceptible and on the rise, some African Americans still believed that the race would benefit by going to the Philippines as colonists. Black settlement of the Philippines was a popular enough notion that by 1903, President Theodore Roosevelt dispatched

T. Thomas Fortune on an expedition to explore the feasibility of mass black emigration to Hawaii, Puerto Rico, and, in particular, the Philippines. Approximately four hundred black Americans settled on the islands during and after the Philippine-American War; most were, at least by Fortune's judgment, fairly prosperous. Fortune was so impressed that he fully endorsed black emigration to the Philippines. He also concluded that only African American labor could tame the islands' landscape into a profitable colony. "It is written on the wall that ultimately, if the American flag remains in the Philippines," Fortune predicted, "the Afro-Americans will have to be drafted to hold it up . . . for the white American does not find either the climate or the people and their ways to his liking. . . . This is no sufficient anchorage . . . in the successful colonization of [a] country." Fortune was so swept up in romantic ideas about empire that in the northern section of Luzon, he posed for formal portraits donning a field costume and hat which bore more than a passing resemblance to the outfits worn by the black cavalrymen who saved the day at San Juan Hill.[54]

Yet when African Americans looked to the Philippines—or Liberia for that matter—as a refuge from racist oppression, colonizationist impulses made them potential oppressors as well. Race man that he was, Fortune apparently saw little inherent contradiction in blacks being either colonists or imperialists. Since African Americans were denied "manhood and citizen rights" in the United States, Fortune swiftly rationalized that the race deserved an opportunity to colonize territories recently acquired by the United States so they too could "enjoy life, liberty and the pursuit of happiness."[55] Fortune's view of the Philippines was not unlike Henry Parks's vision of Africa; for both men, it was possible if not preferable for African Americans to tame new frontiers and attain the heights of manhood beyond American borders.

Tom Fortune and Henry Parks deemed the possibility of black Americans acquiring their own empires as a literal opportunity for racial redemption. Other black Americans approached empire in a literary sense, producing a small wave of historical romances between 1899 and 1910: Pauline Hopkins published the serialized, Pan-Africanist *Of One Blood* (1902-3); Charles Fowler offered a sweeping tale of slavery, the Civil War, Reconstruction, and the Spanish-American War in *Historical Romance of the American Negro* (1902); John Wesley Grant's *Out of the Darkness* (1909) was an unwieldy epic of the "diabolism and destiny" facing a colonized colored race in the post-Reconstruction South. Baptist minister Sutton Griggs was espe-

Portrait of T. Thomas Fortune from "The Filipino: A Social Study in Three Parts,"
Voice of the Negro, *March 1904. By wearing field dress, race journalist Thomas
Fortune visually transformed himself into both military operative and imperial
explorer. Courtesy of General Research and Reference Division, Schomburg
Center for Research in Black Culture, New York Public Library,
Astor, Lenox and Tilden Foundations.*

cially prolific, expounding on race and empire in no less than three novels: *Imperium in Imperio* (1899), *Unfettered* (1902), and *The Hindered Hand* (1905).[56]

Both *Unfettered* and *Imperium in Imperio* contained their share of curious commentary. Part analysis of U.S. incursion in the Philippines, *Unfettered* included a lengthy appendix entitled "Dorlan's Plan" that heartily endorsed "Americanization of the globe" and encouraged African Americans to channel their energies into the Philippines, Hawaii, Cuba, Puerto Rico, and Africa.[57] *Imperium* explored the possibility of a black empire within the United States; the text praised racial purity, invoked social Darwinist thought, and cursed black disfranchisement. Above all, *Imperium* was suffused with muscular rhetoric which boldly proclaimed that "the cringing, fawning, sniffling, cowardly Negro which slavery left, had disappeared, and a new Negro, self-respecting, fearless, and determined in the assertion of his rights [is] at hand."[58]

In *Imperium* both protagonists are "fine specimens of physical manhood" who are forced, over the course of the novel, to compromise their manliness. Belton Piedmont, the "black" hero, is forced to masquerade as a woman, while the threat of racial extinction prevents the mulatto character, Bernard Belgrave, from consummating his love affair with a devoted race woman.[59] Bernard's intended, Viola, commits suicide; her suicide letter invokes social Darwinist concepts about sexuality, racial competition, and processes of extermination:

> Just two years prior to my meeting you, a book entitled "White Supremacy and Negro Subordination" . . . came into my possession. . . . That book proved to me that the intermingling of the races in sexual relationship was sapping the vitality of the Negro race and, in fact, was slowly but surely exterminating the race. . . . While this intermingling was impairing the vital force of our race . . . it was having no such effect on the white race . . . [because] every person having a tinge of Negro blood, the white people cast off. . . . I looked out upon our strong, tender hearted, manly race being swept from the face of the earth by immorality, and . . . [m]y first step was to solemnly pledge to God to never marry a mulatto man.

Viola then bids her lover adieu by begging him to do everything he can to preserve the race, up to and including emigration.[60]

After both ultramasculine protagonists suffer their share of travails, they are reunited in a secret organization—or imperium—which plots to establish a black empire. However, Belton and Bernard's plans for establishing a manly black nation go awry: one is killed, the other loses his grip on reality. *Imperium* forcefully asserted that the denial of black manhood in the United States inevitably led to death or insanity. As a historical romance, moreover, *Imperium* used plot devices similar to those in historical romances produced by white Americans; the genre, as a whole, "spli[t] the subjects of imperial power into gendered positions." *Imperium in Imperio*'s deployment of manhood placed it firmly within a mainstream literary genre.[61]

Literary commentary on masculinity and empire provided a unique opportunity for African American writers to advance highly politicized rebuttals to popular stereotypes about black manhood. In this regard, a short story by poet and magazine publisher James McGirt was singularly notable. McGirt's "In Love as in War" (1907), set during the Philippine-American War, spun the story of a Filipina princess, Quinaldo, who chooses a black sergeant to be her lover over an aristocratic white American lieutenant from Louisiana. Throughout the story, Quinaldo—a name that intentionally evoked Emilio Aguinaldo, leader of Philippine insurgents—swoons whenever she is in close proximity to the virile "Sarge." Their courtship is heated, yet chaste, with Quinaldo and Sarge's mutual desire reaching climax through his tales of conquest:

> They talked over many matters in swift succession, as though they wanted to crowd a lifetime in a few hours. Finally, she became interested in a medal.... "Sarge" [took] it off his breast and [gave] it to her.... He then entertained her with stories of his hair-breadth escapes and his daring encounters with the Indians, as well as in the Spanish-American war.... The princess found herself at times moving, as though she herself were facing the enemy....
>
> When he had described these things to her until she could stand it no longer, she clapped her hands and exclaimed, "Brave! wonderfully brave!"

In contrast to Sarge's calm bravery, Vaughn, the white officer, is a red-faced blue blood, both "defeated and enraged" by the black enlisted man's edge with Quinaldo.[62]

Vaughn is ineffectual—if not effete—whereas Sarge is so manly he arouses passion in every Filipina who espies his glorious physique.[63] Here, the Philippines, as represented in the feminine form of Quinaldo and other women, are more than willing to be possessed by black male bodies. The

Philippines could not only be conquered, McGirt suggested, the territory was also a suitable "wife" capable of sustaining the material and sexual needs of any worthy *black* American man. Put another way, McGirt scripted an alternative to contemporary dynamics of power between black and white men in the American South, and he used sexuality in an imperial setting to do so.

The sad reality was that whether black soldiers were conquerors on the battlefield or in the boudoir, participation in U.S. military efforts abroad did little to change racial dynamics at home. Again, after 1898, outbreaks of racial violence involving returning black veterans and highly publicized racial incidents between black and white soldiers in the Philippines—not to mention reports that some black soldiers defected and joined Filipino insurgents—influenced growing numbers of African Americans to argue that black soldiers should not help white Americans defeat other people of color. To add insult to injury, black soldiers proved their mettle in Cuba and the Philippines only to have their manhood compromised upon their return to the States.

Such a sense of futility led members of the National Afro-American Council to inject a noticeably anti-imperialist tone into its 1899 meeting. Two black anti-imperialist leagues were formed that same year—the league in Chicago even called itself the "Black Man's Burden Society."[64] Black anti-imperialism was anything but universal, however. Classics professor W. S. Scarborough probably spoke for some aspiring and elite men when, in 1901, he argued that Afro-American colonization of "our new possessions" remained the one viable opportunity for "black manhood [to] stand erect and unhindered, and . . . enlarge respect for itself."[65]

But if 1899 was any sort of a watershed in terms of organized, expressed black anti-imperialism, how do we account for Henry Parks's call for what was tantamount to Afro-American imperialism in Africa that same year? Some black Americans—due to convictions that "progress" in Africa benefited Africans and African Americans alike—believed imperialism contained a civilizing component and thus provided race men and women with unparalleled international opportunities. *Alexander's Magazine*, for example, actively promoted Afro-American "development" of Liberia through columns written by Walter F. Walker, vice-president of the Liberian Development Association. Walker and other staff writers especially wanted to reach out to "the manly, the progressive and well equipped men and women of the Negro race [who] want freedom, security in the exercise of manhood rights, just treatment before the law, and opportunities to prove their social efficiency." Throughout its relatively short four-year run, *Alexander's* steadfastly pursued its ideal readership, but the magazine's editorial stance regarding Liberian development changed noticeably by the fall of 1908. The magazine's enthusiasm toward emigration cooled due to a disastrous trip Walker made to Liberia, not because of a mounting sense that Afro-American colonizers might become little more than dark-skinned imperialists.[66]

If emigrationism did not automatically imbue those looking toward Africa with anti-imperialist ideas, Pan-Africanism enabled blacks in the United States and the Caribbean to oppose American and European imperialism as they sought active roles in determining Africa's destiny. The *Colored American*'s Pauline Hopkins and scholar W. E. B. Du Bois both felt stirrings of diasporic kinship at the end of the nineteenth and beginning of the twentieth centuries. As a result, Pan-Africanism found an outlet in each writer's work. In 1900, Trinidad's Henry Sylvester Williams organized the first major Pan-African conference in London to mobilize people of African descent against imperialism and colonialism. African American writer and educator Anna Julia Cooper attended the conference, as did Du Bois; both chafed at the notion that imperialism enabled either civilization or progress.[67]

Given the rather blunt, conquest-hungry language in *Africa: The Problem of the New Century*, it might be difficult if not specious to situate Parks within such a Pan-Africanist camp. Parks dedicated his book to all people of African descent working "hand in hand for mutual good." He clearly believed that racial affinity should compel black Americans to act as counteragents of European imperialism in order to "save the native African from . . . [a miserable] fate."[68] Even further, Parks's evocation of imperial conquest in the name of racial salvation was consistent with viewpoints of black Americans —such as Pauline Hopkins—who simultaneously expressed Pan-African and civilizationist ideas. Still, it is less useful to label Parks a "Pan-Africanist" than it is to assume he could point to Europeans in Africa as justification to fortify black American presence on the continent. Indeed, it was not necessarily a contradiction for race women and men like Hopkins and Parks to embrace imperialism as a providential opportunity for their own uplift work.[69]

Understanding Parks's motives, then, requires situating him within the larger context of the complex, conflicting ways African Americans analyzed imperialism and its impact on people of color. For all the reasons why blacks in the United States opposed certain forms of imperialism, anti-imperialist

African Americans could and did advocate imperialist roles for themselves. Again, Afro-American commentary about Africa became decidedly more anti-imperialist after 1900, but that anti-imperialism was largely directed at white colonists. For example, in 1905, the *Colored American* gleefully predicted that Africans would ultimately defeat any and all European intruders:

> If Africa is not set aside, or rather left alone, to the Africans, it is quite evident that somebody is going to have an abundance of trouble. . . . The natives will rise up against the English and the French in much the same way as they are now rising against the German. . . . We cannot but express the complete satisfaction with which we view the intelligent and patriotic interest the black men of all countries are beginning to show in the status and future of Africa.

> Africa for the Africans, and for the Africans now!

Four years later, an editorial in the same magazine condemned European "lust" for Africa only to call for African Americans—and the United States—to assume a greater role in Liberia. As *Colored American* contributor I. De H. Crooke put it, "Africa for the Africans" was nothing but a hollow cry unless black Americans "colonize[d] and appropriate[d]" the continent's territories and resources.[70] As late as 1913, a familiar argument resurfaced as the New York *Age* chastised black men for not being as aggressive as white men in taking full advantage of Africa. Here, a familiar argument resurfaced: if black men were ever going to thrive as men, if U.S. imperialism was a poor means of fostering black manhood, then black men needed an *African* outlet for their masculinity.[71]

Such a seeming contradiction could have been the product of any number of political realities, motives, or ideas. One explanation rests in Liberia's particular status: the country had long been a virtual ward of the United States, Americo-Liberians and indigenous people were in constant conflict, and the nation's borders were changed on more than one occasion due to wars with France and England. But on another and more likely level, the predominance of racialized theories such as social Darwinism enabled black Americans to abhor "white" imperialist domination in Africa while embracing a claim for themselves. And, given the succession of black consul-generals appointed to Liberia by the U.S. government, African Americans likely expected that an "American" role in Africa would, in reality, be carried out by blacks.[72] After all, if black people were not fit to compete in "white" countries such as the United States, and if Africa was the racial domain for people of African descent, then how inconsistent were the allied positions of the *Colored American*, the *Age*, and Henry Parks?

Considering popular African American attitudes that the race was duty-bound to save Africans from European oppression and given the desire of many black Americans to confer "progress" on Africa by "civilizing" and Christianizing Africans, perhaps Parks's manifesto was something other than rank justification of cultural imperialism. Although it might be tempting to dismiss Parks as a confused crank or self-hating Samaritan, such dismissal would tell us little about Parks or the moment in which he lived. Parks's argument exemplified tensions felt by many black American men who abhorred racial oppression, harbored an allegiance to Africa, and yet desperately wanted to exercise the prerogatives of manhood denied them in the United States. Parks's quest for conquest was, in all likelihood, buttressed by the aura of triumphant black veterans — men who suggested that certain aspects of imperial endeavor could actually bolster feelings of virility and prowess in men in color. Even as growing numbers of African Americans came to view imperialism as threatening the integrity of people of color around the globe, visions of a potential role in Africa enabled aspiring-class and elite black Americans to create new, racialized notions of manhood. In other words, Henry Parks embodied the contradictions and tensions inherent in what many of his contemporaries tellingly labeled the "black man's burden."

The very notion of a "black man's burden" facilitates analysis of gender and race between 1890 and 1910 at the same time that it illuminates why black Americans held myriad opinions about the impact of imperialism on the race's manhood. Rudyard Kipling might have been commemorating war in the Philippines when he wrote "The White Man's Burden," but his phrase was widely appropriated so that it spoke to a range of domestic and international issues. White Americans, such as southerner B. F. Riley, used the notion of a racialized and gendered burden to describe white responsibility "to the Negro Problem." Black Americans often placed the burden squarely on the shoulders of men of color: as H. T. Johnson wryly retorted, "Pile on the Black Man's Burden; His wail with laughter drown; You've sealed the Red Man's problem; and now take up the Brown." Black journalist John E. Bruce — an eventual associate of Marcus Garvey whose Universal Negro Improvement Association promoted its own vision of a black empire in Africa — likewise considered white imperial paternalism as simul-

[THE BLACK MAN'S BURDEN]

taneously ludicrous and tragic. Bruce approached the matter with rueful sarcasm: "It is to laugh—to read of the white man's burden. . . . The white man's burden, self-imposed, will break his back if he is not soon relieved of it. He is the biggest joke in the world today, posing as a *superman*." Howard University professor Kelly Miller shared Bruce's contempt for the "white man's burden," but Miller caustically wondered whether black Americans would "stultify" and "humiliate" the race by supporting imperialism. For Miller, the racial hatred and fear that legitimated segregation and justified lynching were the same as the rationale behind imperial aggression.[73]

Just as Miller condemned the racism implicit in imperialist ideologies and Bruce belittled white men for trying to be ultramasculine, global conquerors, black Americans appropriated and subverted the very notion that the burden was heaviest for any group of men, black or white. "The Black Woman's Burden," for example, appeared in the pages of *Voice of the Negro* and bemoaned sexual victimization of African American women by white— and black—lechers. Similarly, in his take on the ever-appropriated concept, Du Bois addressed the sexual subjugation of colonized women by asserting that women's bodies bore the brunt of "drunken orgies of war." In 1906, a year before his elegy "The Burden of Black Women" was published, Du Bois was less poetic about sex on the imperial front: in an Atlanta University publication, he maintained that "a curious commentary on imperialism" was unfolding due to white soldiers in "foreign service" who spread syphilis and gonorrhea wherever they went.[74] Frances Ellen Harper's "The Burdens of All" went further still—it declared that imperialism created havoc for all humanity.[75]

U.S. and European imperialism certainly affected a vast range of people, and African Americans clearly understood this. However, given the ways in which racialized and gendered concepts informed notions of war and colonial conquest in American life between 1890 and 1910, most black American commentators stressed imperialism's impact on black men. It is no coincidence that the overwhelming majority of these commentators were aspiring-class and elite men: their class status was precarious and they viewed empire as playing a decisive role in stabilizing—or destabilizing—their position vis-à-vis other Americans. However, instead of discussing their situation using class language, these men invoked racialized notions about manhood to express their anxieties.

While many black Americans between 1890 and 1910 believed that campaigns for empire compromised people of color as a whole, imperialism was also construed as a site for a highly racialized and masculinized struggle of the fittest.[76] Imperial efforts in Africa, Cuba, and the Philippines were thus seen as having the potential to serve as figurative and literal fronts where black men could either prove their manhood or openly compete with white men. For Kelly Miller and other African Americans, imperialism was little more than a rigged contest in which black men would inevitably lose. Henry Parks and J. Dallas Bowser saw things in a different light still: they viewed the "black man's burden" as a necessary step in racial redemption, as an inevitable by-product of globalized racial combat, *and* as a morally superior version of imperialism.[77]

The push for empire combined gender and race in provocative ways for Americans who were only decades away from being subjugated and enslaved themselves. Just as race was used at the turn of the century to "remake manhood," imperialism remade and reinforced a gendered racial identity for black American men.[78] Participation in U.S. imperial wars was undoubtedly fraught with contradictions for black American men, but "of all the sites where masculinities are constructed, reproduced, and deployed, those associated with war and the military are some of the most direct."[79] By participating in imperial endeavors as militants and missionaries, African American men could forge masculine identities that were, for the most part, beyond their reach in quotidian life. In a sense, staking a claim to manhood was an attempt to realize social mobility for working-poor, aspiring, and elite black men alike.

Finally, in order to understand why many African Americans continued to embrace imperial roles for themselves in Africa as they became increasingly hostile to U.S. and European imperialism, it is useful to return to the U.S. context. If the period between 1890 and 1910 was an era of "hypermasculinity" in the United States, if the "'psychic crisis'" in the United States during the 1890s was, in fact, "a crisis of manhood," imagine the predicament of African American men.[80] Not only were they emasculated beings according to mainstream discourse, but political disfranchisement, racial violence, and proscribed economic status often prevented them from asserting public claims to manhood; if economic downturns caused "fears of . . . dependency" among white men, those fears were all the more palpable for African American men.[81] Without question, black men possessed integrity, agency, and virility, yet it must have been all but impossible for them to act in the same "hypermasculine" ways as their white contemporaries. In fact, the hypermasculinity of the 1890s might explain why aspiring and elite African American men discussed imperialism in the ways that they did: class was hardly an inconsequential matter, but it nonetheless seems that imperialism's obsession with race—combined with the era's hypermasculinity—led many aspiring and elite men to eschew class politics for a racialized politics of manhood. For all of its contradictions and comprises, imperialism was indeed a problematic arena, but it was an arena in which black men could potentially develop a racial manhood of their own making.

The symbiotic relationship between hypermasculinity and imperialism might also explain the relative absence of African American women in the production of Afro-American discourse on imperialism. Ida Wells, Nannie Burroughs, Pauline Hopkins, and Anna Julia Cooper were certainly not the only black women in the United States to register their views on empire publicly; again, women regaled the feats of black soldiers and some, such as writer Frances Harper, expressed anti-imperialist sentiment.[82] The sheer volume of writing on empire by black men nonetheless suggests that they were more invested in the question of whether imperial endeavors had the power to confer virility and manhood upon the race. Empire was, moreover, a pursuit and domain "presumed to be dominated by males," thus race men took the lead in Afro-American discourse on imperialism.[83]

As the nineteenth century closed and the twentieth opened, African American women frequently faced complex issues of their own surrounding uplift and freedom. These issues would become particularly manifest once concepts regarding racial destiny turned inward after the turn of the century and increasingly focused upon habits, habitats, intraracial relationships, and sexuality. Whereas Afro-Americans continued to debate both empire and emigration into the twentieth century, the sheer prevalence of sex ensured that sundry reform initiatives—popular eugenics, efforts to shape comportment and behavior, attempts to privatize and renovate domestic spaces—would prove another burden for reformers anxious to improve the race. If this particular and more domestic burden had its implications for black men, the burden for race womanhood was anything but negligible. Indeed, as discourses about collective destiny began to prioritize internal dynamics, gendered and sexualized burdens would be thrust upon race womanhood—prepubescent girls, maturing adolescents, young mothers, and matrons alike.

Gendered (manhood) Identity Thogh empire (wars)

3

THE STRONGEST, MOST
INTIMATE HOPE OF THE RACE
SEXUALITY, REPRODUCTION,
AND AFRO-AMERICAN VITALITY

Seven years after Atlanta hosted the 1895 Cotton States Exposition, where Booker Washington conjured up the image of black arms crafting, toting, and casting down buckets, the city was the site of the Negro Young People's Christian and Educational Congress. From the first day, when attendees heard an "Afro-American National Hymn" written by Ida German Carter, to the fourth day, when teachers went to sessions on "the necessity of high moral character," the interdenominational conference was an immense meeting; it encompassed topics as diverse as black mortality, evangelical work in Africa, crime, and the efficacy of benevolent societies. But on Sunday, the final day, women and men held separate "platform meetings" to propose and discuss solutions for delicate "social issues." As the women met at the People's Tabernacle and the men assembled in an auditorium at Piedmont Park on that Sunday morning in August 1902, the day's work for both groups would be, in a sense, sex work. For men, Wilberforce College president Joshua Jones was slated to give a paper on male "crimes" visited upon women, while H. T. Johnson, editor of the *Christian Recorder*, was to describe the moral legacy that rakish fathers bequeathed to their children. Dr. Sarah Jones of Richmond, along with scientist Josephine Silone Yates from Kansas, was scheduled to appear at the Tabernacle to address "physical" matters pertinent to women.[1]

Activist Ariel Serena Bowen was another featured speaker on the women's program, and she believed that "passions running riot" would eventually destroy people of African descent in the United States. Bowen took pains to ensure that the audience at her afternoon session would leave the congress fully capable of recognizing the true dangers of youthful ardor. Freewheeling fornication was not her primary preoccupation, nor did she spend much time preaching that abstinence saved souls as well as bodies. Rather, Bowen was vexed about "child marriage," and she wasted no time outlining why the practice was nothing less than criminal: "It produces physically puny, weak and sickly offsprings. The child-mother is not perfectly developed. The organs are not fully grown. . . . So, too, with the boy-father. . . . This is one of the supreme causes of the large number of emaciated, ill-formed and sickly children with which the race is afflicted . . . [as well as] the high death rate that menaces the race." Bowen's notions mirrored mainstream assumptions that premature sexual activity stunted intellectual development and hastened death.[2] Yet, when Bowen contended that the "high percentage of premature motherhood" among black females compromised "the future stability and prosperity of this race," she was doing more than drawing upon conventional wisdom: by invoking "puny, weak, and sickly" infants she was also addressing the painful reality that African Americans had a markedly high infant mortality rate. If black Americans wanted to be a "truly great people," argued Bowen, then sexual unions among youth simply had to stop.[3]

Ariel Bowen's address abounded with genteel language about the sanctity of the "marriage tie," but it was also built upon strategic — albeit codified — references to the carnal urges responsible for couplings among those barely beyond childhood. In the process of rousing her audience from being too complacent about racial reproduction, in the process of drawing attention to the vitality of future generations, Bowen risked indelicacy and talked about sex. Significantly, the president of the statewide Afro-American division of the Women's Christian Temperance Union in Georgia did not concentrate her energies on moralizing sexual behavior. While Bowen did indeed touch upon the moral implications of early sexual activity and whereas she insisted that labor and education should supplant fornication, her paper was not an out-and-out invective adjuring young people to abstain from intercourse. The overarching, all-important issue for her was that youthful sex resulted in a shoddy product, that "child marriages" kept young people from engaging in the enterprise of race building. Bowen even hinted that for African American children, righteous learning should actually include careful instruction on sexual ethics — or, to invoke her own language, "training for the responsible duty of founding families."[4]

The five-day conference at which Bowen spoke not only provided a space where women and men could actively evaluate sexuality, it culminated with those very evaluations: some attendees fretted over hygiene or urban temptations, some harbored anxieties about clothing and public conduct. Other women and men chose to emphasize moral rectitude by asserting that sexual purity was steadily taking hold among a people just removed from chattel slavery. Overall, then, both organizers and participants of the congress firmly situated sexuality within the "problems and progress" of the race, and in so doing they typified black American reformers at the turn of the century.[5]

Congress participants undoubtedly saw themselves as representative race members that embodied the promise of a people. But if these women and men were representative in certain regards, they were not necessarily typical. Like other African Americans living in postemancipation society, most participants rose from slavery or made their way from otherwise lowly beginnings. Their very attendance at the conference, however, signified access to educational and financial resources beyond the ken of most laboring women and men. As crucial as class status was when it came to reform, uplift work served as a veritable fusion politics uniting African American activists who belonged to different socioeconomic classes yet shared common goals and outlooks; activism in and of itself differentiated the cohort of reformers from women and men who primarily associated sex with leisure, pleasure, marriage, or even trade. Striving black women and men engaged in uplift work did not share the lifestyles or attainments of their more elite brothers and sisters, yet some of their attitudes about domesticity, personal carriage, and sexual behavior could be quite similar. Poorer race members who struggled for daily sustenance were indeed united by economic hardship. Yet, the social attitudes of aspiring women and men who decided to participate in uplift work nonetheless set them apart from working people who spent their spare hours in other ways.

Uplift activists did not speak for all black people, then, yet they dealt with a force that affected virtually every member of the race. Sexuality was not only a factor within individual households but it, along with gender, affected larger questions of labor and citizenship. Moreover, sexuality encompassed a range of relationships and dynamics for African American reformists: choice of sexual partner, courtship, heterosexual intercourse, reproduction, concubinage, miscegenation, rape. Late-nineteenth- and early-twentieth-century reformers occasionally discussed ostensibly gender inappropriate behaviors in ways that suggested sexual inversion or, in rarer cases, insinuated homosexuality. If "nascent models of sexual inversion and homosexuality . . . were entwined . . . with the logic of American scientific racism"—the very scientific racism that spurred reform efforts within the race—Afro-American reformists' discussions of homosexuality remained largely inchoate until the 1920s.[6] Indeed, sexual conduct of a different sort—public comportment, chastity, promiscuity, mating—became a matter of concern for a variety of race institutions. Issues and reforms varied over time, yet sexuality remained "a matter of general interest [and] part of the general discussion of [racial] repression" for women, children, and men living in the wake of Reconstruction.[7]

Sexuality was a paramount concern for other Americans as well. Between 1890 and 1920, decades when "the older Victorian value system was under siege," a range of women and men reassessed "intimate matters."[8] Whether they migrated to cities for greater sexual freedom, chose to limit pregnancies, rejected heterosexuality, or formed a series of erotic partnerships, changes in mores and practices were no less palpable for people at the turn of the century than at any other time in U.S. history. But with social purity campaigns, eugenic theory, settlement work, temperance crusades, and birth control advocacy, as well as increased dissemination of sex information and the coalescence of sexology, sexuality was perhaps more public than ever before.[9]

African Americans broached their own sexuality within this milieu. Black sexuality was particularly charged—so much so that racialized anxieties often devolved into interracial sexual violence, so much so that sexual practices of the black poor and working class caused a fair amount of distress for social strivers within the race.[10] Not only was sexual comportment a significant marker of class status within the race, stereotypes concerning black sexual appetites kept many aspiring and elite race members from engaging in turn-of-the-century social emancipations. These same women and men would nevertheless explore ways in which sex could bolster the literal reproduction of the race, secure a healthy presence in the national body politic, and strengthen the collective integrity of Americans with African heritage.

For a people forced to protect their civil rights, pertinent sexual issues in postemancipation life included lynching, concubinage, and interracial rape; for a people long denied access to resources and facilities, intraracial concerns about sexual health assumed a sense of immediacy as well. In an era when sexual terrorism was an ominous reality for black Americans, at a time when disease and early death cast a pall over many black households, a significant mass of black women and men acted upon the notion that the race's destiny and sexual practices were intertwined.

Self-proclaimed crusaders seized the gauntlet of policing sexual behavior within the race as they poured their energies into ensuring that sex contributed to—rather than detracted from—the work of Afro-American reproduction. The very concept of "racial destiny" emphasized later generations: it implied that biological processes of generation should result in an abundance of vigorous offspring that would, in theory, continue to reproduce a hearty people. Private coupling became public concern in part due to demographic shifts. Beginning in 1890 and lasting until at least 1930, the black population in the United States underwent a massive transformation besides migration and urbanization—the Afro-American birthrate was in flux if not decline. Beyond this trend, infant mortality and disease exacted heavy tolls on black communities throughout the United States. For women and men concerned with the quality and quantity of black people, the era between 1890 and 1930 was an era of crisis. It would prove to be an era of crusades as well. African Americans produced literature about sex, launched grassroots campaigns to promote greater numbers of robust babies, and educated their communities about perilous diseases. Individuals, media, and public forums forged a clear link between group vitality, racial reproduction, and sex; all were instrumental in vivifying that particular link for the Afro-American public.

Reform-minded black women and men proceeded to contend that race progress was contingent upon eradicating vice, increasing the number of "well-born" children, and monitoring sexuality.[11] In the process they drew from contemporary impulses, many of which were built upon eugenic arguments. Eugenic theory was rife with raced, classed, and gendered conceptions of fitness, and its implications were more than a little problematic for black people. But with its basic tenet that sexual behavior was a decisive factor in determining whether children were "well-born," eugenic thought suggested that individuals possessed the potential to improve their offspring through strategic mating. Eugenics further implied that an ethnically, racially, or nationally configured people could ensure their vitality via concerted efforts to impose boundaries and order upon the sexual collective. Thus, whereas African Americans had to contend with a legion of theory that implied all people of color sprung from degenerate stock, they could actually subvert racism within eugenic thought through the guise of uplift. When it came to race progress, furthermore, black women and men found certain eugenic concepts appealing if not pointedly useful. Along these lines, activists such as Ariel Bowen belonged to a black cohort within the American social hygiene movement that "addressed questions of sexuality in order to advance their own standing and . . . that of the entire race."[12]

Afro-Americans—especially the aspiring, middle class, and fairly elite—mobilized social and intellectual resources to alleviate morbidity and channel sexual practices into healthy racial perpetuation. Furthermore, public considerations of black sexuality by African Americans emerged when their very survival was questioned as well as scrutinized. Black reformers were therefore insurgents in that they challenged a plethora of racist notions concerning black sexuality and humanity. But, when these same women and men labored in the name of race uplift, they at times "condemned . . . perceived . . . negative practices and attitudes among their own people."[13] African American sexual politics thus reflected interracial as well as intraracial conflict. "The politics of respectability" could be subversive in contexts where Afro-Americans consciously decided not to allow stereotypes and insults to affect their own measure of self-worth, yet attempts to enforce "respectable" behavior could be oppressive for those black women, men, and children who opted to live by different standards. As much as respectability and uplift were on the minds of a substantial number of black women and men, perhaps concerns about the future—not to mention desires to experience pleasure—resonated with many more.

Racial oppression and mob violence posed terrific threats to the lives of black Americans once Reconstruction ended, but other perils threatened their survival as well. Black women's fecundity appeared to slacken after 1880, while it seemed as though black morbidity levels were skyrocketing due to tuberculosis, pellagra, venereal disease, and other serious ailments. Furthermore, the rate of infant mortality was higher for black children than for any other ethnic group in the United States during the late nineteenth and early twentieth centuries. For certain observers—both white and black—it appeared that Afro-Americans might die out as a distinct "race."

One such observer was particularly influential: Frederick L. Hoffman, a German immigrant and statistician for Prudential Insurance hailed by mainstream pundits as judicious regarding all things racial in the United States. Given his professional standing and supposed impartiality, Hoffman's "Vital Statistics of the Negro," which was published in the *Arena* during the spring of 1892, was at once influential and particularly damning. In this article, Hoffman was willing to grant—on general principle—that statistics on births and deaths were likely to be unreliable, and he acknowledged that projections concerning population growth or the future vitality of any given group could indeed be inaccurate. When it came to the task of exploring whether African Americans were reproducing themselves in a healthy fashion, though, Hoffman cast aside his professed willingness to allow for discrepancies. Instead, he bluntly proclaimed that blacks in the United States were cursed with "race deterioration" brought about by "gross immorality, early and excessive intercourse of the sexes, premature maternity . . . general intemperance . . . [and] susceptibility to venereal diseases." For him, the fate of Afro-Americans was sealed by degenerate "colored females" whose high rates of illegitimacy and stillbirths ensured that blacks in the United States would, in time, "vanish."[14]

Four years later, Hoffman's *Race Traits and Tendencies of the American Negro* drew upon U.S. history, socioeconomic data, material conditions, and census reports in order to assert that black people were dying faster than they were born. He also professed that an excess of deaths over births was a greater problem for Afro-Americans than for any other ethnic group in the nation. In spite of his belief that African American women "were gifted with an abnormally high birth rate," Hoffman still maintained constitutional infirmities among U.S. blacks revealed an incontrovertible fact: "in the struggle for race supremacy the black race is not holding its own."[15] Hoffman's notion that blacks were moribund emerged from social Darwinist tenets concerning the "survival of the fittest," and the major thrust of his work mirrored contemporary beliefs that blacks did not possess the wherewithal to survive outside of slavery.

Hoffman's views were neither unusual nor extreme within majority discourse. For example, a white doctor from Mississippi, H. L. Sutherland, referred to Hoffman as an "impartial observer" in a 1905 address before a southern medical association. Sutherland's speech on the "Destiny of the American Negro" mimicked Hoffman's work in its claim that "marriage is the exception" among Afro-Americans; "their children are brought up in shame . . . [and] not more than 2 per cent. of [N]egro girls preserve their virginity to the age of 12."[16] Here, it is important not to consider Sutherland's writing as distinctly "southern": during the period between 1890 and 1910 — again, an era of national reconciliation and reunion — mainstream attitudes about black sexuality tended to be similar whether the person holding those attitudes was from the South, West, North, Midwest, or East. Moreover, defamatory notions about black sexuality were so pervasive that a recent immigrant like Hoffman could easily publish such views in *Race Traits* under the guise of "objectivity."

The racialist views of Hoffman and Sutherland would be supported in print by at least one Afro-American. William Hannibal Thomas, a descendant of free people of color, penned an especially notorious screed about black morality that was published on the cusp of the new century. His book, *The American Negro*, alleged that "an imperious sexual impulse . . . [in] negro character constitutes the main . . . degeneracy of the race, and is the chief hindrance to [the race's] social uplifting." One of his more provocative examples was an allegation that poor black women routinely excited their male relatives by sashaying about cramped cabins in scanty garments, with "fathers and daughters, brothers and sisters, oblivious of decent social restrictions, abandon[ing] themselves . . . to sexual gratification whenever desire and opportunity arises." The text further insisted it was impossible for black manhood to "respect chaste womanhood."[17]

The American Negro had still more conclusions to offer on black sexuality. According to Thomas, extensive, excessive masturbation among children resulted in "actual carnal knowledge" for a majority before the age of sixteen, and he also maintained widespread infidelity was spreading the scourge of "sexual morbidity" throughout the race. From prostitution to infanticide to abortion, *The American Negro* covered topic after topic as its author — like Hoffman — argued black women were on the road to infertility and insinuated extinction was a real possibility facing Afro-American people. Thomas's writing exceeded tacit acceptance of mainstream notions that lewdness was inscribed upon the innate character of "negroes" in that his work firmly and unrelentingly situated the very history and eventual fate of people of African descent within sexualized, racist canards.[18]

William Hannibal Thomas incensed more than a few of his contemporaries, who promptly censured him for impugning a struggling people, for providing ammunition to detractors, for adding fuel to fire. Booker Washington implied Thomas was "a man without a race," Howard University professor Kelly Miller wrote him off as a pathetic "defamer," and even William Hooper Councill — a conservative race man by almost any standard — felt a fair amount of "disgust" over the publication of Thomas's book. A lesser-known race man, Reverend S. Timothy Tice of Massachusetts, published a sizable pamphlet to rebut and reveal Thomas as "an unscrupulous Negro author . . . appealing to the white race prejudices." In order to substantiate his effort to discredit William Thomas, Tice shored up his text with court records and affidavits that purportedly originated with reliable sources. Two of these documents alleged that, as a student, Thomas impregnated a woman and only *then* saw fit to marry her; another contended that the controversial author was "lecherous."[19]

Tice probably felt justified in his decision to slander Thomas, for whether from within the race or from whites, charges that African Americans were inherently lascivious and degenerate were anything but benign stereotype: they rationalized lynching, justified rape, legitimated segregation, and restricted employment opportunities. Therefore, the act of challenging defamers or highlighting black morality by African American men and women was often about more than controlling the race's image — it was a means of responding to attacks on their collective character and individual bodies. Women were especially vocal and organized in this regard.

Chicago resident Fannie Barrier Williams chose an auspicious moment to voice her discontent with popular concepts of black female sexuality. During the Columbian Exposition of 1893, she addressed the World's Congress of Representative Women and complained that all too often race women were forced to assume defensive positions in order to answer "meanly suggestive" commentary. Significant advances regarding the "moral regeneration of a whole race of women" notwithstanding, Williams and other "representative" African American women found themselves "fervently impatient and stirred by a sense of outrage under the vile imputations of a diseased public opinion." A watershed event two years later reflected their frustration. The formation of an umbrella organization for club women, the National Association of Colored Women, emerged, in part, out of indignation over a scandalous letter "written by a southern editor . . . reflecting upon the moral character of all colored women."[20] When black women — and men — countered oppressive sexual stereotypes or responded to physical assaults, they employed various tactics. One of the most frequently employed strategies was an emphasis on "respectability."[21]

Afro-American claims of respectability typically combined "concern[s] for sexual purity, child rearing, habits of cleanliness and . . . self-improvement." This combination enabled club women and race men to promote certain modes of behavior and instruct their brothers and sisters on how to attain a range of ideals. In addition to being a form of protest for many aspir-

84   [HOPE OF THE RACE]

ing, middling, and elite people, respectability was part of a larger intraracial pedagogy on earning civil rights and gaining self-respect through proper conduct. Along these lines, discussions of respectability advanced specific concepts of acceptable sexuality in that black reformers frequently promoted "respectable reproductive sexuality within the safe confines of marriage" as a viable means of uplifting the masses and working toward black progress.[22]

Yet the political etiquette of respectability was "progressive" in more ways than one. Uplift work placed black reform activists squarely within the Progressive Era, but it also indicated the progression of class stratification within black communities after emancipation. During the last thirty-five years of the nineteenth century, sexual mores increasingly indicated attainment of, or aspiration to, position and status for blacks in the United States in ways that eclipsed antebellum standards for the expected sexual behavior of any given social class. As W. E. B. Du Bois observed in a 1908 Atlanta University study, abolition occasioned a distinct "emergence . . . of successive classes with higher and higher sexual morals."[23] Class stratification among black Americans was thus a major development of postemancipation society; subsequently, sexuality assumed deeply classed meanings.[24]

In turn, this process of class formation after emancipation simultaneously revealed and exacerbated tensions surrounding sexual propriety within the race. Aspiring-class views about sexuality—specifically women's sexuality—could be condescending if not oppressive. For example, as black reformers pushed for intraracial sex reforms in urban settings, many came to view recent migrants as "degenerate." When it came to establishing agencies that both aided and controlled migrant women, "the emergent black bourgeoisie . . . secure[d] . . . personal autonomy in the process of circumscribing [working-class] rights."[25]

The relationship of class, reform, and sexuality was still more complicated. During the first decades of the twentieth century, poor folk often "tolerated" intrusive reform initiatives because at times it benefited them to do so. The pragmatic aspects of reform—namely access to information on sexuality and the potential of intraracial initiatives to improve black health within a segregated society—"were not [necessarily] antagonistic to the interests of the poor." Concepts of respectability could also be integral to "a pre-existing working-class culture" rather than being mere bequests or unwelcome impositions handed down from one class to another. This is not to say that a number of women and men were not angered, insulted, and irked by the sanctimonious tone of moral crusades, nor is it to imply sex reform was a universally embraced, uncontested form of communitarian politics. Attitudes and behaviors between socioeconomic groups definitely clashed—still, that collision did not prohibit black reform efforts from appealing to people from different class backgrounds, nor did it curtail a range of "respectable" African Americans from participating in uplift work.[26]

If the prickly issue of black sexuality deeply informed the intertwined politics of uplift and respectability, during the early twentieth century aspiring and elite activists would increasingly turn to popular scientific concepts to analyze sexuality and reproduction. For this particular cohort, eugenic ideas about achieving "race betterment" through production of well-born children would be especially influential. Eugenic thought attracted considerably more Anglo-Americans than Afro-Americans, and it entered the American mainstream with a vengeance as the nineteenth century closed and the twentieth opened: institutions of higher learning legitimized eugenic concepts by offering coursework on the subject; local eugenics groups proliferated across the nation. Beginning with Indiana in 1907, eugenic sterilization and restrictive marriage laws spread to more than ten states within ten years. Moreover, between 1877 and 1920, more than a dozen "family studies" publicized reproductive histories of so-called "unfit," "mongrelized," and "degenerate" families. Popular hereditarian and eugenic theories were built, in no small part, upon theories of race and class that implied that the poor were more likely to be vicious, that degeneracy plagued certain ethnic groups, and that African Americans lacked positive heritable qualities such as intelligence.[27] Not surprisingly, both strains of thought buttressed rationales behind immigration quotas and antimiscegenation legislation. With conscious manipulation, however, racialist theories could be co-opted in the name of black uplift.

A number of prominent Afro-Americans therefore used arguments regarding how heredity bolstered group vitality; they advocated eugenic solutions and sex regulation as a viable means of lowering black morbidity. Black interest in well-born children—especially among women—stretched back into the late nineteenth century: Dr. Rebecca Crumpler contrasted the ill-effects of excessive "physicking" with the benefits of mating "well" as early as 1883; Frances Ellen Harper explored "the laws of heredity and environment" as each pertained to "enlightened motherhood" nine years later; Selena Sloan Butler, who organized black parent-teacher associations, extolled the hereditarian virtues of domestic environments in 1897. A major journal for club women, the *Woman's Era*, explored questions of "nature or environment" in creating fit people, while one club, the Lucy Thurman

86   [HOPE OF THE RACE]

Union, installed Washington D.C.'s Dr. Carrie Thomas as their "Superintendent of . . . Heredity and Hygiene."[28] Slowly and surely, this interest in popular eugenics would spread to a wider range of Afro-Americans over the next two decades.

One-time Tuskegee instructor Adella Hunt Logan was among those vexed by the notion that too many members of the race thought of sex merely as "the gratification of passion." She dealt with this concern by underscoring the dangers of giving into "unholy feelings" at an Atlanta University conference in 1897, and, in the process, Logan implored race women and men of "all classes" to pay attention to "the claims of prenatal and hereditary influences."[29] Baptist laywoman Sylvia Bryant aired her concerns in public as well. When she addressed the same 1902 Youth Congress where Ariel Bowen gave her paper, Bryant described how disorderly homes, immorality, and careless breeding prevented the production of "a strong healthy race." Club woman Addie Hunton — yet another participant of the congress — believed every child had "a right to the inheritance of the very best of body and soul its parents can bestow." Hunton also echoed Bryant's sentiments when she contended that black women needed to "concentrate their efforts . . . [and] diminish the number of poorly born, poorly bred and deformed children" within the race.[30]

Around the turn of the century, reformists that shared the preoccupations and presumptions of Logan, Hunton, and Bryant ensured that Afro-Americans would have greater access to knowledge about sex and healthy racial reproduction by producing "home manuals." Billed as "educational emancipators" for "the future development of the ambitious colored American," books such as *Life Lines of Success*, *The College of Life*, and *Golden Thoughts on Chastity and Procreation* included detailed advice about sex. These books were aimed at mature readers — or at least those a few years past puberty — and each one devoted considerable space to allaying the worries of young people pondering the duties of marriage for the first time.[31]

Golden Thoughts was notable in terms of its modern and frank approach. Despite the sunny, innocent title, its chapters on adolescence, marriage, and health contained relatively frank advice on everything from masturbation to venereal disease to whether married couples should sleep in the same bed. A black physician from Atlanta, Henry Rutherford Butler, wrote the introduction and urged black women and men to obtain a copy, pore over its contents, and learn about topics "of vital importance to the human family." Butler's endorsement for *Golden Thoughts* went beyond enthusiasm as he vaunted the book as a tool for racial redemption: "This book [comes] . . .

at this most critical period in the existence of the colored American. It brings to my people the golden thoughts on how to perfect themselves in all things social, economical, physical, political and financial. . . . Some good thing can come out of Ethiopia."[32] The text was replete with examples of which sexual proclivities led to destruction: "self abuse" vitiated the young, cross-generational sex produced unfit offspring, excessive intercourse withered genital organs. To animate the text, illustrations and photographs of Afro-Americans in *Golden Thoughts* contrasted desirable and undesirable behavior. There were renderings of pure, innocent youths, sketches of mismatched couples with puny offspring, and series of portraits that contrasted the glowing progeny of the "fit" with the slightly darker-skinned toddlers of the allegedly "unfit." These illustrations—along with an image on the frontispiece of a wholesome family enjoying each other's company in a well-appointed parlor—promoted "bourgeois decorum as an important [part of] emancipatory cultural discourse."[33]

As it identified sexual "intelligence [as] the main hope for the redemption of a stricken race," it seems safe to assume that *Golden Thoughts* was produced solely with the descendants of slaves in mind.[34] But *Golden Thoughts* also appeared under the slightly less euphemistic title of *Social Purity*. This other edition, however, was apparently produced for white Americans. Page by page, line by line, the text in both books was identical; the only appreciable difference was that *Social Purity* had illustrations with white subjects, and its opening pages did not include the introductory comments of Henry Butler.[35] Even further, the married authors of *Golden Thoughts/Social Purity* were apparently not African American.[36] What this implies, in a general sense, is that while contemporary information about sex was marketable to both blacks and whites, the actual information was packaged in oddly segregated forms. Furthermore, it demonstrates that the notion of racial betterment through sexuality held currency for a range of Americans.

However, the phenomenon of *Golden Thoughts/Social Purity* suggests something a little more complex, for both editions contained passages clearly written for a majority audience. Witness the following observation about venereal disease from *Social Purity*: "Its destructiveness has been observed in the past, and there is reason to believe that it is even now threatening the enormous vitality which has given supremacy to the Anglo-Saxon people." The same line appeared verbatim in *Golden Thoughts*. Granted, such a statement can be read as commentary on the perceived station of Euro-Americans or as a means of provoking both races into divergent forms of intragroup action. Given that each edition went on to liken women in

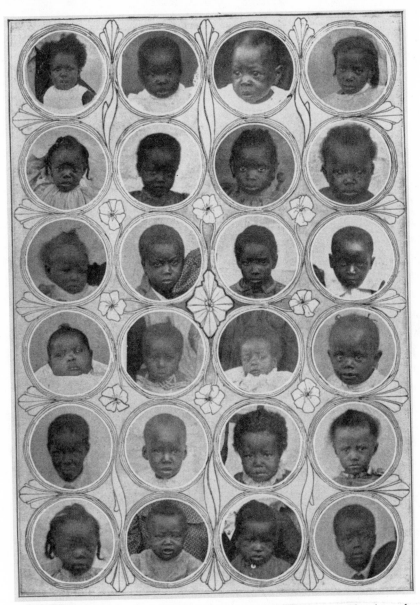

"Children of the Poor and Uneducated," from Golden Thoughts on Chastity and Procreation *(ca. 1903). In contrast to its presentation of cherubic, bright-eyed, sepia-hued children as the product of "pure and intelligent parents,"* Golden Thoughts *associated childhood deprivation and degeneracy with lank looks, anxious faces, and—unintentionally, perhaps—darker complexions. Courtesy of General Research and Reference Division, Schomburg Center for Research in Black Culture, New York Public Library, Astor, Lenox and Tilden Foundations.*

the United States to their fair, rosy-cheeked "English cousins," however, it seems more plausible that much of the text—if not all of it—was initially written with one group of Americans in mind.[37]

Whereas *Life Lines of Success* and *The College of Life* were similarly strange amalgams which fused representations of black progress with writings by white "experts" on reproductive health and sexual protocol, they too represented attempts to bring that information to a black audience. When *Life Lines* proclaimed that sex was the "strongest, most intimate . . . hope of the race," that proclamation happened to be lifted from an ostensibly "white" source. In a society where African Americans did not have easy access to resources, such an insight was most likely appropriated in the name of equal opportunity. As Henry Butler conceded a few years before he endorsed *Golden Thoughts*, "[whites] have the public libraries where they can get and read books on hygiene . . . [whereas] we have no such privileges." For both black reformers and compilers of home manuals, appropriation of mainstream texts was a ready means through which a mass audience of black women and men might be persuaded that sex was not merely for pleasure.[38]

By including text originally aimed at convincing native white couples to produce "well-born" children, moreover, the compilers of Afro-American home manuals clearly believed black people throughout the United States could well benefit from knowledge intended for native white Americans.[39] With higher reported rates of adult morbidity and infant mortality for African Americans, many black reformers were convinced that the race needed the information all the more. Manuals also popularized both contemporary medical language and sex advice among women and men of color. These books were part of an explosion of print media aimed at black Americans around the turn of the century, and they constituted a special niche within the genre of race pride literature. Black women and men seemed to welcome such information, for these books went into multiple editions and were sold by subscription in black newspapers aimed at general audiences.[40] And, as sex information was packaged for African Americans, a range of issues touching upon sexuality increasingly informed activists' discussions of race and destiny.

Placing Afro-American sex literature within historical context and understanding why allied grassroots movements emerged when they did entails a turn to changing demographic trends—especially fertility rates —of the late nineteenth and early twentieth centuries. Birthrates of native-born white and black women in the United States declined with each decade as the nineteenth century ended and continued to do so as the new century progressed. The diminution hardly went unnoticed. Most notably, perhaps, declining birthrates stoked fears about "race suicide," a contemporary expression that encapsulated anxieties about immigration and concerns about women's mobility, increased access to higher education, use of birth control, and reevaluation of motherhood. The race suicide panic "was a backlash, a response to actual changes in birth rate, family structure, and sexual practice." Reactionary as it might have been, the term "race suicide" enjoyed fairly broad circulation, with men such as sociologist Edward Ross and Theodore Roosevelt using it to bemoan the fact that increasing numbers of elite and middle-class native white women embraced "voluntary motherhood" by controlling their own fertility. Most white women bore an average of three babies by 1920 as opposed to five sixty years before; those with a college education tended to have even fewer.[41]

Whereas African American women remained likely to bear more children than native white women, their fecundity experienced an especially sharp drop beginning with the end of Reconstruction and lasting until at least 1930. Black women averaged about seven children on a nationwide basis during the 1870s, whereas three or four children were more typical five decades later. Put another way, the ratio of children under five years old per one thousand African American women between the ages of fifteen and forty-four fell at least 33 percent between 1880 and 1910 alone.[42] Significantly, however, the number of live births varied across class, occupation, and region. Among married women having children around the turn of the century, for example, those in the agricultural South bore up to eight babies, while service workers in the same region might have four. Service workers and middle-class women living in the North and West, in contrast, were likely to bear three children.[43]

Any number of factors contributed to the drop in black women's fecundity, with migration, urbanization, and high levels of participation in the labor force being particularly decisive in the reduction: all three militated against frequent births. Although the majority of the race remained below the Mason-Dixon line, and southern black women's fecundity outstripped that of other African American women, when women migrated out of the South they typically left behind desires for large families. Given that migratory patterns of women and men were generally different, the very process of migration momentarily separated partners and curtailed opportunities for routine sex, thus reducing opportunities for impregnation.[44] Relocation was not the only movement at work, however, since increasing numbers of black women took matters into their own hands by making conscious decisions to limit their pregnancies or delay marriage. Some black women were simply leery of successive childbearing, while others harbored reservations about bringing children into a racially oppressive society. One doctor reported that a few of his "intelligent and upright" patients admitted "they would rather die than . . . bring children into the world to suffer what they had suffered."[45]

By choice or by chance, African American women in the labor force—excluding farm workers—also contributed to fertility reduction, since women who worked outside the home generally had fewer children. Socioeconomic conditions in northern cities probably played a small part in determining the low birthrates of working black women in the urban North, too. As African Americans became urbanized, large families became increasingly impractical due to high costs of living, limited housing stock open to the race, and reduced economic contributions of children to households.[46] Even further, a few financially strapped workers likely engaged in "prenatal infanticide" rather than support yet another child.[47] What one observer dubbed a "mad frenzy to prevent reproduction" on the part of black women included contraceptives, folk medicines, douching, abortifacients, and abstinence. Factors beyond women's control potentially "prevent[ed] reproduction" as well: poverty, hardship, physical stresses endured in a hostile racial climate. Along these lines, pregnant workers engaged in heavy labor might have been especially prone to stillbirths.[48]

Although in-depth reportage on birth control, stillbirths, abortion, and sexual habits was not the stock-in-trade of the Census Bureau, the bureau certainly reported demographic trends and transitions among African American people. The percentage of black people within the national population went from 14.1 percent in 1860 to 9.9 percent in 1920. In terms of rough figures, the 1860 census counted approximately 4,441,000 people of African descent, with a slight increase to 4,880,000 ten years later. By 1880, the black population was at least 6,580,000, while the 1890 enumeration reported about 7,490,000 African Americans. Over 8,833,000 black people lived in the United States at the turn of the century according to official estimates. Yet, those estimates were not necessarily accurate, and three successive decennial counts were sufficiently controversial as to set off racial alarms. An undercount of African Americans in 1870 fueled discussion that blacks were undergoing slow but certain extermination. Oddly enough, a more accurate 1880 census led alarmists to veer toward the opposite extreme and declare that the United States was becoming "Africanized." In 1890, however, another undercount resuscitated extinction theories. If the 1890 census was partially responsible for the last decade of the nineteenth century witnessing "an unparalleled outburst of racist speculation on the impending disappearance of the American Negro," that speculation continued into first decades of the next century.[49]

Afro-Americans both acknowledged and analyzed racial forecasting, with black publications providing a vital forum for dissecting the politics of the census. In 1891, a major race paper of the day published a cogent, opinionated letter from a reader in Searcy, Arkansas:

> One of your contributors is very much perplexed over the decreasing per cent of the Negro population of this country. . . . The question is not so unfathomable. . . . People are populating this country by immigration from Europe . . . [and] in the Southern States. . . . they don't care to give a correct census . . . for general political reasons. . . . I do not say . . . that there is no cause for alarm, for in our cities the per cent of the death rate among us is much greater. This is owing to the unaccountable passion of our [young] men . . . for low pursuits. . . . They are fast vitiating the Negro blood . . . while our women . . . have not learned the proper care of themselves. . . . As much against us as things seem to be, we are gradually developing into a great race.

In his landmark study, *The Philadelphia Negro*, W. E. B. Du Bois offered the more biting observation that any "census which gives a slight indication of the utter disappearance of the American Negro from the earth is greeted with ill-concealed delight."[50]

Not everyone was as blithe as Du Bois in dismissing theories of black extinction. A Baltimore newspaper ran an article with the ominous heading "Necrology of the Negro Race," in which race minister J. Andrew Patterson offered a rather foreboding prognostication: "It has been said by scientists and statisticians that the Negro is dying faster than he is being born. It has also been stated that because of disobedience on the part of parents to prenatal and postnatal laws the majority of the younger generations . . . are and will be inherently weaker than their parents. The foregoing statements being true, it is evident that a race that is dying faster than it is being born, with a majority of the coming generations being poorly born, cannot survive."[51] Patterson's comments—like those of the correspondent from Searcy—sounded a tocsin of impending crisis as they expressed anxiety over sexuality, reproduction, and racial vitality. Whereas their views were dissimilar, neither person discounted the possibility that the race just might be suffering, whether due to lust for "low pursuits" or from disregard of "prenatal and postnatal laws." Even further, black morbidity worried both Patterson and the Arkansan; each writer implied that the race's future was inexorably bound up in altering questionable behaviors and improving compromised bodies.

The *Colored American Magazine* joined the fray over Afro-American vitality and attempted to explore the question from several angles. The journal's print symposium—aptly entitled "Is the Negro Dying Out?"—took on a certain authoritative formality as eleven medical race men offered their expert opinions. With one slight exception, no doctor who appeared in the pages of the *Colored American* concurred with overheated claims of impending black extinction. John Kenney, Booker T. Washington's personal physician, argued it was "granting a great deal" to assume statistics on black Americans were accurate in the first place. Dr. George Cannon pointed out that birthrates during slavery were "abnormal," thus postemancipation rates only seemed low in comparison. U. G. Mason contended births were widely underreported due to so many black women relying on a "'Grannie' who does not know and cares less about the importance of birth reports." Another physician, New York City's Peter Johnson, believed African American population growth was proceeding apace with "undiminished virility": according to Johnson, "race suicide" was a looming issue for white Americans, while black people were actually increasing their ranks through hygiene, sanitation, and improved infant care.[52]

Daniel Hale Williams took yet a different approach. The noted surgeon and founder of Chicago's Provident Hospital plainly stated the race was "not dying out . . . [but] *bleaching* out" and then offered his additional theory that substantial migration and emigration "subtract[ed] from the census figures" of Afro-Americans. Compared to Williams, E. P. Roberts of New York City stood even further apart from other doctors in the symposium. While Roberts conceded that black migration precluded accurate population enumeration, he also argued that "unless the doctrine of healthy living is preached and practiced to a greater extent . . . the race will experience physical deterioration and at least . . . *approach* . . . extinction." For Roberts, the high percentage of "premature marriages" and working women engaged in strenuous labor only exacerbated race deterioration by increasing the likelihood of infant death.[53]

Overall, then, the *Colored American* forum concluded that contemporary analyses of racial reproduction and vitality were highly subjective; eight of the eleven physicians challenged the veracity of statistics and census reports in one way or another. There was indeed ample reason for them to doubt the accuracy of black birth and death figures, since communities throughout the country simply failed to collect such statistics on a systematic basis.[54] Yet, while the overall gist of the symposium was that the race was proliferating rather than waning, many of the participating physicians did feel there was ample room for improvement in terms of reducing morbidity. As E. P. Roberts suggested, perhaps the most important intervention black reform could effect was lowering infant mortality. U. G. Mason was alone among *Colored American* contributors in charging that midwifery was inefficient in terms of reportage of the race's vital statistics. Still, other black health activists who believed infant mortality had to be reduced also fingered "ignorant grannies and meddling old women" as being a major cause of baby death. A few years after Mason blamed midwives for being responsible for compromising the statistical representation of African Americans by failing to report births, one Dr. C. C. Middleton referred to midwives as "high priestess[es] of inefficiency" who delivered babies in filthy conditions, fed them vile concoctions, and caused a host of postnatal physical defects.[55]

As aspiring Afro-Americans and black reformers explored racial vitality, birthrates, and the problem of infant death, some encouraged women to do their duty by having their fair share of healthy babies. Even the hefty and frequently reprinted volume *Progress of a Race* included a section on the birthrate that featured Fisk University professor Eugene Harris's observation that too many black families were having but two or three children. African American women's fecundity was not only "considerably less than it ought to be," Harris decried, but abortion—or "the crime of mothers"— was being practiced with greater frequency in his opinion. On another occasion, he bluntly concluded that "[the] race, like the women of whom Paul once wrote to Timothy, must be 'saved through child-bearing.'"[56] Whether the topic was racial extinction or fecundity, *Progress of a Race* and other black publications contributed to "contemporary analyses of changes in black fertility [that] were . . . concerned with the implications [of these changes] for 'racial survival.'"[57]

If doctors, ministers, educators, club women, and reformist writers participated in allied discussions about the number and quality of black children being born, the phenomenon of "better babies" contests at state fairs and in other venues provides suggestive—if not compelling—evidence of the cross-class appeal of well-born children. "Better babies" contests did not originate with African Americans but rather with the Children's Bureau that was instituted by the U.S. Department of Labor in 1912. The bureau promoted contests and specially designated baby welfare weeks as a means of reaching mothers across the country—regardless of ethnicity, class, region, or race—and encouraging them to learn about hygiene, diet, and infant care. Slides, films, pamphlets, and traveling shows were employed by the bureau as means of educating the largest possible audience; contests at state fairs gave the cause additional exposure. The overall effort became medicalized around 1915 when clinical examinations became a routine component of many competitions. Contests were further institutionalized as the bureau forged local networks consisting of "club women, extension . . . agents, doctors, ministers, and businessmen" to carry out the work of improving the nation's children.[58] The concept of "better babies" might not have been an African American creation, but African American activists carried out the movement with zeal in black communities, often with the assistance of local white officials or state boards of health.

To some extent, concepts regarding infant welfare had already made substantial headway into certain quarters of the black populace before the "better babies" ferment of the 1910s. Dr. Rebecca Crumpler became a pioneer of sorts when she wrote an entire tome devoted to race mothers and their children during the 1880s. Crumpler's *Book of Medical Discourse in Two Parts* was a "common sense" approach to infant care filled with advice on nursing, feeding, and healing babies. She intended it to be both "a primary reader in the hands of every woman" and an agent that would ward off infant death. It is difficult, however, to gauge the success of this early mission; Crumpler apparently sought names of potential buyers then sold and distributed a number of the books herself.[59]

Perhaps more influential precursors to baby welfare activism among African Americans were "mothers' meetings." These local clubs provided women with opportunities to exchange ideas about baby health and attend talks on heredity or morality; they became common institutions among aspiring and middle-class black women during the 1890s. One such convert to the movement, Atlanta University graduate Georgia Swift King, believed frequent infant deaths and persistent reports of declining Afro-American birthrates justified mothers' meetings among as many black women as possible. In 1897, King contended that such meetings were critical sites where "all classes of women . . . even the illiterate" could learn sanitary methods of handling and feeding infants, thus securing "the destiny of the Negro race."[60]

Other club women shared King's convictions. For example, declarations regarding the need for mothers' meetings were integrated into major national platforms, with one such platform "encouraging . . . individual clubs to give time and attention to questions affecting heredity and environments of the children of the race." Members of the Harper Women's Christian Temperance Union in Jefferson City, Missouri, heeded the call and organized their own mothers' meetings; on one occasion before the turn of the century, those in attendance heard a lecture on "child culture." The impetus would only grow over the next decades. Before and after "better babies" competitions were ubiquitous, black women's organizations such as the Federation of Colored Women's Clubs in Chicago and the Woman's Convention of the National Baptist Convention sponsored contests, had their own "child welfare departments," or included baby columns in organizational literature. Black women were therefore instrumental in providing grassroots support for improving the health of children and the quality of their lives.[61]

After 1910, the Afro-American press provided additional publicity for baby welfare events open to black infants. One newspaper in Virginia, the Norfolk *Journal and Guide*, encouraged area readers to "visit the school," "see the plays," view "the stereoptic[o]n," and participate in baby week. The same paper similarly praised organizers in Tarboro, North Carolina, for "cut[ting] out all ideas of a Baby Show" by staging a campaign replete with doctor's examinations, washing and dressing demonstrations, and nutritional instructions. In Tarboro, "lectures and lantern slide talks" by a county official even supplemented exhibits with "placards [about] death rates and eugenics."[62] Efforts such as these—many of which were apparently quite popular—suggest that eugenic notions of racial betterment were introduced to a broad cross-section of the Afro-American populace, as does the emergence of better baby contests at segregated black state fairs in the rural South.

Fairs enticed small landowners and tenant farmers, townspeople and rural dwellers, those who raised livestock and those who bet on horses. Baby contests undoubtedly attracted parents who simply wanted to brag or hoped to win prize money, but they also enabled the promotion of popular eugenics among black Americans. "Better babies" competitions were, moreover, a practical means of reducing infant mortality, a festive way to showcase black development, and an ingenious means of encouraging racial improvement. In 1914, the *Journal and Guide* described the events at a North Carolina fair and proudly reported, "There will be several new features this year, one of which is a 'Better Babies Contest' each day. This unique innovation is supported by the State Board of Health. . . . Hundreds of mothers have indicated their purpose of entering their babies in the contest." After various medical staff inspected and scored the infants, Lenora Slade was declared "State Champion Colored baby" and was awarded a gold medal along with twenty-five dollars. The contest itself was so successful, in fact, that organizers decided to "undertake further and more advanced work along this line" in subsequent years so that black mothers could continue to "go home and remedy . . . what might have been deformities for life" in their children.[63]

Some "deformities" could be corrected, but others were ostensibly the sad legacy of disorderly sexual activity. An appreciable number of black reformers believed "disease and mortality were hereditary liabilities passed down to offspring by sexually licentious parents."[64] "Better babies" were presumably the product of sexual order among parents, thus it is likely that at least some contest organizers encouraged black parents to reevaluate their sexual practices. One baby event in Kansas was held in conjunction with "'fittest family'" competitions that involved screening parents for venereal diseases. Whether or not a majority of black parents who entered their children were themselves tested for sexually transmitted diseases, it is probable that some contests for black babies in the South paid attention to reproductive health given prevailing notions that African American adults were more likely to be stricken with syphilis and gonorrhea.[65]

Black parents also entered their children in competitions throughout the North, Midwest, and West, some of which were integrated.[66] The New York *Age* sponsored an especially large undertaking when it launched a nationwide competition for Afro-American children in 1915. In addition to the New York metropolitan area, entries came from an impressive range of states: Florida, Wisconsin, Missouri, Louisiana, Rhode Island, Oregon, New Mexico, Nebraska. Well over three hundred contenders emerged; as the *Age* published their photographs on the front page, the paper proudly proclaimed their attempt to "arous[e] interest of mothers" successful. Mothers and fathers alike sent letters to New York expressing their satisfaction that the paper's effort was a superior "means of inspiring our people to take better care of the babies."[67]

Alongside one week's photographs, the *Age* reprinted a speech about eugenics given by Dr. John Kenney at Tuskegee Institute. The speech was an assault on moral decay, and it opened with analysis of sexual missteps that would ensue from suggestive dancing. "All too long leaders, educators, preachers, physicians, college presidents, and teachers have winked at this subject," warned Kenney, "while boys and girls are growing up in vicious ignorance and . . . future young mothers are tangoing away the possibili-

Portrait of Gladys Odile Walton, entered in the 1915 New York Age "Better Babies Contest." The Age contest relied heavily on photographs, many of which were studio portraits that suggested material wealth through clothing, toys, furniture, and backdrops. Gladys Walton was one of Gladys Moore Walton and Lester Aglar Walton's two daughters. Her father, a journalist who wrote for the Age and other newspapers, served as United States ambassador to Liberia during the 1930s and 1940s. Courtesy of Photographs and Prints Division, Schomburg Center for Research in Black Culture, New York Public Library, Astor, Lenox and Tilden Foundations.

ties of coming generations amidst unwholesome influences." Kenney was horrified over the possibility that "promiscuous dance" facilitated seductive encounters in which innocent young girls came into contact with "rake[s] and libertine[s]" who were, in all likelihood, infected with sundry social diseases. When it came to persuading prospective parents — especially potential mothers — that moral fortitude was in their own best interest, Kenney believed frank discussion of sexuality and race suicide was nothing less than essential. Accordingly, he upbraided young women who practiced contraception, had abortions, or otherwise went against "nature's decree." John Kenney plainly declared, "we can only perpetuate the race through a healthy childhood" produced by women fit and willing to "perform the duties of wife and mother." The doctor was similarly forthright in his opinion that Afro-American parents should associate eugenic approaches regarding "correct parentage" free from sexually transmitted diseases with sturdy children, reduced infant mortality, and ample racial reproduction. For him, proper social behavior was about more than respectability — it was literally a question of future generations.[68]

For all of the graveness of an item such as the *Age*'s reprint of John Kenney's speech, slightly bizarre and humorous stories about contests occasionally appeared in the black press as well. When a "colored baby" from Newark, New Jersey, was awarded a gold medal over seven hundred other tots during an integrated contest in 1914, for instance, the *Age* chuckled that several white mothers were sufficiently mortified that the contest's promoters scrambled to locate a white child who could "make a better showing." One tongue-in-cheek item in the Chicago *Defender* about a "perfect baby drive" featured six black siblings from California whose father named ice cream as the "source of [their] physical perfection." But as the rather involved, protracted contest sponsored by the *Age* suggests, Afro-American publications could be serious, supportive boosters of the overall endeavor. When the *Competitor* published its own slate of baby and toddler pictures during the summer to 1920, one caption boasted that a tyke named "'Little Jack'" could "capture all the prizes at a Better Baby Show . . . for his bright eyes, plump, well proportioned body, and liking for milk, bread, and eggs."[69]

Even the relatively bourgeois, high-toned *Half-Century Magazine* celebrated "*perfection in babyhood*" by publishing national samplings of baby pictures in 1919 and 1920. Infants were more than "representative American citizens of tomorrow" in the eyes of *Half-Century* editors — crawling, toddling girls and boys would grow up to "guid[e] the destiny of the nation."

The magazine further declared that "better babies are a sign of progress. The future of the race . . . in numerical strength and its physical fitness depends wholly on today's babies. A crop of puny, under-nourished infants could hardly be expected to develop into a race of robust men and women. To give these little folks the proper care . . . and to provide them with sanitary homes . . . may mean years of great sacrifice on the part of . . . the parents of our race." Ignorance had long left black mothers and babies at a disadvantage, the *Half-Century* continued. While race families were larger a mere thirty years before, an abundance of sickly babes born into poverty might have increased infant mortality rates among Afro-Americans: fewer children, the magazine suggested, translated into better babies for all parents regardless of class. The editors quietly implied that "giving every baby a chance" meant, at bare minimum, educating each and every mother about "the proper care of herself and her child." [70]

Such promotion of racial fitness struck a responsive chord due to the spread of grassroots public health movements in many black communities in the World War I era. [71] The Chicago *Defender*—one of the most widely read black weeklies both North and South—responded to the surging interest in health by employing physician A. Wilberforce Williams to write a column about "keep[ing] healthy." [72] Williams, who worked his way from humble beginnings in Monroe, Louisiana, to medical school at Northwestern University, had been a resident at Chicago's black-run Provident Hospital and specialized in treating tuberculosis. Once he started writing for the *Defender*, Williams reliably dispensed information about tuberculosis, influenza, and other ailments each week. [73] In addition to warning tubercular individuals not to marry until well and advising parents to circumcise their sons as a means to "preven[t] masturbation," Williams also devoted a considerable amount of attention to "sexual plagues." [74]

For week upon week in 1913 and in numerous columns over subsequent years, Dr. Williams detailed how sexually transmitted diseases turned healthy young men and women into "damaged goods." Whether this ample coverage was due to high reader demand—as Williams claimed—or simply because he felt there was a crying need, the doctor tackled venereal disease in a direct and sometimes tactless fashion. For example, when pleading with parents of prospective brides and grooms to realize the long-range effects of gonorrhea and syphilis, he wrote: "You would not think of bringing a hog infected with cholera among other healthy hogs. . . . Then, why not for the good of your dear son or daughter, for the good of the unborn— for the good of the race—inquire into the physical condition of those who would enter into the matrimonial alliance, instead of . . . whether the off-spring will be beautiful or not, whether . . . the hair [will be] long or short, straight or kinky[?]" Venereal disease was "responsible for race suicide . . . and sterility," the doctor reasoned. Young men and women needed to be examined, then, with mating and reproduction being reserved for those re-ceiving "clean bill[s] of health." On this rather delicate subject, Williams was more than willing to offend some readers' sense of propriety. He castigated indiscriminate young men, told women to withhold sex from promiscuous partners, urged the afflicted to forego marriage, and counseled young brides who contracted sexually transmitted diseases from their husbands.[75]

Several columns exposed dubious patent medicines that failed to cure venereal disease—let alone much else—and Williams also featured bleak cautionary tales of death and affliction resulting from lack of proper treat-ment. Along these lines, the doctor adroitly used his indignation over par-ents who infected their children to expand his analysis of the ramifications of sexual infirmities. If children were affected, the future of the race was affected. Once the health of too many children was compromised before adolescence there was little hope that black Americans could continue to reproduce in a healthy fashion.[76]

Williams also classed masturbation with venereal disease since he felt both destroyed black youths and vitiated the collective racial body. Accord-ing to the doctor, masturbation was a major cause of sterility and impotence for males as well as females; Williams believed any masturbator who retained reproductive capacity was bound to produce "idiots, epileptics . . . imbe-ciles . . . [and] the hopelessly insane." Once again, he implored mothers and fathers to realize their duty to the race by providing their children with the sort of wholesome sex education that would actively discourage "self-abuse." He also ventured a little further. Wilberforce Williams openly sug-gested that in order to curtail chronic self-abusers, syphilitics, and other supposed defectives from reproducing, every state in the country should "introduce and enforce the Indiana movement and also the Wisconsin and Oklahoma laws in regard to those who should marry." Saying nothing about how such legislation might adversely affect his African American audience, Williams seemed to believe that saving "the flowers of the race" from repro-ductive perils required every effort—even if that meant adopting eugenic statutes.[77]

Williams's preoccupation with venereal disease was hardly personal ec-centricity—when his column featured a "Venereal Drive," it reflected con-temporary claims regarding v.d. and race.[78] Not only did most social hygienists believe African Americans had unusually high rates of syphilis and gonorrhea, most doctors, public health officials, and self-designated authorities singled out venereal disease as the primary cause of black women's decreased fecundity.[79] The surgeon general reported during World War I, furthermore, that black soldiers were twice as likely to have sexually transmitted diseases than their white counterparts.[80] Both black soldiers and civilians were exposed to increasing propaganda about the prevention of sexually transmitted diseases during and after the war. The American Social Hygiene Association (ASHA) was one major agency that acted upon assumptions that African American people required special outreach. In conjunction with the U.S. Public Health Service, the ASHA adapted generic public service announcements for the benefit of "colored boys, girls, men, and women"; the exhibit's posters featured pictures of "fit" Afro-Americans with pithy captions about venereal perils.[81]

Outreach efforts did not stop there, nor were black Americans uninvolved. Wilberforce Williams and other Afro-American physicians, for example, were enlisted to launch public education programs for black soldiers.[82] Physician Charles Victor Roman was exceptional in this regard. Selected by the War Department to carry out grassroots education, he canvassed the South during the spring of 1919 and spoke extensively on the ravages of syphilis and gonorrhea. Roman handed out pamphlets and showed topical films to the reported sum of over 22,000 southern blacks during one tour alone. Whereas his willingness to tour demonstrated a certain commitment to black public health on his part, Roman freely admitted that prevailing medical arguments about blacks and venereal disease were "undoubtedly tinged with prejudice." Roman did not go as far as another race doctor, Julian Lewis, who proclaimed immediately after the war that "venereal diseases are a white man's disease"; still, Roman felt compelled to challenge mainstream medical assumptions regarding sexually transmitted diseases and the rate of infection among African Americans.[83]

Regardless of how he felt about the white medical establishment, Roman—like Wilberforce Williams—worked hard to ensure that sexuality did not compromise black health. In doing so, he was like countless other African Americans who were sex crusaders in service to the race. All told, campaigns for sexual fitness, reproductive health, and child welfare reached unprecedented numbers of black Americans during and immediately after the World War I era. Organizations held sessions where such topics could be discussed; public meeting houses hosted films and lectures. Club women identified venereal disease as a "'pressing problem'" facing the race; they formed a national "Department of Eugenics" in order to "spread the gospel of clean manhood and womanhood." Black reformers additionally joined forces with mainstream movements as race papers publicized occasions such as the National Child Welfare Association's distribution of "educational panels . . . showing healthy, happy and beautiful Negro children."[84] Silent films on sex hygiene were also available. Black women and men with access to movie theaters could view any number of contemporary films on venereal disease, birth control, and eugenics. In Chicago alone, Southside theaters screened sensational photoplays such as *Why I Would Not Marry*, *Where Are My Children?*, *Her Unborn Child*, *End of the Road*, and the film Wilberforce Williams frequently recommended to his readers, *Damaged Goods*.[85]

Admission prices were fairly cheap at nickelodeons but, all the same, class and outlook helped determine who was willing to go to the movies or pay good money for any given film. If tony race folk in urban centers found "picture houses" to be sites of "boisterous recreation" for the working class, it is just as likely that class had something to do with which people were inclined to see something along the lines of *Damaged Goods*. *Damaged Goods* and other films of its ilk were probably considered lurid and tawdry by many "respectable" race folk. Still, aspiring and middling people most likely to be receptive to these films' moralizing, reform-oriented aspects might not have minded being titillated in the process of receiving packaged information about sexual perils.[86]

Other forms of reformist popular culture with decidedly less circulation than motion pictures were consumed by certain black women and men as opposed to others. For instance, Angelina Grimké's short story "The Closing Door" and Mary Burrill's play "They That Sit in Darkness" both attempted to address themes familiar to many black Americans: Grimké addressed the traumatic impact of racial violence on women's mental and reproductive health, while Burrill tackled the physical burdens endured by working mothers. But, given that "The Closing Door" and "They That Sit in Darkness" were both written expressly for the *Birth Control Review*, each piece was really aimed at convincing aspiring women and men that contraception could make significant contributions to racial uplift.[87]

Not only were urban leisure and various forms of popular culture classed phenomena, ideas about uplift sex reform that were promoted through mass media aimed at or produced by black people were deeply classed. The people primed to accept reform-oriented media were typically middling, elite, or aspiring folk. Admittedly, most popular culture consumed by Afro-

Americans during the first decades of the twentieth century was not consumed for its reform matter. When black people enjoyed songs, film, stage acts, and literature with sexualized content during their leisure hours, they were not necessarily looking to appear or become morally upright. Moreover, popular culture—especially blues music and burlesque—actually expanded the public presentation of sexuality in ways that black reformers and uplift activists surely found distasteful. As far as the relationship between sexuality, uplift, and racial reproduction went, however, popular culture was nonetheless one of many means reform-minded women and men deployed in their attempts to convince others that the collective destiny of Afro-Americans indeed depended upon particular sexual behavior and comportment.

Between 1890 and 1920, black thought *writ large* was dominated by debates about racial destiny, and it was during these years—especially around World War I—when sexual behavior and mores underwent profound change in the United States.[88] As white Americans paid more and more attention to issues surrounding sexuality, African Americans did too. This is not to imply that their reasons for doing so were the same: from respectability and uplift to terrorism and miscegenation, sexuality was part and parcel of black ruminations on how to improve the present as well as the future because racial oppression loomed so large and posed very real threats to black lives. If the race was going to have any future at all, African American people would have to direct considerable attention to reproduction, sexuality, and health. Again, terrorism, demographic shifts, and disease provided ample reason for black Americans to worry about their collective vitality and chances for survival.

From Ariel Bowen to Charles Roman, black American women and men interested in racial uplift fought to marshal sexuality so that it contributed to the struggle for self-determination. Whether such action took the form of public speaking, publication of sex manuals, or working toward the production of "better babies," African American attempts to reform sexuality responded to contemporary perceptions about black morbidity and disease levels. As a range of black women and men understood activism to include and even prioritize the literal reproduction of "race," sexuality and health informed Afro-American efforts to secure their future as a distinct and vital people.

The reasons why Afro-American women and men turned to sex in public discourse were varied, but in the end, many of those discussions resulted from worries about whether the race was slowly dying out. Once again, these concerns were partially fueled from racist assumptions, but they also emerged from social phenomena ranging from high infant mortality levels, declining birthrates, disease, and fertility control by black women. African Americans' assessments of sexuality not only emerged when their very survival was under scrutiny, they occurred within the context of massive demographic shifts as well.

And, in addition to black reform efforts and sex literature, public health activism appeared in black communities to help address crisis, upheaval, and change. During the thirty-year span between 1890 and 1920, sex literature, "better babies" contests, and public health activism suggested that the race needed to work on improving itself. "Improvement" meant black women and men should not view sex simply as a means of satisfying carnal urges: having multiple partners was fraught with moral complications, but promiscuity was seen as additionally damnable because it could result in venereal disease. More often than not, preferred behavior was associated with middle-class and aspiring-class values in that it firmly placed sexuality within the realm of marriage and family; and, as more and more black women decided to limit their pregnancies, they were encouraged to bear a healthy number of "well-born" babies by a particular and vocal cohort of racial uplift activists. Combined, all of these phenomena were part of a pronatalist, eugenic trend in African American culture that would culminate in Marcus Garvey's Universal Negro Improvement Association during the 1920s.

Efforts to improve racial stock were undertaken largely by black elites, and these efforts arose from class-based assumptions about sex and vice among the majority of the race. Nonetheless, the appeal of racial betterment through various degrees of sex activism crossed class lines with popular literature, public events, and the press enabling the crossover to occur. Furthermore, a variety of black women and men were receptive to sex reform—especially when such reform was presented as a sign of progress the race had made since slavery. Of course, there was an equally vital alternative discourse about sexuality in music and other forms of popular culture. Black popular culture was indeed a critical site where sex was discussed in terms of skill and endurance, desire and rapture: jokes, songs, and stories touched upon topics ranging from prostitution to incest, infidelity to homosexuality.[89] Yet when sexuality was marshaled in the name of racial betterment, that message had its own special attraction—an attraction that became a preoccupation for reformist women and men. In fact, Afro-American reform-ists' production of texts dealing with sexuality and conduct coincided with sex reform initiatives; these men and women created a vibrant discourse in the process, one riven by assumptions about class, anxieties over comport-ment, and significant gendered tensions.

sexual reformers
health
morals
values
eugenics (improve racial stock)
class
gendered

There is without a doubt a deep-seated feeling in the minds of many that the Negro problem is primarily a matter of morals and manners . . . that Negroes . . . are rude and tho[ugh]tless in manners and altogether quite hopeless in sexual morals.
—*Morals and Manners Among Negro Americans* (1914)

No race under heaven can thrive that does not value character. . . . High and noble aims must be instilled in the rising generation in order to redeem society and save the race.
—Josie Briggs Hall, *Build Character* (1906)

4

THE RIGHTEOUS PROPAGATION OF THE NATION
CONDUCT, CONFLICT, AND SEXUALITY

Racial reproduction and collective destiny were wed on the pages of tracts, manuals, and pamphlets—propagandistic works known alternately as conduct, advice, or prescriptive literature. This singular genre generated idealizations with the power to instruct as it detailed exemplary behavior for readers to copy and perfect. Produced by the aspiring and relatively elite for the masses, prescriptive literature instructed individuals anxious over their own mastery of ostensibly proper behavior and was therefore most likely consumed by aspiring women and men. From at least the early 1890s, conduct literature disseminated purposeful narratives about race women, men, and children, narratives that simultaneously produced and reproduced guidelines to be consumed, circulated, and perpetuated. Such literature also attempted to expand the aspiring class by promoting values befitting the upwardly mobile, by linking comportment and morals to success in life.

Afro-American domestic texts tended to fall in at least one of three categories between 1890 and 1920:

"instructors" such as *Golden Thoughts on Chastity and Procreation* that contained sexual and eugenic advice aimed at mature audiences; "self-educators," "home manuals," and encyclopedic volumes that provided a hodgepodge of general information, history, discourses on progress, and race facts; and advice manuals promoting etiquette and respectable behavior. There was often considerable overlap in a single volume. The *Afro-American Home Manual* (1902) combined subgenres by including race highlights and through offering "rules of etiquette for all occasions" and advice about sex and courtship. The *Manual* also reproduced standard business forms, contracts, wills, and deeds.[1] In a manner similar to the allied genres of "instructors" and "home manuals" containing sexual information, conduct literature transformed advice into knowledge capable of ensuring that black children, women, men, and households would thrive across the generations.

Significantly, prescriptive literature by and for the race emerged during an era when black men were rapidly being disfranchised, when the entrenchment of racial segregation called Afro-American citizenship into question, when African Americans were becoming increasingly literate and black women's fiction was rife with "domestic allegories of political desire."[2] The women and men who produced manuals often de-emphasized electoral politics in the name of building race character as they politicized domestic activity and freighted intraracial interactions with a sense of grave responsibility. With an occasional foreboding title such as *An Evil Router* or simply *Don't*, conduct manuals linked character to collective salvation as they attempted to achieve far more than uplift and respectability for African Americans. The genre enabled authors to articulate concepts that the race shared a destiny, that individuals could impact collective welfare by their purposefulness — or carelessness.

Josie Briggs Hall was at once typical and atypical of Afro-Americans inspired to write conduct literature. Her background as an ambitious yet struggling striver made her representative: born to an industrious family that was among the first cohort of African Americans to own land in Waxahachie, Texas, Josie Briggs was orphaned at eleven and self-sufficient by sixteen; she began a career as a teacher while still a teenager. After her marriage to fellow educator J. P. Hall during the late 1880s, Josie Briggs Hall bore five children and continued to work outside of the home as she juggled the needs of her sizable family. The Texas native also managed to nurture a sense within that the struggles she endured during her youth and young motherhood imbued her with the requisite wisdom to solve racial ills. Hall put this wisdom to

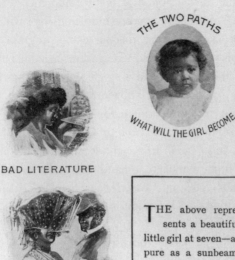

"The Two Paths," from Golden Thoughts on Chastity and Procreation, *(ca. 1903).
Different yet overlapping versions of "The Two Paths"—one for girls, the other for
boys—insinuated that loose living had dire, irreversible consequences. Courtesy of
General Research and Reference Division, Schomburg Center for Research in Black
Culture, New York Public Library, Astor, Lenox and Tilden Foundations.*

work in at least three published works, including two relatively brief tracts, *A Scroll of Facts and Advice* (1905) and *Build Character* (1906).

In addition to another manuscript that was lost in a fire before the turn of the century, Hall also published a full-length book in 1905 that was anything but a small, easily digestible, compact dose of advice. *Hall's Moral and Mental Capsule* was instead a 238-page prescriptive treatise on morals, sexual ethics, and home life that provided its author ample space to offer what were frequently harsh diagnostic observations:

> Yes! my people—descendants of Ham [are] a race whose blood is as impure and habits are as corrupt, as that of any people ever recorded in history. . . . I have compounded a capsule to remove the [illness] . . . by regulating the habits. . . . I have mixed and rolled a series of valuable ingredients together . . . to make a better people and solve the Negro problem. . . . May this capsule bring with it new life to the race, heroic womanhood and stalwart manhood, virtuous girls and industrious boys, worthy parents and better born children.

Hall desired to ease the distress of her people even if that meant calling out many of her brothers and sisters. Her language was dramatic, strident, and at times bordered upon racialist sentiment: Hall assailed men that sat around "on goods-boxes [and] beer-kegs, with nothing to do but slander girls and talk politics," chastised "impure women . . . [on] the streets . . . [that] entice[d] men and boys to enter the slums of debauchery." She lamented the race's being "affected with infectious diseases . . . some of them inherited" and additionally blamed relentless racial oppression for creating an "effete" people prone to "poverty immorality, immorality vice, vice crime, and crime illness." Rather than concluding that the entire race was on the road to ruin, however, Hall provided a moral and educational scheme that would ostensibly invigorate all aspects of Afro-American life. Significantly, Hall's scheme advocated widespread promotion of a "physical arithmetic . . . [to] teach the young people whom to marry, when to marry, and how to marry."[3]

Josie Hall's counsel concerning the "physical arithmetic" of marriage applied to males and females, but as an endorsement printed at the end of the *Capsule* revealed, the author really intended to impress her beliefs upon adolescent girls, young women, and mothers. She was especially worried that "young mothers . . . not old enough . . . [or] strong enough, to battle with the struggles that necessity forces upon them" compromised African American progress. The *Capsule* thus implied that girls who had babies before their time were likely to buckle under further temptation and fail to inculcate their children with moral values beneficial to the collective. These girls—along with young women and men who had children outside of marriage—could not provide "fit examples," nor could they "direct [the] destiny" of the race. For Josie Hall, girl-mothers simply did not contribute to healthy racial reproduction, and unmarried parents bore major responsibility for black degeneration.[4]

Hall's anxieties about adolescent sexuality and fornication emerged from her larger concern with marriage. Hall therefore devoted substantial energy to crafting bleak scenarios of women's marriages to lazy, intemperate, or morally suspect men; she portrayed such unions as woeful affairs riven by sexual infidelities, financial privation, and frequent abandonment. Accordingly, the *Capsule* included entire sections and instructive verse in which the author advised girls not to be promiscuous and women not to marry poorly. Such unions consigned women to backbreaking labor and placed mothers at risk of becoming "physical wrecks" destined to produce "children . . . distressed from the cradle . . . [with] inherited tendencies . . . against their future progress."[5]

The *Capsule* couched racial destiny in hereditarian terms. Its linkage of sexuality and morals to collective welfare and its insinuation that all was not well between black women and men made Hall's text a representative example of its genre in tone as well as purpose. Hall's *Moral and Mental Capsule* and other prescriptive literature forcefully implied that collective progress was contingent upon propriety in intraracial relationships, a propriety that Hall and other reformists believed had not yet developed among the growing Afro-American reading public. Hall was atypical in her position as a woman who authored multiple prescriptive works, yet her desire to contribute to a lasting body of advice literature linked her to a specific cohort of reformists.

Health and advice columns in race periodicals were certainly attempts to shape behavior by means of an ephemeral format, but it was the publication of tracts, manuals, pamphlets, and sermons that created a more permanent body of literature to assist individuals desirous of achieving and performing fitness for collective membership and national citizenship.[6] In newspapers and tracts alike, prescriptive writings suggested that African Americans would enjoy all the prerogatives of citizenship once the race "realized the importance of proper conduct and applied the principles of good management to all aspects of their lives."[7] However, the comparative permanency of bound texts such as *Hall's Moral and Mental Capsule* allowed for the possibility that acquisition of such knowledge might be gradual and that

African Americans would thereby benefit from works that could be passed across generations. Bound texts at once disseminated and codified values: publication and mass production made it easier for authors to reach wider audiences; both phenomena preserved information so that a daughter could receive the same wisdom as her mother.

Whether published lectures and sermons intended to move audiences to action or manuals designed to generate shared sensibilities, advice literature enabled reformist women and men to propagate ideas about behavior, sexual ethics, and "social regeneration." Afro-American conduct literature thus attempted to perpetuate moral ideals as it strove to develop and reproduce a new people. Guidelines within advice literature not only depicted an upright race striving ever upward, but such depictions were, in and of themselves, a form of reproduction not dissimilar to staged studio photographs in which individuals projected desired selves for display and circulation.[8] As print media that frequently included photographs and other images to vivify text and underscore consequences, advice literature imagined African Americans as a people seeking mutually beneficial standards, while multiplying those imaginings with each copy sold, distributed, or shared.

Not only did prescriptive literature propagate standards and imaginings, "reproduction" assumed multiple meanings within the genre: above and beyond biological perpetuation, "reproduction" meant recreating social purist beliefs to fit the needs of Afro-Americans; it entailed spreading those beliefs across an increasingly literate population; it implied character-building among successive generations.[9] Authors were therefore particularly interested in reaching mothers and fathers. "Not only your likeness will be reproduced in your children's forms and faces," one author admonished parent readers, "but your habits will be reproduced also." Indeed, the conduct of each woman and man—whether parent or not—that had contact with children constituted a behavioral "legacy" that at once facilitated race progress and "mould[ed] . . . [children's] destinies."[10] On the street, in the neighborhood, within boarding house and private home alike, adult behavior instructed girls and boys in the ways of womanhood and manhood. Adult comportment provided children with valuable insight, moreover, into how one should represent the race during daily interactions. Adult actions could, moreover, "teach without talking" by providing examples of character, behavior, and morals for children to emulate.[11] Manuals were therefore just as, if not more, likely to be aimed toward adult readership as they were to offer guidance to adolescents and children.

If authors of conduct literature felt the need to comment upon how adults

Lena R. Sherman and students, Mount Pleasant School, Wilkes County, Georgia, 1909. Conduct literature authors, many of whom were former teachers, considered schools a primary site for instruction in morals and comportment. Young teachers such as Lena Sherman encountered students who ranged considerably in age and were, in some cases, parents. Courtesy of Ruth Randall, Albuquerque, New Mexico.

could either guide or corrupt youths, authors wanted to purify households, mold children's behavior, monitor courtship, police leisure activity, and re-form—if not promote—matrimony. Such goals emerged as much out of perceived need as the lived experiences of the authors themselves. Many of women and men who took to dispensing advice on the printed page came from relatively humble backgrounds, endured hardship, and, through dint of their own labor and perseverance, rose to positions of some influence within their respective communities. As individuals who had managed to become upwardly mobile during an era of pervasive racial proscription, these women and men felt that they had earned the right to disseminate instruction to workers, parents, and young adults. Advice literature authored by men was similar to that authored by women in that both male and female authors felt entitled to be blunt about what they perceived to be the failings of other women and men.

Conduct tracts and manuals were allied to sex advice and education literature, yet conduct literature was as preoccupied with public performance as it was concerned with intimate behavior. Public performances of morality and character assumed particular significance for African Americans alive during the entrenchment of racial segregation. Indeed, given sexualized stereotypes about African Americans' alleged propensity toward promiscuity, immorality, and sexual crimes, conduct was freighted with sociopolitical significance for black women, men, and children. The perceived significance of propriety for African Americans resulted in reformist authors approaching sexualized and sexual behavior—kissing, dancing, flirting, infidelity, promiscuity, masturbation, molestation—with language ranging from evasive innuendo to unvarnished depiction. And, as representatives of a race widely considered indiscriminate and promiscuous, Afro-American authors firmly situated sex within the covenant of wedlock: not only was access to legalized marriage a largely postemancipation phenomenon for ex-slaves and their descendants, but as divorce rates doubled in the United States during the Progressive Era,[12] black authors often valorized orderly marital relations as indicative of collective progress.

Whereas Afro-Americans who published texts on the conduct of life likely eschewed graphic discussion of sexuality—whether within marriage or not—as a means to retain their own public appearance as morally upright authorities, the ways in which reformists wrote about conduct and public performances of sexuality would nonetheless change between the 1890s and 1910s. Tracts produced near the turn of the century tended to glorify marital bliss in euphemistic, codified fashion by offering fairly chaste visions of patriarchal order and maternal duty within race households; sexual inferences lurked between lines and behind loaded terms. Conduct literature became increasingly open by the mid-1910s as tracts warned against undue familiarities: one text written by a social purity activist in Kansas chronicled the soul-destroying impact of incest; another advice manual aimed at young girls and young mothers condemned masturbation with genteel language that still made plain to readers what was being discussed. Yet despite changes in how authors addressed sexuality, Afro-American conduct literature produced between 1890 and 1920 politicized conduct as it consistently made "the intimate visible and subject[ed] private activities to scrutiny and classification."[13] Such visibility and scrutiny would reveal a range of conflicts in the process—indeed, these conflicts swirled around sexuality, relationships, and interactions as much as they would shape the very genre itself.

Late-nineteenth- and early-twentieth-century black reformist authors followed the lead of white activists who produced freedmen's primers during and after the Civil War. Primers such as abolitionist and writer Lydia Maria Child's *The Freedman's Book* (1865) and Freedmen's Bureau commissioner Clinton Bowen Fisk's *Plain Counsels for Freedmen* (1866) highlighted which modes of etiquette and behavior would help former slaves navigate freedom's byways and avoid potential pitfalls. In the process, primers aided literacy, promoted faith, instructed readers in the duties of citizenship, and provided idealized examples of manhood and womanhood. For example, Reverend Jared Bell Waterbury's *Friendly Counsels for Freedmen* (1864) adjured former slaves to be industrious, temperate, honest, and godly. Its basic counsel further suggested that African Americans repeat a veritable mantra to themselves on a regular basis: "I will keep my body clean and my house clean, and my children clean; and this will remind me that I must be clean in my thoughts. . . . When I am tempted to impurity, I will say . . . 'How can I do this great wickedness, and sin against God?' I will keep from such vice." *Friendly Counsels* adopted an avuncular, if somewhat patronizing, tone as Waterbury's desire to ease former slaves' transition to free labor resulted in a text that extolled the virtues of exertion, thrift, and upright living. And, in its stern warning that adultery—and, by extension, promiscuity—was a tawdry remnant of slavery, *Friendly Counsels* firmly associated wedded monogamy with progress.[14]

The Freedmen's Book, for its part, contained inspiring biographical sketches, featured an exposition on the "Hour of Freedom" by celebrated abolitionist William Lloyd Garrison, and included a short story by Harriet Beecher Stowe. The primer highlighted perseverance through inclusion of Harriet Jacobs's memorial to her intrepid grandmother; it underscored race achievement by incorporating a variety of works by accomplished Afro-Americans such as Phillis Wheatley, Frances Harper, Frederick Douglass, and Charlotte Forten. Lydia Maria Child dispensed advice throughout the *Freedmen's Book*, too: "Young souls are fed by what they see and hear. . . . You can set them a pure and good example by your conduct and conversation"; "it is morally wrong to indulge in any habits that injure the health . . . of others"; "never allow yourselves to say or do anything in the presence of women of your own color which it would be improper for you to do or say in the presence of the most refined white ladies."[15] Child did not explicitly address adultery or promiscuity, but she did contend that moral instruction was ultimately more important than book learning. Child further argued that sustained demonstrations of virtue by black women, men, and children would slowly erode racism. Between its covers, the *Freedmen's Book* offered readers a potent combination of advice, poetry, exposition, and biography, a mix that provided multiple examples — examples located within in a range of contexts, no less — of how to act, bathe, mate, parent, forge ahead. Child even suggested that freed people's conduct had diasporic consequences in that sloth and moral turpitude on the part of Afro-Americans might compromise emancipation's fruition in Brazil and Cuba.[16]

Primers such as the *Freedmen's Book* presaged advice literature produced by African Americans during the decades immediately preceding and following the turn of the century by steadfastly arguing that routine conduct could either bolster or undermine collective weal. Suffused with an ethos similar to the uplift ideologies that would emerge later in the century, primers of the immediate postemancipation period were suffused with a didactic tone that would later be adopted in a relatively wholesale fashion by black authors anxious to underscore the significance of conduct. These race activists ultimately situated themselves in a position not unlike that assumed by the abolition-minded activists that penned primers: deeply invested mentors willing to broach the unflattering in the name of progress and, if need be, invoke stereotypes to incite the complacent into action. Just as primers provided guidance for the newly freed after the Civil War, pamphlets and manuals produced before and after the turn of the century were intended to help black women and men negotiate "the wilderness of post-Reconstruction."[17] The purpose and tone of post–Reconstruction era prescriptive literature was much the same as that of primers, yet Afro-American authors wrote with an urgency born of a more immediate connection to the intended audience — not to mention keen desires to disassociate themselves from seamy stereotypes associated with the race.

On the pages of conduct literature that began appearing during the 1890s, reformists' desires and needs led them to render patriarchy and moral motherhood as transformative, regenerative forces within black households. Authors eager to make specific arguments about an interconnected web of family and sexuality, womanhood and manhood, purposefully gendered their writings about the potential within and alleged faults of intraracial interaction. There was no neat pattern: both women and men reified motherhood as the primary catalyst for black progress; men as well as women stressed that authoritative fathers were uniquely capable of forging domestic order. Conversely, women reformers placed the onus for intraracial havoc on men that failed to earn a living wage, while race men chastised women they considered either promiscuous or willing to take white lovers. The genre contained its share of gendered admonition as it became a bully pulpit with its own gendered characteristics. Indeed, as the women's club movement coalesced and offered a space in which women read and circulated "club papers" with varied reformist content, men proved to be especially productive in the publication of bound tracts and books.[18]

In 1894, for example, William Reuben Pettiford's *Divinity in Wedlock* tried to inspire male readers on the brink of adulthood to "show [them]-selves men" by accumulating sufficient resources before marriage in order to "secur[e] a home" for their brides. Born almost five decades earlier in North Carolina to free parents, Pettiford lost two wives to sudden death before he was thirty-three years old. It was not until the 1880s and his third marriage to Della Boyd that Pettiford became a father. Despite his travails, Pettiford became a self-made man who believed that black advancement depended upon the heady combination of youth, masculinity, and muscle. *Divinity* appropriately contended that any young man that relied upon the labors of a "plucky young woman" did a disservice to himself, his partner, his race. The Baptist minister tellingly drew upon scripture in order to suggest that black women workers were capable of emasculating the entire Afro-American collective; for Pettiford, racial progress required that women's wages not be black households' primary source of income. Women were critical agents in *Divinity*'s scheme for modern black homes, but only as long as their efforts enabled male authority.[19]

Pettiford did make the seemingly heterodox argument that women were entitled to initiate courtship. He did so out of a belief that the social sphere was woman's sphere, a belief coupled to his conclusion that a prospective bride would pay dearly by choosing poorly. Such an argument on Pettiford's part hewed closely to prescriptive literature convention in that "it was the female participant [in marriage] to whom . . . [authors] addressed their most serious admonitions, for the marriage market seldom offered women an opportunity to renegotiate an adverse exchange."[20] Pettiford's contention that women were just as—if not more—concerned with proper mate selection as were men hardly translated into a conviction on his part that marriage should function as an equal partnership. Once married, Pettiford insisted, a woman was beholden to a sacred duty of wifely submission that demanded she allow her partner in wedlock "to rule" the household; at most, a wife could hope that her moral example and purity might "get her husband to do right." Pettiford even suggested that married men express their commands through intimation to create the illusion that their wives had a voice in household governance. Rendering patriarchy divine law, *Divinity* concocted a particular vision of postemancipation manliness as it maintained that youthful manhood on the cusp of a new century would compensate for the long, regrettable legacy of slavery.[21]

In keeping with the book's avuncular, manly tone, the minister refrained from divulging his own youthful tribulations and connubial traumas in *Divinity in Wedlock* as a means to inspire his readers. Rather, the preface announced: "the object of this pamphlet is to better acquaint the reader with the nature and laws of the marriage institution. . . . It is intended to assist the unmarried in making the proper selection for a suitable companion, and happily mating them for the nuptial journey. . . . While love fills a great space, . . . it is only one of the requisite passports to the matrimonial paradise." Pettiford proceeded to dispense advice about various stages of matrimony beyond courtship: divorce and widowhood were the subjects of two chapters, while the matter of holding on to a partner filled another; the author also offered suggestions as to child rearing and harmonious family life. He had distinct notions of who should marry as well. "Unbelievers," "drunkards," and "loafers" were among those "who should not marry" as were "people . . . in poor health or poor circumstance." Young and old should not intermarry nor should women under twenty or men under twenty-four take a spouse. And, for purposes of creating an upright race home, optimal unions were those between two youthful but mature people in their reproductive prime.[22]

Divinity in Wedlock's exploration of marital sexuality was purposefully obscured by its author, a man of the cloth who had a vested interest in rendering the race as morally unimpeachable and respectable. Quoting scripture throughout *Divinity*—including a revealing reference to I Timothy 5:14, in which young women and widows are advised to marry, have children, and provide no reason for enemies to slander their people—the reverend primarily counseled wives to be virtuous and husbands to remain monogamous. Pettiford was somewhat more forthright in discouraging promiscuity. He urged readers to disassociate themselves from immoral relatives and then condemned "flirts" for encouraging premarital temptation and adultery. If immoral relatives set bad examples for impressionable children and could potentially lead family members astray, "flirts" casually encouraged the sexual attention of others or—even worse—participated in the intimacies of sexual foreplay. Pettiford additionally maintained that "polygamy," "illegal habitation," and "children born out of the wedlock" cut against the law of scripture and reduced the race—especially its mothers—to "moral weaklings."[23]

When Pettiford subtly implied that weaklings begat weaklings, a quiet, lurking subtext of his argument suggested that a morally feeble people would eventually become physically enfeebled. Pettiford accordingly implored his readers to view "the birth of our babies" as a godly mission to occur only within the covenant of marriage. The reverend's theories about mating included vaguely eugenic phrasings concerning the "righteous propagation of the natio[n]," yet he avoided discussion of biological reproduction and instead focused upon the moral training of children. *Divinity in Wedlock* still managed to underscore that the fruit of matrimony built a people despite its lack of overt sex discussion. A book published barely thirty years after the abolition of slavery, *Divinity* was forthright in its argument that mating well and producing upright, healthy children resulted from nothing other than Christian marriage, chaste sexual relations, and proper home life.[24]

If William Pettiford's *Divinity* radiated an ecclesiastic sensibility regarding procreation, other aspiring and elite men felt that they, too, could address unsavory aspects of a racial heritage wrought from bondage by offering advice to readers experiencing the uncertainties of youth or preoccupied with the unpredictable thrills of courting. Lawyer, journalist, politico, and itinerant lecturer Robert Charles O'Hara Benjamin was one such man. Born in St. Kitts in 1855, Benjamin became a U.S. citizen during the 1870s while working as a political organizer in New York City. As much as Benjamin had a passion for politics, the tireless activist threw himself into a productive career as an author and a journalist: he published a slender volume of poems in 1883, released a biography of Toussaint L'Ouverture in 1888, edited a number of newspapers throughout the 1880s, and, in 1894 alone, authored both a "pocket" race history and an antilynching pamphlet.[25] Whereas Benjamin's labors as a writer and political agitator apparently left him little time for working within social reform organizations, he still found an effective means to promote manners and morals—his provocatively entitled pamphlet, *Don't: A Book for Girls*, which predated *Divinity in Wedlock* by three years.

Benjamin was not particularly original when it came to pleading *Don't*. The preface readily admitted that much of the advice manual consisted of "extracts from the press and passages from the writings of eminent authors."

Benjamin nonetheless failed to acknowledge that he was especially indebted to one Oliver Bell Bunce, a white editor whose own *Don't: A Manual of Mistakes and Improprieties more or less prevalent in Conduct and Speech* drew from "established authorities" as well. Both authors' books contained general advice on manners and speech — the volumes shared verbatim passages — yet the two *Don'ts* differed in distinct ways: Bunce's volume was aimed at young, middle-class, white men, whereas Benjamin injected commentary he believed relevant for young women of African descent. More specifically, Benjamin encouraged his female readers not to "slight any [honest] work" as he hinted at new opportunities available to women. Benjamin additionally implied that dubious company — "questionable" women and "profligate" men alike — could easily lead ingenues down into the valley of promiscuous behavior.[26]

Benjamin's version of *Don't* promoted the sort of behavior, morals, carriage, and speech befitting modest young womanhood and, eventually, wedded motherhood. The text pointedly discouraged idleness, flirting, dancing, vindictiveness, backbiting, gossip, and slangy speech. Girls were never to appear "vulgar," "rag-tag," or, even worse, "masculine": "The girl who wears an ulster, who strides, puts her hands in her pockets and imitates the opposite sex in walk and gesture, depr[e]cates and corrupts the delicacy, grace and beauty of the feminine sex. It was never the intention of nature that you should be a man." Since Benjamin was writing when notions about sexual inversion were just starting to transform into medicalized concepts of homosexuality, he stopped sort of suggesting that mannish girls harbored unnatural sexual desires for other females. Rather, by placing his observation about gender performance between reasons why girls should avoid shady associations and arguments regarding how young ladies should interact with the opposite sex, Benjamin wanted to convince his readers that both femininity and selectivity were essential elements of progressive race womanhood.[27]

One of the major reasons that Benjamin wrote — "compiled" might be more accurate — *Don't* was his conviction that girls and women had not received their share of philanthropic largesse given to African Americans since emancipation. Moreover, he believed that young women must be encouraged to become educated and purposeful since they, as mothers, would be responsible for the "future destiny of the race." Benjamin did not outline the specific duties of mothers within households, nor did he advise girls regarding their ostensible obligation to reproduce. And, as much as Benjamin believed that home was woman's "monument," *Don't* took the somewhat unorthodox position that it was better for a woman to remain forever single than to create a dysfunctional household with a drunk, "brute," or "knave." If a young woman did decide to wed, she had better take the time to assess her prospective husband's character. Not only was a bad husband difficult to shed, Benjamin warned, but an "unsteady man before marriage w[ould], after marriage, be like an unsteady lamp—apt to go out nights."[28]

Eight years later, another race man named Elias Woods would not be nearly as bold as Robert Benjamin, who suggested that young women should avoid the altar altogether rather than exchange vows with men of dubious virtue, but Woods's *The Negro in Etiquette: A Novelty* contained its share of foreboding advice on courtship—not to mention amusements likely to arouse youthful passions. The book, like others in its genre, contained previously circulated material: the first part of *The Negro in Etiquette* was initially given as a lecture at Missouri's Lincoln Institute; excerpts of that lecture were then serialized in the St. Louis *Post-Dispatch* prior to the book's actual publication. Woods capitalized upon the apparent popularity of his views on "rules governing degrees of intimacy" by using his book to address both the "giddy school girl" and "courting man" alike on matters both interracial and intraracial. Straightforward prose lent *The Negro in Etiquette* an accessible tone, while illustrations depicting various scenes—a vigilant young woman refusing a potentially lusty kiss, a shady "street corner dude" awaiting innocents, disorderly dancers staggering to a "rag," a frowzy housewife encountering a prim, proper race woman—underscored major points.[29]

Woods's original lecture, "The Gospel of Civility," included relatively general advice on "introductions," "church etiquette," "sidewalk etiquette," and "how to test true love," but it also cautioned against the imminent dangers of dance-hall gyrations.[30] In both original lecture and expanded book, Woods dissuaded youth from swinging their hips to the latest dance crazes: he condemned ragtime as sexually depraved and racially degenerate, claimed that the two-step had the power to "excite animal passions which tend to lead the participants astray," and warned that the cakewalk quickly compromised respectability.[31] The expanded book version, moreover, dismissed potential counterclaims that the cakewalk provided healthy, harmless exercise that even "refined, educated, and wealthy white folks" enjoyed. As far as Woods was concerned, the quotidian sway of prejudice and stereotype meant that the race simply could not afford to indulge in an animalistic dance fad that smacked of degeneracy.[32]

Allegations that African Americans were inherently degenerate—inclined toward political corruption, dishonesty, indolence, promiscuity, rape, and sundry crimes and enervated by constitutional diseases ranging from insanity to tuberculosis—were part and parcel of the environment in which Pettiford, Benjamin, and Woods produced their respective books. At mid-decade, the explosive charge by white editor James Jacks that black women were utterly devoid of virtue catalyzed the formation of the National Association of Colored Women. Frederick Hoffman's *Race Traits and Tendencies of the American Negro* was simultaneously hailed by scientific racialists as providing incontrovertible statistical evidence that African Americans were irredeemable; indeed, the 1890s witnessed a potent coalescence of scientific racialist thought. Moreover, notions of racial degeneracy vitally informed the concurrent erosion of black civil rights. African Americans' status as second-class citizens—the steady proliferation of Jim Crow rail cars throughout the South, disfranchisement at the polls by means of literacy tests and understanding clauses—was not only entrenched during the 1890s, it was codified by the 1896 Supreme Court decision in *Plessy v. Ferguson.*[33]

Black women and men not only challenged segregation and disfranchisement on a routine basis, they refused to accept the mantle of degeneracy in silence. African Americans produced a dizzying array of counternarratives to challenge restrictive legislation and rebut mainstream hypotheses, up to and including the stream of sociological studies that emerged out of Atlanta University during the decade's latter years. The prescriptive writings of Benjamin, Pettiford, and Woods were part and parcel of such normalizing counterdiscourses that humanized the race. Again, prescriptive texts for and by the race predated the 1890s: freed people's primers entreated African Americans to embrace the responsibilities and burdens of free labor; Dr. Rebecca Crumpler's *Book of Medical Discourses* dispensed advice on "How to Marry" and child rearing along with medical guidelines on infant care as early as 1883; educator and conservative race man William Hooper Councill schooled workers on how to "elevat[e] the home life" in 1887's *The Negro Laborer: A Word to Him.* The works that appeared during and after the 1890s, however, formed a politicized and cohesive genre forged in response to a searing firestorm of racist claims that escalated lynching and rationalized disfranchisement and segregation. By their very publication, black conduct manuals suggested that the race contained a better element willing and able to improve themselves—in short, an element that was anything but degenerate.

Still and again, rhetorics of degeneracy vexed and animated the reformists who produced black prescriptive literature: Pettiford pointedly addressed alleged gender role inversion within the race by stressing that black men must head black families; Benjamin dealt with allegations regarding the character and virtue of young black women by writing in a conversational tone that skillfully created a sense that young women were in willing dialogue with his admonitions; Woods, for his part, suggestively challenged the logic of racial segregation by delineating rules that comprised public performances of respectability. These men were motivated to write by perceived intraracial needs, certainly, but these needs spoke to particular issues — relationships of husbands to wives, female purity, public comportment — that lay at the center of mainstream allegations about black degeneracy. The concept of degeneracy not only had gendered valences for authors of Afro-American conduct literature, but authors' concerns about racial reproduction often resulted in texts that focused largely on young women. Even texts aimed at both sexes could nevertheless imply that female behavior was especially capable of perpetuating racial degeneracy.

Damning allegations inspired a Fisk University professor of Hebrew and the Old Testament to publish some of his own sermons dealing with race behavior. Eugene Harris's homiletic tracts were not guides on the conduct of life in the strictest sense, however. *Two Sermons on the Race Problem* (1895) was a jeremiad intended to jar young men into the realization that disease and immorality placed Afro-America at risk of losing a Darwinian struggle for continued existence. *An Appeal for Social Purity in Negro Homes* (1898) adjured young men to protect spouses and female relatives; it sternly advised young women not to "make it hard for the young men to defend" race womanhood.[34] Whereas his works were not completely within the advice genre, Harris appended brief prefaces to both *Two Sermons* and *An Appeal* in which he clearly expressed his intention to inspire exemplary behavior in his readers. *Two Sermons* and *An Appeal* were therefore hybrid texts born of the Fisk professor's anxieties about race morals, anxieties that suffused the very texts he desired "to put . . . into the hands of the young people."[35]

It was *An Appeal*, however, that engaged charges of black degeneracy in sustained fashion by engaging contemporary stereotypes about black women's morals and conduct and then linking women's behavior to racial reproduction. Black women's comportment around white men was of particular concern: the mere exchange of pleasantries between black women and white men led to "infamy and ruin"; flirting was but a "doorway to sexual crimes"; "tolerat[ing] improper liberties" both continued the unsavory sexual heritage of slavery and enabled ongoing "slander" against race women. Whereas Harris refrained from arguing that miscegenation resulted in a physically weakened people, he more than implied that illicit sex between black women and white men compromised the very continuance of African American families. Inviolate women reserved for endogamous marriage made for a progressive race; as important as it was for men to act as protectors, Harris believed it more important for women to police themselves. *An Appeal* was, then, ultimately more of an appeal to women than an appeal on behalf of women.[36]

Another hybrid text appeared four years prior to Eugene Harris's *Appeal*, and it too acknowledged that black women were "tempted by two races"; the author of this earlier text employed an "advice essay formula" as well but to notably different effect. Inasmuch as Gertrude Bustill Mossell's *Work of the Afro-American Woman* (1894) was primarily a literary and intellectual history that served as a corrective to prevailing notions about black women, the text also included a pivotal chapter, "The Opposite Point of View," that offered heterodox guidance for girls and young women. Mossell began the chapter with a subtle entreaty to her contemporaries to cease thinking of courtship as an institutionalized phase of "deception." She argued that if the settled reality of married life paled in comparison to the halcyon days of wooing, that change did not necessarily mean that courting flatteries were any less genuine. In the process, Mossell suggested that viewing courtship as license to deceive might actually contribute to eventual incompatibility between married women and men. Most significantly, the journalist and mother of two young girls challenged typical domestic advice that focused on women's ostensible failings. Mossell not only questioned why so few writers directed their domestic counsel to men—an audience Mossell implied "need[ed] this teaching most"—she encouraged married women to speak their minds rather than practice endless, futile self-abnegation in the name of household harmony.[37]

Overall, "The Opposite Point of View" suggested that Afro-American advice literature was gendered in inequitable ways that buttressed problematical notions about black girls and women. Whereas Mossell ultimately refrained from delineating the very instruction that she insinuated men sorely needed, she boldly challenged the overall thrust of Afro-American advice literature. She did so by relying upon a key trope used frequently within the genre around the turn of the century: careful adjuration that typically made pointed arguments through "genteel Christian rhetoric."[38] Mossell's strategy was successful inasmuch as her "Opposite Point of View" did not prevent a second edition of *Work of the Afro-American Woman* from being published in 1908.[39]

Authors publishing after the turn of the century would adopt tactics similar to Mossell when they addressed relationships between wives and husbands, proper behavior, and sexual purity. Carefully worded appeals animated both Reverend L. T. Christmas's *An Evil Router* (1900) and educator William Noel Johnson's *Common Sense in the Home* (1902). Foreboding title aside, the *Evil Router* was a "[m]issionary [p]amphlet" intended to "medicate" moral derelicts. Christmas provided race activists with a detailed outline to follow when establishing local uplift associations. The teacher and former state legislator avoided detailed discussion of moral lapses and instead stressed that morals, "home relations," and etiquette were essential to collective progress. In contrast, *Common Sense*—innovative in its use of staged photographs yet staid in approach to domestic life—hewed closely to the tone and sensibility of *Divinity in Wedlock*; its chapters stressed the importance of orderly, patriarchal households, home training, and love of race and nation. Johnson's emphasis on moral and physical cleanliness extended beyond advising adults to be exemplars for youths: Johnson implored adults to avoid the "promiscuou[s] kissing of little children," a practice that he contended spread "syphilis and other terrible diseases." Johnson's reference to syphilis was fleeting, yet it still reflected a tentative broadening of topics addressed on the pages of Afro-American conduct literature.[40]

Indeed, black advice literature produced after 1900 became somewhat more willing to touch upon the charged and taboo. This gradual change coincided with the publication of Afro-American home manuals, yet it is difficult to know whether the relative explicitness of texts such as *Golden Thoughts on Chastity and Procreation* had a direct influence on advice literature authors. It is, moreover, difficult to know if the relative explosion in sex education texts aimed at younger readers during the early twentieth century encouraged black writers to embrace a somewhat more open approach to sexuality.[41] Whether as a result of the publication of more explicit material or due to a shift in sexual attitudes, Afro-American advice literature authors began to broach ever more sensitive subjects—albeit in euphemism at times—in the years immediately following the initial publication of *Golden Thoughts* in 1903. The early twentieth century, then, witnessed a slight shift among reformist writers within elite and aspiring race circles regarding the way in which intimate matters were invoked in the name of collective progress.

A children's text published in 1905 was somewhat outside of the slow shift toward candidness, yet its references to gender disorder and inversion nonetheless moved beyond the tight-lipped concern over strutting girls expressed in *Don't. Floyd's Flowers; or, Duty and Beauty for Colored Children* presented the Afro-American reading public with a hundred tales and over seventy-five illustrations to educate, inspire, and guide.[42] Advertised as the "first and only race book of the kind ever written," a book in which Afro-American children could "read of themselves, instead of other children," *Floyd's Flowers* was a moralistic and uplifting children's book published during an era of deepening racial discrimination. The text's author, Silas X. Floyd, eschewed direct discussion of obstacles facing Afro-Americans and instead attempted to inculcate self-reliance along with a quiet sense of race pride in his readers.[43] The illustrations by race artist John Henry Adams — pen and ink illustrations that would largely be replaced by photographs in subsequent editions — simultaneously assisted Floyd's goal and "constituted [a] means of demonstrating black humanity and . . . deservedness."[44]

Illustrations and all, Silas Floyd's text warned girls, boys, and their parents that questionable associates, activities, and character flaws had fretful consequences, and he did so with an appreciable amount of skill. The Atlanta University graduate and one-time contributing editor of the *Voice of the Negro* was a fairly accomplished writer who, by 1905, had already published a biography, a sermon for young men, a brief address, and numerous periodical items. Floyd's writing ability enabled him to use turns of phrase to such effect in *Floyd's Flowers* that he simultaneously imparted morals to children through "clean" stories and warned parents about seamy possibilities — such as children picking up sex information on the streets — between the lines of those stories.[45]

Floyd was notably careful in the way in which he addressed perils facing girls and young women. Indeed, several of his tales with female protagonists avoided direct mention of potential sexual dangers and instead featured innocent, thoughtful, respectful little girls engaged in wholesome activities. The Sunday school organizer's more piquant vignettes addressed "loud," "don't care" girls donning brassy ornaments, tawdry clothes, and "boy's hats." These girls embodied gender disorder: they were far too bold and independent, if not impudent; such pitiable girls "cut . . . foolish capers," behaved poorly in public, attended too many parties, pursued boys, allowed young men to caress them about the waist. Through euphemism, innuendo, and the occasional declaration, *Floyd's Flowers* informed its readers that each and every promiscuous girl was on the road to ruin and would eventually "come to open disgrace[,] . . . die and go to torment." In contrast, modest, orderly, progressive girls were mindful of the impression that they made upon others. A proper girl would even refuse to engage in off-color con-

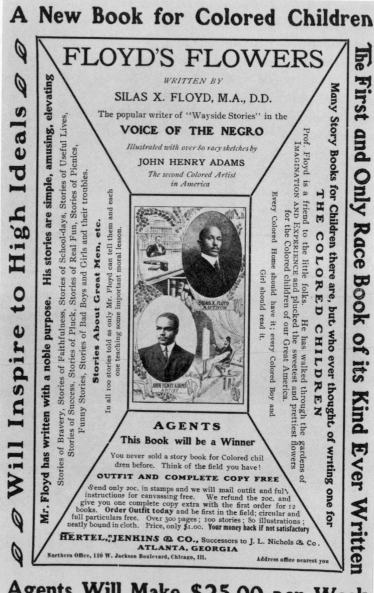

Advertisement for Floyd's Flowers *from* Voice of the Negro, *August 1905. Distinctive in tone and focus,* Floyd's Flowers *was marketed as an unparalleled teaching tool, an inspirational necessity for "every Colored home," and a unique sales opportunity. Courtesy of General Research and Reference Division, Schomburg Center for Research in Black Culture, New York Public Library, Astor, Lenox and Tilden Foundations.*

versations—conversations that, as far as Floyd was concerned, only lured, seduced, and despoiled.[46]

Boys definitely received their share of attention in *Floyd's Flowers*, since Silas Floyd addressed the hazards of young manhood at greater length and with more openness. His text repeatedly underscored that a cursing, cigarette-smoking "rowdy boy"—like the "loud girl"—was a disorderly disgrace headed for an unproductive life of dissipation; he argued that the "school of the street" was such a degenerate influence that it "turn[ed] out the most impure, the most dishonest, and most illiterate boys." Bullies, truants, and urchins were vexing enough, but even more worrisome were effete lads that never ventured out-of-doors for healthy, vigorous games. Silas Floyd hardly hid his disdain for any boy who was "'most a girl": such an unmanly—and, by implication, unnatural—specimen would either perish in youth or spend a warped life as a "male woman . . . hardly fit for anything." Faulty home training was not, as far as Floyd was concerned, necessarily responsible for creating these delicate lads. Still, if "fast" behavior and sartorial androgyny on the part of girls suggested sexual looseness, feminine demeanor on the part of boys indicated an irregularity every bit as problematic as truancy, delinquency, and intemperance. Thus, parents needed to police *what* boys did as much as they needed to monitor *how* boys acted.[47]

Overall, *Floyd's Flowers* blamed careless, habitually absent parents for producing "mannish boy[s]," "womanish girl[s]," and "young flirts" as it tried to instill at least three principles into its young readers. To begin, children determined the future of the race. Uplift also required gender performances by youth that were in line with societal expectations and indicative of heterosexual purity; moreover, each girl and boy had to work hard and be ever vigilant in order to demonstrate fitness for both racial and national life. Through discreet yet ominous language that discouraged promiscuity and gender-inappropriate behavior, *Floyd's Flowers* therefore stressed that both mannerisms and comportment could brand one wayward, if not worthy of insult.[48] This overarching argument by Floyd, along with his more gender-specific messages, hardly went unread or unnoticed: *Floyd's Flowers* was reportedly used as a textbook in some schools; its publisher claimed that 20,000 copies were sold in 1905 alone; at least four reissues or revisions of the book appeared between 1905 and 1925.[49] The *Voice of the Negro* even proclaimed the text "a peculiar blessing at this time when the white man is insisting that color is virtue."[50]

Another book published in 1905 sought to reach audiences with its own set of moral imperatives—Josie Hall's *Moral and Mental Capsule*. The *Cap-*

sule's "unvarnished truth" was intended for a mature audience, and Hall was fairly blunt in identifying what she considered moral failings and lapses in conduct.[51] Despite her ready willingness to castigate adulterous wives, unmarried mothers, and slatternly women, Hall stressed that men were primarily responsible for the "miserable homes" strewn across "four different classes" of Afro-America: "Who will dare to enumerate the hundreds of Negro women whose lives have been crushed, health destroyed, and have lived lives of sorrow; who, by proper care and treatment from husbands, would have made . . . noble wives? When one realizes the unhappy condition of homes caused by unworthy husbands . . . we will not wonder why some women grow desperate and fail to make worthy mothers and live chaste lives." "Proper care" entailed more than consideration or protection: it involved men earning a living wage so women did not have to labor both inside and outside of the home. Hall fretted that male underemployment undermined racial health in more ways than one and, as a result, she argued that underemployment forced women to engage in physically taxing work in order to cover household expenditures while their underemployed partners frequented bordellos and saloons. As did many of her contemporaries, Hall maintained that robust racial reproduction was hindered by the dubious heritage bequeathed by intemperance and by stillbirths brought on by overwork or venereal disease. If, as Hall argued, men with too much time on their hands were prime candidates for infidelity and promiscuity, then the purity of women associated with loafers and gadabouts teetered on the precipice.[52]

Hall further attempted to convince her male readers that if they failed to supply their households with adequate financial support, they cheated women as surely as any philanderer could. A burdened—or abandoned—working woman typically faced limited options when it came to supplementing her income. Hall therefore reasoned that if such a woman strayed from the road of righteous womanhood, a man was probably the one who pushed her off: a husband who deserted the homestead was responsible for creating a grass widow who used sexual favors as currency; a delinquent father created an overtaxed mother who, in desperation, might resort to questionable means of earning money; a hard-working woman who supported a lazy lothario might well be rewarded with either syphilis or gonorrhea for her efforts. Whereas Hall refrained from explicitly connecting promiscuity and venereal affliction, her invocation of "disease" and poor health throughout her discussion of women, marriage, and mating suggested that choosing the wrong man could have dire consequences.[53]

Her strong convictions regarding male culpability notwithstanding, Hall was evenhanded when it came to finding fault and fingering foes. The *Capsule* simultaneously blamed and absolved men as it excoriated women whose sexual behavior did not conform to Hall's standards of propriety. In "The Unfaithful Wife," for example, Hall warned grooms about the perils of entering the state of wedlock with flirtatious women as she emphasized that every young man contemplating marriage needed to realize that it often took sufficient income to "make a virtuous woman." At the same time, however, Hall's verse tried to shame women into prim domesticity. Proclaim as she might that men bore the primary responsibility for ruined homes, "The Unfaithful Wife" highlighted the moral duties — and failings — of women. Hall further underscored women's moral duties in a section aimed at her younger readers. In the "Pinnacle of Fame," Hall urged girls to "reach the pinnacle or die in the ascend[a]ncy"; she detailed seven steps by which girls could stay pure, resist temptation, overcome compromised heredity, persist despite ill-meaning relatives, and embody virtuous young womanhood. Since the race could not "rise higher than its women" as far as Josie Hall was concerned, she was particularly determined to reform the moral expectations that African American girls and women had for themselves.[54]

Hall's Moral and Mental Capsule enabled Josie Briggs Hall to enter the discursive domain of conduct literature — one dominated by male writers — in a way that was both more forceful and more sustained than Gertrude Mossell's intervention in 1894. Hall's treatment of sexuality remained within the realm of innuendo, yet even her insinuations linked marriage to sexuality in ways absent from texts such as *Divinity in Wedlock* and *Common Sense in the Home*. Moreover, the *Capsule*'s 1905 publication date situated it, along with *Floyd's Flowers*, at a crucial juncture when the race was becoming increasingly urbanized, and new concepts regarding the "sexual adolescent" were beginning to emerge within mainstream culture.[55]

By the mid-1910s and the dawn of the First Great Migration, not only had Afro-American club women established urban working girls' homes to protect young women from sexual predators but black reformers began to address adolescents as more explicitly sexual beings that had particular needs and faced specific perils. As mainstream intellectuals, reformers, and psychiatrists shaped emergent discourse on adolescence between 1900 and 1920, adolescence was construed as a life cycle "difficult for boys, . . . treacherous for girls." Maturing boys had their problems to be sure: controlling urges to self-gratify, avoiding venereal disease during sexual experimentation. Developing girls, as Josie Hall was wont to point out, risked being deflowered and ruined; not only was pregnancy a looming possibility for sexually active girls past menarche, but sexual experimentation was not generally considered the rite of passage for unattached adolescent girls that it was for their male counterparts.[56] Early-twentieth-century race reformers other than Josie Hall realized that adolescence had gendered implications, and they would soon add their voices to emergent discourse by producing pamphlets of their own for maturing girls.

One unlikely race reformer was concert singer Emma Azalia Hackley, who traveled throughout the South in order to speak before girls and young women in locales ranging from colleges to backcountry schools. Hackley was a prominent race woman whose lectures reflected class privilege: she emphasized proper expression, tasteful dress, and modest comportment and wished to instruct girls and young women in the ways of "the genteel performance."[57] Still, Hackley did far more than expound the gospel of gentility: she acknowledged—in an upright, respectable, and often euphemistic fashion—that adolescent African American girls had concerns about their own sexuality. Her talks were so popular that she published them as *The Colored Girl Beautiful* in 1916. The book did not include the dicier, "personal" sections from Hackley's public appearances in which she dealt with individual questions, but its chapters on "Love," "Her Relationships with Men," "The Colored Wife Beautiful," and "The Colored Mother Beautiful" touched upon a range of intimate matters.[58]

With a matronly but friendly tone, Hackley informed her readers that they should never view sex as recreation, allow "young men . . . to stroke their bodies," or even worse, "sell" themselves. A maturing, developing girl's "lower nature"—her burgeoning sexual desire—was something "she must conquer or control." Sex was for motherhood, having children was "the chief aim" of marriage, and mothers were nothing less than "health officers" who would "carve the destiny of the race." "The beautiful part about the colored race in America is the future," radiated Hackley. "This race is a growing people . . . [and the] cry of the hour is 'A better breed of babies.' As it takes several generations to breed a prize winner, it is time for the colored race to . . . prepare for the future colored child." She prodded young women to "study . . . the laws of heredity" and encouraged her readers to prize chastity and reproductive health. Emma Hackley also borrowed popular eugenic ideas, translated them into more accessible notions of uplift and betterment, and urged others to work for the future of the race. Not only were young race women to refrain from promiscuity, they were to cherish their wombs as vessels capable of racial regeneration. Hackley even urged mothers to teach their sons "a right idea of the sacred sex organs" so that they would achieve "self mastery . . . even in sleep and recreation." Admonitions regarding temptation, masturbation, better breeding, and all, *The Colored Girl Beautiful* broached sexuality by situating sex within its reproductive capacity.[59] Hackley's approach received praise from one race paper that considered her *Colored Girl Beautiful* as nothing less than "novel," "ideal," and "grand" in spite of its containing language considered "too strong for the girls that ought to read the book."[60]

Two years before publication of *The Colored Girl Beautiful*, a social purity activist presented himself as another concerned friend of young womanhood. Reverend Revels Alcorn Adams had three daughters of his own and was anxious over what he considered "degeneration of the womanhood of the race." His advice manual, *The Negro Girl* (1914), was intended to inspire righteous behavior, offer counsel regarding the dangers facing his readers, and outline adults' responsibilities to young race womanhood. A temperance crusader who would go on to produce tracts decrying syphilis and ragtime, Adams criticized men who were drunkards, abusers, or otherwise errant; he maintained that young men had a duty to protect the chastity of their sisters. Female morality involved more than individual integrity—it involved collective action. As Adams put it, "we must save the girl or lose the race."[61]

The Negro Girl was produced out of a sense of urgency that resulted in direct prose, especially in comparison to the innuendo of *Hall's Moral and Mental Capsule* and the delicacy of Emma Hackley's *Colored Girl Beautiful*. Adams's authorial voice was avuncular and at times gentle. The text sympathetically detailed sexual traps riddling the life paths of black girls—including predatory white men—as it presented one woeful tale after another. His tabulation of perils facing budding race womanhood was replete with anecdotal, "real life" accounts vivifying the tragic experiences of girls ruined by poor heredity and lust, prostitution and abortion, venereal disease and promiscuity, sexual harassment and interracial liaisons. A specific taboo compelled Adams to be particularly frank. Repulsed over sexual crimes perpetrated upon girls by "'male members of the family,'" he spent considerable ink discussing incest and molestation as a despoiler of domestic environments, as a force that pushed girls with no means of support out into the streets. He did so, in part, by including the story of a mother who discovered that her sons had deflowered their sisters along with the narrative of a girl whose father began assaulting her at the age of twelve. Adams even reproduced what he claimed were actual letters written by crestfallen survivors.[62]

The effect was nothing short of dramatic. "I just cannot see our home broken up and . . . disgraced,'" disclosed an anonymous adolescent, "'Oh, Rev. Adams, though it almost kills me, I must confess that it is my own father that has ruined me!'" Another young woman poignantly described how rape and sexual exploitation vitiated her health and broke her will: "'with my body wrecked . . . as the result of the sins of men against me . . . I am almost helpless and entirely hopeless . . . and [might] as well kill myself.'" Not only did such vivid, personal testimony authenticate Adams's insistence that incest and molestation destroyed the psyches and bodies of young women, it assured those carrying similarly shameful burdens that they were not alone. The confessions — doctored or not — also encouraged women to be more vigilant when it came to observing interactions between daughters and brothers-in-law, grandfathers, uncles, siblings, cousins, stepfathers, fathers, and other relatives. Furthermore, the testimonials enabled Adams to drive a critical point home: happenings within one's own household had the potential to push little girls and adolescents toward precipitous physical and moral decline. As much as the section on incest and molestation spoke to girls and women, Adams wanted to jolt "lustful, inhuman" adults into the realization that they deserved nothing less than death for their heinous activities with children.[63]

Revels Adams's *The Negro Girl* was at once a wake-up call to young women and black Americans at large: it addressed the concerns of prepubescent and adolescent girls as it elaborated those concerns to brothers, suitors, fathers, and mothers. Unlike *Don't, Hall's Moral and Mental Capsule*, and *The Colored Girl Beautiful, The Negro Girl* simultaneously attacked the sensitive issue of sexual abuse and addressed housing issues facing an increasingly urbanized African American population. Adams's forthright manner in addressing difficult subjects such as incest and molestation allowed him to appear as a defender of race womanhood. And, whereas he included little extended commentary on patriarchy, Adams stressed that the ideal race man both controlled his sexual impulses and was a teetotaling, hardworking protector of the home.

With its vision of proper behavior for both women and men, Adams's work—along with Pettiford's, Hall's, and others'—instructed African Americans how to live and behave within their communities and within an often hostile world. Afro-American conduct literature addressed a racial collective as it accomplished what mainstream prescriptive literature did: conduct literature for and by African Americans elaborated "the ideal relationship between the individual and . . . society, the obligations of each to the other, and the order of priorities of those obligations."[64] Accordingly, the genre concocted idealized versions of womanhood and manhood for a people anxious to prove their fitness for national citizenship and the franchise. Not all conduct literature directly addressed matters of citizenship or the franchise, however. One of the primary attributes linking the disparate style and substance of black conduct literature produced between 1890 and 1920, then, is the way in which these texts indicated intraracial tensions—not to mention struggles between real men and women. Indeed, advice literature for the race reflected this dynamic along with other salient realities.

As post–Reconstruction era texts that occasionally articulated the relationship between race aspiration and black involvement in the national body politic, Afro-American manuals tended to privilege "a politicized domesticity" over electoral politics. For example, William Noel Johnson announced in *Common Sense in the Home* that it was far better for black women and men to nurture race pride in the home "than to wince and whine and wail about *constitutional rights, ostracism,* and *discrimination.*"[65] *Evil Router* author L. T. Christmas was just as blunt. Christmas, a man who once held elective office in North Carolina, told his readers to "drop politics"; as far as the former legislator was concerned, harmonious marital relations and upstanding morals would "ge[t] the colored race on the proper track of life."[66]

For her part, Josie Hall contended that Afro-American home life suffered terribly in the years following emancipation because race men misspent precious energy obtaining political rights during Reconstruction. Hall's own relationship to politics was conflicted at best. Not only did she distance herself from suffragist aspirations and "women's rights," Hall had once struggled with her husband over his involvement in local governance. Their disagreement ended—by her account at least—with his removal from party politics. "I told him that he should not run any risks," she recalled, "that it was not safe for Negroes to deal too much in politics, for too many dangers threatened their homes." The "risks" Hall alluded to when discussing her own marital discord are not that difficult to imagine: black officials were lynched, intimidated, driven away from their families; women were sexually assaulted, terrorized, and lynched in waves of politically inspired terror. Perhaps Hall had witnessed or experienced retributive mob violence herself; perhaps she lost family members who dared assert their rights at the polls. In the final analysis, Josie Hall resolutely maintained that electoral politics were far more destructive than constructive for Afro-American households—black men, she believed, could best serve their families by eschewing the ballot box.[67]

One of Hall's contemporaries, Scotia Seminary graduate Anne Walker Blackwell, expressed trepidations of her own regarding the franchise. Blackwell was engaged in Women's Christian Temperance Union politics, health activism, and home mission work; her tract, *The Responsibility and Opportunity of the Twentieth Century Woman*, was published during the years leading up to passage of the Nineteenth Amendment. *Responsibility and Opportunity* admonished race women for their "lack of interest" in pressing contemporary issues as it implored African American mothers to "wake up and . . . correct the faults of your children." Blackwell also found fault in white women activists when she questioned the sincerity of white suffragists on the matter of universal woman suffrage. More specifically, Blackwell—who did not consider herself a suffragist—felt that until it was certain that white suffragists would not devise something akin to an exclusionary "'grandmother's clause,'" race women should channel their energies into avenues besides the suffrage movement and focus on domestic reform. Her entreaty regarding the importance of the domestic sphere aside, Blackwell was nonetheless convinced that black women would be more powerful agents of domestic and social change once they possessed the vote.[68] Not all race women considered enfranchisement detrimental to home life, then. A few years after *Responsibility and Opportunity* was published and shortly before *The Colored Girl Beautiful* appeared, Nannie Burroughs urged black women to seize the vote due to her conviction that "the black man does not know the value of the ballot."[69]

The turn toward domesticity on the part of early-twentieth-century African Americans was, in many regards, a surrogate for electoral politics in their quest for self-determination. Politics and politicians were even skewered by some domestic reformers. B. Q. Lee of Pittsburgh likened politicians to reprobates in his attempt to garner support for a "National Home Culture League." "With the great future of the race in the hands of the politician, the sport, the ward heeler, the loafer, and the street walker," Lee contended in 1911, "our doom is sealed. . . . We must be stirred up to a sense of our pressing duty to our homes, our children, our race and our God."[70] Lee's sentiment reveals that when "political options" for Afro-Americans constricted during the late nineteenth and early twentieth centuries, such constriction led many aspiring and petit bourgeois race folk to view conduct, "home[,] and family as the crucial site of race building."[71] Furthermore, the decision of domestic tract writers such as Johnson, Christmas, and Hall to stress the home rather than the poll was part of a larger tactical move by a number of African American women and men who concentrated upon intraracial reform. Significantly, such a turn "from the ballot box to the home . . . was canny political strategy that meshed nicely with the new welfare role of the state."[72]

Not only was the turn toward domesticity political in its own right, the very production of advice literature had its own gendered politics. Aspiring and elite women were heavily invested in domestic reform: women gave speeches at churches, benevolent clubs, and settlement houses; they organized mothers' meetings, engaged in grassroots reform efforts, distributed pamphlets, circulated club papers. Additionally, the circulation of printed "club papers" on subject matter ranging from temperance to public behavior assured "the success of . . . club women's . . . public service projects."[73] Women certainly compiled or authored tracts, pamphlets, and manuals given this flurry of activity. What women of African descent produced, then, could be lost—or yet to be discovered. Josie Hall was nevertheless one of few women to publish an extended domestic tract aimed at instructing readers in the ways of domesticity, let alone provide extensive analysis on the impact of Reconstruction era politics on black households.

The sheer number of men among the authors of extant texts suggests that reform-minded black men saw it as their prerogative to claim a prominent place for themselves in domestic reform through production of domestic tracts. The domestic turn "explicitly increased women's importance at a time when women across the nation campaigned to extend their influence through volunteer activities and the professionalization of social work." Such expansion of women's role within African American communities certainly "threatened" some race men, some of whom were eager to shape a *political* domestic discourse.[74] The perceived threat posed by black women's activity, moreover, apparently informed some black men's decisions to produce domestic texts—the prime example being Pettiford's *Divinity in Wedlock*—that underscored the primacy of patriarchy in uplift politics. Men such as Robert Benjamin and Revels Adams even tried to establish themselves as male authority figures that had the power, the right, to tell black women what to do and how to do it.

The move toward intraracial reform might also be seen as a particular means of political self-preservation for African Americans. Domestic tracts — specifically etiquette books such as E. M. Woods's *The Negro in Etiquette* — were attempts to "increase racial harmony even as the era of Jim Crow laws and racial attacks began." Above and beyond racial conciliation, activist black men probably considered production of domestic texts an alternative avenue for political expression given that their continued engagement in electoral politics could prove deadly. Tragically, one author of a domestic tract found out how dangerous it could be for a man of African descent to engage in electoral politics after 1890. In 1900, six years after he published *Don't*, a gang of Democrats murdered Robert Benjamin for attempting to register black voters in the South.[75]

Just as it would be wrong to suggest that all African Americans decided to abandon electoral politics in favor of a public domestic sphere after 1890, prescriptive literature reflected far more than anxieties, machinations, and conflicts over electoral politics. Conduct literature also delineated distinct classes within the race, often by focusing upon character rather than economic status. Both *Hall's Moral and Mental Capsule* and *Divinity in Wedlock* contained passages describing different "grades of society." Josie Hall maintained that four classes existed within the race; further, she divvied up black women into four additional classes based on industry, behavior, and sexual comportment. Similarly, Pettiford's hierarchical class scheme in *Divinity in Wedlock* presented morality as the primary marker of one's "grade." Pettiford, Hall, and other authors of prescriptive literature were representative of how many black social commentators and authors constructed class difference: wealth was almost incidental to "an amalgam of behavioral criteria and morals, beliefs, and sentiments."[76]

For reformist authors, the production and distribution of prescriptive literature were effective means of promoting specific class values among the masses. The sexual values promoted by manuals were simultaneously idealized and in dialogue with mainstream stereotypes; the manuals themselves included "choice caricatures of subjective . . . assumptions concerning middle-class values" as a means to distance authors and readers from negative attitudes regarding African Americans. Aspiring-class and elite women and men viewed prescriptive literature as a tool that molded behaviors of the upwardly mobile, formed sexual propriety, aided racial progress, and facilitated assimilation to mainstream culture.[77]

Collective progress became all the more difficult during the late nineteenth century, and reform-minded black women and men anxiously wondered whether the aspiring class would flourish or wither during the twentieth century. If mainstream conduct manuals were "written as if they addressed a fairly wide readership with consistent social objectives—a middle-class that was not yet there," black reformist authors penned prescriptive literature out of similar motives. Authors assumed that publication of prescriptive literature for the race—not to mention its consumption—indicated the progressive presence of an expanding aspiring class. They additionally hoped that prescriptive literature would help ensure something that was not at all certain for African Americans: the continuation of aspiring-class, if not elite, values from generation to generation. Advice literature was more than an attempt to *create* class values. Manuals, tracts, and pamphlets were part of an effort by reformers to *reproduce* those values.[78]

Class was a significant factor when it came to prescriptive literature for yet another reason. Prescriptive literature signified and enabled collective uplift in the eyes of reformers, but it simply was not read by all Afro-Americans between 1890 and 1920, many of whom did not have money to spare for books—save the Bible perhaps. Primers and tracts undoubtedly aided black literacy during an era when approximately half of all black Americans were literate. The written gospel of sex reform was not accessible to all women and men, then, and those who consumed prescriptive texts were most likely to be aspiring-class and relatively elite women and men: self-schooled strivers, graduates of colleges and normal schools, church members concerned with self-presentation as well as the salvation of sinners. If mainstream prescriptive literature was generally consumed by people that had disposable income and who hoped that "proper manners and social respectability could be purchased and learned," the same held true for aspiring black women and men.[79]

Overall, not only did Afro-American advice literature provocatively insinuate that conduct reflected class and moral standing, its production reflected specific tensions, anxieties, and conflicts regarding gender and sexuality. As one of many strategies aimed at realizing a positive destiny for black women, children, and men—a destiny inflected by class, politics, gender, and race—prescriptive literature was, moreover, intimately connected to concurrent discussions about home environments and material culture. These discussions would not only involve many of the same assumptions about gender, sexuality, and class, they would firmly situate domestic spaces and material culture within ideologies of collective destiny. Conduct literature, as literature preoccupied with both private and public domains, would even set the stage for new discourses regarding domestic habitats. These discourses about domestic habitats and home life were contemporaneous with conduct literature and even overlapped in some cases. Race reformers were eager to reform the literal spaces in which African Americans lived, and that very preoccupation with physical and moral environments led race women and men to speak about home life in ways outside the purview of most conduct literature. Behavior continued to resonate for African Americans, then, as activists underscored that both personal actions within home environments and concerted efforts to improve residential habitats could result in a healthier race.

In farming, trade and literature,
A people enterprising!
Our churches, schools, and home life
    pure,
Tell to the world we're rising!
—George C. Rowe,
    Progress of a Race (1902)

5

MAKING THE HOME
LIFE MEASURE UP
ENVIRONMENT, CLASS,
AND THE HEALTHY RACE
HOUSEHOLD

If sexuality and conduct were nettlesome issues for African Americans during the late nineteenth and early twentieth centuries, the matter of home life proved just as thorny. The problem of where and how the majority of the race lived dated, at very least, back to the close of the Civil War, when long-awaited freedom rendered slaves "homeless" but at last enabled them to build their own lives. Founding independent households—whether with nuclear, extended, fractured, or reconstituted families—was an ongoing process for postemancipation African Americans who, in many cases, migrated from place to place seeking better opportunities, escape from coercive labor situations, reunions with kin, or new experiences. Yet the matter of land ownership complicated African Americans' ability to establish their own households by the simple fact that legions of black women and men would never own the terrain on which they lived. The effort to establish comfortable homes was further frustrated by the structures and locales typically available to working black Americans. If sharecroppers and tenant farmers frequently had to accept preexisting, ramshackle quarters for housing, other rural workers fared only somewhat better. Some urbanized domestics spent considerable amounts of time boarding with employers; other city dwellers went from year to year boarding with other African Americans; still others rented space in tenements subdivided far beyond original intent.

It is not surprising, then, that those African Americans who owned land and lived in modest or well-appointed houses reflected individual prosperity at the same time they symbolized a more universal gain for the race. It is also not surprising that, due to questions of sanitation and segregation, housing became a pressing political issue: pressing in terms of black health, political in terms of uplift, equity, and civil rights. A primary result of such politicization of housing was that reform-minded women and men actively surveyed homes and home life as part of an attempt to chart the destiny of their people. Activists considered some homes to be showcases where the nation could witness Afro-American advancement; other homes were deemed spare but salubrious; still other domiciles were singled out and subjected to thoroughgoing evaluations that, at times, resulted in calls for their very elimination.

Assessments of black home life dotted the landscape of African American social discourse within a mere generation of slavery's demise. Overriding concerns with moral cleanliness and literal sanitation dominated Afro-American discourse on home life. In 1892, for example, Dr. Halle Tanner Dillon argued that if "injurious habits and customs" were "destroying the life of the race," then every Afro-American home—whether "well-built house" or "humble log-cabin"—needed to become "an altar to Hygeia." Almost five years later, another race physician named Robert Fulton Boyd elaborated upon the concerns expressed by Dillon: "Among a population under the influence of filth, in poorly ventilated houses crowded together in low damp localities, where no rules regulate the habits of eating, drinking, sleeping, clothing, and exercise, the mortality is sure to be great. The infectious diseases here begin, spread, become epidemic, and stalk through the land, carrying death and destruction before them." During the late nineteenth and early twentieth centuries, then, reform-minded women and men equated cramped living quarters with filth, high morbidity levels, and immorality.[1] Black women and men also linked the breakdown of black families to social forces—such as segregation and urbanization—that affected the household.[2] Attempts to adjust domestic habits, reform sexual practices within the home, and create healthy families therefore responded to demographic shifts as well as environmental issues. Early-twentieth-century discourse on black home life reflected a significant moment in class formation among African Americans, as well. A speech given by one Richard Carroll, a man born less than three years before Lincoln issued the Emancipation Proclamation, was emblematic of both preoccupation with cleanliness and slow but steady class stratification.

Sometime during the opening moments of 1898, most likely on the first or second of January, a throng of black women, men, and children gathered in Sumter, South Carolina, for a massive, daylong celebration. It was Emancipation Day, a time of African American jubilation. Perhaps the reported crowd of three thousand participated in a parade, beheld a pageant of some sort, enjoyed musical selections, and feasted on specially prepared foods; games might have entertained restless children while adults engaged in contests of their own. One of the day's main events was a speech by a local minister named Richard Carroll, a man who eschewed politics yet managed to become fairly well known among black and white South Carolinians alike.[3] The featured speaker had a reputation for being a racial conciliator, and his talents were steadily winning him acclaim as an effective orator. As someone who had traveled well beyond his humble plantation beginnings, Carroll was an inspiration for men and women aspiring to better their own condition. When Emancipation Day celebrants assembled to hear Carroll speak, they probably expected the Baptist minister to deliver a rousing sermon commemorating the race's march of progress from bondage to freedom.

What the audience actually heard that day in Sumter, however, was far from congratulatory, celebratory, or even commemorative. Not only did Reverend Carroll declare that black Americans sorely needed to reorganize their priorities, he insinuated that whatever progress had been made since slavery was dubious at best: instead of pragmatic industrial training, questionable educational advances were being attained in "leapfrog style"; too many women and men chose to disdain lowly yet honest labor as discrimination severely limited the number of real opportunities open to black people; inappropriate "aristocratic" class pretensions afflicted the race as a whole. These alleged group faults were serious—at least in Carroll's mind—but he saved a good portion of his rhetorical arsenal to attack still another problem. In "remarkably plain and wholesome" language, the reverend informed the gathered flock that the race literally needed to get its house in order before it could ever hope to secure civil equality: "We will never be the equal of other races unless we cease to live in one room cabins and shanties. It will not do for grandpa, grandma, wife and husband, sons and daughters to sleep in the same room. . . . The house is the greatest institution on earth for good or evil; you can't make a great, good, patriotic and intelligent race if you live in low, wicked, filthy, and ungodly homes." Real progress meant replacing these "defective homes" with "better and larger houses . . . owned and paid for by Negroes." Then and only then, Carroll argued, would black people be fit for the challenge of full-fledged citizenship.[4]

Whether unduly harsh caricature or stark rendition of the dwellings most black women, children, and men actually inhabited, Richard Carroll's contention that living conditions were inseparable from the eventual fate of the race enabled him to stress several interrelated points. First and foremost, he juxtaposed domestic environment with political fitness in order to argue that if the majority of black abodes bred disorder, it was sheer folly for the Afro-American collective to harbor political aspirations. How could the race, he asked, expect to participate in "govern[ing] the country" without having mastered the art of "govern[ing] the home"? The reverend further concluded that black home-owning folk were at once the "best citizens" and the "poor[est] politicians." According to him, Afro-Americans that worked unstintingly at improving their lot could live in relative harmony with Anglo-Americans because their industriousness was likely to keep them too occupied to seek public office or agitate for civil rights.[5]

Carroll stopped short of declaring that black Americans had absolutely no business in politics. Rather, he asserted that the race needed to establish clear priorities. Owning homes, improving existing structures, acquiring property, and eradicating domestic chaos were particularly essential since each achievement or action demonstrated industry, upward mobility, and civilization. Implicit within this message was a notion that the benefits of electoral politics could be elusive and fleeting whereas constructive work performed within the race, *on the race*, possessed transformative potential. Erecting homes and fashioning an orderly home life thus assumed dual significance: to build for self was to construct superior environments that would create a physically sounder people; to build for race was to accord self-determination precedence over integration into the American body politic.[6]

Beyond whatever statement Carroll wished to make about the stance black Americans should take toward voting, office holding, and civil rights, his deliberate evocation of an extended family stuffed into a cabin underscored the material poverty endured by a majority of African Americans at the end of the nineteenth century. Thirty-five years might have passed since the abolition of slavery, but many black southerners still inhabited dwellings

A woman, two men, and three children outside a cabin in or near Jacksonville, Florida, 1886. For race men such as Richard Carroll, who fretted that cabins incubated sexual depravity, small cabin-based households led by industrious "happy fathers" could indicate collective progress. Courtesy of Photographs and Prints Division, Schomburg Center for Research in Black Culture, New York Public Library, Astor, Lenox and Tilden Foundations.

hauntingly similar to slave cabins — if not former slave quarters themselves.[7] By labeling these dwellings "filthy" as well, Carroll implied that cabins were anything but tidy. Perhaps there was a negligible degree of truth in his implication — many cabins had dirt floors and were thus constantly dusty since the relative or complete lack of windows prevented easy ventilation. Limited space, a major issue facing African American households, posed other serious problems: it resulted in crowding, frustrated the separation of social reproduction from bodily functions, and complicated sanitation.

Yet cleanness was not all that Richard Carroll had on his mind when he uttered the word "filthy." His suggestive evocation of women, men, and children sleeping in a single room night after night punctuated the possibility that "filth" could easily characterize moral atmosphere as well. For example, Carroll's deft characterization of one-room cabins as "ungodly" drew attention to the possibility that more than a few black girls and boys grew up being both proximate to and aware of the sexual activity of adults. Unlike William Hannibal Thomas, who would deploy a more denigratory, scabrous tone to characterize the sexual atmosphere of cabins in *The American Negro* two years later, Reverend Carroll channeled his disgust over cabins—and, by extension, homes of the black poor—into a jeremiad that he probably hoped would spur listeners into believing domestic reform would forever wash away a serious charge leveled against black women, children, and men: that environment rendered the race retrogressive, diseased, and sexually degenerate.[8]

The public face of black residences—especially those in the rural South—was often a rough aesthetic combining rudimentary construction, swept dirt yards, and tools, along with debris from household manufacture. Household manufacture provided needed goods and offset low wages, yet black homes and yards that served as literal sites of production were incongruous with the bourgeois domesticity found in middle-class dwellings inhabited by native whites.[9] Such exteriors smacked of degeneration and poverty for someone such as Richard Carroll who wanted the race to present a progressive front to the American public. For him, where and how people lived was an indicator of socioeconomic standing and health. Distinctively homey surroundings were the "foundation of society, morality, and religion," thus it was high time for the race to advance beyond slave-like, preindustrial conditions and emulate the houses and home life of other Americans. Carroll was loath to see his people affect pretensions, yet he also found certain realities created by poverty repugnant. His jeremiad therefore reflected a desire for collective mobility as it revealed class-bound assumptions within uplift politics.[10]

As Carroll's cautionary speech suggests, the seemingly benign subject of housing elicited anxious commentary among a certain cadre of postemancipation black Americans. Why, though, did he single out cabins and then stigmatize them as dirty dens of iniquity? How many African American people actually lived in cabin homes? Moreover, how many boys and girls slept commingled with adults, with each other?

Richard Carroll linked the overall status and disposition of the race to cabins for reasons both strategic and contemporary. Cabins—as both structural reality and racialized imaginary—signified material want and suggested physical privation; they hearkened back to the antebellum era, conjured up sexualized phantoms of slavery. An overwhelming majority of black Americans still resided in the rural South, therefore cabins retained a certain saliency for many members of the race; modest rural quarters were part of most African Americans' past lives whether they currently resided in a cottage, alley, frame house, or tenement. Cabins were even important tropes in race literature. Katherine Davis Chapman Tillman, for example, produced dramatic plays—*Thirty Years of Freedom, Aunt Betsy's Thanksgiving,* and *Fifty Years of Freedom, or From Cabin to Congress*—that traced her characters' rise from "rude Southern cabin[s]" to respectable spaces and stations. Not only was the literary symbolism of cabins potent because of cabins' very familiarity to black readers, aspiring-class readers of race literature had either experienced or wanted to experience the residential mobility idealized by Tillman and other writers.[11] Since "the cabin" resonated with so many African Americans, the call to reform them ostensibly applied to, or had ramifications for, the entire race.

Uplift activists emphasized several strategies for black advancement beyond domestic reform. Most activists considered education vital in developing a capable people, religion critical in fostering moral fortitude, and individual industry essential to collective accumulation of property and wealth. But since home life arguably had a decisive impact upon people's school attendance, church involvement, and work ethic, it is not surprising that post-emancipation reformers highlighted the ways in which domestic domains bequeathed an overarching heritage to the race. And, given popular theories associating blackness, sexual degeneracy, and the possibility of racial extinction, activists approached domestic reform with a certain sense of urgency. For race women and men environment was just as important as heredity—healthy racial reproduction relied as much upon wholesome settings free from vice's taint as upon orderly sexual relations.

As African American migration and urbanization increased, discourse about race homes embraced a welter of contemporary concepts regarding the relationship between environment, home life, and character. The Progressive Era abounded with notions that the cultural, physical, and moral climate contained within any four walls directed the trajectory of a person's life. For example, euthenics—an early-twentieth-century "science of controllable environment" inspired by eugenics—maintained that home surroundings influenced whether or not a baby would be "well-born." As euthenic theory had it, a child with excellent genes could be adversely affected by compromising habitats over the course of a lifetime; conversely, a wholesome home life could improve the overall hereditary package of a child from a fair or even weak genetic background. Put another way, if seamy surroundings could breed promiscuity and dissipation among the fit and unfit alike, domestic purity could ensure that someone from a humble background still became an upright, productive citizen.[12] Such theories powerfully shaped African American visions of residences and home life.

Euthenic theories at once shaped African American visions of home life and promoted systematic domestic rehabilitation efforts within the race. In 1913, for example, Nannie Helen Burroughs, the pragmatic president of the National Training School for Women and Girls, observed "in Washington City there is much talk about getting the seventeen thousand Negroes out of the alleys. To the student of euthenics, who believes that the shortest cut to health is by creating a clean environment in which to live. . . . [one must first] 'get the alley' out of the seventeen thousand Negroes, and [then] it will be an easy task to get them out of the alley." For uplift activists, "getting the alley out of the Negroes" entailed changing more than people's habits—it meant encouraging black women and men to view the home as a primary agent in racial progress.[13] Manners and cleanliness were certainly desirable, as were "dress, personal behavior, and public behavior," but changes in each would mean little if domestic spaces failed to promote physical as well as moral health.[14]

Such conviction led activists to address a range of issues. Some activists argued that homes were not only endowed with cultural, social, and political significance; these reformers embraced the notion that material culture within homes had the power to mold youth, promote race pride, and secure black self-determination. Additionally, activists made provocative insinuations about the relatively routine practice of boarding in order to suggest that homes with boarders incubated a sexual degeneracy that compromised both children and the collective at large. If boarding was partially a phenomenon that emerged out of urbanization, urbanization also led activists to embrace public health initiatives in order to address conditions within and surrounding race residences. As migration and urbanization reshaped black households and neighborhoods, the question of home life came to inform early sociological studies by African Americans as well.

Between 1890 and 1920, then, black discourse about domestic spaces maintained that the weal or woe of African Americans was bound up in the purification of home environments. Activists adjured the race to realize that larger homes could facilitate a necessary privatization of intimate matters, that domestic sexual order would portend a blessed future for a struggling people, that neighborhoods should be orderly and clean. Whereas reform-minded black Americans could eradicate neither discrimination nor segregation, they did believe that it was within their power to create better habitats for a healthier, more wholesome people. As Women's Christian Temperance Union and home mission activist Anne Walker Blackwell declared in the years leading up to the First Great Migration, "making the home life measure up to the highest ideal" would ensure that "this race of ours . . . take[s] its rightful place among the other races of the world."[15] In short, for some women and men, home life seemed more pressing than ever.

Less than two months after Richard Carroll issued his cautionary words in South Carolina, Mary Church Terrell addressed a meeting of the National American Women's Suffrage Association where she outlined the domestic reform work being performed by members of the National Association of Colored Women (NACW). She skillfully asserted that if white women felt compelled to launch a variety of domestic initiatives, a crying need for similar efforts existed among women "from whom shackles have but yesterday fallen." As president of the NACW, Terrell's immersion in black social activism enabled her to testify that race women across the United States were heeding the call of reform. Their "vigorous crusade[s]" were proceeding apace: "Believing that it is only through the home that a people can become . . . truly great, the National Association of Colored Women has entered that sacred domain. Homes, more homes, better homes, purer homes is [our] text . . . [and the] work of bringing the light of knowledge and the gospel of cleanliness to [our] benighted sisters . . . has been conducted with signal success." Terrell skirted around sexualized aspects of family life, but she nonetheless shared Carroll's conviction that cramped living arrangements were, by and large, detrimental to Afro-American progress.[16]

Women of the NACW surveyed physical interiors, assessed intraracial habits, and slated race households for renovation. Creating morally and physically sound black families, according to the NACW's official line at least, required an overhaul of home environments deemed "destructive of virtue." Women in Chicago, for example, used home visitations as a means of lecturing parents who sent their children to bars to fetch beer; the Women's Loyal Union distributed low-priced pamphlets on "The Sanctity of the Home" as an attempt to "reach the masses" in Manhattan and Brooklyn. Other club women instructed their sisters—many of whom were decidedly less privileged than these reform activists—in hygienic domestic arts, while still other clubs offered "talks on social purity and the proper method of rearing children." Granted, when Terrell described how the NACW's "gospel of cleanliness" covered the moral as well as the material, she took pains to stress that many black mothers required assistance due to poverty and not pathology. Still, as much as women of the NACW acted out of empathy and decided conviction, their very assumption that "benighted sisters" needed to be enlightened underscores the reality that club women typically believed uplift

uplift → *class*

meant transferring aspiring-class—if not elite—values to working-class and working-poor black Americans.[17]

If Mary Terrell used discreet, class-coded language to call for housing reform, in 1902, Baptist activist Sylvia Bryant offered an alarmist observation similar to that made by Richard Carroll four years earlier. Whereas she cast the matter in slightly more explicit terms than either Terrell or Carroll, Bryant shared their conviction that home life determined the race's future. Race homes, in the aggregate, indicated a people at risk in the eyes of the "efficient," "forceful" home missions worker: "There is a fearful responsibility resting upon the homes from which the future generations must emanate. . . . One of the greatest evils of our race is the crowding of from six to a dozen persons in one room. How can we produce a race free from social evil [with] this? Separate your boys and girls." The underlying urgency in Bryant's observation reflected no small amount of angst over the impact crowding had on children's sexuality. Not only were single-room shanties likely to provide precocious sex education for little girls and boys who could see or hear adult sexual activity, densely populated sleeping quarters could literally foster incestuous behavior among maturing, curious youth. "Impure" homes bred "impure" youths; in turn, contaminated youths were bound to produce a polluted race. Hyperbolic or not, Bryant's fretful message emerged out of a frustration over structural limitations facing black Americans who often had no choice but to make do with what little they had.[18]

Indeed, the concerns of Bryant, Terrell, and Carroll reflected contemporary housing realities faced by African Americans. Less than a quarter of all black people in the United States owned the spaces where they lived, slept, and died in 1900; that statistic would change little by 1930. A majority of African Americans were tenants or renters, and at least 15 percent of all black households took in boarders, often to "help pay [rent]."[19] Well over three decades after emancipation, a majority of black Americans still lived within walls owned by others. Even further, the prevalence of tenancy, renting, and boarding meant that a fundamental part of quotidian life remained beyond the control of most black women, men, and children. Such control was vital for a liminal people: ownership provided literal insulation from the threat of eviction, while the ability to install sanitary facilities or expand existing quarters was largely predicated upon whether one owned the premises in question. Owning a home was more than possessing a title—home ownership was one and the same with security and could determine comfort as well as health. Black reformers were acutely aware of the residential vulnera-

150   [HOME LIFE]

bility of most Afro-Americans; they therefore treasured home ownership and linked it to black advancement. But since most African Americans could not afford to own or build their own home, many reform activists decided to speak to the broader issue of home life.

Post–Reconstruction era tracts were one means by which activists advocated home ownership and offered domestic advice. In 1887, for example, William Hooper Councill wrote a tract called *The Negro Laborer* in which he suggested that strikes placed undue stress on black households. Councill's work also contained pithy advice pertaining to the organization and administration of working-class households. Councill admonished laboring men to preserve the sanctity of home and the "comliness of manhood" by assuming the role of respectable, responsible patriarch; in part, this entailed avoiding dubious forms of leisure, especially "the dram shop [and] the house of prostitution." As Councill would have it, one of the most important things black men could do besides realizing their potential as workers was to work toward home ownership; if a working man could not afford to buy, then he should improve and expand his family's existing home. In Councill's opinion, the race would never "make much progress" until black homes had private chambers and working-poor families stopped "occupying the same bed." [20]

As the nineteenth century closed and the twentieth opened, Afro-Americans tended to invoke a critical, almost dogmatic whiggishness that implied collective progress would occur once the race took pains to realize and correct common missteps. Two turn-of-the-century tracts illustrate this tendency on the part of reformers. In *An Evil Router*, the Reverend L. T. Christmas chided African Americans for allowing themselves to be "humbugged by all kinds of quackery, nostrums, and . . . foolish schemes" aimed at realizing individual as well as collective prosperity. Emigration and politics were particularly problematic as far as Christmas was concerned. For him, the surest hope for racial progress rested "not in Africa . . . Cuba . . . Oklahoma . . . [or] in any party" but in reforming Afro-American habits and homes. Christmas's twenty-six-page *Router* stressed the primacy of domesticity and provided guidelines for the formation of instructional associations where the masses could learn domestic hygiene as well as "how, whom, and when" to marry. [21]

William Noel Johnson's *Common Sense in the Home* contained somewhat different notions about the relationship between black advancement and home life than did the *Router*, but it too argued that African Americans had made their share of mistakes since emancipation. Johnson—who, like Christmas, was a former teacher—worried that the lack of proper home training in many black homes was producing "unruly and untruthful children." Parents needed to serve as role models for their children; adults had to realize that it was their domestic duty to cultivate race pride in girls and boys by displaying images of accomplished Afro-Americans, promoting race literature, and relaying the intrepid feats of past and present heroes. Johnson further ventured that careless talk and gossip within the household caused a "lack of unity which so retards race progress" as he maintained that a modern approach to domestic governance was essential. As a Progressive Era text, Johnson's *Common Sense* pointed out that if "good government" was a desideratum of the times, the "right government of . . . homes" would provide the primary "basis upon which to build our future greatness."[22]

Notions that African American homes were inexorably linked to black progress proliferated within domestic tracts produced by people such as Johnson and Christmas whether authors bemoaned the supposed moral, spiritual, and physical diseases invading working-class domiciles or cheered the slight yet discernible emergence of bourgeois residences. No matter how pessimistic the assessment of "dwellings of our people"—up to and including dreary predictions about the connection between poor housing stock and high mortality rates—there was almost always a slightly optimistic sense among uplift activists. In other words, these activists generally clung to the hope that if reform crossed the thresholds of black homes, group progress would only be a matter of time.

For Euphemia Kirk of the *Colored American*, men had as much a "duty" to the domestic sphere as women. She considered working men who were "too stingy to marry and establish a home" race traitors. Kirk used her column on one occasion in 1900 to portray well-paid, educated black bachelors as slackers who allowed "the ignorant and vicious to increase the population for us." Another journalist believed that too many race folk encouraged young wives to stabilize black households by catering to their husbands. Gertrude Mossell was troubled that virtually every item published in the black press on domestic life "invariably pointed [at] . . . women," and she was irked when "conservatives" absolved men of any responsibility for domestic weal. There were significant differences between the two women's overall arguments, including the fact that Mossell's analysis was informed by a nascent feminism while Kirk's critique was inflected with palpable class bias. Still, both women pointedly suggested that black men had domestic responsibilities that extended well beyond their ability to earn a living.[23]

For his part, social purity activist Revels Adams was disgusted with club women, professionals, and "women of the upper class" who failed to rally their resources to build "working girls' homes." In *The Negro Girl*, Adams painted a bleak, if suggestive, picture of the living spaces inhabited by working women: "Many . . . girls live in homes where they are constantly in association with men and women 'roomers' who are unfit for any decent person's association; many live in homes where men and boys . . . insult them [while] . . . many sleep in rooms without doors and men may enter these rooms and gaze at them while asleep; they must share the bath room and toilet with men and women of all classes. . . . [All the] while the average Negro school teacher spends all she makes for clothes and a vacation." Curiously silent on the efforts of Victoria Earle Matthews, who founded New York City's White Rose Mission in 1897 and club women in Chicago who established a Phyllis Wheatley Home after the turn of the century, Adams railed against women more concerned with material possessions and leisure than with the plight of working, cast-out, or exploited girls. He even criticized church ladies who demonstrated frenzied, public concern over the souls of people abroad while neglecting their own children at home. In short, selfish—or self-involved—black women were an affront to the race; they "sin[ned]" because they failed to uplift their "little sisters." Revels Adams could certainly be empathetic toward the sorrows endured by some women, but he also could be dismissive, and perhaps ignorant, of choices made by others.[24]

As suggested by his less than flattering depiction of rooming houses, one economic decision made by a number of African American home-owning parents vexed Adams: the practice of earning income by taking in boarders. Boarding not only helped recent migrants assimilate to town or city life, black home-owners also benefited in that "lodging could actually enhance family stability by permitting women to earn money while remaining at home with their children."[25] Social and economic benefits aside, the letting of rooms disturbed Adams because he accepted aspects of euthenic thought that suggested domestic spaces shaped character and bequeathed a lasting legacy to children. Euthenic theory called for the maintenance of sanitary conditions that would enable "race improvement through . . . [r]ight living conditions"; it cast moral hygiene as an imperative element of optimal domestic environments by insinuating that "habits of the mind as well as of body" were ostensibly forged "in healthy physical and moral environments."[26]

The problem with accepting strangers into one's household, then, was that unscrupulous boarders might contaminate moral climate, introduce a variety of unsanitary, undesirable practices, *and* imperil children's bodies.

Not only might boarders engage in sexual activities with unsupervised children, the sexual undercurrents of boarding presented another problem. Roomers might also tempt parents: Adams was particularly concerned about mothers who associated indiscriminately with male lodgers in front of their daughters. Adams shared other social purists' heated notions about "the lodger evil," and his jeremiad on conduct—with evocative language, alarming examples, heart-wrenching testimony and all—made readers pointedly aware of problems one could invite into the household by simply letting rooms to persons unknown.[27]

Domestic literature such as *The Negro Laborer*, *An Evil Router*, *Common Sense in the Home*, and *The Negro Girl* were—as objects—material culture that signified racial achievement as well as individual aspiration when placed in the home. Since domestic texts were considered a progressive literature, a number of texts produced for home consumption celebrated race progress by publishing the latest statistics on black home ownership. *Sparkling Gems of Race Knowledge Worth Reading* (1897), *Progress of a Race* (1897), and *Lamp of Wisdom* (1898), all highlighted race industry, attainment, and thrift by reporting the number of homes owned by black Americans, property values, and personal savings. *Sparkling Gems* even inserted photographs comparing "the hut of a slave" with "the home of a freeman"—said "freeman" happened to be Robert Church, the wealthy father of leading club woman Mary Church Terrell.[28] Not only did *Sparkling Gems* make it a point to enumerate "Negro wealth by states,"[29] uplift-minded men and women clearly realized that wealth could enable African Americans to acquire markers of prosperity. Aspiring and elite uplift activists knew that money could improve the physical appearance of race homes. They also believed that attractive homes and the comportment of their residents signified civilized black prosperity to the broader culture. Thus, attempts to improve race homes and modify Afro-American conduct were allied aspects of intraracial reform activity.

If attractive exteriors and comportment were considered evidence of an advancing race, Afro-American domestic texts themselves indicated a people that had come far since emancipation. Tracts and manuals were integral components of an African American discourse on home life, yet that discourse was itself rapidly turning to new, scientific ways of assessing the organization of domestic spaces. One young African American scholar who embraced environmentalist theories would be particularly responsible for expanding discourse on black households. This same scholar would also come to conclusions about morality, home life, and class stratification among African Americans that echoed—somewhat eerily—many of the same conclusions offered by reformers, pamphleteers, and conduct literature authors.

Not only did a distinct genre of tracts and manuals on Afro-American home life coalesce between 1890 and 1920, that very coalescence coincided with the emergence of formal sociological study in the United States. "Sociology" emerged as a term and concept during the 1850s; fifty years later, at least nine major research institutions had sociology departments.[30] Newly trained sociologists, many of whom were imbued with Progressive sensibilities, turned to urban centers and rural sites to study structural life: organizations, institutions, and domestic arrangements all became viable areas of inquiry for scholars bent on exploring how people ordered daily existence.

Given the turn-of-the-century perception that a "Negro Problem" loomed large and considering that uplift was a mission of sorts among aspiring race activists, Afro-Americans became both subjects and conductors of sociological studies. In contrast to the uneven style and often impressionistic substance of Reuben Pettiford's *Divinity in Wedlock*, Josie Hall's *Moral and Mental Capsule*, and Revels Adams's *The Negro Girl*, sociological investigations emerged from fieldwork, included empirical data, and pushed the scrutiny of black homes and home life in striking new directions. Sociologically inflected studies, including ones by prominent white liberal Mary White Ovington and Columbia-trained black sociologist George Edmund Haynes, detailed material conditions as they charted major demographic shifts such as migration and urbanization. As much as sociological studies contained their share of moralizing, their deployment of social science helped entrench environmentalist notions regarding Afro-American health, character, and destiny.[31]

The consummate scholar W. E. B. Du Bois either conducted or oversaw some of the most notable new work. His stewardship of many Atlanta University investigations, essays on housing in the *Southern Workman*, and work for the U.S. Bureau of Labor covered country, town, and city.[32] Significantly, when assessing housing and home life in these investigations, Du Bois catalogued the diversity of Afro-American living arrangements and concluded that environmental factors placed much of the race at risk; for him, surroundings had the power to subvert efforts of parents, even conscientious ones "[who] strive hard to protect the home."[33]

Du Bois acknowledged human agency, then, yet he also stressed that environments molded individuals. As it ~~was in reform~~ broadsides written by other race men and women, the term "environment" was broadly construed throughout Du Bois's work, so that it accounted for neighborhoods along with individual homes, physical structures as well as economic factors, moral atmospheres in addition to health conditions. Such an inclusive vision made Du Bois's research euthenic, as did his stock conclusion that better environments made for a better people. Moreover, one of his major pieces of scholarship deployed popular euthenic concepts as social science methodology.

The Philadelphia Negro was, despite its immediate disclaimer that "sociological research . . . [was] liable to inaccuracies," an exhaustive exploration of employment, institutions, and households. The fieldwork upon which it was based extended over a sixteen-month period when Du Bois himself visited household after household armed with questions that informants probably found tedious, baffling, and perhaps intrusive.[34] Du Bois was not responsible for selecting Philadelphia as a research site, since the study was commissioned by eugenic-minded liberal and Progressive members within the University of Pennsylvania community; this particular cohort was concerned about supposed pathologies among the city's black residents. Still, as primary investigator, Du Bois made the project his own by seizing the opportunity to issue a jeremiad on the obstacles standing in the way of collective black progress.[35] The impediments Du Bois fingered were environmental factors both beyond and within the control of black people: racism, neighborhood character, and home life.

The specific environment captured in the pages of *The Philadelphia Negro* was the city's Seventh Ward. At the turn of the century the Seventh was a predominantly black district where different socioeconomic classes bumped shoulders and native Pennsylvanians encountered recent transplants from the Upper South along with a few immigrants from the Caribbean. Other wards citywide—particularly the Fifth and Thirteenth—cropped up throughout *The Philadelphia Negro* as key referents when it came to the subjects of black illiteracy, occupations, health, and class, but it was the Seventh that emerged as the primary site where "nearly all the Negro problems" converged. What had been a historic district for free blacks before the Civil War appeared to be teetering between opportunity and depravity by 1899:

It is a thickly populated district of varying character. . . . The houses are mostly brick, some wood, not very old, and in general uncared for rather than dilapidated. . . . There is an abundance of political clubs [and] . . . [the street] corners, night and day, are filled with Negro loafers . . . gamblers, thieves and prostitutes. . . . [Other habitués include] stevedores, porters, laborers and laundresses. . . . On small streets . . . [there] is a curious mingling of respectable working people . . . with . . . the semi-criminal class. . . . On the larger streets, there live many respectable colored families . . . with a fringe of more questionable families.

The Seventh's diversity provided a convenient microcosm where a variety of people and race institutions coexisted, where boundaries between "respectable," "questionable," and "criminal" seemed neither fixed nor definite. With the comparatively low earning power of its black men, an uneven sex ratio, and abundance of boarders, the ward presented its share of challenges for someone with Du Bois's assumptions about sexuality and proper home life.[36]

Du Bois bluntly believed that "the mass of the Negro population" was afflicted with an unfortunate predilection for "sexual looseness"—a predilection that could "be traced to bad home life in most cases." Not only did Du Bois presume that promiscuity resulted from poor heredity, he linked unfavorable economic conditions—namely low wages—to high rates of cohabitation and desertion. And, if the actual percentage of African Americans who were married approached the percentage of married whites, Du Bois nevertheless maintained that the stable, monogamous union was "a comparatively new institution" for the race. Analysis of black sexuality in *The Philadelphia Negro* both "reflect[ed] the norms of turn-of-the-century middle-class propriety" and betrayed Du Bois's own "troubling ambivalence" regarding gender, sex, and the organization of black households.[37]

If a certain ambivalence—one that occasionally bordered on open condescension—regarding sexual behavior of the masses characterized *The Philadelphia Negro*, a similarly conflicted sensibility would suffuse future sociological and ethnographic work by Du Bois, especially his articles on race housing that appeared in the *Southern Workman*. Derived from fieldwork largely conducted by Atlanta University students and published between July 1901 and February 1902, the six-part *Southern Workman* series on the "problem of housing the Negro" categorized black homes in both the rural and urban South.[38] The series richly described interiors, exteriors, and neighborhoods as stark illustrations and photographs vivified text; each article was a miniature manifesto detailing how shoddy homes produced a shoddy people. Du Bois argued throughout the series that the race was indeed beginning to achieve domestic integrity. The young scholar nonetheless felt that there was ample reason for "the candid student" of human conditions to study black home life, since he personally believed that the vast majority of African American homes remained "disturbed and debauched." With such a perspective as its driving assumption, the series went on to expose health problems, criticize negligent parents, bemoan financial improvidence, curse segregation and, not surprisingly, demonize cabins.[39]

Du Bois began the series by hearkening back to Africa in order to suggest that, over time, bondage in the United States warped the simple but relatively wholesome domestic customs of enslaved Africans and their descendants. Like many of his peers, Du Bois pointedly claimed that slavery obliterated sexual ethics among the race, weakened family ties, and resulted in household chaos. Unlike most of his contemporaries, however, Du Bois delineated two types of North American slavery and then maintained that the shift from a "patriarchal" to a "commercial" form dealt a mortal blow to African American home life by removing slaves from the watchful benevolence of masters. Distanced from so-called civilizing influences and left to their own devices, "sexual looseness and debauchery . . . spread among the slave[s]." Once the moral climate of black households was thus compromised, personal habits, physical conditions, and general hygiene veered toward degeneracy. Bondage's legacy reverberated throughout postemancipation Afro-America and created domestic environments among the black masses of the South that were, in Du Bois's eyes, bleak, barren, dysgenic, and "disgusting."[40]

For Du Bois the situation hardly improved with emancipation. The third installment in the *Southern Workman* series began by admitting that the Freedmen's Bureau did indeed enable a few people to acquire land and build modest houses. This essay on the "home of the country freedman" conceded that town migration inspired some freedpeople to erect cottages with a couple of rooms, but it also contended that "at least one-third" of the race embarked upon new lives in spaces that were, for all intents and purposes, unfortunately familiar one-room cabins. Although people living in one room were not a majority and many of them were tenant farmers who had to accept whatever accommodations landlords provided, Du Bois proceeded to analyze cabins as though they determined the very character of Afro-American homes in the rural South. He did so largely because rustic cabins smacked of slavery and, as such, were vexing remnants of an unpleasant past.[41]

One-room cabins easily became "veritable pest house[s]" whenever poor ventilation, few hygienic facilities, insufficient insulation, and inadequate nutrition conspired to create a tubercular environment. Overcrowding only made a bad situation worse: "Sometimes married sons or daughters continue to live at home, thus introducing a second or third family. . . . The migration of young men in search of work . . . brings in a class of male lodgers. As a result many families entirely outgrow the physical home and use it only for sleeping. . . . Of real group family life there is . . . little, and in this absence of group training . . . there develop untold evils." Du Bois chose not to emphasize the potential communal benefits of residing under one roof for extended families, nor did he acknowledge that "lodgers" might very well be extended family members. He also failed to mention that boarders generated income and could provide various forms of social support within the household. In other words, Du Bois overlooked real and potential benefits of households with members beyond the nuclear family in order to portray transiency as a major peril facing postemancipation households. Whether on the part of young marrieds, extended family members, or migrant labor, he believed that transiency was a health threat largely because it introduced additional bodies into environments with limited resources and few hygienic facilities. Those additional bodies further complicated strategies to maintain a modicum of privacy in houses without discrete chambers.[42]

To begin, married children who failed to establish their own households contributed to domestic instability by disrupting nuclear family units—their parents' and their own. Boarders were problematic because they interrupted, if not commercialized, family space; Du Bois found the very practice of boarding unsettling since, in theory, lodgers could initiate girls and boys into sexual activity.[43] Even if resourceful parents managed to shield children from nudity, sex, and lodgers, Du Bois concluded that households with transients usually failed at the enterprise of upright home training: "diminutive single-room dwellings" replete with revolving residents were bound to send youths "into the world sadly lacking in that finer sense . . . which it is the peculiar province of the home to impart." As he did in *The Philadelphia Negro*, Du Bois basically concluded that moral turpitude did not result from so-called inherent race traits; rather, structural and material conditions were responsible, as was an absence of home training.[44]

In a magazine with a distinct southern orientation, W. E. B. Du Bois argued that a decisive portion of the region's homes failed to provide beneficial environments for the race and its youth. For him, life in rural districts neither ensured health nor protected morals: the airy, sunny climate did little for people who lived in stuffy, packed residences; the relative absence of commercialized leisure hardly eliminated temptations that might be presented by crowding, lodging, and young male transients.

There were certainly black families in the South that fared better than cabin dwellers in both space and circumstance. In terms of home ownership alone, for example, almost 350,000 black southerners—about 21 percent—owned their residences in 1900, less than half of which were mortgaged. Some of these homes were cabins, and some owners had married children or boarders living with them. Yet people who earned income sufficient to purchase property were likely to have resources to build additions or equip their homes with modest comforts. Of course some renters lived in better surroundings than did owners, but for African Americans living at the turn of the century, autonomy from landlords was no small accomplishment. All the same, owners and renters presented a different set of worries for Du Bois since quite a few working-class and aspiring people who either owned or rented decidedly nicer housing stock were apparently growing dissatisfied with "country districts" that were "bare, dull, unlovely places." Many of these people—much to Du Bois's chagrin—were all too willing to leave decent homes for urban centers and the unknown. If cabins were incubators for disease and immorality, rural areas in and of themselves could breed a discontent that drove people to pack their bags.[45]

Migration was a major phenomenon affecting postemancipation black households, then. Du Bois was quick to acknowledge the positive side of this particular phenomenon as he happily reported that town migration inspired industrious migrants to erect frame cottages and acquire a few comfortable furnishings. As an added bonus, one-room domiciles were somewhat of a rarity in towns and cities. Only 17 out of 262 families resided in a single room in one Virginia community where a "building association" empowered people to build their own homes. Further south, "thrifty Negroes [bought] homes on installment" in Covington, Georgia, while almost three thousand families in Atlanta lived in houses with four or more rooms. Less than seven hundred of Atlanta's black families were crammed into a single chamber.[46]

Relocation to towns and cities made it possible for many people to better their lot, but urban life could undermine home life, too. The same Georgia community praised for installment plans also had sundry diversions that discouraged temperance and siphoned needed dollars from household budgets. These "dives" provided questionable forms of leisure in the forms of "gambling" and "disorder," a euphemism for sexual transactions that occurred at certain watering holes. Du Bois feared that the overall character of "village slums" and "pestilential . . . [city] alleys" functioned as a vortex that sucked the weak into lives of crime. He also worried that seasonal labor patterns that created transiency in the country caused "idleness and loafing" in urban centers.[47]

Whether urbanization, idleness, and criminality were actually linked is up for debate, but at the turn of the century black underemployment in towns and cities was clearly gendered and sexualized. African American women either equaled or outnumbered black men in most major southern cities, with men being more likely to be engaged in irregular work with erratic income. And, while women tended to earn lower wages, men's underemployment made women's participation in the paid labor force a virtual necessity for nonrural married and cohabiting couples. Urbanization provoked considerable anxiety for observers concerned with the state of patriarchy in black households, and those anxieties extended well beyond women's participation in the workforce. Howard University's Kelly Miller was, for one, impressed with the industry of urban women, but he was nevertheless disturbed by a "surplus" number of females in cities. Miller was convinced that city living consigned black women to lives of "perpetual spinsterhood," and he believed an excess of women over men fostered moral and economic climates that undercut the integrity of manhood: a "preponderance" of women allegedly encouraged prostitution; the easy availability of jobs for women allowed them to be both financially and sexually independent of men. The professor mentioned nothing about how uneven sex ratios could facilitate homosociality and homosexuality, but his dual distress over "spinsterhood" and "sordid city association" might have been built, in part, upon concerns regarding surplus women who decided they could do without men in every aspect of their lives.[48]

Du Bois shared some of Miller's concerns. The "loafing" mentioned by Du Bois referred to slack periods experienced by male day laborers, but Du Bois also thought fornication, promiscuity, and paid sex were integral parts of "idleness" in black communities with uneven sex ratios. After all, the unstated assumptions swirling around "loafing," "idleness," "crime," and "vice" in the *Southern Workman* articles were previously spelled out in *The Philadelphia Negro*, in which Du Bois explicitly linked each word with prostitution, cohabiting, and—most importantly—women supporting underemployed and unemployed men.[49]

Beyond his concerns about how migration reconfigured gender and sexuality within the race, Du Bois contended that the lives of new migrants and established city dwellers alike were profoundly shaped by segregation. Jim Crow streetcars complicated travel between different areas of town; residential segregation created densely populated neighborhoods as it prevented race folk from seeking housing wherever they wished. Not only were "respectable people" forced to live in dubious areas, the concurrence of increased migration and entrenched segregation strained housing stock. Migration, as it were, was Janus-faced.[50]

Du Bois poignantly underscored the duplicitous aspects of urbanization by arguing that one of the graver by-products of migration to towns and cities was increased morbidity: "The high death-rate of the Negro is directly traceable to . . . [urban] slum districts. In the country, the Negro death-rate is probably as low as . . . the whites. In the healthy wards of Northern cities the Negro death rate is low; but in the alleys of Charleston, which are probably the vilest human habitations in a civilized land, the wretched inmates die in droves, while the country complacently calculates on that abnormal basis the probable extinction of black folk in America." Southern municipal governments typically failed to pave sidewalks or provide adequate drainage in predominantly black areas, so sanitation was often a *neighborhood* issue. A structure with multiple rooms and windows might be perpetually dusty simply because it was wedged between adjacent houses on a dirt road. Furthermore, it was possible for an owner or renter to keep their own home clean yet still be exposed to raw sewage and contaminated water; a domicile might have few residents but be located in an area congested by recent migrants to such a degree that backyard privies no longer provided adequate waste disposal. Du Bois's claim that "poor houses and poor home customs" exacerbated the black death rate was accurate insofar as it fingered derelict housing, but the urban death rate was not a question of African American sloth. Rather, the volatile mix of discrimination, poverty, and rapid demographic transitions exacerbated morbidity levels; the fact that infrastructure in most black neighborhoods sagged under the weight of a constant influx of new migrants hardly helped matters.[51]

But urban life meant neither certain death nor unmitigated misery for Afro-American people. Migration made it possible for individuals and families to earn higher wages or escape sharecropping; it also provided access to expanded educational, institutional, and cultural life. Urbanization allowed people to pool resources in dynamic new ways as it created discrete black communities that, in turn, strengthened the tenuous position of race professionals. Moreover, cities and towns contained a phenomenon indicative of class stratification: the appearance of larger homes — some commodious and well appointed—belonging to Afro-Americans. Du Bois was almost effusive about the trend. Whereas middling folk and the elite did not occupy the same sort of spaces, towns and cities were nevertheless sites where "Negro homes fully equal to the homes of . . . [similarly positioned] whites" existed. And, whereas the homes of black urban professionals were indeed a statistical minority, these race homes still signified "extraordinary accomplishment for a single generation"—an accomplishment as rooted in individual initiative as possessing collective ramifications.[52]

In stark contrast to the rough-hewn, disorderly log cabins bemoaned by Du Bois in earlier installments, the urban homes praised in the final *Southern Workman* article were visions of bourgeois comfort: "[One] home . . . is a frame house two stories high, with eight rooms. . . . Two rooms are papered, the rest white finished. There is a double parlor with piano, a dining-room and a kitchen on the first floor, four bedrooms and a bath on the second. The furniture is good and all the rooms are carpeted. . . . [Another house has] . . . a parlor set, table, sofa, four chairs and a piano . . . a dining-room with a nice dining table, three chairs, a refrigerator and sideboard." These homes and others—some with finished woodwork, glass windows, running water, gas jets, painted walls, and tiled fireplaces—were not only modern, they showcased black gentility and highlighted the race's fitness for civilization. Such homes were occasionally located in neighborhoods that, due to the vagaries of segregation, housed bordellos; this unsavory possibility aside, Du Bois concluded that "a strong beautiful family life"—one free from sexual irregularities, vice, and dubious moral atmosphere—was present in the "decen[t] and even luxuriou[s]" homes of the middling and elite. In other words, despite red-light districts, segregation, and even high morbidity rates, the progress of the race was evident in cities.[53]

The *Southern Workman* articles—for all their ethnographic, sociological trappings—failed to detail the impact of occupation and income on housing options available to the race. The installments did, however, provide ample evidence of class stratification; a few offered suggestive commentary on whether household organization reflected sexual mores among poorer Afro-Americans. Whereas it is difficult to know how many African American reformers actually read any or all of the installments, the *Workman* series did represent the emergence of an environmentalist approach to African American domestic spaces that was moored in social activist assumptions regarding dissipation and regeneration. Du Bois's series accomplished something else in the process: it documented migration and urbanization, two massive demographic shifts among African American people

Women, a man, and children on a house porch, Atlanta, Georgia, 1899 or 1900.
Photographs from albums assembled by W. E. B. Du Bois for the 1900 Paris
Exposition evocatively suggested that aspiring and elite African Americans epitomized
fitness for the demands of a new century. The Negro American Family *(1908)*
contained a different photograph of this house, which it identified as the "residence of
a Negro lawyer." Courtesy of the Library of Congress, Prints and Photographs
Division, LC-USZ62-69915.

that spurred race activists to rehabilitate space and surroundings in new, health-minded ways. More specifically, reformist women and men would embark upon public health initiatives aimed at improving segregated, over-crowded neighborhoods.

People of African descent were on the move as the twentieth century opened: before 1900, black migration within the South was heavy, with African Americans traveling from state to state, pushing westward, and set-tling within New South cities. Moreover, from 1900 to 1920 alone, the number of blacks in urban areas nationwide rose from 23 to 34 percent. The overwhelming majority of the race remained South in the early decades of the century, yet well over one million black women, men, and children participated in various forms of migration and urbanization during those years.[54] A predominant factor behind black migration and urbanization was a desire on the part of black people to improve their lives financially and socially. Whether tenant farmers, low-paid household workers, semiskilled industrial labor, or marginalized professionals, black women, men, and children forged new lives during the early twentieth century. They did so, in part, by finding new homes. Yet as more black Americans left old homes for new ones, certain conditions endured—one common problem with both rural and urban housing was packed sleeping quarters—while new conditions emerged.[55] One of these new conditions resulted from a rather different sort of crowding.

Residential segregation, especially in urban centers, became more entrenched throughout the United States between 1900 and 1920. By restricting both mobility and choice, segregation created densely populated all-black neighborhoods in cities such as Chicago and Detroit.[56] The quotidian practice and environmental impact of Jim Crow notably varied from region to region. Many southern cities had numerous pockets where black residences were concentrated in addition to districts where a few African Americans—including live-in servants—lived interspersed with whites. Somewhat ironically, industrial northern cities that attracted black migrants immediately before and during the First Great Migration often tended to have highly entrenched patterns of residential segregation.[57] The net result was hauntingly similar across wide sections of the United States despite regional variation: segregation exacted a literal toll on black lives. Morbidity levels were excessively high in the back alleys of southern cities, within poorly ventilated northern tenements, and around industrial midwestern "black belts."

In Chicago—the metropolis with "the highest level of segregation of any city in the North" during the early twentieth century—*Defender* columnist Dr. A. Wilberforce Williams addressed urban sanitary conditions on a regular basis throughout the 1910s.[58] With his characteristic directness that emerged from both accessible language and blunt observation, Williams informed his readers that "tuberculosis germs breed best in damp, dark, crowded, poorly ventilated houses"; he urged readers to report any "neighbor . . . contented to live amid dirt and filth" to their local health department. He implored readers to realize that "home pride, civic and community pride . . . begets self-pride," described the attributes of "the sanitary home" in detail, and educated urban "newcomers" about maintaining their health in cities.[59] The *Defender* was not alone in its move to connect health and urban environments. In 1913, another race paper took a slightly different approach by arguing that urban housing discrimination ensured African Americans were cordoned off "in unhygienic sections, unfit for lower species of creation . . . where one child out of every three dies before its first year is completed."[60]

Not all Afro-American newspapers agreed upon how and where residential segregation appeared. Southern race editors often overlooked Jim Crow housing practices within their own region when they attempted to convince readers that northern migration was synonymous with segregation. As Norfolk's *Journal and Guide* flatly proclaimed, "[we have] several times expressed the opinion that segregation and unwholesome living conditions would follow wherever any considerable number of the [race settle] in the North."[61] Justified or not, the association between "unwholesome living conditions," segregation, and migration northward was relatively common after 1910; reform activists typically believed that urbanization presented real challenges for racial uplift.

As the race became more and more urbanized, concepts of degeneracy often turned on the problem of amusement and black youth. "Home training," in particular, was promoted as a means of policing cheeky boys and truant girls who roamed the streets.[62] For example, when Rosetta Douglass Sprague discussed the task facing contemporary black parents, she noted that the race sorely needed "homes in which purity can be taught [rather than] hovels that are police-court feeders."[63] Like other black social commentators, Sprague seemed to acknowledge that modest home amusements paled in comparison to sundry temptations and commercialized forms of leisure in urban centers; she also seemed to believe that parents had some control over how their children chose to amuse themselves as long as the domestic environment available to those children was one of "purity."

Still, it was undoubtedly difficult for urban black parents to control every aspect of the environments in which their children grew to maturity. Not only did red-light districts tend to be proximate to all-black neighborhoods, segregation affected the quality of housing stock available to Afro-Americans. Sanitation and hygiene warranted as much, if not more, attention as did moral purity in many black neighborhoods. Granted, some race women and men argued that all-black neighborhoods fostered rather than hindered respectability,[64] but both experience and conviction led many more people to contend that—from sanitation to housing stock to overall environment—black households were indeed compromised by segregation.

This is not to imply that black women, men, and children had no control

Clean-up campaign, Chicago, April 1919. National Negro Health Week encouraged participation in community upkeep efforts — some of which were affiliated with initiatives not limited to African Americans — such as this YMCA tin can drive that reportedly enlisted hundreds of energetic girls and boys. Courtesy of Photographs and Prints Division, Schomburg Center for Research in Black Culture, New York Public Library, Astor, Lenox and Tilden Foundations.

over their surroundings: in addition to personal initiative, Afro-American reform activists, health officials, and welfare workers were quick to respond to the problems they believed were posed by segregated urban environments in addition to derelict rural housing. Black Virginians began holding "Clean-Up Days" in 1910 and within a few years, members of the Hampton-based Negro Organization Society worked in conjunction with Virginia's Board of Health to distribute free "Health Handbook[s] for Colored People" throughout the state. Not only did a 1913 edition of the Chicago *Defender* declare Clean-Up Day "the beginning of an organized movement," by the end of the decade at least one "colored" YMCA in Chicago staged a "clean-up campaign" that mobilized black children to collect rubbish in Southside streets and alleys.[65]

The efforts of African Americans in Virginia and Illinois reflected well over a decade of public health organizing. Health-related organizations, events, and initiatives began appearing in black communities across the country shortly after the turn of the century, a time when African Americans "developed mechanisms to take care of themselves," more black nurses and doctors were being trained, and black hospitals were steadily emerging around the country.[66] As early as 1907, men from "the best class of colored people" in New York City established the Alpha Physical Culture Club. Club women in Atlanta began sponsoring health clinics before 1910, and Chicago women launched pure milk and fresh air campaigns shortly thereafter. In addition, members of the all-black National Medical Association (established 1895) convened on a regular basis throughout the early twentieth century, the *Defender* began publishing a weekly health column in 1913, and race activists in Muskogee, Oklahoma, mobilized their own public health campaign a year later. Health-consciousness gained a degree of acceptance and popularity among African Americans during the early twentieth century; such consciousness came about, in part, through the demands created by migration, segregation, and urbanization.[67]

By the time Booker T. Washington decided to push for a weeklong national health observance among the race, then, many black communities were already mobilizing on their own behalf. In a 1915 report to the trustees of Tuskegee Institute, Washington explained that he wanted to "reac[h] a large proportion of the ten million colored people" and encourage formation of community "clean-up committees" that would engage in "the thorough cleaning of premises . . . including dwellings, yards, [and] outbuildings." Although Washington's report was predicated upon the notion that the black masses needed instruction in basic sanitation, varied plans for official conservation of black health quickly materialized and enjoyed a solid measure success nationwide. In certain communities, black women, men, and children could even attend their own church in order to hear "special health sermons." Following the first National Negro Health Week, the National Medical Association even promoted a "Public Health Sunday" as a means to "spread the gospel of good health."[68]

If Booker T. Washington was not singularly responsible for the success of community-based public heath initiatives among African Americans, the flurry of grassroots activity laid critical foundations that enabled National Negro Health Week to be embraced by black communities. The efficaciousness and rapidity with which National Negro Health Week was realized was largely due to preexisting and continuing work by black women. Over a decade prior to the inauguration of Health Week, club women engaged in home visitations, and clubs sponsored "talks on sanitary and hygienic science." These women were, moreover, among the first race activists to engage in public health campaigns within black communities, and they hardly ceased their activity once Health Week was instituted. Women's organizations — notably the National Association of Colored Women's Clubs and the National Association of Colored Graduate Nurses — were among the leading race institutions responsible for establishing Health Week nationwide. Still, activist women — like activist men — engaged in such activity for complicated reasons, including "a personal stake in the 'improvement' of the poor because of the potential effects on their own status." Just as the Wizard of Tuskegee's class assumptions informed his activism, the same was true for black women organizers on the local level who "occasionally verged on victim-blaming when they stressed changes in individual behavior as the solution to improved black health." [69]

National leadership and grassroots activists did more than point fingers at other African Americans: they equated filth with segregation; newspapers were quick to trumpet their cause and disseminate information about Health Week. In columns, editorials, and brief notices, race papers throughout the United States alerted communities about special activities, provided instructions on how to clean yards as well as interiors, and vaunted individual fitness as a means of insuring collective health.[70] For example, the New York *Amsterdam News* announced, "the issue of health should be a matter of serious consideration with the entire race. Despite the lying assertions . . . that the colored people are dying out, the facts show us as being on the increase, but not half as fast as a healthy race should be. . . . Our people are forced by prejudice and its servant, segregation, to live in . . . unsanitary houses. . . . Observe the Health Week all the year round!" The *Journal and Guide* tried to remind its readers about the benefits of improved health by publishing an eye-catching sidebar that was at once simple and direct: "Remember the three deadly 'D's — dirt, disease, death. . . . Clean homes and clean streets mean fewer flies, better babies, happier children, happier people." For his part, Wilberforce Williams cheered the impetus behind National Negro Health Week as "the very thing that . . . [the *Defender*] has been advocating for nearly three years." The St. Louis *Argus* gave Health Week its own hearty endorsement when staff writers linked the effort to self-respect, increased overall health, and even the eradication of racial discrimination.[71] For all of their enthusiasm, columnists and editors occasionally delivered unflattering opinions of working-class and working-poor blacks with shocking bluntness. One Atlanta *Independent* writer coolly assessed the alleged "ignorance" of the black masses: "by all means . . . [they] should be taught the lesson of cleanliness in the home" as well as "the importance of taking care of their bodies."[72]

As uncomplimentary as it was, the item in the *Independent* reflected a larger Afro-American discourse about neighborhood and home environments in that it focused upon culture and values. Its commentary suggested that class status could indicate degeneracy, that poor homes were likely to be unhealthy homes. If items such as the one published in the *Independent* came off as being condescending editorial as to why black communities could benefit from clean-up campaigns, public health campaigns in and of themselves were predicated on assumptions similar to those held by race activists who produced domestic tracts. Health activism might have stressed personal as well as collective initiative, but it, like domestic tracts and environmentalist studies of black home life, stressed that the race sorely needed to work on improving itself. As public health activists looked for ways to "work and talk to the people . . . and not . . . at the people," as reformers acknowledged that stereotypes about unhealthy black residences enabled "'Jim Crowism,'" the home remained a site where women, men, and children could renovate their habitats as well as their habits.[73]

In 1922, black sociologist and "sometime professor" at Fisk University George Edmund Haynes displayed no small amount of pride when he pointed out that well over ten thousand homes were owned by African American families when the Emancipation Proclamation was signed almost six decades earlier. With freedom, Haynes observed, "those who had been united as slaves sought legal and ecclesiastical sanction in marriage and reëstablished . . . family hearts upon the ashes of the slave cabin"; an increasing number of African Americans acquired property as race homes grew "in stability, in purity, in culture, and in [their] power to mold a potential people." One- and two-room cabins still housed black families during the first decades of the twentieth century, but they now existed alongside multiroom dwellings with facilities and furnishings, wallpaper and decorations, race papers and books.[74]

Proud though he might be, Haynes was a social scientist attuned to the problems facing early-twentieth-century households. Southern municipalities typically neglected to provide public utilities and services to segregated black enclaves; "red light districts of whites" were often adjacent to African American residences both South and North; economic immiseration and poor health taxed the energies of black women, men, and children throughout the nation. Although World War I temporarily increased the wages available to black working families, wages fell when the war was over and could no longer support what was becoming "the Negro's standard of living." Yet the sociologist still managed to feel somewhat optimistic since at least one major aspect of African American life had improved markedly since the last century. As Haynes noted in his book, *The Trend of the Races*, Americans of the early twentieth century could find ample "evidence of Negro progress . . . by looking at . . . Negro homes."[75]

Black households and home life had, if nothing else, undergone marked change by the early 1920s. While Haynes's earlier study, *Negro New-Comers in Detroit, Michigan* (1918), reflected anxieties that emerged out of migration—the "lodger evil" being one of them—*The Trend of the Races* covered dynamics encountered by unprecedented numbers of African Americans who experienced urbanization, migration, and ever increasing residential segregation.[76] A flurry of intraracial reform activity addressed these demographic shifts; reform spoke to pressing issues facing black households and reflected a belief on the part of activists that black home life was beginning to indicate collective progress. Change manifested itself in other ways as well. On one level, sociological study on African Americans confirmed the existence of different economic classes and modes of living within the race. On another level, prescriptive domestic literature advised the growing cohort of upwardly mobile black folks how they should order their households. In certain critical regards, George Haynes's optimism about black home life reflected the culmination of an era, an era when discourse on domestic spaces was at once prominent and politicized.

Concepts regarding home environments emanated largely from aspiring-class, prominent, or otherwise privileged Afro-Americans. The majority of extant observations on domesticity obscure divergent views from poor and working-poor people, yet this very obfuscation underscores a critical point. Poor African Americans were not only absent from the production of this discourse, the overwhelming majority of this rhetoric reflected a desire for collective upward mobility on the part of the race. If, as Du Bois claimed, it was not until the turn of the century that black people—as a group—had the stability and resources to establish either humble or comfortable homes,[77] then aspirations to better those homes among some African Americans after 1900 reflected increased intraracial class stratification. Furthermore, by 1920, both the slight increase in black home ownership and improvements in black home environments reflected that stratification.

As the twentieth century opened, then, "making the home life measure up" /was as much about addressing very real, often problematic material conditions—overcrowding, segregation, bad sanitation—as it was about articulating the desire for an upwardly mobile and moral respectability for the race. The discussion about home environments resulted in part from contemporaneous social science findings that advanced the notion that environment was responsible for the literal character of a people. Moreover, public health initiatives aimed at addressing environment and Afro-American well-being—health columns in race papers, clean-up campaigns, "public health Sunday[s]"—existed, in large part, due to earlier reform networks established by club women, nurses, doctors, and local activists. Notions about environment continued to inform discourse focused upon black conduct as well. T. S. Boone's 1921 pamphlet, *Paramount Facts in Race Development*, put it bluntly: if it was true that white Americans justified segregation by associating the race with disorderly homes, "disease, filth, and noise," it was also true that for African Americans "ENVIRONMENT HAS ITS STAIN."[78]

Just as class-based notions informed activists' ideas about proper environment and Afro-American domestic literature contained various assumptions regarding class, discourse on black homes and racial character also reflected deeply held notions regarding womanhood, manhood, and proper sexual activity. Racialized theories of domestic disorder and contamination were fraught with gendered notions. Black women in particular found themselves in an oxymoronic position: they were simultaneously caricatured by white Americans as diseased contaminants *and* characterized by Afro-Americans as primary agents in regenerating the race's home life.[79] Since it was commonly assumed that the race's home life was firmly within the provenance of womanhood, women were expected to steer youths from urban vice, keep errant husbands in check, and maintain a sanitary home environment for the sake of producing better children. Women not only bore the brunt for enacting reform within Afro-American households, then, they were singled out as primary targets of reform—in terms of attitude, conduct, and activism.[80] Indeed, black girls and women would continue to be considered both agents and targets of reform, and such a focus upon women would certainly be evident in heated intraracial discussions on material culture, miscegenation, and even nationalism.

Domestic spaces / reform
Home cleanliness / ownership
Neighborhood pride

Gendered

172   [HOME LIFE]

Class stratified reform

If, perchance, a black . . . doll finds its way into [the] home . . . [a] child's first impulse is either to discard it . . . or make it the servant of [a] white doll. Thus . . . is the baleful work of slavery made evident.
—Nathan B. Young,
  A.M.E. Church Review (1898)

No toy you can buy for a small colored girl will instill more of self-respect in her — unconsciously — than a colored doll. Burn up the others.
—"Negro Dolls," *Christian Recorder* (1921)

6

THE COLORED DOLL IS A LIVE ONE! MATERIAL CULTURE, BLACK CONSCIOUSNESS, AND CULTIVATION OF INTRARACIAL DESIRE

Because of a doll, six-year-old Maud Evangeline Gary had an auspicious future ahead of her — at least her mother believed that this was the case. Maud Gary's doll was ordinary in many respects: it was clothed, had combable hair, and was roughly the size of a small toddler. Maud likely spent hours on end playing with the companion "she love[d] very dearly"; the little girl might have taken her playmate with the pleasant, welcoming face nearly everywhere she went. Whatever she did with her doll, Maud probably did not suspect that her mother had an ulterior motive for giving it to her. Her mother confessed, "I do not allow her to play with [white] dolls only [those] of her own race. I am trying to make her a race woman by daily teaching her to love whatever belongs to the colored race. . . . The only way to make race-loving men and women is to start in early childhood." For Maud's mother, the important thing was not that Maud adored her toy but that the girl played with a colored doll: a colored doll kept her daughter out of city streets, a colored doll taught "race love," a colored doll would help ensure that Maud grew up to become a respectable woman partnered with a black man. Maud's acquisition of black consciousness went beyond the dolls that she cradled. Her mother was additionally convinced that "every mother should surround their children with pictures and literature of our race." Maud Gary, then, was surrounded by a comprehensive home culture built upon race pride, objects reflective of Afro-American ability and appearance, and conscious effort to foster intraracial desire.[1]

Maud's mother was so certain that such race training gave her daughter a decided edge in life that she decided to enter the little girl in a "better babies" contest. Sometime during July or August 1915, she composed a hope-filled letter, tucked a snapshot of daughter and doll into an envelope, and sent off her entry to the contest sponsor, the New York *Age*. Part beauty contest, part eugenic undertaking, the *Age*'s better "baby" initiative focused upon infants as well as children up to the age of twelve. The *Age* proudly announced that the contest showcased "future men and women of the race" as it encouraged black parents to take an interest in the "sanitary and hygienic precautions" that constituted the recently defined science of "baby culture." The leading Afro-American newspaper endeavored mightily to make mothers and fathers more mindful of their children's diet and exercise. Readers were quick to respond to this strategic initiative by sending letters, entries, and feedback to the *Age*. Shortly after Maud's picture and her mother's letter were published, another *Age* reader enthusiastically wrote the paper in order to endorse the use of "Negro dolls," "colored pictures," and "Sunday School cards representing colored characters" as a means of ensuring that African Americans understood eugenics entailed "race pride."[2] For this reader, a consciously eugenic version of race pride produced better children, strengthened Afro-American identity, and enabled a positive collective destiny.

The story of Maud Evangeline Gary and her doll reflects a historical moment when African Americans—especially aspiring, middling, and elite people—considered the steady proliferation of healthier home environments and "better babies" within black communities as evidence that the race had made spectacular strides since emancipation. But Maud's story is part of other tales as well. As a child born in the first decade of the twentieth century, Maud Gary was playing with toys during an era when race reformers turned their attention to children, when black consciousness assumed new salience among aspiring-class women and men, when reformists viewed proper conduct as essential to race progress. Maud Gary carried around her

[THE COLORED DOLL]

doll at a time when race women and men made a connection between the toys with which children played and their impending entrance into adolescence, sexuality, and mate selection. And, Maud's mother was a consumer who consciously decided to purchase a "colored" toy at a time when aspiring and working-class African Americans had more expendable income and access to mass-produced goods.

Demographic developments were partially responsible for the very appearance of material culture aimed at and produced by African Americans. Urbanization after the turn of the century provided better labor opportunities that, in turn, increased the number of African Americans with expendable income. Growing black literacy rates additionally expanded the market for race products in that once more children, women, and men could read billboards and print ads, then more people were likely to consider buying race literature and other forms of black material culture. Advertisements in race publications therefore reached an increased number of potential buyers as the percentage of literate black women, men, and children surpassed 50 percent during the early decades of the twentieth century. These advertisements did more than sell commodities: they promoted race pride and, at times, peddled ideas that neatly meshed with reformist discourse about black domestic spaces. Many of these same advertisements tried to convince potential buyers that specific items were essential for the proper home training of black girls and boys.

If advertisements were critical to the emergence of black consumer culture, consumer culture itself was contingent upon technological advances. Technology facilitated the manufacture of affordable mass-market goods, goods that increased the production of advertising. Critical technological advances in mass printing and innovations in advertising—refinements in lithography that led to the explosion of colorful trading cards during the 1870s and 1880s, greater reliance on memorable slogans and copy during the 1880s and 1890s—made products seem all the more appealing and enticing.[3] It was not until the early twentieth century, however, that Afro-American publications and the advertisements in them became more visually sophisticated. Not only did ads with better graphics help generate a niche-market of African Americans but that niche market appeared toward the end of a period in which technology greatly expanded consumer culture in the United States.

Late-nineteenth- and early-twentieth-century U.S. consumer culture was rife with derogatory portrayals of black people on trading cards, on packaging, and in the form of toys, souvenirs, stereographs, and everyday articles. Since African Americans generally found these items distasteful if not harmful, many black women and men felt the need to counteract offensive images and objects with items that promoted pride, self-love, and black consciousness.[4] One such race woman in Chicago, a Mrs. Mack, penned a purposeful missive to the *Half-Century* in which she championed objects of race pride:

> White people do not fill their houses with pictures of Colored people. . . . They cover their walls with pictures of their own race. If, occasionally they do use a picture of a Colored person it is usually in a ridiculous role . . . or doing menial labor. . . . At present I have no pictures on my walls . . . that haven't Colored people in them. And I don't allow a ridiculous picture of a Colored person in my house. . . . I have purchased pretty Colored dolls for my children so that they will learn to love and respect heroes and beauties of their own color.

Suggestive in its implication that limited, unflattering, or denigrating depictions of Afro-Americans were just as, if not more, damaging than the absence of positive images, Mack's letter underscored that "colored" material culture stood counterposed to the "menial" and the "ridiculous," which for Mack included both "eating watermelon" and outlandish dress. This juxtaposition on her part powerfully emphasized the fact that race consumers had options — options that at once uplifted the collective and challenged the problematic. And when Mack urged other *Half-Century* readers to pressure shops into stocking "beautiful Colored pictures" and to consider seriously giving their children "Colored dolls," she articulated specific ways in which black women and men could simultaneously empower themselves and shape their children's most personal and deep-seated tastes, preferences, and cravings.[5]

Mack's own wish for her children — and other race children, for that matter — to "love and respect their own color" was as much reflective of race pride as it was indicative of a broader concern with child's play among individuals concerned about the future of African Americans. Race-conscious individuals put aside nickels, dimes, and quarters in order to purchase the new "colored" pictures, books, and toys as activists and parents offered pointed rationales for why these items were necessary. Whereas race activists considered a range of material culture beneficial, one object in particular was accorded a unique transformative power in enabling children to become race-conscious adults who would go on to produce their own upright offspring. As the twentieth century opened and progressed, both aspiring

[THE COLORED DOLL]

and "representative" women and men believed that children could learn life lessons without being endowed with precocious knowledge, that material culture could simultaneously serve the goals of home training, "race" training, and the disciplining of desire. For reformers and parents who believed that playthings could have a decisive impact on the minds, bodies, psyches, and predilections of children, dolls were unrivaled in their ability to shape collective destiny.

Material culture and race consciousness converged with a reformist preoccupation over sexuality to make the colored doll an exemplary racial tool —one that ostensibly supported Afro-American industry, facilitated self-love, and enabled proper intraracial conduct. Dolls became possessed with a power to influence children's sexuality and eventual sexual preferences: reformers imbued them with eugenic properties and the ability to ensure racial purity; one educator claimed that dolls could help reduce or even stop lynching. In order to understand why educators, reformers, and parents forged provocatively potent connections between material culture and sexuality, dolls and racial reproduction, toys and collective well-being, it is necessary to reconstruct the history of the inanimate, sepia companions that little girls like Maud Gary caressed and cherished.

During the early twentieth century, black reformers considered the placement of certain forms of material culture within domestic spaces to be a symbol of collective progress. Ideally, for purposes of racial uplift, homes were supposed to be classrooms providing constant instruction to children through an array of examples disseminated by thoughtful parents and adult relatives. Just as churchgoing folk might imbue religious faith in their daughters and sons or education-minded people might inspire members of their household on to academic achievement, chaste mothers and fathers allegedly set the moral compass of children. Spiritual guidance, ambition, and restrained sexual behavior were valued within a range of black households, including the homes of aspiring, middling, and elite race families. For many of these families and for more than a few reform-minded race activists, home life and collective progress were more than connected: collective progress was all but contingent upon domestic uplift. Given that the bulk of black reform discourse demonized certain domestic arrangements—especially crowding and boarding—for their supposed detrimental impact on sexuality, it is not surprising that race reformers believed home training should account for sex, sexual ethics, and reproducing the collective.

According to this vision of black advancement and racial destiny, the domestic sphere was one sphere over which African Americans exacted some measure of control. Destitute, struggling, working-class, and aspiring-class parents could all strive to provide their children every advantage within their means; every parent could do *something* to enrich the home environment. The seemingly simple task of hanging "a few good pictures" of prominent Afro-Americans on one's walls could enable children in the lowliest homes to learn about the race's achievements.[6] If what the race's youth learned at home had broad implications and if domestic spaces were seats of learning, then material culture within those spaces would facilitate uplift, progress, and, indeed, self-love. The mere ability to purchase material culture was, however, largely restricted to households with at least a modicum of expendable income—those households composed of solid working-class, middling, and representative families.

The presence of material culture in domestic spaces gained new significance for black women, men, and children around the turn of the century. Activists and advertisements alike claimed that items featuring Afro-American images, leaders, and achievement brought "a gleam of joy . . . [to the] eyes," imparted a "new hope . . . [to the] soul," and made "the heart of every race-lover beat faster."[7] Books were cherished since literacy was closely associated with collective progress. Race reformers thus promoted books as a potent tool in the crusade to uplift, enlighten, and transform the black masses. Although these reform-minded women and men typically realized that working black families might not have the resources to purchase books, their realization was usually overwhelmed by their conviction that black mothers and fathers were duty-bound to place race literature in the home.

In 1902, for example, race woman Julia Layton Mason advised black parents that "no matter how humble [their] home" they should nonetheless "strive to start a good library . . . [and] secure the books that have been written by our own people." Similarly, a 1906 advertisement in *Voice of the Negro* urged every "Negro family in the South" to obtain their own copy of the pricey, four dollar *Afro-American Home Manual*: not only did this "grand" morocco-bound volume "dea[l] with topics of vital interest to the colored people," its pages were filled with "timely and scholarly articles" intended to educate race readers.[8] Books were valued for their contents and for what they could teach, but they were also important—to both reformers and willing, able buyers—as objects that represented black aspiration and ability. Along with other forms of material culture in the home, books were a representative item that could uplift an individual who both possessed a longing to be transformed and an urge to support "authors . . . of our own flesh and blood."[9] As with Afro-American conduct tracts and manuals, race literature sought to reproduce class-bound values; while conduct literature stressed behavior that mirrored restrained, ostensibly bourgeois sexuality, race literature promoted a range of achievement that might lead to class mobility.

Mobility and progress were contingent upon race literature in the eyes of writer-physician Dr. Monroe A. Majors. In 1918, the author of *Noted Negro Women: Their Triumphs & Activities* contended that race women and men should endeavor to "make a few big authors and poets of our own"; he maintained that production of history texts was "essential . . . in the formation of races." As much as Majors considered it imperative for black Americans to buy and read race literature, he also believed that Afro-American texts—the "rich fruit of . . . race heritage"—would fail to realize their full potential without "a deal of race pride to go with them." Books were certainly critical agents in terms of what they could instill and in their ability to influence readers' self-image, thought, consciousness, and conduct. Still, as Majors pointed out, books alone did not generate "better pride." Race pride was additionally produced through environment and representations; race pride was inculcated in children through nurture, education, and play. More than a decade before Majors equated race pride with African Americans "occupy[ing] their place in the circle of nations," activists considered how nurture, education, and play shaped girls, boys, and collective destiny. And, if Majors focused on literature, poetry, and history during the 1910s— a time when history became professionalized among African Americans— some of his immediate activist and intellectual predecessors developed an allied preoccupation with dolls.[10]

Black Americans were cognizant of the varied potential of dolls as early as the 1890s. For example, during an 1891 tour of Sierra Leone when AME bishop Henry McNeal Turner noticed that the only dolls available had white faces, Turner concluded that exciting market possibilities existed for black American innovators willing to produce the "millions of colored dolls" sought by "African ladies . . . want[ing] black, brown, and yellow dolls."[11] Others would, in time, share Turner's belief that black dolls could play a key role in economic self-determination. Most Afro-American women and men who promoted colored dolls before 1910, however, echoed lawyer Edward Johnson's sentiment that dolls were an integral part of "spur[ring] our race to properly teach itself." If, as Johnson put it in 1894, the prevalence of "bad representations" made the need for positive images pressing, then it was of utmost importance for black girls and boys to be given toys and texts that "correspond[ed]" with the actual achievements, conditions, and appearance of the race. Within four years, one of Johnson's contemporaries, Nathan Young, was relieved that race parents were "wisely beginning" to place "Negro doll[s]" in their homes for the "edification" of children.[12]

The importance that Johnson and Young attached to dolls as means of socialization placed both men within a larger cultural trend. If, by the 1890s, the antebellum view that dolls were practical tools that helped girls learn to sew had subsided, white middle-class parents increasingly believed that dolls helped girls "imitate social ritual[s] of polite society." Adults in the United States—specifically white women doll makers, maternalists, and reformers—actively began to promote dolls as a means to instruct children about "social relationships." Adults increasingly assumed that children formed emotional attachments to dolls as well. Changes in doll production enabled this shift on the part of adults and children in that the "progressive juvenilization in . . . dolls' appearance" that occurred over the latter nineteenth century made it more likely that children would actually identify with these particular toys. As adults came to expect that most forms of child's play with dolls mimicked parenting and fostered desires for domesticity, children were increasingly encouraged to engage in a fantasy life involving dolls. With a little imagination, girls could become little mothers and boys little fathers as their nurturing arms transformed dolls into "babies." Doll play became all the more associated with gender role socialization in the process: both girls and boys acted in nurturing—and aggressive ways—toward dolls, yet "boys often assumed authoritative public roles such as doctor, preacher, and undertaker to sick, dying, and dead dolls." Dolls were associated with domesticity, then, but they also assumed significance as implements that guided children as they learned to negotiate intimate relationships, gender performance, and social roles.[13]

Changing beliefs and expectations over the function of dolls within the broader culture informed Afro-American discourse in provocative ways. Race-conscious individuals such as Edward Johnson and Nathan Young became more explicit—albeit incrementally—about what they believed dolls could accomplish. Johnson himself, who by 1900 had produced a history of African Americans for school children as well as an account of black soldiers in the Spanish-American War, returned to the matter of what dolls could do for race children in 1908. In an article entitled "Negro Dolls for Negro Babies," the lawyer cum author opined that "one of the best ways to teach Negro children to respect their own color would be to see to it that the children be given colored dolls. . . . In most cases they prefer white dolls . . . but this idea could easily be removed. . . . To give a Negro child a white doll means to create in it a prejudice against its own color, which will cling to it through life." More than inconsequential child's play, the use of white-skinned dolls "sow[ed] . . . seeds of discontent" and bred self-loathing that irrevocably warped black children's outlook. Self-hatred hindered race progress; hatred of one's complexion translated into the inability to be attracted to somebody else of similar hue. Without saying as much, Johnson was able to get the message across that learning to "respect [one's] own color" during childhood was intimately tied to the eventual selection of sexual partners. His text mentioned neither illicit interracial sex nor so-called bastardization, yet provocative insinuations were nevertheless shot through his text: all one had to do was ponder the full implications of self-hatred implanted at an early age.[14]

Johnson's article in the *Colored American* was published just as race-conscious women and men were beginning to rally around the notion of black dolls for black children. Before 1900, dark-skinned dolls, in and of themselves, did not possess automatic appeal among black children, let alone their parents. Stereotyped images and normalized portrayals of black women and men as servants were so ubiquitous that realistic toys produced in the United States that approximated the actual appearance of African American children were at once novelty and rarity.[15] For black parents who possessed expendable income to purchase toys, choices were few: either white-skinned dolls or "'Darky Head,'" "'Mammy,'" "'Topsy,'" and "'Dusky Dude'" playthings provided by factories and department stores catering to mainstream tastes.[16] Undoubtedly, a people barely two generations removed from bondage did not relish the idea of their children playing with what were essentially kerchiefed plantation figures and, even worse, "demon[s] or caricature[s]."[17]

Homemade dolls were always an option since women—black and white alike—produced black rag dolls. Whereas middle-class white women doll makers in the United States produced black dolls during the late nineteenth century, these dolls tended to be "mammy" and "servant" rag or stockinet dolls that were considerably popular among middle-class white children.[18] The rag dolls that black mothers produced for their children were likely well-used and cherished items. Yet, if African American children and parents were going to reject commercial white dolls, attractive black ones needed to be mass-produced and the reasons for purchasing these new dolls sufficiently dramatized.

The artistic and technological development that enabled production of mass-market, lifelike colored dolls did not occur in the United States but in Europe. During the late 1880s, German doll makers began using unglazed porcelain, which is known as bisque; they modeled dolls' features from life, used an array of brown tints, and pioneered the mass production of attractive, lifelike colored dolls. German factories did indeed produce stereotypical black dolls during this period, but nonetheless, their innovations resulted in the creation of dolls that resembled African American children.[19] When realistic colored dolls finally emerged on the U.S. market around the turn of the century, then, most were imported from Europe. U.S.-based E. M. S. Novelty Company, for example, sold imported colored dolls during the 1910s for use in "emancipation celebrations, bazaars, fairs."[20] Since U.S. doll makers would not match the technological and aesthetic innovation of German companies until World War I, those African Americans who sold commercial colored dolls during the early decades of the century often went through considerable efforts to import their product.

The mere existence of lifelike colored dolls hardly ensured that they would become familiar and coveted items in black households, however. Imported dolls of any hue were expensive, therefore middle-class and elite consumers, the majority of whom were native-born whites, were their primary purchasers. Working-class children—especially the sons and daughters of immigrants—played far less with commercially produced dolls because their parents generally could not afford them. Similarly, for African Americans, imported as well as domestically produced dolls could carry a "prohibitive" price tag.[21]

It took initiative on the part of one of Afro-America's largest institutions to make colored dolls more accessible to black consumers and to popularize the notion that colored dolls shaped black children's self-esteem. Shortly after the turn of the century, the National Baptist Convention (NBC) launched several efforts to promote colored dolls.[22] Black Baptists first passed a resolution in 1908 encouraging members of the denomination to give children nothing but brown-skinned doll babies. Baptist women began organizing "'Negro Doll Clubs'" around 1914; along these lines, the NBC sponsored well-timed "doll bazaars" for the Christmas trade. Black Baptists also owned and operated the National Negro Doll Company (NNDC), which opened in 1908. The company sent at least one representative on a promotional tour around the United States, while company president Richard H. Boyd did some traveling of his own by crossing the Atlantic in order to establish business relationships with doll makers in Germany. While in Europe,

Boyd either procured dolls or learned about manufacturing high-quality bisque products; Boyd likely accomplished both tasks, since the NNDC eventually manufactured their own product from their Nashville headquarters.[23]

The *Age* proclaimed the National Baptist Convention's sundry efforts to promote colored dolls "a timely and mighty step in the right direction." Not only did celebration of the race's likeness mean certain progress for black Americans, such a "sensible change in Negro sentiment for Negro toys and ornaments w[ould] profoundly affect Negro nature." The *Age* editorial further commented that the NBC's endeavor would have a stronger impact on home training if used in conjunction with race pictures and calendars. In one brief news item, the *Age* advanced key concepts about home life and its components: images and items contained within households shaped "Negro nature"; those same images and items possessed the power to alter the race's overall sociopolitical trajectory.[24]

When the *Age* additionally decried unwitting promotion of "foreign standards of beauty and culture," it pointed to the attendant pitfalls awaiting young folks without making any direct reference to gender. Danger presumably existed for both sexes. Prizing whiteness might result in girls succumbing to white men's flatteries, while boys might develop a risky preference for white females. The underlying message, then, was that something as simple as a doll could reduce concubinage, miscegenation, black-on-white rape, and lynching. The paper did not specifically mention sex, but just as Edward Johnson spoke volumes through carefully crafted prose, the editorial subtly communicated the message that race dolls were particularly powerful toys.

The NNDC publicized its own claims regarding the potent utility of colored dolls. NNDC advertisements suggested that if other races were "teach-[ing] their children . . . object lessons" through dolls, then dolls would enable black children's "higher intellectual" development as well. The company's illustrated brochures proclaimed that "our dolls vividly portray the smart set, as is often referred to in society and news items."[25] As the NNDC would have it, their dolls had three distinct properties: they shaped children's thinking, fostered respectability, and provided a class-based example of what the race could achieve. By pricing their toys as low as fifty cents and one dollar, moreover, the NNDC placed colored dolls within closer reach of aspiring families. Lower-end NNDC dolls were not necessarily cheap, but they were certainly less expensive than other commercial dolls, both imported and domestic.[26]

Over the course of the 1910s, the NNDC began to have competitors as a range of companies—white-owned as well as race-operated—plied their wares on the pages of Afro-American publications. The E. M. S. Novelty Company tried to lure customers by announcing to *Crisis* readers that "THE COLORED DOLL IS A LIVE ONE."[27] Both Gadsden Doll Company and Berry & Ross advertised in the *Crisis* as well as the Chicago *Defender*. Gadsden Company ads made no mention of whether the company was black-owned or -operated; Berry & Ross, however, was a race concern that produced dolls fashioned by its two women founders, Evelyn Berry and Victoria Ross.[28] Another Afro-American woman, Theresa Cassell, headed the Chicago-based National Colored Doll and Toy Company (NCDTC). Significantly, many of these companies appeared on the scene during and immediately after World War I, when imported colored dolls became difficult, if not impossible, to procure. The NCDTC, for one, experienced problems with its "source of supply" during the war, yet the company was able to stay in operation all the same. In July 1919, the *Half-Century*—where the NCDTC advertised— featured a profile on Cassell in which the magazine noted the entrepreneur's conviction "that Colored children should be taught to cherish the . . . beauty of a brown skin . . . [and] the wave of curly hair." One of Cassell's supporters, Evelyn Jones of Tulsa, promptly wrote in to the *Half-Century* to praise the magazine for drawing race consumers' attention to the NCDTC. Jones informed other *Half-Century* readers that Tulsa's blacks were swayed by Cassell's vision and efforts; she also confessed that her own baby "crie[d] all the time for a New 'Tolored' Doll" from the NCDTC.[29]

One of the attributes that made Gadsden, Berry & Ross, and NCDTC dolls "live" was their resolute rejection of stereotype. As one Berry & Ross advertisement put it, New Negroes did not want "old time, black face, red lip aunt Jemima colored dolls but dolls well made and truly representative of the race in hair and features." Alvah Bottoms of Chicago concurred. She was appalled by "'dancing coon'" and "'Aunt Jemima'" toys that reinforced notions that "all colored men are fit for is to . . . amuse white people . . . [and] colored women are fit only for servants." At a time when racist portrayals of African Americans were all too common in the United States, at a moment when black consciousness was on the rise, colored dolls and the companies that made them were in vogue. That vogue was no meaningless fad.[30]

In addition to colored dolls appealing to race-conscious individuals for what they were not, the message that such dolls were synonymous with respectability would have been especially attractive to urban aspiring-class parents. This group of mothers and fathers was most likely to be concerned with the detrimental impact that employers, boarders, and street denizens might have on their children's sexuality. Working parents could not be sure about the nature of their children's interactions with other adults, but they could counteract environmental stressors by placing certain objects within the home. Giving a black child a black doll might not prevent that child from being molested by an adult, but it might keep that child from seeking intimate relationships with whites upon reaching sexual maturity: a black doll might keep a daughter from succumbing to the advances of an employer, a son from indulging in pleasures offered at black-and-tan watering holes. The benefit of black consciousness for the working and aspiring class, then, was that racial sensibilities might help future race women and men resist interracial sex and remain within the bounds of respectability.

Colored dolls found an unlikely champion in a relatively obscure black educator from Oklahoma named J. H. A. Brazelton. An ardent believer in developmental psychology, Brazelton was sufficiently concerned about the current cast and direction of racial reproduction that he self-published *Self-Determination, The Salvation of the Race* in 1918. With a frontispiece bearing the likeness of Thomas Jefferson, his book touched upon subjects ranging from segregation and disfranchisement to the Spanish-American War and the Great War. The most striking feature of *Self-Determination* was its unrelenting insistence that domestic influences and material culture decided the race's future.[31]

Self-Determination was as much a "plea for character building in our race-variety" as it was a treatise on how Afro-Americans should maintain ethnic distinctiveness: "I am trying to show . . . that black children are born with honor and integrity; that our mothers, not thinking psychologically and sociologically, take away the honor and integrity of our children by . . . certain devices in the cradle. . . . Heredity counts for naught in these matters . . . and ideals count for everything in the history of a race-variety. So, if we want honor and integrity in our race-variety, we must begin in the cradle to fix the next generation." Although Brazelton recognized that structural conditions forced many adults to expend considerable energy on the material support of their families—which meant, of course, that they spent limited time at home—he still believed that parents needed to seize control of domestic influences. Schools and teachers might possess the power to correct "the faults of . . . Afro-American homes," but the obverse was just as true: a dubious home life could obliterate progressive strides acquired through education. Public education could also backfire. According to Brazelton, standard textbooks that lionized the exploits of white Americans subjected black children to "spiritual slavery"—he even believed textbooks had a hand in "maintain[ing] illegal amalgamation." If the race was going to sustain itself, its distinctiveness, and its honor, home life had to be carefully administered.[32]

Proper administration of the household required use of race images, texts, and "devices," namely dolls. Believing most ethnic groups partook in material culture that reflected themselves, Brazelton unfavorably compared black Americans to Puerto Ricans and Filipinos who, although colonized, allegedly had the foresight to "use their own dolls." Brazelton offered no real proof that residents of U.S. territories either possessed or created hued dolls. Concrete evidence was beside the point, however: the mere implication that African Americans lagged behind other peoples mattered most. Such comparison made the race seem retrograde and suggested that failure to remove white dolls from black homes resulted in diminished probity of children who already belonged to a people considered morally suspect in mainstream society. In other words, no one could afford to underestimate the power of a seemingly benign toy since something as simple as a doll could prevent collective advancement.[33]

For J. H. A. Brazelton, dolls were a "powerful . . . silent force in the world" that should, in their own right, be looked upon as "children . . . [and] the monuments of our souls." His poetic turn of phrase likening dolls to babies offered the compelling suggestion that children viewed dolls as friends, loved and cherished them, considered them daughters or sons when playing house. Since girls and boys developed deep attachments to these companions in miniature, once an Afro-American child began to "love and embrace" a white doll, God-given integrity diminished along with a "desire [to] . . . live forever."[34]

Self-Determination and self-preservation were one and the same for the teacher from Oklahoma. With his conviction that material culture enabled black children to perpetuate and build up the race, Brazelton went so far as to argue that dolls possessed a eugenic component which helped remove "defects of body and sense-organs."[35] This argument on Brazelton's part was similar to earlier contentions by white women doll makers—including Martha Chase, who produced Chase Sanitary Dolls—that dolls could help "'produce a generation of Better Babies'" through promoting scientific motherhood along with health and domestic hygiene.[36] Brazelton, like other reform-minded African Americans, drew from eugenic discourse in order to connect children's weal to racial health.

Brazelton departed somewhat from the argument offered by Chase and her maternalist contemporaries, who tended to view dolls as a means "to teach infant hygiene to working-class mothers and their children."[37] Brazelton neither discussed whether dolls could shape black women's hygienic habits nor did he stop at claiming that the eugenic benefits of colored dolls were limited to dolls' purported benefit to their possessors' bodies. Dolls, Brazelton maintained, played a key role in shaping racial reproduction and determining race purity. Brazelton summoned compelling language to declare "the Afro-American doll . . . a double-barrelled shot gun that will destroy in PEACE both illegal amalgamation and the first cause of lynch law." For him, miscegenation was slow, creeping genocide: "According to the census of the United States, there are 3,000,000 mulattoes in the country today. . . . We shall have to wait for the next census to find out whether . . . the rate of increase of mulattoes is greater than the rate of increase of blacks. . . . I want the integrity of my race-variety sustained to the eternities. . . . I want illegal amalgamation stopped now." With his concerns about racial reproduction, Brazelton was quick to name whom he felt was ultimately responsible for such an alarming state of affairs—African American mothers. He insisted that too many mothers failed to realize that infants possessed an innate craving to "see continued existence," thus they unwittingly warped impressionable little minds by foisting white dolls upon their tykes. As far as Brazelton was concerned, black mothers created children who craved whiteness from infancy and would continue to do so upon reaching sexual maturity.[38]

What Edward Johnson gently inferred and the *Age* quietly intimated a decade earlier, J. H. A. Brazelton boldly stated: black dolls ensured racial purity. Whereas neither Johnson nor the anonymous editorial writer specified how doll play affected either sex, Brazelton proposed that dolls shaped the sexuality of the entire race. *Self-Determination* implied that dark-skinned dolls imbued little girls with the wish to become mothers of their own sepia-toned babies, that they primed infant boys to value blackness. As if to underscore that both sexes did indeed play with dolls, the Oklahoman alternated between gendered pronouns in his text as he connected toys, home training, and predilections for interracial sex. In the course of doing so, he reproached women for their alleged role in perpetuating miscegenation. And, whereas Brazelton drew upon statistics compiled by Afro-American sociologist Monroe Work to substantiate his own assertion that 75 percent of those lynched were actually "charged with offenses other than that unmentionable crime," Brazelton nonetheless maintained that black-on-white rape motivated the practice of lynching. Brazelton also concluded that misguided home training induced the remaining 25 percent to assault white females. Accordingly, he implied that if black parents could not prevent mob violence from affecting their families, they could at least make sure that their sons were not exposed to rosy-cheeked, flaxen-haired dolls.[39]

Brazelton rendered his argument in such stark fashion to arouse a sense of urgency in his readers. Who, after all, would want to risk giving their son a toy that might ultimately lead to his murder? What decent parent would want his or her own carelessness to result in a daughter seeking illicit interracial sex? Brazelton expected his audience to be aspiring-class people like himself, and he therefore addressed their anxieties as well as their hopes. He realized that the many African Americans who led somewhat tenuous lives wanted to bequeath an honorable heritage to their children, if nothing else. Put another way, parents who could not afford a commodious home might be able to put aside a few pennies at a time and eventually buy their child a "Negro doll" for twenty-nine cents.[40] Domestic material culture certainly took other forms—such as race histories, novels, and portraits—but dolls played a particular role in black home reform in that they ostensibly had a direct influence on morality, sexuality, and racial reproduction. As J. H. A. Brazelton endeavored to suggest, dolls could prove just as critical as separate bedrooms when it came to home training and morality.

Brazelton was more than a lone voice out in Oklahoma. He embodied a growing sentiment among aspiring women and men who consumed African American material culture after the war; his arguments came during a period of especially prominent display and availability of Negro dolls. As a major Afro-American periodical observed within two years of the publication of Brazelton's book, black dolls were "fast becoming the fashion among our people."[41] This "fashion" was evident in race publications with aspiring, middling, and elite readership. The *Half-Century* ran a photograph of a little girl and her little brown doll on its cover in 1920. Almost three years later, the *Half-Century*'s cover for its November–December issue, provocatively captioned "Her Choice," featured a race girl lovingly cradling a race doll in her arms—as a rejected white doll lay askew at the child's feet, no less. The growing visibility of black dolls was supplemented by African Americans' interest in doll making as a fortuitous opportunity to cultivate black consciousness and turn a profit. North Carolina's Afro-American Novelty Shop of Wilmington attempted to win customers with ad in the *Competitor* promoting itself as the "only colored wholesale and retail doll mail order house in this section." Berry & Ross pitched their "Famous Brown Skin Dolls" on

Advertisement for Berry & Ross, Inc., Chicago Defender, *April 5, 1919.
Started by two African American women and eventually connected to the Universal Negro Improvement Association, Berry & Ross ingeniously promoted "colored dolls" by associating their product with "sound" financial, industrial, familial, and racial investments. Courtesy of General Research and Reference Division, Schomburg Center for Research in Black Culture, New York Public Library, Astor, Lenox and Tilden Foundations.*

numerous levels to *Defender* readers: the Harlem-based firm claimed that their products encouraged self-love in children, provided economic self-determination for adults, and offered significant employment opportunities for black women. Parents could also purchase ten-dollar shares for their children—on the "Liberty loan easy payment plan," no less. The company even promoted Victoria Ross and Evelyn Berry as role models that could help children realize "the real value of Negro industry to the Race."[42]

Other outfits, including New York City's Otis H. Gadsden Company, packaged their dolls as part of a larger project in race pride, one that incorporated portraits of black soldiers and calendars featuring children "for home use." Chicago's National Colored Doll & Toy Company even tried to entice little boys by advertising toy replicas of World War I helmets along with miniature toy gas masks. Any lucky boy who managed to save up $1.35 could imagine himself "go[ing] over the top" just like the 369th Colored Infantry, whose heroic efforts in France earned them both the nickname of the "Hell Fighters" and the coveted Croix de Guerre. Therefore, by marketing toy war paraphernalia, the National Colored Doll & Toy Company could capitalize on the 369th's fame and recoup wartime losses at the same time that little boys could imagine themselves ferocious warriors and race heroes.[43]

Dolls and other forms of material culture that reflected race pride assumed various meanings and uses, some of which were explicitly political. One of the largest political movements ever among African Americans—among members of the greater black Atlantic community, really—advocated black dolls during the 1920s. Members of Marcus Garvey's Universal Negro Improvement Association (UNIA) considered black dolls integral to realizing the goals of black nationalism, and Garveyites pushed dolls in connection with their larger cultural program. When, for example, the UNIA staged an Educational and Commercial Exposition in 1922, the association announced that it would distribute black dolls to winners of its better babies contest.[44]

Moreover, Garveyites such as Estelle Matthews held convictions strikingly similar to those of J. H. A. Brazelton. Matthews, the Lady President of her division in Philadelphia, begged mothers in the movement to realize that they held the very destiny of the race in their hands. Matthews stressed that a good "race mother" was a vigilant molder of children's minds:

You talk race purity, and yet, by the white pictures on your walls . . . you are teaching your children to love and idolize the other race. By the white dolls in the arms of your baby girls you are teaching them to love and honor white babies, and when these girls grow into womanhood naturally they will believe it more honorable to be the mothers of white babies than black babies. . . . By the white tin soldiers in the hands of your little boys you are teaching them to be serfs and slaves for the other race. . . . It is the babies in the cradle who will be the true Garveyites of tomorrow.

Matthews fervently believed that race mothers needed to shape little ones by controlling influences within the home, by actively promoting race pride, by "teach[ing] the instincts of Garveyism" from the cradle well into adolescence. In the process, women would serve as critical agents in promoting black consciousness as they realized the movement's primary aim of black self-determination. Tellingly, Estelle Matthews came to the conclusion that black dolls would train race girlhood to "believe the highest joy is to love and honor their own black men."[45]

Not only did the Garveyite newspaper "plu[g] the sale of black dolls," the UNIA's Negro Factories Corporation began manufacturing dolls once the association acquired Berry & Ross in late 1922.[46] Whether UNIA dolls were identical to those produced by Berry & Ross is open to question, but it is clear that active Garveyites were both subtly and outwardly urged to purchase UNIA dolls as a means of training their children in the very values of the movement.[47] One UNIA division in Ohio proudly reported the desirable outcome of its outreach activity: "Little Thelma Miller, eight years old, is very fond of her little colored doll. . . . She has never had the opportunity and pleasure of playing with no other doll except a colored doll. [Thelma] is a real Garveyite."[48]

As colored dolls helped transform little girls like Thelma Miller into "real Garveyites," movement girls played with dolls whose features suggested racial intermixture, a phenomenon that the UNIA deeply opposed. The Universal Negro Improvement Association—especially its leader, Marcus Garvey—condemned interracial sex and was preoccupied with racial purity. Ironically, the overwhelming majority of distributors and companies that advertised in the UNIA's *Negro World* and other race publications marketed dolls to African Americans that were "high brown," "light-brown," or even "mulatto." The hair atop black dolls' heads was yet another matter. During the 1920s, firms typically offered colored dolls with "long flowing curls" or "nice straight hair." The cascading locks of a colored doll often reached and occasionally passed its buttocks. Black consumers had other options, but those options were somewhat limited: the Gadsden Doll Company was one of few companies to offer a doll with dark "natural hair" that can best be described as tightly curled; dolls produced by the UNIA's own Negro Factories Corporation had "brown skin."[49]

However limited, colored dolls represented a range of Afro-American looks, thus stalwart Garveyites could find the occasional doll that did not seem to vaunt a racially mixed ideal. For African Americans concerned with inculcating race pride in their children—including Garveyites in the United States, both native-born and immigrant—even a sepia-toned, silken-haired doll could promote black consciousness, police predilections, and ensure racial boundaries when compared to a white doll with golden tresses. For these people, dolls were a means to influence sexuality among both prepubescents and adolescents. Indeed, if Estelle Matthews and J. H. A. Brazelton expressed concerns about both boys and girls in terms of self-concept and intimate cravings, dynamics of race and reproduction resulted in gender-specific anxiety. Put another way, Maud Gary and Thelma Miller had something in common other than being little black girls alive during the first decades of the twentieth century: both were given colored dolls that were intended to inculcate them with a black consciousness that would, in time, shape their most intimate urges and choices.

There is little coincidence that black dolls became popular among aspiring, middling, and elite African Americans during the early decades of the twentieth century. Industrialization, migration, and urbanization transformed various forms of black leisure by providing growing numbers of African Americans with greater options along with increased opportunities to earn expendable income. Organizations such as the Negro Society for Historical Research (1912) and the Association for the Study of Negro Life and History (1915) started popularizing historically based versions of black consciousness as they professionalized the writing of race history. Prescriptive literature aimed at the working and aspiring classes promoted specific values and behaviors as reform-minded activists argued that the race should carefully place objects within domestic spaces as a means of uplift. Indeed, the production of prescriptive literature during the early twentieth century coincided with the appearance of children's publications: from the books *Floyd's Flowers* and *Unsung Heroes* to periodicals such as *Our Boys and Girls* and the *Brownies' Book*, Afro-American children's literature preached the virtues of good conduct, self-respect, and "race pride."[50] Furthermore, since over half of the race had achieved literacy by 1900, more

African Americans were reading newspapers and, as a result, advertising reached more black women, men, and children.

Changing demographic trends besides rising literacy rates informed how race-conscious men and women came to view texts, pictures, and toys — particularly dolls — as implements that shaped identity, behavior, and pre-dilection. Birthrates of native-born black women in the United States de-clined with each decade as the nineteenth century ended and continued to do so as the new century progressed. Whereas African American women were likely to have more children than native-born white women, their fe-cundity experienced a sharp drop beginning with the end of Reconstruction and lasting until at least 1930.[51] A number of factors contributed to the drop in black women's fecundity: migration, urbanization, and high levels of par-ticipation in the labor force all militated against frequent births.[52] Increasing numbers of black women made conscious decisions to limit pregnancies or delay marriage as well.[53]

As more black women had fewer children, aspiring, middling, and elite people had ample opportunity to read about changes in the African Ameri-can birthrate. Black newspapers and magazines frequently ran stories about census statistics and race; they published analyses of what shrinking num-bers meant as the percentage of blacks within the national population went from a little over 14 percent in 1860 to not quite 10 percent in 1920. Such a decrease might seem insignificant today, but at the end of the nineteenth and beginning of the twentieth centuries, the decrease resulted in impassioned claims that African Americans faced extinction.[54] What was perceived as a precipitous drop in the black birthrate stoked fears about "race suicide" among a range of black people and organizations.[55] Above and beyond any anxieties that certain black people had concerning the number and quality of offspring produced by intraracial — not to mention interracial — unions, demographic transitions deeply influenced the ways in which many reform-ers and activists construed what black consciousness should entail.

The sharp drop in the black birthrate was significant in creating the very market for colored dolls in two different ways. First, if smaller family size ostensibly enabled parents to devote more attention and resources to the raising of each child, and if race reformers occasionally criticized working black mothers for not paying sufficient attention to their offspring, Afro-American doll discourse spoke to reformist, class-bound expectations that black parents could take an active role in shaping their children's identi-ties, intellects, and tastes.[56] Second, during the era of the "New Woman,"

Corner in a teacher's home, New Orleans, Louisiana, ca. 1899. Education-minded women and men imbued with race pride valued books for their content and as material objects. Courtesy of the Library of Congress, Prints and Photographs Division, LC-USZ62-51558

the possibility that young black girls would grow into women who either shunned marriage or opted out of motherhood altogether was disturbing for women and men vested in racial perpetuation.

Significantly, late-nineteenth- and early-twentieth-century anxieties over race suicide coexisted with both a nascent black consciousness movement and increased availability of commercially produced material culture that positively reflected the race's appearance and achievement. There were strong links between black consciousness, Afro-American material culture, and the wishes of people such as J. H. A. Brazelton to see their "race variety sustained to the eternities." As much as self-respect and love were part and parcel of an individual's internal sense of esteem, material culture that countered racist mainstream stereotypes buttressed race pride by instructing, edifying, enlightening. Popular and material culture inspired not only through its ability to subvert endemic negative portrayals of the race but also if African Americans were the producers of commercial items. In 1921, for example, an ad for the Black Swan label not only argued that "every school child" should listen to records by "high class colored singers," it also stressed that Black Swan records were "made by Colored People" instead of by a "Jim Crow annex to a white concern."[57] Advertisements for race histories, calendars, pictures, and toys did not always reveal whether a company was black-owned or black-run. Companies such as Berry & Ross, however, made it a point to inform consumers that race women and men were in charge—and even to suggest that selling race products contributed to collective progress.

It is within this overall context that mass-produced and mass-marketed black dolls informed intraracial debates about collective destiny. The sale and promotion of colored dolls attempted to shape children's sexuality at a time when lynching and rape posed serious threats to racial well-being. As commentators, activists, and eventually Garveyites expressed concerns about birthrates, miscegenation, and mob violence, advertisements promoted colored dolls as devices that could ensure racial purity by teaching children "respect for one's self and for one's own kind."[58] The decision of parents (often mothers) to give their children—daughters especially— Afro-American material culture was an attempt to patrol desire in that dolls were seen as tools that influenced young Afro-Americans to select sexual partners within the race, produce children within endogamous heterosexual marriages, and eschew miscegenation.

Not every woman, man, or Afro-American publication committed to racial progress or preservation emphasized the power of dolls to shape self-image and conduct. In the mid-1910s, *Golden Thoughts on Chastity and Procreation* captioned a photograph with a black girl cradling a white doll as "Maternal Instinct." The 1922 edition of the *New Floyd's Flowers* contained a photograph of a black girl playing with white dolls; the text's one image of a child playing with a seemingly nonwhite doll was retouched so that the doll only appeared "colored." Neither *Golden Thoughts* nor *New Floyd's Flowers* connected dolls to consciousness or predilection. Out of the two, only *New Floyd's Flowers* contained textual discussion of the power of dolls, and what Silas Floyd did write vaunted domestic life, skills, and the acquisition of maternal feeling.[59] Reform-minded African Americans associated doll play with a more general promotion of maternity and the home, then, but the specific discourse surrounding the utility of colored dolls primarily underscored that children's toys shaped consciousness, identity, and the most personal of tastes.

The colored doll was indeed a live one, especially given anxieties over miscegenation and racial destiny—anxieties that existed from the immediate postemancipation period up into the 1920s. The women who expressed their opinions to race publications about toys they gave to their children and the men who expounded upon why parents should purchase colored dolls did so when more than a few African American activists had something to say about interracial sex and its impact on the race. Commentators ultimately did more than suggest that mothers had a special duty as consumers to purchase colored dolls and maintain that it was particularly critical to shape girls' sexuality, then. These commentators made their contentions as heated considerations of miscegenation raged among other African American intellectuals, activists, and reformers — contemporaries whose assessments would, more often than not, also prioritize ways in which girls' and women's behavior needed to be controlled in the name of racial preservation.

material culture
Dolls
domestic Influence affect
races
Future

race mothers imbve
race pride into children

7

A BURDEN OF RESPONSIBILITY
GENDER, "MISCEGENATION," AND RACE TYPE

When she addressed the Hampton Negro Conference in July 1898, Victoria Earle Matthews issued an ominous warning for young, southern women planning to migrate to the urban North without protection of family and friends: their naivete could result in their ending up as prostitutes. "Sporting and disreputable" men and women routinely preyed upon "green," innocent "crops"; shady "employment bureau[s]" made it their business to funnel "untrained and inexperienced workers" into unsavory situations. To compound matters, the limited financial resources of many incoming female migrants forced them to seek lodging in houses that boarded men in the same rooms as women. Although Matthews's own migration was markedly different—she arrived in New York City from Virginia during the early 1870s along with her mother and siblings—the journalist's experience as a reformer gave her insight into the perils of which she spoke. Matthews was on a mission motivated, in part, by anxiety over miscegenation: "By various sophistries, many refined, educated girls, particularly mulattoes and fair quadroons, are secured for the diversion of young Hebrews (the identity of their offspring is easily lost among Afro-Americans). These girls are led to believe they will get permanent work in stores and public service. . . . So our 'tenderloins' are filled." A former slave who could easily be mistaken as white, Victoria Matthews provided no concrete evidence to support her claim that Jewish immigrants fueled a sex trade involving fair-skinned women of African descent. Whether she had evidence or not, the crusading reformer was resolute in her conviction that it was better for young race women to "starve" below the Mason-Dixon line than to be subject to the wiles of "strangers."[1]

When Victoria Earle Matthews established the White Rose Mission in New York in 1897 as a means to shelter and shepherd new arrivals so that they would not wind up "heart broken, disgraced young creature[s]," it was not unusual for her contemporaries to connect interracial sex to a host of phenomena. It was also not unusual for African Americans to make a variety of assertions about racial intermixture itself. In fact, around the time Victoria Matthews offered her curious argument that "Hebrew" blood was "easily lost among Afro-Americans"—an assertion that implied Jewish immigrants occupied a liminal racial status neither white nor black—another former slave named Wesley Gaines worried that too many African Americans coveted "white blood."[2]

In his 1897 book, *The Negro and the White Man*, Wesley Gaines situated the issue of miscegenation within the larger question of collective destiny: "Many have claimed that there are but three destinies possible to the negro, viz., extinction, emigration and amalgamation. . . . The facts furnished by the latest statistics show that the negro, instead of dying out, is increasing with wonderful rapidity. . . . The negro does not take to [emigration]. . . . The amalgamation theory is the only one of these which has a basis of probability." Gaines devoted an entire chapter of his tome to "Amalgamation" and another to the "Intermarriage Question." Not only did he agree with Matthews that the "exposure" of girls seeking employment too often resulted in interracial sex, the AME bishop believed that "sin" and "ignorance" allowed miscegenation to continue. Gaines believed that too many white men maintained black concubines, but he also felt that too many women of African descent wanted to bear light-skinned children. Gaines did not necessarily think anti-intermarriage laws were desirable; in fact, he felt that their very existence compromised the race by rendering black women with white lovers into "adultress[es]" and their children into "bastard[s]." A man who preferred to see his race retain its "integrity," Gaines came to what he considered a "dreaded" conclusion: that "interblending of the races" was "no longer a theory, but well-nigh an accomplished fact."[3]

For all the different ways in which African Americans could approach the question of their own destiny—social, political, physical—the very matter of "race" was significant in and of itself, since racial fusion with whites was a viable, looming possibility. Commentators harbored any one or a combination of four specific anxieties: that interracial sex was steadily diluting the race; that damaging intraracial fissures based on color had emerged; that men's tendency to fetishize light skin, fine features, and glossy hair compromised morals; that too many women were contributing to a steady whitening of African Americans. Not only were such anxieties expressed in ways that were at once alarmist and highly gendered, but the overall cast of Afro-American discourse on miscegenation during the late nineteenth and early twentieth centuries could be gendered in somewhat inequitable fashion.

A Georgia minister named G. W. Johnson, for example, railed that women who bragged about their white lovers compromised collective advancement and were thus no longer worthy of protection. In an 1897 article on "Race Evils," Johnson was less than sympathetic as he associated prating women with unscrupulous individuals who procured girls for the amusement of white men; he likened both contingents to "lepers" and pronounced their associates "unclean." Johnson was clear in his convictions: because certain women fueled mainstream stereotypes regarding black female promiscuity, any woman who flaunted her illicit affairs with men outside of the race deserved to suffer nothing less than the ignominious sting of ostracism.[4] Club woman Addie Hunton diverged markedly from Johnson's argument, but she, too, felt that women had a particular responsibility when it came to limiting interracial sex and mixture: "Upon the Negro woman rests a burden of responsibility peculiar in its demands. It is not similar to that borne by any other woman. . . . Questions of morals among inferior and superior races have settled themselves largely by amalgamation . . . but the Negro woman must tear herself away from the sensual desires of the men of another race who seek only to debase her." Hunton's opinion—originally offered within the confines of the 1902 Negro Young People's Christian and Educational Congress in Atlanta—certainly reflected an overarching concern on her part with challenging mainstream perceptions that black women were loose women. Addie Hunton also wanted to convince her sisters that a "burden" rested on their shoulders, one that contained all the volatility of race, gender, and sex.[5]

Such anxieties and motivations deeply informed how African Americans discussed the impact of interracial sex upon the collective, but Afro-American discourse on miscegenation was nonetheless varied: scholars attempted to take an anthropological approach to the matter; journals cele-brated the emergence of a new "race type." Concepts regarding both "race type" and "miscegenation" were fraught during the late nineteenth and early twentieth centuries and apprehensions regarding the very hue of Afro-America were at once palpable and potent. The women and men who shared concerns similar to those expressed by Hunton, Johnson, Gaines, and Mat-thews would use a host of gendered arguments to vivify their claims about racial intermixture — claims that routinely associated miscegenation with women, claims overwhelmingly focused on women as reproducers of the race.[6]

If the very act of interracial sex pulsed with tawdry, seamy conno-tations in mainstream culture, its referents had a sordid history all their own. Antebellum abolitionists were discredited by their critics through pruri-ent accusations that the former sought — craved, even — sexual "amalgama-tion" of the races. Throughout much of the nineteenth century, especially the latter decades, "social equality" functioned as a convenient euphemism for much interracial interaction, whether casual socializing or carnal inter-lude.[7] "Melaleukation" and "miscegenation" first appeared in a Civil War–era pamphlet that was an elaborate hoax designed by northern Democrats to cast racialized, sexualized aspersions upon the Republican Party prior to the election of 1864.[8] Although the neologism "melaleukation" was a spe-cific reference to fusion of black and white, "miscegenation" would come to signify a variety of black/white sexual relationships: marriage, consensual liaisons, concubinage, coerced intercourse, rape.[9] Yet another neologism, "mongrelization," aroused particular anxieties for southern Redeemers; its bestial overtones would hold particular salience for twentieth-century ar-chitects of racial segregation.[10]

During the decade immediately following Reconstruction, black women and men rarely invoked the phantasm of "mongrelization." They were in-stead more likely to speak of "race absorption," "race assimilation," "inter-marriage," or even "social equality" and "amalgamation." "Social equality" resonated among race activists due to its deep association with charged mainstream arguments regarding Afro-American ambition, education, and political aspiration. Significantly, when African American men fought steady disfranchisement after 1877, white commentators — many of whom were male Democrats in the South — frequently equated black men's fervent claims to political rights with a pulsating desire for sexual access to white women. Indeed, if in the wake of Reconstruction, "'social equality' existed only in the negative" for many white Americans (especially white southerners), the term was problematic as well for a number of African Americans, largely because commentators of color tended to invoke it in order to suggest "a lack of race pride."[11] Whereas "social equality" had eclipsed "amalgamation" within mainstream usage during the late nineteenth century, race activists still continued to invoke "amalgamation" when discussing interracial mixture. Moreover, within Afro-American discourse, commentators did not automatically shun the word "miscegenation" due to its problematic origin and connotations; that particular coinage gained currency among African American activists and intellectuals only around the turn of the century.

More important than phraseology, however, was *how* Afro-American reformers, intellectuals, and activists broached the subject. There certainly existed a long-standing internal creed by which race women and men refused publicly to "concede that the descendants of planters were superior to the descendants of slaves on both sides." African Americans were often loath to discriminate against one another, and families frequently contained an array of skin tones, hair textures, and features. Still, intraracial stratification did exist, and skin color was not irrelevant to that stratification.[12]

Afro-American commentators therefore invoked hierarchies based on skin color as one means to explore the intraracial dynamics occasioned by miscegenation. In 1877, for example, fledgling journalist John Edward Bruce wrote a scathing satire of the colored elite in Washington, D.C., that provided glimpses into social hierarchies within the race. Bruce skewered women and men who took obvious pride in their non-African ancestry and "wouldn't be caught dead with an ordinary Negro." He mocked women and men who traced their ancestors back to "William the Silent," and upbraided vain creatures who fished for compliments on their glossy, straight hair. The relatively dark-skinned former slave might have been making sport of District "sersiety," but in the process, Bruce documented the rigidification of social distinctions within the race based on phenotype and ancestry. Indeed, such distinctions were a conspicuous aspect of Afro-American socializing in the District: Washington was, along with Charleston, New Orleans, Philadelphia, and Cleveland, a "blue vein" capital.[13]

Bruce not only contended that intraracial segregation applied to courtship and marriage, he leveled the sensational charge that some parents sought grooms for their daughters across the color line by offering financial incentives to "white m[e]n of low degree."[14] The provocative allegation implied that color-conscious individuals would go to any length to lighten their family line; such bartered love smacked of prostitution.[15] Above and beyond suggesting that interracial marriages were most likely to involve lower-class whites, Bruce—who, by the end of the century would be glowingly referred to as "the prince of Negro correspondents"—insinuated that such unions tended to emerge out of dubious, pathetic motivations.[16]

Satire aside, Bruce's decision to target marriage was strategic. Marriage was an intimate part of African Americans' efforts to reorganize their lives following the abolition of slavery in the United States. From former slaves who formalized existing relationships to members of the black elite who claimed that the race's future depended upon wedlock, marriage was perceived as both a personal act and as an institution with ramifications for the entire Afro-American collective.[17] Orderly homes, personal behavior, and thrift supposedly indicated black people's readiness for full participation in the national body politic, thus marriage could ostensibly obliterate the sexual legacies of slavery, especially concubinage. Moreover, expositions about marriage provided a space where postemancipation women and men could detail what they believed were the responsibilities and ramifications of mate selection for members of the race. These very expositions contained their share of discussion on intermarriage and miscegenation as well at a time when antimiscegenation laws were at once enacted and challenged.[18]

John Bruce's vetting of Washington's "'fust families'" contained a barbed wit that bordered on cutting insult, yet Bruce was not alone in resorting to rhetorical flourish in order to make a point. Reverend Emanuel King Love, for one, offered some intriguing remarks of his own within an Emancipation Day address in Savannah, Georgia. The message of the day was racial unity. Perhaps inspired by the vagaries of local debates over integration, Love invoked Frederick Douglass's 1884 second marriage to a white woman named Helen Pitts as a means of registering his avowed disapproval of "amalgamation whether legal or illegal."[19] Love—an ex-slave and "Baptist of the deepest dye" who had enjoyed marked success as the pastor of a 5,000-member church—believed that Douglass's marriage set a poor example for other race men. More specifically, Douglass's marriage to Pitts prompted Love to fret that a number of striving men might begin to think that they, too, were entitled to a white wife if and when they became successful. As far as Love was concerned, the lengthy history of white men despoiling black women made marrying out of the race utterly unnecessary. Not only could black men "afford to oppose" intermarriage, but Love additionally argued that race men had "a garden with a larger variety from which to choose the flower of life's joy. [We] can get a wife . . . as black as dye, as white as they are made and of various colors all between. No other race is so highly favored by nature." Reverend Love evidently did not think that color consciousness might undermine racial unity: endogamous marriage was essential, and a woman of African descent was a race woman whether her complexion was alabaster or ebony. For Love, the sort of unity required for collective progress entailed eschewing social equality and what he called "miscegeneration" as much, if not more, than reading race papers and patronizing race businesses. In other words, any "sensible," race-loving man would desire nothing other than "to marry his own women [as] they are good enough for him."[20]

Not all of Love's contemporaries would agree that skin color was irrelevant when it came to marriage within the race. This issue appears to have become especially contentious after 1890, the year of the Census Bureau's first and only attempt to parse the race into "negroes," "mulattoes," "quadroons," and "octoroons."[21] Wesley Gaines was distressed over the premium he felt black men placed having upon fair wives. Gaines, who believed that the "social future of the colored race" depended upon "the marriage relation," was convinced that racially mixed men and women tended to intermarry to the point of separation; such exclusiveness was, he argued, one of the most divisive dynamics among African Americans. Journalist T. Thomas Fortune was also vexed over the matter of mate selection, but for decidedly different reasons. Fortune—who took considerable pride in his own Native American, European, and African heritage—archly criticized cleric Alexander Crummell and academicians J. W. Cromwell and Daniel Culp for being prominent, dark-skinned men "who clamor[ed] . . . loudly and persistently for the purity of Negro blood" yet married visibly mixed women. Culp's wife, Fortune claimed, was "so white that no one would suspect that she was an Afro-American."[22] If, as such logic went, the "Negro race type" was going to be perpetuated, was it not the duty of dark to marry dark so as to wash away the sexual ignominy of slavery?

Slavery, with its legacy of concubinage and its variegation of Afro-American complexion, was the starting point for C. M. E. bishop Lucius Holsey of Georgia. In his 1898 essay "Amalgamation or Miscegenation," Holsey did not outline an ethics regarding intraracial marriage but instead touched upon the question of interracial marriage. Holsey broached the issue by contending that "the way amalgamation has been brought about in these Southern States is enough to make the bushmen in the wild jungles blush with shame." Holsey then made it a point to underscore that interracial sex—

Studio portrait of a young couple, Norfolk, Virginia, ca. 1900. Intraracial diversity provoked animated, often contentious debate when race women and men discussed intimate partnerships. Courtesy of Photographs and Prints Division, Schomburg Center for Research in Black Culture, New York Public Library, Astor, Lenox and Tilden Foundations.

in and of itself—was not a sin against nature. Holsey's religious convictions did, however, lead him to argue that "sodomy" was sinful because it was not reproductive; these convictions enabled him to contrast nonreproductive sex with the very fact children could result from interracial unions. Indeed, beyond his desire to prove that all people belonged to a common humanity, Holsey even acknowledged that "craving, heaving, and impulsive passion" on the part of diverse humans the world over made intermixture likely and even inevitable. Holsey nevertheless deployed similarly evocative language—"unbridled lusts," "villainy," "sought after and . . . debased"—to underscore that forced sex between white men and black women was part and parcel of what he considered an ongoing "damnable miscegenation." The primary problem with most interracial liaisons for Holsey, then, was that they were illicit unions borne of an oppressive social hierarchy as opposed to legal marriages.[23]

Holsey did not limit his public exposition to contentions regarding marriage and miscegenation. In 1903, when he delivered a speech before a national conference on "the race problem," Holsey provocatively suggested that Afro-Americans should contemplate territorial separation. After explaining the difference between separatism and emigration, Holsey told his audience that disfranchisement of African American men thoroughly "degrade[d] and destroy[ed] . . . respectable and decent manhood," with the entire race rendered "but a little short of abject slavery" as civil rights eroded. Oppression embittered black males and prevented them from being both active citizens and full-fledged men in the South, he continued, thus the only means of providing the race with ample opportunity was to eliminate interracial contact altogether. African American people were therefore, in Lucius Holsey's mind, entitled to all-black territories within national borders.[24]

Holsey then proceeded to outline how sovereign race havens would do far more than eliminate strife between black and white men: they would liberate women of color from being "corrupted and despoiled of their procreative sanctity" by predatory white men. Restricted access to women's sexuality was about more than freeing women from the threat of rape or restoring the prerogatives of masculinity to race men. In the eyes of the bishop, the very reproduction of Afro-American people was imperiled. Holsey—who was himself the fair-haired, fair-eyed product of a master-slave relationship—flatly informed his audience that white male lust was turning black people into "a race of weaklings and effeminates in moral, mental, and physical health." With his next breath, Holsey pointedly asked, "[How can] a people . . . become wise, upright and healthy . . . while their mothers, daughters and sisters are polluted in their genital powers?"[25]

With his pointed observation that "genital powers" could raise the race to sublime heights or subject it to hellish lows, Holsey forcefully suggested that rape, concubinage, and miscegenation compromised racial reproduction. Granted, Lucius Holsey alluded to sexual integrity as only part of a broader plan to secure black political rights, yet he clearly considered sex and reproduction vital elements in the struggle for black autonomy. Holsey's rhetoric about liaisons between black women and white men resulting in "weaklings"—not to mention "mongrels"—further implied that miscegenation equaled degeneracy. The bishop had offered a similar theory about miscegenation before: at an Atlanta University conference in 1896 he asserted that tuberculosis was more likely to strike members of the race with "white blood in their veins." By 1903, however, he opted to stress that sexuality was linked inexorably to "the destiny of a great African race" in the United States. Beyond Holsey's belief that legal intermarriage could potentially produce "a stronger, a longer lived . . . more . . . homogeneous race," he remained convinced that the prevailing moral cast of interracial sex throughout the U.S. South insulted black men, wrecked black women, and propelled the entire race down a path of destruction.[26] Finally, Holsey selectively borrowed hereditarian concepts in the name of black salvation, as did other reform-minded men and women.[27]

Whereas Holsey combined political, territorial, and hereditarian concepts to condemn what was typically referred to as "illegal amalgamation," Nannie Helen Burroughs addressed miscegenation and intraracial sexual dynamics in a manner reminiscent of John Bruce. The National Baptist Convention activist opened her 1904 article "Not Color But Character" by forcefully linking skin bleaching and hair straightening to a general "Negrophobia" that pervaded U.S. culture; she did so as a means of introducing her argument that individuals, families, and churches within the race were succumbing to the scourge of "colorphobia." Burroughs saved her most biting observations, however, for a specific predilection based upon color: "I have seen black men have fits about black women associating with white men, and yet these same men see more to admire in a half-white face owned by a characterless, fatherless woman than in faces owned by thoroughbred, legal heirs to the throne. . . . The man who puts color as the first requisite in his choice . . . invariably gets nothing but color, but the man who puts character first, always gets a woman."[28] Burrough's insinuation that such men were fools was characteristic of her no-holds-barred expository style, as was her larger assessment of a problematic intraracial double standard. She evoked the well-worn postemancipation refrain that race women were morally bound to shun sexual relationships with white men in order to highlight the irony that certain African American men attempted to benefit from the very relationships they were wont to condemn. Like most of her contemporaries, Burroughs failed to comment upon whether there existed a class of race women who sought near-white black men, yet she nevertheless exposed a troublesome hypocrisy, one that could assail women for engaging in interracial sex yet fetishize the fair daughters of such unions.

Burroughs's contemporary Anna Borden offered similarly pointed commentary. Borden published an essay, "Some Thoughts for Both Races to Ponder Over," in a pro-intermarriage text by an iconoclastic white man named John James Holm. In that essay, Borden—who was a teacher active on the lecture circuit—matter of factly stated that any racial chauvinist "proud of [his] black face" should "not amalgamate with a yellow or white complexioned colored woman and thereby 'degrade' [his] offspring with foreign blood."[29] A relatively obscure race woman from Alabama named Sophia Cox Johnson tendered yet another view. In an essay about mothers' meetings and other attempts to uplift "the colored woman on the plantation," Johnson "achingly notice[d]" the presence of strikingly diverse complexions within single households. "What differences in the color of families!," Johnson bemoaned. "Brothers and sisters from the darkest shades of ebony to the fairest of the fair calling the same woman mother!"[30] Although Holsey was troubled by the power that white men wielded over concubines of color, and while Burroughs and Borden critiqued black men for their personal tastes, Johnson was disturbed that immoral, hierarchical sexual relationships during slavery had managed to create color hierarchies within families.

At a time when African American women novelists routinely crafted variations on "the marriage plot," Burroughs's, Borden's, and Johnson's concerns stood apart from those of novelist Pauline Hopkins, whose work frequently revolved around the romantic tribulations of beleaguered, racially mixed heroines. Hopkins explored miscegenation in more sustained, albeit fictional, fashion than Burroughs, Borden, or Johnson. Hopkins's novel *Contending Forces* (1900) offered hereditarian arguments about miscegenation as it condemned concubinage and questioned whether mulattoes would face eventual extinction; her serialized tale, *Of One Blood* (1902–3), dealt with passing and insinuated that miscegenation had so complicated family bloodlines as to result occasionally in accidental incest. As African American women such as Hopkins turned to fiction to explore the tangled, inter-racial sexual legacies of slavery, as novelists and the occasional club woman noted that the phenomenon of racial passing could easily result in white women and men wedding "African[s] in disguise," women such as Bur-roughs and Borden were atypical in their use of the essay form to challenge the romantic inclinations of some race men.[31]

Indeed, beyond utilizing the genres of fiction and essay as a means to assess the complications occasioned by racial intermixture, women also ad-vanced arguments regarding what their sisters could do to check misce-genation. In 1904, for example, Louisiana club woman Sylvania Williams maintained that women who actively taught "race integrity" in the home did "more to preserve the purity of the Caucasian race than all the laws against miscegenation and for segregation." Two years later, Deaconness Annie Hall was distressed that "the Chinaman" had become the "latest fad" among young girls who attempted to attract suitors by wearing flashy clothes. Hall flatly contended that such girls needed to "discipline" themselves in pub-lic for the sake of the race.[32] Emma Azalia Hackley addressed the matter of discipline as well by stressing other aspects of what women should at-tempt to control. On the pages of *The Colored Girl Beautiful* (1916), Hackley stressed that Afro-American mothers needed to make sure that their sons eventually married women "of [their] mother's race." Hackley was forth-right in acknowledging her belief that African Americans were a "mixed race" that should "have pride in [their] black as well as . . . white blood," yet she nonetheless thought it imperative that women teach their children to "improve racial stock" by marrying within the race.[33]

Male activists concerned with halting miscegenation detailed imperatives of their own, imperatives that typically centered on the theme of protection. Fisk University professor Eugene Harris was as willing to chastise young men who failed to protect women as he was to condemn young women who "ma[d]e it hard" for their brothers to do so. Black males who concocted reasons as to why they could not prevent white men from maintaining black concubines or procuring black prostitutes were themselves poor excuses for men in the eyes of novelist David Bryant Fulton. In a 1912 pamphlet that contrasted the sexual prohibitions facing black men with the liberties rou-tinely taken by white men, Fulton insisted that Afro-Americans could not "boast of education or wealth" as long as black women were "under the con-trol and domination of the men of another race." Fulton, also known by his nom de plume, "Jack Thorne," made a similar argument in one of his novels. *Hanover* implied that "unholy minglings of Shem and Ham" in southern "harems" continued due to the castrating effects of racial oppression; the fictionalized account of the 1898 Wilmington, North Carolina, race riot even included a passage in which a quadroon concubine takes up arms in order to disperse gangs of white men bent on assaulting black women. In both fiction and social tract, Fulton got his message across: race women could no longer be "willingly surrender[ed] . . . to the enemy."[34]

For his part, social purity activist Revels Alcorn Adams shared Emma Hackley's conviction that parents had specific duties, but Adams—like Harris and Fulton—couched those duties under the rubric of chivalry and protection. In *The Negro Girl*, a book that preceded Hackley's by two years, Adams urged parents to think twice about sending their daughters into the labor force, where they would encounter "evil[,] designing white men, whose only thought is to make them their prey." He relayed the tragic tales of two "nearly white" teenaged girls who were the "unwelcome child[ren]" of white women and black men, grew up in white families, and had no black male relatives to watch over them; both girls, according to Adams, wound up being despoiled by randy white men, one of whom was an employer. Adams told these stories, in part, to argue that all race women—regardless of their origin—deserved protection. Adams also insisted that black men should be prepared to die each and every time they stepped up to defend a race woman.[35]

Some men chose to make arguments about interracial sex that had little to do with protection, including one well-regarded scholar at a prominent race institution. William Scarborough of Wilberforce University was married to a white woman, and he found notions of racial purity—not to mention much of the intraracial debate about miscegenation—highly specious. Afro-American veins already coursed with blood from "every nation that ha[d] set its foot upon [the] shores" of the United States; thus, as far as Scarborough was concerned, it was ludicrous for the race to attempt to maintain its "integrity." Future citizens of the United States, he predicted, would be "neither black, white, red, [or] yellow." What was the point, then, of race women and men trying to halt an inexorable process?[36]

Scarborough's coolly rational approach to miscegenation reflected an important trend of the early twentieth century. As surely as some African Americans felt uneasy about miscegenation, other individuals—and even some institutions—attempted to approach the matter through the methodologies and language provided by emerging sciences. Indeed, William Scarborough offered his argument that the race included representatives of the most "complex mixture on the earth" in the wake of a major attempt to catalogue intraracial diversity. During the early twentieth century, reformers such as Emma Hackley and Revels Adams maintained that race men and women should do something to prevent miscegenation, but they did so at a time when other African Americans chose to assess the outcome of intermixture that had already occurred.

The opening pages of Atlanta University's 1906 study *The Health and Physique of the Negro American* contained intriguing evidence about the composition of the race. There, a series of head shots captured the virtually expressionless yet pleasant faces of over fifty young women and men, all attractive, under twenty-one years of age, and clothed in conservative yet stylish fashion. The serious, occasionally pensive faces prodded readers to reflect upon the subjects' future prospects as the grouping of individuals by phenotype lead readers' minds in a slightly different direction. All of the head shots were arranged on plates that, in succession, contrasted "unmixed types" with "blended types": the "very dark brown" complected were placed alongside those who were merely "brown"; "Negroes" were juxtaposed with "Mulattoes"; "Quadroons" were featured next to "White Types with Negro Blood." Accompanying text detailed variations in hue, hair texture, facial features, and build with descriptors such as "fair," "crisp," "prognathous," and "stocky"; adjectives ranging from "vivacious" to "plodding" described each person's disposition and presumed intelligence. With twenty-four individuals presumed to be more or less "full-blooded," twenty-five whose attributes provided visible documentation of interracial sex, and at least seven who might be mistaken as white, the plates suggested that, on the cusp of a new century, the race had broken down into discernible types.[37]

Beyond the compelling photographic evidence that graced its opening pages, *The Health and Physique of the Negro American* explored—among a number of topics—the slave trade, birth and mortality rates, alcoholism, syphilis, tuberculosis, and psychology. The study even compared brain weights among African Americans possessing varying degrees of Euro-American ancestry; that it was possible to make such comparisons within the race seemed an intriguing and noteworthy development. Such intraracial comparison was a compelling means to showcase the stunning diversity that was Afro-America. "In America," an uncredited author explained, "we have brought to our very thresholds representatives of a great historic race. . . . We have had going on beneath our very eyes an experiment in race-blending

Head shots from Health and Physique of the Negro American *(1906). These photographs, originally from Du Bois's 1900 Paris Exposition albums, showcased variations in skin color, features, and hair. Anthropology, hereditarianism, and environmentalist assumptions informed Du Bois's commentary about his young subjects. Courtesy of the Library of Congress, Prints and Photographs Division, LC-USZ62-124715, LC-USZ62-124755, and LC-USZ62-124711.*

such as the world has nowhere seen before, and we have today living representatives of almost every possible degree of admixture." The writer not only believed dispassionate study of "race mixture" in the United States was long overdue, that same author — in all likelihood the study's editor, W. E. B. Du Bois, whose own bloodline was quite complicated — was thoroughly convinced such study could dismantle prevailing notions that miscegenation produced degenerate offspring.[38]

Those African Americans who had the chance to skim or read *Health and Physique* upon its release were people likely to be concerned about the race as a collective. The report boldly attempted to demolish theories regarding black degeneracy, and readers likely sought confirmation that the race was comprised of prime physical specimens. Readers probably pored over both photographs and text as they wondered how the subjects' lives would turn out or visualized how any offspring the subjects might have would look. *The Health and Physique of the Negro American* must have piqued a certain curiosity among people alive at the beginning of a new century: what would the future of African Americans be — and *look* like? Would the "blended" mate with the "unmixed," resulting in a sepia race? Would a so-called intermediate race emerge, apart from whites yet distinct from blacks? Or, would Afro-Americans become fairer and fairer with each new generation until the race was thoroughly blanched?

In the years leading up to and following *Health and Physique*'s publication, estimates regarding the percentage of Afro-Americans who had either European or Native American ancestors—or both—were legion. Shortly before the 1890 census classified approximately 15 percent of the race as "mulatto," noted author Charles Chesnutt argued that more than half of the race was "of mixed blood." Over a decade later, journalist T. Thomas Fortune believed 30 percent was more accurate; Pauline Hopkins ventured in her novel *Contending Forces* (1900) that "no such thing as an unmixed black on the American continent" still existed; Missouri club woman Maria P. Williams offered the more conservative estimate of 20 percent. The editor of *Health and Physique* concurred with Tom Fortune. "At least one-third of the Negroes of the United States have recognizable traces of white blood," Du Bois averred. "It is quite possible that the mulattoes form an even larger percentage than this, but I should be greatly surprised to find that they formed a smaller proportion."[39] *The Health and Physique of the Negro American*'s attempt to catalogue the range of skin colors, features, and hair textures possessed by the descendants of slaves reflected, then, a piqued concern about racial composition among African Americans.

Health and Physique was neither the first attempt by African Americans to describe race types in a scientific fashion nor was it the last. As early as 1881, John Patterson Sampson applied the study of phrenology to "mixed races"; Joseph Hayne, a one-time dean of theology, published a "natural history of the Hametic race" in 1894 in which he differentiated mulattoes from a host of other intermixtures.[40] Sampson's *Mixed Races: Their Environment, Temperament, Heredity, and Phrenology* was aimed at a general readership and included a sketch that attempted to capture the contours of a mixed Afro-American's skull. Hayne took a broader view of race types by attempting to categorize racially mixed persons in the United States, Caribbean, Europe, and Asia. Not only did Hayne brook orthodoxy by referring to quadroons as "terceroon[s]" and octoroons as "quateroon[s]," he took pains to note that whereas someone with a black parent and a mulatto parent was a "griffe or zambo," the offspring of a "black and terceroon" would be considered a "quateroon saltratas." Given Hayne's inclusion of quotation marks in his text, his unusual terminology appeared to come from another source, as did his brief observations regarding the coloring of genitals in racially mixed individuals.[41] The terminology might not have been his own, yet Hayne acknowledged a significant phenomenon all the same: "mixture" could also occur when two people of African descent mated.

Relatively few people created their own lexicons denoting degrees of intermixture, and phrenology was a passing fad. In comparison, the anthropological approach demonstrated by *Health and Physique* proved more durable. The National Association for the Advancement of Colored People (NAACP) commissioned a pamphlet exploring miscegenation from noted Columbia University anthropologist Franz Boas in 1912; the pamphlet's partial purpose was to debunk notions that either "the Negro" or "the mulatto" were inferior beings. Above and beyond the NAACP's initiative in seeking out Franz Boas, Caroline Bond Day began conducting a detailed "anthropometric" study of miscegenation in 1919. Day had studied under a number of social scientists, including W. E. B. Du Bois; like Du Bois, she hailed from a racially mixed family. When Day's *Study of Some Negro-White Families in the United States* was published by Harvard University during the early 1930s, it contained an exhaustive set of genealogies (including those of her own relatives) and anthropometric measurements, along with a photographic chart of hair samples intended to indicate degree of intermixture.[42]

Even when the stalwart race paper, the *Age*, launched a beauty contest in the summer of 1914, its editors quickly proclaimed that their contest had a noble aesthetic goal: the challenging of "caricatures and exaggerations" as well as the determining of a new and "ideal race type." An enthusiastic reader named Demond Lewis sent in an engaged letter that at once praised the merits of the contest and provided feedback on how it should be judged: "I modestly suggest that the committee that has the important [t]ask of deciding such an interesting and vital task select as a standard . . . a distinctly American-Negro type. . . . From this type could be illustrated in historical and scientific order various fusing and variations from the basi[c] American-Negro type . . . until the Negro element is *nil.*" The *Age* agreed with Lewis. Their work would be challenging, and if the contest actually revealed a predominant type, it would "approximate the composite American type . . . [since] the amalgamation of races has gone so far."[43] Lewis sent in yet another missive in which he outlined a "scientific" set of five categories indicating degree of intermixture. Not only did Lewis's categories hew closely to those outlined eight years earlier in *Health and Physique*, but the *Age*'s editorial response to Lewis stressed that their contest had "set the ethnology students of the race to work."[44] Another reader, a woman who actually submitted her photograph for consideration, confessed that she was hard pressed to place herself in any particular category given her African, Irish, French, and Native American heritage.[45] In the end, the paper selected fifteen women from around the nation, and, indeed, those selected represented a diverse range of looks—even if that diversity veered toward the lighter end of the racial spectrum.[46]

By publishing the photos of sepia beauties week after week, the *Age* did not launch a scholarly endeavor, nor was its contest imbued with the same political purpose as was *Health and Physique*. Still, the *Age* contest was a popular manifestation of the notion that the race was undergoing a transformation worthy of scrutiny, however superficial and sexualized. Other race publications, including the *Crisis* and *Half-Century*, routinely featured photographs of beautiful young women, and the *Half-Century* ran its own beauty contests in addition to invoking the language of "racial type." The *Age* even returned to the matter in 1919 when it published a photograph of "war relief" nurses and urged readers to acknowledge and appreciate Afro-American beauty by placing such inspirational photographs in their homes.[47] Whereas the *Age*'s vaunting of race beauty had its admirable qualities, the paper's focus on women and beauty worked to reinforce a deep, preexisting association of women with miscegenation.

All told, efforts by the *Age*, Atlanta University, the NAACP, and individuals ranging from Joseph Hayne to Caroline Bond Day represented how interest in phenotypic changes wrought by miscegenation became institutionalized during the late nineteenth and early twentieth centuries. These attempts to explore the physical impact of miscegenation were, moreover, attempts to rationalize and even celebrate a phenomenon that elicited a host of fears— fears that involved class as well as race, fears that had been clearly articulated by African Americans anxious that the race might slowly fade to white, fears that focused upon women's actions as well as their attributes.[48]

As varied as African Americans' discussions about miscegenation were, many invoked self-control on the part of women or advocated protection of women by men; a few even suggested ostracism for those black women and men who crossed the sexual color line. In an oppressive climate where mob violence sought to castrate black men figuratively and literally, at a time when black women had little recourse if they were raped or otherwise sexually exploited, discussions touching upon miscegenation often assumed anxious, heated, heavily gendered tones. Victoria Matthews and Annie Hall worried that young women in urban centers might either become the sexual prey of immigrants or even seek immigrants as lovers. Thomas Fortune, Nannie Burroughs, and Anna Borden all criticized self-professed race men for choosing light-skinned partners. David Fulton and Revels Adams feared that black men might not risk death in order to prevent white men from satiating themselves through the bodies of black women.

As producers and subjects, African American men were hardly absent from intraracial discourse on miscegenation. Still, throughout the post-emancipation and Progressive eras, intraracial discourse focused on women —their exploitation, their complicity, their phenotypical attributes—in a sustained fashion that ultimately placed a burden of sorts on women of African descent. Black women's bodies critically informed sociopolitical assessments of miscegenation in yet another way: Ida B. Wells, the tireless antilynching activist who did not hesitate to broach hypocrisies within mainstream viewpoints about interracial sex was herself marked by white commentators as a "'saddle-colored Sapphira.'"[49]

During the decades when dubious antimiscegenation laws proliferated —forty-one states had legislation prohibiting interracial sex and/or marriage by 1914—African Americans had ample reason to harbor trepidation.[50] At varying junctures between 1888 and 1916, Aaron Mossell, Archibald Grimké, Alexander Walters, and Daniel Murray all maintained that statutes aimed at restricting the desires of black men actually maintained the sexual exploitation of black women by white men.[51] And, when a debate raged in Ohio regarding a proposed anti-intermarriage bill during the early 1910s, an item printed in the Cleveland *Gazette* opined: "That 'Separate Marriage' laws are failures, is a well-known fact. But how they promote immorality, is not so well known. White men in the south . . . know that anti-intermarriage laws of their states make marriage, with the Colored girls or women they seduce, impossible. . . . Naturally, they regard every good-looking Colored girl or woman . . . as their prey, 'governing' their passions accordingly."[52] While the *Gazette* reiterated arguments that African Americans had been making since Reconstruction, the editor of another Ohio paper, Wendell Phillips Dabney, focused upon the impact of such legislation on both race men and women. Dabney's pamphlet, *The Wolf and the Lamb*, invoked Aesop's fables as a means of analyzing interracial sex and mixture: he argued that "Negro men occup[ied] the place of the poor lamb" and that white men bore responsibility "for any mingling between Negro men and white women." Dabney further contended that states without laws prohibiting interracial marriage had the lowest incidence of such unions; he insisted that African Americans desired "race purity." All and the same, the editor and one-time government worker strongly insinuated that the race's integrity and "honor" were dependent upon "the keeping of its women" since antimiscegenation laws had no intention of protecting black women. In toto, the *Wolf and the Lamb*'s text and photographs—five of which included women and two with men—spoke to the highly gendered quality of debates over intermarriage and mixture as it suggested that racial destiny and the protection of women were inextricably linked.[53]

Again, male sexuality was not altogether overlooked when African Americans discussed miscegenation, and some commentators connected black men's social decisions to racial reproduction. For example, the Boston-based lawyer George Ruffin acknowledged that some light-skinned men who passed were having children by white wives; when Howard University's Kelly Miller insisted that light-skinned men could "more easily conceal their negroid origin," he implied that such men had less to worry about when it came to sex and reproduction than did "female mulattoes."[54] Nonetheless, given that black men of varied hue could be lynched if merely accused of having carnal knowledge of a white woman, intraracial consideration of African American male sexuality and miscegenation tended not to explore whether errant black men diluted the race—or whether passing men were raising ostensibly "white" families—but rather emphasized the stunning array of women within the race from which black men could select sexual partners. Gendered anxieties over interracial sex were surely built upon an "anxious concern to stabilize racial identity through paternity," but that very stability was contingent upon the gendered division of reproduction—a division in which women's labor assumed a certain primacy.[55]

Finally, in a climate of racial violence that included rape as well as lynching, at a time when antimiscegenation laws left black women vulnerable, it is not surprising that reformers, journalists, ministers, and activists who wanted to control miscegenation focused upon intraracial sexuality generally and African American women specifically. For individuals concerned about the state of the race, it was not only important that women had babies but whether they had babies as the result of intraracial relationships. Grown women as well as teenaged girls were therefore urged to shun white lovers—and race men were expected to see that they did so—because racial reproduction was viewed as occurring primarily through women. If miscegenation had indeed thrust a "burden of responsibility" upon African

Americans, those responsibilities were often gendered so that women and men were encouraged to think about ways that their most intimate actions affected the entire collective. Such dynamics and expectations would become potently manifest in one of the largest mass movements of people of African descent in U.S. history—the transnational, diasporic, nationalist Universal Negro Improvement Association.

miscegenation
interacial sex / marriage
racial hierarchy based on skin color
race purity

Fears of fading white over time

*Slavery brought upon us the curse of many colors
within the Negro race, but that is no reason why
we . . . should perpetuate the evil; hence instead of
encouraging a wholesale bastardy in the race, we feel
that we should now set out to create a race type and
standard of our own which . . . in the future could
be recognized and respected as the true race type.*
—*Philosophy and Opinions of Marcus Garvey* (1923)

WHAT A PURE, HEALTHY,
UNIFIED RACE CAN ACCOMPLISH
COLLECTIVE REPRODUCTION AND
THE SEXUAL POLITICS OF BLACK
NATIONALISM

A provocative and somewhat disturbing piece of news graced the pages of the official propaganda organ of Marcus Garvey's Universal Negro Improvement Association during the spring of 1922. In early April, the *Negro World* reported that a contingent of African American men in Sylvester, Georgia, had come across a black woman and white man who were "maintaining improper relations." This chance meeting did more than raise a few eyebrows: it raised the black men's collective dander, and they quickly assumed intimidating postures; the overwhelmed white paramour managed to escape the wrath of the small posse as overt threats flared into active pursuit. The *Negro World* failed to divulge just how involved the couple actually was when their privacy came to an abrupt end, but the turn of events that followed the chase suggest that coitus had indeed been interrupted.[1]

With one attempt to mete out physical punishment foiled, the race men remained sufficiently riled to seek

out their wayward sister next. They subsequently lectured her on the "sanctity of Negro womanhood," white men's sexual excesses during slavery, and
the lynchings of black men accused of "look[ing] hard" at white women.
Verbal assault then became bluntly physical as the mob gave the woman "a
severe whipping" in order to "impress her . . . with their 'determination to
preserve race purity.'" Of course we cannot know whether she eventually
rejected her lover as the result of being brutalized by angry vigilantes, but
from the pages of the *Negro World*, we do know that the involved parties allegedly appeared in court the next day. The presiding judge fined the white
man $20, the woman was ordered to pay $15, and each assailant had to come
up with $5. One witness, according to reports, wryly mused, "Guess it was
worth $5 to teach her a lesson," as the judge either adjourned court or turned
to the next case on the docket.[2]

Why would a black nationalist newspaper consider this story news-
worthy? For one, black men terrorizing a white man in a small southern
town during the 1920s challenged racialized patterns of daily life endured
by many people of African descent; what transpired in Sylvester could ostensibly embolden one segment of the *Negro World*'s readership to guard
their communities with manly resolve. But why was the article drafted so
as to suggest that intraracial violence—between a group of men and a lone
woman at that—could amount to collective uplift?[3] If we think about the
UNIA as a back-to-Africa scheme, or if we analyze the movement solely in
terms of Garvey as man and myth, this scandal-tinged human interest story
appears to be little more than tantalizing filler. However, if we embed what
happened that night in Georgia within the fundamental principles of Garveyism, a potentially trivial news item takes on emblematic proportions.

Although the *Negro World* covered a variety of international, national,
and local issues, column space was primarily reserved for the tenets of the
Universal Negro Improvement Association. Marcus Garvey established
the UNIA as a nonpolitical benevolent society in his native Jamaica during
the summer of 1914, but the movement failed to garner much attention or
gather sufficient momentum.[4] The itinerant printer with a knack for elocu-
tion subsequently emigrated to Harlem in 1916, and by 1919 his movement
called for racial consolidation, "founding a great nation," and African redemption.[5] Over the next six years the association peaked in membership,
influence and notoriety, for once the movement became explicitly political, Garveyism touched the raw nerves of aspiring-class, working-class, and
working-poor blacks across the United States, the Caribbean, and Africa.
The regional variety of UNIA branch divisions within the United States alone

reflected both the magnitude of African American migration and the rapid spread of Garveyism: locals existed in southwestern, Rocky Mountain, and southern states as well as in New England, the Middle Atlantic, the Pacific Northwest, and the Midwest. Although most African American divisions were concentrated in urban centers, several locals sprang up in small towns and rural hamlets as well.[6]

The UNIA's motto of "One God! One Aim! One Destiny!" simultaneously captured the movement's spirit and spoke to a long-standing tradition of Afro-American discourse on racial destiny. The sentiment endowed within movement slogan "race first" provocatively indicated critical motivations behind Garveyism: "Reasonably interpreted it means that in the situation of racial strife . . . Negroes should give preference to members of their own . . . so as to conserve their resources . . . to combat those forces that oppose them."[7] The dictum of "race first" was, moreover, inclusive in that it was intended to apply to manifold aspects of black life. From the eradication of socioeconomic oppression to the acquisition of political power, from the promotion of collective endeavor to the inculcation of self-love, racial chauvinism shaped the UNIA's economic, industrial, cultural, and social programs for group preservation. The emphasis on staying within the group had still more personal ramifications. To begin, Garveyites could not realize any of their goals without the actual biological perpetuation of the race. If the UNIA was to be successful in promoting—and ultimately creating—a strong, healthy nation, sexuality had to be monitored and controlled so that it benefited the race; if that nation were to be "black," Garveyites would need to enforce racial purity as well. As both ideology and practice, then, "race first" applied to the sex lives of Garveyites and, by extension, all people of African descent—including the unfortunate woman in Sylvester.

Given that "race first" was an organizing principle of the UNIA and since it had a sexual cast, it is not surprising that there were other occasions when either Marcus Garvey or his followers dealt with intimate matters. A few months after it reported the events in Georgia, the *Negro World* reprinted a speech that Garvey gave in Harlem during which he justified his infamous summit meeting with Edward Young Clarke, Imperial Wizard of the Ku Klux Klan. Garvey's speech maintained that in the course of his meeting with Clarke, the two men had agreed that their respective members needed to safeguard racial purity through actively policing the sexual conduct of others. Boasted Garvey, "The Universal Negro Improvement Association is carrying out that doctrine splendidly. When I arrived at Baton Rouge . . . I was visited by the president and some officers of the near-by division. They

brought me this report: . . . seven white men came into a colored neighborhood . . . [and were found] at midnight sleeping in homes where they had
no business. . . . [Men of the UNIA] flogged them and drove them out of the
neighborhood." Afterward, these ardent race men went before a white judge
who not only belonged to the Klan but also released them with the blessing
to "do some more of that."[8] Doing "more of that" likely involved subsequent
surveillance of girls and women in those homes, since well-timed nocturnal
interventions had the potential to disrupt continued interracial couplings.
Sustained harassment and ostracism could compel a woman to abandon certain sexual practices—at least momentarily. Regardless of whether the men
in Baton Rouge actually continued to take matters into their own hands,
Garvey highlighted the initial incident in order to drive home a pointed argument: black men needed to flex their muscles and "strike back on white
men trying to get too close to black women."[9] While Garvey desired that all
black people seize control over "the social question of race," he wanted the
UNIA to assume the vanguard of safeguarding "the purity of the black race
not only down South, but all through the world."[10]

The staff of the *Negro World* could have omitted the portion about Louisiana without altering Garvey's overall message. Yet it was purposefully included for—like the dispatch from Georgia—the lesson of Baton Rouge
was that if sustained, quotidian maintenance of racial purity entailed physical intervention on occasion, then black men should take it upon themselves
to prevent interracial sex through force or, if need be, outright violence.
Women's role in preserving racial purity was broached somewhat differently in UNIA rhetoric: Garveyite women were urged to influence their sisters
through example; they could sway men through reason or perhaps denun-
ciation. A few women sought notably more proactive ways of discouraging
white men. The *Negro World* relayed a report about black women who, during the late months of 1925, had allegedly lynched a lone white "libertine"
in order to prevent coerced sexual congress. Over a year earlier, one reader
from Philadelphia sent a letter to the *Negro World* in order to solicit aid in
her quest to hunt down a white man who tried to molest her daughter. The
girl's mother, Nellie Edwards, sought a confrontation with the assailant, and
she pointedly expressed her wish to be the one who "riddle[d] him with
bullets."[11] These reports aside, the *Negro World* never so much as intimated
that livid race matrons could, or should, horsewhip a black man for enjoying
an illicit rendezvous with a white woman.

Such an overarching emphasis on race purity was neither incidental nor
fleeting, for speeches, editorials, and letters vetted the subject, while al-

most half of the UNIA's nine basic doctrines opposed miscegenation. Published in 1924, the eight-point "What We Believe" also opened with a call for "the uniting and blending of all Negroes into one strong, healthy race" and swiftly warned of racial suicide. Notably, "What We Believe" made sure to distinguish between types of interracial liaisons by labeling both "rich blacks marrying poor whites" along with "rich or poor whites taking advantage of Negro women" as inimical to the enterprise of race building. An explicit desire for total racial purity was yet another tenet, while an allied point called for self-determination and nationhood via "social and political physical separation."[12] Moreover, Garvey's pamphlet *Aims and Objects* decried "mongrelization" as it called upon "off-Colored people" to "re-establish the purity of their own race."[13] Rather than being tertiary or even secondary to Garveyism, homogenizing the race was part and parcel of core movement ideology.

The particular brand of antimiscegenationist thought which permeated Garveyite ideology translated into action and shaped a broad range of relationships. Yet the UNIA's maintenance of racial purity primarily resulted in prescriptive—if not proscriptive—gender roles. Gender not only shaped the contours of any given member's responsibility to the race, sexual accountability was parsed inequitably and experienced differently among female and male members of the collective. Movement discourse encouraged women to monitor sexuality, yet as women, they were usually the targets of protection, coercion, and control. Men, on the other hand, were chided for having carnal appetites that led them to stray beyond the race, but they were more typically exhorted to stand tall, "be men," and guard the sexual integrity of black women.

This is not to say that husbands, brothers, and sons were not held accountable for their actions: female delegates at one major convention spoke out against men who looked beyond the race for social companionship and spent an entire afternoon chastising those who "had very little regard for their wom[en]."[14] And, relationships involving black men and white women were certainly considered taboo. One member, Richard Tate, urged women to "keep tab[s] on your Negro men." Male sexual impulses needed to remain within the confines of blackness as a matter of fundamental practice, for if too many men chose women without African heritage as partners, the Atlanta resident reasoned, "large numbers of [our women will] die old maids." Tate's remarkably pithy March 1925 letter to the *Negro World* clearly labeled the erotic proclivities of some of his brothers as detrimental to the enterprise of race building, but the letter also spoke to black female sexu-

"Rebecca, Augusta, and Rosa, Emancipated Slaves from New Orleans," 1863.
Editorials, articles, and letters in the UNIA's Negro World *associated interracial*
heterosexual relationships (especially those involving girls and women of African
descent) with slavery, concubinage, exploitation, and rape. During the 1920s, the
question of racial purity was of signal importance to Garveyites based in the United
States. Courtesy of Photographs and Prints Division, Schomburg Center for Research
in Black Culture, New York Public Library, Astor, Lenox and Tilden Foundations.

ality in that Tate implied suitable husbands could be found if women would only "rally to Garveyism . . . where the Negro [man] can see more attraction within his race than any other." Richard Tate's comment about "old maids" reflected an anxiety that any intraracial benefit to be derived from black female sexuality might go unfulfilled. Viewed another way, his quick comment on how women should make themselves available for display suggested that it was up to women to do whatever was necessary to catch, hold, and wed a man.[15]

Although Tate remained silent about couplings between black women and white men, that silence nonetheless spoke to black women's sexuality because it ironically underscored that female indulgence in forbidden love was all but out of the question. This particular opprobrium existed for at least two reasons: liaisons between black women and white men conjured up slavery with its sexualized hierarchy, a hierarchy which undoubtedly left a number of black men feeling somewhat impotent well into the twentieth century. Deeply gendered notions about racial reproduction additionally implicated women as primary conduits for both pollution and dilution. Tate, then, likely harbored fears about black women's role in perpetuating miscegenation and their potential to thwart the realization of the UNIA's goals.

Women could—and did—harbor similar apprehensions to those expressed by Richard Tate. Less than two months after Tate aired his views, Eva Aldred Brooks penned an article about comparative birthrate statistics, ethnic distinctiveness, evolutionary law, and racial extermination. "The world today is thinking in terms of self-determination," Brooks observed, "[and we] see . . . other races within the Caucasian group . . . doing their utmost to perpetuate themselves." Brooks was deeply chagrined that black people were not doing the same and was especially irked over women who lacked race pride. Then she cut to the quick: "Is it not true . . . that many of our women and girls deem it an honor to be the mistress of some white man rather to be the wife of one of her own race? It is the duty of every Negro woman to put an end to this abomination. . . . If we allow these conditions to exist, a weak-kneed progeny shall arise. . . . If we correct the abuses of the race we shall see within a short while what a pure, healthy, unified race can accomplish." The very deed of interracial sex was, for Brooks, highly problematic, but she did not consider the actual deed more damaging than its potential outcome: being a white man's mistress was an "abomination" largely because it compromised optimal race reproduction by limiting the numbers of robust "black" babies born. Both sexuality and motherhood were thus central to realizing the movement's nationalist project for Brooks,

[A PURE, HEALTHY, UNIFIED RACE]

but as she claimed an active role for women in realizing a grand collective destiny, she also blamed women for hindering racial health and unity. Eva Brooks's views were anything but aberrant. Rather, Brooks's strategic gendered and sexualized interpretation of "race first" was shared by many other members of the UNIA.[16]

For all the anxieties that it produced, interracial sex was but one means through which matters pertaining to gender, copulation, and reproduction seeped into Garveyism. The columns of the *Negro World* and the UNIA's political program systematically dealt with gender issues along with a range of sexual topics as Garveyites—rank and file members as well as movement leaders—assessed sex in terms of nationhood, gradual racial purification, popular eugenic theory, and the possibility of extinction. But since racial reproduction was, to a large degree, contingent upon the issue of heterosexual intercourse, the sexuality of women faced extensive scrutiny. Thus, it is through the sexualized, gendered implications of the UNIA's program for race betterment that the incidents in Georgia and Louisiana must be viewed and Garveyites' rhetoric of progress and degeneration must be analyzed. Understanding the sexual politics of racial reproduction within the black nationalist program of the UNIA also entails highlighting intraracial dynamics, and it particularly requires close consideration of the places accorded women by the movement.

Modeled after late-nineteenth- and early-twentieth-century fraternal orders,[17] the Universal Negro Improvement Association operated under the basic assumption that males and females had separate arenas and different functions.[18] Within the movement, "women had an important economic function" as fund-raisers, workers, and stock-holders; some women were even able to "ac[t] . . . in autonomous 'male' ways."[19] Still, the movement institutionalized the reinforcement of gender roles. The movement's constitution established juvenile programs that served the dual purpose of being primers in Garveyism and gender-specific activity: young girls prepared for homemaking while little boys engaged in industrial education; teenaged girls received instruction in hygiene and "domestic science" as adolescent boys were ushered into the political infrastructure of the association through military training.[20] Sex-segregated activity continued into adulthood, with most UNIA women—whether they channeled their energies into auxiliary work or participated in general forums—finding themselves in situations that mirrored places in the home.[21] As men formulated movement policy in meetings and practiced military maneuvers in the streets, women served as support staff, provided food at UNIA functions, and discussed their role during special "ladies' days." Even the militaristic women's Motor Corps, whose members received basic training in automobile repair, was formed primarily to "assist the [male] Universal African Legions in the performance of their duties."[22] Garveyism inspired girls and women to contribute their energies toward collective uplift, but the form of their contribution assumed a different design than it did for boys and men.[23]

All the same, girls and women were engaged participants who joined the UNIA in numbers equal to males as Garveyism altered their perceptions of self and surroundings.[24] Gertrude Hawkins of Maryland sold the *Negro World* and felt compelled to write the paper about the impact the movement was having on her young life: "My parents are . . . trying to get an organization of the Universal Negro Improvement Association at a church out here by us, and everyone my parents meet they tell them about this organization. . . . I am only ten years old . . . and I see where we need a state and a home for ourselves." Violet McCracken was another youthful convert. At sixteen, McCracken stood before her local in Muskogee, Oklahoma, and beseeched those present to "work with all the zeal and interest that behooves us to better the condition of the Negro race." Women in their twenties and beyond felt similarly committed: Rosetta Stenson believed the movement was uniquely capable of elevating the race; Mary Carter prayed that she would not die until Garveyites delivered Africa; members in New Orleans avowed "[the UNIA] is our church, our clubhouse, our theatre, our fraternal order, and our school," and that none would "forsake it while we live [and] neither will our men."[25]

When it came to being active in terms of political discourse, however, women faced resistance sufficient enough to prompt open frustration with their assigned functions. For example, when Garveyism was at its crest in the United States, the association held annual conventions in Harlem where members had major opportunities to discuss pertinent issues, exchange ideas, and influence each other's thought. At the raucous 1922 International Convention, during which internecine struggles and street brawls erupted, a contingent of women literally seized the floor on the last day to protest their status in the movement. Victoria Turner, a delegate from St. Louis, presented a lengthy list of women's grievances ranging from the paucity of women in "important offices . . . [and] initiative positions" to the existing leadership structure of women's auxiliaries. When Turner stepped down, other women took the floor and testified that they were "being curbed to a great extent" by men of the UNIA. Significantly, some of these women served

UNIA officers 2nd Lt. J. Harris, 2nd Lt. Hagor T. Wallace, and Lt. Israel Dinezy, undated. Uniforms, rituals, rank, and discipline were critical components of the UNIA's gendered vision of racial redemption. Courtesy of Photographs and Prints Division, Schomburg Center for Research in Black Culture, New York Public Library, Astor, Lenox and Tilden Foundations.

in atypical capacities—such as field organizer—and they apparently faced questions about their "competence" and "conduct"; even among these dissenters, at least one still believed that if women performed certain organizational tasks, men would fail to take them seriously and even question their claims on respectable femininity.[26]

There were, then, exceptional movement women who stood apart from rank and file women with families, husbands, or children, but by and large, women who served in atypical capacities were single, otherwise unattached, or past childbearing age. International Organizer and Assistant President-General Henrietta Vinton Davis was an older woman without children; the manager of UNIA's printing plant, Lyllian Galloway, was young and unmarried.[27] Amy Jacques Garvey was in yet another category still: a prolific, talented, and politically astute writer who all but led the UNIA while Garvey was imprisoned for mail fraud, Amy Jacques gained her prominence, to some degree, from being Marcus's second wife. Maymie De Mena—one of few married women with a high profile in the movement—understood her own relative power was somewhat of an anomaly. De Mena's rueful assessment of gender roles in the UNIA was that "women were given to understand that they were to remain in their places, which meant nothing more than [being] a Black Cross Nurse or a general secretary of [a] division."[28]

De Mena's comments—along with those made by protesters in 1922—underscore how even women with unusual visibility could feel constrained by the province allowed women within organizational structure. Prominent UNIA women were skilled and often charismatic. Yet "the success of Davis, De Mena, and Jacques as UNIA leaders was seemingly owing not only to their own merit as strong intellects and forceful organizers but to their perceived status as Garvey's representatives—a status that prevented them from being seen as 'real' leaders in their own right."[29] Not surprisingly, then, female participation in ostensibly nonpolitical activity was a different matter. Many women in the UNIA therefore chose to underscore their centrality to the movement by invoking social roles, by naming motherhood a key site of nation building.

This strategy is not surprising given that the movement lauded black parenthood in general but glorified race motherhood specifically: the UNIA chaplain provided print sermons regaling selfless madonnas, the *Negro World* offered constant commentary on maternal contributions to race building, festive Mother's Day programs became gala events.[30] At one Mother's Day observance, women were encouraged to view motherhood as "the noblest career in which a woman can succeed," and even men were prodded to "pay greater respect to women and more attention to production of off-spring." Predictably, it would be women who received more than their share of prodding to procreate that May afternoon as Chaplain General George Carter flatly told his audience that real women—true women—longed to reproduce. Although he assured listeners that women played a quintessential role in "put[ting] over [our] program," the chaplain general more than implied that motherhood should be their primary contribution.[31] Carter's particular approach to extolling black mothers might not have appealed to every woman who heard him speak, yet his views nevertheless echoed those held by a number of women. At the same time that men such as Carter could derive benefits from encouraging women to embrace childbearing along with domesticity, women could also have a special stake—both rhetorically and literally—in representing motherhood as a political locus of racial reproduction.

Philadelphia's Lady President Estelle Matthews was one such woman who politicized mother work. When she begged her sisters to heed the call of motherhood and determine the destiny of future race women and men, for instance, she decided to couch her plea in "the redemption of Africa." Matthews chose not to pressure women to have more children but instead stressed that girls and boys forever bore the imprint of racial instruction received at mother's knee. Women could therefore act as critical agents in realizing the movement's aims by turning the home into a place that reinforced race pride on a daily basis. More specifically, she urged women to be highly selective in choosing images to adorn their walls; Matthews even more emphatically urged women to give their children toys that celebrated blackness.[32]

Estelle Matthews's expansive view of mothering was certainly in sync with movement ideologies that expressly politicized attainment of a "pure" racial integrity. Upholding motherhood in such a fashion was ultimately problematic, however: Matthews's promotion of race motherhood augmented the importance of a familiar, familial role, but it also detracted from other political or creative aspirations a woman might harbor. And, if the primary function of a UNIA woman was to bear fruit and nurture the collective, then reproductive capacity arguably set women apart as objects of special concern. Since the political realm of the movement was cordoned off as the domain of men, the movement spent considerably less time promoting men's familial roles or responsibilities beyond encouraging them to provide adequate financial support, "respect women," and, in the words of member Hannah Nichols, "practice self-control."[33] Both women and men of the UNIA would find ways to locate motherhood in new arenas, however. And they would do so, in part, by invoking scientific motherhood, racial reproduction, and popular eugenics.

Garveyite concepts about racial reproduction were in many regards distinct, although they mirrored contemporary currents of thought. For instance, when members of the UNIA chose to apply scientific principles to the production of future redeemers of Africa, they certainly drew from modern notions about hygiene, but they also turned to popular eugenic theories. Eugenics, a voice for progress throughout the early twentieth century, sprang from social Darwinism, which argued that "natural selection" irreversibly rendered certain racial groups less "fit" to compete in the struggle of life. Unlike its progenitor, however, eugenic theory held that through regulation of heredity, environment, and sexuality, racial stock could actually be improved. Such improvement could, theoretically, be realized in at least three ways: the "unfit" could bear a limited number of offspring or be sterilized altogether; the "best elements" could be induced to reproduce at a prolific rate in order to combat racial degeneration; all prospective parenthood could be encouraged to create the best babies possible.[34] In the United States, the eugenics movement was based on classist, nativist, and racist assumptions and had obvious ideological limitations for people of African descent. Eugenicist theory influenced a diverse range of black intellectuals nevertheless: the NAACP's W. E. B. Du Bois and Howard University's Kelly Miller were concerned that the "masses" were more fecund than the "classes"; socialist activist Chandler Owen and educator Mary Burrill both felt birth control could improve the quality of children born to the race.[35] Not only did a range of black writers invoke "metaphorical eugenics" during the 1920, but "uplift ideology adapt[ed] quite readily to the period's characteristic eugenic thinking."[36]

Garveyites and Garveyism were no exception. Whereas most Garveyites were downright leery of sterilization—not to mention birth control—men and women of the movement appropriated popular eugenic vernaculars concerning heredity and physical improvement which, in turn, reinforced the UNIA's concept on the relationship between sexuality and race first.[37] During the 1924 convention, the relevance of eugenics for black people was tackled in at least one session when physician—and loyal Garveyite—J. J. Peters offered his observation that "in the interest of the next generation . . . [we must] banish prudery and mock modesty . . . and give pr[o]creation more eugenic attention." Two men who offered allied opinions followed Peters:

one speaker was a doctor who described how venereal disease compromised reproductive health; the other commentator claimed that the problems sexually transmitted ailments presented to the race were largely due to black men who slept with "women of other races."[38]

The *Negro World* was also instrumental in filtering popular eugenics into routine movement discourse. On its women's page, "Our Women and What They Think," Amy Jacques Garvey regularly deployed eugenic arguments in editorials on motherhood and "childlife." In one of her more subtle offerings, Jacques Garvey wrote

> Much needs to be done as yet before motherhood and childhood will be placed upon the scientific basis where the very best results can reasonably be expected in the production of best and brightest type of manhood and womanhood. . . . We shall hardly be able to meet the growing need for a properly trained childhood . . . for many years to come. . . . [But I am] proud of the splendid work our women have done in the home and school and church . . . and [I] have faith to hope that they will do better work in the coming days.[39]

Eugenicist concepts appeared in a number of general articles as well.[40] Lester Taylor contributed an especially lengthy discourse on racial reproduction in which he pointedly suggested that the race needed to give the breeding of children serious consideration:

> Show me a race that sets a high premium on childbearing and that strives ever to improve the quality of children it produces, and I will show you a race destined to outnumber, overcome, and survive all other races . . . in the game of life. Show me, on the other hand, a race . . . careless of the quality of the children it produces . . . [and I] will show you a race doomed . . . [to produce] an ever increasing percentage of abortions and deformities, of cowards and weaklings . . . a race doomed to disappear.

Tropical climates enabled people of African descent to double their numbers within the relatively short span of forty years, Taylor claimed, and the reproduction of the race suffered in North America due to economic pressures as well as racist sterilization practices. Ample replenishment of North American blacks therefore required "clean, orderly sexual relations" and the production of "high physical and mental types" who would secure black people's place at "the vanguard of human progress."[41]

Taylor was hardly alone in his conviction that life entailed racial competition, that when it came to reproducing the race, quality counted as much if not more—than quantity. Carrie Mero Leadett, a secretary for the Black Star Line who joined the movement in 1919, used her discourse on maternal responsibility to assert that the race could ill afford "children who [were] physically, mentally, and morally unfit for life's struggle." Leadett then urged all women devoted to the cause to produce "100 per cent." babies capable of winning full-fledged racial competitions. If the black nationalist program of the UNIA was to succeed, she concluded, the production of "high physical and mental types" was nothing less than vital.[42]

If Leadett's convictions were slightly trenchant, Marcus Garvey's views could veer toward the alarmist. "The Negro is dying out, and he is going to die faster . . . in the next fifty years," Garvey warned. "[And] if we do not seriously reorganize ourselves as a people . . . our days in civilization are numbered."[43] Garvey also told a 1921 New York audience that if black people failed to preserve themselves and pay attention to declining birthrates, nothing short of "doom" awaited.[44] It is not completely clear whether Garvey actually believed the race was dying out, but he manipulated the concept of extermination to push sex, the black birthrate, and collective health as critical items on the "race first" agenda. He was successful: UNIA members debated whether blacks were on the verge of extinction as they discussed the significance of census figures, venereal disease, and sex reform.[45]

Such reform and "reorganization" entailed active redirection of sexual activities so that they resulted in prolific, eugenic childbearing within the confines of an endogamous marriage. Along with Garvey, many adherents of the movement were often preoccupied with the possibility of extinction because they held widespread, contemporary assumptions about how birth control, venereal disease, promiscuity, and premarital sex ultimately led to race suicide. Their interest in comparative birthrate statistics was, furthermore, shared by a range of intellectuals and politicians in the United States, where the majority of UNIA locals existed during the 1920s. While some American pundits worried that white, native-born women were lagging dangerously behind in their rate of childbirth, many had a perverse fixation with the birthrates of European immigrants, and more still with those of women of African descent. Ironically, while census figures from the U.S. government did not necessarily support claims that African Americans faced extinction, census data fueled racial and ethnic comparisons nonetheless.

According to the U.S. Census Bureau, the number of African Americans nearly doubled between 1870 and 1920. Between 1900 and 1910 alone, the decennial increase in black population was around 11 percent; the aggregate figure of approximately ten million people of African descent translated into about 10 percent of the total population in 1910. In contrast, whites—both native and immigrant—comprised over 80 percent of the total population. Whereas these percentages did not deviate all that much from those reported in previous decennial counts, the black birthrate continued to be in sharp decline in comparison to native-born white or immigrant women. Not only were more and more black women limiting their pregnancies, but between 1910 and 1920, the influenza epidemic was especially harsh on black communities, which—again, in comparison to other ethnic groups—had higher overall mortality rates. Whether due to birth control, morbidity, war, migration, or careless census enumerators, the 1920 census announced that African Americans entered the third decade of the century as less than 10 percent of the national total. Black people in the United States might not have been moribund, but to many observers, it certainly appeared that the race was stagnant and in decline.[46]

To exacerbate matters, economic immiseration vitiated urban communities such as Washington, D.C., Baltimore, New York, New Orleans, Philadelphia, Detroit, and Chicago.[47] These cities had particularly large black populations and housed some of the largest UNIA branches. Not surprisingly, locals in large cities frequently responded to the demands of urban life through providing a variety of business enterprises that created jobs and offered services: some divisions offered soup kitchens for the unemployed or provided sleeping quarters for homeless black men and women; the "Liberty Halls" of other locals gave out information about affordable lodging.[48] Movement programs therefore addressed the consumer demands in black communities and provided pragmatic solutions to material needs. Such pragmatism hardly meant that facilities and programs were not aimed at realizing the movement's ideology, however.

The response of Garveyites to disease and morbidity was at once pronounced and pragmatic. In an attempt to bridge ideology and reality, the Universal Negro Improvement Association stood prepared to combat needless deaths in black communities through public education; *Negro World* health columns offered plain talk about disease, hygiene, and prevention; while women in Black Cross auxiliaries lectured and demonstrated the latest sanitary methods. Black Cross Nurses provided a range of grassroots services in their communities, many oriented toward alleviating symptoms of poverty. Despite the grittiness of some of the work the Black Cross performed within communities, nurses were idealized in the iconography of the movement which presented them as angels of mercy draped in white, as intraracial missionaries bearing the light of knowledge.[49] Whether their routine duties actually veered toward the messianic or the mundane, women of the auxiliary prioritized outreach work—especially among mothers of the race. In addition to the Black Cross maintaining "baby health stations" that were staffed by women ready to dole out advice, the auxiliary promoted eugenic concepts of scientific motherhood and counseled women to patronize black health workers rather than risk being "tampered with by prejudiced white doctors."[50] Even further, a Black Cross Nurse from Chicago, Clara Morgan, contributed a regular column directed at mothers in the *Negro World*; there she circulated the U.S. Child Welfare Department's "ABCs of Child Welfare," regularly advised women on how to improve their household habits, and promoted the idea that creating a "more intelligent and better Negro motherhood" should top the UNIA's agenda.[51]

But prioritizing the reproductive development and destiny of the race was a complex matter. For one, improving racial stock could well involve increasing and purifying that stock as much as it could upgrading the living conditions of black people to a respectable if not bourgeois standard—whether such a standard was actually attainable is another matter. For another, it was one thing to issue rhetorical calls for increased racial reproduction but quite another to influence actual reproductive choices. UNIA members might not have demanded that their sisters bear children, but they certainly tried to inspire, if not shame, childless women into action.

As a result, typical UNIA rhetoric about collective perpetuation was littered with blunt pronouncements as well as veiled phrases signifying the evils of delayed childbearing and birth control. Amy Jacques simply proclaimed that birth control suited whites rather than blacks.[52] Hubert Cox, a *Negro World* staffer, condemned birth control as inherently contrary to "correct" sexual impulses that resulted in children. Whereas Cox maintained that both men and women possessed an "[innate] desire for children," he declared that women who practiced birth control as a means of accessing contemporary liberties were doing far more than harming themselves. His words of warning were at once foreboding and fantastic: "[Currently women] desire the freedom from motherhood and in consequence, we are on the brink of active racial suicide. The penalty that nature exacts is very severe. The suppression of restriction of innate desire for children by women result[s] in hysteria, melancholy, nervousness, unhappiness . . . disease and an early grave." Cox, for his part, actively associated contraception with women's independence and their eschewing of reproduction as the primary means of serving both family and race. Men who shunned fatherhood were not much better off in his mind: a childless man was at risk of degenerating into a murderer or facing "self-debasement, masturbation, deadening of conscience, corruption of heart . . . suicide or untimely death."[53]

Like Jacques Garvey and Cox, Black Cross Nurse Kate Fenner disapproved of contraception, and she accepted the notion that mothers were rightfully assigned the difficult task of "build[ing] up a pure black generation." However, Fenner also believed that black men had all but prostituted women of the race. She wryly concluded that once they started acting manly, ceased hiding "behind [women's] skirts," and did their "duty as men . . . there [would] be no cause for the other side to preach birth control among black women."[54] But whether it was Fenner chastising men for irresponsible behavior or Cox conjuring up future torments for women who used contraception, prevailing movement ideology considered birth control inimical to a progressive black nation.[55] Unlike Margaret Sanger and other proponents of birth control who viewed contraception as having a positive eugenic effect,[56] movement rhetoric consistently suggested that birth control was a dysgenic, or negative, drain on racial reproduction. For the purposes of the UNIA, racial degeneration could be minimized through proper sexual conduct, not birth control. Some of its members would even hint that birth control led to debilitating perversions.

If Hubert Cox argued that the "restriction of innate desire for children" led to "self-debasement," a few Garveyites ventured further and dealt with homosexuality.[57] Direct references to lesbians and gay men were rare if not absent from the pages of the *Negro World*, but veiled messages that could ostensibly be interpreted as applying to homosexuality relied upon the language of perversion and degeneration. One contributor, however, was clearly homophobic and was not afraid to condemn people who were not heterosexual. As he bemoaned social forces he believed to be warping black youth, John Houghton harshly critiqued interracial sex. But another sexual interaction vexed him more: "Some of the older women of the race . . . have a way of discouraging young girls, and endeavor to fill the places of men—for most of them prefer that they die maidens. . . . If this condition continues and this immoral practice of some of our women and men keeps up . . . race extinction within a given period of time [is inevitable]." Houghton's focus upon lesbianism echoed Richard Tate's fears about "old maids," and he further intimated that lesbians played a role in leading black people down the road to race suicide. Granted, Houghton implicated gay men as well, but by the gendered tone of his self-labeled exposé, he clearly considered lesbianism the greater danger.[58]

When Garveyites inveighed that the race had to produce better children and more children, their arguments were gendered in such a way that women's sexuality was the focal point of discussion. Furthermore, appropriations of eugenic theories, anxieties over racial purity, worries about black women's fecundity, and fears about homosexuality fortified the existing gendered structure of the UNIA: in toto, these concerns reinforced a notion that men and women had distinct and separate racial responsibilities. Members of the organization outlined varied characteristics of race manhood and race womanhood in striking detail, but perhaps the most important and sustained manipulation of gendered concepts in the UNIA was the reification of racial motherhood. Members did discuss the duties and responsibilities of fathers and men, yet the concept of racial fatherhood was not as clearly or extensively articulated.[59] Both the *Negro World* and the movement behind it simply paid more attention to issues surrounding black women's sexuality. Black men who strayed from the race were derided, but women might be forced to endure assault for their transgressions. Again, men might sire mixed-race children, but women, the literal bearers of the race, were expected to view race motherhood as their primary duty in the struggle for self-determination.

If it was indeed the case that "no race could rise higher than its motherhood," it was just as true that the UNIA's ideal of race motherhood entailed a degree of struggle, if not sacrifice.[60] Maida Springer Kemp's mother, for example, was an immigrant from Panama who ran a New York City beauty shop; a single parent, she was an active Garveyite throughout the 1920s as well. In describing her own childhood, Kemp recalled that when her "mother marched as a Black Cross Nurse . . . she had [me] by the hand and I went to meetings because there were no babysitters. . . . Wherever [my mother] went, I went."[61] Kemp's mother might have been unusually energetic and enterprising, but in one critical regard, her life was typical— multiple demands commanded the lives of most black women. It is unlikely, therefore, that the majority of women in the UNIA could single-mindedly focus on motherhood or avoid work outside of the home.

Given that many black men were chronically underemployed and not all black households were structured around nuclear families, certain UNIA beliefs were moored as much in assumptions of class as of gender. Furthermore, not all black people chose to be sexually active within the confines of a heterosexual, intraracial marriage or relationship. Irrespective of the realities and choices facing Garveyites—female and male, working-poor and middling, U.S.-born and immigrant—movement ideology viewed sexuality as a means to foster racially "pure" black families, encourage a bold and potent manhood, create a progressive childhood, and enforce a maternally virtuous womanhood. And as much as these ideological lenses created a holistic vision where both men and women were integral to African redemption, women were considered particularly responsible for reproducing the race.

Whereas Garveyism might have been radical in some respects, it contained an abiding conservatism in that the movement and its attendant ideology sought to conserve people of African descent as a distinct "race."[62] Furthermore, members of the Universal Negro Improvement Association resorted to fairly rigid, conservative gender conventions in pursuit of this aim. If the UNIA's "retreat from radicalism" occurred as soon as Garvey "resorted to the ideology of racial purity" in the early 1920s, such a contention implies that Garveyites' embrace of antimiscegenationist beliefs was somehow incongruous with the movement's initial aim of sustained race building.[63] Linking the pursuit of racial purity to political retreat without interrogating the politics implicit within a racial purist vision obscures how Garveyism is similar to other nationalisms as it elides the ways in which gender and sexuality are crucial informants to nationalist projects such as the UNIA.

Similarly, if we go back to the incidents in Georgia and Louisiana, consider them as the ideology of racial purity in action, and leave it at that, then our ability to understand the significance of those incidents is severely compromised. In and of itself, merely noting the existence of racial purist ideology neither explains why the UNIA institutionalized gender-specific functions and activity nor fully contextualizes the race purist cast of Garveyite pronatalism. It also, frankly, does not account for *whose* sexuality was affected most and *why* sexuality was part and parcel of the politics of racial destiny.

In order to understand why racial purist thought emerged as a critical component of the Garvey movement's vision of racial destiny it is therefore essential to assess how assumptions about gender within the UNIA—or, for that matter, the gendered warp and woof of nationalist politics generally—encouraged Garveyites to zero in on sexuality. Nationalisms tend to prioritize the preservation and perpetuation of ethnic, religious, or national groups.[64] On some level, then, nationalisms are also concerned with biological, social, and "racial" processes of reproduction.[65] The politics of Garveyism must therefore be scrutinized in ways that fully engage theories of sexuality within other nationalisms; scholars of black nationalism must continue to interrogate the gendered, sexualized politics of racial reproduction.[66]

Garveyites assessed black people's sexuality in light of contemporary exigencies as well as historical discourses on black sexuality. Throughout much of the history of the United States, a value-laden dialogue about black sexuality has existed. Not all Garveyites that lived in the United States or contributed to the *Negro World* during the UNIA's peak—including Amy Jacques Garvey, Maymie De Mena, Marcus Garvey, and countless others—were native-born, but many were deeply influenced by U.S. racial discourses. Most significantly, late-nineteenth- and early-twentieth-century stereotypes about black sexuality worked in conjunction with assertions that slavery tainted gender roles among people of African descent and compounded the already complex ways in which Garveyites viewed their own sexuality. The mere possibility that blacks could not achieve the "sexual purity . . . [needed] to survive and develop" therefore led Garveyites to search for their own solutions. Some of those very solutions, however, were somewhat reactionary when it came to gender and sexuality in that they drew upon popular eugenics and looked toward pronatalist solutions for race building.[67] Garveyites embraced eugenics as a sexual corrective for the race at large, then, due to perceived needs, problematic stereotypes, and material realities.

If the eugenic and pronatalist strains in movement rhetoric reveal that Garveyites' expectations for sexual behavior carried additional implications for women, then a major question bears revisiting: why were women singled out? The divergent ways in which women and men experienced the racial purist impetus behind Garveyism emerged from the social, biological, and gendered division of labor involved in having children. Women do more than have babies, they "reproduc[e] the race"; their sexual activities are a source of greater anxiety as a result.[68] And if "those who are preoccupied with the 'purity' of the race [are also] preoccupied with the sexual relationships between members of different collectivities,"[69] the ideology of Garveyism contained such a preoccupation. The movement, in other words, placed the blame for miscegenation at the feet of black women, if not in their beds.

If we simply consider that the movement's constitution institutionalized sex-specific responsibilities and functions, then gender might seem merely a consideration that shaped how Garveyites organized meetings and activities. Once we also consider that members of the UNIA were concerned with both racial purity and black women's reproductive function, that prolific and eugenic childbearing was considered a primary duty for race women, it becomes all but impossible to assert that male and female Garveyites truly shared the same purpose in the movement's overarching vision of "One God! One Aim! One Destiny!"[70] By examining the programs and precepts of Garveyites with gender and sexuality in mind, it is abundantly clear that in the quest for racial redemption and black nationhood, the UNIA might have had one God and one aim, but men and women in the movement had somewhat separate destinies.

Race First

Sexual politics of racial reproduction

UNIA intentional? reinforced? gender roles

quality of race "Race First" Agenda

EPILOGUE
THE CROSSROADS
OF DESTINY

In 1928, when Garveyism was on the wane
in the United States, the *Negro World* tried to rouse
its readers to action by publishing a trenchant editorial on black self-determination and its less than
appealing alternatives. Its argument was straightforward. "No race can grow fat . . . that feeds on the
crumbs that fall from the tables of others," ventured
the *Negro World*, "nor can a race gain political and economic sufficiency . . . [when] jostled and beaten and
cheated by a hostile majority." If people of African descent wanted to thrive and avoid further degeneration,
they had to act fast and pour their energies into the
UNIA. The *Negro World* vivified their editorial by pair-
ing it with a provocative cartoon that pictured a well-
dressed, youthful "New Negro" standing at a crossroads where six fates merged. With his gaze firmly
fixed upon the UNIA's sunlit road "to nationhood" and
his back toward avenues of "political death" and "race
suicide," the young man faced possible descents into
"economic distress," "mental paralysis," and "slavery."
The forward-looking young man—unaccompanied
by either woman or child—would presumably not
tarry at the crossroads but instead ascend the "manhood path to liberty and light." Editorial and cartoon
did more than suggest that black people should look
to Africa for collective redemption; the juxtaposition
underscored that a "manhood path" provided leadership and unfettered opportunity. As the *Negro World*
would have it, then, the "crossroads of destiny" was

"At the Crossroads," editorial cartoon from the Negro World, *April 14, 1928. If both African Americans' embrace of Garveyism and the language of "racial destiny" waned after 1930, the notion that collective fate and fortune were gendered did not. Courtesy of General Research and Reference Division, Schomburg Center for Research in Black Culture, New York Public Library, Astor, Lenox and Tilden Foundations.*

both male proving ground and racial position as the 1920s came to a close.[1]

African Americans did indeed stand at a crossroads, but not quite in the manner envisioned by the *Negro World*. As part—albeit a sizable part—of Garveyism's Afro-Atlantic constituency, blacks in the United States were a half-century removed from the end of Reconstruction and more than six decades past emancipation. Arguments about racial destiny had dominated and shaped Afro-American thought since the late nineteenth century. As racial segregation continued and deepened during the twentieth century, black women, men, and children would continue to think of themselves as a collective; black women and men would continue to debate amongst themselves about empire, sexuality, conduct, home life, and interracial sex; black children would continue to read race histories and embrace material culture that reflected black achievement and appearance. Liberia—and even emigration—continued to engage African Americans into the 1930s, though with less furor than when black women and men pooled their resources to purchase the *Azor* and flooded the American Colonization Society with correspondence decades before.[2] Intraracial discourse and politics were nevertheless in the process of transformation by the 1920s, a transformation that, ironically, began to occur as racial destiny concepts and strategies reached their apogee in Garveyism.

In 1920, for example, Robert L. Vann proclaimed in the inaugural issue of his short-lived magazine, the *Competitor*, that the race was becoming "interested in themselves—not as Negroes especially, but as Americans." Vann, an attorney and journalist whose Pittsburgh *Courier* would eclipse Robert Abbott's Chicago *Defender* by the end of the 1930s, shared some of Abbott's assumptions: vital though it was to fight mightily against racial proscription, segregation, and discrimination, critical though it was to have race pride, it was sheer folly to embrace nationalist politics of the sort espoused by the UNIA. Certainly, African Americans had called for the "Americanism" of the race long before 1920. Black abolitionists invoked the Americanness of slaves and free people as a means to rebut claims made by colonizationists that the United States was a "white" nation. A range of race commentators simultaneously argued for full inclusion in the U.S. body politic and harbored deep beliefs that black people had a distinct destiny throughout the nineteenth century and into the twentieth. Still, Vann's conviction that "the Negro has determined . . . to be an American" would prove prescient.[3]

When, for example, James Weldon Johnson maintained in 1934 that the "most feasible and most worthwhile . . . course" for African Americans "to follow . . . leads to our becoming an integral part of the nation, with the same rights and guarantees that are accorded to other citizens," his sentiments had similar implications as did Robert Vann's pronouncement: it was time for African Americans to be all the more assertive in laying claim to the perquisites of American citizenship; it was time, perhaps, to focus on a somewhat different form of collective destiny.[4] If African Americans' adoption of the "doctrine 'We Are All Americans'" potentially resulted in what one commentator feared was woeful "loss of all . . . racial identity" among young black women and men, the black press, for one, would nonetheless invoke and promote Americanism on an increasing basis up to and after 1930.[5]

Preoccupations over racial destiny did not altogether disappear, however, especially as the Nation of Islam emerged, in part, out of the remnants of the UNIA during the 1930s.[6] Furthermore, the shift away from the rhetorics of racial destiny was neither abrupt nor wholesale within Afro-American discourse. In 1934, the Forty-Ninth State movement called for "a new state . . . wherein colored people . . . [would] have an opportunity to work out their own destiny." A year later, the short-lived, Harlem-based periodical *Education* contained an article that identified poor housing, infant mortality, and venereal disease as conditions that compromised the "destiny of the Negro."[7] Debates about racial reproduction continued as well: two men— one from Minnesota, the other from Texas—presented opposing opinions on the "physical future of the Negro" on the pages of the *Crisis*; women and men continued to debate the desirability of interracial marriage and sex as anxieties over whether the race was "doomed to absor[p]tion" still vexed; during the summer of 1932, the *Birth Control Review* published a symposium in which race leaders contended that "quality and not mere quantity" would ensure progressive racial survival.[8] As late as 1937, pundit Thomas Kirksey even revisited late-nineteenth-century claims that "American Negro Racial Destiny" had three distinct possibilities—"amalgamation, extermination, and emigration."[9] Indeed, African Americans continued to focus upon many of the same issues as had Progressive Era race activists largely because exclusion, discrimination, and oppression remained palpable, dynamic, distorting forces in their quotidian lives.

As much as there was continuity in the issues that animated intraracial discourse during the 1930s, and whereas African Americans remained, as black Communist Louise Thompson acknowledged, "a people struggling for freedom," Afro-American discourse began to shift due to the decade's particular exigencies.[10] When the Chicago *Defender* published its own editorial cartoon in 1934 depicting yet another lone man standing at a crossroads, it posed similar collective possibilities—"intermarriage," "back to Africa," "back to the farm," "higher education," and a "49th state"—as had the *Negro World*. The *Defender*'s "crossroad puzzle," however, was less resolute and more ambiguous in which choice would lead to horizons of "success." The dark overtones also implied that the future for African Americans was ominously tenuous at a time when women, men, and children throughout the nation found themselves in the midst of a crushing economic depression whose dynamics were, in the words of one Mississippi woman, partially responsible for sending "our people . . . to untimely graves."[11]

The uncertainty and hardship presented by the Great Depression were indeed a crossroads for the race. Above and beyond President Franklin

Roosevelt's creation of a "Black Cabinet" and the Democratic Party's overtures to the race, the sociopolitical landscape was changing for descendants of Africans living in the United States. The National Association for the Advancement of Colored Peoples's attempt to secure Congressional passage of a federal antilynching bill foundered, yet its legal strategy to dismantle segregation in higher education gathered considerable force. A. Philip Randolph's Brotherhood of Sleeping Car Porters placed African Americans squarely within organized labor; at mid-decade, the National Negro Congress mobilized an array of black workers and organizations into a unified base of collective agitation for civil rights and economic recovery; black club women became more actively engaged with state and national politics with the formation of the National Council of Negro Women in 1935. On a decisively different front, interracial corps of Communists defended the Scottsboro Nine and organized agricultural workers within the South's Black Belt. Radical left politics not only made inroads into black communities, but the very presence of an active and vocal Communist Party encouraged some race editors to at once critique and defend democracy as practiced—and unfulfilled—in the United States.[12]

Concerns over black people's collective future would hardly disappear in the midst of such upheaval and change. Despite vicissitudes of the times, the crossroads at which they stood, race women and men knew that African Americans could, as Nannie Helen Burroughs put it, "work out [their] own salvation." Six decades of institution building would sustain the struggle; six decades of organizing assured activists that they had the wherewithal to devise strategies for collective survival and progress; six decades of debate proved that African Americans could withstand internal tension and dissent. The material realities of immiseration, moreover, ensured that black activists and reformers would continue to participate in a range of intraracial work. If African Americans became somewhat less anxious over the literal reproduction of the race and the very term "racial destiny" resonated less and less after 1930, the politics of racial destiny left a legacy all the same: the strategies and rhetorics of racial destiny ultimately resulted in preoccupations with women's gender performances and sexual choices, and those preoccupations were part and parcel of the masculinization of African American activism that began during the 1890s and became all the more palpable from the 1930s onward. And, significantly, the politics of racial destiny both enabled and informed the ways in which gender and sexuality shaped black activism up until the 1970s.[13]

Whereas it would be ahistorical to assert that gender and sexuality shaped

Afro-American existence, letters, and protest in the same ways after 1930 as during the decades following Reconstruction, it would be erroneous to claim that gender and sexuality were any less central to middle- and late-twentieth-century black life, thought, and politics. Both the Second World War and the Second Great Migration resulted in "social dislocation and . . . introduce[d] new tensions . . . that disrupted family life." As wartime and postwar economies provided black women with higher wages, those higher wages enabled black women to improve their individual and familial lot by granting them greater independence and allowing them to leave unsatisfactory relationships.[14] Throughout this period, the rhetoric of racial manhood spurred individual men "to reclaim the mantle of black manhood" as it powerfully informed what would become the modern civil rights movement. Without doubt, the movement pointedly called attention to the discrimination faced and the oppression endured by all African Americans. The movement nevertheless "spelled disaster . . . for organizations or movements that privileged female autonomy over racial solidarity . . . [in that placing] gender consciousness ahead of race consciousness was judged inherently selfish, divisive, and inimical to the race."[15] During the late 1960s, Black Power activists further valorized virile manhood in the wake of the controversial assertion that African American people were warped and hindered by "black matriarchy." Certain nationalists promoted feminine submissiveness as others demonized birth control as genocide; interracial sex remained controversial among some activists; black feminists challenged sexist dynamics within intraracial relationships, called attention to the coerced sterilization of black women, and even faced the need to confront homophobia among their own ranks.[16]

A deep desire to understand the end of the twentieth century and the opening of the twenty-first has prodded me to write about gender, sexuality, and reform during the late nineteenth and early twentieth centuries. When I began this project well over a decade ago, I typically heard two distinct yet eerily connected warnings: one, that the evidence I wanted to find simply did not exist; the other that drawing attention to intraracial tensions was a dangerous, undesirable undertaking that could only aid and abet racist charges that deep, gendered animosities pervade black communities. If there was indeed intriguing, provocative, and ample evidence to be discovered—and happily there was—the last thing that I wanted to do was provide historical grist for racist phantasms about my own people. I persisted with this project because I believed it important to write a historically based account of how profoundly gender and sexuality have shaped black thought and activism.

I persisted because, as I have argued elsewhere, it is my conviction that "silence might actually enable" inaccurate notions about gender, sexuality, and African Americans. The fact that I was in graduate school when Anita Hill's decision to accuse Clarence Thomas of sexual harassment resulted in overheated, incredible arguments about black women being traitors to the race only underscored the importance of undertaking a history of gender, sexuality, and black thought. Although "themes of collective survival, community mobilisation, and institution building are of signal importance to the field" of African American history, it is essential that historians analyze dynamics of intraracial tension—not to mention how, where, and why that tension involved an imbrication of gender, sexuality, and class.[17]

Hopefully, this work has accomplished at least one thing: a recasting of late-nineteenth- and early-twentieth-century African American thought that reveals the centrality of gender, sexuality, and anxieties about collective reproduction. Within these pages, I have endeavored to uncover the implications of African Americans' efforts to improve their fortunes, sociopolitical standing, health, homes, and selves. I have tried to address tensions within the race over appropriate gender roles, moral codes, and sexual behaviors. By focusing on racial reproduction, it has been my desire to highlight how discussions about the decline in African American women's fecundity could be agitated and fretful.

I selected certain subjects in order to make a particular point about the trajectory of racial destiny concepts, mainly that preponderant emphases on reforming gender and sexuality within arguments about racial destiny were ultimately conservative in that they sought to preserve Americans of African descent. In turn, this conservatism fueled beliefs that black women's sexuality needed to be monitored because their reproductive labor ultimately determined collective destiny. A primary legacy of efforts to ensure the racial future of African Americans during the late nineteenth and early twentieth centuries, then, was a conservative black nationalism that stressed racial reproduction, racial purity, and women's roles as mothers. In other words, if race was destiny, so were gender and sexuality.

Given the overall and particular thrust of my argument, then, I hope that this book speaks to those interested in questions of gender, sexuality, morality, and, indeed, nationalism. *Righteous Propagation* is a historical study that assesses dynamics during decades immediately before and after the beginning of the last century, but it also speaks to highly charged arguments and phenomena concerning race, gender, sexuality, and destiny during the late twentieth century. The 1980s and 1990s were heady for reasons other than a range of volatile discussions about census categories, sexual preference, welfare reform, reproductive rights, and AIDS. The resurgence of black nationalist politics via the Nation of Islam and Louis Farrakhan, ever-persistent arguments regarding the supposed amorality of the "black underclass," and racialized controversies over intelligence, merit, and affirmative action all left distinct marks upon the sociopolitical and cultural landscapes of the 1980s as well as the 1990s. Such discourses, debates, and phenomena appear to be retaining remarkable saliency into the new millennium. For the moment, at least, historians shall need to continue interrogating why and how many people remain convinced that gender, sexuality, class, "race," and "nation" indicate the potential, character, and future prospects of individuals as well as collectivities. We are all standing at yet another crossroads.

NOTES

PROLOGUE

1. Annie Williams (Baltimore, Md.) to William Coppinger, March 15, 1878, American Colonization Society Papers, Manuscript Division, Library of Congress, Washington, D.C. (hereafter ACS Papers), ser. 1A, vol. 230; Williams to Coppinger, March 20, 1878, ACS Papers, ser. 1A, vol. 230.

2. Williams to Coppinger, March 20, 1878, ACS Papers, ser. 1A, vol. 230.

3. "Testimony of Henry Adams," in *Report and Testimony of the Select Committee of the United States Senate to Investigate the Causes of Removal of the Negroes from the Southern States to the Northern States* (Washington, D.C.: Government Printing Office, 1880), 2:178; cited in Nell Irvin Painter, *Exodusters: Black Migration to Kansas after Reconstruction* (New York: Knopf, 1977), 77.

   The observation that Adams was "marked for assassination" — in addition to biographical information on the activist — may be found in Painter, *Exodusters*, 71–81.

4. Significantly, "colonization" had varied and shifting connotations throughout the nineteenth century for African Americans. During the antebellum period, many African American activists disparagingly discussed "colonization" in the context of white nationalists' desires to remove Negroes from the United States to Liberia under the auspices of the American Colonization Society. But, after Reconstruction, the term "colonization" — as well as "emigration" — came to signify migration within the South or United States. As Nell Painter observes of 1870s grassroots movements, "since it was envisioned that large numbers of Blacks would go together and settle together, that process was termed 'colonization.'. . . Thus, 'colonization' was synonymous with collective pioneering." See Painter, *Exodusters*, 83 n. 3.

5. Henry Adams (New Orleans, La.) to William Coppinger, July 9, 1879, ACS Papers, ser. 1A, vol. 233; Adams (Shreveport, La.) to Coppinger, November 16, 1878, ACS Papers, ser. 1A, vol. 233; Adams (New Orleans, La.) to Coppinger, July 17, 1879, ACS Papers, ser. 1A, vol. 236; Adams (Shreveport, La.) to Rutherford B. Hayes, January 5, 1878, ACS Papers, ser. 1A, vol. 230.

6. Neither Williams nor Adams is listed on a comprehensive roster of emigrants sent to Liberia by the ACS between 1865 and 1904. Williams possibly married and then migrated under her husband's surname; it is just as likely that she never emigrated, since the society was reluctant to send single female emigrants. According to Nell Painter, Henry Adams sent his last letter to the ACS in 1884 when he was living in New Orleans. See *Exodusters*, 105.

7. Born into slavery in Maryland almost twenty-five years before the Civil War, Amanda Berry Smith knew "nothing about the experience" of slavery due largely to her father, Samuel Berry, who manumitted his large family by incremental purchase after buying himself. Sam Berry's determined industry combined with the spiritual fortitude of Mariam Matthews Berry to imbue their eldest daughter with strength, yet Amanda faced hardship nonetheless. In 1854 she married at age seventeen to find herself wedded to a man whose taste for distilled spirits left him "profane and unreasonable." An infirmity nearly killed Amanda a year into her marriage; within a decade, her husband—from whom she had become estranged—died while a Union soldier. During a second, rocky marriage to James Smith that took her to New York City, sheer desperation led Amanda to remain temporarily in the employ of slatternly women who "were not straight." Smith buried four out of her five children as well. See Amanda Smith, *An Autobiography: The Story of the Lord's Dealings with Mrs. Amanda Smith, the Colored Evangelist* (Chicago: Meyer & Brother, 1893), iv, 17–23, 42, 57–63, 66–68, 122–24.

Additional biographical information may be found in Darlene Clark Hine, Elsa Barkley Brown, and Rosalyn Terborg-Penn, eds., *Black Women in America: An Historical Encyclopedia*, 2 vols. (Bloomington: Indiana University Press, 1994), 2:1072–73.

8. Smith, *Autobiography*, 286–99, 331–42, 466, 502. See also Hallie Q. Brown, comp. and ed., *Homespun Heroines and Other Women of Distinction* (Xenia: Aldine Publishing, 1926. Reprint, New York: Oxford University Press, 1988), 128–32.

While in Liberia, Smith weathered recurring, debilitating bouts of "acclimating fever." "Acclimating fever"—also referred to as "African fever" in numerous letters to the American Colonization Society by prospective emigrants to Liberia—was a folk name for malaria.

9. Smith, *Autobiography*, iii, 331–465.

As with the majority of race literature produced between 1878 and 1930, it is somewhat difficult to ascertain number of copies sold and actual readership of Smith's *Autobiography*. One contemporary source, however, claimed that the book enjoyed "wide sale." See H. F. Kletzing and W. H. Crogman, *Progress of A Race, or, The Remarkable Advancement of the Afro-American Negro* (Atlanta: J. L. Nichols, 1898. Reprint, New York: Negro Universities Press, 1969), 575.

10. Smith, *Autobiography*, 414–15.

11. Ibid., 415–17; italics in original. For a description of Smith's own arrival in Cape Palmas (on or around February 19, 1885) see pages 431–36.

Smith's narrative is not strictly chronological, therefore it is difficult to ascertain exactly when the reception in Cape Palmas occurred. Moreover, she does not provide so much as a vague reference as to month or season. Based on emigrant rosters published in the *African Repository*, the seventieth and seventy-first annual reports of the American Colonization Society, and Peter Murdza's exhaustive inventory of emigrants to Liberia after 1864, I believe that Smith must be referring to a sizable group of emigrants that left New York City on October 30, 1886, and arrived in Cape Palmas in late December; with the exception of one lone party from Florida, the entire contingent hailed from South Carolina. Given that this expedition was about twice the size of another that departed in March 1887 and since Smith's narrative underscores that the particular group of emigrants arriving in Cape Palmas was rather "large," she must be referring to the emigrants who sailed in October.

Significantly, descriptors within emigrant rosters (e.g., family position, age, occupation) released by the American Colonization Society can be problematic given that ACS agents apparently manipulated information regarding emigrants. For example, the promotional organ of the American Colonization Society — revealingly titled *The African Repository* — published selective information regarding emigrants sent. See Peter J. Murdza Jr., *Immigrants to Liberia, 1865 to 1904: An Alphabetical Listing*, Liberian Studies Research Working Paper No. 4, University of Delaware (Newark: Liberian Studies Association in America, 1975), 43; *African Repository* 63, no. 1 (January 1887): 28–29; ibid., no. 2 (April 1887): 63; *The Annual Reports of the American Colonization Society*, Vols. 64–71 (Reprint, New York: Negro Universities Press, 1969).

12. See, for example, her discussion of the fate met by an outspoken "Moses" from the South Carolina contingent named "Mr. Massie." Smith, *Autobiography*, 416–17.

13. Ibid., 458, 451–52.

14. Ibid., 451–52, 459–61.

   What Smith did or did not explicitly address in her narrative reflected both her times and her chosen profession. For example, she not only invoked nativist arguments concerning Polish, Jewish, Italian, Irish, and German immigrants to the United States during the late nineteenth century, she also spoke disdainfully of the habits, cleanliness, and overall "enlighten[ment]" of African American "new-comers" to Liberia. Finally, her conviction that racial oppression gave black Americans an even greater claim to membership in U.S. civil society reflected her time as well, in that a range of contemporary race women and men made similar assertions. Refer to pages 451–63 of her *Autobiography*.

15. Edwin S. Redkey, *Black Exodus: Black Nationalist and Back-to-Africa Movements, 1890–1910* (New Haven: Yale University Press, 1969).

16. "Testimony of Henry Adams," 101–214, esp. 104.

17. For important views on African American intellectual history or concepts of racial destiny between 1880 and 1930, see Rayford W. Logan, *The Negro in American Life and Thought: The Nadir, 1877–1901* (New York: Dial Press, 1954); August Meier, *Negro Thought in America, 1880–1915: Racial Ideologies in the Age of Booker T. Washington* (Ann Arbor: University of Michigan Press, 1963); George M. Fredrickson, *The Black Image in the White Mind: The Debate on Afro-American Character and Destiny, 1817–1914* (New York: Harper & Row, 1971);

Mia Bay, *The White Image in the Black Mind: African American Ideas about White People, 1830–1925* (New York: Oxford University Press, 1999); Richard Gray, "The Black Manifest Destiny as Motivation for Mission During the Golden Age of Black Nationalism" (Ph.D. diss., Fuller Theological Seminary, 1996).

18. Reginald Horsman, *Race and Manifest Destiny: The Origins of American Racial Anglo-Saxonism* (Cambridge: Harvard University Press, 1981), 1–6, 9–24, 116–38, 187–207, 298–303, esp. 9, 1.

19. Ibid., 25–42, passim.

20. Frederick Douglass, *The Claims of the Negro, Ethnologically Considered. An Address, Before the Literary Societies of Western Reserve College at Commencement, July 12, 1854* (Rochester: Lee, Mann, 1854); William Wells Brown, *The Black Man: His Antecedents, His Genius, and His Achievements* (New York: Thomas Hamilton, 1863); Henry Highland Garnet, *The Past and the Present Condition, and the Destiny of the Colored Race: A Discourse Delivered on the Fifteenth Anniversary of the Female Benevolent Society of Troy, New York* (Troy, N.Y.: Steam Press of J. C. Kneeland, 1848); Martin R. Delany, *The Condition, Elevation, Emigration, and Destiny of the Colored People of the United States* (Philadelphia: Martin R. Delany, 1852); Mary A. Shadd, *A Plea for Emigration: or, Notes of Canada West, in its Moral, Social, and Political Aspect: With Suggestions Respecting Mexico, W. Indies and Vancouver's Island* (Detroit: George W. Pattison, 1852); James T. Holly, *A Vindication of the Capacity of the Negro Race for Self-Government and Civilized Progress as Demonstrated by the Historical Events of the Haytian Revolution* (n.p., 1857). For revealing analysis of racialist thinking among African Americans before 1880, see Bay, *The White Image*, 13–37, 38–111. For illuminating discussion of ideological differences—one that notes Delany's deployment of "destiny"— between Delany and Douglass, see Robert S. Levine, *Martin Delany, Frederick Douglass, and the Politics of Representative Identity* (Chapel Hill: University of North Carolina Press, 1997), 58–98.

21. As Wilson Jeremiah Moses notes, the abolitionist and women's rights advocate produced work that "contain[ed] a biblically inspired perception of African Americans as a people with a special God-given mission and destiny." Tellingly, whereas Stewart's speeches strongly invoke a collective past, present, and future, she does not—as an activist of the early 1830s—literally use the term "destiny." See Moses, ed., *Classical Black Nationalism: From the American Revolution to Marcus Garvey* (New York: New York University Press, 1996), 90. For Stewart's speeches, see Marilyn Richardson, ed., *Maria W. Stewart, America's First Black Woman Political Writer* (Bloomington: Indiana University Press, 1987).

22. Whereas I believe that black people's ideas regarding their future as a collective were not always "nationalist," Wilson J. Moses situates concepts of collective destiny firmly within what he refers to as a "classical" black nationalist tradition. Refer to Wilson Jeremiah Moses, "National Destiny and the Black Bourgeois Ministry," in *The Wings of Ethiopia: Studies in African American Life and Letters*

(Ames: Iowa State University Press, 1990), 159–77, esp. 160, 174; Moses, "Introduction," in *Classical Black Nationalism*, 1–42.

23. Nira Yuval-Davis, "Gender and Nation," *Ethnic and Racial Studies* 16, no. 4 (October 1993): 621–32, esp. 623.

24. Relevant discussions of "racial destiny" between 1880 and 1930 are far too numerous to cite, but the following represent major and extended analyses: Alexander Crummell, "The Destined Superiority of the Negro," in *The Greatness of Christ and Other Sermons* (New York: Thomas Whittaker, 1882), 332–52; Rebecca Lee Crumpler, *A Book of Medical Discourses* (Boston: Cashman, Keating, 1883); Samuel Chapman, *Destiny of the Black Man* ([Muldrow?], Indian Territory: [1897?]); Pauline Hopkins, *Contending Forces: A Romance Illustrative of Negro Life North and South* (Boston: Colored Co-Operative Publishing, 1900); John Wesley Grant, *Out of the Darkness, or Diabolism and Destiny* (Nashville: National Baptist Publishing Board, 1909); Kelly Miller, "The Land of Goshen," in *Race Adjustment: Essays on the Negro in America* (New York: Neale Publishing, 1908), 154–67; Kelly Miller, "The Physical Destiny of the American Negro," in *Out of the House of Bondage: A Discussion of the Race Problem* (New York: Thomas Y. Crowell Company, 1914); Amy Jacques Garvey, ed., *Philosophy and Opinions of Marcus Garvey* (New York: Universal Publishing House, 1923–25).

Invocations of "racial destiny" in secondary literature may be found in Gail Bederman, *Manliness and Civilization: A Cultural History of Gender and Race in the United States, 1880–1917* (Chicago: University of Chicago Press, 1995), 178; and Kevin K. Gaines, *Uplifting the Race: Black Leadership, Politics, and Culture in the Twentieth Century* (Chapel Hill: University of North Carolina Press, 1996), 111.

25. I find Nell Painter's observation about race and class terminology in the late nineteenth and early twentieth centuries quite instructive and suggestive. She argues that "[a]lthough the word *class* almost never appeared in turn-of-the-century writing about the South, the hierarchy of racism expressed a clear ranking of classes, in which the word *white*, unless modified, indicated a member of the upper class, and *black*, unless modified, equaled impoverished worker." See Nell Irvin Painter, "'Social Equality' and 'Rape' in the Fin-de-Siecle South," *Southern History across the Color Line* (Chapel Hill: University of North Carolina Press, 2002), 113.

My decision to use "aspiring class" partially reflects Glenda Gilmore's argument that "middle class" was a term "never used" by "leading black men and women" as well. Moreover, both Kevin Gaines and Stephanie Shaw invoke the term "rising" when discussing educated strivers; Gaines further speaks of "aspiring and middle class members of racialized . . . populations." See Glenda Elizabeth Gilmore, *Gender and Jim Crow: Women and the Politics of White Supremacy in North Carolina, 1896–1920* (Chapel Hill: University of North Carolina Press, 1996), xix; Gaines, *Uplifting the Race*, 246, 259; Stephanie J. Shaw, *What a Woman Ought to Be and to Do: Black Professional Women Workers during the Jim Crow Era* (Chicago: University of Chicago Press, 1996), 80.

26. For analyses along these lines, see Sandra Gunning, *Race, Rape, and Lynching: The Red Record of American Literature, 1890–1912* (New York: Oxford University Press, 1996); Patricia A. Schechter, *Ida B. Wells-Barnett and American Reform, 1880–1930* (Chapel Hill: University of North Carolina Press, 2001); and Hannah Rosen, "'Not That Sort of Women': Race, Gender, and Sexual Violence during the Memphis Riot of 1866," *Sex, Love, Race: Crossing Boundaries in North American History*, ed. Martha Hodes (New York: New York University Press, 1999), 267–93.

27. Works that address and debunk these stereotypes include Herbert G. Gutman, *The Black Family in Slavery and Freedom, 1750–1925* (New York: Pantheon, 1976); Fredrickson, *Black Image in the White Mind*; John D'Emilio and Estelle Freedman, *Intimate Matters: A History of Sexuality in America* (New York: Harper & Row, 1988); Beverly Guy-Sheftall, *Daughters of Sorrow: Attitudes Toward Black Women, 1880–1920* (New York: Carlson Publishing, 1990); Anthony S. Parent Jr. and Susan Brown Wallace, "Children and Sexual Identity Under Slavery," *Journal of the History of Sexuality* 3, no. 3 (January 1993): 363–401.

28. Political, religious, medical, and reformist commentaries on racial oppression and destiny frequently invoked gender and sexuality—as well as morality. Examples include Rev. Emanuel K. Love, "Oration Delivered on Emancipation Day, January 2, 1888" (n.p., n.d.); Wesley J. Gaines, *The Negro and the White Man* ([Philadelphia?]: A.M.E. Publishing House, 1897); Lucius Henry Holsey, "Race Segregation," *How to Solve the Race Problem. The Proceedings of the Washington Conference on the Race Problem in the United States*, ed. Jesse Lawson (Washington, D.C.: Beresford Printer, 1904. Reprint.,Chicago: Afro-Am Press, 1969); Mrs. A. W. [Anne Walker] Blackwell, *The Responsibility and Opportunity of the Twentieth Century Woman* (n.p., ca. 1910); Dr. Charles Victor Roman, "The Negro Woman and the Health Problem," *The New Chivalry—Health*, Southern Sociological Congress; Houston, Texas, May 8-11, 1915, ed. James E. McCulloch (Nashville: Southern Sociological Congress, 1915), 393–405.

29. Critical texts that explore uplift, dissemblance, and respectability include Darlene Clark Hine, "Rape and the Inner Lives of Black Women in the Middle West: Preliminary Thoughts on the Culture of Dissemblance," *Signs* 14, no. 4 (Summer 1989): 912–20; Evelyn Brooks Higginbotham, *Righteous Discontent: The Women's Movement in the Black Baptist Church, 1880–1920* (Cambridge: Harvard University Press, 1993); Gaines, *Uplifting the Race*; Shaw, *What a Woman Ought to Be*; Deborah Gray White, *Too Heavy a Load: Black Women in Defense of Themselves, 1894–1994* (New York: W. W. Norton, 1999); Victoria W. Wolcott, *Remaking Respectability: African American Women in Interwar Detroit* (Chapel Hill: University of North Carolina Press, 2001).

Important analyses of gender and/or sexuality include the following: James

Oliver Horton, "Freedom's Yoke: Gender Conventions among Antebellum Free Blacks," *Feminist Studies* 12, no. 1 (Spring 1986): 51–76; Nell Irvin Painter, "'Social Equality,' Miscegenation, Labor, and Power," in *The Evolution of Southern Culture*, ed. Numan V. Bartley (Athens: University of Georgia Press, 1988), 47–67; Jim Cullen, "'I's a Man Now': Gender and African American Men," in *Divided Houses: Gender and the Civil War*, ed. Catherine Clinton and Nina Silber (New York: Oxford, 1992), 76–91; Hazel V. Carby, "Policing the Black Woman's Body in an Urban Context," *Critical Inquiry* 18, no. 4 (Summer 1992): 738–55; Claudia Tate, *Domestic Allegories of Political Desire: The Black Heroine's Text at the Turn of the Century* (New York: Oxford University Press, 1992); Christina Simmons, "African Americans and Sexual Victorianism in the Social Hygiene Movement," *Journal of the History of Sexuality* 4, no. 1 (July 1993): 51–75; Karen V. Hansen, "'No *Kisses* Is Like Youres': An Erotic Friendship between Two African American Women during the Mid-Nineteenth Century," *Gender and History* 7, no. 2 (August 1995): 153–82; Gilmore, *Gender and Jim Crow*; Tera W. Hunter, *To 'Joy My Freedom: Southern Black Women's Lives and Labors After the Civil War* (Cambridge: Harvard University Press, 1997); Leslie A. Schwalm, *A Hard Fight for We: Women's Transition from Slavery to Freedom in South Carolina* (Urbana: University of Illinois Press, 1997); Martha Hodes, *White Women, Black Men: Illicit Sex in the Nineteenth Century South* (New Haven: Yale University Press, 1997); Siobhan B. Somerville, *Queering the Color Line: Race and the Invention of Homosexuality in American Culture* (Durham: Duke University Press, 2000); Maurice O. Wallace, *Constructing the Black Masculine: Identity and Ideality in African American Men's Literature and Culture, 1775–1995* (Durham: Duke University Press, 2002).

For further discussion of African Americanist scholarship on gender and sexuality, see Michele Mitchell, "Silences Broken, Silences Kept: Gender and Sexuality in African American History," *Gender & History* 11, no. 3 (November 1999): 433–44.

30. Gender and sexuality certainly influenced the creation of all-black communities as well as scriptural notions about the future of the race; sex and gender had decisive impacts on organized religion, the political environment during and after Reconstruction, and disfranchisement. Refer to M. Elaine Roland, "A Land Where You Can Be Free: Gender, Black Nationalism, and the All-Black Towns of Oklahoma" (Ph.D. diss., University of Michigan, Ann Arbor, forthcoming); Laura Edwards, *Gendered Strife and Confusion: The Political Culture of Reconstruction* (Urbana: University of Illinois Press, 1997); Elsa Barkley Brown, "Negotiating and Transforming the Public Sphere: African American Political Life in the Transition from Slavery to Freedom," *Public Culture* 7, no. 1 (Fall 1994): 107–46; Gilmore, *Gender and Jim Crow*.

Ethiopianism emerged from scripture (Psalms 68:31) that suggested people of African descent — referred to in the Bible as "Egypt" and "Ethiopia" — would eventually thrive despite various trials and tribulations. And, as Wilson Moses points out, Ethiopianism was also predicated upon "a cyclical view of history — the idea that the ascendancy of the white race was only temporary, and that . . . divine providence . . . was working to elevate the African peoples." See Wilson J. Moses, *The Golden Age of Black Nationalism, 1850–1925* (New York: Oxford University Press, 1988), 23–24; Moses, "Introduction," in *Classical Black Nationalism*, 16.

CHAPTER ONE

1. Social Darwinist theory sharply implied that black people were such unfit subjects for civilization that African Americans were ultimately susceptible to complete extermination at the hands of Anglo-Saxons. Furthermore, George Fredrickson points out that the "notion that a racial 'struggle for supremacy' was inevitable so long as blacks and whites tried to inhabit the same soil in a state of freedom" dated back to the early 1830s when Alexis de Tocqueville toured the United States. See George M. Fredrickson, *The Black Image in the White Mind: The Debate on Afro-American Character and Destiny, 1817–1914* (New York: Harper & Row, 1971), 228–55, esp. 229. For allied discussion, see Reginald Horsman, *Race and Manifest Destiny: The Origins of American Racial Anglo-Saxonism* (Cambridge: Harvard University Press, 1981).

My reason for placing "Anglo-Saxon," "Alpine," and "Nordic" in quotation marks is based on my observation that these terms, in social Darwinist thought, typically connoted something in addition to region of origin and ethnic heritage: each one conjured up the apex of whiteness and the heights of civilization.

2. James Dubose (Orchard Knob, Tenn.) to William Coppinger, September 15, 1889, American Colonization Society Papers, Manuscript Division, Library of Congress, Washington, D.C. (hereafter ACS Papers), ser. 1A, container 275, vol. 276.

3. Thomas H. Cox (Benton Co., Miss.) to William Coppinger, October 1, 1891, ACS Papers, ser. 1A, container 281, vol. 285.

Prospective emigrants also compared the potential for freedom in Oklahoma, Kansas, and western states to Liberia. See James A. Miller (San Souci, Ark.) to Coppinger, September 9, 1891, ACS Papers, ser. 1A, container 281, vol. 284; Henry Adams (New Orleans, La.) to Coppinger, July 9, 1879, ACS Papers, ser. 1A, container 236; [J. W.?] Harvey (Helena, Ark.) to Coppinger, September 12, 1891, ACS Papers, ser. 1A, container 281, vol. 284.

4. Sucheng Chan, *Asian Americans: An Interpretive History* (New York: Twayne Publishers, 1991), 3–23, esp. 4; Tom W. Shick, *Behold the Promised Land: A History of Afro-American Settler Society in Nineteenth-Century Liberia* (Baltimore: Johns Hopkins University Press, 1980), 135.

5. Henry Adams (New Orleans, La.) to William Coppinger, November 16, 1878, ACS Papers, ser. 1A, container 233.

6. For representative reasons given by prospective emigrants, see John Wilson Jr.

(Rockville, Ind.) to William Coppinger, June 2, 1884, ACS Papers, ser. 1A, container 254; W. L. Ransom (Buffalo, Tex.) to J. Ormond Wilson, March 3, 1894, ACS Papers, ser. 1A, container 288, vol. 294; Thomas J. Fields (Nacogdoches, Tex.) to Coppinger, January 22, 1883, ACS Papers, ser. 1A, container 250; [A. Freeney?] (Mobile, Ala.) to Wilson, April 28, 1894, ACS Papers, ser. 1A, container 288, vol. 293.

7. James Harris (St. Louis, Mo.) to J. Ormond Wilson, February 5, 1894, ACS Papers, ser. 1A, container 288, vol. 294. See also Rev. R. L. Davis (Samantha, Ala.) to William Coppinger, August 31, 1891, ACS Papers, ser. 1A, container 281, vol. 284.

8. Thomas Fields (Nacogdoches, Tex.) to William Coppinger, January, 22, 1883, ACS Papers, ser. 1A, container 250; W. H. Holloway (Randall, Ark.) to Coppinger, July 6, 1891, ACS Papers, ser. 1A, container 280, vol. 284; W. H. Holloway (Randall, Ark.) to Coppinger, November 11, 1891, ACS Papers, ser. 1A, container 282, vol. 285; James A. McHenry (Vian, Indian Territory) to J. Ormond Wilson, January 1, 1898, ACS Papers, ser. 1A, container 287, vol. 292.

   For reference to Bishop Turner, see G. W. Walter, M.D., to Coppinger, [March 14, 1891?], ACS Papers, ser. 1A, container 279, vol. 282. Significantly, Edwin Redkey points out that Turner's "name was mentioned by many who wrote to the Colonization Society" in *Black Exodus: Black Nationalist and Back-to-Africa Movements, 1890–1910* (New Haven: Yale University Press, 1969), 172.

9. For diversity of opinion among relatively elite race men regarding African emigration, see "Symposium: 'What Should be the Policy of the Colored American Toward Africa,'" *A.M.E. Church Review* 2, no. 1 (July 1885): 68–75; T. Thomas Fortune, "Will the Afro-American Return to Africa?," *A.M.E. Church Review* 8, no. 4 (April 1892): 387–91; C[harles] S[pencer] Smith, *Glimpses of Africa: West and Southwest Coast* (Nashville: Publishing House A.M.E. Church Sunday School Union, 1895); William H[enry] Heard, *The Bright Side of African Life* ([Nashville?]: A.M.E. Publishing House, 1898. Reprint, New York: Negro Universities Press, 1969). In her *Autobiography*, Amanda Smith was one of few race women—save Ida B. Wells, perhaps—to offer sustained commentary on emigration. See *An Autobiography: The Story of the Lord's Dealings with Mrs. Amanda Smith, the Colored Evangelist* (Chicago: Meyer & Brother, 1893) and "Amanda Smith's Letter," *Voice of Missions* 3, no. 7 (July 1895): 2.

10. Nell Irvin Painter, *Exodusters: Black Migration to Kansas after Reconstruction* (New York: Norton, 1977), 141–45; Redkey, *Black Exodus*, 32–34, 70–71; August Meier, *Negro Thought in America, 1880–1915* (Ann Arbor: University of Michigan Press, 1966), 59–68. See also Gilbert A. Williams, *The Role of the "Christian Recorder" in the African Emigration Movement, 1854–1902* (Austin: Association for Education in Journalism and Mass Communications, 1989).

11. J. P. Barton (Talledega, Fla.) to William Coppinger, July 2, 1889, ACS Papers, ser. 1A, container 275, vol. 276.

12. Barton (Talledega, Fla.) to Coppinger, July 2, 1889, ACS Papers, ser. 1A, container 275, vol. 276.

13. See Sheldon H. Harris, *Paul Cuffe, Black America, and the African Return* (New York: Simon & Schuster, 1972).

14. William Lloyd Garrison, *Thoughts on African Colonization*, Part II (Boston: Garrison and Knapp, 1832. Reprint, New York: Arno Press, 1968), 9.

15. P. J. Staudenraus, *The African Colonization Movement, 1816–1865* (New York: Columbia University Press, 1961), esp. 17 and 251; Fredrickson, *Black Image in the White Mind*, 6–21, esp. 21. See also Marie Tyler McGraw, "The American Colonization Society in Virginia, 1816–1832: A Case Study in Southern Liberalism" (Ph.D. diss., George Washington University, 1980).

16. "Address of Rev. Elijah R. Craven, D.D.," *Fifty-Fourth Annual Report of the American Colonization Society; with the Proceedings of the Annual Meeting and of the Board of Directors, January 17 and 18, 1871* (Washington: American Colonization Society, 1871), 28–36, esp. 34.

17. Fredrickson, *Black Image in the White Mind*, 16; Rev. Robert M. Luther, D.D., *Reasons For Existence: The Annual Discourse, Delivered at the Seventy-Second Annual Meeting of the American Colonization Society, Held in the First Baptist Church, Washington, D.C.* (Washington, D.C.: Published by Request of the Society, 1889), 9, 7.

    For a more benign, benevolent statement of the society's purposes during the postbellum era, see "Our Mission," *African Repository* (hereafter *AR*) 50, no. 2 (February 1874): 47. A general account of colonization efforts during Reconstruction may be found in Willis Dolmond Boyd, "Negro Colonization in the Reconstruction Era, 1865–1870," *Georgia Historical Quarterly* 40, no. 4 (December 1956): 60–82.

18. Bruce Dorsey, "A Gendered History of African Colonization in the Antebellum United States," *Journal of Social History* 34, no. 1 (Fall 2000): 77–103, esp. 78, 83–84.

19. Howard Holman Bell, *A Survey of the Negro Convention Movement, 1830–1861* (New York: Arno Press, 1969), 29–34.

20. [A Colored Female of Philadelphia], "Emigration to Mexico," *The Liberator* 2, no. 4 (January 28, 1832): 14, reprinted in *Early Negro Writing, 1760–1837*, ed. Dorothy Porter (Boston: Beacon Press, 1971), 292–93; Maria W. Stewart, "An Address Delivered At The African Masonic Hall" (February 27, 1833), *Maria W. Stewart, America's First Black Woman Political Writer: Essays and Speeches*, ed. Marilyn Richardson (Bloomington: Indiana University Press, 1987), 61, 64.

21. Jane Rhodes, *Mary Ann Shadd Cary: The Black Press and Protest in the Nineteenth Century* (Bloomington: Indiana University Press, 1998), 28.

22. Consult "Call for a National Convention of Colored Men" and "Succeeding Conventions," in M. R. Delany, *Official Report of the Niger Valley Exploring Party*

(New York: Thomas Hamilton, 1861), 5–8. Further discussion of emigration conventions—and the convention movement at large—may be found in Bell, *Survey of the Negro Convention Movement*.

In 1854, Mary Bibb was the National Emigration Convention's Second Vice President; in 1856, both Bibb and Shadd were on the Convention's Board of Publications. See "Black Women in the United States: A Chronology," in Darlene Clark Hine, Elsa Barkley Brown, and Rosalyn Terborg-Penn, eds., *Black Women in America: An Historical Encyclopedia*, 2 vols. (Bloomington: Indiana University Press, 1992), 2:1312. For discussion of women delegates at these conventions, see Dorsey, "A Gendered History of African Colonization," 93.

23. Wilson Jeremiah Moses, *The Golden Age of Black Nationalism, 1850–1925* (New York: Oxford University Press, 1988), 27, 35. Moses further notes that immediately preceding passage of the Fugitive Slave Act, the "National Negro Convention movement . . . took a strong stand against colonization . . . while taking an occasional interest in emigration." Ibid., 34–35. See also Moses' tremendously useful and succinct "Introduction" in his edited volume *Liberian Dreams: Back to Africa Narratives from the 1850s* (University Park: The Pennsylvania State University Press, 1998) as well as Floyd J. Miller's *The Search for a Black Nationality: Black Emigration and Colonization, 1787–1863* (Urbana: University of Illinois Press, 1975).

24. Dorsey, "A Gendered History of African Colonization," 92.

25. Mary A. Shadd, *A Plea for Emigration: or, Notes of Canada West, in its Moral, Social, and Political Aspect: With Suggestions Respecting Mexico, W. Indies and Vancouver's Island* (Detroit: Printed by George W. Pattison, 1852); Martin Robinson Delany, *The Condition, Elevation, Emigration and Destiny of Colored People of the United States: Politically Considered* (Philadelphia: Published by the Author, 1852); James T. Holly, *A Vindication of the Capacity of the Negro Race for Self-Government and Civilized Progress, as Demonstrated by Historical Events of the Haytian Revolution* (New Haven: Afric-American Printing Co., 1857).

26. Martin R. Delany, *Official Report of the Niger Valley Exploring Party* (New York: Thomas Hamilton, 1861). For analysis of Delany's complex, somewhat contradictory views on African American removal to Africa, see Robert M. Kahn, "The Political Ideology of Martin Delany," *Journal of Black Studies* 14, no. 4 (June 1984): 415–40, esp. 418–19 and 435–36. For invaluable commentary that further contextualizes Delany's views on emigration and colonization, see Robert S. Levine, *Martin Delany, Frederick Douglass, and the Politics of Representative Identity* (Chapel Hill: University of North Carolina Press, 1997).

27. Rhodes, *Mary Ann Shadd Cary*, 34, 137–39. For Shadd's comments, see her "Introductory Remarks" in *A Plea for Emigration*.

28. William Nesbit, *Four Months in Liberia; or, African Colonization Exposed* (Pittsburgh: J. T. Shyrock, 1855. Reprint. New York: Arno Press, 1969), esp. 27, 46–

50; Samuel Williams, *Four Years in Liberia: A Sketch of the Life of the Reverend Samuel Williams... Together with an Answer to Nesbit's Book* (Philadelphia: King & Baird, Printers, 1857. Reprint. New York: Arno Press, 1969), esp. 23, 61, 19.

In the introduction to the Arno reprint *Two Black Views of Liberia* (a volume which combines Nesbit and Williams), Edwin Redkey notes that Williams charged Nesbit "attacked Liberia because he needed money from the sale of the book and because he came under the influence of [Martin] Delany." "Introduction," vi–ii.

29. "Liberian Independence Day at Savannah, Ga.," *AR* 51, no. 9 (September 1865): 273; *AR* 55, no. 4 (October 1879): 115–17, esp. 116.

30. "Fortieth Anniversary Celebration," *AR* 63, no. 4 (October 1887): 117–18, esp. 118; "Liberia Day at New Orleans," *AR* 63, no. 2 (April 1887): 53–56, esp. 55. The same article reports that child celebrants sang a song that would become an anthem of sorts for Marcus Garvey's Universal Negro Improvement Association— "From Greenland's Icy Mountains." Descriptions of other Liberia Days include "Liberian Independence Day at Savannah, Ga.," *AR* 51, no. 9 (September 1865): 273; "Celebration at New Orleans," *AR* 59, no. 4 (October 1883): 121. Additional commentary on how Liberia Day galas could "sti[r] up considerable enthusiasm on the subject of colonization" may be found in *AR* 55, no. 4 (October 1879): 115–17, esp. 116. For reference to Henry Adams, see *AR* 51, no. 9 (October 1883): 121.

Apparently, African Americans in New Orleans maintained a fairly committed tradition of celebrating Liberia's Independence Day—as late as 1894, J. Wesley Pierce informed the ACS that "thair has been for some years a very healthy feeling in this section for the Liberian Republic." J. Wesley Pierce (New Orleans, La.) to J. Ormond Wilson, August 8, 1894, ACS Papers, ser. 1A, container 286, vol. 291; see also Pierce to Wilson, July 22, 1894, ACS Papers, ser. 1A, container 286, vol. 291.

31. Testimony of Willis Johnson, Columbia, South Carolina, July 3, 1871, and Testimony of Charlotte Fowler, Spartanburgh, South Carolina, July 6, 1871, in *A Documentary History of the Negro People in the United States: From the Reconstruction Era to 1910*, ed. Herbert Aptheker (New York: Citadel Press, 1951), 2:572–76.

32. "The African Emigrant's Song," *AR* 51, no. 1 (January 1875): 28. The stanzas quoted here are the first two of three. See also her "Come Over and Help Us," *AR* 50, no. 12 (December 1874): 325. Martin herself might have remained in Columbia instead of emigrating; see *AR* 62, no. 1 (January 1886). Given the *African Repository*'s interracial reader and subscriber base, it is possible that Martin was a southern white woman who supported emigration. As I have been unable to ascertain her first and maiden names, it is also difficult to know whether she had previously emigrated only to return to the United States on a temporary or permanent basis.

33. Alfred Brockenbrough Williams, *The Liberian Exodus* (Charleston: News & Courier, 1878), 11; italics in original. Not only did Williams refer to stories of

persecution as a fantastic "outrage mill," he clearly did not believe said "honest looking colored man." Although Williams's coverage is peppered with racist judgments, it remains a valuable firsthand account of the expedition: for example, the reporter notes class differences among emigrants. See Williams, *The Liberian Exodus*, 11, 3, 9.

34. Melinda Meek Hennessey, "Racial Violence during Reconstruction: The 1876 Riots in Charleston and Cainhoy," in *Black Freedom/White Violence, 1865–1900*, ed. Donald G. Nieman (New York: Garland Publishing, 1994), 186–98, esp. 192; "That Ship," *Christian Recorder*, March 7, 1878, 2; "African Movement," *Christian Recorder*, April 18, 1878, 1. For powerful analysis of the sexualized nature of mob violence immediately after the Civil War, see Hannah Rosen, "'Not That Sort of Women': Race, Gender, and Sexual Violence during the Memphis Riot of 1866," in *Sex, Love, Race: Crossing Boundaries in North American History*, ed. Martha Hodes (New York: New York University Press, 1999), 267–93.

35. George B. Tindall, *South Carolina Negroes, 1877–1900* (Columbia: University of South Carolina Press, 1952), 153–68, esp. 154–56; Letter, *AR* 53, no. 2 (April 1877): 38. Whereas the LEA was an independent effort, its organizers did correspond with the ACS. See Tindall, *South Carolina Negroes*, 158.

   South Carolinians formed a decisive majority within the LEA, but a few emigrants were from Georgia, North Carolina, Florida, and Alabama. See Williams, *The Liberian Exodus*, 31–32.

36. "Consecration of the Exodus Bark 'Azor'" and "The Ark of the 'Exodus,'" *Christian Recorder*, April 4, 1878, 1.

   Another source claimed the *Azor* was a former slave ship used "in the fruit trade between Boston and the Azore Islands." See Rev. Thomas S. Malcom, "Is it Suitable for Emigrants?," *AR* 55, no. 1 (January 1879): 19–22, esp. 19.

37. *AR* 54, no. 4 (October 1878): 125; Tindall, *South Carolina Negroes*, 160; *AR* 54, no. 3 (July 1878): 77–78. For biographical information on some LEA leaders (as well as other post–Reconstruction era emigrationists who were former officeholders) see Eric Foner, ed., *Freedom's Lawmakers: A Dictionary of Black Officeholders during Reconstruction* (New York: Oxford University Press, 1993).

   According to most secondary sources, the *Azor* left Charleston Harbor with 206 people. However, Williams reported a total of 274, Harrison Bouey claimed there were 256, and another contemporary report—one that relayed the story of unhappy emigrants who returned to the United States in 1879—claimed 370 sailed. Williams, *The Liberian Exodus*, 32; Harrison Bouey, "The Azor Passengers," *AR* 56, no. 6 (October 1880): 109–10, esp. 110; "Home From Liberia," *Herald* (New York, N.Y.), November 19, 1879, 5.

   Whatever the actual total, George Tindall points out the number of people desiring to go exceeded available space. See "The Liberian Exodus of 1878," *South Carolina Historical Magazine* 53, no. 3 (July 1952): 133–45, esp. 139.

38. Williams, *The Liberian Exodus*, 5–8, 13, 33, 21. For insight—albeit skewed and

incomplete—into how the emigrants felt about Williams and his work, see *The Liberian Exodus*, 8, 13, 27.

39. "The Exodus," *AR* 55, no. 2 (April 1879): 36–37; "Statement of Captain Richardson," *AR* 56, no. 1 (January 1880): 24–26; "Movements of the Azor," *AR* 54, no. 4 (October 1878): 125; "The Bark Azor," *AR* 56, no. 3 (July 1880): 67–68; "The Azor Passengers," *AR* 56, no. 2 (April 1880): 37–38.

40. "Home from Liberia," *Herald*, November 19, 1879, 5. There are at least three reasons the *Herald* story assumed the tone it did: A. B. Williams had already primed the reading public to think of the *Azor* expedition as a complete failure; tabloid tales of scandal sell papers; and, during the late 1870s and early 1880s—the early years of national reconciliation—a report of black mismanagement was probably more palatable than an account of success in a land governed by Americo-Liberians and African Americans. Black emigrants who decided to stick it out in Liberia knew that their detractors had ulterior motives and some made concerted efforts to offer pointed rebuttals.

41. "Hon. Daniel B. Warner," *AR* 57, no. 7 (July 1881): 107; "The Azor Emigrants," *AR* 56, no. 2 (April 1880): 58–59; "Death of President Warner," *AR* 57, no. 5 (April 1881): 52; "Ex-President Warner," in *Sixty-Fourth Annual Report of the American Colonization Society* (Washington, D.C.: American Colonization Society, 1881), 18; Tindall, *South Carolina Negroes*, 165–67.

42. D. B. Warner (Monrovia, Liberia) to William Coppinger, June 8, 1878, ACS Papers, ser. 1B, container 18; Warner to Coppinger, August 5, 1979, ACS Papers, ser. 1B, container 19; Warner to Coppinger, August 12, 1878, ACS Papers, ser. 1B, container 18.

43. Bouey, "The Azor Passengers"; "The Azor and Passengers," *AR* 57, no. 2 (February 1881): 19–20; "Ten Years in Liberia," *AR* 65, no. 4 (October 1889): 121–22. Both William Henry Heard (U.S. consul general to Liberia during the 1890s) and Henry McNeal Turner were also among those who claimed that *Azor* emigrants had managed to make a way for themselves in Liberia. See Heard, *Bright Side of African Life*, 15, 26; Papers of Henry McNeal Turner, Manuscript Division, Moorland-Spingarn Collection, Howard University, folder 13, 1–2.

   For additional information on the Irons family, consult "A Talk With a Returned Emigrant," *AR* 61, no. 4 (October 1885): 120–22; "Dr. Blyden in Charleston," *AR* 66, no. 1 (January 1890): 28–29; Letter to Bishop Turner, *Voice of Missions* 1, no. 1 (January 1893): 3; Debra Lynn Newman, "The Emergence of Liberian Women in the Nineteenth Century" (Ph.D. diss., Howard University, 1984), 176–79.

44. "Exodus Movement in Arkansas," *AR* 54, no. 1 (January 1878): 29–30; "Contemplated Exodus," *AR* 54, no. 2 (April 1878): 35–37; Painter, *Exodusters*, 139.

   One of the more publicized of these independent efforts, the Liberia Exodus Arkansas Colony, would be markedly less successful than the Liberia Exodus

Association. See Adell Patton Jr., "The 'Back-to-Africa' Movement," *Arkansas Historical Quarterly* 51, no. 2 (Summer 1992): 164–77.

45. I. W. Penn (Augusta, Ark.) to William Coppinger, April 10, 1891, ACS Papers, ser. 1A, containers 279 and 280, vols. 282 and 283.

46. *AR* 54, no. 2 (April 1878): 35–37.

According to an annual report of the ACS, the petition by the Emigration Aid Society was presented in the House of Representatives in late October, 1877. See *Sixty-First Annual Report of the American Colonization Society* (Washington, D.C.: American Colonization Society, 1878), 9–10.

47. "First Impressions in Liberia," *AR* 54, no. 3 (July 1878): 90–91; "Education," *AR* 56, no. 2 (April 1880): 43–44; "Experience and Observation," *Sixty-Fifth Annual Report of the American Colonization Society* (Washington, D.C.: American Colonization Society, 1882), 7–8; Sherwood Capps (Brewerville, Liberia) to William Coppinger (October 28, 1878), ACS Papers, ser. 1B, vol. 19, pt. 2. It should be noted that the last source erroneously states that Capps emigrated in 1877: in actuality, he sailed from New York Harbor on January 2, 1878. See "Roll of Emigrants," *AR* 54, no. 2 (April 1878): 53; and Murdza, *Immigrants to Liberia*, 12.

48. This estimate is drawn from "Emigrants Sent By the American Colonization Society," *Sixty-Ninth Annual Report of the American Colonization Society* (Washington, D.C.: American Colonization Society, 1886), 24. However, it is important to realize that this figure is considerably lower than early postbellum totals; refer to Murdza, "Introduction," in *Immigrants to Liberia*, i–ii.

49. Redkey, *Black Exodus*, 6–7.

50. "Minutes of the Board of Directors," *AR* 63, no. 2 (April 1887): 49–51; *Seventieth Annual Report of the American Colonization Society* (Washington, D.C.: American Colonization Society, 1887), 7–9. See also "Memorial From the Descendants of Africa," *AR* 66, no. 2 (April 1890): 49–51.

51. *Seventieth Annual Report of the American Colonization Society*, 8–9; Painter, *Exodusters*, 185–205. For consideration of how some Exodusters became interested in emigration—as well as discussion that not all Exodusters were millenarian— see Painter, *Exodusters*, 256–61, 205–56.

52. *AR* 66, no. 2 (April 1890): 46–47. For capsule summaries of each bill, consult "Governmental Action," *Seventy-Third Annual Report of the American Colonization Society* (Washington, D.C., 1890), 6–7. Reference to yet another bill introduced in late 1889 by "Mr. Thompson of Ohio" may be found in "Half a Million Desire to Go," *AR* 66, no. 2 (April 1890): 51–52. See also Redkey, *Black Exodus*, 47.

53. Redkey, *Black Exodus*, 59–72; *Official Compilation of Proceedings of the Afro-American League National Convention, Held at Chicago, January 15, 16, 17, 1890* (Chicago: J. C. Battles and R. B. Cabbell, 1890), 28, 16, 37, 38.

54. Fortune edited the New York *Age*, Cooper the Indianapolis *Freeman*, Mitchell

the Richmond *Planet*, and Chase the Washington *Bee*. I borrow the term "best men" from Glenda Gilmore's *Gender and Jim Crow: Women and the Politics of White Supremacy in North Carolina, 1896–1920* (Chapel Hill: University of North Carolina Press, 1996), 61–89.

It is important to note that the league's proceedings refer to "ladies" in attendance but do not name any of the women who were there. Since Ferdinand Barnett was there, one could surmise that Ida Wells-Barnett—along with many of her contemporaries in the club movement—was also involved with the league. Kevin Gaines identifies Wells-Barnett as one of the "dissident black leaders" responsible for establishing the league. Gaines, *Uplifting the Race: Black Leadership, Politics, and Culture in the Twentieth Century* (Chapel Hill: University of North Carolina Press, 1996), 29.

55. By the turn of the century, Heard served as Liberian consul general during the Cleveland Administration. Heard presided over the Colored National Emigration Association and became involved in Charles Alexander's Liberian Development Association after the turn of the century.

Predictably, perhaps, Heard's mentor Henry McNeal Turner was among the few African Americans who publicly supported the Butler Bill. The bishop even suggested that emigration bills could be considered reparations since the United States owed "the colored race forty billions of dollars anyway." See "A Colored Bishop on Emigration," *AR* 66, no. 2 (April 1890): 54–55.

56. B. J. Kirkland (Valdosta, Ga.) to William Coppinger, November 11, 1889, ACS Papers, ser. 1A, container 275, vol. 277; "The Colored Emigrating Society," ACS Papers, ser. 1A, container 276, vol. 279; J. S. Daniels (Pine Bluff, Ark.) to Coppinger, January 26, 1890, ACS Papers, ser. 1A, container 276, vol. 278.

57. Some ACS correspondents observed that rumors about emigrants being sold into slavery were commonplace; the possibility that these rumors existed in connection with the Butler Bill is speculation on my part. See A. L. McCoy (McAlpin, Fla.) to William Coppinger, November 10, 1889, ACS Papers, ser. 1A, container 275, vol. 277; and John Williams (W. Atlanta, Ga.) to Coppinger, September 24, 1891, ACS Papers, ser. 1A, container 281, vol. 284.

Edwin Redkey points out that the appearance of the colonization bills in 1890 was due to a recent Federal Elections Bill (also known as a "force bill") by the Republican Party that was an effort to ensure black men would retain the franchise. See Redkey, *Black Exodus*, 59–61.

58. L. A. Johnson and Henry Baily (Rich, Miss.) to William Coppinger, January 3, 1891, ACS Papers, ser. 1A, container 279, vol. 282; Thos. Patterson and W. H. Jackson (Stephens, Ark.) to Coppinger, January 3, 1891, ACS Papers, ser. 1A, container 279, vol. 282.

59. Cornelius Smith (W. Baton Rouge Parish, La.) to William Coppinger, March 2, 1883, ACS Papers, ser. 1A, container 250. Brief discussion of underground activity may be found in Painter, *Exodusters*, 92.

For evidence of mass meetings, see "Convention!" (broadside), ca. 1878, ACS Papers, ser. 1A, container 233; "Notice! Notice! The Colored Citizens of Ouachita and Adjoining Counties" (broadside), ca. fall 1890, ACS Papers, ser. 1A, container 278, vol. 281; Colored Colonization Association broadside, ca. 1891, ACS Papers, ser. 1A, container 280, vol. 283.

60. See, for example, Samuel Chapman, *Constitution of the Liberian Emigration Clubs*; *Destiny of the Black Man* ([Muldrow?], Indian Territory: [1897?]), 13-14.

61. Mary E. Jackson (Atlanta, Ga.) to William Coppinger, June 16, 1891, ACS Papers, ser. 1A, container 280, vol. 283; Jackson to Coppinger, May 20, 1891, ACS Papers, ser. 1A, container 280, vol. 283; Ines Dargan (Morrilton, Ark.) to Coppinger, February 21, 1891, ACS Papers, ser. 1A, container 279, vol. 282; "Letter from Dr. Wade About the Steamship," *Voice of Missions* 1, no. 3 (March 1893): 1.

The reference to the women's organization in New Orleans appears in Reverend Thomas S. Malcom, "Is it Suitable for Emigrants?," *AR* 55, no. 1 (January 1879): 19-22, esp. 20. It is, however, important to realize that since the ACS published the *African Repository* and because the society had a vested interest in portraying emigrationism as a popular movement, it is possible that the ACS inflated the numbers of people who wanted to emigrate. In other words, the actual number of members in the women's organization in New Orleans might have been considerably lower.

62. Here, I take my lead from Elsa Barkley Brown's persuasive article on postbellum African American public spheres, "Negotiating and Transforming the Public Sphere," where she contends black women were vital political actors in the years immediately after slavery. She further notes that by the end of the century women's political viability had eroded somewhat, leading them to "attemp[t] to retain space they traditionally had held in the immediate postemancipation period." Brown, "Negotiating and Transforming the Public Sphere: African American Political Life in the Transition from Slavery to Freedom," *Public Culture* 7, no. 1 (Fall 1994): 107-46. See also Dorsey, "A Gendered History of African Colonization."

63. J. N. Walker (Denver, Colo.) to William Coppinger, October 4, 1889, ACS Papers, ser. 1A, container 275, vol. 277; [S. A.?] Billingslea (Providence, R.I.) to Coppinger, August 28, 1894, ACS Papers, ser. 1A, container 288, vol. 294. The original, full name of Walker's club was the "Western African Emigration Society." See *AR* 63, no. 4 (October 1887): 118-19.

64. Joseph Hunter (Roland, Ark.) to William Coppinger, February 3, 1891, ACS Papers, container 279, vol. 282; V. J. E. Granger Sr. (Paulding, Miss.) to J. Ormond Wilson, September 12, 1894, ACS Papers, container 286, vol. 291; W. M. Hall (Jackson, Ga.) to Wilson, April 24, 1895, ACS Papers, container 287, vol. 293; Paul Garrett (Chicago, Ill.) to Wilson, May 25, 1897, ACS Papers, container 286, vol. 292; "Information About Going to Liberia," ACS Papers, ser. 1A, container 283, vol. 286.

65. Redkey, *Black Exodus*, 47-58, esp. 49, 52; Edward Wilmot Blyden, "The Call of

Providence to the Descendants of Africa in America," in *Liberia's Offering* (New York: John A. Gray, 1862), 67–91, esp. 68. For more on Blyden's views regarding racial intermixture, see Edward Wilmot Blyden, "On Mixed Races in Liberia," in *Annual Report of the American Colonization Society* (Washington, D.C.: Smithsonian Institution, 1871), 386–89; Hollis R. Lynch, *Edward Wilmot Blyden: Pan-Negro Patriot* (London: Oxford University Press, 1964).

66. J. W. Turner et al. (Poplar Grove, Ark.) to William Coppinger, August 30, 1891, ACS Papers, ser. 1A, container 281, vol. 284; G. W. Lowe (Holly Grove, Ark.) to Coppinger, September 12, 1891, ACS Papers, ser. 1A, container 281, vol. 284; W. W. Caldwell (Poplar Grove, Ark.) to Coppinger, September 30, 1891, ACS Papers, ser. 1A, container 281, vol. 284; Redkey, *Black Exodus*, 110–11.

67. *AR* 63, no. 2 (April 1887): 49–51; *AR* 66, no. 2 (April 1890): 49–51; Redkey, *Black Exodus*, 47, 73, 150–70; *Voice of Missions* 1, no. 9 (September 1893): 2; J. Fred Rippy, "A Negro Colonization Project in Mexico," *Journal of Negro History* 6 (January 1921): 66–73; Mozell C. Hill, "The All-Negro Communities of Oklahoma: The Natural History of a Social Movement," *Journal of Negro History* 3, no. 1 (July 1946): 254–68; Norman L. Crockett, *The Black Towns* (Lawrence: Regents Press of Kansas, 1979). See also M. Elaine Roland, "A Land Where You Can Be Free: Gender, Black Nationalism, and the All-Black Towns of Oklahoma" (Ph.D. diss., University of Michigan, Ann Arbor, forthcoming).

   Late nineteenth-century Afro-Americans rarely used the term "nationalism" but instead spoke of "nationalization" or "Negro nationality"; when discussing the possibility of carving a black nation out of the United States, they occasionally used "segregation."

68. William Fairly (Laurinburg, N.C.) to William Coppinger, December 25, 1889, ACS Papers, ser. 1A, container 275, vol. 277.

69. Redkey, *Black Exodus*, 7; [C. H. Hafer?] (England, Ark.) to William Coppinger, April 20, 1891, ACS Papers, ser. 1A, container 280, vol. 283; J. W. Harvey (Helena, Ark.) to Coppinger, September 21, 1891, ACS Papers, ser. 1A, container 281, vol. 284; R. F. Green (Metropolis City, Ill.) to J. Ormond Wilson, November 24, 1892, ACS Papers, ser. 1A, container 288, vol. 294.

70. Ollie [Olive] Edwards (Columbus, Ga.) to William Coppinger, ca. July 1889, ACS Papers, ser. 1A, container 275, vol. 276; Application of Edwards Family, ca. July 1889, ACS Papers, ser. 1A, container 275, vol. 276; Edwards to Coppinger, September 11, 1889, ACS Papers, ser. 1A, container 275, vol. 276.

71. Edwards to Coppinger, January 13, 1890, ACS Papers, ser. 1A, container 276, vol. 278; Edwards to Coppinger, July 13, 1890, ACS Papers, ser. 1A, container 272, vol. 280; Edwards to Coppinger, February 23, 1890, ACS Papers, ser. 1A, container 276, vol. 278; Edwards to Coppinger, October 25, 1890, ACS Papers, ser. 1A, container 278, vol. 281.

   Apparently, the Edwards family made it to Liberia safely. The last piece of correspondence I have been able to locate regarding Ollie Edwards is a letter in which her niece asks Coppinger about her aunt's health and whereabouts; Coppinger assured her "Mr. & Mrs. Edwards and children . . . safely and duly arrived at Grand Bassa, Liberia." See Julia Adams (Columbus, Ga.) to William Coppinger, July 7, 1891, ACS Papers, ser. 1A, container 280, vol. 283; Coppinger to Adams, July 10, 1891, ACS Papers, ser. 2, container 35.

72. See, for example, Emma Jones (Elizabeth City, N.C.) to William Coppinger, March 26, 1878, ACS Papers, ser. 1A, container 230; Jones to Coppinger, April 28, 1879, ACS Papers, ser. 1A, container 235; Jones to Coppinger, January 5, 1880, ACS Papers, ser. 1A, container 238; Jones to Coppinger, November 10, 1883, ACS Papers, ser. 1A, container 253.

73. Ollie [Olive] Edwards to William Coppinger, October 5, 1890, ACS Papers, ser. 1A, container 278, vol. 281; W. Carter Payne (Warrenton, Ga.) to J. Ormond Wilson, January 9, 1893, ACS Papers, container 288, vol. 294.

For evidence that people received information via lectures and word of mouth, see E. W. Edwards (Bushnell, Fla.) to William Coppinger, October 7, 1889, ACS Papers, ser. 1A, container 275, vol. 277; and H. H. Rhoads (Bushnell, Fla.) to Coppinger, [October 6?], 1889, ACS Papers, ser. 1A, container 275, vol. 277. See also Thomas Taylor's letter for an example of someone who wanted to "subscribe for a paper so I can learn something about this Negro Exodus." Thomas Taylor (Turner, Ark.) to Coppinger, ca. December 1891, ACS Papers, ser. 1A, container 282, vol. 285.

74. "Information About Going to Liberia," 4.

75. For discussion of this subject, consult Newman, "The Emergence of Liberian Women," 199–204.

76. Nellie Richardson (Boston, Mass.) to William Coppinger, October 9, 1883, ACS Papers, ser. 1A, container 253; Richardson to Coppinger, November 19, 1883, ACS Papers, ser. 1A, container 253.

Sample female emigrants' occupations were culled from the ACS Papers, ser. 1A, containers 275–85.

77. David Green & J. W. Sessions (Washington Co., Ga.) to J. Ormond Wilson, February 6, 1895, ACS Papers, ser. 1A, container 288, vol. 294.

78. Georgia E. L. Patton, "Brief Autobiography of a Colored Woman," *Liberia* 3 (November 1893): 78–79; S. W. McLean (Chambers Co., Ala.) to William Coppinger, April 11, 1891, ACS Papers, ser. 1A, container 280, vol. 283.

79. H. C. Cade (Camden, Ark.) to William Coppinger, January 18, 1891, ACS Papers, ser. 1A, container 279, vol. 282; C. W. Wofford (Camden, Ark.) to Coppinger, September 13, 1890, ACS Papers, ser. 1A, container 278, vol. 280; Mary J. Evans (Muldrow, Indian Territory) to Coppinger, December 31, 1891, ACS Papers, ser. 1A, container 282, vol. 285.

80. Gemel B. H. Rutherford (Memphis, Tenn.) to William Coppinger, February 10, 1884, ACS Papers, ser. 1A, container 254. "A Talk With a Returned Emigrant," *AR* 61, no. 4 (October 1885): 120–22.

81. Lenwood Davis asserts that "economics was the predominate reason Blacks wanted to go to Liberia." Whereas I think this was certainly the case with many prospective emigrants, I believe Davis underplays the sway of other powerful factors. See Lenwood G. Davis, "Black American Images of Liberia, 1877–1914," *Liberian Studies Journal* 6, no. 1 (1975): 53–72, esp. 55.

82. George Giles (Pittsburgh, Pa.) to William Coppinger, January 10, 1883, ACS Papers, ser. 1A, container 250; Coppinger to Giles, January 13, 1883, ACS Papers, ser. 2, container 30; Newman, "The Emergence of Liberian Women," 85.

83. F. M. Gilmore et al. (Pastoria, Ark.) to William Coppinger, April 15, 1891, ACS Papers, ser. 1A, container 280, vol. 283; James Dubose to Coppinger, February 12, 1891, ACS Papers, ser. 1A, container 279, vol. 282.

84. "A Nut for the Negro Philosophers to Crack," *Voice of Missions* 2, no. 5 (May 1894): 2.

85. Redkey, *Black Exodus*, 177–79. Although I agree with Redkey that Turner controlled the *Voice*, I disagree with his assessment that the paper was little more than the bishop's "mouthpiece." Examples of antiemigrationist views and topical items include Bishop B. F. Lee, "The Negro is not a Scullion Here," *Voice of Missions* 2, no. 11 (November 1894): 1; and "Glorious Future for Mankind," *Voice of Missions* 2, no. 7 (July 1894): 2.

86. "About Going to Africa," *Voice of Missions* 2, no. 1 (January 1894): 3. The notice ran from December 1893 until at least September 1894.

87. Henry McNeal Turner, Convention Call, *Voice of Missions* 1, no. 8 (August 1893), quoted in Redkey, *Black Exodus*, 184; T. McCants Stewart, *Liberia: The Americo-Liberian Republic. Being Some Impressions of the Climate, Resources, and People, Resulting from Personal Observations and Experiences in West Africa* (New York: Edward O. Jenkins' Sons, 1886), 12, 76–77, 82.

88. F. [S.?] Marion (Columbus, Miss.) to William Coppinger, March 24, 1883, ACS Papers, ser. 1A, container 250; Peter Lawrence (Boston, Mass.) to Coppinger, February 28, 1884, ACS Papers, ser. 1A, container 254; W. Carter Payne (South Philadelphia, Pa.) to J. Ormond Wilson, n.d., ACS Papers, ser. 1A, container 288, vol. 294; John Carter (Fox Lake, Wisc.) to Coppinger, November 21, 1883, ACS Papers, ser. 1A, container 253; Carter to Coppinger, November 24, 1883, ACS Papers, ser. 1A, container 253; *AR* 67, no. 1 (January 1891): 31.

89. Neither Murdza's *Immigrants to Liberia, 1865 to 1904* nor emigrant inventories published by the American Colonization Society include a Carter family consisting of a woman with children after John Carter's departure in 1890.

There are a few possibilities as to the fate of the rest of John Carter's family. His wife and children most likely stayed in the United States in the event that John established a new household with another woman after he emigrated, if he died in Liberia before his family could join him, or if Carter became a returnee shortly after his arrival in Africa. It is also possible that after John Carter sailed, the family might have fallen upon hard times or decided against emigrating. Even if the rest of the Carter family remained committed to the idea of going to Liberia, passionate emigrationists such as James Dubose never left the United States because poverty prevented them from so doing. Negative publicity could also have discouraged Mrs. Carter and the children: newspaper articles about death, dissipation, and derelict settlements in Liberia were especially effective in rattling prospective emigrants, eroding their resolve, and influencing them to remain stateside. If this was the case, then the Carter household might have been permanently fractured.

90. Emigrants desiring to return to the United States turned to the ACS for assistance. For a detailed example of such correspondence, see May Withers et al. (Cape Mount, Liberia) to William Coppinger, April 29, 1889, ACS Papers, ser. 1B, vol. 26, pt. 2.

91. Anna Logan (Atlanta, Ga.) to William Coppinger, February 23, 1891, ACS Papers, ser. 1A, container 279, vol. 282; Logan to Coppinger, ca. March 1891, ACS Papers, ser. 1A, container 279, vol. 282; See also W. W. Watkins (Atlanta, Ga.) to Coppinger, October 16, 1891, ACS Papers, ser. 1A, container 281, vol. 285; Madison Stones (Atlanta, Ga.) to Coppinger, ca. June 1891, ACS Papers, ser. 1A, container 280, vol. 283.

92. Logan to Coppinger, ca. August 3, 1891, ACS Papers, ser. 1A, container 281, vol. 284; Coppinger to Logan, August 6, 1891, ACS Papers, ser. 2, container 35; Logan to Coppinger, October 2, 1891, ACS Papers, ser. 1A, container 281, vol. 284; clipping, ACS Papers, ser. 1A, container 281, vol. 284; Logan to Coppinger, October 8, 1891, ACS Papers, ser. 1A, container 281, vol. 284.

93. Redkey, *Black Exodus*, 154.

94. Ibid., 155–62.

95. Ibid., 162–69; clipping, ACS Papers, ser. 1A, container 281, vol. 284.

96. Redkey, *Black Exodus*; see also *AR* 63, no. 2 (April 1887): 49–51, esp. 50.

97. D. E. Brown (Laurens Co., Ga.) to J. Ormond Wilson, September 7, 1894, ACS Papers, ser. 1A, container 288, vol. 294; Wesley John Gaines, *The Negro and the White Man* ([Philadelphia?]: A.M.E. Publishing House, 1897. Reprint, New York: Negro Universities Press, 1969), 203–12, esp. 211.

98. "Black Women in the United States: A Chronology," 2:1317; William E. Bittle and Gilbert Geis, *The Longest Way Home: Chief Alfred C. Sam's Back-to-Africa Movement* (Detroit: Wayne State University Press, 1964).

99. Symposium on Emigration, *Freeman* (Indianapolis, Ind.), November 25, 1893, 2–6. For additional commentary regarding Wells, see Patricia A. Schechter, *Ida B. Wells-Barnett and American Reform, 1880–1930* (Chapel Hill: University of North Carolina Press, 2001), 173–74.

100. W. S. Scarborough, "The Exodus — A Suicidal Scheme," *Christian Recorder*, January 3, 1878, 4; W. H. Crogman (Atlanta, Ga.) to William Coppinger, December 10, 1883, ACS Papers, ser. 1A, container 253; W. H. Crogman, "Negro Education — Its Helps and Hindrances. Delivered Before the National Teachers' Asso-

ciation, at Madison, Wis., July 16, 1884," *Talks for the Times*, 2nd ed. (Cincinnati: Jennings & Pye, 1896), 55–56.

101. Symposium on Emigration, 2–6; John Wright, "A Plea for Africa," *Freeman*, April 2, 1892, 2.

Redkey observes that out of thirty-nine participants, twenty-two rejected emigration outright; he also provides a rather thorough account of Turner's convention where approximately "800 delegates joined a throng of local blacks to hear Bishop Turner's opening address." *Black Exodus*, 183–94.

Representative antiemigrationist sentiment includes Rev. Emanuel K. Love, "Oration Delivered on Emancipation Day, January 2, 1888" (n.p., n.d.), 6; Rev. R. F. Hurley, "Why We Should Not Go to Africa," *Christian Recorder*, February 21, 1878, 1; Rev. Andrew J. Chamber, "American Versus Africa," *Christian Recorder*, March 7, 1878, 1; Rev. T. E. Knox, "The Negro is at Home Here," *Christian Recorder*, May 15, 1890, 5.

102. Redkey, *Black Exodus*, 7; Painter, *Exodusters*, 88.

103. As quoted in W. H. Holloway (Randall, Ark.) to William Coppinger, July 6, 1891, ACS Papers, ser. 1A, container 280, vol. 284.

CHAPTER TWO

1. H[enry] B[lanton] Parks, *Africa: The Problem of the New Century; The Part the African Methodist Episcopal Church is to have in its Solution* (New York: A.M.E. Church, 1899), 5, 8–9, 20. The brief biographical information used here is from Horace Talbert's *The Sons of Allen* (Xenia, Ohio: Aldine Press, 1906), 212–14.

2. Parks assumed the post in 1896; see Talbert, *The Sons of Allen*, 214.

For general overviews of African American viewpoints on European imperial campaigns in Africa, see Sylvia Jacobs, *The African Nexus: Black American Perspectives on the European Partitioning of Africa, 1880–1920* (Westport, Conn.: Greenwood Press, 1981), and Elliott P. Skinner, *African Americans and U.S. Policy toward Africa, 1850–1924: In Defense of Black Nationality* (Washington, D.C.: Howard University Press, 1992). For a detailed, rich history of the A.M.E. Church and its complex relationship to South—and, to a lesser degree, West—Africa, see James T. Campbell, *Songs of Zion: The African Methodist Episcopal Church in the United States and South Africa* (New York: Oxford University Press, 1995).

3. The work of Walter L. Williams and Kevin Gaines provides relevant and detailed commentary on black Americans' varied, often conflicted concepts of Africa: see Williams, "Black Journalism's Opinions about Africa during the Late Nineteenth Century," *Phylon: The Atlanta University Review of Race and Culture* 34, no. 3 (September 1973): 224–35; Williams, *Black Americans and the Evangelization of Africa, 1877–1900* (Madison: University of Wisconsin Press, 1982); Gaines, "Black Americans' Racial Uplift Ideology as 'Civilizing Mission': Pauline E. Hopkins on Race and Imperialism," in *Cultures of United States Imperialism*, ed.

Amy Kaplan and Donald E. Pease (Durham: Duke University Press, 1993), 433–55.

4. The actual language used by Fortune is revealing and worth quoting at length:

> If the conquest of Africa shall proceed in the next seventy-five years as it has done in the past twenty-five, the whole continent will be under European control. . . . The vast population of Africa will be brought under Christian influences [and the] . . . demoralizing heterogeneousness which now prevails over the whole continent will give place to a pervading homogeneity in language, in religion, and in government. . . .
>
> The inevitable destiny of the European whites in Africa is absorption and assimilation by the African blacks as surely as the ultimate destiny of the African blacks in the United States is absorption and assimilation by the American whites. . . . Here we absorb and assimilate the Indian, the European, the Asiatic and the African and grow strong in mental and physical prowess in the process. . . . The nationalization of Africa will proceed along the same lines.

T. Thomas Fortune, "The Nationalization of Africa," *Africa and the American Negro: Addresses and Proceedings on the Congress of Africa*, ed. J. W. E. Bowen (Atlanta: Gammon Theological Seminary, 1896), 199–204, esp. 201, 203–4. For a summary of Fortune's editorials on Africa published during the previous decade, see Jean M. Allman and David R. Roediger, "The Early Editorial Career of Timothy Thomas Fortune: Class, Nationalism and Consciousness of Africa," *Afro-Americans in New York Life and History* 6, no. 2 (July 1982): 39–52.

5. Ida B. Wells, "Afro-Americans and Africa," *A.M.E. Church Review* 9, no. 1 (July 1892): 40–44, esp. 41; S. H. Johnson (Lawrence, Kans.), "Negro Emigration: A Correspondent Portrays the Situation and the Benefit to be Derived by Emigration," *Freeman* (Indianapolis, Ind.), March 26, 1892, 3; Parks, *Africa: The Problem of the New Century*, 20–22.

6. Parks, *Africa: The Problem of the New Century*, 29–30, 41. For a similar argument regarding the A.M.E. Church as a conqueror — by a non-member, no less — see Mrs. N. F. [Gertrude] Mossell, "'Will the Negro Share The Glory That Awaits Africa?,'" *Christian Recorder*, January 4, 1893, 3.

7. Parks, *Africa: The Problem of the New Century*, 7, 20, 48, 8–9.

8. Ibid., 7.

9. Richard Hofstadter, *Social Darwinism in American Thought: 1860–1915* (New York: G. Brazilier, 1959); August Meier, *Negro Thought in America, 1880–1915* (Ann Arbor: University of Michigan Press, 1966); J. Edward Chamberlin and Sander L. Gilman, eds., *Degeneration: The Dark Side of Progress* (New York: Columbia University Press, 1985).

10. Michael Adas, *Machines as the Measure of Men: Science, Technology, and Ideologies of Western Dominance* (Ithaca: Cornell University Press, 1989), 272–75, 292–318. For works that explore the slipperiness of race during the late nineteenth

and early twentieth centuries, see Matthew Frye Jacobsen, *Whiteness of a Different Color: European Immigrants and the Alchemy of Race* (Cambridge: Harvard University Press, 1998); and Matthew Pratt Guterl, *The Color of Race in America, 1900–1940* (Cambridge: Harvard University Press, 2002).

11. For commentary on the gendered subtexts of imperialism, race, and civilization in turn-of-the-century American thought, see Gail Bederman, *Manliness and Civilization: A Cultural History of Gender and Race in the United States, 1880–1917* (Chicago: University of Chicago Press, 1995); for analysis of the connections between race, social Darwinism, and imperialism, see Jan Bremen, ed., *Imperial Monkey Business: Racial Supremacy in Social Darwinist Theory and Colonial Practice* (Amsterdam: VU University Press, 1990).

12. Adas, *Machines as the Measure of Men*, 14.

13. Parks, *Africa: The Problem of the New Century*, 20–21. Michael Adas points out the significance of railroads during much of the nineteenth century: "More than any other technological innovation, the railway . . . dramatized the gap . . . between the Europeans and all non-Western peoples." He further points out that nineteenth-century "mission stations came to be viewed as centers for the dissemination of technical skills and . . . scientific learning." See Adas, *Machines as the Measure of Men*, 221, 207.

14. Parks, *Africa: The Problem of the New Century*, 8–9, 22, 40–41, 43. For observations of Turner, see *Respect Black: The Writings and Speeches of Henry McNeal Turner*, ed. Edwin S. Redkey (New York: Arno Press, 1971), 124, 159. For critical analysis of the civilizationist suppositions of social Darwinism in this context, see Gaines, "Black Americans' Racial Uplift Ideology," 433–55, esp. 438; and Williams, "Black Journalism's Opinions about Africa," 230.

15. For analysis of black women's political activism during these years, see Evelyn Brooks Higginbotham, *Righteous Discontent: The Women's Movement in the Black Baptist Church, 1880–1930* (Cambridge: Harvard University Press, 1993); Glenda Elizabeth Gilmore, *Gender and Jim Crow: Women and the Politics of White Supremacy in North Carolina, 1896–1920* (Chapel Hill: University of North Carolina Press, 1996); Stephanie J. Shaw, *What a Woman Ought to Be and to Do* (Chicago: University of Chicago Press, 1996); Deborah Gray White, *Too Heavy a Load: Black Women in Defense of Themselves, 1894–1994* (New York: Norton, 1999); Patricia A. Schechter, *Ida B. Wells-Barnett and American Reform, 1880–1930* (Chapel Hill: University of North Carolina Press, 2001).

16. Patricia Schechter argues that "by 1900, the space for black women in national leadership had shrunk." Whereas the nationalization of the club movement during the late 1890s certainly indicates an expansion of black women's place in intraracial politics, Schechter's contention is nevertheless suggestive when one considers the relative paucity of women's voices in key intraracial debates. See Schechter, *Ida B. Wells-Barnett and American Reform*, 4.

17. See, for example, Willard B. Gatewood Jr., "Negro Troops in Florida, 1898,"

Florida Historian Quarterly 49, no. 1 (July 1970): 1–15; Willard B. Gatewood Jr., "Black Americans and the Quest for Empire, 1898–1903," *Journal of Southern History* 38, no. 4 (November 1972): 545–66; Willard B. Gatewood Jr., *Black Americans and the White Man's Burden, 1898–1903* (Urbana: University of Illinois Press, 1975); Richard E. Welch Jr., *Response to Imperialism: The United States and the Philippine-American War, 1899–1902* (Chapel Hill: University of North Carolina Press, 1979), 101–16; Kevin Gaines and Penny von Eschen, "Ambivalent Warriors: African Americans, U.S. Expansionism, and the Legacies of 1898," *Culture Front* 8 (Spring 1998): 63–64, 73–75.

18. George M. Fredrickson, *The Black Image in the White Mind: The Debate on Afro-American Character and Destiny, 1817–1914* (New York: Harper & Row, 1971); James Horton, "Freedom's Yoke: Gender Conventions among Antebellum Free Blacks," *Feminist Studies* 12, no. 1 (Spring 1986): 51–76, esp. 53.

19. Quotation from Ida B. Wells, *Voice of Missions*, 2, no. 6 (June 1894): 2. Wells — a tireless antilynching activist — was especially adept at using concepts of race, manhood, and civilization in her speeches against lynching. See Gail Bederman, "'Civilization,' the Decline of Middle-Class Manliness, and Ida B. Wells's Anti-lynching Campaign (1892–94)," *Radical History Review* 52 (Winter 1992): 5–30.

20. Elsa Barkley Brown offers powerful commentary on past and present tendencies to view lynching as largely a "masculine experience." See Brown, "Imaging Lynching: African American Women, Communities of Struggle, and Collective Memory," *African American Women Speak Out on Anita Hill–Clarence Thomas*, ed. Geneva Smitherman (Detroit: Wayne State University Press, 1995), 100–124, esp. 101–2.

21. Henry McNeal Turner, "Essay: The American Negro and the Fatherland," *Africa and the American Negro: Addresses and Proceedings on the Congress of Africa . . .*, ed. J. W. E. Bowen (Atlanta: Gammon Theological Seminary, 1896), 195–98, esp. 197. Italicized portions in original.

22. Wesley J. Gaines, *The Negro and the White Man* ([Philadelphia?]: A.M.E. Publishing House, 1897), 156. See also Reverend Emanuel K. Love, "Oration Delivered on Emancipation Day" (January 2, 1888), Daniel A. P. Murray Pamphlet Collection, Library of Congress, Washington, D.C.; Jack Thorne [David Bryant Fulton], *A Plea for Social Justice for the Negro Woman* (New York: Lincoln Press Association, 1912).

23. Norman Vance, *The Sinews of the Spirit: The Ideal of Christian Manliness in Victorian Literature and Religious Thought* (Cambridge: Cambridge University Press, 1985), 1.

24. See David Leverenz's discussion of Frederick Douglass in Leverenz, *Manhood and the American Renaissance* (Ithaca: Cornell University Press, 1989).

25. Lucy V. Norman, "Can a Colored Man Be a Man in the South?," *Christian Recorder*, July 3, 1890, 2; Henry McNeal Turner, "The American Negro and the Fatherland," 195–98, esp. 195. Italicized portions in original.

26. Edwin S. Redkey, *Black Exodus: Black Nationalist and Back-to-Africa Movements, 1890–1910* (New Haven: Yale University Press, 1969).

27. I. W. Penn (Augusta, Ark.) to William Coppinger, April 10, 1891, American Colonization Society Papers, Manuscript Division, Library of Congress, Washington, D.C. (hereafter ACS Papers), container 280, vol. 283.

28. Mary E. Jackson (Atlanta, Ga.) to William Coppinger, May 20, 1891, ACS Papers, container 280, vol. 283. Around the time she wrote this letter to Coppinger, Jackson became involved in an independent colonization society; see also Jackson (Atlanta, Ga.) to Coppinger, June 16, 1891, ACS Papers, container 280, vol. 283.

29. Lewis Lee (Bolivar Co., Miss.) to J. Ormond Wilson, October 23, 1894, ACS Papers, container 286, vol. 291; John Lewis (Toledo, Ohio) to Wilson, January 31, 1893, ACS Papers, container 288, vol. 294; R. A. Wright (Wadley, Ga.) to Wilson, February 26, 1894, ACS Papers, container 286, vol. 291; F. M. Gilmore (Pastoria, Ark.) to William Coppinger, April 15, 1891, ACS Papers, container 280, vol. 283; James Dubose (Orchard Knob, Tenn.) to Coppinger, February 12, 1891, ACS Papers, container 279, vol. 282.

   For discussion of Liberia as an "open door" for those of "pioneer spirit," see Francis H. Warren, "The Upbuilding of Liberia, West Africa," *Alexander's Magazine* 2, no. 10 (February 1907): 183–85, esp. 183; and T. McCants Stewart, "A Letter to the Editor," *Alexander's Magazine* 3, no. 3 (July 1907): 173–75, esp. 173.

   R. A. Wright was, it seems, able to find success in Africa: in addition to practicing law in Greenville, Liberia, Wright farmed and served as a representative in the Liberian legislature. R. A. Wright (Greenville, Liberia) to J. Ormond Wilson, July 7, 1897, ACS Papers, ser. 1B, vol. 27, pt. 2; Wright to Wilson, May 8, 1899, ACS Papers, ser. 1B, vol. 27, pt. 2.

30. C. H. J. Taylor, *Whites and Blacks, or The Question Settled* (Atlanta: Jas. P. Harrison, 1889), 39, 33–34, 37. Biographical data on Taylor is provided in "Short Review of the Career of the Late C. H. J. Taylor and Favorable Mention of his Widow, Mrs. Julia A. Taylor," *Broad Ax* (Chicago, Ill.), January 2, 1904, 3.

31. "Amanda Smith's Letter," *Voice of Missions* 3, no. 7 (July 1895): 2.

32. Levi J. Coppin, "Editorial: What Shall We Do?," *A.M.E. Church Review* 10, no. 4 (April 1894): 549–57, esp. 551–52.

33. J. H. Harris (Conway, Ark.) to William Coppinger, August 5, 1891, ACS Papers, container 281, vol. 284.

34. For one example of this line of argument, see Reverend June Moore, quoted in "Made a Fortune in Liberia," *Liberia Bulletin*, no. 9 (November 1896), 84–86; A. L. Ridgel (Monrovia, Liberia) to J. Ormond Wilson, ACS Papers, June 1, 1894, container 286, vol. 291, reel 143. Underlining in original document.

35. Benjamin W. Arnett, "Africa and the Descendants of Africa: A Response in Behalf of Africa," *A.M.E. Church Review* 11, no. 2 (October 1894): 231–38. esp. 233.

36. J. H. Smyth, "The African in Africa and the African in America," *Africa and the American Negro: Addresses and Proceedings of the Congress on Africa . . . In*

Connection with the Cotton States and International Exposition: December 13–15, 1895, ed. J. W. E. Bowen (Atlanta: Gammon Theological Seminary, 1896), 69–83, esp. 74, 77.

37. Interestingly, V. G. Kiernan points out that "a large part of the army defeated at Adowa in 1896 was composed of men from . . . Afric[a]." See Kiernan, *Imperialism and Its Contradictions*, ed. Harvey J. Kaye (New York: Routledge, 1995), 83.

38. Mrs. C. C. [Sarah Dudley] Pettey, *A.M.E.Z. Church Quarterly* 7 (April 1897): 30. Pettey contributed a regular column for women in the *Star of Zion*, was married to A.M.E. Zion bishop Charles Calvin Pettey, and died before the twentieth century was a decade old. Glenda Gilmore's *Gender and Jim Crow* contains detailed insight into Pettey's life and work.

39. Jim Cullen, "'I's a Man Now': Gender and African American Men," *Divided Houses: Gender and the Civil War*, ed. Catherine Clinton and Nina Silber (New York: Oxford, 1992), 76–91, esp. 77; Gaines and von Eschen, "Ambivalent Warriors," 64. For compelling analysis of the interplay between race and revolution in Cuba during this period, see Ada Ferrer, *Insurgent Cuba: Race, Nation, and Revolution, 1868–1898* (Chapel Hill: University of North Carolina Press, 1999).

40. *Weekly Blade* (Parsons, Kans.), July 9, 1898; *Colored American* (Washington, D.C.), April 30, 1898; *American* (Coffeyville, Kans.), May 7, 1898. For a sampling of African American opinions on U.S. imperialism, see George P. Marks III, comp. and ed., *The Black Press Views American Imperialism (1898–1900)* (New York: Arno Press, 1971).

41. *Bee* (Washington, D.C.), May 21, 1898, 5. This notice of Burroughs's speech, "Should the negro take part in the Spanish-American trouble," is a summary; thus, the text quoted above might not be Burroughs's actual wording.

42. Sergeant M. W. Saddler, letter dated July 30, 1898, to the Indianapolis *Freeman*; reprinted in Willard B. Gatewood Jr., *"Smoked Yankees" and the Struggle for Empire: Letters from Negro Soldiers, 1898–1902* (Urbana: University of Illinois Press, 1971), 55–57.

43. Booker T. Washington et al., *A New Negro for a New Century* (Chicago: American Publishing House, 1900), 40–41; Amy Kaplan, "Black and Blue on San Juan Hill," *Cultures of United States Imperialism*, ed. Amy Kaplan and Donald E. Pease (Durham: Duke University Press, 1993), 219–36, esp. 226.

44. Remarks of Kenneth Robinson from W. H. Crogman, "The Negro Soldier in the Cuban Insurrection and Spanish-American War," *Progress of a Race or the Remarkable Advancement of the American Negro, From the Bondage of Slavery, Ignorance, and Poverty to the Freedom of Citizenship, Intelligence, Affluence, Honor and Trust*, revised and enlarged, ed. J. L. Nichols and William H. Crogman (Naperville, Ill.: J. L. Nichols, 1925), 131–45, esp. 137–38. For additional arguments that black troops "saved" the Rough Riders, refer to Herschel V. Cashin et al., *Under Fire with the Tenth U.S. Cavalry* (New York: F. Tennyson Neely, 1899).

45. Theophilus G. Steward, *The Colored Regulars in the United States Army* (Phila-

delphia: A.M.E. Book Concern, 1904), illustration of material circulated by "the Patriotic Colored Women of Brooklyn, N.Y.," between pp. 230 and 231; Stella A. E. Brazeley, "The Colored Boys in Blue," in *The Spanish-American War Volunteer*, ed. W. Hillary Coston (Middletown: Mount Pleasant Printery, 1899); Katherine Davis Chapman Tillman, "A Tribute to Negro Regiments," *Christian Recorder*, June 9, 1898, and "The Black Boys in Blue," *Recitations* (Philadelphia: A.M.E. Book Concern, 1902). Both poems are reprinted in *The Works of Katherine Davis Chapman Tillman*, ed. Claudia Tate (New York: Oxford University Press, 1991), 146, 188–89.

For other perspectives on heroism in war, see "Peter Purity: . . . A word about Black Heroes," *Broad Ax* (Salt Lake City, Utah), January 7, 1899, 4; Lena Mason, "A Negro In It," in *Twentieth Century Negro Literature or, A Cyclopedia of Thought on the Vital Topics Relating to the American Negro*, ed. D. W. Culp (Naperville, Ill.: J. L. Nichols, 1902), 447.

46. Crogman, "The Negro Soldier in the Cuban Insurrection," 135–44; "W. A. B.," and "The Rough Rider 'Remarks,'" *World*, August 22, 1898, reprinted in Cashin, *Under Fire with the Tenth U.S. Cavalry*, 277–79; Miles V. Lynk, *The Black Troopers, or The Daring Heroism of The Negro Soldiers in the Spanish-American War* (Jackson, Tenn.: Lynk Publishing, 1899), 18, 69–70.

Gatewood summarizes the formation and deployment of black "immune" regiments; see "Introduction," in *Smoked Yankees*, 11.

47. Washington, *A New Negro for a New Century*, esp. 47–48.

48. *Colored American*, ca. 1899; quoted in Gatewood, *Smoked Yankees*, 237. *American Citizen* (Kansas City, Kans.), April 28, 1899, and *Reporter* (Helena, Ark.), February 1, 1900; both quoted in Marks, *The Black Press Views American Imperialism*, 124–25, 167.

49. Sergeant M. W. Saddler, letter dated November 18, 1899, to the Indianapolis *Freeman*; reprinted in Gatewood, *Smoked Yankees*, 247–49.

50. Edward L. Ayers, *The Promise of the New South: Life after Reconstruction* (New York: Oxford University Press, 1992), 333.

51. Gatewood, *Smoked Yankees*, 88–89, 85.

52. Kaplan, "Black and Blue on San Juan Hill," 235.

53. For critical scholarly assessments of the Wilmington Massacre and its sociopolitical impact, see David S. Celeski and Timothy Tyson, eds., *Democracy Betrayed: The Wilmington Riot of 1898 and Its Legacy* (Chapel Hill: University of North Carolina Press, 1998).

54. T. Thomas Fortune, "The Filipino: A Social Study in Three Parts," *Voice of the Negro* 1, no. 3 (March 1904): 93–99, esp. 96–97.

55. T. Thomas Fortune, "The Filipino: Some Incidents of a Trip Through the Island of Luzon," *Voice of the Negro* 1, no. 6 (June 1904): 240–46, esp. 246.

56. Pauline Hopkins, *Of One Blood: or, the Hidden Self*, in *The Magazine Novels*

of *Pauline Hopkins*, ed. Hazel V. Carby (New York: Oxford, 1988), 441–621; Charles H. Fowler, *Historical Romance of the American Negro* (Baltimore: Press of Thomas & Evans, 1902); J[ohn] W[esley] Grant, *Out of the Darkness; or, Diabolism and Destiny* (Nashville: National Baptist Publishing Board, 1909); Sutton E. Griggs, *Imperium in Imperio* (Cincinnati: Editor Publishing, 1899. Reprint, New York: Arno Publishing, 1969); Sutton E. Griggs, *Unfettered: A Novel; with Dorlan's Plan* (Nashville: Orion Publishing, 1902); Sutton E. Griggs, *The Hindered Hand* (Nashville: Orion Publishing, 1905).

57. Griggs, *Unfettered*, 256–57, 275.

58. Griggs, *Imperium in Imperio*, 62.

59. Ibid., 132–35, 173–74.

60. Ibid., 173–75. The work referred to in the "suicide letter" is by Dr. John H. Van Evrie. See J. H. Van Evrie, M.D., *White Supremacy and Black Subordination, or, Negroes a Subordinate Race, And (So-Called) Slavery its Normal Condition* (New York: Van Evrie, Horton, 1868), esp. 149–67.

61. Amy Kaplan, "Romancing the Empire: The Embodiment of American Masculinity in the Popular Historical Novel of the 1890s," *American Literary History* 2, no. 4 (Winter 1990): 659–90, esp. 672. Despite its many interpretive strengths, Kaplan's article bypasses African American work. For analysis of McGirt, Griggs, and other contemporaneous black writers, see James Robert Payne, "Afro-American Literature of the Spanish-American War," *Melus* 10, no. 3 (Fall 1983): 19–32, esp. 27–29. Analysis of Griggs's *Imperium* may also be found in the following: Ayers, *The Promise of the New South*, 371; Kevin K. Gaines, *Uplifting the Race: Black Leadership, Politics, and Culture in the Twentieth Century* (Chapel Hill: University of North Carolina Press, 1996), 54, 114–15, 124–25.

62. James E. McGirt, "In Love as in War," *Triumphs of Ephraim* (Philadelphia: McGirt Publishing, 1907), 63–76, esp. 71, 75. For background on how the United States successfully ousted Aguinaldo, who served as president of the Philippine Republic from 1899 to 1901, see Welch, *Response to Imperialism*.

63. McGirt, "In Love as in War," 75.

64. Kelly Miller, "Immortal Doctrines of Liberty Ably Set Out by a Colored Man; The Effect of Imperialism Upon the Negro Race," *Springfield Republican*, September 7, 1900. Reprinted in *The Anti-Imperialist Reader: A Documentary History of Anti-Imperialism in the United States: From the Mexican War to the Election of 1900*, ed. Philip S. Foner and Richard C. Winchester (New York: Holmes and Meier Publishers, 1984), 1:176–80, esp. 180. Also see Gatewood, "Black Americans and the Quest for Empire," 545–66, esp. 559.

65. W. S. Scarborough, "The Negro and Our New Possessions," *Forum* 31, no. 3 (May 1901): 341–49, esp. 347.

66. Walter F. Walker, "News about Liberia and Africa Generally," *Alexander's Magazine* 5, no. 3 (January 15, 1908): 66–67, esp. 67; Walter F. Walker, *Alexander's*

Magazine 6, no. 4 (August 1908): 162–66. Apparently, Walker eventually emigrated to Liberia and became secretary to the republic's president. See "Liberian President Warns Immigrants," *Age* (New York, N.Y.), July 9, 1914, 1.

67. Hazel V. Carby, "Introduction," in *The Magazine Novels of Pauline Hopkins*, xlv; Gaines, "Black Americans' Racial Uplift Ideology," 436. For additional insights on how Du Bois's anti-imperialism evolved over the span of his long and prolific public life, see Helene Christol, "Du Bois and Expansionism: A Black Man's View of Empire," *Anglo-Saxonism in U.S. Foreign Policy: The Diplomacy of Imperialism, 1899–1919*, ed. Serge Ricard and Hélène Christol (Aix-en-Provence: Publications de l'Université d'Aix-en-Provence, 1991), 49–63.

68. The full quote from the title page reads "two races hand in hand for mutual good." Parks, *Africa: The Problem of the New Century*, title page.

69. For an elaboration of this argument, see Gaines, "Black Americans' Racial Uplift Ideology," 437, 440.

70. "Africa for the Africans," *Colored American Magazine* 9, no. 3 (September 1905): 470–71; "The Grab for Liberia and Her Needs," *Colored American Magazine* 17, no. 2 (August 1909): 118–22; I. De H. Crooke, "Africa for Africans," *Colored American Magazine* 15, no. 2 (February 1909): 101–2. For more along these lines, see "Still Fighting in Africa," *Colored American Magazine* 9, no. 6 (December 1905): 663–64.

71. *Age*, March 13, 1913, and November 13, 1913; Tuskegee Institute News Clipping File, ser. 1, main file, reel 2, frames 13 and 333.

72. Skinner, *African Americans and U.S. Policy toward Africa, 1850–1924*.

73. B. F. Riley, *The White Man's Burden* (Birmingham: B. F. Riley, 1910), title page; H. T. Johnson, "The Black Man's Burden," *Broad Ax* (Salt Lake City, Utah), April 15, 1899, 4; John E. Bruce, "The White Man's Burden" (ca. 1910; italics in original), reprinted in *The Selected Writings of John Edward Bruce: Militant Black Journalist*, comp. and ed. Peter Gilbert (New York: Arno Press, 1971), 97–98, esp. 97; Miller, "Immortal Doctrines of Liberty."

   In *Imperial Leather: Race, Gender and Sexuality in the Colonial Conquest* (New York: Routledge, 1995), Anne McClintock points out that the international concept of a "white man's burden" could be at once racist and crassly commercial; she notes that Pears' Soap used Kipling's phrase as eye-catching advertising copy. See McClintock, *Imperial Leather*, 32–33.

74. W. E. B. Du Bois, "The Burden of Black Women" (1907) reprinted in *W. E. B. Du Bois: A Reader*, ed. David Levering Lewis (New York: Henry Holt, 1995), 291–93. His comment about venereal disease may be found in W. E. Burghardt Du Bois, ed., *The Health and Physique of the Negro American* (Atlanta: Atlanta University Press, 1906), 69. Daniel Webster Davis, "The Black Woman's Burden," *Voice of the Negro* 1, no. 7 (July 1904): 308.

75. Frances Ellen Watkins Harper, "The Burdens of All" (ca. 1900); reprinted in *A*

Brighter Coming Day: A Frances Ellen Watkins Harper Reader, ed. Frances Smith Foster (New York: Feminist Press, 1990), 390.

76. Bederman, *Manliness and Civilization*, 171.

77. For further commentary on African American reworkings of Kipling's [in]famous line, Gatewood, *Black Americans and the White Man's Burden*, 183–86.

78. Bederman, *Manliness and Civilization*, 5.

79. Dennis H. J. Morgan, "Theatre of War: Combat, the Military, and Masculinities," *Theorizing Masculinities*, ed. Harry Brod and Michael Kaufman (Thousand Oaks: Sage Publications, 1994), 165. Relevant texts include Mark C. Carnes and Clyde Griffen, eds., *Meanings for Manhood: Constructions of Masculinities in Victorian America* (Chicago: University of Chicago Press, 1990); Jeff Hearn and David Morgan, eds., *Men, Masculinities, and Social Theory* (London: Unwin Hyman, 1990); Michael Kimmel, *Manhood in America: A Cultural History* (New York: Free Press, 1996); Harry Stecopoulos and Michael Uebel, eds., *Race and the Subject of Masculinities* (Durham: Duke University Press, 1997); Darlene Clark Hine and Earnestine Jenkins, eds., *A Question of Manhood: A Reader in US Black Men's History and Masculinity* (Bloomington: Indiana University Press, 1999).

80. Clyde Griffen, "Reconstructing Masculinity from the Evangelical Revival to the Waning of Progressivism: A Speculative Synthesis," in *Meanings for Manhood*, 183–204, esp. 199; Bederman, *Manliness and Civilization*, 170–215; Kristin Hoganson, *Fighting for American Manhood: How Gender Politics Provoked the Spanish-American and Philippine-American Wars* (New Haven: Yale University Press, 1998), 11–12.

81. Hoganson, *Fighting for American Manhood*, 12.

82. Frances E. W. Harper, " 'Do Not Cheer, Men Are Dying,' " Richmond *Planet* (reprinted from the *Christian Recorder*), December 3, 1898.

83. Adas, *Machines as the Measure of Men*, 13.

CHAPTER THREE

1. *Souvenir: Official Program and Music of the Negro Young Peoples' Christian and Educational Congress, Held August 6–11, 1902, Atlanta, Ga.* (Nashville: National Baptist Publishing Board, ca. 1902), esp. 87–90.

The reason for my ambiguity regarding whether certain papers were actually delivered at the conference is that not all of the papers listed within the official program actually appear in the published proceedings of the congress, I. Garland Penn and J. W. E. Bowen, eds., *The United Negro: His Problems and His Progress, Containing the Addresses and Proceedings [of] the Negro Young People's Christian and Educational Congress, Held August 6–11, 1902* (Atlanta: D. E. Luther Publishing, 1902). There are at least three plausible reasons: some of scheduled speakers were absent or unable to present; they failed to submit drafts to Penn and Bowen; or, the editors simply decided not to publish certain contributions.

2. See, for example, John S. Haller Jr., "From Maidenhood to Menopause: Sex Education for Women in Victorian America," *Journal of Popular Culture* 6, no. 1 (1972): 49–69, esp. 55.

3. Ariel Serena [Mrs. J. W. E.] Bowen, "Child Marriage a Social Crime—Its Remedy," in Penn and Bowen, *The United Negro*, 451–53. During the 1880s and 1890s, Bowen taught at Tuskegee Institute and Clark University; a musician and singer, she was "busily engaged in . . . reform work" throughout her marriage to prominent race man (and Negro Youth Congress organizer) John Bowen. See "Mrs. Ariel Serena Hedges Bowen," in *Twentieth Century Negro Literature, or A Cyclopedia of Thought on the Vital Topics Relating to the American Negro*, ed. D. W. Culp (Naperville, Ill.: J. L. Nichols, 1902), 264–65, reverse of photograph.

4. Bowen, "Child Marriage a Social Crime," 452–53; *Souvenir*, 86.

5. For examples of papers other than those listed in text, refer to *Souvenir*, esp. 87, 89, 90. Here, the phrase quoted in text is a direct reference to the subtitle of *The United Negro*.

6. Whereas the argument regarding whether, how, and when African American reformers discussed inversion and homosexuality is my own, here I am quoting and drawing upon Siobhan Somerville's argument in *Queering the Color Line: Race and the Invention of Homosexuality in American Culture* (Durham: Duke University Press, 2000), 39.

7. Elsa Barkley Brown, "Negotiating and Transforming the Public Sphere: African American Political Life in the Transition from Slavery to Freedom," *Public Culture* 7, no. 1 (Fall 1994): 107–46, esp. 140 n. 59. I must note that Brown's original emphasis differs slightly from the interpretation I offer here. To begin with, she specifically refers to changing notions about "sexual danger" during Reconstruction and the post-Reconstruction era. Whereas Brown contends that black discourse about sexuality shifted from an overarching anger over sexual violence to "a more clearly gendered discourse . . . where violence against men was linked to state repression and . . . violence against women became a matter of specific interest, increasingly eliminated from the general discussions," I feel that her comments nonetheless evoke the wide-ranging significance of sexuality in Afro-American life after slavery.

8. John C. Fout, "Introduction," in *American Sexual Politics: Sex, Gender, and Race since the Civil War*, ed. John C. Fout and Maura Shaw Tantillo (Chicago: University of Chicago Press, 1993), 1–16, esp. 3; John D'Emilio and Estelle B. Freedman, *Intimate Matters: A History of Sexuality in America* (New York: Harper & Row, 1988), 171–235.

9. General historiography on sexuality in the United States during the late nineteenth and early twentieth centuries includes John C. Burnham, "The Progressive Era Revolution in American Attitudes toward Sex," *Journal of American History* 59, no. 4 (March 1973): 885–908; David J. Pivar, *Purity Crusade: Sexual Morality and Social Control, 1868–1900* (Westport, Conn.: Greenwood Press,

1973); Linda Gordon, *Woman's Body, Woman's Right: A Social History of Birth Control in America* (New York: Penguin Books, 1977); Patricia J. Campbell, *Sex Education Books for Young Adults, 1892–1979* (New York: R. R. Bowker, 1979); Barbara Epstein, "Family, Sexual Morality, and Popular Movements in Turn-of-the-Century America," in *Powers of Desire: The Politics of Sexuality*, ed. Ann Snitow, Christine Stansell, and Sharon Thompson (New York: Monthly Review Press, 1983), 117–30; Carroll Smith-Rosenberg, *Disorderly Conduct: Visions of Gender in Victorian America* (New York: Alfred A. Knopf, 1985); Christina Simmons, "Modern Sexuality and the Myth of Victorian Repression," in *Passion and Power: Sexuality in History*, ed. Kathy Peiss and Christina Simmons with Robert A. Padgug (Philadelphia: Temple University Press, 1989), 157–77; Ann du Cille, "'Othered' Matters: Reconceptualizing Dominance and Difference in the History of Sexuality in America," *Journal of the History of Sexuality* 1, no. 1 (July 1990): 102–27; Jesse F. Battan, "'The Word Made Flesh': Language, Authority, and Sexual Desire in Late Nineteenth-Century America," in Fout and Tantillo, *American Sexual Politics*, 101–22; George Chauncey, *Gay New York: Gender, Urban Culture, and the Making of the Gay Male World, 1890–1940* (New York: Basic Books, 1994); Somerville, *Queering the Color Line.*

10. For particular commentary about African American sexuality during this period, see Nell Irvin Painter, "'Social Equality,' Miscegenation, Labor, and Power," in *The Evolution of Southern Culture*, ed. Numan V. Bartley (Athens: University of Georgia Press, 1988), 47–67; Hannah Rosen, "'Not That Sort of Women': Race, Gender, and Sexual Violence during the Memphis Riot of 1866," in *Sex, Love, Race: Crossing Boundaries in North American History*, ed. Martha Hodes (New York: New York University Press, 1999), 267–93; Willard B. Gatewood Jr., *Aristocrats of Color: The Black Elite, 1880–1920* (Bloomington: Indiana University Press, 1990); Darlene Clark Hine, "Rape and the Inner Lives of Black Women in the Middle West: Preliminary Thoughts on the Culture of Dissemblance," *Signs* 14, no. 4 (Summer 1989): 912–20; Gail Bederman, "'Civilization,' the Decline of Middle-Class Manliness, and Ida B. Wells's Antilynching Campaign (1892–94)," *Radical History Review* 52 (Winter 1992): 5–30; Hazel V. Carby, "Policing the Black Woman's Body in an Urban Context," *Critical Inquiry* 18, no. 4 (Summer 1992): 738–55; Ann du Cille, *The Coupling Convention: Sex, Text, and Tradition in Black Women's Fiction* (New York: Oxford University Press, 1993), 30–65; Martha Hodes, "The Sexualization of Reconstruction Politics: White Women and Black Men in the South after the Civil War," *Journal of the History of Sexuality* 3, no. 3 (January 1993): 402–17; Robyn Wiegman, "The Anatomy of Lynching," *Journal of the History of Sexuality* 3, no. 3 (January 1993): 445–67.

Analyses of sexuality during slavery include Deborah Gray White, *Ar'n't I a Woman?: Female Slaves in the Plantation South* (New York: W. W. Norton, 1985), as well as Anthony S. Parent Jr. and Susan Brown Wallace, "Childhood and Sexual Identity under Slavery," in Fout and Tantillo, *American Sexual Poli-*

tics, 19–58. Relevant commentary pertaining to the U.S. South may be found in Peter W. Bardaglio, *Reconstructing the Household: Families, Sex, and the Law in the Nineteenth-Century South* (Chapel Hill: University of North Carolina Press, 1995). Moreover, Sander L. Gilman offers relevant analysis of Western—specifically European—concepts of black sexuality in *Difference and Pathology: Stereotypes of Sexuality, Race, and Madness* (Ithaca: Cornell University Press, 1985), 109–27.

11. The sociological studies spearheaded by Atlanta University epitomize this trend. Relevant titles are *Mortality Among Negroes in Cities* (Atlanta: Atlanta University Press, ca. 1896); *Social and Physical Condition of Negroes in Cities* (Atlanta: Atlanta University Press, 1897); *The Health and Physique of the Negro American* (Atlanta: Atlanta University Press, 1906); *Morals and Manners Among Negro Americans* (Atlanta: Atlanta University Press, 1914).

12. Christina Simmons, "African Americans and Sexual Victorianism in the Social Hygiene Movement, 1910–1940," *Journal of the History of Sexuality* 4, no. 1 (July 1993): 51–75, esp. 53.

13. Evelyn Brooks Higginbotham, *Righteous Discontent: The Women's Movement in the Black Baptist Church, 1880–1920* (Cambridge: Harvard University Press, 1993), 198.

14. Frederick L. Hoffman, "Vital Statistics of the Negro," *Arena* 29 (April 1892): 529–42, esp. 534, 542.

15. Frederick L. Hoffman, *Race Traits and Tendencies of the American Negro* (New York: Macmillan, 1896), 33–148, passim, esp. 59 and 148. In his discussion of history, Hoffman referred to Afro-American colonization and emigration efforts; he even wrote William Coppinger of the American Colonization Society requesting information about the "aims and work of your organization." Frederick L. Hoffman (Hampton, Va.) to William Coppinger, May 13, 1892, American Colonization Society Papers, container 283, vol. 286.

    Kelly Miller published a lengthy rebuttal to Hoffman in conjunction with the American Negro Academy. See Miller, "A Review of Hoffman's *Race Traits and Tendencies of the American Negro*," *American Negro Academy Occasional Papers, No. 1* (Washington, D.C.: American Negro Academy, 1897. Reprint, New York: Arno Press, 1969), 3–36.

16. Hoffman, *Race Traits*, 52, 55; H. L. Sutherland, "The Destiny of the American Negro," 2. The Sutherland pamphlet may be found in the Library of Congress's Daniel A. P. Murray Pamphlets Collection, Rare Book and Special Collections Division.

    George Fredrickson provides vital historical context pertaining to Hoffman and like-minded thinkers in *The Black Image in the White Mind: The Debate on Afro-American Character and Destiny, 1817–1914* (New York: Harper & Row, 1971), esp. 228–55.

17. William Hannibal Thomas, *The American Negro: What He Was, What He Is, and*

What He May Become. A Critical and Practical Discussion (New York: Macmillan, 1906), 173–207, passim, esp. 176–79. See also John David Smith's biography of Thomas, *Black Judas: William Hannibal Thomas and The American Negro* (Athens: University of Georgia Press, 2000).

18. Thomas, *The American Negro*, 180–84, 190–93.

19. Booker T. Washington, book review, *Outlook* 67 (March 30, 1901): 733–36; Kelly Miller, "The Negro's Part in the Negro Problem," in *Race Adjustment: Essays on the Negro in America* (New York: Neale Publishing, 1908. Reprint, New York: Arno Press, 1968), 96; W. H. Councill, "The American Negro: An Answer," *Southern History Association Publications* 6 (1902): 40–44; S. Timothy Tice, *The American Negro: What He Was, What He Is, and What He May Become; A Critical and Practical Rejoinder to William Hannibal Thomas* ([Cambridgeport?]: J. Frank Facey, 1901), 5, 45, 48.

For interpretation of Councill as a "notorious accommodator" and "unctuous sycophant," see August Meier, *Negro Thought in America, 1880–1915* (Ann Arbor: University of Michigan Press, 1966), 77, 110, 209–20.

20. Fannie Barrier Williams, "The Intellectual Progress of the Colored Women of the United States Since the Emancipation Proclamation," in *The World's Congress of Representative Women: A Historical Resume for Popular Circulation of the World's Congress of Representative Women, Convened in Chicago on May 15, and Adjourned on May 22, 1893, Under the Auspices of the Woman's Branch of the World's Congress Auxiliary*, ed. May Wright Sewall (Chicago: Rand, McNally, 1894), 696–711, esp. 702–4; *A History of the Club Movement Among the Colored Women of the United States of America; As Contained in the Minutes of the Conventions, Held in Boston, July 29, 30, 31, 1895, and of the National Federation of Afro-American Women, Held in Washington, D.C., July 20, 21, 22, 1896* (n.p., 1902), 4, Ida B. Wells Papers, Special Collections, University of Chicago, box 5, folder 13.

In 1896, the National Association of Colored Women was established when the National Federation of Afro-American Women and the National League of Colored Women consolidated forces. Further, detailed discussion of club women's assaults on sexual stereotypes as well as overarching analyses of the club movement may be found in the following: Paula Giddings, *When and Where I Enter: The Impact of Black Women on Race and Sex in America* (New York: Bantam Books, 1984); Wilson J. Moses, "Domestic Feminism, Conservatism, Sex Roles, and Black Women's Clubs, 1893–1896," *Journal of Social and Behavioral Sciences* 24, no. 4 (Fall 1987): 166–77; Dorothy Salem, *To Better Our World: Black Women in Organized Reform, 1890–1920* (New York: Carlson Publishing, 1990); Stephanie J. Shaw, "Black Women and the Creation of the National Association of Colored Women," in *"We Specialize in the Wholly Impossible": A Reader in Black Women's History*, ed. Darlene Clark Hine, Wilma King, and Linda Reed (New York: Carlson Press, 1995). Also relevant is Beverly Guy-Sheftall's *Daughters of*

Sorrow: Attitudes toward Black Women, 1880–1920 (New York: Carlson Publishing, 1990).

21. The relationship between sexual behavior, "respectability," and class aspirations for postbellum black Americans has been richly documented by a number of historians. See, for example, Wilson Jeremiah Moses, "Sexual Anxieties of the Black Bourgeoisie in Victorian American: The Cultural Context of W. E. B. Du Bois' First Novel," in *The Wings of Ethiopia: Studies in African American Life and Letters* (Ames: Iowa State University Press, 1990); Gatewood, *Aristocrats of Color*; Higginbotham, *Righteous Discontent*; Stephanie J. Shaw, *What a Woman Ought to Be and to Do: Black Professional Women Workers during the Jim Crow Era* (Chicago: University of Chicago Press, 1996); Kevin K. Gaines, *Uplifting the Race: Black Leadership, Politics, and Culture in the Twentieth Century* (Chapel Hill: University of North Carolina Press, 1996); Victoria W. Wolcott, "'Bible, Bath, and Broom': Nannie Helen Burroughs's National Training School and African American Racial Uplift," *Journal of Women's History* 9, no. 1 (Spring 1997): 88–110. See also Michele Mitchell, "Silences Broken, Silences Kept: Gender and Sexuality in African American History," *Gender and History* 11, no. 3 (November 1999): 433–44, esp. 437–38.

22. Gaines, *Uplifting the Race*, 12, 45, 78.

23. *The Negro American Family* (Atlanta: Atlanta University Press, 1908), 37. Wilson Jeremiah Moses also cites this quote in his analysis of Du Bois's views on sexuality in "Sexual Anxieties of the Black Bourgeoisie in Victorian American," 248.

24. Higginbotham, *Righteous Discontent*, 187–88. Also see James Oliver Horton, "Freedom's Yoke: Gender Conventions among Antebellum Free Blacks," *Feminist Studies* 12, no. 1 (Spring 1986): 51–76.

25. This argument is drawn, in large part, from Hazel Carby's pioneering article on African Americans, sexuality, and urban sites. Although Carby primarily assesses efforts of women like Jane Edna Hunter, I feel that her analysis is more than fitting in this context. In terms of her decision to focus upon women reformers, Carby contends that it was black *female* sexuality which was "variously situated as a threat to the progress of the race; as a threat to the establishment of a respectable urban black middle class . . . as a threat to the formation of black masculinity in an urban environment." See Carby, "Policing the Black Woman's Body," 738–55, esp. 745, 746, 741.

26. Susan L. Smith, "Welfare for Black Mothers and Children: Health and Home in the American South," *Social Politics* 4, no. 1 (Spring 1997): 49–64, esp. 50; Wolcott, "'Bible, Bath, and Broom,'" 89.

   Related analyses which provide additional historical context for assertions made here may be found in the following texts: Simmons, "African Americans and Sexual Victorianism"; Tera W. Hunter, *To 'Joy My Freedom: Southern Black Women's Lives and Labors after the Civil War* (Cambridge: Harvard University Press, 1997); Victoria W. Wolcott, *Remaking Respectability: African American*

Women in Interwar Detroit (Chapel Hill: University of North Carolina Press, 2001).

27. Daniel J. Kevles, *In the Name of Eugenics: Genetics and the Uses of Human Heredity* (New York: Knopf, 1987), 59, 69, 74–75, 100, 106–12; Mark Haller, *Eugenics: Hereditarian Attitudes in American Thought* (New Brunswick, N.J.: Rutgers University Press, 1963), 6; Nicole Hahn Rafter, *White Trash: The Eugenic Family Studies, 1877–1919* (Boston: Northeastern University Press, 1988), 1–31. Also see J. Edward Chamberlin and Sander L. Gilman, eds., *Degeneration: The Dark Side of Progress* (New York: Columbia University Press, 1985).

28. Rebecca [Lee] Crumpler, *A Book of Medical Discourses in Two Parts* (Boston: Cashman, Keating, 1883), 9; Frances E. W. Harper, "Enlightened Motherhood: An Address by Mrs. Frances E. W. Harper, Before the Brooklyn Literary Society, November 15th, 1892" (n.p., n.d.); Selena Sloan Butler, "Heredity," *Spelman Messenger*, June 1897, quoted in Higginbotham, *Righteous Discontent*, 66; Mary V. Bass, "Nature or Environment," *Woman's Era* 2 (1895): 6–7; *A History of the Club Movement*, 77.

A revealing discussion of "illegitimacy," eugenics, and children's importance to the future of black Americans can also be found in Lucy C. Laney, "Address Before the Women's Meeting," in *Social and Physical Conditions of Negroes in Cities. Report of an Investigation Under the Direction of Atlanta University: And Proceedings of Problems Concerning Negro City Life, Held at Atlanta University, May 25–26, 1897* (Atlanta: Atlanta University Press, 1897), 55–57.

29. Adella Hunt Logan, "Prenatal and Hereditary Influences," in *Social and Physical Conditions of Negroes*, 37–40, esp. 39 and 40. One reviewer praised Logan for refusing to "shrink from telling plain and solemn truths" and dealing with them in "a simple, direct manner." Review, *Southern Workman* 26, no. 10 (October 1897): 206–7.

30. Sylvia C. J. [Mrs. P. J.] Bryant, "How Can Mothers and Fathers Teach Their Sons and Daughters Social Purity," in Penn and Bowen, *The United Negro*, 439–40; Addie W. Hunton, "A Pure Motherhood the Basis of Racial Integrity," in ibid., 433–35, esp. 434–35.

Twenty years later, novelist Sutton Griggs would be far more blunt than Bryant, Hunton, or Logan. He opined that the race needed "to make disposition of its waste matter" if it ever wanted to enjoy an exalted future. See Sutton E. Griggs, *Science of Collective Efficiency* (Memphis: National Public Welfare League, c. 1921), 20. Griggs also spoke at the 1902 Negro Young People's Congress; he participated in a symposium on "The Negro's Contribution to His Own Development." See *Souvenir*, 67. For an example of a race activist questioning popular invocations of heredity and race, see W. E. B. Du Bois, "Heredity and the Public Schools," in *Pamphlets and Leaflets by W. E. B. Du Bois*, ed. Herbert Aptheker (White Plains, N.Y.: Kraus-Thomson, 1986), 45–52.

31. Henry Davenport Northrop, Joseph R. Gay, and I. Garland Penn, *The College of*

Life, or Practical Self-Educator (Chicago: Chicago Publication and Lithograph Co., 1895); Joseph R. Gay, *Life Lines of Success; A Practical Manual of Self-Help for the future development of the ambitious Colored American* (Chicago: Howard, Chandler, 1913); Professor and Mrs. J. W. Gibson, *Golden Thoughts on Chastity and Procreation Including Heredity, Prenatal Influences, Etc., Etc.: Sensible Hints and Wholesome Advice for Maiden and Young Man, Wife and Husband, Mother and Father* (Naperville, Ill.: J. L. Nichols, 1903 and 1914).

32. H[enry] R[utherford] Butler, "Introduction," in Gibson and Gibson, *Golden Thoughts*, 1. Butler trained at Meharry Medical College and was, incidentally, the husband of Selena Sloan Butler.

33. Claudia Tate, *Domestic Allegories of Political Desire: The Black Heroine's Text at the Turn of the Century* (New York: Oxford University Press, 1992), 4.

34. Gibson and Gibson, "Preface," in *Golden Thoughts*, 5.

35. Professor and Mrs. J. W. Gibson, *Social Purity, or The Life of the Home and Nation; Including Heredity, Prenatal Influences, Etc. Etc. An Instructor, Counselor and Friend for the Home* (New York: J. L. Nichols, 1903).

36. Although my research on the Gibsons has yielded precious little information, from all appearances, John Gibson, at least, was white. As one of the legions of editors who worked on *Progress of a Race*, his photograph appears in more than one edition of that book (ca. 1900–1912). Moreover, he is openly identified as "white" in these editions. Thus far, I have uncovered only one reference to Gibson as "Negro." See *Voice of the Negro* 4, no. 1 (January and February 1907): back cover.

37. Gibson and Gibson, *Social Purity*, 323, passim. Refer to the same pages in *Golden Thoughts* for text cited.

38. Gay, *Life Lines of Success*, 258; H. R. Butler, "Negligence A Cause of Mortality," in *Mortality Among Negroes in Cities* (Atlanta: Atlanta University Press, 1896), 20–25, esp. 25.

39. Furthermore, *Golden Thoughts* culled data from the same "noted specialists" used by compilers of general audience books. See T. W. Shannon, *Eugenics, or The Laws of Sex Life and Heredity* (Marietta: S. A. Mullikin, ca. 1904); and B. G. Jefferis and J. L. Nichols, *Safe Counsel, or Practical Eugenics* (Naperville, Ill.: J. L. Nichols, 1922).

40. Joseph Gay's *Life Lines of Success*, for one, was advertised in the pages of the Chicago *Defender*. See *Defender*, July 14, 1914, 3.

It is worth noting here that the 1913 edition of *Life Lines of Success* was simultaneously published under the title of *Progress and Achievements of the 20th Century Negro* (n.p., 1913). Similarly, *The College of Life* was reissued as the *Afro-American Home Manual and Practical Self-Educator* in 1902. As John D'Emilio and Estelle Freedman have pointed out, multiple editions of "guides to sexual health . . . revealed how hungry Americans were about the meaning of sexuality." D'Emilio and Freedman, *Intimate Matters*, 72.

41. Gordon, *Woman's Body, Woman's Right*, 137, 48. For statistics of college graduates — specifically Seven Sisters alumnae — see Louise Michele Newman, ed., *Men's Ideas/Women's Realities: "Popular Science," 1870–1915* (New York: Pergamon Press, 1985), 105–24, esp. 114–15.

For an overview of Progressive Era reformers' fixation on ethnicity, nativity, race, and birthrates, see Miriam King and Steven Ruggles, "American Immigration, Fertility, and Race Suicide at the Turn of the Century," *Journal of Interdisciplinary History* 22, no. 3 (Winter 1990): 347–69. King and Ruggles argue against conventional wisdom that the birthrate of immigrant women exceeded that of native white women by asserting "the much heralded 'breeding power' of ethnics at the turn of the century was an illusion." Furthermore, King and Ruggles maintain that children of immigrants had even *lower* birthrates than their white contemporaries who were the children of native-born Americans. King and Ruggles, "American Immigration, Fertility, and Race Suicide," 364, 352. Along similar lines, Daniel J. Kevles connects anxieties over immigrants' fecundity to the popularity of eugenics during the late nineteenth and early twentieth centuries. See *In the Name of Eugenics*, 72.

Primary sources which discuss birthrates include John S. Billings, "The Diminishing Birth Rate in the United States," *Forum* 15, no. 4 (June 1893): 467–77; J. McKeen Cattell, "The Causes of the Declining Birth Rate," and Walter F. Willcox, "Differential Fecundity," in *Proceedings of the First National Conference on Race Betterment: January 8, 9, 10, 11, 12, 1914, Battle Creek, Michigan* (n.p.: Race Betterment Foundation, ca. 1914), 67–72, 79–89.

42. Reynolds Farley, *Growth of the Black Population: A Study of Demographic Trends* (Chicago: Markham Publishing, 1971), 56–57; [U.S. Department of Commerce, Bureau of the Census], *Negro Population, 1790–1915* (Washington, D.C.: Government Printing Office, 1918. Reprint, New York: Kraus Reprint Co., 1969), 286; Ansley J. Coale and Norfleet W. Rives Jr., "A Statistical Reconstruction of the Black Population of the United States 1880–1970: Estimates of True Numbers By Age and Sex, Birth Rates, and Total Fertility," *Population Index* 39, no. 1 (January 1973): 3–36, esp. 26.

Whereas I do not explore the various methods demographers use to compute fertility rates here, it is important to note that a variety of methods for determining fertility exist, including backward projection to obtain total fertility rates, computation of woman-child ratios, and estimation of gross-reproduction rates. It is equally important to point out that despite a variety of methods, and despite discrepancies in actual findings, virtually every approach suggests that the drop in black women's fecundity was both undeniable and substantial. Discussion of various approaches may be found in Farley, *Growth of the Black Population*, 51–56, 102–4; Jamshid Momeni, "Black Demography: A Review Essay," in *Demography of the Black Population in the United States: An Annotated Bibliography with a*

Review Essay (Westport, Conn.: Greenwood Press, 1983), 13–14; Robert Higgs, *Competition and Coercion: Blacks in the American Economy, 1865–1914* (London: Cambridge University Press, 1977), 15–17.

43. Herman Lantz and Lewellyn Hendrix, "Black Fertility and the Black Family in the Nineteenth Century: A Re-Examination of the Past," *Journal of Family History* 3, no. 3 (Fall 1978): 251–61, esp. 256. Lantz and Hendrix cite data pertaining to the number of children ever born to cohorts of women from *Sixteenth Census of the United States (1940): Population. Differential Fertility, 1940 and 1910* (Washington, D.C.: Government Printing Office, 1945).

Unfortunately, in the 1940 exploration of differential fertility, the Census Bureau ascertained women's class status according to their husband's occupation; I assume that a majority of the African American women polled worked outside of the home. For brief commentary on fertility differentials by class and region, refer to Momeni, "Black Demography," 16.

44. Stewart E. Tolnay, "Family Economy and the Black American Fertility Transition," *Journal of Family History* 11, no. 3 (July 1986): 272–77; Darlene Clark Hine, "Black Migration to the Urban Midwest: The Gender Dimension, 1915–1945," in *Hine Sight: Black Women and the Re-Construction of American History* (Brooklyn: Carlson Publishing, 1994), 59–86.

For analysis of fertility in the South—which Lantz and Hendrix consider "a high fertility region for both races"—see Lantz and Hendrix, "Black Fertility and the Black Family," 254–56; Stanley L. Engerman, "Black Fertility and Family Structure in the U.S., 1880–1940," *Journal of Family History* 2, no. 2 (June 1977): 117–38, esp. 124. Tolnay offers similar observations, though he largely distinguishes between rural and urban rather than by region; see Stewart Emory Tolnay, "The Fertility of Black Americans in 1900" (Ph.D. diss., University of Washington, 1981).

Statistics regarding migration and regional concentrations of African Americans may be found in Daniel M. Johnson and Rex R. Campbell, *Black Migration in America: A Social Demographic History* (Durham: Duke University Press, 1981), 73–74.

45. Charles V[ictor] Roman, "The American Negro and Social Hygiene," *Journal of Social Hygiene* 7 (January 1921): 41–47, esp. 45. Here, Roman's comments reflect a concern—not all that unlike Edward Ross's and Theodore Roosevelt's—that the "intelligent" shunned parenthood while the "masses" proliferated. For a later example of an educated race woman questioning the wisdom of African Americans bringing children into the world in light of racism and discrimination, see Cecelia Eggleston, "What a Negro Mother Faces" (1938), reprinted in *A Documentary History of The Negro People in the United States, 1933–1945*, ed. Herbert Aptheker (Secaucus, N.J.: Citadel Press, 1974), 291–97.

I eschew arguments that suggest lower black birthrates primarily resulted from "impaired fecundity" due to "biological" factors. Such views were, perhaps, most popular with demographers during the early 1970s. Another take on the "impaired fecundity" thesis is contained within *Labor of Love, Labor of Sorrow* where historian Jacqueline Jones observes that the "decline in black fertility . . . [was] probably due in part to the poor health of rural women and their families." Health was likely a factor for many women, yet I believe that "changes in the social fabric of the Black population" (migration, education, urbanization, decreased utility of children within a sharecropping context, labor participation of women, conscious childlessness) probably had greater overall impact. Jacqueline Jones, *Labor of Love, Labor of Sorrow: Black Women, Work and the Family, from Slavery to the Present* (New York: Vintage Books, 1986), 88, 123; Tolnay, "The Fertility of Black Americans in 1900," 23.

46. Again, for regional statistics, see Lantz and Hendrix, "Black Fertility and the Black Family," 254–56; Engerman, "Black Fertility and Family Structure," 127.

47. Eugene Harris, "The Physical Condition of the Race; Whether Dependent Upon Social Conditions or Environment," in *Social and Physical Condition of Negroes*, 19–28, esp. 25. Another of Harris's euphemisms for abortion was "the crime of mothers." See H. F. Kletzing and W. H. Crogman, eds., *Progress of a Race: or, The Remarkable Advancement of the American Negro* (Atlanta: J. L. Nichols, 1898), 281–82.

48. Dr. H. F. Gamble, "Infant Mortality," *Colored American Magazine* 7, no. 10 (October 1904): 630–33, esp. 633; Butler, "Negligence a Cause of Mortality," 21.

Reynolds Farley completely discounts any role that contraception might have had in lowering black women's fecundity; I am far more swayed by the argument of Joseph McFalls and George Masnick, who persuasively contend that many Afro-Americans "undoubtedly perceived [a] need and . . . practiced birth control." See Joseph McFalls and George Masnick, "Birth Control and Fertility of the U.S. Black Population, 1880 to 1980," *Journal of Family History* 6, no. 1 (Spring 1981): 89–106. Additional observations about black views on and practices of birth control during the time period under consideration are located in Jessie May Rodrique's "The Afro-American Community and the Birth Control Movement, 1918–1942" (Ph.D. diss., University of Massachusetts, 1991). For primary evidence that suggests that literature aimed at upwardly mobile and elite race members contained discussion of family limitation, see Gibson and Gibson, *Golden Thoughts*, 361–62.

49. Fredrickson, *Black Image in the White Mind*, 238–47, esp. 246–47.

For decennial statistics pertaining to the African American population, see *Negro Population, 1790–1915*, 21–27, esp. 25; [U.S. Department of Commerce, Bureau of the Census], *Negroes in the United States, 1920–32* (Washington, D.C.: Government Printing Office, 1935), 1, 2, 13. In *Negroes in the United States*, the Census Bureau conceded that both the 1870 and 1890 enumerations undercounted African Americans; adjustments estimate that the 1870 census should have accounted for about 5,392,000 black Americans and the 1890 census

7,760,000. Useful analysis of African American population growth rates per decade—along with adjusted figures and percentages—may be found in Momeni, "Black Demography," 5–7.

50. [C. J.], "Prohibited from Drinking Water," *Freeman* (Indianapolis, Ind.), August 15, 1891, quoted in Willard B. Gatewood Jr., ed., "Arkansas Negroes in the 1890s: Documents," *Arkansas Historical Quarterly* 33, no. 4 (Winter 1974): 293–325, esp. 306–9; W. E. B. Du Bois, *The Philadelphia Negro: A Social Study* (1899. Reprint, New York: Schocken Books, 1967), 387.

Discussions about the census in the Afro-American press include "As to the Negro's Future," *Gazette* (Raleigh, N.C.), February 12, 1898, 1; "The Twelfth Census," *Colored American* (Washington, D.C.), March 17, 1900, 15; "Negroes Constitute Tenth of Population," *Courier* (Pittsburgh, Pa.), November 18, 1911, 1; "Negroes in the 1910 Census," *Defender* (Chicago, Ill.), July 27, 1912, 1; "Census Bureau and Negro Facts," *Age* (New York, N.Y.), October 15, 1914, 1.

51. "Necrology of the Negro Race," *Afro-American Ledger* (Baltimore, Md.), August 6, 1910. I am indebted to Steven A. Reich for bringing this key item to my attention.

52. "Is the Negro Dying Out? (A Symposium)," *Colored American Magazine* 15, no. 1 (January 1909): 659–80, esp. 659, 670, 672, 680, 678.

A primary source that provides capsule biographies of some doctors who participated in the *Colored American*'s forum is John Kenney's *The Negro in Medicine* (n.p., ca. 1912).

53. "Is the Negro Dying Out?," 663–64, 670–71.

54. Analysis of black health activists' efforts to standardize birth and death registration may be found in Susan L. Smith, *Sick and Tired of Being Sick and Tired: Black Women's Health Activism in America, 1890–1950* (Philadelphia: University of Pennsylvania Press, 1995).

55. "The Mortality of the Colored People and How to Reduce It," *Afro-American Encyclopaedia; or the Thoughts, Doings, and Sayings of the Race*, comp. James T. Haley (Nashville: Haley and Florida, 1896), 64–70, esp. 69; "'Better Babies,' An Address Delivered by Dr. C. C. Middleton at Health Week Observance at Urban League Headquarters," *Savannah Tribune*, April 3, 1915, Tuskegee Institute News Clippings File (hereafter Tuskegee File), ser. 1, main file, reel 4, frame 240.

56. Kletzing and Crogman, *Progress of a Race*, 281–82; Harris, "The Physical Condition of the Race," 25. Whereas other scholars have identified Harris as white, the introduction to the Atlanta University study *Social and Physical Condition of Negroes* states that all essays "were written exclusively by colored men and women" (3). Moreover, Harris self-identifies as black in two pamphlets that he authored. See Eugene Harris, *An Appeal for Social Purity in Negro Homes: A Tract* (Nashville: n.p., 1898), and Harris, *Two Sermons on the Race Problem, Addressed to Young Colored Men, By One of Them* (Nashville: n.p., 1895).

57. Engerman, "Black Fertility and Family Structure," 117.

58. Marilyn Irvin Holt, *Linoleum, Better Babies and the Modern Farm Woman, 1890–1930* (Albuquerque: University of New Mexico Press, 1995), 111–13.

Holt observes that, despite the bureau's intentions to serve all children, one of its critics was Kelly Miller. As Holt points out, Miller wondered whether the bureau accounted for the possibility that black babies—the descendants of former slaves—might not be adequately served by programs and approaches that ignored the physical legacy of racial oppression (116).

Additional analysis on infant welfare campaigns may be found in Richard A. Meckel, *Save the Babies: American Public Health Reform and the Prevention of Infant Mortality* (Baltimore: Johns Hopkins University Press, 1990).

59. Crumpler, *Book of Medical Discourses*, 1, 3, 4. The doctor also devoted a brief chapter about "how to marry": there, she advised that early and advanced marriages alike created "weakly children"; she further proclaimed that "a union of persons whose parents are of unmixed blood, and whose statures are nearly in proportion, usually turns out well" (6).

For evidence that she sold books herself, see handwritten note from Crumpler to a "Mrs. Stone" (ca. April 1884) inserted behind frontispiece of copy at the National Library of Medicine, Bethesda, Maryland.

60. Georgia Swift King, "Mothers' Meetings," in *Social and Physical Conditions of Negroes*, 61–62.

61. Margaret Murray Washington, "Club Work as a Factor in the Advance of Colored Women," *Colored American Magazine* 11, no. 2 (August 1906): 83–90, esp. 85; *A History of the Club Movement*, 15; Higginbotham, *Righteous Discontent*, 150–84, esp. 176–80; "Eleven Babies Win Prizes at Baby Show," *Defender*, July 13, 1918.

The information cited in the text regarding the Harper WCTU may be found in *A History of the Club Movement*, 5. Another primary source on club women and mothers' meetings is Josephine Silone Yates, "Kindergartens and Mothers' Clubs," *Colored American Magazine* 8, no. 6 (June 1905): 304–11.

In commenting on the beginnings of the child welfare movement in the United States, Alisa Klaus points out that women—Julia Lathrop and Florence Kelley, for example—were critical in establishing and staffing children's welfare agencies, including the U.S. Children's Bureau. In addition to her observation that the "baby-health contest was invented by two Iowa club women purportedly inspired by the effectiveness of the livestock show in improving the breeding of cattle," Klaus also notes that Janie Porter Barrett's settlement house "sponsored an annual Baby Day beginning in 1909." See Alisa Klaus, "Depopulation and Race Suicide: Maternalism and Pronatalist Ideologies in France and the United States," in *Mothers of a New World: Maternalist Politics and the Origins of Welfare States*, ed. Seth Koven and Sonya Michel (New York: Routledge, 1993), 188–212, esp. 191, 203, 206.

62. "Baby Week—Last Call," *Journal and Guide* (Norfolk, Va.), May 5, 1917; "Spe-

cial Features for Baby Week," *Journal and Guide*, April 28, 1917; "Baby Welfare Week A Success in Tarboro," *Journal and Guide*, June 30, 1917. For provocative evidence of black club women's more forthright embrace of eugenics during the 1920s, see "Child Welfare and Mat[e]rnity" (1928), in *Records of the National Association of Colored Women's Clubs, 1895–1992*, ed. Lillian Serece Williams (Bethesda, Md.: University Publications of America, 1993), reel 7, frames 00355–58. I am immensely grateful to Jennifer Pettit for bringing this report to my attention.

It should be noted that the Children's Bureau declared 1918 "Children's Year." As the Chicago *Defender* announced in May of that year, "all over the land the first fundamental step is being made to build up a nation of strong, fine, happy young men and women by saving and protecting the babies and children." "Campaign for Better Babies," *Defender*, May 18, 1918. I sincerely thank Wallace D. Best for alerting me to this article.

63. "Carolina Fair Opens Monday," *Journal and Guide*, October 24, 1914; Tuskegee File, ser. 1, main file, reel 2, frame 895. "N.C. Fair Was Great Success," *Journal and Guide*, November 14, 1914; Tuskegee File, ser. 1, main file, reel 2, frame 896. "Interest in 'Better Babies,'" *Journal and Guide*, November 21, 1914, Tuskegee File, ser. 1, main file, reel 2, frame 919.

Apparently, the contest aroused similar interest the next year. See "State Fair Next Week," *Journal and Guide*, October 23, 1915, Tuskegee File, ser. 1, main file, reel 4, frame 176.

64. Gaines, *Uplifting the Race*, 45.

65. Holt, *Linoleum, Better Babies*, 117–18. Although Holt does not mention race, it seems likely that the Kansas contest was for white families. Additional commentary on the eugenic content of baby and "fit family" contests is offered in Kevles, *In the Name of Eugenics*, 59, 61–62. General historical analysis that touches upon African Americans and v.d. may be found in Allan M. Brandt, *No Magic Bullet: A Social History of Venereal Disease in the United States Since 1880* (New York: Oxford, 1985), esp. 116, 157–58.

66. For evidence of baby contests in the North, Midwest, and West, see "700 Babies After Medal," *Age*, ca. March 18, 1914, Tuskegee File, ser. 1, main file, reel 2, frame 934; "Eleven Babies Win Prizes At Baby Show," *Defender*, July 13, 1918; and "Little People of the Month," *Brownies' Book* 1, no. 4 (April 1920): 116.

67. "Photos From All Sections of U.S.," *Age*, August 19, 1915; "Interested in Better Babies," *Age*, July 22, 1915; "Instructions about Photos," *Age*, July 29, 1915; "Just Four Weeks More of Contest," *Age*, August 5, 1915.

68. "Baby Culture for the Aid of Better Babies," *Age*, August 12, 1915.

Scheduled to run photographs from July 22 to September 2, 1915, the paper continued to publish them long after the competition had ended; moreover, the *Age* did not even announce winners until April of 1916. Winners were presented with silver cups which, incidentally, were not awarded until July 1916 due to "war conditions." "Babies Who Win Prizes," *Age*, April 6, 1916; "Prize Babies Will Get Cups," *Age*, July 6, 1916.

69. "700 Babies After Medal," *Age*, ca. March 18, 1914, Tuskegee File, ser. 1, main file, reel 2, frame 934. The controversy in Newark was covered by at least one black paper in the South; see "Colored Baby Won," *Planet* (Richmond, Va.), March 21, 1914, Tuskegee File, ser. 1, main file, reel 2, frame 926; "Six Tots in one Family— 100 Per Cent," *Defender*, July 27, 1918; *Competitor* 2, no. 1 (July 1920): 58–59, esp. 58.

   I thank Wallace Best for providing me with a copy of the rather interesting item out of the *Defender*.

70. "Citizens of Tomorrow," *Half-Century Magazine*, April 1919, 11 (italics in original); "Future Leaders in the Affairs of Men," *Half-Century Magazine*, March 1920, 8–9.

71. Smith, *Sick and Tired*.

72. James R. Grossman assesses the circulation of the *Defender* in *Land of Hope: Chicago, Black Southerners and the Great Migration* (Chicago: University of Chicago Press, 1981), 74–88.

   In addition to Williams's column in the *Defender*, at least two other black newspapers carried regular health columns during the mid-1910s: Dr. Lloyd E. Bailer's "Health Hints" appeared in the *Sun* (Kansas City, Mo.), Tuskegee File, ser. 1, main file, reel 4, frame 248; Dr. J. W. Pierce contributed "Health Talks" to the *Journal and Guide*.

73. Williams wrote his column from about 1913 until around 1929. For biographical information, see *Who's Who of the Colored Race: A General Biographical Dictionary of Men and Women of African Descent. Vol. One: 1915*, ed. Frank Lincoln Mather (Reprint, Detroit: Gale Research Co., 1976), 1:284. An especially interesting source that includes a small section on Williams ("The Rise of a Surgeon") is located in the Special Collections at the University of Illinois–Chicago; see *The Negro in Chicago, 1779 to 1929, Vols. 1–2* (Chicago: Washington Intercollegiate Club and International Negro Student Alliance, 1929), 116–17.

74. A. Wilberforce Williams, "Dr. A. Wilberforce Williams Talks on Preventive Measures, First Aid Remedies, Hygienics, and Sanitation," *Defender*, April 8, 1916, 8; ibid., October 14, 1916, 12.

75. A. Wilberforce Williams, "Keep Healthy," *Defender*, October 25, 1913, 4. For claims regarding reader demand, see ibid., February 14, 1914, 4; for columns where Williams answered questions from readers who were infected, see "Keep Healthy" columns (which were given various headings over the years) for February 14, 1914; March 28, 1914; and August 15, 1914.

   Williams's reference to "damaged goods" refers to a contemporary book that was realized both as a play and silent film; see his column from January 22, 1916; and separate advertisement for *Damaged Goods*, *Defender*, January 1, 1916, 6.

76. Examples of Williams's treatment of children and venereal disease are located within columns from May 24, 1913; October 18, 1913; August 1, 1914; May 11, 1918. He also wrote on child welfare and promoted baby week; consult April 25, 1914; November 20, 1915; June 24, 1916; June 30, 1917; June 8, 1918; August 17, 1918.

77. Williams, "Keep Healthy," *Defender*, November 8, 1913, 4. The column for May 18, 1918, contains additional commentary by Williams on restrictive marriage laws.

78. Examples of Williams's "Venereal [Disease] Drive" columns may be found in the following issues of the *Defender*: May 11, 1918; May 18, 1918; May 25, 1918; June 1, 1918; June 15, 1918. See also "Dr. A. Wilberforce Williams Talks on . . . Venereal Plague—138,000 Cases Among Our Young Men in the Army—What Are You Going to Do About It?," *Defender*, September 21, 1918, 16.

79. McFalls and Masnick, "Birth Control and Fertility," 90; Jessie Rodrique, "The Black Community and the Birth-Control Movement," in *Unequal Sisters: A Multi-Cultural Reader in U.S. Women's History*, ed. Ellen Carol Du Bois and Vicki L. Ruiz (New York: Routledge, 1990), 333.

80. "A Campaign Among Negroes," *Journal of Social Hygiene* 5 (1919): 630–31, esp. 630. Other primary discussions of venereal affliction and black Americans include Arthur B. Spingarn, "The Health and Morals of Colored Troops," *Crisis* 16 (1918): 166, 168; Arthur B. Spingarn "The War and Venereal Disease Among Negroes," *Journal of Social Hygiene* 4 (1918): 333–46; Franklin O. Nichols, "Some Public Health Problems of the Negro," *Journal of Social Hygiene* 8 (1922): 281–85.

81. [The American Social Hygiene Association], "The Keeping Fit Exhibit for Negro Boys and Young Men" (New York City: American Social Hygiene Association, ca. 1919). Records of the American Social Health Association, folder 171: 8, Social Welfare History Archives, University of Minnesota Libraries. SWHA Archivist David Klaassen very kindly supplied me with facsimiles of exhibition literature.

82. *The Negro in Chicago, 1779 to 1929, Vols. 1–2*, 117; "Educational Campaign Against Venereal Diseases," *Tribune* (Philadelphia, Pa.), September 28, 1918, Hampton University News Clippings File, item 267, no. 2, frame 139.

83. "A Campaign Among Negroes," 631; Charles V[ictor] Roman, "The American Negro and Social Hygiene," *Journal of Social Hygiene* 7 (1921): 41–47, esp. 43; Dr. Julian Lewis, "Health Talks," *Half-Century Magazine* 7, no. 3 (September 1919): 10.

Significantly, Christina Simmons makes the observation that in black social hygiene work during the late 1910s, "the voices of male professional experts dominated the discourse." Simmons, "African Americans and Sexual Victorianism," 58. This certainly appears to be the case in terms of v.d. canvassing during the Great War.

84. "At the Y.M.C.A. Headquarters," *Defender*, April 12, 1913, 5; "Begin Campaign

for Negro Child Welfare," *Age*, January 21, 1921, 8; "The Glorious Task of 'Lifting As We Climb,'" *Competitor* 3, no. 1 (January/February 1921): 39–43, esp. 39; "National Federation of Women's Clubs: The President Announces Heads of Departments," *Competitor* 2, no. 3 (November 1920): 211–14, esp. 212.

85. For ads and summaries of the dramas mentioned in text, see "Unhappily Wed," *Defender*, February 22, 1919, 13; "Where Are My Children," ibid., October 28, 1916, [8?]; "Her Unborn Child," ibid., June 22, 1918, 4; "End of the Road," ibid., June 28, 1919, 8. An intriguing primary study that provides context for *End of the Road* and *Damaged Goods*—a study partially conducted among four gender and race segregated groups—is Karl S. Lashley and John B. Watson, "A Psychological Study of Motion Pictures in Relation to Venereal Disease Campaigns," *Journal of Social Hygiene* 7 (1921): 181–219. Interestingly, such films were screened abroad as well: Gail Hershatter notes that both *Damaged Goods* and *End of the Road* were shown in Shanghai. See Hershatter, *Dangerous Pleasures: Prostitution and Modernity in Twentieth-Century Shanghai* (Berkeley: University of California Press, 1997), 228.

86. Mary Carbine, "'The Finest Outside the Loop': Motion Picture Exhibition in Chicago's Black Metropolis, 1905–1928," *Camera Obscura: A Journal of Feminism and Film Theory* 23 (May 1990): 8–41, esp. 14 and 17. For fascinating analysis of eugenics in popular culture, see Martin S. Pernick, *The Black Stork: Eugenics and the Death of "Defective" Babies in American Medicine and Motion Pictures Since 1915* (New York: Oxford University Press, 1996).

87. Angelina W. Grimké, "The Closing Door," *Birth Control Review* 3, no. 9 (September 1919): 10–14; Angelina W. Grimké, "The Closing Door," *Birth Control Review* 3, no. 10 (October 1919): 8–12; Mary Burrill, "They That Sit in Darkness: A One-Act Play of Negro Life," *Birth Control Review* 3, no. 9 (September 1919): 5–8.

88. Fout, "Introduction," in *American Sexual Politics*; Simmons, "African Americans and Sexual Victorianism"; George Chauncey Jr., "Christian Brotherhood or Sexual Perversion?: Homosexual Identities and the Construction of Sexual Boundaries in the World War I Era," in *Hidden From History: Reclaiming the Gay and Lesbian Past*, ed. Martin Bauml Duberman, Martha Vicinus, and George Chauncey Jr. (New York: Penguin, 1989), 294–317.

89. Lawrence W. Levine, *Black Culture and Black Consciousness: Afro-American Folk Thought from Slavery to Freedom* (New York: Oxford University Press, 1977), 242–44, 275–82, 332–34. Whereas I would qualify his contention that late nineteenth and early twentieth century "Afro-Americans were often freer to express . . . [sexual] truths for the simple reason that they had less stake in the preservation of the sexual myths of the larger society" (282), Levine's work remains invaluable. Equally invaluable is Hazel V. Carby's "'It Jus Be's Dat Way Sometime': The Sexual Politics of Women's Blues," in *Unequal Sisters*, 238–49.

CHAPTER FOUR

1. Joseph R. Gay and I. Garland Penn, *Afro-American Home Manual and Practical Self-Educator Showing What to Do and How to Do It, Being a Complete Guide to Success in Life* (n.p.: 1902); the *Afro-American Home Manual* was first published as *The College of Life or Practical Self-Educator* (Chicago: Chicago Publication and Lithograph Co., 1895).

2. Claudia Tate, *Domestic Allegories of Political Desire* (New York: Oxford University Press, 1992). Tate explicitly situates conduct literature and "domestic novels" as part of the same historical moment; see *Domestic Allegories*, 4, 110, 183–84.

3. Josie B[riggs] Hall, *Hall's Moral and Mental Capsule: For the Economic and Domestic Life of the Negro, As a Solution of the Race Problem* (Dallas: Rev. R. S. Jenkins, 1905), 5, 10, 7, 15–16, 2, 20. Hall had apparently written another book entitled *Precious Thoughts of the Present and Future*, which was lost in a fire as Hall was finishing it during the 1890s. See *Hall's Moral and Mental Capsule*, 1. I am grateful to Leslie K. Dunlap who brought the fascinating and obscure *Capsule* to my attention.

   Biographical data on Hall appears in the introductory pages of the *Capsule* (v–vi) and additional information on her may be found in *Who's Who Among the Colored Baptists of the United States*, ed. Samuel William Bacote (Kansas City, Mo.: Franklin Hudson Publishing, 1913), 1:258–60. This entry claims that Hall's book enjoyed "a wide circulation . . . by thousands of people—both white and colored—who have attempted to solve the so-called race problem."

4. Hall, *Hall's Moral and Mental Capsule*, 45–47.

5. Ibid., 236, 45–46, 54–89. Here, I focus on Hall's comments regarding marriage, but another key aspect of her text is "The Pinnacle of Fame," where she outlined the ideal life path for "Negro girl[s]." There, she contended that all girls—regardless of class or occupation—could be virtuous and thus "erase the stigma that's now attached to the name of Negro womanhood." See 112–27, esp. 123–24.

   On a somewhat related note, Hall announced that while she had little interest in the question of "Woman's Rights" (155–57), earlier in the text (65) she nevertheless observed that "[if] the same dishonor was attached to male debauchers, which stigmatizes women . . . would there not be a better state of affairs in society?"

6. In *Forgotten Readers*, literary scholar Elizabeth McHenry contends that texts and "literary societies . . . worked . . . to create citizens in black communities throughout the United States." I take McHenry's argument in a slightly different direction by asserting that conduct manuals performed a similar function by serving as primers. More specifically, I draw upon Saidiya Hartman's critical identification of primers as textbooks on citizenship. See McHenry, *Forgotten Readers: Recovering the Lost History of African American Literary Societies* (Durham: Duke University Press, 2002), 19; Saidiya V. Hartman, *Scenes of Subjection: Terror, Slavery,*

and Self-Making in Nineteenth-Century America (New York: Oxford University Press, 1997), 128–29, 133.

Nicole Stanton quite thoughtfully alerted me to the existence of McHenry's work as I was writing this chapter; I sincerely thank her for doing so.

7. Hartman, *Scenes of Subjection*, 129; Tate, *Domestic Allegories of Political Desire*, 4.

8. Sandra Gunning made a compelling and fascinating observation about Afro-American texts constituting a form of collective reproduction similar to photographs during a conversation in August 2002, for which I am extremely grateful.

9. For incisive commentary on the significance of "character development"—especially for parents who harbored professional aspirations for their children—within the race, see Stephanie J. Shaw, *What a Woman Ought to Be and to Do: Black Professional Women Workers during the Jim Crow Era* (Chicago: University of Chicago Press, 1996), 13–40, esp. 15, 16, 20.

10. Eugene Harris, *An Appeal for Social Purity in Negro Homes: A Tract* (Nashville: [University Press?], 1898), 2; Hall, *Hall's Moral and Mental Capsule*, 101–2, 44.

11. William Noel Johnson, *Common Sense in the Home* (Cincinnati: Press of Jennings & Pye, 1902), 54.

12. Elizabeth Lunbeck, *The Psychiatric Persuasion: Knowledge, Gender, and Power in Modern America* (Princeton, N.J.: Princeton University Press, 1994), 256.

13. M. E. Melody and Linda M. Peterson, *Teaching America about Sex: Marriage Guides and Sex Manuals from the Late Victorians to Dr. Ruth* (New York: New York University Press, 1999), 4.

14. Hartman, *Scenes of Subjection*, 125–63, esp. 128–29; Clinton B[owen] Fisk, *Plain Counsels for Freedmen: In Sixteen Brief Lectures* (Boston: American Tract Society, 1866), 59–64, esp. 61; J[ared] B[ell] Waterbury, *Friendly Counsels for Freedmen* (New York: American Tract Society, 1864), esp. 27, 19–20, 28–29, 14–15.

15. L[ydia] Maria Child, *The Freedmen's Book* (Boston: Ticknor and Fields, 1865), 206–18, 221–22, 249, 270–71. Saidiya Hartman notes that not only were freed people's primers used as textbooks, but Child's work was "generally considered too incendiary for use in many Southern schools because she encouraged the freed to leave work situations where they were not respected and directly addressed the ravages of slavery." See Hartman, *Scenes of Subjection*, 236 n. 13.

16. Child, *The Freedmen's Book*, 223–24, 270.

17. I borrow this phrase from Claudia Tate, *Domestic Allegories of Political Desire*, 3–22.

18. For analysis of the content and purpose of club papers, see McHenry, *Forgotten Readers*, 207–19.

19. W[illiam] R[euben] Pettiford, *Divinity in Wedlock: That State of Existence that Most Thoroughly Develops the Deepest and Best Passions of the Soul* (Birmingham: Roberts & Son, 1894), 27–31. Pettiford's construction of proper, wedded black manhood hews closely to what Elizabeth Lunbeck calls "the respectable masculinity of the breadwinner." See Lunbeck, *The Psychiatric Persuasion*, 230.

20. Tate, *Domestic Allegories of Political Desire*, 197. Pettiford clearly makes an argument along these lines; see *Divinity in Wedlock*, 64–65.

21. Pettiford, *Divinity in Wedlock*, 12, 19–20, 61–67, 69, 77–78, 32. It is especially revealing that Pettiford's chapter for husbands is entitled "Hints to the Husband" (68–75), while the one for wives is given the graver heading "God's Advice to the Wife" (61–67).

22. Pettiford, *Divinity in Wedlock*, 5–6, 33–40, 56, 59.

On page 60, the author makes an oblique reference to his own "very peculiar history" regarding marriage; this reference follows Pettiford's assertions that husbands must be able to provide for their wives. According to William Simmons, Pettiford's first marriage occurred when he was twenty-two; Simmons further suggests that despite ample initiative on his part, Pettiford's young manhood was one of economic hardship. See William J. Simmons, *Men of Mark: Eminent, Progressive, and Rising* (Cleveland: Geo. M. Rewell, 1887), 460–65. Brief references to Pettiford's later years as prosperous race man may be found in Robin D. G. Kelley, *Hammer and Hoe: Alabama Communists during the Great Depression* (Chapel Hill: University of North Carolina Press, 1990), 3, 108.

23. Pettiford, *Divinity in Wedlock*, 56, 11–13, 23–25, 64–65, 51–55.

Patricia J. Campbell makes the revealing observation that during the late nineteenth century "flirting" also connoted what "later sex educators were to call . . . 'petting.'" Campbell further notes that late nineteenth-century authors often argued that flirting on the part of young women resulted in frustrated young men seeking sexual release with prostitutes. See Campbell, *Sex Guides: Books and Films About Sexuality for Young Adults* (New York: Garland Publishing, 1986), 37.

24. Pettiford, *Divinity in Wedlock*, 91–93, 52–53. The author also detailed proper roles for wives and husbands, described the ideal regulation of home life, and delineated social classes among the race. Pettiford's "classes" were predicated upon economic standing *and* moral turpitude. See *Divinity in Wedlock*, 7–13.

25. Rayford W. Logan and Michael R. Winston, eds., *Dictionary of American Negro Biography* (New York: W. W. Norton, 1982), 39–40; I[rvine] Garland Penn, *The Afro-American Press and Its Editors* (Springfield, Mass.: Willey, 1891); Robert C[harles] O['Hara] Benjamin, *Poetic Gems* (Charlottesville, Va.: Peck & Allan, 1883); R[obert] C[harles] O['Hara] Benjamin, *The Life of Toussaint L'Ouverture . . . with a Historical Survey of Santo Domingo* (Los Angeles: Evening Express Co., c. 1888); R[obert] C[harles] O['Hara] Benjamin, *Benjamin's Pocket History of the American Negro: A Story of Thirty-One Years, from 1863 to 1894* (Providence: Marion Trint, 1894); R[obert] C[harles] O['Hara] Benjamin, *Southern Outrages: A Statistical Record of Lawless Doings* ([Los Angeles?]: n.p., 1894).

According to one source, Benjamin authored at least seven more works by the end of the century. See Kletzing and Crogman, *Progress of a Race, or The Remarkable Advancement of the Afro-American Negro* (Atlanta: J. L. Nichols, 1898. Reprint, New York: Negro Universities Press, 1969), 578.

26. R[obert] C[harles] O['Hara] Benjamin, *Don't: A Book for Girls* (San Francisco: Valleau & Peterson, 1891); Oliver Bell Bunce ["Censor"], *Don't: A Manual of Mistakes and Improprieties more or less prevalent in Conduct and Speech* (New York: D. Appleton, 1883), 23; Benjamin, *Don't*, 16–17, 29, 33–35.

Mia Bay not only alerted me to the existence of Benjamin's work, she graciously provided me with a copy of his version of *Don't*. I became aware of Bunce's book through John F. Kasson's *Rudeness and Civility: Manners in Nineteenth-Century Urban America* (New York: Hill and Wang, 1990), 52.

27. Benjamin, *Don't*, 13, 29–30, 20–23, 34; George Chauncey Jr., "From Sexual Inversion to Homosexuality: The Changing Medical Conceptualization of Female 'Deviance,'" in *Passion and Power: Sexuality in History*, ed. Kathy Peiss and Christina Simmons with Robert A. Padgug (Philadelphia: Temple University Press, 1989), 87–117, esp. 88.

For discussion of homosexual experimentation and sex play among children and adolescents during the early twentieth century, see Lunbeck, *The Psychiatric Persuasion*, 233–34, 295–98. For analysis that situates the emergence of concepts regarding homosexuality within the racially charged atmosphere in which black men and women produced conduct literature, see Siobhan B. Somerville, *Queering the Color Line: Race and the Invention of Homosexuality in American Culture* (Durham: Duke University Press, 2000), 15–38.

28. Benjamin, *Don't*, 43–44, 8, 10, 36–45, 73–76.

29. E[lias] M[c Sails] Woods, *The Negro in Etiquette: A Novelty* (St. Louis: Buxton & Skinner, 1899), 9, 63, 32, 47, 152.

30. See ibid., 9, 13–61.

31. Ibid., 48–49, 131–33.

32. Ibid., 131, 133.

33. A number of African American women's historians have commented upon James Jacks's slanderous remarks about black women while Ida Wells was in England on a second antilynching tour; a succinct, rather effective account may be found in Deborah Gray White, *Too Heavy a Load: Black Women in Defense of Themselves, 1894–1994* (New York: W. W. Norton, 1999), 21–55. Classic statements on rampant discourses linking blacks with pathology include George M. Fredrickson, *The Black Image in the White Mind: The Debate on Afro-American Character and Destiny, 1817–1914* (New York: Harper & Row, 1972), 228–82; Sander L. Gilman, *Difference and Pathology: Stereotypes of Sexuality, Race, and Madness* (Ithaca: Cornell University Press, 1985); Nancy Stepan, "Biological Degeneration: Races and Proper Places," in *Degeneration: The Dark Side of Progress*, ed. J. Edward Chamberlin and Sander L. Gilman (New York: Columbia University Press, 1985), 97–116. For documents that illuminate the context in which disfranchisement and segregation occurred (including an excerpt from Hoffman's *Race Traits*), see *"Plessy v. Ferguson": A Brief History with Documents*, ed. Brook Thomas (Boston: Bedford Books, 1997).

34. Eugene Harris, *Two Sermons on the Race Problem, Addressed to Young Colored Men, By One of Them* (Nashville: University Press, 1895), 7; Harris, *An Appeal for Social Purity*, 5.

35. Harris, *An Appeal for Social Purity*, 2.

36. Ibid., 8, 10–11, 15–16.

37. Mrs. N. F. [Gertrude Bustill] Mossell, *The Work of the Afro-American Woman*, 2nd ed. (Philadelphia: Geo. S. Ferguson, 1908. Reprint, New York: Oxford University Press, 1988), 116–25, esp. 116 and 119, 123. Here, I borrow Joanne Braxton's phraseology regarding Mossell's invocation of advice literature in *The Work of the Afro-American Woman*; see Braxton's introduction to the Oxford reprint edition, xxxvi–xxxvii.

38. Braxton, "Introduction," in ibid., xxxvi.

39. The second edition appears to be unrevised as it contains no information regarding events that happened—or texts published—after 1894, the original publication date.

40. L. T. Christmas, *An Evil Router from all the Walks of Life—from the Cradle to the Grave. A Panacea for Racial Frictions and a Crowning Benediction to Humanity* . . . (Raleigh: Presses of Edwards & Broughton, 1900), 3, 5, 12–13; Johnson, *Common Sense in the Home*, 50–68, 187–88.

41. For a brief argument regarding the appearance of sex education texts aimed specifically at youthful readers, see Campbell, *Sex Guides*, 15.

42. Advertisement, *The Voice* 3, no. 7 (July 1906): back cover. Published originally as the *Voice of the Negro* when based in Atlanta, the journal's title was shortened once it began to be published in Chicago.

43. Thomas G. Dyer contends that *Floyd's Flowers* may be considered a "schoolbook written for black children . . . [that was] intended to introduce young blacks to aspects of their culture and history." Dyer acknowledges that the text had a "strong moral tone" but he primarily analyzes ways in which *Floyd's Flowers* encouraged girls and boys both to learn about race heroes and to persevere in the face of mounting racial oppression. See Dyer, "An Early Black Textbook: *Floyd's Flowers or Duty and Beauty for Colored Children*," *Phylon* 37, no. 4 (Fourth Qtr., 1976): 359–61, esp. 359.

44. Maurice O. Wallace, *Constructing the Black Masculine: Identity and Ideality in African American Men's Literature and Culture, 1775–1995* (Durham: Duke University Press, 2002), 83.

45. Dyer, "An Early Black Textbook," 359. Floyd's publications include *National Perils: An Address delivered at Atlanta, Georgia, Monday, January 2, 1899* (Augusta, Ga.: Georgia Baptist Print, ca. 1899); *Prodigal Young Men: A Sermon to Young Men at Tabernacle Baptist Church, Augusta, Georgia, Sunday night, January 28, 1900* (Augusta, Ga.: Georgia Baptist Print, 1900); *Life of Charles T. Walker* (1902. Reprint, New York: Negro Universities Press, 1969).

46. Silas X. Floyd, *Floyd's Flowers; or, Duty and Beauty For Colored Children, Being One Hundred Short stores Gleaned From the Storehouse of Human Knowledge and Experience . . .* (Atlanta: Hertel, Jenkins, 1905. Reprint, New York: AMS Press, 1975), 46–50, 309–11, 252–53, 229.

   As did a number of his contemporaries who were social reformers, Silas Floyd attended the 1902 Negro Young People's Christian and Educational Congress; he also contributed a column to *Voice of the Negro* for a brief time. A brief biography of Floyd may be found in *Souvenir: Official Program and Music of the Negro Young Peoples' Christian and Educational Congress, Held August 6–11, 1902, Atlanta, Ga.* (Nashville: National Baptist Publishing Board, ca. 1902), 183.

47. Floyd, *Floyd's Flowers*, 51–53, 96–99, 219, 250–53. Dyer briefly argues that Floyd "gave special attention to male misbehavior." See Dyer, "An Early Black Textbook," 360.

48. Floyd, *Floyd's Flowers*, 250–53, passim.

   Ironically, in 1918, an anonymous *Defender* subscriber from Georgia suggested that Silas Floyd was the last man in any position to offer advice to the race: "I've known [Floyd] all my life and he is not a decent man morally. He is what I would call a white people's nigger." *Defender* (Chicago, Ill.), February 16, 1918, 10.

49. Advertisement, *The Voice* 3, no. 7 (July 1906): back cover. *Floyd's Flowers* was reissued in 1909 by Chicago's Howard, Chandler publishing house, and the Austin Jenkins Company in Washington, D.C., published revised versions of the books under at least three different titles: *Short Stories for Colored People Both Old and Young* (1920), *The New Floyd's Flowers: Short Stories for Colored People Old and Young* (1922), and *Charming Stories for Young and Old* (1925). Moreover, Austin Jenkins published a version of *Floyd's Flowers* as the second part of its *National Capital Book of Etiquette* during the early 1920s. See *Crisis* 22, no. 6 (October 1921): 285; *Crisis* 24, no. 6 (October 1922): 283.

50. Review of *Floyd's Flowers*, *Voice of the Negro* 2, no. 10 (October 1905): 722.

51. Hall, *Hall's Moral and Mental Capsule*, 237. It should be noted that the *Capsule* includes writings by other authors as well; I have endeavored only to quote from portions that appear to have been produced by Hall herself.

52. Ibid., 54–70, esp. 65–66.

   An example of domestic whiggishness, Hall's "What a Wonderful Progress!" commemorates uplift; this poem proudly highlights the race's movement from "huts into cottages." See pages 182–83.

53. Ibid., 155–57, 48, 57, 61.

54. Ibid., 67–70, 112–37.

55. For commentary on the emergence of the "sexual adolescent" at the turn of the century, see Jeffrey P. Moran, *Teaching Sex: The Shaping of Adolescence in the 20th Century* (Cambridge: Harvard University Press, 2000), 1–22.

56. Lunbeck, *The Psychiatric Persuasion*, 187–94, esp. 187–89. In addition to her

critical argument regarding anxieties over the "hypersexual woman" (185–208), Lunbeck's work is particularly suggestive in terms of her assertion that adolescence is a deeply gendered concept.

57. See Willard B. Gatewood's chapter "The Genteel Performance" in his *Aristocrats of Color: The Black Elite, 1880–1920* (Bloomington: Indiana University Press, 1990), 187–209; specific reference to Hackley appears on 184–85, 198, 208. My own interpretation of Hackley differs somewhat from Gatewood's, yet I certainly agree with him that, in *The Colored Girl Beautiful*, Hackley unequivocally links the progress of the privileged to the progress of the poorer. See Gatewood, *Aristocrats of Color*, 208.

58. Emma Azalia Hackley, *The Colored Girl Beautiful* (Kansas City, Mo.: Burton Publishing, 1916), 10–11, 61–67, 109–13, 169–78, 181–206.

59. Ibid., 61, 63, 64, 195, 194, 181–82, 17–18, 183, 201–2.

60. For the review cited in the text, see the *Freeman* (Indianapolis, Ind.), [August 4?], 1917, Tuskegee Institute News Clippings File, ser. 1, main file, reel 6, frame 72.

61. Rev. R[evels] A[lcorn] Adams, *The Negro Girl* (Kansas City, Kans.: Independent Press, 1914), dedication, title page, 12–20, 87, 82, 24, 58, 110–19, 63–65, 77, 87, 102, 100. With the exception of *The Negro Girl* and *The Social Dance* (Kansas City, Kans.: Published by the Author, 1921), Adams's other tracts are difficult to find and may no longer be extant; the Library of Congress's copy of *Syphilis — The Black Plague* (Kansas City, Kans.: Published by the Author, 1919) appears to be lost. Still, the cover of *The Social Dance* refers to his other works, *Fighting the Ragtime Devil* and *Exalted Manhood*.

62. Adams, *Negro Girl*, 32, 94–97.

63. Ibid., 97–101.

64. Regina Lois Wolkoff, "The Ethics of Sex: Individuality and the Social Order in Early Twentieth-Century American Sexual Advice Literature" (Ph.D. diss., University of Michigan, Ann Arbor, 1974), 3.

65. Johnson, *Common Sense in the Home*, 142–43. Italics in original.

66. Christmas, *An Evil Router*, 7–8, 24.

67. Hall, *Hall's Moral and Mental Capsule*, 173–74, 155–57, 128–36, esp. 133–34. Although mere speculation on my part, it is possible that Hall connected painful losses of her childhood to the political activity of her elders. See ibid., vi; Samuel William Bacote, ed., *Who's Who Among the Colored Baptists of the United States* (Kansas City, Mo.: Franklin Hudson Publishing, 1913), 1:258–60, esp. 258.

For primary testimony on the maelstrom swirling about black political involvement during and after Reconstruction, see Herbert Aptheker, ed., *A Documentary History of the Negro People in the United States. Vol. II: From the Reconstruction Era to 1910* (New York: Citadel Press, 1951), 572–99. See also Donald G. Nieman, ed., *Black Freedom/White Violence, 1865–1900* (New York: Garland Publishing, 1994).

68. Anne Walker [Mrs. A. W.] Blackwell, *The Responsibility and Opportunity of the Twentieth Century Woman* (n.p., ca. 1910), 9, 5, 3, 12.

Blackwell was corresponding secretary for the Woman's Home and Foreign Missions Society; her husband was A.M.E. Zion preacher George Lincoln Blackwell. While it is somewhat difficult to ascertain the contours and demands of Blackwell's own household—her two children were deceased by 1915—she believed every woman should work toward improving home life: her own or that of the collective. For additional biographical data see Frank Lincoln Mather, *Who's Who of the Colored Race: A General Biographical Dictionary of Men and Women of African Descent* (Reprint, Detroit: Gale Research Co., 1976), 1:27–28.

69. N[annie] H[elen] Burroughs, "Black Women and Reform," in "Votes for Women: A Symposium by Leading Thinkers of Colored America," *Crisis* 10, no. 4 (August 1915): 187. A number of women expressing their viewpoints in this issue of the *Crisis* argued that the vote—especially in the hands of women—was essential for the maintenance of black women's virtue and the protection of African American households.

Whereas her position might have eventually changed, Hall was hostile to woman suffrage in 1905. See "Woman's Rights," in *Hall's Moral and Mental Capsule*, 155–57.

70. B. Q. Lee, "National Home Culture League to Solve Problem," *Pittsburgh Courier*, June 17, 1911.

71. Kevin K. Gaines, *Uplifting the Race: Black Leadership, Politics, and Culture in the Twentieth Century* (Chapel Hill: University of North Carolina Press, 1996), 12.

72. Tate, *Domestic Allegories of Political Desire*, 20; Glenda Elizabeth Gilmore, *Gender and Jim Crow: Women and the Politics of White Supremacy in North Carolina, 1896–1920* (Chapel Hill: University of North Carolina, 1996), 152–53.

73. McHenry, *Forgotten Readers*, 202.

74. Gilmore, *Gender and Jim Crow*, 152–53.

75. Kasson, *Rudeness and Civility*, 54; Logan and Winston, *Dictionary of American Negro Biography*, 39–40. Unfortunately, the *Dictionary of American Negro Biography* is one of few sources that mention Benjamin's untimely demise. Other biographical accounts of Benjamin's life are Delilah L. Beasley, *The Negro Trail Blazers of California* (Los Angeles: Times Mirror Printing and Binding House, 1919), 195–96; Simmons, *Men of Mark*, 991–94. See also Winston James, *Holding Aloft the Banner of Ethiopia: Caribbean Radicalism in Early Twentieth-Century America* (London: Verso, 1998), 11–12.

Benjamin was reportedly involved in at least three violent confrontations with white men in Alabama years before he was murdered. For a description of these encounters, see the introduction to Benjamin's *Southern Outrages: A Statistical Record of Lawless Doings*, 5–7.

76. Hall's four classes of women were as follows: honest, put-upon wives—women

that might be physical wrecks due to hard labor—coupled to a no-good man; home-wreckers and single mothers; unfaithful, idle, and immoral women; and "model" wives of men earning a living wage. *Hall's Moral and Mental Capsule*, 54–70; Pettiford, *Divinity in Wedlock*, 7–13; Adolph L. Reed Jr., *W. E. B. Du Bois and American Political Thought: Fabianism and the Color Line* (New York: Oxford University Press, 1997), 37. See also W. E. B. Du Bois, *The Philadelphia Negro: A Social Study* (Philadelphia: University of Pennsylvania Press, 1899. Reprint, Philadelphia: University of Pennsylvania Press, 1996), 168–92, 310–11.

77. Tate, *Domestic Allegories of Political Desire*, 3–22; John S. Haller Jr., "From Maidenhood to Menopause: Sex Education for Women in Victorian America," Journal of Popular Culture 6, no. 1 (1972): 66. For analysis of Civil War-era primers that is particularly relevant to the subject at hand, see Hartman, *Scenes of Subjection*, 125–63.

78. Nancy Armstrong, "The Rise of the Domestic Woman," in *The Ideology of Conduct: Essays in Literature and the History of Sexuality*, ed. Nancy Armstrong and Leonard Tennenhouse (London: Methuen), 187; Ronald G. Walters, ed., *Primers for Prudery: Sexual Advice to Victorian America* (Baltimore: Johns Hopkins University Press, 2000), xiii.

79. Kasson, *Rudeness and Civility*, 43.

CHAPTER FIVE

1. Halle T[anner] Dillon, "Practical Physiology," *A.M.E. Church Review* 9, no. 2 (October 1902): 183–88, esp. 184, 186; R[obert] [Fulton] Boyd, "The Mortality of the Race," *A.M.E. Church Review* 13, no. 3 (January 1897): 280–86, esp. 283. Whereas the *A.M.E. Church Review* cites Boyd as "R. S. Boyd," I believe that this is a typographical error on their part. Given that the *Review* published a photograph of Boyd along with "The Mortality of the Race," it is possible to discern that the author is indeed Robert Fulton Boyd. For a profile of Boyd featuring the same photograph, see John William Gibson and W. H. Crogman, *Colored American From Slavery to Honorable Citizenship* (Atlanta: J. L. Nichols, ca. 1903), 586–88. This text is also known as *Progress of a Race*.

2. Secondary works that touch upon black women and men's efforts to reform the health of the race during the period under consideration include Dorothy Salem, *To Better Our World: Black Women in Organized Reform, 1890–1920* (Brooklyn: Carlson Publishing, 1990); Linda Gordon, "Black and White Visions of Welfare: Women's Welfare Activism, 1890–1945," *Journal of American History* 78, no. 2 (September 1991): 559–90; Christina Simmons, "African Americans and Sexual Victorianism in the Social Hygiene Movement, 1910–40," *Journal of the History of Sexuality* 4, no. 1 (July 1993): 51–75; Susan L. Smith, *Sick and Tired of Being Sick and Tired: Black Women's Health Activism in America, 1890–1950* (Philadelphia: University of Pennsylvania Press, 1995); Susan L. Smith, "Welfare for Black

Mothers and Children: Health and Home in the American South," *Social Politics* 4, no. 1 (Spring 1997): 49–64.

3. In addition to being a minister and lecturer, Carroll served as an Army chaplain during the Spanish-American War. Beginning in 1913, he began work as an "Evangelist to Negroes of the South" under the aegis of the Southern Baptist Convention's Home Mission Board. Rev. J. J. Pipkin, *The Story of a Rising Race: The Negro in Revelation, In History and In Citizenship* (n.p.: N. D. Thompson Publishing Company, 1902. Reprint, Freeport, N.Y.: Books For Libraries Press, 1971), 51; Clement Richardson, *National Cyclopedia of the Colored Race* (n.p., 1919), 449.

Apparently, local whites found Carroll—and his views—relatively palatable. Even the state's rabidly racist senator, Benjamin Tillman, reportedly acknowledged Carroll was "'highly thought of by the white people of South Carolina.'" Carroll's commitment to interracial cooperation might have emerged from his own multi- or biracial background—he was either the son or grandson of a white slaveholder. See Arthur B. Caldwell, *History of the American Negro*, South Carolina Edition (n.p.: A. B. Caldwell, 1919), 310–13, esp. 311.

4. "Carrol[l] Advises the Race," *Gazette* (Raleigh, N.C.), January 15, 1898, 4.

Not only did the *Gazette* excerpt Carroll's address, the editorial comment does not indicate how much—or little—of what Carroll actually said was printed. It is also important to note that the *Gazette* failed to publish the exact date of Sumter's Emancipation Day celebration. Although observations of Emancipation Day varied around the United States, it is safe to assume that if Carroll spoke in January, the Sumter gala occurred on New Year's Day. See William H. Wiggins Jr., *O Freedom!: Afro-American Celebrations* (Knoxville: University of Tennessee Press, 1987), xvii–xx, esp. xix.

5. "Carrol[l] Advises the Race," 4.

6. Ibid., 4.

7. At the turn of the century, more than a few aspiring-class and elite African Americans equated features of rural black homes—from size to quality, family life to economic hardship—with slave dwellings. In 1901, for example, W. E. B. Du Bois observed that "even to this day, there is a curious bareness and roughness in the ordinary Negro home, the remains of an uncouthness which in slavery times made the home anything but a pleasant lovable place." W. E. B. Du Bois, "The Problem of Housing the Negro, II. The Home of the Slave," *Southern Workman* 30, no. 9 (September 1901): 486–93, esp. 492.

8. William Hannibal Thomas, *The American Negro: What He Was, What He Is, and What He May Become. A Critical and Practical Discussion* (New York: Macmillan, 1906).

9. For analysis of late nineteenth- and early twentieth-century concepts of orderly households, see Martha Banta, *Taylored Lives: Narrative Productions in the Age of Taylor, Veblen, and Ford* (Chicago: University of Chicago Press, 1993), esp. 205–71.

10. "Carrol[l] Advises the Race," 4.

In terms of Carroll's overarching vision of domesticity, industrial education, politics, and race reform, Kevin Gaines offers relevant commentary: "The problem with *racial* uplift ideology [was] . . . one of unconscious internalized racism. . . . Building black homes and promoting family stability came to displace a broader vision of uplift as group struggle for citizenship and material advancement." Gaines, *Uplifting the Race: Black Leadership, Politics, and Culture in the Twentieth Century* (Chapel Hill: University of North Carolina Press, 1996), 6.

11. Claudia Tate, ed., *The Works of Katherine Davis Chapman Tillman*, (New York: Oxford University Press, 1991), 301–8, 315–40, 341–88. In *Domestic Allegories of Political Desire*, Tate makes the intriguing observation that *Fifty Years of Freedom* is a somewhat deceptive title: "[It] suggests optimism in that the hero moves from a lowly cabin to congress, [but] Tillman's placement of the action into a self-contradictory time frame undermines that optimism." Tate, *Domestic Allegories of Political Desire: The Black Heroine's Text at the Turn of the Century* (New York: Oxford University Press, 1992), 18.

Elsewhere, Tate suggests Tillman's take on racial progress was tempered by the "harsh reality of segregation at the turn of the century, a time when the promises of Reconstruction proved false." Tate, "Introduction," in *The Works of Katherine Davis Chapman Tillman*, 3–62, esp. 52.

12. A notable example of how euthenicists attempted to coalesce these concepts into a "science" is Ellen H. Richards's *Euthenics: The Science of Controllable Environment; a Plea for Better Living Conditions as a First Step Toward Higher Human Efficiency* (Boston: Whitcomb & Barrows, 1910). See also Lester F. Ward, "Eugenics, Euthenics, and Eudemics," *American Journal of Sociology* 18, no. 6 (May 1913): 737–54.

13. Nannie Helen Burroughs, [National Baptist Convention], *Thirteenth Annual Report of the Executive Board and Corresponding Secretary of the Woman's Convention* (Nashville: National Baptist Publishing Board, 1913), 15. Quoted in Evelyn Brooks Higginbotham, *Righteous Discontent: The Women's Movement in the Black Baptist Church, 1880–1920* (Cambridge: Harvard University Press, 1993), 203.

14. For revealing commentary about the formation of a "Dress Well Club" in response to black migration to Detroit, see Victoria W. Wolcott, *Remaking Respectability: African American Women in Interwar Detroit* (Chapel Hill: University of North Carolina Press, 2001), 56–58.

15. Anne Walker [Mrs. A. W.] Blackwell, *The Responsibility and Opportunity of the Twentieth Century Woman* (n.p., ca. 1910), 12.

Inasmuch as Blackwell vaunted home life, she was loath to see women reduced to domestic "drudge(s)." Blackwell urged "capable women of the race to take up every question that tends toward the uplift and betterment of conditions." She implored black women to engage in temperance work and called for mothers to protect children from sites of urban leisure. She further urged women to "counteract the influence of . . . selfish and ambitious men" in black churches. See *Responsibility and Opportunity*, 1, 5, 6, 8, 9, 13.

16. Mary Church Terrell, "The Progress of Colored Women; An address delivered before the National American Women's Suffrage Association . . . February 18, 1898, on the occasion of its Fiftieth Anniversary" (Washington: Smith Brothers, 1898), 10–11. Ida B. Wells Papers, Special Collections, University of Chicago, box 5, folder 13.

17. Resolutions; July 22, 1896, in *A History of the Club Movement Among the Colored Women of the United States of America* (n.p., 1902), 47, Ida B. Wells Papers, box 5, folder 13; Katie V. Carmand, "Report of the Women's Loyal Union of New York and Brooklyn," in *A History of the Club Movement*, 14; Records of the National Association of Colored Women's Clubs, pt. 1, reel 1, frames 164–65; Terrell, "The Progress of Colored Women," 10–11, Ida B. Wells Papers, box 5, folder 13.

    Susan Smith offers similar analysis of club women in *Sick and Tired*, 17–32, esp. 17–19.

18. Sylvia C. J. Bryant [Mrs. P. J.], "How Can Mothers and Fathers Teach Their Sons and Daughters Social Purity," in *The United Negro: His Problems and His Progress, Containing the Addresses and Proceedings [of] the Negro Young People's Christian and Educational Congress, Held August 6–11, 1902*, ed. I. Garland Penn and J. W. E. Bowen (Atlanta: D. E. Luther Publishing, 1902), 439–40.

    Mention—albeit scant—of Bryant's activity in the Baptist Church may be found in the following sources: Lewis G. Jordan, *Negro Baptist History* (Nashville: Sunday School Publishing Board, National Baptist Convention, 1930), 393; Thomas Oscar Fuller, *History of the Negro Baptists of Tennessee* (Memphis: Haskins Print, ca. 1936), 145. See also Higginbotham, *Righteous Discontent*, esp. 157.

19. [U.S. Department of Commerce, Bureau of the Census], *Negro Population: 1790–1915* (Washington, D.C.: Government Printing Office, 1918. Reprint, New York: Kraus Reprint Co., 1969), 459; [U.S. Department of Commerce, Bureau of the Census], *Negroes in the United States, 1920–32* (Washington, D.C.: Government Printing Office, 1935), 253; George Edmund Haynes, *Negro New-comers in Detroit: A Challenge to Christian Statesmanship; A Preliminary Survey* (New York: Home Missions Council, 1918. Reprint, New York: Arno Press, 1969), 21.

20. William Hooper Councill, *The Negro Laborer: A Word to Him* (Huntsville: R. F. Dickson, 1887), 10, 15–21.

21. Rev. L. T. Christmas, *An Evil Router From All the Walks of Life—From Cradle to Grave—A Panacea for Racial Fitness and a Crowning Benediction to Humanity* (Raleigh: Edwards and Broughton, 1900), 4–15.

22. William Noel Johnson, *Common Sense in the Home* (Cincinnati: Press of Jennings and Pye, 1902), 9–11, 145, 66–68.

23. Euphemia Kirk, "The Woman's World" [column], *Colored American* (Washington, D.C.), February 17, 1900, 6–7; Gertrude Bustill [Mrs. N. F.] Mossell, *The*

Work of the Afro-American Woman, 2nd ed. (Philadelphia: Geo. S. Ferguson, 1908), 115–25.

24. Rev. R[evels] A[lcorn] Adams, *The Negro Girl* (Kansas City, Kans.: Independent Press, 1914), 33, 74–75, 22–23. For commentary on men without "a sense of their duty to the womanhood of the race," see pages 80–83.

Victoria Matthews expressed her convictions regarding the need of black people to take initiative in establishing institutions for the "young and unfriended" in a paper excerpted in the *Southern Workman* 28, no. 9 (September 1898): 173–74; primary evidence of black working girls' homes may be found in *Efforts for Social Betterment among Negro Americans* (Atlanta: Atlanta University Press, 1909), 100–103. A general history that contextualizes the efforts of black women who established working girls' homes is Dorothy Salem's *To Better Our World*.

25. James R. Grossman, *Land of Hope: Chicago, Black Southerners, and the Great Migration* (Chicago: University of Chicago Press, 1989), 133.

26. Richards, *Euthenics*, vii–x, 81, 44.

27. Adams, *The Negro Girl*, 23, 29–33.

For a reference to reformers who decried the "lodger evil," see Grossman, *Land of Hope*, 133.

28. James T. Haley, comp., *Sparkling Gems of Race Knowledge Worth Reading* (Nashville: J. T. Haley, 1897), 185–90, frontispiece; W. H. Councill, *Lamp of Wisdom; or, Race History Illuminated. A Compendium of Race History Comprising Facts Gleaned From Every Field for Millions of Readers* (Nashville: J. T. Haley, 1898), 34–36, 130; H. F. Kletzing and W. H. Crogman, eds., *Progress of a Race, or The Remarkable Advancement of the Afro-American Negro* (Atlanta: J. L. Nichols, 1897), 160–62, 627–28.

Pride over race homes was no incidental aspect of race pride literature. In 1915 during the celebration of the "Lincoln Jubilee," the *Michigan Manual of Freedman's Progress* included a richly illustrated section on "Negro Home and Property Owners." Many of the featured residences were spacious frame houses. See *Michigan Manual of Freedman's Progress*, comp. Francis H. Warren (Reprint, Detroit: John M. Green Publisher, 1985), 146–93.

29. Haley, *Sparkling Gems*, 54–55.

30. Historical commentary on the beginnings of the discipline—and its "early white sociological fraternity"—may be found in Edwin D. Driver and Dan S. Green, eds., *W. E. B. Du Bois on Sociology and the Black Community* (Chicago: University of Chicago Press, 1978), 1–48, esp. 39–48. See also Michael B. Katz and Thomas J. Sugrue, eds., *W. E. B. Du Bois, Race, and the City: "The Philadelphia Negro" and Its Legacy* (Philadelphia: University of Pennsylvania Press, 1998), esp. 17–30.

31. Mary White Ovington, *Half a Man: The Status of the Negro in New York* (New York: Longmans, Green, 1911); George Edmund Haynes, *The Negro at Work in New York City* (New York: Longmans, Green, 1912); Haynes, *Negro New-comers*

in Detroit; George Edmund Haynes, *The Trend of the Races* (New York: Council of Women for Home Missions and Missionary Education Movement of the United States and Canada, 1922). See also Richard R. Wright Jr., "The Economic Condition of Negroes in the North: I. Home Ownership and Savings Among the Negroes of Philadelphia," *Southern Workman* 36, no. 12 (December 1907): 665–76; Kelly Miller, *Race Adjustment: Essays on the Negro in America* (New York: Neale Publishing, 1908).

32. Du Bois summarized the work at Atlanta University in "The Atlanta Conferences," *Voice of the Negro* 1, no. 9 (March 1910): 85–90. See also *Social and Physical Condition of Negroes in Cities* (Atlanta: Atlanta University Press, 1897); W. E. Burghardt Du Bois, "The Problem of Housing the Negro, I. The Elements of the Problem," *Southern Workman* 30, no. 7 (July 1901): 390–95; W. E. B. Du Bois, "The Negroes of Farmville, Virginia: A Social Study," U.S. Department of Labor, *Bulletin* 14, no. 3 (January 1898).

Du Bois's early sociological work and his years in Atlanta are covered by David Levering Lewis in *W. E. B. Du Bois: Biography of a Race, 1868–1919* (New York: Henry Holt, 1993), 179–237. See also Driver and Green, *W. E. B. Du Bois on Sociology*, 9–17, as well as Katz and Sugrue, *W. E. B. Du Bois, Race, and the City*, esp. 1–37.

33. W. E. Burghardt Du Bois, ed., *The Negro American Family; Report of a Social Study made principally by the College Classes of 1909 and 1910 of Atlanta University . . . together with the Proceedings of the 13th Annual Conference for the Study of the Negro Problems, held at Atlanta University on Tuesday, May the 26th, 1908* (Atlanta: Atlanta University Press, 1908. Reprint, New York: Negro Universities Press, 1969), 60.

34. W. E. B. Du Bois, *The Philadelphia Negro: A Social Study; Together with a Special Report on Domestic Service by Isabel Eaton* (Philadelphia: University of Pennsylvania Press, 1899; Reprint, Philadelphia: University of Pennsylvania Press, 1996), esp. 2, 400–410.

35. Adolph L. Reed Jr., *W. E. B. Du Bois and American Political Thought: Fabianism and the Color Line* (New York: Oxford University Press, 1997) 28; Lewis, *W. E. B. Du Bois: Biography of a Race*, 188; Elijah Anderson, "Introduction to the 1996 Edition of *The Philadelphia Negro*," in Du Bois, *The Philadelphia Negro*, xiv–xx.

36. Du Bois, *The Philadelphia Negro*, 73–82, 88, 124–25, 147–63, 309, 58–65, esp. 58 and 60. See also Reed, *W. E. B. Du Bois and American Political Thought*, 29.

Du Bois was quick to note that "considerable social distinction" existed among black Philadelphians regarding region of origin. In other words, southerness was stigmatized to a sufficient degree in the city that Du Bois speculated many residents, when asked, preferred to claim "a Northern birthplace" even if their origins were below the Mason-Dixon Line. See *The Philadelphia Negro*, 73 n. 1.

37. Du Bois, *The Philadelphia Negro*, 72, 67, 166, 192; Reed, *W. E. B. Du Bois and American Political Thought*, 28, 31.

38. Du Bois did acknowledge the role of student researchers in gathering data for the series. See "The Laboratory in Sociology at Atlanta University," *Annals of the American Academy of Political and Social Science* 21 (May 1903): 503-5. Reprinted in Driver and Green, *W. E. B. Du Bois on Sociology*, 61-64, esp. 63.

39. Du Bois, "The Problem of Housing the Negro, I," 391; Du Bois, "The Problem of Housing the Negro, II," 486-93, esp. 492-93; Du Bois, "The Problem of Housing the Negro, III. The Home of the Country Freedman," *Southern Workman* 30, no. 10 (October 1901): 535-42, esp. 539-40; Du Bois, "The Housing of the Negro, VI. The Southern City Negro of the Better Class," *Southern Workman* 31, no. 2 (February 1902): 65-72, reprinted in Herbert Aptheker, ed., *Writings by W. E. B. Du Bois in Periodicals*, 1:135-38, esp. 137.

  The *Southern Workman* series and some of its illustrations would later be integrated into a major discussion on housing in an Atlanta University study. See Du Bois, *The Negro American Family*, 42-96.

40. Du Bois, "The Problem of Housing the Negro II," 486, 488-90, 492.

41. Du Bois, "The Problem of Housing the Negro, III," 537-39.

42. Ibid., 538-41.

  In his analysis of alley houses in Washington, D.C., James Borchert offers a similar analysis of lodging as James Grossman's *Land of Hope*; Borchert also points out that "boarders" could actually be family members. He further argues "taking a boarder meant incorporating another person into the family; it also meant that aid and support were reciprocal. . . . [Furthermore, boarding typically] had established guidelines which helped to mitigate . . . disrupting influences." James Borchert, *Alley Life in Washington: Family Community, Religion, and Folklife in the City, 1850-1970* (Urbana: University of Illinois Press, 1980), 80-81.

43. Du Bois outlined the sexual aspects of boarding in *The Philadelphia Negro* (194-95). Although speculation on my part, it is fairly probable that Du Bois disapproved of entire families who boarded with other families. Reform-minded race folk like Du Bois typically found boarding families problematic and disturbing. One race paper argued that lodging men were but "grain[s] of sand," women who boarded became lazy, "flippant . . . gossip[s]," and children in boarding houses lost "the best part of their rightful inheritance . . . home association." See "Make a Home, Girls," *American Citizen* (Kansas City, Kans.), March 15, 1901.

44. Du Bois, "The Problem of Housing the Negro, III," 540.

  Not only did Du Bois maintain crowding was a greater problem in the country than in the city, he attempted to demonstrate just how widespread one-room cabins actually were: "in one black belt county, out of 1474 Negro families . . . 761 lived in 1 room, 560 in 2 rooms, 93 in 3 rooms and 60 in 4 or more rooms." In addition, some rural homes with two "rooms" were, in reality, single chambers with suspended lofts. Ibid., 540; Du Bois, "The Problem of Housing the Negro, IV.

The Home of the Village Negro," *Southern Workman* 30, no. 11 (November 1901): 601–4, esp. 602.

45. [U.S. Department of Commerce, Bureau of the Census], *Negro Population: 1790–1915* (Washington, D.C.: Government Printing Office, 1918. Reprint, New York: Kraus Reprint Co., 1969), 461; Du Bois, "The Problem of Housing the Negro, III," 542.

46. Du Bois, "The Problem of Housing the Negro, IV," 602–3; Du Bois, "The Problem of Housing the Negro, V. The Southern City Negro of the Lower Class," *Southern Workman* 30, no. 12 (December 1901): 688–93, esp. 691.

47. Du Bois, "The Problem of Housing the Negro, IV," 603; Du Bois, "The Problem of Housing the Negro, V," 689, 692–93.

Du Bois made explicit mention of prostitution only in terms of how segregation tended to place bordellos in black neighborhoods, but his objection to urban "disorder" mostly likely included sex workers; see Du Bois, "The Housing of the Negro, VI," reprinted in Aptheker, *Writings by W. E. B. Du Bois in Periodicals*, 137.

Commentary on how early twentieth-century leisure spots could double as sites where prostitutes met clients may be found in Kevin J. Mumford, *Interzones: Black/White Sex Districts in Chicago and New York in the Early Twentieth Century* (New York: Columbia University Press, 1997), 96–97.

48. Jacqueline Jones, *Labor of Love, Labor of Sorrow: Black Women, Work and the Family, from Slavery to the Present* (New York: Vintage, 1985), 110–51; Kelly Miller, "Surplus Negro Women," *Race Adjustment* (New York: Neale Publishing Company, 1908), 168–78. See also Miller, "The City Negro," in *Race Adjustment*, 119–32.

49. Du Bois, *The Philadelphia Negro*, 192–93.

Du Bois did not explore the ratio of women to men in the *Southern Workman*. However, when arguing that Philadelphia had an "unusual excess of females," he openly acknowledged his intellectual debt to an essay Kelly Miller published under the auspices of the American Negro Academy. As Sharon Harley points out, he also referred to Miller's work in *The Negro American Family*. Du Bois, *The Philadelphia Negro*, 53 n. 2; Sharon Harley, "For the Good of Family and Race: Gender, Work, and Domestic Roles in the Black Community, 1880-1930," *Signs* 15, no. 21 (Winter 1990): 336–49, esp. 343 n. 16.

Here, it is also crucial to note that between 1880 and 1930, black females were reported as outnumbering black males in the general African American population. Labor migration undoubtedly skewed decennial enumerations but, all the same, females reportedly outnumbered males as far back as 1840, and most observers during the late nineteenth and early twentieth centuries accepted the "fact" that African American females predominated. However, black men supposedly outnumbered black women in certain northern and western regions. See

[U.S. Department of Commerce, Bureau of the Census], *Negroes in the United States: 1920–32* (Washington, D.C.: Government Printing Office, 1935), 78. An important regional variation appeared in the North and West where there were more black men. Figures for 1880, 1890, 1900, and 1910 — most likely not adjusted for undercounts — reflecting regional variation may be found in [U.S. Department of Commerce, Bureau of the Census], *Negro Population: 1790–1915* (Washington, D.C.: Government Printing Office, 1918. Reprint, New York: Kraus Reprint Co., 1969), 150.

50. Du Bois, "The Problem of Housing the Negro, V," 691–92. Analysis of how segregation created densely populated urban pockets such as Chicago's "black belt" may be found in Grossman, *Land of Hope*, esp. 123–60.

51. Du Bois, "The Problem of Housing the Negro, V," 692, 690; Du Bois, "The Housing of the Negro, VI," reprinted in Aptheker, *Writings by W. E. B. Du Bois*, 138.

52. Du Bois, "The Housing of the Negro, VI," reprinted in Aptheker, *Writings of W. E. B. Du Bois*, 135–36.

53. Ibid., 136, 138.

54. Daniel M. Johnson and Rex R. Campbell, *Black Migration in America: A Social Demographic History* (Durham: Duke University Press, 1981), 62–68, 73. During this period, Earl Lewis estimates there were "roughly 1.5 million" black outmigrants from the South. See Earl Lewis, "Connecting Memory, Self, and The Power of Place in African American Urban History," *Journal of Urban History* 21, no. 3 (March 1995): 347–71, esp. 349.

55. For analysis of how urban and rural, southern and northern living quarters differed, refer to Jacqueline Jones, *Labor of Love, Labor of Sorrow: Black Women, Work and the Family, from Slavery to the Present* (New York: Vintage, 1986), 182–90.

56. A revealing image of "some of the hovels in which the Colored inhabitants of large cities are forced to live" may be located in *Half-Century Magazine* 7, no. 2 (August 1919): 6.

57. Urban historian Kenneth Kusmer's observations about regional variation in residential segregation are worth quoting at length:

> There were differences between southern cities and the large northern metropolises at the turn of the century. In the South, the enclaves of blacks were greater in number in any given city and more dispersed. Furthermore, there were substantially more blacks living outside these clusters . . . than in the large northern urban areas. . . . [Also], the older, slow-growing southern cities — such as New Orleans, Charleston, and Mobile — retained the . . . pattern of racial intermingling in residency much longer than did New South cities like Atlanta. . . . [Before World War I,] the level of segregation of blacks in a particular city was closely related to the community's urban structure. Segregation

was highest in the fully developed large industrial centers of the North and lowest in the languishing gulf port cities of the South.

See Kenneth L. Kusmer, "The Black Urban Experience in American History," in *The State of Afro-American History: Past, Present, and Future*, ed. Darlene Clark Hine (Baton Rouge: Louisiana State University Press, 1986), 91–122, esp. 109–10.

58. Ibid., 109–10.

59. Suellen Hoy, *Chasing Dirt: The American Pursuit of Cleanliness* (New York: Oxford University Press, 1995), 117–21, esp. 119. For examples from Williams's columns cited in the text, see the following columns: A. Wilberforce Williams, "Dr. A. Wilberforce Williams Talks on Preventive Measures, First Aid Remedies, Hygienics, and Sanitation," *Defender* (Chicago, Ill.), May 1, 1915, 2; ibid., August 29, 1914, 8; "Keep Healthy," *Defender*, August 20, 1913, 4; "Dr. A. Wilberforce Williams Talks on . . . ," *Defender*, May 8, 1915, 2; ibid., April 14, 1914, 8; ibid., August 15, 1917, 12; ibid., September 22, 1917, 12.

60. "Meeting the Crisis: Race Distinction and Segregation—Duty to Our Children," *Reliance* (Boston, Mass.), November 22, 1913, Tuskegee Institute News Clippings File (hereafter Tuskegee File), ser. 1, main file, reel 2, frame 0361.

61. "Segregation Following Northern Migration," *Journal and Guide* (Norfolk, Va.), April 28, 1917.

62. See, for example, "The Future of the Race Dependent Upon the Restrictions and the Home-Training of the Unit of the Race," Tuskegee File, ser. 1, main file, reel 1, frame 26.

63. Rosetta Douglass Sprague, quoted in *A History of the Club Movement Among the Colored Women of the United States of America* (n.p., 1902), 36. Ida B. Wells Papers, box 5, folder 13.

64. *Bee* (Washington, D.C.), November 10, 1917, 4.

65. "Virginia Has Health Campaign," *Defender*, March 22, 1913; [Photograph], "Chicago YMCA, Clean-Up Campaign, 1919," Jesse Alexander Photo Collection, Schomburg Center for Research in Black Culture, Photographs and Prints Collection. For additional information on the distribution of health handbooks, see "Handbook on Health Issued in Virginia," *Age* (New York, N.Y.), April 22, 1914, Tuskegee File, ser. 1, main file, frame 933.

66. Vanessa Northington Gamble, *Making a Place for Ourselves: The Black Hospital Movement, 1920–1945* (New York: Oxford University Press, 1995), 3–34, esp. 10–11.

67. "The Origin and Growth of the Alpha Physical Culture Club" (ca. 1907), Hampton University Newspaper Clippings File, item 267, no. 1, frame 10; Smith, *Sick and Tired*, 24–25, 29–30, 36–39; "Negroes Discuss Problems of Health," *Age-Herald* (Birmingham, Ala.), May 9, 1913, Hampton University Newspaper Clippings File, item 267, no. 1, frame 74; "A Preventable Death Rate," *National Baptist Union Review*, Tuskegee File, ser. 1, main file, reel 2, frame 947; "The Conserva-

tion of Negro Health," [*American Oklahoma?*], March 20, 1914, Tuskegee File, ser. 1, main file, frame 933.

68. Booker T. Washington, "The Principal's Report to the Board of Trustees of Tuskegee Institute," May 31, 1915, *The Booker T. Washington Papers*, ed. Louis R. Harlan et al. (Urbana: University of Illinois Press, 1984), 13:298–314, esp. 303–4; "Nation to Observe Negro Health Week," *New York Press*, March 21, 1915, Hampton University Newspaper Clippings File, item 267, no. 1, frame 25; Williams, "Keep Healthy," *Defender*, August 21, 1915, 2.

69. *A History of the Club Movement*, 77–78; "Great National Health Week," *Defender*, January 24, 1915, Tuskegee File, ser. 1, main file, reel 4, frame 226; Smith, *Sick and Tired*, 17–32, esp. 18, 2.

70. Dr. Lloyd E. Bailer, "Health Hints: National Negro Health Week, March 21–27," *Sun* (Kansas City, Mo.), March 20, 1915, Tuskegee File, ser. 1, main file, reel 4, frame 248.

71. "The Health Crusade," *Amsterdam News* (New York, N.Y.), February 5, 1915, Tuskegee File, ser. 1, main file, reel 4, frame 220; "Dirt, Disease, Death," *Journal and Guide*, April 21, 1917; "Dr. A. Wilberforce Williams Talks on . . . ," *Defender*, April 3, 1915, 8; "National Health Week," *Argus* (St. Louis, Mo.), March 9, 1915.

    In 1917, as a tribute to Booker Washington, National Negro Health Week was moved to April—the month of Washington's birth—following his death in 1915. There was no Health Week in 1916. See Smith, *Sick and Tired*, 43–45.

72. "National Negro Health," *Independent* (Atlanta, Ga.), March 20, 1915, Tuskegee File, ser. 1, main file, reel 4, frame 220.

73. Williams, "Keep Healthy," *Defender*, August 21, 1915, 2; Williams, "Dr. A. Wilberforce Williams Talks On . . . ," *Defender*, April 3, 1915, 8.

74. Haynes, *The Trend of the Races*, 41–46.

75. Ibid., 41–46.

76. See Haynes, *Negro New-Comers in Detroit*, 21–27.

77. W. E. B. Du Bois, "The Problem of Housing the Negro, I," 93.

78. T. S. Boone, *Paramount Facts in Race Development* (Chicago: Hume Quick Print, 1921), 8, 9, 1.

79. Higginbotham, *Righteous Discontent*, 202. Tera Hunter dissects the portrayal of black women—particularly domestics and laundresses—as "conveyors of germs" in *To Joy My Freedom: Southern Black Women's Lives and Labors After the Civil War* (Cambridge: Harvard University Press, 1997), 187–218, esp. 196.

80. See "Woman Must Take Courage," *Courier* (Pittsburgh, Pa.), April 8, 1911, 8.

CHAPTER SIX

1. "The Contest Now Has Three Weeks," *Age* (New York, N.Y.), August 12, 1915, 1, 3. Unfortunately, the *Age* did not publish the name of Maud's mother, who may not have been married or whose surname might not have been Gary. As awkward

as it is to label the mother with indirect referents, I do not wish to assume that she was known as "Mrs. Gary."

2. "*Age* Contest for Better Babies," *Age*, July 15, 1913, 1, 3; "Just Four More Weeks of Contest," *Age*, August 5, 1915, 1–2; "Baby Culture for the Aid of Better Babies," *Age*, August 12, 1915, 1, 3; "Interested in Better Babies," *Age*, July 22, 1915, 1; "Diamond Rings for 175 Babies," *Age*, August 26, 1915, 1, 5.

3. For revealing commentary on gender, race, and innovations in advertising in the United States, see Marilyn Maness Mehaffy, "Advertising Race/Raceing Advertising: The Feminine Consumer (-nation), 1876–1900," *Signs* 23, no. 1 (Autumn 1997): 131–74. See also Kenneth W. Goings, *Mammy and Uncle Mose: Black Collectibles and American Stereotyping* (Bloomington: Indiana University Press, 1994), 10–11.

4. Goings, *Mammy and Uncle Mose*, 1–18; Paul R. Mullins, *Race and Affluence: An Archaeology of African America and Consumer Culture* (New York: Kluwer Academic/Plenum Publishers, 1999), 41–48, 155–83.

5. Mrs. M. Mack, "Too Many White Pictures," [letter to "The People's Forum"], *Half-Century Magazine* 7, no. 4 (November 1919): 21. Kenneth Goings suggests that popular culture depiction of black women and men as servants worked to reinforce and naturalize racial subordination. See *Mammy and Uncle Mose*.

6. Julia Mason Layton, "How the Colored Woman Can Make Home More Attractive," in *The United Negro: His Problems and His Progress, Containing the Addresses and Proceedings [of] the Negro Young People's Christian and Educational Congress, Held August 6–11, 1902*, ed. I. Garland Penn and J. W. E. Bowen (Atlanta: D. E. Luther Publishing, 1902), 441–42, esp. 442; Haley, *Sparkling Gems*, 82. For representative samples of how pictures and pamphlets were marketed as tools that inculcated or strengthened black consciousness, see "Pictures for the Home, Office or School . . . Inspiring—Educative—A Stimulus to Race Pride," *Defender* (Chicago, Ill.), May 17, 1919, 6; "Race Pride: What Do You Teach Your Boy or Girl?," [Douglas Specialties advertisement], *Defender*, June 14, 1919, 12; "Colored Man No Slacker," [Hanzel Sales Co. advertisement], *Voice of the Negro* 3, no. 1 (January 1906), advertisement section; "Why Don't You Get Acquainted with Your Race?," [Progressive Book Co. advertisement], *Half-Century Magazine* 11, no. 2 (November 1921): 13.

7. Nathan B. Young, "A Race Without an Ideal; What Must It Do to Be Saved? or, The Negro's Third Emancipation," *A.M.E. Church Review* 15, no. 2 (October 1898): 605–17; "The Newest Thing In the Publishing World," [Advertisement], *Voice of the Negro* 4, no. 4 (April 1907): advertisement section.

8. Layton, "How the Colored Woman," 442; *Voice of the Negro* 3, no. 6 (June 1906): advertisement section; Joseph R. Gay and I. Garland Penn, *Afro-American Home Manual and Practical Self-Educator Showing What to Do and How to Do It Being a Complete Guide to Success in Life* (n.p.: 1902).

9. "Standard Books by Negro Authors," [Advertisement], *Half-Century Magazine* 5, no. 5 (December 1918): advertisement section.

10. Dr. M[onroe] A[lphus] Majors, "Why We Should Read Books Written by the Negro," *Half-Century Magazine* 4, no. 6 (June 1918): 13. For Majors's own work of race history, see *Noted Negro Women: Their Triumphs and Activities* (Jackson, Tenn.: M. V. Lynk Publishing House, 1893). Biographical information on Majors may be found in Frank Lincoln Mather, ed., *Who's Who of the Colored Race: A General Biographical Dictionary of Men and Women of African Descent* (Chicago: F. L. Mather, 1915), 1:183.

    Stephen Gilroy Hall provides an overview of the race history movement in "'To Give a Faithful Account of the Race': History and Historical Consciousness in the African American Community" (Ph.D. diss., The Ohio State University, 1999).

11. Bishop Henry McNeal Turner, [Letter from Freetown, Sierra Leone], November 16, 1891, in Edwin S. Redkey, *Respect Black: The Writings and Speeches of Henry McNeal Turner* (New York: Arno Press, 1971), 107–11, esp. 110.

12. *Minutes of the American Association of Educators of Colored Youth: Session of 1894, held at Baltimore, Maryland, July 24, 25, 26, 27, 1894,* Daniel A. P. Murray Pamphlet Collection, Library of Congress, Washington, D.C.; Young, "A Race Without an Ideal," 608.

13. Miriam Formanek-Brunell, *Made to Play House: Dolls and the Commercialization of American Girlhood, 1830–1930* (New Haven: Yale University Press, 1993), 7–11, 19, 20, 61–63, 71, 30. Not all child's play with dolls mimicked nurturing aspects of domesticity: Formanek-Brunell points out that during the late nineteenth and early twentieth centuries, children often mutilated doll bodies or staged elaborate "funerals" for them. For commentary on the various meanings of "playing house" during this period, see *Made to Play House,* 5–6, 15–34; for analysis of how gender impacted doll making in the United States, see 35–60, 61–89, 90–116. Commentary on toys and gender role socialization during the early twentieth century may be found in Carroll W. Pursell Jr., "Toys, Technology, and Sex Roles in America, 1920–1940," in *Dynamos and Virgins Revisited: Women and Technological Change in History*, ed. Martha Moore Trescott (Metuchen, N.J., and London: Scarecrow Press, 1979), 252–67.

14. E. A. Johnson, "Negro Dolls for Negro Babies," *Colored American Magazine* 14, no. 10 (November 1908): 583–84, esp. 583. The works by Johnson mentioned in the text are *A School History of the Negro Race in America from 1619 to 1890: with a short introduction as to the origin of the race; also a short sketch of Liberia*, rev. ed. (Chicago: W. B. Conkey, 1893); *A History of the Negro Soldiers in the Spanish-American War* (Raleigh: Capital Publishing, 1899).

15. See Patikii and Tyson Gibbs' *Collector's Encyclopedia of Black Dolls* (Paducah, Ky.: Collector Books, 1989).

16. Doris Y. Wilkinson, "The Doll Exhibit: A Psycho-Cultural Analysis of Black Female Role Stereotypes," *Journal of Popular Culture* 21, no. 2 (Fall 1987): 19–29, esp. 22–23; Myla Perkins, *Black Dolls: An Identification and Value Guide, 1820–1991* (Paducah, Ky.: Collector Books, 1995), 57–58.

17. Young, "A Race Without an Ideal," 608.

18. During the late nineteenth and early twentieth centuries, a "large number of black dolls [were] created by middle-class white mothers." Around the turn of the century, many white children preferred to play with black rag dolls since "African American women played an increasingly significant role in the rearing of middle-class [white] children." See Formanek-Brunell, *Made to Play House*, 73, 28–29. Rag dolls from this era were also made from mass-produced commercial patterns. See Perkins, *Black Dolls*, 59–60.

    At least one black man, a Georgian named Leo Moss, made black dolls (largely as an avocation) during the late nineteenth and early twentieth centuries. See Perkins, *Black Dolls*, 12–18.

19. Formanek-Brunell, *Made to Play House*, 28–29, 73. For an example of a black doll made by a leading U.S. woman dollmaker, Martha Chase, see Myla Perkins, *Black Dolls: An Identification and Value Guide, Book II* (Paducah, Ky.: Collector Books, 1995), 12. For evidence that black rag dolls were used as "servants" during white children's play, see the stereopticon image reproduced in Perkins, *Black Dolls, Book II*, 39.

    It is worth noting that French and British doll makers produced "realistic" colored dolls during this period, but in far fewer numbers than German factories; see Perkins, *Black Dolls*, 19. For examples of "servant" and "savage" dolls produced in Germany, see illustrations in *Collector's Encyclopedia of Black Dolls*, 63, 74.

20. Mary Hillier, *Dolls and Doll-makers* (London: Weidenfeld and Nicolson, 1968), 175–83, esp. 175–76; Jan Foulke, *13th Blue Book: Dolls and Values* (Grantsville, Md.: Hobby House Press, 1997), 52–55; "The Colored Doll Is a Live One," [E. M. S. Novelty advertisement], *Crisis* 6, no. 3 (October 1913): 255.

21. Formanek-Brunell, *Made to Play House*, 15–16, 60, 89, 167–68. Whereas Formanek-Brunell's observations about the cost of domestic dolls are discussed within the context of white consumers in the United States, her observations about the relative expense of many domestically produced dolls is quite instructive here.

22. Evelyn Brooks Higginbotham, *Righteous Discontent: The Women's Movement in the Black Baptist Church, 1880–1920* (Cambridge: Harvard University Press, 1993), 166, 194.

23. "Thousands of Negro Dolls," November 9, 1911, Tuskegee Institute News Clippings File, ser. 1, main file, reel 1, frame 162; Higginbotham, *Righteous Discontent*, 194. Higginbotham notes that NNDC dolls were manufactured in Nashville,

while W. D. Weatherford reports that the company's dolls were initially made in Germany. See Weatherford, *The Negro From Africa to America* (New York: George H. Doran, 1924), 427.

24. "Negro Dolls," *Age*, October 8, 1908, 4.

25. "Give the Child a Doll," [National Negro Doll Company advertisement], *Crisis* 2, no. 3 (August 1911): 131; Excerpts of the NNDC catalog mentioned herein are reproduced in Perkins, *Black Dolls*, 22–23.

26. "Give the Child a Doll," 131; "National Negro Doll Company's Special Price List of Negro Dolls for the Christmas Season, 1911–1912," [National Negro Doll Company advertisement], *Crisis* 3, no. 2 (December 1911): 50.

   Formanek-Brunell speaks to the affordability of commercial dolls when she points out that, in 1905, mass-market "Campbell Kid dolls . . . sold for only one dollar . . . more than [working-class] families . . . could afford." *Made to Play House*, 109.

27. "The Colored Doll Is a Live One," [E. M. S. Novelty Co. advertisement], *Crisis* 6, no. 5 (October 1913): 255. Although I have yet to find conclusive evidence, I suspect that not all companies that sold black dolls were black-run or employed African Americans; it is not clear, for example, whether Otis H. Gadsden or E. M. S. Novelty were race concerns.

28. "Doll Concern Sells Stock on E-Z Payment Basis," *Defender*, May 10, 1919, 4. Berry & Ross was incorporated in 1918; see Formanek-Brunell, *Made to Play House*, 150, 220 n. 32.

29. "In the Limelight," *Half-Century Magazine* 7, no. 1 (July 1919): 9, 19; Evelyn Jones, "The Doll Manufacturer," [letter to "The People's Forum"], *Half-Century Magazine* 7, no. 2 (August 1919): 21.

30. "Colored Dolls for Your Children," [Berry & Ross advertisement], *Crisis* 17, no. 4 (February 1919): 202; Alvah L. Bottoms, "Objectionable Toys," [letter to "The People's Forum"], *Half-Century Magazine* 8, no. 1 (January 1920): 17. For an argument that racist " 'Nigger' " books were harmful to white children, see Alice Evans, "Sowing the Seeds of Prejudice," [letter to "The People's Forum"], *Half-Century Magazine* 7, no. 6 (December 1919): 17.

31. J[ames] H[enry] A[ugustus] Brazelton, *Self-Determination: The Salvation of the Race* (Oklahoma City: The Educator, 1918), frontispiece, 254–58, 34, 45.

32. Ibid., 21, 19–20, 15, 25–26. Reference to Brazelton's age may be located on page 25.

33. Ibid., 18, 15. That the struggle for "self-determination" was an issue for both black Americans and imperial subjects was apparently lost on Brazelton; he seemed more intent on suggesting that African Americans lagged behind white Americans *and* colonized people in U.S. territories. Throughout the book, he distinguishes between various "race-varieties" as well. See, for example, ibid., 24.

34. Ibid., 48, 13.

35. Ibid., 34, 14, 74. Additional hereditarian assertions are made on page 23; more comments regarding "illegal amalgamation" are located on page 26.

36. Formanek-Brunell, *Made to Play House*, 4, 85–89.

37. Ibid., 87.

38. Brazelton, *Self-Determination*, 250–53, 76–77. Interestingly, the educator also insists that the image of a "white Santa Claus" was damaging; see pages 15, 17–18, 251. For specific commentary on the "psychology of the doll," see page 18. For an example of a "Brown-Skin Santa" in Afro-American popular culture, see *Half-Century Magazine* 1, no. 5 (December 1916): cover.

39. Brazelton, *Self-Determination*, 77, 251–53.

40. Prices for black dolls typically ranged from as little as twenty-nine cents to as much as eight dollars. See advertisements cited herein for prices.

41. "Negro Dolls," *Christian Recorder*, December 22, 1921, Tuskegee Institute News Clippings File, ser. 1, main file, reel 14, frame 716.

42. "Her First Birthday," *Half-Century Magazine* 8, no. 1 (January 1920): cover; "Her Choice," *Half Century Magazine* 13, no. 3 (November–December 1922): cover; "Colored Dolls," [Afro-American Novelty Shop advertisement], *Competitor* 2, no. 3 (October–November 1920): 228; "Doll Concern Sells Stock"; "An Appeal to 12,000,000 Americans," [Berry & Ross advertisement] *Defender*, April 19, 1919, 2.

43. "Colored Dolls," [Berry & Ross advertisement], *Defender*, April 5, 1919, 17; "Now Selling on the Liberty Loan Installment Plan," [Berry & Ross advertisement], *Defender*, May 10, 1919, 4; "An Appeal to 12,000,000 Americans"; "Dolls, Dolls," [Otis H. Gadsden advertisement], *Crisis* 16, no. 6 (October 1918), 309; "Dolls—Dolls," [Otis H. Gadsden advertisement], *Crisis* 18, no. 5 (September 1919), 269. For a pointed example of how doll companies appealed to race pride, see "A Colored Child Should Have a Colored Doll," [Art Novelty Co. advertisement], *Negro World* (New York), November 22, 1924, 9.

Both Berry & Ross and the Gadsden Company produced "girl" and "boy" dolls. The National Colored Doll & Toy Company of Chicago sold the miniature gas masks. See "Boys! Go Over the Top," [National Colored Doll & Toy Company advertisement], *Half-Century Magazine* 7, no. 1 (July 1919): 14.

As early as the 1920s, writers chronicled the rise of realistic black dolls. In 1924, W. D. Weatherford noticed that "fifty years ago . . . Negroes wanted white dolls for their children because white carried with it the idea of privilege and advancement. It is significant that this is now changed, that the Negro doll carries with it the sense of race pride and race achievement." See Weatherford, *The Negro from Africa to America*, 427–28. See also Bruno Lasker, *Race Attitudes in Children* (New York: Henry Holt, 1929), 220–21. In discussing organizations responsible for popularizing black dolls, Weatherford mentions the National Baptist Convention, while Lasker mentions the Garvey movement.

44. "Words—Words—Words," *Negro World*, October 14, 1922, 10; "Exhibitors: Annual Fair and First Educational and Commercial Exposition," *Negro World*, November 4, 1922, 10.

45. Estelle Matthews, "Message for the Negro Women of the World," *Negro World*, February 4, 1922, 11.

46. See Report by Special Agent P-138, in *The Marcus Garvey and Universal Negro Improvement Association Papers*, ed. Robert A. Hill (Berkeley: University of California Press, 1983), 539–41, esp. 541 n. 3. The UNIA even promoted dolls in its public events. See, for example, "Words—Words—Words"; and "Exhibitors: Annual Fair and First Educational and Commercial Exposition."

    The connection between Berry & Ross and Marcus Garvey is odd indeed. Berry & Ross's president, H. S. Boulin—who, like Garvey, hailed from Jamaica—was initially hostile to the Universal Negro Improvement Association during the organization's early existence; as agent "P-138," Boulin informed on Garvey for the Federal Bureau of Investigation. By 1921 or 1922, however, Boulin was on friendly terms with Garvey. All the same, the reason and terms for the sale of Berry & Ross to the UNIA are not clear—neither Boulin, Berry, nor Ross appeared to have ever joined the organization.

47. See "Negro Dolls with Brown Skin," [advertisement], *Negro World*, December 30, 1922, 10.

48. E. David Cronon, *Black Moses: The Story of Marcus Garvey and the Universal Negro Improvement Association* (Madison: University of Wisconsin Press, 1955), 175.

49. For evidence of the UNIA's advocacy of racial purity, see Marcus Garvey, "Purity of Race," in *Philosophy and Opinions of Marcus Garvey or, Africa for the Africans*, 2 vols., comp. Amy Jacques Garvey (Reprint, Dover, Mass.: Majority Press, 1986), 1:37. For references to skin tone and hair type in doll advertisements, see the following examples: "Beautiful Colored Doll Free," [J. Griffith Art Company advertisement], *Crisis* 7, no. 4 (February 1914): 205; "The Colored Doll is a Live One," 255; "Dolls! Dolls!," [Otis H. Gadsden advertisement], *Defender*, September 28, 1918, 5; "Colored Dolls," [Berry & Ross advertisement], *Age*, August 30, 1919; "A Negro Child Should Have a Negro Doll," *Negro World*, August 2, 1924, 16.

50. Elizabeth Ross Haynes's *Unsung Heroes* (New York: Du Bois and Dill, 1921) was a race history for children. Silas X. Floyd's *Floyd's Flowers, or Duty and Beauty for Colored Children* (Washington, D.C.: Hertel, Jenkins, 1905) was revised, expanded, and reissued at least two times between its original publication date and 1925.

    In August 1919, the *Defender* contained a short squib announcing the publication of *Our Boys and Girls*, a "unique little monthly . . . [that] appeals especially to our boys and girls and is distinctive in the journalistic world of our Race." See *Defender*, August 30, 1919, 4. See also advertisement in *The Crusader* 2, no. 1 (September 1919): 32. "Distinctive" though it might have been, the magazine no longer appears to be extant. The only runs of *Our Boys and Girls* that I have been able to locate are mainstream, ostensibly "white" magazines; these include *Oliver Optic's Magazine: Our Boys and Girls* (1867–1875) and a range of magazines—

published in locales ranging from Pennsylvania to Missouri to California—entitled *Our Boys and Girls* published between the 1870s and the 1940s.

W. E. B. Du Bois and A. G. Dill published the *Brownies' Book*, which they advertised as being "for the Children of the Sun"—from 1920 to 1921; see *Brownies' Book* 1, no. 2 (February 1920): frontispiece.

51. Reynolds Farley, *Growth of the Black Population: A Study of Demographic Trends* (Chicago: Markham Publishing, 1971), 56–57; [U.S. Department of Commerce; Bureau of the Census], *Negro Population, 1790–1915* (Washington, D.C.: Government Printing Office, 1918. Reprint, New York: Kraus Reprint Co., 1969), 286; Ansley J. Coale and Norfleet W. Rives Jr., "A Statistical Reconstruction of the Black Population of the United States 1880–1970: Estimates of True Numbers by Age and Sex, Birth Rates, and Total Fertility," *Population Index* 39, no. 1 (January 1973): 3–36; Herman Lantz and Lewellyn Hendrix, "Black Fertility and the Black Family in the Nineteenth Century: A Reexamination of the Past," *Journal of Family History* 3, no. 3 (Fall 1978): 251–61; Stanley L. Engerman, "Black Fertility and Family Structure in the U.S., 1880–1940," *Journal of Family History* 2, no. 2 (June 1977): 117–38; Stewart Emory Tolnay, "The Fertility of Black Americans in 1900" (Ph.D. diss., University of Washington, 1981).

52. Stewart E. Tolnay, "Family Economy and the Black American Fertility Transition," *Journal of Family History* 11, no. 3 (July 1986): 272–77; Darlene Clark Hine, "Black Migration to the Urban Midwest: The Gender Dimension, 1915–1945," in *Hine Sight: Black Women and the Re-Construction of American History* (Brooklyn: Carlson Publishing, 1994), 59–86; Jacqueline Jones, *Labor of Love, Labor of Sorrow: Black Women, Work and the Family, from Slavery to the Present* (New York: Vintage Books, 1986), 88, 123.

53. Key secondary works on African Americans and birth control include Joseph McFalls and George Masnick, "Birth Control and Fertility of the U.S. Black Population, 1880 to 1980," *Journal of Family History* 6, no. 1 (Spring 1981): 89–106; Jessie May Rodrique, "The Afro-American Community and the Birth Control Movement, 1918–1942" (Ph.D. diss., University of Massachusetts, 1991).

54. George Fredrickson, *The Black Image in the White Mind: The Debate on Afro-American Character and Destiny* (New York: Harper & Row, 1971), 238–47, esp. 246–47.

For decennial statistics pertaining to African Americans, see *Negro Population, 1790–1916*, 21–27, esp. 25; [U.S. Department of Commerce; Bureau of the Census], *Negroes in the United States, 1920–1932* (Washington, D.C.: Government Printing Office, 1935), 1, 2, 13. Useful analysis of African American population growth rates per decade—along with adjusted figures to account for undercounts during the late nineteenth century—may be found in Jamshid Momeni, "Black Demography: A Review Essay," in *Demography of the Black Population in the United States: An Annotated Bibliography with a Review Essay* (Westport, Conn.: Greenwood Press, 5–7).

55. Refer to Kevin K. Gaines, *Uplifting the Race: Black Leadership, Politics, and Culture in the Twentieth Century* (Chapel Hill: University of North Carolina Press, 1996), 120–27.

Of course, race suicide was a hotly discussed issue among native-born white Americans as well. See, for example, Linda Gordon, *Woman's Body, Woman's Right: A Social History of Birth Control in America* (New York: Grossman, 1976), 136–58; and Louise Michele Newman, ed., *Men's Ideas/Women's Realities: "Popular Science," 1870–1915* (New York: Pergamon Press, 1985), 105–24, esp. 114–15.

56. Formanek-Brunell, *Made to Play House*, 65; Sharon Harley, "For the Good of Family and Race: Gender, Work, and Domestic Roles in the Black Community, 1880–1930," *Signs* 15, no. 2 (Winter 1990): 336–49, esp. 341–42.

57. "Every School Child," [Black Swan/Pace Phonograph Corporation advertisement], *Crisis* 23, no. 2 (December 1921): 92. For detailed discussion of Black Swan Records, see David Suisman, "Co-workers in the Kingdom of Culture: Black Swan Records and the Political Economy of African American Music," *Journal of American History* 90, no. 4 (March 2004): 1295–324.

58. "A Colored Child Should Have a Colored Doll." See also "Colored Dolls for Your Children"; "Inspiration: Give Your Child a Negro Doll," [Unique Doll Exchange advertisement], *Negro World*, September 22, 1928, 10.

59. See John William and Mrs. John William Gibson, *Golden Thoughts on Chastity and Procreation* (Naperville, Ill.: J. L. Nichols, ca. 1914), plate between 360–61. For the images from Silas X. Floyd's *The New Floyd's Flowers* (Washington, D.C.: Austin Jenkins, 1922), see "Mary and Her Dolls" and "Dolly's Hungry."

CHAPTER SEVEN

1. Victoria E. Matthews, "Some of the Dangers Confronting Southern Girls in the North," *Hampton Negro Conference, Number 11, July 1898* (Hampton, Va.: Hampton Institute Press, [1898?]), 62–69. Matthews's surname is, at times, cited as "Mathews" in both primary and secondary sources. For biographical information on Matthews, see Hallie Quinn Brown, comp. and ed., *Homespun Heroines and Other Women of Distinction* (Xenia, Ohio: Aldine Publishing, ca. 1926), 208–16; Elizabeth Lindsay Davis, *Lifting as They Climb* (Nashville: National Association of Colored Women, 1933), 21–22; Monroe A. Majors, *Noted Negro Women: Their Triumphs and Activities* (Jackson, Tenn.: M. V. Lynk Publishing House, 1893), 211–13; Lawson A. Scruggs, *Women of Distinction: Remarkable in Works and Invincible in Character* (Raleigh, N.C.: L. A. Scruggs, 1893), 30–32.

2. Wesley John Gaines, *The Negro and the White Man* ([Philadelphia?]: A.M.E. Publishing House, 1897. Reprint, New York: Negro Universities Press, 1969), 155. Relevant commentary on the slipperiness of racial categories around the turn of the century may be found in Matthew Pratt Guterl, *The Color of Race in America, 1900–1940* (Cambridge: Harvard University Press, 2002), esp. 14–67.

3. Gaines, *Negro and the White Man*, 151–53, 155, 162; for the chapters mentioned

within the text, consult pages 151–60 and 161–67. A contemporaneous argument that comes to some of the same conclusions regarding Afro-American women's aesthetic preferences and reproduction may be found in Thomas Nelson Baker, "Ideals," *Alexander's Magazine* 2, no. 5 (September 1906): 23–29, esp. 28.

4. Rev. G. W. Johnson, "Race Evils," in *Sparkling Gems of Race Knowledge Worth Reading*, comp. James T. Haley (Nashville: J. T. Haley, 1897), 62–67, esp. 64–65. For a later example of a woman making this very argument, see Mildred Miller, "No Excuse for Immoral Living: Marry," *Defender* (Chicago, Ill.), April 13, 1912, 8.

5. Addie W. Hunton, "A Pure Motherhood the Basis of Racial Integrity," in *The United Negro: His Problems and His Progress, Containing the Addresses and Proceedings [of] the Negro Young People's Christian and Educational Congress, Held August 6–11, 1902*, ed. I. Garland Penn and J. W. E. Bowen (Atlanta: D. E. Luther Publishing, 1902), 433–35, esp. 434.

Nell Irvin Painter illuminates why race activists tended to focus on women in "'Social Equality' and 'Rape' in the Fin-de-Siecle South," *Southern History across the Color Line* (Chapel Hill: University of North Carolina Press, 2002), 112–33, esp. 128–30. For allied analyses — albeit with a different focus — see Thelma Jennings, "'Us Colored Women Had to Go Through a Plenty': Sexual Exploitation of African American Slave Women," *Journal of Women's History* 1, no. 3 (Winter 1990): 45–74; and Hélène Lecaudey, "Behind the Mask: Ex-Slave Women and Interracial Sexual Relations," in *Discovering the Women in Slavery: Emancipating Perspectives on the American Past*, ed. Patricia Morton (Athens: University of Georgia Press, 1996), 260–77.

6. Kevin K. Gaines asserts that "for the black South, miscegenation was synonymous with the rape of black women by white men." Gaines's observation further clarifies why intraracial debates about miscegenation frequently involved considerations of black women's sexuality. See Gaines, *Uplifting the Race: Black Leadership, Politics, and Culture in the Twentieth Century* (Chapel Hill: University of North Carolina Press, 1996), 58, 122.

7. Leslie M. Harris, "From Abolitionist Amalgamators to 'Rulers of the Five Points': The Discourse of Interracial Sex and Reform in Antebellum New York City," in *Sex, Love, Race*, ed. Martha Hodes (New York: New York University Press, 1999), 191–212. Examples of how amalgamation was deployed in the late nineteenth century may be found in Alex[ander] Crummell, *The Race Problem in America* (Washington, D.C.: William R. Morrison, 1889); Rev. A. A. Burleigh, "Prohibition and the Race Problem," *A.M.E. Church Review* 3, no. 3 (January 1887): 287–92; L[ucius] H. Holsey, "Amalgamation or Miscegenation," in *Autobiography, Sermons, Addresses, and Essays of Bishop L. H. Holsey* (Atlanta: Franklin Printing and Publishing, 1898), 233–38.

For Afro-American expositions on social equality in primary documents, refer to the following: William Hooper Councill, *The Negro Laborer: A Word to Him*

(Huntsville: R. F. Dickson, 1887), 25–27; William Pickens, "Social Equality," *Voice of the Negro* 3, no. 1 (January 1906): 25–27; W[illiam] S. Scarborough, "Race Integrity," *Voice of the Negro* 4, no. 5 (May 1907): 197–202; "Social Equality," *Crisis* 8, no. 2 (June 1914): 72–73; W. E. B. Du Bois, "President Harding and Social Equality," *Crisis* 23, no. 2 (December 1921): 53–56; *Negro Yearbook: An Annual Encyclopedia of the Negro, 1921–1922* (Tuskegee: Tuskegee Institute, ca. 1922), 46–53; W. E. B. Du Bois, "Social Equality," *Crisis* 35, no. 2 (February 1928): 61–62.

Critical historical context may be found in a number of works, including Nell Irvin Painter, "'Social Equality,' Miscegenation, Labor, and Power," in *The Evolution of Southern Culture*, ed. Numan V. Bartley (Athens: University of Georgia Press, 1988), 47–67; Gaines, *Uplifting the Race*, 47–66; Martha Hodes, *White Women, Black Men: Illicit Sex in the 19th-Century South* (New Haven: Yale University Press, 1997), 146–208.

8. David Goodman Croly and George Wakeman, *Miscegenation: The Theory of the Blending of the Races* (New York: H. Dexter, Hamilton, ca. 1863). See also *Miscegenation indorsed by the Republican Party* (New York: s.n., 1864); and Samuel Sullivan Cox, *Miscegenation or Amalgamation: Fate of the Freedman* (Washington, D.C.: Office of *The Constitutional Union*, 1864).

9. For a political history of the emergence of the term "miscegenation," see Stanley Kaplan, "The Miscegenation Issue in the Election of 1864," *Journal of Negro History* 34, no. 3 (July 1949): 274–343.

10. Frank G. Ruffin, "White or Mongrel?: A Pamphlet on the Deportation of Negroes from Virginia to Africa" (1890), in *Emigration and Migration Proposals*, ed. John David Smith (New York: Garland Publishing, 1993); Theodore G. Bilbo, *Take Your Choice: Separation or Mongrelization* (Poplarville, Miss.: Dream House Publishing, 1947).

11. Martha Hodes, "The Sexualization of Reconstruction Politics: White Women and Black Men in the South after the Civil War," *Journal of the History of Sexuality* 3, no. 3 (January 1993): 402–17; Gaines, *Uplifting the Race*, 59; Hodes, *White Women, Black Men*, 147–75; Painter, "'Social Equality' and 'Rape,'" 112–13. For additional relevant analyses, consult the following: Elsa Barkley Brown, "Negotiating and Transforming the Public Sphere: African American Political Life in the Transition from Slavery to Freedom," *Public Culture* 7, no. 1 (Fall 1994): 107–46; Glenda Elizabeth Gilmore, *Gender and Jim Crow: Women and the Politics of White Supremacy in North Carolina, 1896–1920* (Chapel Hill: University of North Carolina Press, 1996); Laura F. Edwards, *Gendered Strife and Confusion: The Political Culture of Reconstruction* (Urbana: University of Illinois Press, 1997); and Hannah Rosen, "The Gender of Reconstruction: Rape, Race, and Citizenship in the Postemancipation South" (Ph.D. diss., University of Chicago, 1999).

12. Painter, "'Social Equality' and 'Rape,'" 127.

13. John E. Bruce, "Washington's Colored Society" (n.p., 1877), 12–14, 23–24, 27, 21.

A copy of this manuscript may be found in the John E. Bruce Papers at the Schomburg Center for Research in Black Culture (New York, N.Y.). For discussion of cities with concentrations of light-skinned African Americans, see Willard B. Gatewood Jr., *Aristocrats of Color: The Black Elite, 1880–1920* (Bloomington: Indiana University Press, 1990).

14. Bruce, "Washington's Colored Society," 13–14.

Despite Bruce's hope that "Washington's Colored Society" would find a "place on the centre table of every well regulated family" (21) the audience for his work was likely limited to associates and relatives. The manuscript apparently did not appear in print until black sociologist E. Franklin Frazier quoted liberally from it over sixty years later. See Gatewood, *Aristocrats of Color*, 377 n. 52.

15. For commentary along these lines, see Gaines, *Uplifting the Race*, 57.

16. William Hooper Councill also believed that interracial relationships were more likely to occur between the "substratum of both races," as did Bishop J. W. Smith. See Councill, *The Negro Laborer*, 27; Smith, "All Human Blood Is Alike — Intermarriage," in John James Holm, *Holm's Race Assimilation, Or The Fading Leopard's Spots: A Complete Scientific Exposition of the Most Tremendous Question that has ever confronted two races in the world's history* (Naperville and Atlanta: J. L. Nichols, 1910), 511–18, esp. 516–17.

Reference to Bruce's standing as a journalist may be found in Charles Alexander, *One Hundred Distinguished Leaders* (Atlanta: Franklin Printing and Publishing, ca. 1899), 57.

17. For relevant literature on the significance of marriage after emancipation, see Laura F. Edwards, "'The Marriage Covenant is at the Foundation of all Our Rights': The Politics of Slave Marriages in North Carolina after Emancipation," *Law and History Review* 14, no. 1 (Spring 1996): 81–124; Ira Berlin, Steven F. Miller, and Leslie S. Rowland, "Afro-American Families in the Transition from Slavery to Freedom," *Radical History Review* 42 (1988): 89–121; Barry A. Crouch, "The 'Chords of Love': Legalizing Black Marital and Family Rights in Postwar Texas," *Journal of Negro History* 79, no. 4 (Fall 1994): 334–51; Sharon Harley, "For the Good of Family and Race: Gender, Work and Domestic Roles in the Black Community, 1880–1930," *Signs* 15, no. 2 (Winter 1990): 336–49; Susan A. Mann, "Slavery, Sharecropping, and Sexual Inequality," *Signs* 14, no. 4 (Summer 1989): 774–98; Amy Dru Stanley, *From Bondage to Contract: Wage Labor, Marriage, and the Market in the Age of Slave Emancipation* (Cambridge: Cambridge University Press, 1998).

18. Saidiya V. Hartman, *Scenes of Subjection: Terror, Slavery, and Self-Making in Nineteenth-Century America* (New York: Oxford University Press, 1997), 164–206; Charles F. Robinson II, "The Antimiscegenation Conversation: Love's Legislated Limits (1868–1967)" (Ph.D. diss., University of Houston, 1998); Peter W. Bardaglio, "Shamefull Matches: The Regulation of Interracial Sex and Marriage in the South before 1900," in Hodes, *Sex, Love, Race*, 121–38; Rachel F. Moran,

Interracial Intimacy: The Regulation of Race and Romance (Chicago: University of Chicago Press, 2001).

19. E[manuel] K[ing] Love, "Oration Delivered on Emancipation Day, January 2, 1888" (n.p., n.d.), 5, 7. Love briefly mentions a recently defeated "Glenn Bill" in Georgia that opposed racially integrated schools; I can only speculate that Georgia state legislators argued that interracial marriages were an undesirable by-product of school integration.

20. Ibid., 7; E. R. Carter, *Biographical Sketches of Our Pulpit* (Atlanta: J. P. Harrison, 1888), 155–57, esp. 157; William J. Simmons, *Men of Mark: Eminent, Progressive, and Rising* (Cleveland: G. M. Rewell, 1887), 481–83.

21. According to historian Joel Williamson, the U.S. Census Bureau "never attempted to make such distinctions again." See Williamson, *New People: Miscegenation and Mulattoes in the United States* (Baton Rouge: Louisiana State University Press, 1995), 112. Presumably, the bureau did not feel that there was a reliable way to determine "proportion of Negro blood." *Negro Population, 1790–1915*, 207–8.

22. Gaines, *Negro and the White Man*, 147, 155–56, 184; T. Thomas Fortune, "The Latest Color Line," *Liberia*, Bulletin No. 11 (November 1897): 60–65, esp. 65.

23. Holsey, "Amalgamation or Miscegenation," 233–38, esp. 233–34, 237. Critical biographical information on Holsey, along with a physical description of the bishop, may be found in Glenn T. Eskew, "Black Elitism and the Failure of Paternalism in Postbellum Georgia: The Case of Bishop Lucius Henry Holsey," *Journal of Southern History* 58, no. 4 (November 1992): 637–66.

It is not completely clear whether Holsey meant "sodomy" to indicate same-sex intimacy or bestiality. Moreover, Holsey's varied convictions about sexuality did not result in his offering a lengthy condemnation of rape in this text.

24. Lucius Henry Holsey, "Race Segregation," in *How to Solve the Race Problem: The Proceedings of the Washington Conference on the Race Problem in the United States*, ed. Jesse Lawson (Washington: Beresford Printer, 1904. Reprint, Chicago: Afro-Am Press, 1969), 40–58, esp. 45.

For writings submitted to the Atlanta *Constitution*, see "Bishop Holsey on the Race Problem," (Atlanta: n.p., ca. 1899), Daniel A. P. Murray Pamphlets Collection, Rare Book and Special Collections Division, Library of Congress, Washington, D.C. Also see Lucius Henry Holsey, *Autobiography, Sermons, Addresses, and Essays of Bishop L. H. Holsey* (Atlanta: Franklin Printing and Publishing, 1898). Here, it is also important to note that "segregation" is, at times, roughly equivalent to "separatism" in Holsey's thought.

25. Holsey, "Race Segregation," 50–51.

Significantly, Holsey was a major figure in the short-lived Colored National Emigration Association that was spearheaded, in large part, by Bishop Henry McNeal Turner. See Edwin S. Redkey, *Black Exodus: Black Nationalist and Back-to-Africa Movements, 1890–1910* (New Haven: Yale University Press, 1969), 252–86, esp. 271.

Glenn Eskew contends that the bishop viewed his white father "[w]ith muted contempt." See Eskew, "Black Elitism," 637–66, esp. 639.

26. Holsey, "Race Segregation," 41, 48, 51. For his opinions about tuberculosis, see "Remarks of Bishop L. H. Holsey," in *Mortality Among Negroes in Cities. Proceedings of the Conference for Investigations of City Problems Held at Atlanta University, May 26–27, 1896* (Atlanta: Atlanta University Press, 1896), 46.

27. The distinction between hereditarianism and eugenics is that hereditarian thought emerged, more or less, out of genetic experiments by August Weismann and Gregor Mendel whereas eugenics primarily emerged from Francis Galton's social Darwinist ideas regarding the reproduction of human beings. Hereditarianism—through postulation that genetic material passed down from one generation to another was immutable—challenged notions that nurturance had the power to alter heredity ("nature vs. nurture"). Finally, eugenics—in its popular as opposed to "scientific" form—was slightly more concerned with *active creation* of better people. All the same, late nineteenth- and early twentieth-century eugenic ideas were clearly influenced by hereditarian thought, especially in terms of ostensibly eugenic statutes such as sterilization law and prohibitive legislation regarding marriage. See Nancy Leys Stepan, *"The Hour of Eugenics": Race, Gender, and Nation in Latin America* (Ithaca: Cornell University Press, 1991), 22–26; Daniel J. Kevles, *In the Name of Eugenics: Genetics and the Uses of Human Heredity* (New York: Alfred A. Knopf, 1985), 8–19.

Like Holsey, Adella Hunt Logan also expressed hereditarian sentiments. Curiously, however, Logan invokes race within an essay on heredity, but she does not deal explicitly with heredity and miscegenation—curious because Logan was multiracial herself. See Logan, "Prenatal and Hereditary Influences," in *Social and Physical Condition of Negroes in Cities. Report of an Investigation Under the Direction of Atlanta University* . . . (Atlanta: Atlanta University Press, 1897), 37–40. A later invocation of hereditarian thought (albeit somewhat brief) within Afro-American assessments of miscegenation may be found in Sarah D. Brown, *Color Trees and Tracks* (Chicago: Published by the Author, 1906), 17.

28. Nannie H. Burroughs, "Not Color But Character," *Voice of the Negro* 7, no. 1 (July 1904): 277–79, esp. 277.

29. Anna D. Borden, "Some Thoughts for Both Races To Ponder Over," in Holm, *Holm's Race Assimilation*, 497–504, esp. 498.

30. Sophia Cox Johnson, "The Colored Woman on the Plantation; And How She Is Raised By Progress Made," in Holm, *Holm's Race Assimilation*, 504–11.

31. Ann du Cille, *The Coupling Convention: Sex, Text, and Tradition in Black Women's Fiction* (New York: Oxford University Press, 1993); Pauline E. Hopkins, *Contending Forces: A Romance Illustrative of Negro Life North and South* (Boston: Colored Co-Operative Publishing, 1900. Reprint, New York: Oxford University Press, 1988); Pauline E. Hopkins, *Of One Blood; or, The Hidden Self in The Magazine Novels of Pauline Hopkins* (New York: Oxford University Press,

1988), 441–621. *Of One Blood* was originally serialized in the *Colored American Magazine* from November 1902 until November 1903.

For the quote about "African[s] in disguise," see Fannie Barrier Williams, "Perils of the White Negro," *Colored American Magazine* 13, no. 6 (December 1907): 421–23, esp. 423. For commentary on passing and intimate relationships as explored in black women's fiction, see Claudia Tate, *Domestic Allegories of Political Desire* (New York: Oxford University Press, 1992), esp. 197–99. Commentary on the ways in which other Afro-American—female as well as male—novelists used fiction to analyze miscegenation's impact may be found in the following: Painter, "'Social Equality' and 'Rape,'" 127–28; Gaines, *Uplifting the Race*, 54, 120, 123–24; Edward L. Ayers, *The Promise of the New South: Life after Reconstruction* (New York: Oxford University Press, 1992), 366–71; and Sandra Gunning, *Race, Rape, and Lynching: The Red Record of American Literature, 1890–1912* (New York: Oxford University Press, 1996).

32. Sylvania F. Williams, "The Social Status of the Negro Woman," *Voice of the Negro* 1, no. 7 (July 1904): 298–300, esp. 299; Annie E. Hall, "What Can the Colored Woman Do to Improve the Street Railroad Dep[o]rtment," in *The United Negro*, 454–56, esp. 454. It should be noted that the *Voice of the Negro* cites Williams's name as both "Sylvanie" and "Sylvania."

33. Emma Azalia Hackley, *The Colored Girl Beautiful* (Kansas City, Mo.: Burton Publishing, 1916), 165–201, esp. 199, 197. Hackley's views on intermarriage may be found in Hackley, "How the Color Question Looks to an American in France," *A.M.E. Church Review* 23, no. 3 (January 1907): 210–15.

34. Eugene Harris, *An Appeal for Social Purity in Negro Homes: A Tract* (Nashville: n.p., 1898), 5, 8; Jack Thorne [David Bryant Fulton], *A Plea for Social Justice for the Negro Woman*, Occasional Paper No. 2, Negro Society of Historical Research (New York: Lincoln Press Association, 1912), esp. 2–4, 6, 7, 9; Jack Thorne [David Bryant Fulton], *Hanover; or The Persecution of the Lowly. A Story of the Wilmington Massacre* (n.p.: M. C. L. Hill, ca. 1900. Reprint, New York: Arno Press, 1969), 53–54, 35.

35. R[evels] A[lcorn] Adams, *The Negro Girl* (Kansas City, Kans: Independent Press, 1914), 66–67, 76–77, 80–81, 91.

36. Scarborough, "Race Integrity," 200–201; Gatewood, *Aristocrats of Color*, 178.

37. W. E. Burghardt Du Bois, ed., *The Health and Physique of the Negro American: Report of a Social Study made under the direction of Atlanta University; together with the Proceedings of the Eleventh Conference for the Study of the Negro Problems . . . May the 29th, 1906* (Atlanta: Atlanta University Press, 1906), plates A–H and 1–48; 31–36.

38. Ibid., 27, 29.

39. [U.S. Department of Commerce; Bureau of the Census], *Negro Population, 1790–1915* (Washington, D.C.: Government Printing Office, 1918. Reprint, New York: Kraus Reprint Co., 1969), 207–8; Charles Chesnutt, "What is a White Man?,"

Independent 41 (May 30, 1889): 5–6; [T.] Thomas Fortune, "Race Absorption," *A.M.E. Church Review* 18, no. 1 (July 1901): 54–66, esp. 59; Hopkins, *Contending Forces*, 151; Maria P. Williams, *My Work and Public Sentiment* (Kansas City, Mo.: Burton Publishing, 1916); Du Bois, *Health and Physique*, 30.

40. John Patterson Sampson, *Mixed Races: Their Environment, Temperament, Heredity, and Phrenology* (Hampton, Va.: Normal School Steam Press, 1881); Joseph E. Hayne, *The Black Man; or, The Natural History of the Hametic Race* (Raleigh, N.C.: Edwards & Broughton, 1894).

41. Hayne, *The Black Man*, 2–38, esp. 32.

42. Franz Boas, *The Real Race Problem From the View of Anthropology* (New York: Publications of the National Association for the Advancement of Colored People, ca. 1912); Caroline Bond Day, *A Study of Some Negro-White Families in the United States* (Cambridge: Peabody Museum of Harvard University, ca. 1932).

   Adele Logan Alexander points out that Caroline Bond Day began research for *A Study of Some Negro-White Families* around 1919 and that Day had once been taught by Du Bois. See Alexander, *Homelands and Waterways: The American Journey of the Bond Family, 1846–1926* (New York: Pantheon, 1999), 342–78, esp. 349, 375–78. Refer also to "Harvard University Anthropologist Makes Preliminary Report of Study," *Amsterdam News* (New York, N.Y.), June 11, 1930.

43. "More Interest in Race Beauty," *Age* (New York, N.Y.), August 20, 1914, 1; "Ideal Type of Negro Beauty," ibid., August 6, 1914, 1–2; "The Making of a Race Type," ibid., August 20, 1914, 4. See also "Women's Beauty Will Win Prizes," ibid., July 23, 1914, 1.

44. "Hard Task for Beauty Judges," ibid., August 27, 1914, 1–2.

45. ". . . Wants 'Chosen Fifteen,'" ibid., September 17, 1914, 1.

46. "Decision of Judges in Beauty Contest," ibid., October 1, 1914, 4; "The Chosen Fifteen," ibid., October 14, 1914, 1.

47. "Members of the Women's War Relief, Syracuse, N.Y.," ibid., May 17, 1919, 1; "Racial Types," ibid., May 17, 1914, 4. For examples of how the *Half-Century* employed the rhetoric of type, see "Types of Racial Beauty," *Half-Century Magazine* 6, no. 6 (June 1919), and "Who is the Prettiest Colored Girl in the United States?," *Half-Century Magazine* 10, no. 3 (May–June 1921), 15.

48. An observation that such anxieties involved class may be found in Gaines, *Uplifting the Race*, 120–27.

49. Patricia A. Schechter, *Ida B. Wells-Barnett and American Reform, 1880–1930* (Chapel Hill: University of North Carolina Press, 2001), 81–120, esp. 105.

50. The literature on antimiscegenation legislation is varied and ranges from legal to intellectual to cultural history. A now-classic statement on the matter is Peggy Pascoe, "Miscegenation Law, Court Cases, and Ideologies of 'Race' in Twentieth-Century America," *Journal of American History* 83, no. 1 (June 1996): 44–69. See also Robinson, "The Antimiscegenation Conversation"; Werner Sollors, ed., *Interracialism: Black-White Intermarriage in American History, Literature, and*

Law (Oxford: Oxford University Press, 2000); Moran, *Interracial Intimacy*; and Earl Lewis and Heidi Ardizzone, *Love on Trial: An American Scandal in Black and White* (New York: W. W. Norton, 2001).

51. Aaron Mossell, "The Unconstitutionality of The Law Against Miscegenation," *A.M.E. Church Review* 5, no. 2 (October 1888): 72–79; Testimony of Archibald Grimké, *Intermarriage of Whites and Negroes in the District of Columbia and Separate Accommodations in Street Cars For Whites and Negroes in the District of Columbia. Hearing Before the Committee on the District of Columbia. House of Representatives, Sixty-Fourth Congress, First Session . . . February 11, 1916* (Washington, D.C.: Government Printing Office, 1916), 3–19; Bishop Alexander Walters, "Miscegenation and Its Baneful Effects," in Holm, *Holm's Race Assimilation*, 486–88, esp. 488; Daniel Murray, "Race Integrity—How to Preserve It in the South," *Colored American Magazine* 11, no. 6 (December 1906): 369–77, esp. 370.

John D'Emilio and Estelle B. Freedman point out that African Americans made such arguments during the early stages of Reconstruction. See D'Emilio and Freedman, *Intimate Matters: A History of Sexuality in America* (New York: Harper & Row, 1988), 104–7. For further scholarly analysis along these lines, see Tate, *Domestic Allegories of Political Desire*, 271 n. 13; Martha Hodes, *White Women, Black Men*, 148–49, 165–67; Bardaglio, "'Shamefull Matches,'" 112–38, esp. 113. For information regarding when laws were passed, see Randall Kennedy, "The Enforcement of Anti-Miscegenation Laws," in Sollors, *Interracialism*, 140–62, esp. 144.

52. "Do Not Stop Miscegenation," *Gazette* (Cleveland, Ohio), March 22, 1913, 2. For contemporaneous comment on the attempt of various states to enact such laws during the decade, see "Bills Against Intermarriage Being Introduced in Various Legislatures," *Age*, January 23, 1913, 1; "Intermarriage," *Crisis* 5, no. 6 (April 1913): 296–97; "The Next Step," *Crisis* 6, no. 2 (June 1913): 79. Many such attempts were unsuccessful: see "Afro-American Cullings," *Gazette*, April 19, 1913, 1; and "Ohio Sustains Human Rights," *Gazette*, May 3, 1913, 1.

53. W[endell] P[hillips] Dabney, *The Wolf and the Lamb* (Cincinnati: W. P. Dabney, ca. 1913), 5, 7, 9, 10. Biographical information on Dabney may be found in W. P. Dabney, *Cincinnati's Colored Citizens* (Cincinnati: Dabney Publishing, ca. 1926), 360; and Joseph J. Boris, *Who's Who in Colored America: A Biographical Dictionary of Notable Living Persons of Negro Descent in America* (New York: Who's Who in Colored America Corp., 1927), 51. For evidence that Dabney was active in fighting anti-intermarriage legislation, see "A Little Pile of Books and Pamphlets," *Crisis* 7, no. 4 (February 1914): 201; and "Anti-Intermarriage Bills," *Crisis* 31, no. 5 (March 1926): 232.

Of course, during the 1910s, sensationalist outrage over the sexual adventures and choices of "black pugilist" Jack Johnson were an ever-present informant to attempts to pass anti-intermarriage laws. See "Spoiling Good Work," *Gazette*,

July 12, 1913, 2; "Jack Johnson Again," *Age*, December 12, 1912, 4; "Aftermath of Johnson Muss," *Age*, December 19, 1912, 1; "Intermarriage," *Crisis* 5, no. 4 (February 1913): 180–81.

54. George L. Ruffin, "A Look Forward," *A.M.E. Church Review* 2, no. 1 (July 1885): 29–33, esp. 31–32; Kelly Miller, "The Physical Destiny of the American Negro," *Out of the House of Bondage: A discussion of the Race Problem* (New York: Thomas Y. Crowell, 1914), 42–59, esp. 57. Interestingly, Ruffin contended that passing women were even more responsible for infusing black blood into white America.

55. Gaines, *Uplifting the Race*, 126.

CHAPTER EIGHT

1. "Georgia Negroes Whip Woman to Impress Race Purity," *Negro World* (hereafter *NW*), April 1, 1922, 2.

2. Ibid. Sylvester might not have had a UNIA division when this incident occurred, but a local did exist by 1926. See Mary Gambrell Rolinson, "The Universal Negro Improvement Association in Georgia: Southern Stronghold of Garveyism," in *Georgia in Black and White: Explorations in the Race Relations of a Southern State, 1865–1950*, ed. John C. Inscoe (Athens: University of Georgia Press, 1994), 202–24, esp. 204.

3. This *Negro World* article—in my reading, at least—does not contain the slightest hint that this assault was unwarranted or excessive, and the inclusion of the speech allegedly given on the occasion is rather revealing: "the angry mob read a certain lecture to the woman on 'race purity.'. . . 'A new day has dawned and there will be no toleration of any liaison between colored women and white men. The times are changing; these are not days when Negro women could not protect themselves and were at the mercy of the white man's lust. There is no excuse at this day and time for Negro women to maintain clandestine relationships with white men.'" "Georgia Negroes Whip Woman."

   Hazel V. Carby's work on sexual policing provides a provocative analytical prism through which to view this incident. See Carby, "Policing the Black Woman's Body in an Urban Context," *Critical Inquiry* 18, no. 4 (Summer 1992): 738–55.

4. Monographs on Garvey and Garveyism include Edmund Cronon, *Black Moses: Marcus Garvey and the Universal Negro Improvement Association* (Madison: University of Wisconsin Press, 1953); Theodore Vincent, *Black Power and the Garvey Movement* (San Francisco: Ramparts Press, 1971); Tony Martin, *Race First: The Ideological and Organizational Struggles of Marcus Garvey and the Universal Negro Improvement Association* (Westport, Conn.: Greenwood Press, 1976); Judith Stein, *The World of Marcus Garvey: Race and Class in Modern Society* (Baton Rouge: Louisiana State University Press, 1986); Ula Yvette Taylor, *The Veiled Garvey: The Life and Times of Amy Jacques Garvey* (Chapel Hill: University of North Carolina Press, 2002).

5. See volume 1 of Robert A. Hill, ed., *The Marcus Garvey and Universal Negro Improvement Association Papers*, 7 vols. (Berkeley: University of California Press, 1983–86, 1989–90) (hereafter Hill, *Garvey Papers*), esp. 384. For a detailed elaboration of early political aims of the UNIA, see "Declaration of Rights of the Negro Peoples of the World" (ca. 1920), in Hill, *Garvey Papers*, 2:571–80; for an articulation of the UNIA's racial nationalism, see "Universal Negro Catechism" (ca. 1921), in Hill, *Garvey Papers*, 3:302–20. Robert Hill outlines the political shifts of the UNIA in his "General Introduction," in *Garvey Papers*, 1:xxxv–xc.

   Here, it is important to note that when Marcus Garvey decided to relocate to the United States, he was part of a steady stream of black immigrants from South America, Central America, and the Caribbean. David Hellwig notes that this stream crested in the mid-1920s; his work further chronicles tensions between African Americans and recent black arrivals. See David J. Hellwig, "Black Meets Black: Afro-American Reactions to West Indian Immigrants in the 1920s," *South Atlantic Quarterly* 77, no. 2 (Spring 1978): 206–24.

   For critical analysis of radicalism and Caribbean migration to the United States, see Winston James, *Holding Aloft the Banner of Ethiopia: Caribbean Radicalism in Early Twentieth-Century America* (London: Verso, 1998). Relevant analysis may also be found in Charles V. Carnegie, "A Politics of Transterritorial Solidarity: The Garvey Movement and Imperialism," in *Postnationalism Prefigured: Caribbean Borderlands* (New Brunswick: Rutgers University Press, 2002), 145–75.

6. The movement's constitution established that seven or more people could form a chapter. "Constitution and Book of Laws," (Article I, Section IV), in Hill, *Garvey Papers*, 1:257. Tony Martin provides a comprehensive roster of UNIA branches in North, Central, and South America, as well as the Caribbean, Africa, and Great Britain in an appendix (*Race First*, 361–73). Mary Rolinson's work contains critical insight into smaller divisions located in the American South; she asserts that "Garvey gave inspiration to latent black consciousness in isolated rural communities." Rolinson, "The Universal Negro Improvement Association in Georgia," 203.

7. "RACE FIRST!," *NW*, July 26, 1919, reprinted in Hill, *Garvey Papers*, 1:468–70, esp. 469.

8. "Hon. Marcus Garvey Tells of Interview with Ku Klux Klan," *NW*, July 15, 1922, reprinted in Hill, *Garvey Papers*, 4:707–15, esp. 709, 713, and 714. Along these lines, Nancy MacLean's *Behind the Mask of Chivalry: The Making of the Second Ku Klux Klan* (New York: Oxford University Press, 1994) provides highly relevant analysis of the Klan's intraracial policing of sexuality and morality.

   Garvey also forged unlikely relationships with at least two other white supremacists in addition to Clarke over the question of racial purity: John Powell, founder of the Anglo-Saxon Clubs of America, and Earnest Sevier Cox, author of *White America*. Refer to J. David Smith, "John Powell and Marcus Garvey:

The Peculiar Alliance," in *The Eugenic Assault on America: Scenes in Red, White, and Black* (Fairfax, Va.: George Mason University Press, 1993), 23–35; William A. Edwards, "Racial Purity in Black and White: The Case of Marcus Garvey and Earnest Cox," *Journal of Ethnic Studies* 15, no. 1 (Spring 1987): 117–42.

9. Speech by Marcus Garvey (original title unknown), *NW*, July 15, 1922, reprinted in Hill, *Garvey Papers*, 4:707–15.

Even with its publication of Garvey's desideratum that black men must "strike back on white men," the *Negro World* would also acknowledge that doing so often resulted in a less than desirable outcome. In the spring of 1921, for example, the paper publicized the case of W. T. Bowman, a Mississippi teacher who had been attacked by a mob upon expelling a 17-year-old schoolgirl whose lover was a local white man. See "Southern Mob Whips Negro Teacher," *NW*, April 23, 1921, 1.

10. Garvey made this argument about the "social question of race" while discussing President Warren Harding's aversion to "social equality." Speech by Marcus Garvey (original headline unknown), *NW*, November 5, 1921, reprinted in Hill, *Garvey Papers*, 4:141–51, esp. 145. For remainder of text quoted here, see *Garvey Papers*, 4:714.

11. "The Women Lynched the White Libertine," *NW*, December 29, 1923, 4. Interestingly, the writer observed that "if the Negro women of Fayette County did lynch the white libertine for insulting one of their number, they have done more . . . than any Negro man has done in Fayette County." Given that the *Negro World* article opens with the disclosure that they knew about this event because of a reader, however, it is possible that the women themselves did not belong to the UNIA. For the item on Nellie Edwards, see "Moral Leper Attempts to Assault Negro Child," *NW*, July 19, 1924, 2.

The *Negro World* followed the unsuccessful campaign to pass the Dyer Anti-Lynching Bill during the early 1920s and featured brief items about lynching. One such item, "An Eye for An Eye" (May 27, 1922, 4), decried lynching as it implored "black men [to] rise en masse and wage war on the licentious violators of black womanhood!" For a statement suggesting that combating lynching entailed maintenance of race purity, see "Negro Race Purity" (July 12, 1930, 4).

12. Marcus Garvey, "What We Believe," in *The Philosophy and Opinions of Marcus Garvey or, Africa for the Africans*, 2 vols., comp. Amy Jacques Garvey (Reprint, Dover, Mass.: Majority Press, 1986), 2:81. The remaining three points refer to universal rights, black pride, and "the spiritual Fatherhood of God and the Brotherhood of Man."

13. Marcus Garvey, *Aims and Objects of Movement for Solution of Negro Problem Outlined* (New York: Press of the Universal Negro Improvement Assocation, 1924), 3, 6.

14. "Convention Report," *NW*, September 2, 1922, reprinted in Hill, *Garvey Papers*, 4:934–42, esp. 936 and 939.

15. Richard Tate, "Negro Men Should Marry Negro Women," *NW*, March 7, 1925.

16. Eva Aldred Brooks, "A Pure, Healthy, Unified Race, Plea of Women," *NW*, May 23, 1925, 7. A similar call for race "standardization" may be found in "Black Peoples Must Dignify Own Homogeneity" (September 28, 1929, 2).

17. Fraternal orders were familiar institutions in late nineteenth- and early twentieth-century America, and their popularity reflected, in part, an attempt to reestablish "traditional" order during an era when gender constructions and sexual relationships were in a state of flux. According to Mary Ann Clawson's provocative work on fraternalism, one of the foremost reasons behind brotherhoods as social institutions was to "make [men] aware of their separation from women, and thus to enforce the exercise of masculine power." Mary Ann Clawson, *Constructing Brotherhood: Class, Gender, and Fraternalism* (Princeton, N.J.: Princeton University Press, 1989), esp. 131–35 and 178. Since most brotherhoods routinely excluded blacks, African American men typically participated in segregated offshoots of mainstream orders. The link between fraternal orders and Garveyism is explored in Robert Hill's introduction to the first volume of the *Garvey Papers*, lx–lxiii.

18. Arguably, these same notions could be considered "bourgeois" and/or "conservative." One of the first works to assert that black nationalist politics are inclined toward "bourgeois conservatism" rather than being inherently working-class, militant, or radical is Wilson Jeremiah Moses' *The Golden Age of Black Nationalism: 1850–1925* (New York: Oxford University Press, 1988), esp. 5–31.

19. Barbara Bair, "'Ethiopia Shall Stretch Forth Her Hands Unto God': Laura Kofey and the Gendered Vision of Redemption in the Garvey Movement," in *A Mighty Baptism: Race, Gender, and the Creation of American Protestantism*, ed. Susan Juster and Lisa MacFarlane (Ithaca: Cornell University Press, 1996), 38–61, esp. 46.

20. The only juvenile group for both girls and boys was the "Infant Class" for ages 1 to 7; it provided "Bible Class and Prayer" along with schooling on UNIA doctrine, the Black Star Line, Negro Factories Corporation, and African history "in story book fashion." Older juveniles also studied race history and were indoctrinated in "race pride and love." See "Rules and Regulations for Juveniles," Articles I–IV, in Hill, *Garvey Papers*, 3:770–72.

21. Men could participate in women's groups to a limited degree, but women were prohibited, according to the constitution, from engaging in any activities designated specifically for men. See "Rules and Regulations for Universal African Legions of the U.N.I.A. and A.C.L.," Articles I, III, VI, IX, and XI, XVIII, in Hill, *Garvey Papers*, 3:755–59; "Rules and Regulations Governing the Universal African Black Cross Nurses," Articles I–V, in Hill, *Garvey Papers*, 3:766–68; "Rules and Regulations Governing the Universal African Motor Corps," Articles I–IV, in Hill, *Garvey Papers*, 3:769.

Although other interpretations of the UNIA differ from my own in several regards, critical discussions of women and gender in the UNIA include Mark Matthews, "Our Women and What They Think: Amy Jacques Garvey and the *Negro World*," in *Black Women in United States History*, ed. Darlene Clark Hine (New York: Carlson Publishing, 1990), 7:866–78; William Seraile, "Henrietta Vinton Davis and the Garvey Movement," in Hine, *Black Women in United States History*, 8:1073–91; Tony Martin, "Women in the Garvey Movement," in *Garvey: His Work and Impact*, ed. Rupert Lewis and Patrick Bryan (Trenton, N.J.: Africa World Press, 1991), 67–72; Honor Ford-Smith, "Women and the Garvey Movement in Jamaica," in Lewis and Bryan, *Garvey: His Work and Impact*, 73–86; Barbara Bair, "True Women, Real Men: Gender, Ideology, and Social Roles in the Garvey Movement," in *Gendered Domains: Rethinking Public and Private in Women's History*, Essays From the Seventh Berkshire Conference on the History of Women, ed. Dorothy O. Helly and Susan M. Reverby (Ithaca: Cornell University Press, 1992), 154–66; Ula Yvette Taylor, "The Veiled Garvey: The Life and Times of Amy Jacques Garvey" (Ph.D. diss., University of California, Santa Barbara, 1992); Karen S. Adler, "'Always Leading Our Men in Service and Sacrifice': Amy Jacques Garvey, Feminist Black Nationalist," *Gender & Society* 6, no. 3 (September 1992): 346–75; Martin Anthony Summers, "Nationalism, Race Consciousness, and the Construction of Black Middle Class Masculinity during the New Negro Era, 1915–1930" (Ph.D. diss., Rutgers University, 1997); Ula Y. Taylor, "'Negro Women are Great Thinkers as Well as Doers': Amy Jacques-Garvey and Community Feminism in the United States," *Journal of Women's History* 12, no. 2 (Summer 2002): 104–26; Taylor, *The Veiled Garvey*.

22. In addition to yearly conventions that formally allotted time for "Women's Industrial Exhibits" where culinary feats, handicrafts, and fashions were proudly displayed, sex-specific activities occurred on the local level as well. The bulk of *Negro World* reports on women's activities in local UNIA divisions mentioned conversations on women's loyalty and duty to the cause; the *Negro World* frequently gave reviews of local "Ladies' Days" on its "News and Views of U.N.I.A. Divisions" page. The following citations provide but a *few* examples: "Boston Div. Celebrates Ladies' Day," *NW*, April 1, 1922, 9; "Wonderful Program Rendered by Ladies of Oakland, Cal., Division," *NW*, March 3, 1923, 4; "Ladies' Day Observed at Denver, Col., Division," *NW*, April 8, 1922, 8; "Wonderful Pageant Given By Women's Department of New Haven Division of U.N.I.A.," *NW*, July 16, 1921, 9. Also see "U.N.I.A. in New Orleans on the Upward March," *NW*, February 19, 1921, 8; "Ladies Stage Great Program at U.N.I.A. Mass Meeting in Oakland, Cal.," *NW*, January 20, 1923, 7; "The Baltimore, Md., U.N.I.A.," *NW*, October 1, 1921, 11. For quote on the function of the Motor Corps, see "Rules and Regulations Governing the Universal African Motor Corps," in Hill, *Garvey Papers*, 3:769.

23. Revealing analysis of how Garveyite women viewed their position in the movement—including an argument about women of African descent and "community feminism"—may be found in Taylor, "'Negro Women are Great Thinkers.'"

24. Hill maintains that the earliest years of the UNIA witnessed virtual parity in male

and female membership. Such parity would soon change: in early 1922, at the apex of Garveyism's popularity and influence, Marcus Garvey was indicted for mail fraud. FBI agents had monitored Garvey and UNIA activities for well over two years; the federal government alleged, among many things, that Garvey's flagship project, the Black Star Line, was an illegitimate business enterprise and that Garvey abused the mails for purposes of extortion. After serving a three-month portion of his five-year sentence in 1923, Garvey was finally imprisoned at Atlanta's Tombs Prison in 1925. In 1927, he was released only to be expeditiously deported to Jamaica. It was not until the movement was in decline that its membership came to be overwhelmingly dominated by women. Phone interview with Robert Hill, November 1990.

In contrast, Beryl Satter maintains that the UNIA was always predominantly male; see Satter, "Marcus Garvey, Father Divine and the Gender Politics of Race Difference and Race Neutrality," *American Quarterly* 48, no. 1 (March 1996): 43–76.

25. Gertrude Hawkins letter, *NW*, January 12, 1924, 10; "Sixteen-Year Old Colored Girl Addresses Oklahoma Division," *NW*, August 27, 1921, 11; "African Redemption Fund," *NW*, October 1, 1921, 3; Editorial letter, *NW*, October 1, 1921, 6; "New Orleans Division in Letter to Mayor Defends the U.N.I.A.," *NW*, March 24, 1923, 8.

In an interview conducted in 1978, Audley Moore recalled that when she lived in New Orleans during the early 1920s, she heard Garvey speak in person; that very first encounter inspired Moore to become a fast and ready adherent to the principles of Garveyism. See Cheryl Townsend Gilkes, "Interview with Audley (Queen Mother) Moore," *The Black Women Oral History Project* (Cambridge: Schlesinger Library, Radcliffe College, 1978), 9–10.

26. Hill, *Garvey Papers*, 4:1037–38. Robert Hill and Theodore Vincent offer further comment on these women; see Hill, *Garvey Papers*, 4:xxxv; and Vincent, *Black Power and the Garvey Movement*, 124–25.

Barbara Bair's analysis of this conflict is particularly useful; Bair, "True Women, Real Men," 160–61. Mark Matthews, Beryl Satter, and Karen Adler (who focuses mostly on the rift between Amy Jacques and Marcus) also explore more general tensions between women and men in the movement: Matthews, "'Our Women and What They Think,'" 11–12; Satter, "Marcus Garvey, Father Divine," 51; Adler, "'Always Leading Our Men,'" 354–66.

Further details of the crises that marred the 1922 convention may be found in Hill, *Garvey Papers*, 4:xxxi–xxxv.

27. Davis had been married during the 1880s. Whereas it is not altogether clear whether Galloway was a practicing Garveyite, she did, at very least, refer to the UNIA's minister of industries and labor, Ulysses S. Poston, as her "'boss.'" Presumably, then, the two worked together; thus Galloway was familiar with some of the movement's basic tenets and was also willing to work for the UNIA. "Thriv-

ing Business Enterprises of the Universal Negro Improvement Association," *NW*, July 8, 1922, 3.

28. M. L. T. De Mena, "Part Women Must Play in the Organization," *NW*, January 23, 1926, 7. A woman who served the UNIA in a variety of capacities, De Mena was from Nicaragua and had a daughter (who also was a Garveyite). De Mena apparently was affiliated with Father Divine during the 1930s. Robert A. Hill, ed., *Marcus Garvey: Life and Lessons, a Centennial Companion to the Marcus Garvey and Universal Negro Improvement Association Papers* (Berkeley: University of California Press, 1987), 376–77; Satter, "Marcus Garvey, Father Divine," 51.

29. In her account of the assassination of Laura Adorkor Kofey, Barbara Bair provides a chilling example of what happened to one woman who seized unusual power for herself within the movement. For quote cited in text and for information on Kofey, see Bair, "True Women, Real Men," 163.

30. Examples of typical paeans to race motherhood may be found in George Carter, "Weekly Sermon," *NW*, May 13, 1922, 6; and Carrie Mero Leadett, "The Obligations of Motherhood," *NW*, March 29, 1924, 10.

31. "The Women of the Race are Lauded in Liberty Hall on Observance of Mother's Day," *NW*, May 17, 1924, 3.

32. Estelle Matthews, "Message for the Negro Women of the World," *NW*, February 4, 1922, 11. For an extended argument along these lines, see J. H. A. Brazelton, *Self-Determination: The Salvation of the Race* (Oklahoma City: Educator, 1918).

   Useful examination of how a range of women politicized motherhood during the late nineteenth and early twentieth centuries appears in Eileen Boris's "The Power of Motherhood: Black and White Activist Women Redefine the Political," in *Mothers of a New World: Maternalist Politics and the Origins of Welfare States*, ed. Seth Koven and Sonya Michel (New York: Routledge, 1993), 213–45.

33. Examples include "The Hand that Rocks the Cradle," *NW*, July 5, 1924, 12; Hannah Nichols, "Lady Delegate . . . Demands Single Standard for All," *NW*, August 23, 1924, 16; Kate Fenner, "Negro Men Must Beard the Lion," *NW*, March 25, 1922, 3. One article, "The Glory of Fatherhood," somewhat stands out in that it claims that a man who is not a father is merely "half a man." However, this piece contains no specific reference to people of African descent and might not have been written by a member of the movement; it could also have been pulled from another periodical. See Mrs. Walter Ferguson, "The Glory of Fatherhood," *NW*, December 25, 1926, 8.

34. Although Charles Darwin was never involved in the movement that adopted his name, social Darwinism evolved into a broadly influential movement following publication of the *Origin of Species* (1859). In turn, it begat eugenics, which advocated active engagement in eradicating "degenerate" elements from society. Social Darwinists and eugenicists alike favored a host of legislation, from immigration quotas to antimiscegenation laws to enforced sterilization.

   Historical analyses of race, ethnicity, social Darwinism and/or eugenics include Richard Hofstadter, *Social Darwinism in American Thought: 1860–1915* (New York: G. Braziller, 1959); Thomas Gossett, *Race: The History of an Idea in America* (New York: Schocken Books, 1963); Mark Haller, *Eugenics: Hereditarian Attitudes in American Thought* (New Brunswick, N.J.: Rutgers University Press, 1963); Daniel J. Kevles, *In the Name of Eugenics: Genetics and the Uses of Human Heredity* (New York: Alfred A. Knopf, 1985); Edward J. Larson, *Sex, Race, and Science: Eugenics in the Deep South* (Baltimore: Johns Hopkins University Press, 1995); Martin S. Pernick, *The Black Stork: Eugenics and the Death of "Defective" Babies in American Medicine and Motion Pictures since 1915* (New York: Oxford University Press, 1996); Lisa Lindquist Dorr, "Arm in Arm: Gender, Eugenics, and Virginia's Racial Integrity Acts of the 1920s," *Journal of Women's History* 11, no. 1 (Spring 1999): 143–66; Gregory Michael Dorr, "Assuring America's Place in the Sun: Ivey Foreman Lewis and the Teaching of Eugenics at the University of Virginia," *Journal of Southern History* 66, no. 2 (May 2000): 257–96; and Wendy Kline, *Building a Better Race: Gender, Sexuality, and Eugenics from the Turn of the Century to the Baby Boom* (Berkeley: University of California Press, 2002).

For the connection between race, gender, eugenics, nationalism, and empire, see Nancy Leys Stepan, *"The Hour of Eugenics": Race, Gender, and Nation in Latin America* (Ithaca: Cornell University Press, 1991); Alexandra Minna Stern, "Buildings, Boundaries, and Blood: Medicalization and Nation-Building on the U.S.-Mexico Border, 1910–1930," *Hispanic American Historical Review* 79, no. 1 (February 1999): 41–81; Alexandra Minna Stern, "Responsible Mothers and Normal Children: Eugenics, Welfare, and Nationalism in Post-Revolutionary Mexico, 1900–1940," *Journal of Historical Sociology* 12, no. 4 (Fall 1999): 369–97; and Laura Briggs, *Reproducing Empire: Race, Sex, Science, and U.S. Imperialism* (Berkeley: University of California Press, 2002).

35. W. E. B. Du Bois, "Opinion," Annual Children's Number, *Crisis* 24, no. 6 (October 1922): 247–53; Kelly Miller, "The Eugenics of the Negro Race," *Scientific Monthly* 5, no. 1 (July 1917): 57–59; Chandler Owen, "Women and Children of the South," *Birth Control Review* 3, no. 9 (September 1919): 9 and 20; Mary Burrill, "They That Sit in Darkness: A One-Act Play of Negro Life," *Birth Control Review* 3, no. 9 (September 1919): 5–8. See also W. E. B. Du Bois, "The Damnation of Women," in *Writings*, ed. Nathan Huggins (New York: Literary Classics, 1986), 952–68; and Chandler Owen, "Marriage and Divorce," *Messenger* 5, no. 3 (March 1923): 629–31. Other black intellectuals who wrote on eugenics include Theodore Burrell, "Negro Womanhood—An Appeal," *Crusader* 2, no. 11 (July 1920): 18; J. A. Rogers, "The Critic," *Messenger*, April 1925, 165–66; E. Franklin Frazier, "Eugenics and the Race Problem," *Crisis* 31, no. 2 (December 1925): 91–92.

36. Daylanne English, "W. E. B. Du Bois's Family *Crisis*," *American Literature* 72, no. 2 (June 2000): 291–319, esp. 298 and 311.

37. Tony Martin observes that "Garvey's belief in the necessity for self-reliance led

him occasionally to speak in the language of Social Darwinism" (*Race First*, 32), while Wilson Moses assesses how social Darwinism influenced black nationalist ideology during the late nineteenth and early twentieth centuries (*Golden Age of Black Nationalism*, 27).

The following sources illuminate how Garvey appropriated social Darwinist concepts: "Report of UNIA Meeting" (original headline unknown), *NW*, November 1, 1919, reprinted in Hill, *Garvey Papers*, 2:138-42, esp. 139-40; Editorial letter by Marcus Garvey, *NW*, May 8, 1920, reprinted in Hill, *Garvey Papers*, 2:330-31; Marcus Garvey, "Shall the Negro Be Exterminated?," in *Philosophy and Opinions*, 1:63-67; Marcus Garvey, "Blazing the Trail of African Redemption," *NW*, May 5, 1923, 1. Also see "Women Who Refuse Responsibility of Parenthood Traitors to Race," *NW*, July 12, 1924, 12. This particular editorial—which was reprinted from the *New York Times*—in "Our Women and What They Think" contains classist, eugenic injunctions to "women of intelligence and culture" to bear children.

Several Garveyites mouthed the language of social purity as well. Although the Progressive Era was effectively over by the time the UNIA took off in the United States, the redress of social "impurities" remained on the agenda of American reformers, educators, writers, and politicians. Examples of social purist language in the UNIA include "We Must Maintain A High Standard of Morality," *NW*, August 2, 1924, 4; Hannah Nichols, "Lady Delegate . . . Demands Single Standard for All," *NW*, August 23, 1924, 16; Florence Bruce, "The Great Work of the Negro Woman Today," *NW*, December 18, 1924, 8; "Convention Report," August 12, 1924, in Hill, *Garvey Papers*, 5:717-22. Relevant commentary on social purity may be found in Christina Simmons, "African Americans and Sexual Victorianism in the Social Hygiene Movement, 1910-1940," *Journal of the History of Sexuality* 4, no. 1 (1993): 51-75, esp. 53; Linda Gordon, *Woman's Body, Woman's Right: A Social History of Birth Control in America* (New York: Grossman, 1976), 116-58.

38. "Convention Report," August 12, 1924, in Hill, *Garvey Papers*, 5:717-22.

39. "The Hand that Rocks the Cradle." Also see "More Attention Given to Our Child Life," *NW*, May 31, 1924, 10.

40. In one article written exclusively for the *Negro World*, black bibliophile Arthur Schomburg went as far to assert that European and American scientists poached the concept from ancient African cultures; "Arthur A. Schomburg Pays a Tribute to [the] African Woman," *NW*, April 2, 1921, 7. For other examples, see "The Question of Race Superiority," *NW*, October 8, 1921, 4; and "The World Suffers from Shortage of Big Minds," *NW*, October 22, 1921, 6.

41. Lester Taylor, "Children and the Race," *NW*, October 29, 1921.

42. Carrie Mero Leadett, "The Obligations of Motherhood," *NW*, March 29, 1924, 10. Also see Mrs. W. Waldron Pitt, "A Woman's Appeal to Ethiopian Women," *NW*, January 6, 1923, 6.

43. Marcus Garvey, "Speech Delivered at Carnegie Hall," in *Philosophy and Opinions*, 2:101–2. Refer to the following as well: Garvey, "Shall the Negro Be Exterminated?," 1:64; Marcus Garvey, "Garvey Quotes Hearst and Other White Writers Who Believe Negro is Slowly, Inevitably Diminishing in Numbers . . . ," *NW*, December 3, 1921, reprinted in Hill, *Garvey Papers*, 4:221–28; "Race Extinction," *NW*, May 20, 1922, 4; Kelly Miller, "Educated Negroes Said Not to Marry and Raise Large Families," *NW*, February 7, 1925.

Some Garveyites invoked Native Americans when they discussed the possibility of genocide; one such example is Ida Jacques, "Fate of Red Indians Should Be a Warning to Negroes," *NW*, January 24, 1925. A group of Garveyites in Kansas went in a different direction: they associated the threat of extinction with a need to leave the United States for Africa. See [Alfred D. House?] et al. to Earnest Sevier Cox; Earnest Sevier Cox Papers, Special Collections, Perkins Library, Duke University, Durham, N.C., box 3, folder 1929–1930.

44. Speech by Marcus Garvey (original title unknown), *NW*, September 10, 1921; reprinted in Hill, *Garvey Papers*, 4:26.

45. See, for example, "Report of Committee on 'The Future of the Negro in America,'" *NW*, September 9, 1922; reprinted in Hill, *Garvey Papers*, 4:1017–21.

An especially compelling counterargument to Garvey's appears in A[rnold] H[amilton] Maloney, "Maloney Says Negro Race is Not Doomed to Extinction," *NW*, September 16, 1922, 3. Maloney, a professor at Wilberforce University who would later publish *Race Leadership* (Xenia: Aldine Publishing House, 1924), also provided one of the only articles in the *Negro World* to advocate miscegenation. See "Miscegenation Only Local Alternative to Social and Economic Serfdom—Maloney," *NW*, June 17, 1922, 2.

46. For detailed, comparative statistics, refer to *Negro Population, 1790–1915*, 22–24, 283–87; also refer to *Negroes in the United States, 1920–32*, 1–2.

Mainstream epidemiology during the late nineteenth and early twentieth centuries consistently supported the view that black children, women, and men were anything but vital. Examples of arguments that venereal disease and tuberculosis were especially prevalent among blacks may be found in Frederick L. Hoffman, *Race Traits and Tendencies of the American Negro* (New York: Macmillan, 1896); Mary White Ovington, *Half a Man: The Status of the Negro in New York* (New York: Longmans, Green, 1911); Mark J. White, "Report of the Committee on Venereal Diseases of the State and Provincial Health Authorities," *American Journal of Public Health* 13 (1923): 723–37.

47. Health-related coverage in the *Negro World* appeared on a fairly regular basis: Dr. B. S. Herben, "Are You Strong for the Race?" (April 7, 1923, 3); "Negro Race Needs More Medical Men Among the People" (July 28, 1923, 9); "Saving Our Children" (November 10, 1923, 8); "Negro City Death Rate" (December 8, 1923, 7); "Life Expectation of Negroes is Much Greater" (July 5, 1924, 7); "Com-

municable Diseases and Health and Wealth" (April 18, 1925, 10); "Birth Rate is Lowest Recorded in America" (December 19, 1925, 5); "Eugenics and Civilization" (September 11, 1926, 7); "Alarming Rise in Negro Death Rate Reported" (July 16, 1927, 2).

48. In *Garvey and Garveyism* (Kingston: United Printers, 1963), Amy Jacques Garvey recorded that the UNIA's "Liberty Halls, wherever located, served the needs of the people. . . . Public meetings . . . concerts and dances were held. . . . Notice boards were put up where one could look for a room, a job." *Garvey and Garveyism*, 91. John Charles Zampty, a Trinidadian who belonged to the UNIA local in Detroit, remembered that his division ran "'laundries, restaurants, shoe shine parlors, drugstores, and . . . even . . . theaters.'" See Jeannette Smith-Irvin, comp. and ed., *Footsoldiers of the Universal Negro Improvement Association (Their Own Words)* (Trenton, N.J.: Africa World Press, 1989), 11.

49. In particular, the *Negro World* periodically ran an idealized image of a nurse with the following caption: "carrying the torch of knowledge about health and rightful living for the enlightenment of our people . . . and eradicating the fatalistic theory that disease is God-sent." *NW*, March 31, 1923.

50. Josephine Spence, "Black Cross Nurses Trained to Care for Mothers and Babies," *NW*, November 1, 1924, 10. See also Isabella Lawrence's "Conservation of Child Life a Race Duty," *NW*, August 2, 1924, 12.

51. Morgan's column was entitled "Universal African Black Cross Nurses Child Welfare Department." For examples cited in text, please see "ABCs of Child Welfare," *NW*, February 4, 1922, 8; and *NW*, July 15, 1922, 6.

52. Amy Jacques Garvey, "Listen Women!," *NW*, April 9, 1927, 7.

53. Hubert Cox, "Birth Control Condemned as Heinous, Corrupted, Inhuman," *NW*, January 14, 1922, 7.

54. Katie Fenner, "Negro Men Must Beard the Lion in Its Den," *NW*, March 25, 1922, 3; Fenner, "Woman, Lovely Woman," *NW*, September 9, 1922, 10. Lucius Lenan-Lehman of California was sufficiently incensed by Fenner's opinions that he wrote a pointed rebuttal to her "Negro Men." See Lucius Lenan-Lehman, "Mrs. Katie Fenner," *NW*, September 30, 1922, 8.

55. Also refer to Benito Thomas, "Advocates of Birth Control Flayed," *NW*, April 4, 1925, 10; as well as "Birth Control Called Crime," in "Our Women and What They Think," *NW*, November 7, 1925, 7. In 1934, at the Seventh International Convention of the UNIA in Kingston, Jamaica, Garveyites unanimously approved a moratorium on the practice of birth control for all women of African descent. *The Black Man* 1, no. 6 (November 1934): 34. See also Jessie M. Rodrique, "The Black Community and the Birth-Control Movement," in *Unequal Sisters: A Multi-Cultural Reader in U.S. Women's History*, ed. Ellen Carol Du Bois and Vicki L. Ruiz (New York: Routledge, 1990), 333–44, esp. 336.

56. Margaret Sanger, *Woman and the New Race* (New York: Blue Ribbon Books,

1920). For arguments about the relationship between contraception and eugenics, see Gordon, *Woman's Body, Woman's Right*, 116–35.

57. For insight on African Americans' attitudes about homosexuality during the Harlem Renaissance, see Daphne Duval Harrison, *Black Pearls: Blues Queens of the 1920s* (New Brunswick, N.J.: Rutgers University Press, 1988), 14, 53, 103–4; and Eric Garber, "A Spectacle in Color: The Lesbian and Gay Subculture of Jazz Age Harlem," in *Hidden From History: Reclaiming the Gay and Lesbian Past*, ed. Martin Bauml Duberman, Martha Vicinus, and George Chauncey Jr. (New York: New American Library, 1989), 318–31. Refer also to Siobhan B. Somerville, *Queering the Color Line: Race and the Invention of Homosexuality in American Culture* (Durham: Duke University Press, 2000). An overview of interracial sexuality—one that explores same-sex desire—during this period may be found in Kevin J. Mumford, *Interzones: Black/White Sex Districts in Chicago and New York in the Early Twentieth Century* (New York: Columbia University Press, 1997).

58. John Houghton [also Haughton], "The Plight of Our Race in Harlem, Brooklyn, and New Jersey," *NW*, April 21, 1923, 8. Also see J. C. Cake, "Sex Truths," *NW*, May 19, 1923, 8. In addition, Benito Thomas's and Hubert J. Cox's language of social evil may be interpreted as references to homosexuality; Thomas, "Advocates of Birth Control Flayed"; and Cox, "Birth Control Condemned."

59. For examples of how black manhood was discussed by male and female Garveyites, see R. T. Brown, "A Call to Negro Manhood," *NW*, September 23, 1922, 9; Amelia Sayers Alexander, "A Brave Man Betrayed," *NW*, March 14, 1925, 7; P. L. Burrows, "Black Man's Duty to His Women," *NW*, August 16, 1924, 16.

Works that explore reifications of motherhood in nationalist ideologies include Deborah Gaitskell and Elaine Unterhalter, "Mothers of the Nation: A Comparative Analysis of Nation, Race, and Motherhood in Afrikaner Nationalism and the African National Congress," in *Woman-Nation-State*, ed. Nira Yuval-Davis and Floya Anthias (New York: St. Martin's Press, 1989), 58–78; Leila J. Rupp, "Mother of the *Volk*: The Image of Women in Nazi Ideology," *Signs* 3, no. 2 (Winter 1977): 362–79; Leslie Lynn King, "Gender, Nation, Pronatalism: Encouraging Births in France, Romania, and Israel" (Ph.D. diss., University of Illinois, Urbana-Champaign, 1998); and Taylor, "'Negro Women are Great Thinkers.'"

60. It is critical to note that using the word "sacrifice" in this context is not a presentist, feminist rendering of the past given that articles in the *Negro World* by both women and men frequently coupled that very word to motherhood. See Laura Thomas, "Living for Others," *NW*, June 14, 1924, 12; and Hubert Cox, "The Women of the Race," *NW*, January 21, 1922, 8. For an elaboration of the "double-edged" nature of motherhood as used in the context of political struggle, see Patricia Stamp, "Burying Otieno: The Politics of Gender and Ethnicity in Kenya," *Signs* 16, no. 4 (Summer 1991): 843–44; also refer to Patricia Hill-Collins's discussion of black women and motherhood in *Black Feminist Thought: Knowledge,*

Consciousness and the Politics of Empowerment (New York: Routledge, 1991), 115–37, esp. 132.

61. Elizabeth Balanoff, "The 20th Century Trade Union Woman: Vehicle For Social Change. Oral History Interview with Maida Springer Kemp, International Ladies Garment Workers Union," in *The Black Women Oral History Project* (Cambridge: Schlesinger Library, Radcliffe College, 1978), 6.

62. Moses, *Golden Age of Black Nationalism*; Stein, *The World of Marcus Garvey*. Additional commentary on racial conservatism may be found in Kevin K. Gaines, *Uplifting the Race: Black Leadership, Politics, and Culture in the Twentieth Century* (Chapel Hill: University of North Carolina Press, 1996), 120–27.

63. Robert Hill, "Introduction," in *Philosophy and Opinions of Marcus Garvey*, ed. Amy Jacques Garvey (New York: Atheneum, 1992), lxxxiv.

64. George L. Mosse, *Nationalism and Sexuality: Middle-Class Morality and Sexual Norms in Modern Europe* (Madison: University of Wisconsin Press, 1985). Refer also to Andrew Parker et al., eds., *Nationalisms and Sexualities* (New York: Routledge, 1992); Margaret Jolly, "Motherlands? Some Notes on Women and Nationalism in India and Africa," *Australian Journal of Anthropology* 5, nos. 1–2 (Winter-Spring 1994): 41–59; Nilanjana Chatterjee and Nancy E. Riley, "Planning an Indian Modernity: The Gendered Politics of Fertility Control," *Signs* 26, no. 3 (Spring 2001): 811–45; and Jennifer A. Nelson, "'Abortions under Community Control': Feminism, Nationalism, and the Politics of Reproduction among New York City's Young Lords," *Journal of Women's History* 13, no. 1 (Spring 2001): 157–80. A complex statement on the complex relationship between feminisms, ethnicities, and nationalisms is Daiva K. Stasiulis, "Relational Positionalities of Nationalisms, Racisms, and Feminisms," in *Between Woman and Nation: Nationalisms, Transnational Feminisms, and the State*, ed. Caren Kaplan, Norma Alarcón, and Minoo Moallem (Durham: Duke University Press, 1999), 182–218.

65. Floya Anthias and Nira Yuval-Davis, "Introduction," in *Woman-Nation-State*, 1–15, esp. 7–8.

In addition to acknowledging that "reproduction" refers to a range of processes (child-bearing, material production, maintenance of citizenry, replication of "national" groups), Yuval-Davis and Anthias offer a theoretical etymology of "reproduction" as an analytical term that is worth quoting at length:

> A word of caution is necessary in relation to the use of the term "reproduction." We consider this concept as problematic on more than one ground. First of all, its use in the literature includes many and indeed inconsistent meanings, from a definition of women's biological role to explanations of the existence of social systems over time. . . . Even more importantly, the term "reproduction" has been criticised as being tautological on the one hand, often implicitly assuming that "reproduction" takes place, and static on the other hand, therefore unable to explain growth, decline, and transformation processes. (7–8)

I view reproduction as dynamic, as a means through which people, households, identities, and "race" are both created and maintained. See Michele Mitchell, "Commentary," *Cuban Studies* 33 (2002): 124–28.

66. Such work has been underway for some time and includes E. Frances White, "Africa on My Mind: Gender, Counterdiscourse, and African American Nationalism," *Journal of Women's History* 2, no. 1 (Spring 1990): 73–97; Wahneema Lubiano, "Black Nationalism and Black Common Sense: Policing Ourselves and Others," in *The House That Race Built: Black Americans, U.S. Terrain,* ed. Wahneema Lubiano (New York: Pantheon, 1997), 232–52; Summers, "Nationalism, Race Consciousness, and the Constructions of Black Middle Class Masculinity"; and Tracye Ann Matthews, "'No One Ever Asks What a Man's Place in the Revolution Is': Gender and Sexual Politics in the Black Panther Party, 1966–1971" (Ph.D. diss., University of Michigan, Ann Arbor, 1998).

67. George M. Fredrickson, *The Black Image in the White Mind: The Debate on Afro-American Character and Destiny, 1817–1914* (New York: Harper & Row, 1971), 251. Refer to John D'Emilio and Estelle B. Freedman's *Intimate Matters: A History of Sexuality in America* (New York: Harper & Row, 1988) for further analysis of race and sexuality.

68. Mariana Valverde, "'When the Mother of the Race Is Free': Race, Reproduction, and Sexuality in First-Wave Feminism," in *Gender Conflicts: New Essays in Women's History,* ed. Franca Iacovetta and Mariana Valverde (Toronto: University of Toronto Press, 1992), 3–26, esp. 4.

69. Nira Yuval-Davis, "Gender and Nation," *Ethnic and Racial Studies* 16 (1993): 621–32, esp. 628.

70. This central movement proclamation was frequently printed in the pages of the *Negro World* and also appeared on parade banners.

EPILOGUE

1. "At the Crossroads," [editorial cartoon], and "On to Nationhood," [editorial], *Negro World,* April 14, 1928, 4. For allied commentary, see "Race's Destiny Not to be Trifled With, Marcus Garvey Warns The Self-Seeking," *Negro World,* February 18, 1928, 1.

2. For examples of African American discussion of Liberia during the 1930s, see Theodore G. Vincent, ed., *Voices of a Black Nation: Political Journalism in the Harlem Renaissance* (San Francisco: Ramparts Press, 1973), 312–21. Evidence of emigrationist desire during the 1930s may be found in a "Petition" issued by the American Negro African Movement in 1933; see "The American Negro African Movement," in *A Documentary History of the Negro People in the United States, 1933–1945,* ed. Herbert Aptheker (Secaucus, N.J.: Citadel Press, 1974), 10–11.

3. Robert L. Vann, "Why This Magazine," *Competitor* 1, no. 1 (January 1920): 2. For an additional editorial declaration regarding Americanism, see "A Misnomer," *Competitor* 1, no. 2 (February 1920): 3–4. Significantly, the *Competitor* publicized

the National Association of Colored Women's "American Citizenship Department"; see "America Must Mean Equal Training and Opportunity For All," *Competitor* 3, no. 3 (May 1921): 26. Theodore Vincent situates the *Competitor* within what he terms the "New Negro press" of the Harlem Renaissance. See Vincent, *Voices of a Black Nation*, 26.

4. James Weldon Johnson, *Negro Americans, What Now?* (New York: Viking Press, 1934), 98.

5. Andrew G. Paschal, "Negro Youth and the Lost Ideals," *Crisis* 39, no. 2 (February 1932): 49, 69; Vincent, *Voices of a Black Nation*, 35. Vincent suggests that the black press's embrace of Americanism emerged out of the promise of the New Deal. However, the Great War—and the specter of "Bolshevism"—was also decisive in leading some African Americans to embrace Americanism during the postwar period as "the only way to eventually secure full recognition of citizenship." See Sergeant John R. Williams, "Americanism of the Negro," *Competitor* 1, no. 5 (June 1920): 25–28, esp. 28. Revealing commentary on the contradictions and tensions of Americanism for African Americans during the 1930s and 1940s may be found in Barbara Dianne Savage's *Broadcasting Freedom: Radio, War, and the Politics of Race, 1938–1948* (Chapel Hill: University of North Carolina Press, 1999).

6. See Dean E. Robinson, *Black Nationalism in American Politics and Thought* (Cambridge: Cambridge University Press, 2001), for provocative analysis of black nationalism during the twentieth century.

7. "For a 49th (All Black) State," in Aptheker, *Documentary History*, 84–90, esp. 86; A. George Daly, M.D., "The Negro and the Present Social Order," *Education* 1, no. 3 (September 1935): 2–3.

8. "The Physical Future of the Negro," *Crisis* 40, no. 1 (January 1933): 7; "Inter-Marriage: A Symposium," *Crisis* 37, no. 2 (February 1930): 50–67; "Inter-Marriage: A Symposium," *Crisis* 37, no. 3 (March 1930): 89–91; Leslie Best, "Is the American Negro Doomed to Absorbtion?" (sic), *Education* 1, no. 2 (May 1935): 4, 8; *Birth Control Review: A Negro Number* 16, no. 6 (June 1932). Inasmuch as the *Birth Control Review* symposium had distinct eugenic overtones, some race commentators dismissed eugenic premises during the late 1920s and early 1930s. A particularly pithy dismissal may be found in "That Eugenic Baby," *The Light and Heebie Jeebies* 4, no. 43 (September 15, 1928), 4.

9. Thomas Kirksey, *Where is the American Negro Going?* (Chicago: Prairie State Press, 1937), 113–18.

10. Louise Thompson, "Southern Terror," *Crisis* 41, no. 11 (November 1934): 327–28, esp. 328.

11. "A Crossroad Puzzle," [Editorial cartoon], *Defender* (Chicago, Ill.), November 10, 1934; located in the Clipping File of the Schomburg Center for Research in Black Culture, frame 000846; "Discrimination on WPA," in *Black Women in White America: A Documentary History*, ed. Gerda Lerner (New York: Vintage, 1992), 398–405, esp. 402.

12. See, for example, "Negro Editors on Communism: A Symposium of the American Negro Press," *Crisis* 39, no. 4 (April 1932): 117–19; ibid., no. 5 (May 1932): 154–56, 170. Incisive commentary on radical politics among African Americans during the 1930s may be found in Robin D. G. Kelley, *Hammer and Hoe: Alabama Communists during the Great Depression* (Chapel Hill: University of North Carolina Press, 1989); and Rod Bush, *We Are Not What We Seem: Black Nationalism and Class Struggle in the American Century* (New York: New York University Press, 1999).

13. My argument here is informed by the following: Elsa Barkley Brown, "Negotiating and Transforming the Public Sphere: African American Political Life in the Transition from Slavery to Freedom," *Public Culture* 7, no. 1 (Fall 1994): 107–46; Deborah Gray White, *Too Heavy a Load: Black Women in Defense of Themselves, 1894–1994* (New York: W. W. Norton, 1998); Victoria W. Wolcott, *Remaking Respectability: African American Women in Interwar Detroit* (Chapel Hill: University of North Carolina Press, 2001), 207–40; Patricia A. Schechter, *Ida B. Wells-Barnett and American Reform, 1880–1930* (Chapel Hill: University of North Carolina Press, 2001); and Jonathon Scott Holloway, *Confronting the Veil: Abram Harris Jr., E. Franklin Frazier, and Ralph Bunche, 1919–1941* (Chapel Hill: University of North Carolina Press, 2002).

14. Jacqueline Jones, *Labor of Love, Labor of Sorrow: Black Women, Work and the Family, from Slavery to the Present* (New York: Vintage Books, 1986), 254; Gretchen Lemke-Santangelo, *Abiding Courage: African American Migrant Women and the East Bay Community* (Chapel Hill: University of North Carolina Press, 1996), 114–17.

15. Marilynn S. Johnson, "Gender, Race, and Rumours: Re-examining the 1943 Race Riots," *Gender & History* 10, no. 2 (August 1998): 252–77, esp. 72; White, *Too Heavy a Load*, 174. Nuanced, detailed commentary on gender politics in the movement during the 1960s may be found in Barbara Ransby, *Ella Baker and the Black Freedom Movement: A Radical Democratic Vision* (Chapel Hill: University of North Carolina Press, 2003).

16. Incisive analytical overviews of gender and sexuality in late twentieth-century activism and thought may be found in Deborah Gray White, *Too Heavy a Load*, and E. Frances White, "Africa on My Mind: Gender, Counterdiscourse, and African-American Nationalism," *Journal of Women's History* 2, no. 1 (Spring 1990): 73–97. Provocative commentary on how birth control was considered genocide by some black activists during the late 1960s and early 1970s may be found in Toni Cade, "The Pill: Genocide or Liberation?," in Cade, ed., *The Black Woman: An Anthology* (New York: Signet, 1970), 163–69.

17. Michele Mitchell, "Silences Broken, Silences Kept: Gender and Sexuality in African-American History," *Gender & History* 11, no. 3 (November 1999): 433–44, esp. 440.

BIBLIOGRAPHY

Primary Sources

MANUSCRIPT AND MICROFILM COLLECTIONS

American Colonization Society Papers. Manuscript Division, Library of Congress. Washington, D.C.

Claude A. Barnett Papers. Chicago Historical Society. Chicago, Ill.

John E. Bruce Papers. Schomburg Center for Afro-American Culture, New York Public Library. New York, N.Y.

Nannie Helen Burroughs Papers. Manuscript Division, Library of Congress. Washington, D.C.

Earnest Sevier Cox Papers. Special Collections, Perkins Library, Duke University. Durham, N.C.

Hampton University News Clippings File (microfilm). Alexandria, Va.: Chadwyck-Healey, 1988.

Liberian Consular Records. National Archives. Washington, D.C.

Kelly Miller Papers. Moorland-Spingarn Research Center, Howard University. Washington, D.C.

Daniel A. P. Murray Pamphlets Collection. Rare Book and Special Collections Division, Library of Congress. Washington, D.C.

Daniel Alexander Payne Murray Papers. Manuscript Division, Library of Congress. Washington, D.C.

Records of the National Association of Colored Women's Clubs, 1895–1992 (microfilm), ed. Lillian Serece Williams. Bethesda, Md.: University Publications of America, 1993.

Schomburg Center for Research in Black Culture Clippings File (microfilm). New York: New York Public Library; Alexandria, Va.: Chadwyck-Healey, 1974.

Mary Church Terrell Papers. Moorland-Spingarn Research Center, Howard University. Washington, D.C.

Henry McNeal Turner Papers. Moorland-Spingarn Research Center, Howard University. Washington, D.C.

Tuskegee Institute News Clippings File (microfilm). Tuskegee: The Institute, [1899–1966]; Sanford, N.C.: Microfilming Corporation of America, 1976.

Carter Godwin Woodson Papers. Manuscript Division, Library of Congress. Washington, D.C.

NEWSPAPERS AND PERIODICALS

A.M.E. Church Review

African Repository

Age (New York, N.Y.)

Alexander's Magazine

Broad Ax (Salt Lake City, Utah, and
   Chicago, Ill.)

Brownies' Book

Christian Recorder

Colored American (Washington, D.C.)

Colored American Magazine

Competitor

Constitution (Atlanta, Ga.)

Courier (Pittsburgh, Pa.)

Crisis

Defender (Chicago, Ill.)

Forum

Freeman (Indianapolis, Ind.)

Gazette (Cleveland, Ohio)

Gazette (Raleigh, N.C.)

Half-Century Magazine

Journal and Guide (Norfolk, Va.)

Liberia Bulletin

Negro World (New York, N.Y.)

Planet (Richmond, Va.)

Southern Workman

Voice of Missions

Voice of the Negro

GOVERNMENT PUBLICATIONS

U.S. Bureau of the Census. *Historical Statistics of the United States: Colonial Times to 1970*. Washington, D.C.: Government Printing Office, 1975.

U.S. Department of Commerce, Bureau of the Census. *Negro Population. 1790–1915*. Washington, D.C.: Government Printing Office, 1918. Reprint, 1969.

U.S. Department of Commerce, Bureau of the Census. *Negroes in the United States, 1920–1932*. Washington, D.C.: Government Printing Office, 1935.

BOOKS, PAMPHLETS, ARTICLES, AND SPEECHES

Adams, R[evels] A[lcorn]. *The Negro Girl*. Kansas City, Kans.: Independent Press, 1914.

Afro-American League. *Official Compilation of Proceedings of the Afro-American League National Convention held at Chicago*. Chicago: J. C. Battles & R. B. Cabbell, 1890.

Alexander, Charles. *One Hundred Distinguished Leaders*. Atlanta: Franklin Printing and Publishing, 1899.

American Colonization Society. *Annual Reports*. Reprint, New York: Negro Universities Press, 1969.

American Negro Academy. *Occasional Papers: 1–22*. New York: Arno Press, 1969.

Anderson, Arthur A. *Prophetic Liberator of the Coloured Race of the United States of America: Command to His People*. New York: New York Age Print, 1913.

Atlanta University. *Social and Physical Condition of Negroes in Cities. Report on an Investigation Under the Direction of Atlanta University: And Proceedings of the Second Conference for the Study of Problems Concerning Negro City Life, Held at Atlanta University, May 25–26, 1897*. Atlanta: Atlanta University Press, 1897.

Benjamin, R[obert] C[harles] O['Hara]. *Don't: A Book for Girls*. San Francisco: Valleau & Peterson, 1891.

Blackwell, Anne E. Walker [Mrs. A. W.] *The Responsibility and Opportunity of the Twentieth Century Woman*. N.p., ca. 1910.

Blyden, Edward Wilmot. *The African Problem and Other Discourses Delivered in America in 1890*. London, 1890.

Bowen, Ariel Serena [Mrs. J. W. E.] "Child Marriage A Social Crime — Its Remedy." In *The United Negro: His Problems and His Progress, Containing the Addresses and Proceedings [of] the Negro Young People's Christian and Educational Congress, Held August 6–11, 1902*, edited by I. Garland Penn and J. W. E. Bowen, 451–53. Atlanta: D. E. Luther Publishing, 1902.

Bowen, John Wesley Edward. *An Appeal to the King*. Atlanta: [Gammon Theological Seminary?], c. 1895.

Bowen, J. W. E. *What Shall the Harvest Be? A National Sermon; or, a Series of Plain Talks to the Colored People of America, on their Problems*. [Washington, D.C.?]: Press of the Stafford Printing Co., ca. 1892.

———, ed. *Africa and the American Negro . . . Addresses and Proceedings of the Congress on Africa . . . In Connection with the Cotton States and International Exposition: December 13–15, 1895*. Atlanta: Gammon Theological Seminary, 1896.

Brazelton, J[ames] H[enry] A[ugustus]. *Self-Determination: The Salvation of the Race*. Oklahoma City: Educator, 1918.

Bruce, John E. *The Blot on the Escutcheon; An Address Delivered before the Afro-American League . . . at the Second Baptist Church, Washington D.C., April 4, 1890*. Washington: R. L. Pendleton, 1890.

Bruce, John E. *The Making of a Race*. New York: s.n., 1922.

Burks, George H. *Future: Containing Great Lectures on the Future of the Colored Race, Nat Turner's Insur[r]ection, the New Insur[r]ection*. New Albany: Will A. Dudley, 1890.

Burrill, Mary. "They That Sit in Darkness: A One-Act Play of Negro Life." *Birth Control Review; Special Number — The New Emancipation: The Negroes' Need for Birth Control, As Seen By Themselves* 3, no. 9 (September 1919): 5–8.

Cashin, Herschel V., et al. *Under Fire With the Tenth U.S. Cavalry*. New York: F. Tennyson Neely, 1899.

Chapman, Samuel. *Destiny of the Black Man. Constitution of the Liberian Emigration Clubs*. [Muldrow?], Indian Territory: [1897?]

Chase, Thomas N., ed. *Mortality Among Negroes in Cities. Proceedings of the Conference for Investigation of City Problems, held at Atlanta University, May 26–27, 1896*. Atlanta: Atlanta University Press, 1896.

Christmas, Rev. L. T. *An Evil Router From All the Walks of Life — From the Cradle to the Grave — A Panacea for Racial Frictions and a Crowning Benediction to Humanity*. Raleigh: Edwards & Broughton, 1900.

Coston, W. Hilary. *The Spanish-American War Volunteer*. Middletown, Pa.: Mount
Pleasant Printery, 1899.

Councill, W[illiam] H[ooper]. *Lamp of Wisdom; or, Race History Illuminated.*
A Compendium of Race History Comprising Facts Gleaned From Every Field For
Millions of Readers. Nashville: J. T. Haley, 1898.

———. *The Negro Laborer: A Word to Him*. Huntsville, Ala.: R. F. Dickson, 1887.

Crogman, William H. *Talks For the Times*. Atlanta: Franklin Printing and
Publishing, 1878.

Crummell, Alex[ander]. *Africa and America: Addresses and Discourses, by Rev. Alex.*
Crummell. Springfield, Mass.: Willey & Company, 1891. Reprint, New York:
Negro Universities Press, 1969.

———. *Destiny and Race: 1840–1898*. Edited by Wilson J. Moses. Amherst:
University of Massachusetts Press, 1992.

———. *The Future of Africa: Being Addresses, Sermons, Etc, Etc., Delivered in the*
Republic of Liberia. New York: Charles Scribner, 1862. Reprint, Detroit: Negro
History Press, 1969.

———. "The Social Principle Among a People, and its Bearing on Their Progress
and Development. A Discourse, Delivered on Thanksgiving Day, November 25,
1875."

Crumpler, Rebecca Lee. *A Book of Medical Discourses, In Two Parts*. Boston:
Cashman, Keating, 1883.

Culp, D[aniel] W[allace]. *Twentieth Century Negro Literature or, a Cyclopedia of*
Thought. Naperville, Ill.: J. L. Nichols, 1902.

Dancy, John C. "How to Save Our Youth." In *The United Negro: His Problems and*
His Progress, edited by I. Garland Penn and J. W. E. Bowen, 475–76. Atlanta:
D. E. Luther Publishing, 1902.

Du Bois, W. E. B. "Heredity and the Public Schools: A Lecture Delivered under the
Auspices of the Principals' Association of the Colored Schools of Washington,
D.C." In *Pamphlets and Leaflets by W. E. B. Du Bois*, compiled and edited by
Herbert Aptheker, 46–52. White Plains, N.Y.: Kraus-Thomson, 1986.

———. *The Philadelphia Negro: A Social Study. Together with a Special Report on*
Domestic Service by Isabel Eaton. Philadelphia: University of Pennsylvania Press,
1899. Reprint, Philadelphia: University of Pennsylvania Press, 1996.

———. *Writings*. Edited by Nathan Huggins. New York: Literary Classics, 1986.

———, ed. *The Health and Physique of the Negro American. Report of a Social*
Study made under the direction of Atlanta University; together with the
Proceedings of the Eleventh Conference for the Study of the Negro Problems, held
at Atlanta University, on May the 29th, 1906. Atlanta: Atlanta University Press,
1906.

———, ed. *The Negro American Family. Report of a Social Study made principally*
by the College Classes of 1909 and 1910 of Atlanta University, under the patronage
of the Trustees of the John F. Slater Fund; together with the Proceedings of the 13th

*Annual Conference for the Study of the Negro Problems, held at Atlanta University
on Tuesday, May the 26th, 1908.* Atlanta: Atlanta University Press, 1908.

———, ed. *Some Efforts of American Negroes for their Own Social Betterment.*
Atlanta: Atlanta University Press, 1898.

Du Bois, W. E. B., and Augustus Granville Dill, eds. *Morals and Manners Among
Negro Americans. Report of a Social Study made by Atlanta University under the
patronage of the Trustees of the John F. Slater Fund; with the Proceedings of the
18th Annual Conference for the Study of the Negro Problems, held at Atlanta
University, on Monday, May 26th, 1913.* Atlanta: Atlanta University Press, 1914.

Ferris, William H. *The African Abroad; or, His Evolution in Western Civilization.*
2 vols. New Haven: Tuttle, Morehouse & Taylor Press, 1913.

Floyd, Silas X. *Floyd's Flowers, or Duty and Beauty for Colored Children.*
Washington, D.C.: Hertel, Jenkins, 1905.

Fortune, Timothy Thomas. *Black and White: Land, Labor and Politics in the South.*
New York: Fords, Howard & Hulbert, 1884. Reprint, New York: Arno Press,
1968.

Fowler, Charles H. *Historical Romance of the American Negro.* Baltimore: Press of
Thomas & Evans, 1902. Reprint, New York: Johnson Reprint Corporation, 1970.

Frazier, E. Franklin. "Eugenics and the Race Problem." *Crisis* 31, no. 2 (December
1925): 91–92.

Gaines, Wesley J. *The Negro and the White Man.* [Philadelphia?]: A.M.E. Publishing
House, 1897. Reprint, New York: Negro Universities Press, 1969.

Garvey, Amy Jacques, comp. *The Philosophy and Opinions of Marcus Garvey or,
Africa for the Africans.* 2 vols. Reprint, Dover, Mass.: Majority Press, 1986.

Gay, Joseph R. *Progress and Achievements of the 20th Century Negro . . . A Handbook
for Self-Improvement Which Leads to Greater Success.* N.p.: 1913.

Gibson, John William, and Mrs. John William. *Golden Thoughts on Chastity and
Procreation Including Heredity, Prenatal Influences, etc., etc. . . .* Washington,
D.C.: Austin Jenkins, ca. 1914.

———. *Social Purity, or The Life of the Home and Nation; Including Heredity,
Prenatal Influences, Etc., Etc.; an Instructor, Counselor and Friend for the Home.*
New York: J. L. Nichols, 1903.

Gibson, J. W., and W. H. Crogman. *Progress of a Race or The Remarkable
Advancement of the Colored American.* Rev. and enl. ed. Naperville, Ill.: J. L.
Nichols, ca. 1912.

Grant, J[ohn] W[esley]. *Out of the Darkness, or Diabolism and Destiny.* Nashville:
National Baptist Publishing Board, 1909.

Griggs, Sutton E. *Guide to Racial Greatness; or, The Science of Collective Efficiency.*
Memphis: National Public Welfare League, ca. 1921.

———. *The Hindered Hand.* Nashville: Orion Publishing, 1905.

———. *Imperium in Imperio.* Cincinnati: Editor Publishing, 1899. Reprint,
Miami: Mnemosyne Publishing, 1968.

———. *Life's Demands; or, According to Law*. Memphis: National Public Welfare League, ca. 1916.

———. *Light on Racial Issues*. Memphis: National Public Welfare League, 1921.

———. *Overshadowed. A Novel*. Nashville: Orion, 1901.

———. *Pointing the Way*. Nashville: Orion, 1908.

———. *The Story of My Struggles*. Memphis: National Public Welfare League, 1914.

———. *Unfettered. A Novel; with Dorlan's Plan*. Nashville: Orion, 1902. Reprint, New York: AMS Press, 1971.

Grimké, Archibald H. "The Sex Question and Race Segregation." *American Negro Academy Occasional Papers, Nos. 18–19*. Washington, D.C.: American Negro Academy, ca. 1915.

Guthrie, James M. *Campfires of the Afro-American; or, The Colored Man as a Patriot, Soldier, Sailor, and Hero, In the Cause of Free America: Displayed in Colonial Struggles, in the Revolution, The War of 1812, and in Later Wars, Particularly the Great Civil War—1861–5, and the Spanish-American War—1898: Concluding With an Account of the War with the Filipinos—1899* . . . Philadelphia: Afro-American Publishing, 1899. Reprint, New York: Johnson Reprint Corporation, 1970.

Hackley, Emma Azalia Smith. *The Colored Girl Beautiful*. Kansas City, Mo.: Burton Publishing, 1916.

Haley, James T., comp. *Afro-American Encyclopedia; or, The Thoughts, Doings, and Sayings of the Race*. Nashville: Haley and Florida, ca. 1895.

———. *Sparkling Gems of Race Knowledge Worth Reading*. Nashville: J. T. Haley, 1897.

Hall, A[lonzo] L[ouis]. *The Ancient, Medieval, and Modern Greatness of the Negro*. Memphis: Stiker Print, [1907?]

Hall, Josie B[riggs]. *Build Character*. Mexia: Houx's Printery, 1906.

———. *Hall's Moral and Mental Capsule: For the Economic and Domestic Life of the Negro, As a Solution of the Race Problem*. Dallas: Rev. R. S. Jenkins, 1905.

———. *A Scroll of Facts and Advice*. Mexia: Houx's Printery, 1905.

Hampton Agricultural and Vocational Institute. *Annual Report, Hampton Negro Conference*. Nos. 2–16. July 1898–1912. Hampton: Hampton Institute Press, ca. 1891–1912.

Harper, Frances E. W. *Enlightened Motherhood. An Address before the Brooklyn Literary Society, November 15, 1892*. N.p., n.d.

Harris, Eugene. *An Appeal for Social Purity in Negro Homes: A Tract*. Nashville: [University Press?], 1898.

———. *Two Sermons on the Race Problem Addressed to Young Colored Men, By One of Them*. Nashville: University Press, 1895.

Hartshorn, W[illiam] N[ewton]. *An Era of Progress and Promise, 1863–1910*. Boston: Priscilla Publishing, 1910.

Haynes, George Edmund. *The Trend of the Races*. New York: Council of Women for Home Missions and Missionary Education Movement of the United States and Canada, 1922.

Heard, William H. *The Bright Side of African Life*. Philadelphia: A.M.E. Publishing House, 1898. Reprint, New York: Negro Universities Press, 1969.

Hoffman, Frederick L. *Race Traits and Tendencies of the American Negro*. American Economic Association, 1896.

Holm, John James. *Holm's Race Assimilation, or the Fading Leopard's Spots. A Complete Scientific Exposition of the Most Tremendous Question that has ever confronted two races in the world's history*. Naperville, Ill.: J. L. Nichols, 1910.

Holsey, Lucius Henry. "Amalgamation or Miscegenation." *Autobiography, Sermons, Addresses, and Essays of Bishop L. H. Holsey, D.D.* Atlanta: Franklin Printing and Publishing, 1898.

———. "Bishop Holsey on the Race Problem." N.p.: August 1899.

———. "Race Segregation." In *How to Solve the Race Problem. The Proceedings of the Washington Conference on the Race Problem in the United States . . .* , edited by Jesse Lawson, 40–58. Washington, D.C.: Beresford Printer, 1904. Reprint, Chicago: Afro-Am Press, 1969.

Hopkins, Pauline E. *Contending Forces: A Romance Illustrative of Negro Life, North and South*. Boston: Colored Co-operative Publishing, 1900.

———. *Of One Blood*. Reprinted in *The Magazine Novels of Pauline Hopkins*. New York: Oxford University Press, 1988.

———. *A Primer of Facts Pertaining to the Early Greatness of the African Race and the Possibility of Restoration by Its Descendants*. Cambridge: P. E. Hopkins, 1905.

Hunton, Addie W. "A Pure Motherhood the Basis of Racial Integrity." In *The United Negro: His Problems and His Progress*, edited by I. Garland Penn and J. W. E. Bowen, 433–35. Atlanta: D. E. Luther Publishing, 1902.

Johnson, Edward A. *History of Negro Soldiers in the Spanish-American War*. Raleigh: Capital Publishing, 1899.

———. *Light Ahead for the Negro*. New York: Grafton Press, ca. 1904.

———. "Negro Dolls for Negro Babies." *Colored American Magazine* 14, no. 10 (November 1908): 583–84.

Johnson, H. T. "The Hereditary Effects of the Immorality of the Father Upon the Children." In *The United Negro: His Problems and His Progress*, edited by I. Garland Penn and J. W. E. Bowen, 468–70. Atlanta: D. E. Luther Publishing, 1902.

Johnson, William Noel. *Common Sense in the Home*. Cincinnati: Press of Jennings and Pye, 1902.

Kenney, John A. *The Negro in Medicine*. Tuskegee: Tuskegee Institute Press, ca. 1912.

King, Georgia Swift. "Mother's Meetings." In *Social and Physical Conditions of Negroes in Cities*, 61–62. Atlanta: Atlanta University Press, 1897.

Kletzing, H. F., and W. H. Crogman, eds. *Progress of a Race, or The Remarkable Advancement of the Afro-American Negro*. Atlanta: J. L. Nichols, 1898. Reprint, New York: Negro Universities Press, 1969.

Laney, Lucy C. "Address Before the Women's Meeting." In *Social and Physical Conditions of Negroes in Cities*, 55–57. Atlanta: Atlanta University Press, 1897.

Lawson, Jesse, ed. *How to Solve the Race Problem*. Washington: Beresford Printer, 1904.

Lichtenberger, J. P., ed. *The Negro's Progress in Fifty Years. The Annals*. 1913. Reprint, New York: Negro Universities Press, 1969.

Logan, Adella Hunt. "Methods of Restraining Pre-Natal and Hereditary Influences." In *Social and Physical Condition of Negroes in Cities*, 37–41. Atlanta: Atlanta University Press, 1897.

Love, Emanuel K. "Oration Delivered on Emancipation Day, January 2, 1888." N.p., n.d.

Lynk, Miles V. *The Black Troopers, or The Darling Heroism of The Negro Soldiers in the Spanish-American War*. 1899. Reprint, New York: AMS Press, 1971.

Majors, M[onroe] A[lphus]. *Noted Negro Women; Their Triumphs and Activities*. Jackson, Tenn.: M. V. Lynk Publishing House, 1893.

Matthews, Victoria Earle. "The Value of Race Literature: An Address (1895)." Reprint, *The Massachusetts Review* 27 (Summer 1986): 170–85.

McGirt, James Ephraim. *Avenging the Maine, A Drunken A. B., and Other Poems*. 3rd rev. and enl. ed. Philadelphia: George F. Lasher, Printer and Binder, 1901. Reprint, Freeport, N.Y.: Books for Libraries Press, 1970.

———. *The Triumphs of Ephraim*. 1907. Reprint, Freeport, N.Y.: Books for Libraries Press, 1972.

Miller, Kelly. "Eugenics of the Negro Race." *Scientific Monthly* 5, no. 1 (July 1917): 57–59.

———. *The Everlasting Stain*. Washington, D.C.: Associated Publishers, 1924. Reprint, New York: Arno Press, 1969.

———. *Out of the House of Bondage: A Discussion of the Race Problem*. New York: Thomas Y. Cowell, 1914.

———. "The Primary Needs of the Race: An Address." Washington: Howard University Press, 1899.

———. *Race Adjustment: Essays on the Negro in America*. New York: Neale Publishing, 1908. Reprint, New York: Arno Press, 1969.

Moton, Robert R. *Some Elements Necessary to Race Development*. Hampton, Va.: Press of the Hampton Normal and Agricultural Institute, 1913.

National Federation of Afro-American Women. *A History of the Club Movement Among the Colored Women of the United States of America*. N.p., 1902.

Nesbit, Willliam. *Four Months in Liberia: or African Colonization Exposed*. Pittsburgh: J. T. Shryock, 1855. Reprint, New York: Arno Press, 1969.

Parks, H[enry] B[lanton]. *Africa: The Problem of the New Century; The Part the*

African Methodist Episcopal Church is to have in its Solution. New York: AME
Church, 1899.

Parris, Oswald Z. *The Nationalism of the New Negro*. Newport News, Va.: O. Z.
Parris, 1920.

Penn, I[rvine] Garland. *Afro-American Home Manual and Practical Self-Educator
Showing What To Do and How To Do It Being a Complete Guide to Success in Life
. . . With Articles by Professor I. Garland Penn and many other distinguished men
of the African Race*. Atlanta: Phillips-Boyd, 1902.

———. *The Afro-American Press and its Editors*. Springfield, Mass.: Willey, 1891.

———. *Souvenir: Official Program and Music of the Negro Young People's Christian
and Educational Congress*. Washington, D.C.: Congress, 1906.

Penn, I[rvine] Garland, and J. W. E. Bowen, eds. *The United Negro: His Problems
and His Progress, Containing the Addresses and Proceedings of the Negro Young
People's Christian and Educational Congress*. Atlanta: D. E. Luther Publishing,
1902.

Pettiford, W. R. *Divinity in Wedlock: That State of Existence that Most Thoroughly
Develops the Deepest and Best Passions of the Soul*. Birmingham: Roberts & Sons,
1894.

Pipkin, J. J. *The Story of a Rising Race; the Negro in Revelation, in History, and in
Citizenship*. St. Louis: N. D. Thompson Publishing, 1902.

Richards, Ellen H. *Euthenics: The Science of Controllable Environment; A Plea for
Better Living Conditions As a First Step Toward Higher Human Efficiency*.
Boston: Whitcomb & Barrows, 1910.

Robb, Frederic H., ed. *The Negro in Chicago, 1779 to 1929*. 2 vols. Chicago:
Washington Intercollegiate Club and International Negro Student Alliance, 1929.

Roberts, W[illiam] K. *An African Canaan for the American Negro. Information on
Liberia For Intending Negro Emigrants. — The Necessary Preparation for the
Journey and How to Succeed as a Colonist*. Birmingham: Leslie Bros., 1896.

Roman, Charles Victor. *A Knowledge of history is conducive to racial solidarity, and
other writings. . . .* Nashville: Sunday School Union Print, 1911.

———. *Medical Essays: 1896–1925*. N.p., n.d.

———. "The Negro Woman and the Health Problem." *The New Chivalry —
Health*. Southern Sociological Congress, Houston, Texas. May 8–11, 1915. Edited
by James E. McCulloch. Nashville: Southern Sociological Congress, 1915,
392–405.

Rowe, George C. "The Aim of Life: Live, Learn, Labor, Love: Annual Address
Delivered at Claflin University, Orangeburg, S.C., April 26, 1892." 2nd ed.
Charleston: Kahrs and Welch, 1892.

Scott, Rev. J. H. "The Hereditary Effects of the Immorality of the Father Upon the
Children." In *The United Negro: His Problems and His Progress*, edited
by I. Garland Penn and J. W. E. Bowen, 470–71. Atlanta: D. E. Luther
Publishing, 1902.

Scottron, Samuel Raymond. "Chinese vs. Negroes as American Citizens." Brooklyn: Brooklyn Eagle, 1899.

Shorter, Susan I. *The Heroines of African Methodism*. Jacksonville, Fla.: Chew, 1891.

Simmons, William J. *Men of Mark: Eminent, Progressive, and Rising*. Cleveland: Geo. M. Rewell, 1887.

Smith, Amanda [Berry]. *An Autobiography: The Story of the Lord's Dealings with Mrs. Amanda Smith, The Colored Evangelist. Containing an Account of Her Life Work of Faith, and Her Travels in America, England, Ireland, Scotland, India and Africa, As An Independent Missionary*. Chicago: Meyer & Brother, 1893. Reprint, New York: Oxford University Press, 1988.

Steward, T[heophilus] G[ould]. *The Colored Regulars In the United States Army*. Philadelphia: A.M.E. Book Concern, 1904.

Stewart, T. McCants. *Liberia: The Americo-African Republic. Being Some Impressions of the Climate, Resources, and People, Resulting from Personal Observations and Experiences in West Africa*. New York: Edward O. Jenkins' Sons, 1886.

Taylor, C. H. J. *Whites and Blacks, or, The Question Settled*. Atlanta: Jas. P. Harrison, 1889.

Taylor, George E. *A National Appeal: Addressed to the American Negro and the Friends of Human Liberty*. . . . Oskaloosa, Iowa: National Colored Men's Protective Association of America, 1892.

Thomas, William Hannibal. *The American Negro: What He Was, What He Is, and What He May Become. A Critical and Practical Discussion*. New York: Macmillan, 1901.

Thorne, Jack. [David Bryant Fulton]. *Hanover; or, The Persecution of the Lowly. A Story of the Wilmington Massacre*. M. C. L. Hill, ca. 1899. Reprint, New York: Arno Press, 1969.

———. *A Plea for Social Justice for the Negro Woman*. Negro Society of Historical Research, Occasional Paper 2. New York: Lincoln Press Association, 1912.

Tice, S. Timothy. *The American Negro: What He Was, What He Is, and What He May Become; A Critical and Practical Rejoinder to William Hannibal Thomas*. [Cambridgeport?]: J. Frank Facey, 1901.

Tillman, Katherine Davis Chapman. *The Works of Katherine Davis Chapman Tillman*. Edited by Claudia Tate. New York: Oxford University Press, 1991.

Turner, Henry McNeal. *Respect Black: The Writings and Speeches of Henry McNeal Turner*. Compiled and edited by Edwin S. Redkey. New York: Arno Press, 1971.

———. "A Speech on the Present Duties and Future Destiny of the Negro Race." September 2, 1872. [Savannah, Ga.?]: Lyceum, 1872.

Walker, Charles Thomas. *The Colored Men for the 20th Century*. New York: J. P. Wharton, 1899.

Ward, Lester F. "Eugenics, Euthenics, and Eudemics." *American Journal of Sociology* 18, no. 6 (May 1913): 737–54.

Warren, Francis H., comp. *Michigan Manual of Freedmen's Progress*. Detroit: [Freedmen's Progress Commission?], 1915. Reprint, Detroit: John M. Green, 1985.

Washington, Booker T. *The Booker T. Washington Papers*. 13 vols. Edited by Louis Harlan. Urbana: University of Illinois Press, 1972–1984.

———. *The Future of the American Negro*. Reprint, New York: Haskell House Publishers, 1968.

Washington, Booker T., et. al. *A New Negro for a New Century*. Chicago: American Publishing House, 1900. Reprint, New York: Arno Press, 1969.

Washington, Booker T., W. E. B. Du Bois, T. Thomas Fortune, et al. *The Negro Problem: A Series of Articles by Representative American Negroes of Today*. New York: J. Pots, 1903.

Washington, Margaret Murray [Mrs. Booker T.] "The Negro Home and the Future of the Race." In *Democracy in Earnest: The Southern Sociological Congress, 1916–1918*, edited by James McCulloch, 334–41. Washington, D.C.: Southern Sociological Congress, 1918.

Wells-Barnett, Ida B. *Selected Works of Ida B. Wells-Barnett*. Compiled by Trudier Harris. New York: Oxford University Press, 1991.

Williams, Alfred Brockenbrough. *The Liberian Exodus. An Account of Voyage of the First Emigrants in the Bark "Azor" and Their Reception at Monrovia With a Description of Liberia. . . .* Charleston: News and Courier, 1878.

Williams, Samuel. *Four Years in Liberia. A Sketch of the Life of the Rev. Samuel Williams. With Remarks on the Missions, Manners and Customs of the Natives of Western Africa. Together with an Answer to Nesbit's Book*. Philadelphia: King & Baird, 1857. Reprint, New York: Arno Press, 1969.

Woods, E[lias] M[cSails]. *The Negro In Etiquette: A Novelty*. St. Louis: Buxton & Skinner, 1899.

Secondary Sources

ARTICLES, BOOKS, AND DISSERTATIONS

Adas, Michael. *Machines as the Measure of Men: Science, Technology, and Ideologies of Western Dominance*. Ithaca: Cornell University Press, 1989.

Alter, Peter. *Nationalism*. Translated by Stuart McKinnon-Evans. London: Edward Arnold, ca. 1989.

Anderson, Benedict. *Imagined Communities: Reflections on the Origin and Spread of Nationalism*. Rev. ed. New York: Verso, 1991.

Anthias, Floya, Nira Yuval-Davis, and Harriet Cain, eds. *Racialized Boundaries: Race, Nation, Gender, Colour, and Class and the Anti-Racist Struggle*. New York: Routledge, 1992.

Aptheker, Herbert. "Consciousness of Negro Nationality to 1900." In *Toward Negro*

Freedom, edited by Herbert Aptheker, 104–11. New York: New Century Publishers, 1956.

Armstrong, Nancy. "The Rise of the Domestic Woman." In *The Ideology of Conduct: Essays on Literature and the History of Sexuality*, edited by Nancy Armstrong and Leonard Tennenhouse, 96–141. London: Methuen, 1987.

Ayers, Edward L. *The Promise of the New South: Life after Reconstruction*. New York: Oxford University Press, 1992.

Bair, Barbara. "True Women, Real Men: Gender, Ideology, and Social Roles in the Garvey Movement." In *Gendered Domains: Rethinking Public and Private in Women's History*, edited by Dorothy O. Helly and Susan Reverby, 154–66. Ithaca: Cornell University Press, 1992.

Baker, Lee. *From Savage to Negro: Anthropology and the Construction of Race, 1896–1954*. Berkeley: University of California Press, 1998.

Bardaglio, Peter W. *Reconstructing the Household: Families, Sex, and the Law in the Nineteenth-Century South*. Chapel Hill: University of North Carolina Press, 1995.

Bay, Mia. *The White Image in the Black Mind: African American Ideas about White People*. New York: Oxford University Press, 1999.

Bederman, Gail. *Manliness and Civilization: A Cultural History of Gender and Race in the United States, 1880–1917*. Chicago: University of Chicago Press, 1995.

Bell, Howard H[olman]. "Negro Nationalism in the 1850s." *Journal of Negro Education* 35, no. 1 (Winter 1966): 100–104.

———. *A Survey of the Negro Convention Movement: 1830–1861*. New York: Arno Press, 1969.

Berry, Mary Frances, and John W. Blassingame. *Long Memory: The Black Experience in America*. New York: Oxford University Press, 1982.

Bethel, Elizabeth Rauh. *The Roots of African-American Identity: Memory and History in Antebellum Free Communities*. New York: St. Martin's Press, 1999.

Bittle, William E., and Gilbert Geis. *The Longest Way Home: Chief Alfred C. Sam's Back-to-Africa Movement*. Detroit: Wayne State University Press, 1964.

Bland, Lucy, and Laura Doan, eds. *Sexology in Culture: Labelling Bodies and Desires*. Chicago: University of Chicago Press, 1998.

Blumin, Stuart M. *The Emergence of the Middle Class: Social Experience in the American City, 1760–1900*. New York: Cambridge University Press, 1989.

Bock, Gisela. "Racism and Sexism in Nazi Germany: Motherhood, Compulsory Sterilization, and the State." *Signs* 8, no. 3 (Spring 1983): 400–421.

Borchert, James. *Alley Life in Washington: Family, Community, Religion, and Folklife in the City, 1850–1970*. Urbana: University of Illinois Press, 1980.

Boris, Eileen. "The Power of Motherhood: Black and White Activist Women Redefine the 'Political.'" In *Mothers of a New World: Maternalist Politics and the Origins of the Welfare State*, edited by Sonya Michel and Seth Koven, 213–45. New York: Routledge, 1993.

Boyd, Willis Dolmond. "Negro Colonization in the Reconstruction Era, 1865–1870."
    Georgia Historical Quarterly 40, no. 4 (December 1956): 360–82.
Brandt, Allan M. *No Magic Bullet: A Social History of Venereal Disease in the United
    States since 1880.* New York: Oxford University Press, 1985.
Bremen, Jan, ed. *Imperial Monkey Business: Racial Supremacy in Social Darwinist
    Theory and Colonial Practice.* Amsterdam: VU University Press, 1990.
Brink, Elsabe. "Man-made Women: Gender, Class, and the Ideology of the
    Volksmoeder." In *Women and Gender in Southern Africa to 1945*, edited by
    Cherryl Walker, 273–92. London: James Currey, 1990.
Brooks, Evelyn. "Feminist Theology of the Black Baptist Church, 1880–1900." In
    Class, Race and Sex: The Dynamics of Control, edited by Amy Swerdlow and
    Hanna Lesinger, 31–59. Boston: G. K. Hall, 1983.
Brown, Elsa Barkley. "Negotiating and Transforming the Public Sphere: African
    American Political Life in the Transition from Slavery to Freedom." *Public
    Culture* 7, no. 1 (Fall 1994): 107–46.
Bruce, Dickson D., Jr. *Black American Writing from the Nadir: The Evolution of a
    Literary Tradition, 1877–1915.* Baton Rouge: Louisiana State University Press,
    1989.
Byrd, W. Michael, and Linda A. Clayton. *A Medical History of African Americans
    and the Problem of Race: Beginnings to 1900.* Vol. 1 of *An American Health
    Dilemma.* New York: Routledge, 2000.
Campbell, James T. *Songs of Zion: The African Methodist Episcopal Church in the
    United States and South Africa.* New York: Oxford University Press, 1995.
Campbell, Karlyn Kohrs. "The Rhetoric of Radical Black Nationalism: A Case
    Study in Self-Conscious Criticism." *Central States Speech Journal* 22, no. 3
    (Fall 1973): 151–60.
Campbell, Patricia J. *Sex Education Books for Young Adults, 1892–1979.* New York:
    R. R. Bowker, 1979.
Carby, Hazel V. "'On the Threshold of Woman's Era': Lynching, Empire, and
    Sexuality in Black Feminist Theory." *Critical Inquiry* 12, no. 1 (Autumn 1985):
    262–77.
———. "Policing the Black Woman's Body in an Urban Context." *Critical Inquiry*
    18, no. 4 (Summer 1992): 738–55.
Carlisle, Rodney. *The Roots of Black Nationalism.* Port Washington, N.Y.: Kennikat
    Press, 1975.
Carnes, Mark C. *Secret Ritual and Manhood in Victorian America.* New Haven: Yale
    University Press, 1989.
Carnes, Mark C., and Clyde Griffen, eds. *Meanings For Manhood: Constructions of
    Masculinity in Victorian America.* Chicago: University of Chicago Press, 1990.
Caulfield, Sueann. *In Defense of Honor: Sexual Morality, Modernity, and Nation in
    Early-Twentieth-Century Brazil.* Durham: Duke University Press, 2000.

Chamberlin, J. Edward, and Sander L. Gilman, eds. *Degeneration: The Dark Side of Progress*. New York: Columbia University Press, 1985.

Chatterjee, Partha. *The Nation and Its Fragments: Colonial and Post Colonial Histories*. Princeton, N.J.: Princeton University Press, 1993.

Cimbala, Paul A. *Under the Guardianship of the Nation: The Freedmen's Bureau and the Reconstruction of Georgia, 1865–1870*. Athens: University of Georgia Press, 1997.

Cimbala Paul A., and Randall M. Miller, eds. *The Freedmen's Bureau and Reconstruction: Reconsiderations*. New York: Fordham University Press, 1999.

Clancy-Smith, Julia Ann, and Frances Goude, eds. *Domesticating the Empire: Race, Gender, and Family Life in French and Dutch Colonialism*. Charlottesville: University of Virginia Press, 1998.

Clawson, Mary Ann. *Constructing Brotherhood: Class, Gender, and Fraternalism*. Princeton, N.J.: Princeton University Press, 1989.

Coale, Ansley J., and Norfleet W. Rives Jr. "A Statistical Reconstruction of the Black Population of the United States 1880–1970: Estimates of True Numbers by Age and Sex, Birth Rates, and Total Fertility." *Population Index* 39, no. 1 (January 1973): 3–36.

Cohen, William. *At Freedom's Edge: Black Mobility and the Southern White Quest for Racial Control, 1861–1915*. Baton Rouge: Louisiana State University Press, 1991.

Cooper, Frederick, Thomas C. Holt, and Rebecca J. Scott. *Beyond Slavery: Explorations of Race, Labor, and Citizenship in Postemancipation Societies*. Chapel Hill: University of North Carolina Press, 2000.

Cooper, Frederick, and Ann Laura Stoler, eds. *Tensions of Empire: Colonial Cultures in a Bourgeois World*. Berkeley: University of California Press, 1997.

Cullen, Jim. "'I's a Man Now': Gender and African-American Men." In *Divided Houses: Gender and the Civil War*, edited by Catherine Clinton and Nina Silber, 76–91. New York: Oxford University Press, 1992.

Cronon, E. David. *Black Moses: The Story of Marcus Garvey and the Universal Negro Improvement Association*. Madison: University of Wisconsin Press, 1955.

Dailey, Jane, Glenda Elizabeth Gilmore, and Bryant Simon, eds. *Jumpin' Jim Crow: Southern Politics from Civil War to Civil Rights*. Princeton, N.J.: Princeton University Press, 2000.

Davis, Lenwood G. "Black American Images of Liberia, 1877–1914." *Liberian Studies Journal* 6, no. 1 (1975): 53–72.

———. "The Politics of Black Self-Help in the United States: A Historical Overview." In *Black Organizations*, edited by Lennox S. Yearwood, 37–50. Washington, D.C.: University Press of America, 1980.

Dean, David M. *Defender of the Race: James Theodore Holly, Black Nationalist Bishop*. Boston: Lambeth Press, 1979.

D'Emilio, John, and Estelle B. Freedman. *Intimate Matters: A History of Sexuality in America*. New York: Harper & Row, 1988.

Dodson, Jualynne. "Nineteenth-Century A.M.E. Preaching Women: Cutting Edge of Women's Inclusion in Church Polity." In *Women in New Worlds: Historical Perspectives on the Wesleyan Tradition*, edited by Hilah F. Thomas and Rosemary Skinner Keller, 1:276–92. Nashville: Abingdon Press, 1981.

Draper, Theodore. *The Rediscovery of Black Nationalism*. London: Secker & Warburg, 1971.

Driver, Edwin D., and Dan S. Green, eds. *W. E. B. Du Bois on Sociology and the Black Community*. Chicago: University of Chicago Press, 1978.

Du Bois, W. E. B. *Black Reconstruction in America, 1860–1880*. New York: Atheneum, 1972.

duCille, Ann. *The Coupling Convention: Sex, Text, and Tradition in Black Women's Fiction*. New York: Oxford University Press, 1993.

———. "'Othered' Matters: Reconceptualizing Dominance and Difference in the History of Sexuality in America." *Journal of the History of Sexuality* 1, no. 1 (July 1990): 102–27.

———. *Skin Trade*. Cambridge: Harvard University Press, 1996.

Edwards, Laura F. *Gendered Strife and Confusion: The Political Culture of Reconstruction*. Urbana: University of Illinois Press, 1997.

Engerman, Stanley L. "Black Fertility and Family Structure in the U.S., 1880–1940." *Journal of Family History* 2, no. 2 (June 1977): 117–38.

English, Daylanne. "W. E. B. DuBois's Family *Crisis*." *American Literature* 72, no. 2 (June 2000): 291–319.

Epps, Archie. "A Negro Separatist Movement of the Nineteenth Century." *Harvard Review* 4, no. 1 (1966): 69–87.

Ferrer, Ada. *Insurgent Cuba: Race, Nation, and Revolution, 1868–1898*. Chapel Hill: University of North Carolina Press, 1999.

Fields, Barbara J. "Ideology and Race in American History." In *Region, Race and Reconstruction: Essays in Honor of C. Vann Woodward*, edited by J. Morgan Kousser and James M. McPherson, 143–77. New York: Oxford University Press, 1982.

Formanek-Brunell, Miriam. *Made to Play House: Dolls and the Commercialization of American Girlhood, 1830–1930*. Baltimore: Johns Hopkins University Press, 1998.

Foner, Eric. *Reconstruction: America's Unfinished Revolution, 1863–1877*. New York: Harper & Row, 1988.

Fout, John C., and Maura Shaw Tantillo, eds. *American Sexual Politics: Sex, Gender and Race since the Civil War*. Chicago: University of Chicago Press, 1993.

Frankel, Noralee, and Nancy S. Dye, eds. *Gender, Class, Race, and Reform in the Progressive Era*. Lexington: University Press of Kentucky, 1991.

Fraser, Gertrude Jacinta. *African American Midwifery in the South: Dialogues of Birth, Race, and Memory*. Cambridge: Harvard University Press, 1998.

Fredrickson, George M. *The Black Image in the White Mind: The Debate on Afro-American Character and Destiny, 1817–1914*. New York: Harper & Row, 1971.

Freedman, Estelle B. "Sexuality in Nineteenth-Century America: Behavior, Ideology, and Politics." *Reviews in American History* 10, no. 4 (December 1982): 196–215.

Gaines, Kevin K. *Uplifting the Race: Black Leadership, Politics, and Culture in the Twentieth Century*. Chapel Hill: University of North Carolina Press, 1996.

Gaitskell, Deborah, and Elaine Unterhalter. "Mothers of the Nation: A Comparative Analysis of Nation, Race, and Motherhood in Afrikaner Nationalism and the African National Congress." In *Woman-Nation-State*, edited by Nira Yuval-Davis and Floya Anthias, 58–78. London: Macmillan Press, Ltd., 1989.

Gamble, Vanessa Northington. *Making a Place for Ourselves: The Black Hospital Movement, 1920–1945*. New York: Oxford University Press, 1995.

Garvey, Amy Jacques. *Garvey and Garveyism*. Kingston: United Printers, 1963.

Garvin, Roy. "Benjamin or 'Pap' Singleton and His Followers." *Journal of Negro History* 33, no. 1 (January 1948): 7–23.

Gatewood, Willard B. *Aristocrats of Color: The Black Elite, 1880–1920*. Bloomington: Indiana University Press, 1990.

———. *Black Americans and the White Man's Burden*. Urbana: University of Illinois Press, 1975.

———. *"Smoked Yankees" and the Struggle for Empire: Letters from Negro Soldiers, 1898–1902*. Fayetteville: University of Arkansas Press, 1987.

Geiss, Imanuel. *The Pan-African Movement: A History of Pan-Africanism in America, Europe and Africa*. New York: Africana Publishing, 1974.

Geertz, Clifford. "Ideology as a Cultural System." In *Ideology and Discontent*, edited by David E. Apter, 47–76. London: Free Press of Glencoe, 1964.

Genovese, Eugene. "The Legacy of Slavery and the Roots of Black Nationalism." With Commentary by Herbert Aptheker, C. Vann Woodward, and Frank Kofsky. *Studies on the Left* 6, no. 6 (November/December 1966): 2–61.

Gilmore, Glenda Elizabeth. *Gender and Jim Crow: Women and the Politics of White Supremacy in North Carolina, 1896–1920*. Chapel Hill: University of North Carolina Press, 1996.

Gordon, Linda. *Woman's Body, Woman's Right: A Social History of Birth Control in America*. New York: Grossman, 1976.

Gordon, Michael. "From an Unfortunate Necessity to a Cult of Mutual Orgasm: Sex in American Marital Education Literature, 1830–1940." In *Studies in the Sociology of Sex*, edited by James M. Henslin, 53–77. New York: Appelton-Century-Crofts, 1971.

———. "Sex Manuals: Past and Present." *Medical Aspects of Human Sexuality* 5 (September 1971): 21–37.

Gossett, Thomas F. *Race: The History of an Idea in America*. New York: Schocken Books, 1963.

Green, Dan S., and Edwin D. Driver, eds. *W. E. B. Du Bois on Sociology and the Black Community*. Chicago: University of Chicago Press, 1978.

Gunning, Sandra. *Race, Rape, and Lynching: The Red Record of American Literature, 1890–1912*. New York: Oxford University Press, 1996.

Gutman, Herbert. *The Black Family in Slavery and Freedom, 1750–1825*. New York: Pantheon Books, 1976.

Guy-Sheftall, Beverly. *Daughters of Sorrow: Attitudes Toward Black Women, 1880–1920*. New York: Carlson Publishing, 1990.

Hahn, Steven. *The Roots of Southern Populism: Yeoman Farmers and the Transformation of the Georgia Upcountry, 1850–1890*. New York: Oxford University Press, 1984.

Hall, Jacquelyn Dowd. "'The Mind That Burns in Each Body': Women, Rape, and Racial Violence." In *Powers of Desire: The Politics of Sexuality*, edited by Ann Snitow, Christine Stansell, and Sharon Thompson, 328–49. New York: Monthly Review Press, 1983.

Hall, Raymond L. *Black Separatism in the United States*. Hanover, N.H.: University Press of New England, 1978.

Hall, Stephen Gilroy. "'To Give a Faithful Account of the Race': History and Historical Consciousness in the African-American Community, 1827–1915." Ph.D. diss., Ohio State University, 1999.

Haller, Mark A. *Eugenics: Hereditarian Attitudes in American Thought*. New Brunswick, N.J.: Rutgers University Press, 1963.

Handlin, Oscar. *Race and Nationality in American Life*. Boston: Little, Brown, 1957.

Harding, Sandra, ed. *The "Racial" Economy of Science: Toward a Democratic Future*. Bloomington: Indiana University Press, 1993.

Harley, Sharon. "For the Good of Family and Race: Gender, Work, and Domestic Roles in the Black Community, 1880–1930." *Signs* 15, no. 2 (Winter 1990): 336–49.

Hartman, Saidiya V. *Scenes of Subjection: Terror, Slavery, and Self-Making in Nineteenth-Century America*. New York: Oxford University Press, 1997.

Haws, Robert, ed. *The Age of Segregation: Race Relations in the South, 1890–1945*. Jackson: University Press of Mississippi, 1978.

Higginbotham, Evelyn Brooks. *Righteous Discontent: The Women's Movement in the Black Baptist Church, 1880–1920*. Cambridge: Harvard University Press, 1993.

Higham, John. *Strangers in the Land: Patterns of American Nativism, 1860–1925*. New York: Atheneum, 1968.

Hill, Robert A., ed. *The Marcus Garvey and Universal Negro Improvement Association Papers*. 7 vols. Berkeley: University of California Press, 1983–86, 1989–90.

Hine, Darlene Clark, and Earnestine Jenkins, eds. *A Question of Manhood: A Reader in U.S. Black Men's History*. Bloomington: Indiana University Press, 1999.

Hobsbawm Eric J. *Nations and Nationalism Since 1780: Programme, Myth, Reality*. New York: Cambridge University Press, 1990.

Hodes, Martha. "The Sexualization of Reconstruction Politics: White Women and

Black Men in the South after the Civil War." *Journal of the History of Sexuality* 3, no. 3 (January 1993): 402–17.

————. *White Women, Black Men: Illicit Sex in the Nineteenth Century South*. New Haven: Yale University Press, 1997.

————, ed. *Sex, Love, Race: Crossing Boundaries in North American History*. New York: New York University Press, 1999.

Hofstadter, Richard. *Social Darwinism in American Thought: 1860–1915*. New York: G. Braziller, 1959.

Holloway, Jonathan Scott. *Confronting the Veil: Abraham Harris Jr., E. Franklin Frazier, and Ralph Bunche, 1919–1941*. Chapel Hill: University of North Carolina Press, 2002.

Holt, Marilyn Irvin. *Linoleum, Better Babies, and the Modern Farm Woman, 1890–1930*. Albuquerque: University of New Mexico Press, 1995.

Holt, Thomas C. *Black Over White: Negro Political Leadership in South Carolina during Reconstruction*. Urbana: University of Illinois Press, 1979.

Horsman, Reginald. *Race and Manifest Destiny: The Origins of American Racial Anglo-Saxonism*. Cambridge: Harvard University Press, 1981.

Horton, James Oliver. "Freedom's Yoke: Gender Conventions among Antebellum Free Blacks." *Feminist Studies* 12, no. 1 (Spring 1986): 51–76.

Howell, Joel D., and Catherine G. McLaughlin. "Race, Income, and the Purchase of Medical Care by Selected 1917 Working-Class Urban Families." *Journal of the History of Medicine and Allied Sciences* 47 (October 1992): 439–61.

Hoy, Suellen. *Chasing Dirt: The American Pursuit of Cleanliness*. New York: Oxford University Press, 1995.

Hunter, Tera W. *To 'Joy My Freedom: Southern Black Women's Lives and Labors after the Civil War*. Cambridge: Harvard University Press, 1997.

Hyam, Ronald. *Empire and Sexuality: The British Experience*. Manchester: Manchester University Press, 1990.

Jacobs, Sylvia. *The African Nexus: Black American Perspectives on the European Partitioning of Africa, 1880–1920*. Westport, Conn.: Greenwood Press, 1981.

Jacobsen, Matthew Frye. *Whiteness of a Different Color: European Immigrants and the Alchemy of Race*. Cambridge: Harvard University Press, 1998.

Johnson, Daniel M., and Rex R. Campbell. *Black Migration in America: A Social Demographic History*. Durham: Duke University Press, 1981.

Jones, Jacqueline. *Labor of Love, Labor of Sorrow: Black Women, Work, and the Family, from Slavery to the Present*. New York: Vintage Books, 1986.

Kaplan, Amy. "Romancing the Empire: The Embodiment of American Masculinity in the Popular Historical Novel of the 1890s." *American Literary History* 2, no. 4 (Winter 1990): 659–90.

Kaplan, Amy, and Donald E. Pease, eds. *Cultures of United States Imperialism*. Durham: Duke University Press, 1993.

Katz, Michael B., and Thomas J. Sugrue, eds. *W. E. B. Du Bois, Race, and the City:*

"The Philadelphia Negro" and Its Legacy. Philadelphia: University of Pennsylvania Press, 1998.

Kelley, Robin D. G. *Hammer and Hoe: Alabama Communists during the Great Depression*. Chapel Hill: University of North Carolina Press, 1990.

———. *Race Rebels: Culture, Politics, and the Black Working Class*. New York: Macmillan, ca. 1994.

Kemilainen, Aira. *Nationalism: Problems Concerning the Word, the Concept and Classification*. Jyvaskyla: Kustantajat, ca. 1964. Reprint, New York: Meridian, 1970.

Kevles, Daniel J. *In the Name of Eugenics: Genetics and the Uses of Human Heredity*. New York: Knopf, 1987.

King, Leslie Lynn. "Gender, Nation, Pronatalism: Encouraging Births in France, Romania, and Israel." Ph.D. diss., University of Illinois, Urbana-Champaign, 1998.

King, Miriam, and Steven Ruggles. "American Immigration, Fertility, and Race Suicide at the Turn of the Century." *Journal of Interdisciplinary History* 20, no. 3 (Winter 1990): 347–69.

Kinney, James. *Amalgamation!: Race, Sex, and Rhetoric in the Nineteenth-Century American Novel*. Westport, Conn.: Greenwood Press, 1985.

Kiple, Kenneth F. *The African Exchange: Toward a Biological History of Black People*. Durham: Duke University Press, 1987.

Kohn, Hans. *The Idea of Nationalism: A Study in Its Origins and Background*. New York: Macmillan, 1944.

———. *Nationalism: Its Meaning and History*. Rev. ed. Princeton, N.J.: D. Van Nostrand, 1965.

Kousser, J. Morgan. *The Shaping of Southern Politics: Suffrage Restriction and the Establishment of the One-Party South*. New Haven: Yale University Press, 1974.

Lantz, Herman, and Lewellyn Hendrix. "Black Fertility and Black Family in the Nineteenth Century." *Journal of Family History* 3, no. 3 (Fall 1978): 251–61.

Larson, Edward J. *Sex, Race, and Science: Eugenics in the Deep South*. Baltimore: Johns Hopkins University Press, 1995.

Lawson, Ellen N. "Sarah Woodson Early: 19th Century Black Nationalist 'Sister.'" In *Black Women in American History*, edited by Darlene Clark Hine, 3:815–26. New York: Carlson Publishing, 1990.

Lemelle, Sidney, and Robin D. G. Kelley, eds. *Imagining Home: Class, Culture, and Nationalism in the African Diaspora*. London: Verso, 1994.

Leverenz, David. *Manhood and the American Renaissance*. Ithaca: Cornell University Press, 1989.

Levine, Lawrence W. *Black Culture and Black Consciousness: Afro-American Folk Thought from Slavery to Freedom*. New York: Oxford University Press, 1977.

Lewis, David Levering. *W. E. B. Du Bois: Biography of a Race, 1868–1919*. New York: Henry Holt, 1993.

Lewis, Earl. *In Their Own Interests: Race, Class, and Power in Twentieth-Century Norfolk, Virginia*. Berkeley: University of California Press, 1991.

Lewis, Earl, and Heidi Ardizzone. *Love on Trial: An American Scandal in Black and White*. New York: W. W. Norton, 2001.

Litwack, Leon F. *Trouble in Mind: Black Southerners in the Age of Jim Crow*. New York: Alfred A. Knopf, 1998.

Logan, Rayford W. *The Negro in American Life and Thought: The Nadir, 1877–1901*. New York: Dial Press, 1954.

Lunbeck, Elizabeth. *The Psychiatric Persuasion: Knowledge, Gender, and Power in Modern America*. Princeton, N.J.: Princeton University Press, 1994.

Lynch, Hollis R. *Edward Wilmot Blyden, Pan-Negro Patriot, 1832–1912*. London: Oxford University Press, 1967.

MacLean, Nancy. *Behind the Mask of Chivalry: The Making of the Second Ku Klux Klan*. New York: Oxford University Press, 1994.

Magubane, Bernard Makhosezwe. *The Ties That Bind: African-American Consciousness of Africa*. Trenton, N.J.: Africa World Press, 1987.

Martin, Tony. *Race First: The Ideological and Organizational Struggles of Marcus Garvey and the Universal Negro Improvement Association*. Westport, Conn.: Majority Press, 1976.

Masur, Katharine. "Reconstructing the Nation's Capital: The Politics of Race and Citizenship in the District of Columbia, 1862–1878." Ph.D. diss., University of Michigan, 2001.

McDaniel, Antonio. *Swing Low, Sweet Chariot: The Mortality Cost of Colonizing Liberia in the Nineteenth Century*. Chicago: University of Chicago Press, 1995.

McFalls, Joseph, and George Masnick. "Birth Control and Fertility of the U.S. Black Population, 1880 to 1980." *Journal of Family History* 6, no. 1 (Spring 1981): 89–106.

McGlynn, Frank, and Seymour Drescher, eds. *The Meaning of Freedom: Economics, Politics, and Culture after Slavery*. Pittsburgh: University of Pittsburgh Press, 1992.

McHenry, Elizabeth. *Forgotten Readers: Recovering the Lost History of African American Literary Societies*. Durham: Duke University Press, 2002.

Meckel, Richard A. *Save the Babies: American Public Health Reform and the Prevention of Infant Mortality*. Baltimore: Johns Hopkins University Press, 1990.

Mehlinger, Louis. "The Attitude of the Free Negro Toward African Colonization." *Journal of Negro History* 1, no. 3 (July 1916): 271–301.

Meier, August. "The Emergence of Negro Nationalism." *Midwest Journal of Political Science*. Part I (Winter 1951–52): 96–104; Part II (Summer 1953): 95–111.

———. *Negro Thought in America, 1880–1915: Racial Ideologies in the Age of Booker T. Washington*. Reprint, Ann Arbor: University of Michigan Press, 1988.

Melody, M. E., and Linda M. Peterson, eds. *Teaching America about Sex: Marriage*

Guides and Sex Manuals from the Late Victorians to Dr. Ruth. New York: New York University Press, 1999.

Miller, Floyd J. *The Search for a Black Nationality: Black Emigration and Colonization*. Urbana: University of Illinois Press, 1975.

Mjagkij, Nina. *Light in the Darkness: African Americans and the YMCA, 1852–1946*. Lexington: University Press of Kentucky, 1994.

Moses, Wilson Jeremiah. *The Golden Age of Black Nationalism, 1850–1925*. New York: Oxford University Press, 1988.

————. *The Wings of Ethiopia: Studies in African-American Life and Letters*. Ames: Iowa State University Press, 1990.

Mosse, George L. *Nationalism and Sexuality: Respectability and Abnormal Sexuality in Modern Europe*. New York: Howard Fertig, 1985.

Mumford, Kevin J. *Interzones: Black/White Sex Districts in Chicago and New York in the Early Twentieth Century*. New York: Columbia University Press, 1997.

Neiman, Donald G. *Promises to Keep: African-Americans and the Constitutional Order, 1776 to the Present*. New York: Oxford University Press, 1991.

Nelson, Dana D. *National Manhood: Capitalist Citizenship and the Imagined Fraternity of White Men*. Durham: Duke University Press, 1998.

Newman, Debra Lynn. "The Emergence of Liberian Women in the Nineteenth Century." Ph.D. diss., Howard University, 1984.

Newman, Louise Michele. "The Birth Rate Question." In *Men's Ideas/Women's Realities: "Popular Science," 1870–1915*, edited by Louise Michele Newman, 105–24. New York: Pergamon Press, 1985.

————. *White Women's Rights: The Racial Origins of Feminism in the United States*. New York: Oxford University Press, 1999.

Odem, Mary E. *Delinquent Daughters: Protecting and Policing Adolescent Female Sexuality in the United States, 1885–1920*. Chapel Hill: University of North Carolina Press, 1995.

Ofari, Earl. *Let Your Motto Be Resistance: The Life and Thought of Henry Highland Garnet*. Boston: Beacon, 1972.

Ownby, Ted. *Subduing Satan: Religion, Recreation, and Manhood in the Rural South, 1865–1920*. Chapel Hill: University of North Carolina Press, 1990.

Painter, Nell Irvin. *Exodusters: Black Migration to Kansas after Reconstruction*. New York: Knopf, 1977.

————. "'Social Equality,' Miscegenation, Labor, and Power." In *The Evolution of Southern Culture*, edited by Numan V. Bartley, 47–67. Athens: University of Georgia Press, 1988.

————. *Southern History across the Color Line*. Chapel Hill: University of North Carolina Press, 2002.

Parker, Andrew, Mary Russo, Doris Sommer, and Patricia Yaeger, eds. *Nationalisms and Sexualities*. New York: Routledge, 1992.

Pascoe, Peggy. "Miscegenation Law, Court Cases, and Ideologies of 'Race' in

Twentieth-Century America." *Journal of American History* 83, no. 1 (June 1996): 44–69.

Peck, Ellen, and Judith Senderowitz, eds. *Pronatalism: The Myth of Mom and Apple Pie*. New York: Thomas Y. Crowell Company, 1974.

Pernick, Martin S. *The Black Stork: Eugenics and the Death of "Defective" Babies in American Medicine and Motion Pictures since 1915*. New York: Oxford University Press, 1996.

———. "Defining the Defective: Eugenics, Aesthetics, and Mass Culture in Early-Twentieth Century America." In *The Body and Physical Difference: Discourses of Disability*, edited by David T. Mitchell and Sharon L. Snyder, 89–110. Ann Arbor: University of Michigan Press, 1997.

———. "Taking Better Babies Contests Seriously." *American Journal of Public Health* 92, no. 5 (May 2002): 707–8.

Pinkney, Alphonso. *Red, Black and Green: Black Nationalism in the United States*. New York: Cambridge University Press, 1976.

Pivar, David J. *Purity Crusade: Sexual Morality and Social Control, 1868–1900*. Westport, Conn.: Greenwood Press, 1973.

Record, Wilson. "The Negro Intellectual and Negro Nationalism." *Phylon: The Atlanta University Review of Race and Culture* 10, no. 10 (October 1954): 10–18.

Redkey, Edwin S. *Black Exodus: Black Nationalist and Back-to-Africa Movements: 1890–1910*. New Haven: Yale University Press, 1969.

Reed, Adolph L., Jr. *W. E. B. Du Bois and American Political Thought: Fabianism and the Color Line*. New York: Oxford University Press, 1997.

Rhodes, Jane. *Mary Ann Shadd Cary: The Black Press and Protest in the Nineteenth Century*. Bloomington: Indiana University Press, 1998.

Robinson, Dean. *Black Nationalism in American Politics and Thought*. Cambridge: Cambridge University Press, 2001.

Rodrique, Jessie M. "The Black Community and the Birth-Control Movement." In *Unequal Sisters: A Multi-Cultural Reader in U.S. Women's History*, edited by Ellen Carol Du Bois and Vicki L. Ruiz, 333–44. New York: Routledge, 1990.

Rosen, Hannah. "The Gender of Reconstruction: Rape, Race, and Citizenship in the Postemancipation South." Ph.D. diss., University of Chicago, 1999.

Rupp, Leila J. "Mother of the *Volk*: The Image of Women in Nazi Ideology." *Signs* 3, no. 2 (Winter 1977): 362–79.

Russett, Cynthia Eagle. *Sexual Science: The Victorian Construction of Womanhood*. Cambridge: Harvard University Press, 1989.

Salem, Dorothy. *To Better Our World: Black Women in Organized Reform, 1890–1920*. New York: Carlson Publishing, 1990.

Saville, Julie. *The Work of Reconstruction: From Slave to Wage Laborer in South Carolina, 1860–1870*. Cambridge: Cambridge University Press, 1994.

Schechter, Patricia A. *Ida B. Wells-Barnett and American Reform, 1880–1930*. Chapel Hill: University of North Carolina Press, 2001.

Schwalm, Leslie A. *A Hard Fight for We: Women's Transition from Slavery to Freedom in South Carolina*. Urbana: University of Illinois Press, 1997.

Scott, Rebecca J. *The Abolition of Slavery and the Aftermath of Emancipation in Brazil*. Durham: Duke University Press, 1988.

———. *Slave Emancipation in Cuba: The Transition to Free Labor, 1860–1899*. 1985. Reprint, Pittsburgh: University of Pittsburgh Press, 2000.

Shaw, Stephanie J. *What a Woman Ought to Be and to Do: Black Professional Women Workers during the Jim Crow Era*. Chicago: University of Chicago Press, 1995.

Shick, Tom W. *Behold the Promised Land: A History of Afro-American Settler Society in Nineteenth-Century Liberia*. Baltimore: Johns Hopkins University Press, 1977.

Simmons, Christina. "African Americans and Sexual Victorianism in the Social Hygiene Movement, 1910." *Journal of the History of Sexuality* 4, no. 1 (July 1993): 51–75.

Smith, Anthony D. *Theories of Nationalism*. 2nd ed. New York: Holmes & Meier Publishers, 1983.

Smith, John David. *Black Judas: William Hannibal Thomas and "The American Negro."* Athens: University of Georgia Press, 2000.

Smith, Shawn Michelle. *American Archives: Gender, Race, and Class in Visual Culture*. Princeton, N.J.: Princeton University Press, 1999.

Smith, Susan L. *Sick and Tired of Being Sick and Tired: Black Women's Health Activism in America, 1890–1950*. Philadelphia: University of Pennsylvania Press, 1995.

———. "Welfare for Black Mothers and Children: Health and Home in the American South." *Social Politics* 4, no. 1 (Spring 1997): 49–64.

Smith-Rosenberg, Carroll. *Disorderly Conduct: Visions of Gender in Victorian America*. New York: Knopf, 1985.

Sollors, Werner, ed. *The Invention of Ethnicity*. New York: Oxford University Press, 1989.

Somerville, Siobhan B. *Queering the Color Line: Race and the Invention of Homosexuality in American Culture*. Durham: Duke University Press, 2000.

Stanley, Amy Dru. *From Bondage to Contract: Wage Labor, Marriage, and the Market in the Age of Slave Emancipation*. Cambridge: Cambridge University Press, 1998.

Staudenraus, Philip J. *The African Colonization Movement, 1816–1865*. New York: Columbia University Press, 1961.

Stecopoulos, Harry, and Michael Uebel, eds. *Race and the Subject of Masculinities*. Durham: Duke University Press, 1997.

Stein, Judith. "'Of Mr. Booker T. Washington and Others': The Political Economy of Racism in the United States." *Science and Society* 38, no. 4 (Winter 1974/75): 422–63.

———. *The World of Marcus Garvey: Race and Class in Modern Society*. Baton Rouge: Louisiana State University Press, 1986.

Stepan, Nancy Leys. *"The Hour of Eugenics": Race, Gender, and Nation in Latin America*. Ithaca: Cornell University Press, 1991.

Stoler, Ann Laura. "Making Empire Respectable: The Politics of Race and Sexual Morality in 20th-Century Colonial Cultures." *American Ethnologist* 16, no. 4 (November 1989): 634–60.

Stuckey, Sterling. *Slave Culture: Nationalist Theory and the Foundations of Black America*. New York: Oxford University Press, 1987.

Summers, Martin Anthony. "Nationalism, Race Consciousness, and the Constructions of Black Middle Class Masculinity during the New Negro Era, 1915–1930." Ph.D. diss., Rutgers University, 1997.

Tate, Claudia. *Domestic Allegories of Political Desire: The Black Heroine's Text at the Turn of the Century*. New York: Oxford University Press, 1992.

Tate, Gayle T. "Black Nationalism: An Angle of Vision." *Western Journal of Black Studies* 12, no. 1 (Spring 1988): 40–48.

Taylor, Ula Y[vette]. "'Negro Women Are Great Thinkers as well as Doers': Amy Jacques-Garvey and Community Feminism in the United States, 1924–1927." *Journal of Women's History* 12, no. 2 (Summer 2000): 104–26.

———. *The Veiled Garvey: The Life and Times of Amy Jacques Garvey*. Chapel Hill: University of North Carolina Press, 2002.

Terborg-Penn, Rosalyn. "Black Male Perspectives on the Nineteenth-Century Woman." In *The Afro-American Woman*, edited by Sharon Harley and Rosalyn Terborg-Penn, 28–42. Port Washington, N.Y.: Kennikat Press, 1978.

Thornborough, Emma Lou. *T. Thomas Fortune: Militant Journalist*. Chicago: University of Chicago Press, 1972.

Tindall, George Brown. *South Carolina Negroes: 1877–1900*. Columbia: University of South Carolina Press, 1952.

Tolnay, Stewart E. "Family Economy and the Black American Fertility Transition." *Journal of Family History* 11, no. 3 (July 1986): 272–77.

———. "The Fertility of Black Americans in 1900." Ph.D. diss., University of Washington, 1981.

———. "Trends in Total and Marital Fertility for Black Americans, 1866–1899." *Demography* 18, no. 4 (November 1981): 443–63.

Ullman, Sharon R. *Sex Seen: The Emergence of Modern Sexuality in America*. Berkeley: University of California Press, 1997.

Vance, Norman. *The Sinews of the Spirit: The Ideal of Christian Manliness in Victorian Literature and Religious Thought*. Cambridge: Cambridge University Press, 1985.

von Eschen, Penny. *Race against Empire: Black Americans and Anticolonialism, 1937–1957*. Ithaca: Cornell University Press, 1997.

Wallace, Maurice O. *Constructing the Black Masculine: Identity and Ideality in African American Men's Literature and Culture, 1775–1995*. Durham: Duke University Press, 2002.

Walters, Ronald G. *Primers For Prudery: Sexual Advice to Victorian America.* Englewood Cliffs, N.J.: Prentice-Hall, 1974.

Weiss, Sheila Faith. *Race Hygiene and National Efficiency: The Eugenics of Wilhelm Schallmayer.* Berkeley: University of California Press, 1987.

Welch, Richard E., Jr. *Response to Imperialism: The United States and the Philippine-American War, 1899–1902.* Chapel Hill: University of North Carolina Press, 1979.

West, Lois A., ed. *Feminist Nationalism.* New York: Routledge, 1997.

White, Deborah Gray. *Ar'n't I a Woman?: Female Slaves in the Plantation South.* New York: W. W. Norton, 1987.

———. "The Cost of Club Work, the Price of Black Feminism." In *Visible Women: New Essays on American Activism*, edited by Nancy A. Hewitt and Suzanne Lebsock, 247–69. Urbana: University of Illinois Press, 1993.

———. "The Slippery Slope of Class in Black America: The National Council of New Women and the International Ladies' Auxiliary to the Brotherhood of Sleeping Car Porters—A Case Study." In *New Viewpoints in Women's History: Working Papers from the Schlesinger Library Fiftieth Anniversary Conference, March 4–5, 1994*, edited by Susan Ware, 180–95. Cambridge: Arthur and Elizabeth Schlesinger Library on the History of Women in America, 1994.

———. *Too Heavy a Load: Black Women in Defense of Themselves, 1894–1994.* New York: W. W. Norton, 1998.

White, E. Frances. "Africa on My Mind: Gender, Counter Discourse, and African-American Nationalism." *Journal of Women's History* 2, no. 1 (Spring 1990): 73–97.

Wiebe, Robert H. *The Search for Order, 1877–1920.* New York: Hill and Wang, 1968.

Williams, Walter L. "Black Journalism's Opinions about Africa during the Late Nineteenth Century." *Phylon: The Atlanta University Review of Race and Culture* 34, no. 3 (September 1973): 224–35.

Williamson, Joel. *New People: Miscegenation and Mulattoes in the United States.* New York: Free Press, 1988.

Wolcott, Victoria W. *Remaking Respectability: African American Women in Interwar Detroit.* Chapel Hill: University of North Carolina Press, 2001.

Wolkoff, Regina Lois. "The Ethics of Sex: Individuality and the Social Order in Early Twentieth Century American Sexual Advice Literature." Ph.D. diss., University of Michigan, 1974.

Woodward, C. Vann. *Origins of the New South, 1877–1913.* Baton Rouge: Louisiana State University Press, 1951.

———. *The Strange Career of Jim Crow.* 2nd rev. ed. New York: Oxford University Press, 1966.

Yuval-Davis, Nira. *Gender and Nation.* London: Sage Publications, 1997.

Yuval-Davis, Nira, and Floya Anthias, eds. *Woman-Nation-State*. New York: Macmillan, 1989.

Zelinsky, Wilbur. *Nation into State: The Shifting Symbolic Foundations of American Nationalism*. Chapel Hill: University of North Carolina Press, 1988.

Zeugner, John. "A Note on Martin Delany's *Blake* and Black Militancy." *Phylon: The Atlanta University Review of Race and Culture* 32, no. 1 (First Quarter 1971): 98–105.

INDEX

Boulin, H. S., 320 (n. 46)

Bowen, Ariel Serena, 77, 78, 81, 87, 105, 280 (n. 3)

Bowen, John W. E., 279 (n. 1), 280 (n. 3)

Bowser, J. Dallas, 74

Boyd (Pettiford), Della, 118

Boyd, Richard H., 182, 183

Boyd, Robert Fulton, 142, 304 (n. 1)

Brazelton, James Henry Augustus, 185–88, 190, 192, 194, 318 (nn. 32, 33); and comparative views on African Americans and colonized peoples, 186, 318 (n. 33); and "psychology of the doll," 186, 319 (n. 38); on eugenic component of dolls, 186, 187

Brazely, Stella, 63

Brazil, 117

Brooks, Eva Aldred, 224, 225

Brotherhood of Sleeping Car Porters, 245

Brown, D. E., 47

Brown, William Wells, 8

Brownies' Book, 192, 321 (n. 50)

Bruce, John Edward, 72, 73, 201–2, 206, 325 (n. 16)

Bryant, Sylvia C. J., 87, 150, 285 (n. 30), 307 (n. 18)

Bunce, Oliver Bell, 121, 299 (n. 26)

Burrill, Mary, 104, 230

Burroughs, Nannie Helen, 10, 75, 148, 206, 208, 245, 275 (n. 41); on black men's participation in Spanish-American War, 62; on black women, men, and the franchise, 136; euthenic views of, 148; on interracial hierarchies, 206–7; on mate selection and skin color, 215

Butler, Henry Rutherford, 87, 88, 90, 286 (n. 32)

Butler, Matthew, 33

Butler, Selena Sloan, 86, 286 (n. 32)

Butler Bill, 33, 34, 264 (nn. 55–57)

Cabins, 143–47, 158, 160, 170, 310 (n. 44)

Cade, H. C., 41

Cannon, George, 94

Capps, Sherwood, 31, 41, 263 (n. 47)

Carr, J. W., 48

Carroll, Richard, 143–46, 149, 150, 305 (nn. 3, 4); on domesticity, education, politics, and reform, 306 (n. 10)

Carter, George, 229

Carter, Ida German, 76

Carter, John, 44–45, 268 (n. 89); and fate of Carter family, 44–45, 268 (n. 89)

Carter, Mary, 226

Cassell, Theresa, 184

Census. *See* United States Census Bureau

Chapman, Samuel, 35

Chase, Martha, 186; as producer of black dolls, 317 (n. 19)

Chase, W. Calvin, 33, 264 (n. 54)

Chase Sanitary Dolls, 186

Chesnutt, Charles, 212

Child, Lydia Maria, 116, 117, 297 (n. 15)

Christian Recorder, 43, 60

Christmas, L. T., 126, 135, 137, 151, 152

Church, Robert, 154

Circumcision, 101

Citizenship, 8, 18, 20, 21, 33, 48, 65, 79, 100, 109, 112, 116, 123, 135, 144, 147, 202, 205, 243, 296 (n. 6), 306 (n. 10), 345 (n. 5)

Civil War, 8, 21, 22, 61, 64, 65, 116, 117, 141, 156, 200

Clark, Jackson, 29

Clarke, Edward Young, 220

Class distinctions, 9–10, 78, 79, 123, 138–39, 157, 171, 298 (n. 24), 303 (n. 76)

Class formation, 85, 139, 143

Class stratification, 10, 14, 85, 143, 154–55, 162–63, 171

Dargan, Ines, 35

Dargan, James, 35

Darwin, Charles, 337 (n. 34)

Davis, Henrietta Vinton, 228, 336 (n. 27)

Day, Caroline Bond, 213, 214; as student of W. E. B. Du Bois, 213, 329 (n. 42)

Defender (Chicago, Ill.), 100, 101, 165, 167, 168, 190, 244, 293 (nn. 72, 73)

Degeneracy, 10, 15, 43, 81–86, 122–24, 146, 166, 170, 211, 225

Delany, Martin, 8, 22, 23, 252 (n. 20), 259 (n. 26), 260 (n. 28); participation in National Emigration Conventions, 22; disapproval of Liberia as site for emigration, 23; support of *Azor* movement, 26

De Mena, Maymie, 228, 238, 337 (n. 28)

Democrats, 26, 29, 33, 48–49, 59, 138, 200, 245

Dill, A. G., 321 (n. 50)

Dillon, Halle Tanner, 142

Disfranchisement, 5, 54, 56, 62, 67, 74, 109, 299 (n. 33)

Divinity in Wedlock (Pettiford), 118–20, 126, 131, 137, 138, 155

Divorce, 115, 119, 122

Dolls, 173, 174, 175, 176, 177, 179–92, 193, 195, 196, 316 (n. 13), 317 (nn. 18, 19, 21, 23), 318 (nn. 26, 27), 319 (nn. 38, 40, 43), 320 (n. 46)

Domestic reform, 9, 75, 136, 142–63, 169, 170, 171, 172

Don't: A Book for Girls (Benjamin), 109, 120–22, 127, 138

Douglass, Frederick, 8, 116, 202, 252 (n. 20), 273 (n. 24)

Du Bois, W. E. B., 9, 171, 311 (n. 49); anti-imperialist views of, 70, 73, 278 (nn. 67, 74); and Pan-Africanism, 70; on sexuality and morals, 85, 284 (n. 23), 310 (n. 43); on census statistics and claims regarding racial extinction, 93; range of sociological work, 155; and *The Philadelphia Negro*, 156–57, 310 (n. 43); and series on housing in *The Southern Workman*, 157–63; and *Health and Physique of the Negro American*, 211; estimate of racial intermixture among African Americans by, 212; as teacher of Caroline Bond Day, 213, 329 (n. 42); and eugenicist theory, 230; on rural black homes, 305 (n. 7), 310 (n. 44); early sociological work of, 309 (n. 32); and student researchers, 310 (n. 38); on urban crowding, 310 (n. 44); on prostitution and segregation, 311 (n. 47); on uneven sex ratios in Philadelphia, 311 (n. 49); as publisher (with A. G. Dill) of *Brownies' Book*, 321 (n. 50)

Dubose, James, 17, 39, 42, 43, 59

E. M. S. Novelty Company, 182, 184

Edwards, Jerry, 39, 267 (n. 71)

Edwards, Nellie, 221

Edwards, Ollie (Olive), 15, 38–40, 45, 266 (n. 71)

Electoral politics, 14, 18, 24, 25–26, 109, 135–38, 144, 151

Ellis, W. H., 37

Emancipation, 7, 11, 15, 24, 41, 57, 85, 117, 121, 135, 144, 150, 151, 154, 158, 174, 202, 325 (n. 17)

Emancipation Day, 143, 182, 202, 305 (n. 4)

Emancipation Proclamation, 143, 170

Emigration, 3–7, 8, 18–49, 55, 59–60, 67, 75, 151, 198, 205, 243, 249 (nn. 4, 6), 250 (n. 11), 256 (n. 3), 257 (n. 9), 259 (n. 26); and single women, 4, 31, 39–40, 45, 267 (n. 75), 270 (n. 101), 282 (n. 15); and gender, 18, 19–

sex and intermixture, 58, 198–99; on
mate selection and skin color, 203
Galloway, Lyllian, 228, 336 (n. 27)
Galton, Francis, 327 (n. 27)
Gamble, H. F., 92
Garnet, Henry Highland, 8
Garrison, William Lloyd, 116
Garvey, Amy Jacques, 238, 341 (n. 48);
leadership position in the UNIA of,
228; eugenic thought of, 231; disapproval of birth control, 234; rift with
Marcus Garvey, 336 (n. 26)
Garvey, Marcus, 72, 190, 191, 218,
228, 232, 238, 331 (n. 4); and eugenic trend in black thought, 106;
advocacy of racial purity by, 191,
220–21, 222, 237, 333 (n. 10); founding of UNIA, 219; on black men as
protectors of black women, 220–
21, 333 (n. 9); relationships with
white supremacists, 220, 332 (n. 8);
imprisonment of, 228, 336 (n. 24);
beliefs regarding racial extinction,
232; immigration to United States,
332 (n. 5); indictment for mail fraud,
336 (n. 24); rift with Amy Jacques
Garvey, 336 (n. 26); social Darwinist
views of, 338 (n. 37)
Garveyism, 219, 220, 222, 224, 225, 226,
230, 237, 238, 241–42, 331 (n. 4), 334
(n. 17), 336 (n. 24). See also Garveyites; Universal Negro Improvement
Association
Garveyites, 220, 221, 225, 226, 230,
233, 235, 236, 237, 238, 239, 335
(n. 23), 339 (n. 37). See also Garveyism; Universal Negro Improvement
Association
Gary, Maud Evangeline, 173–74, 177,
192; mother of, 173–74, 175, 314 (n. 1)
Gaston, Benjamin, 47
Gibson, John W., 88, 286 (n. 36)

Gibson, Mrs. John W., 88
Gibson, R. L., 33
Giles, George, 42
*Golden Thoughts on Chastity and Pro-
creation* (Gibson and Gibson), 87–
90, 109, 110, 126, 195, 286 (n. 39).
See also Social purity
Gonorrhea, 73, 101, 103, 130
Grant, John Wesley, 65
Green, David, 40
Griggs, Sutton E., 65, 67, 277 (n. 61);
eugenic views of, 285 (n. 30)
Grimké, Angelina, 104
Grimké, Archibald, 215
Guam: U.S. intervention in, 61

Hackley, Emma Azalia, 132–33, 208,
209; eugenic and hereditarian views
of, 132; influence of class on social
views of, 132; on mate selection, 208;
on miscegenation, 210, 328 (n. 33)
Haines, J. C., 24
Half-Century Magazine, 100, 101, 176,
184, 188, 214
Hall, Annie, 208, 215
Hall, J. P., 109
Hall, Josie Briggs, 10, 109, 111–12, 129–
32, 134, 135, 137, 155, 296 (nn. 3, 5),
301 (nn. 51, 52); on respective failures of husbands and wives, 130–31;
on impact of Reconstruction-era
politics on black households, 135–
36, 137, 302 (n. 67); on intraracial
class distinctions, 138, 303 (n. 76);
on woman suffrage, 303 (n. 69)
Hall's Moral and Mental Capsule, 111–
12, 129–31, 133, 134, 138, 155, 296
(n. 3)
Hampton Negro Conference, 197
Harper, Frances Ellen, 116; anti-
imperialist views of, 73, 75; hereditarian thought of, 86

Harris, Eugene, 124, 125, 209; on African American birth rate, 95; on black men as protectors of black women, 124, 208; on black women's conduct, 124, 125, 208; on interracial sex, 124–25; racial identity of, 290 (n. 56)

Harris, James, 18

Hawaii, 17, 67; U.S. intervention in, 51, 61

Hawaiians, 51

Hawkins, Gertrude, 226

Hayes, Rutherford B., 5, 14

Hayne, Joseph, 212, 213, 214

Haynes, Elizabeth Ross, 320 (n. 50)

Haynes, George Edmund, 155, 170–71

Health and Physique of the Negro American, 210–14

Heard, William Henry, 33, 262 (n. 43), 264 (n. 55)

Henderson, T. W., 48

Hereditarianism, 44, 86, 87, 93, 96, 97, 132, 206, 285 (n. 30), 327 (n. 27)

Her Unborn Child (film), 104

Heterosexuality, 79, 195, 225, 236

Hill, Anita, 247

Hoffman, Frederick L., 81–83, 123, 282 (nn. 15, 16)

Holloway, W. H., 19

Holly, James T., 8, 23; participation in National Emigration Conventions, 22; disapproval of Liberia as site for emigration, 23

Holm, John James, 207

Holsey, Lucius H., 10, 203, 205, 206, 207, 326 (nn. 23, 24, 25); on interracial sex, 203, 205; on racial intermixture, 205; on sexuality and racial segregation, 205–6; on sodomy, 205, 326 (n. 23); hereditarian thought of, 206; on intermarriage, 206

Home life, 111, 119, 126, 131, 133–34, 136, 139, 140, 141–43, 145, 148–60, 156–60, 163, 170–72, 174, 177–78, 298 (n. 24), 303 (n. 68), 305 (n. 7)

Home ownership, 144, 150, 151, 154, 160, 163, 170, 308 (n. 28)

Home training, 126, 135, 152, 159, 166, 177

Homophobia, 246

Homosexuality, 10, 79, 106, 121, 129, 161, 235, 236, 280 (n. 6), 299 (n. 27), 342 (nn. 57, 58); lesbians, 235

Hood, J. W., 48

Hopkins, Pauline, 65, 75, 207, 208; civilizationist ideas of, 70; and Pan-Africanism, 70; literary explorations of miscegenation, 207; and estimates of racial intermixture among African Americans, 212

Houghton, John, 235

Hunter, Jane Edna, 284 (n. 25)

Hunton, Addie, 87, 199, 200, 285 (n. 30)

Hypermasculinity, 74–75

Immigration, 7, 17–18; and quotas, 86

Imperialism, 7, 13, 14, 49, 51–56, 60, 61, 64, 65, 68, 69–75, 270 (n. 1), 271 (n. 4), 278 (n. 74); and manhood, 54; and masculinity, 55, 68, 73; and manhood, 56, 61, 74; and hypermasculinity, 74–75

Incest, 10–11, 12, 83, 133–34, 150, 207

Infanticide, 83

Infant mortality, 10, 11, 77, 80, 90, 94, 95, 96, 97, 100, 101, 106, 244

Influenza, 101, 233

Intermarriage, 42, 44, 202–3, 205–6, 207, 215–16, 222, 244, 326 (n. 19), 328 (n. 33); and skin color, 203, 215, 216

Intermixture, 67, 205–6, 208, 210, 211, 212, 213, 266 (n. 65)

Racial terminology, 8, 16, 212–13, 256 (n. 1)

Randolph, A. Philip, 245

Rape, 10, 11, 33, 41, 43, 49, 73, 79, 80, 84, 123, 134, 183, 187, 195, 200, 205, 206, 214, 326 (n. 23)

Reconstruction, 3, 7, 10, 11, 13, 14, 16, 24, 26, 31, 35, 79, 81, 91, 135–37, 215, 242, 258 (n. 17), 302 (n. 67), 306 (n. 11), 330 (n. 51)

Republicans, 5, 14, 24, 34, 49, 64

Respectability, 4, 11, 12, 13, 42, 56, 79, 81, 84–86, 100, 105, 109, 119, 122, 124, 139, 166, 172, 174, 183, 184, 185, 254 (n. 29), 284 (nn. 21, 25)

Responsibility and Opportunity of the Twentieth Century Woman, The (Blackwell), 136

Rice, Monroe, 33

Richardson, Nellie, 40

Ridgel, A. L., 60

Riley, B. F., 72

Roberts, E. P., 94, 95

Robinson, Kenneth, 62, 63

Roman, Charles Victor, 92, 103, 105, 288 (n. 45)

Rooming. *See* Boarding

Roosevelt, Franklin, 244–45

Roosevelt, Theodore, 62, 64, 91, 288 (n. 45)

Ross, Edward, 91, 288 (n. 45)

Ross, Victoria, 184, 190; and UNIA, 320 (n. 46)

Ruffin, George, 216, 331 (n. 54)

Rutherford, Gemel, 42

Saddler, M. W., 62, 64

Sam, Alfred, 47

Samoa: U.S. intervention in, 61

Sampson, John Patterson, 212

Sanger, Margaret, 235

Sanitation, 145, 149, 150, 158, 159, 162, 164, 165, 166, 167, 168, 169, 172, 174

Scarborough, William S., 48, 69, 209

Schomburg, Arthur (Arturo), 339 (n. 40)

Segregation, 61, 73, 84, 85, 88, 123, 124, 138, 141, 162, 163, 164, 168, 169, 170, 172, 208, 245, 299 (n. 33), 306, (n. 11), 311 (n. 47); residential, 162, 165–66, 170, 171, 312 (nn. 50, 57)

Self-Determination, The Salvation of the Race (Brazelton), 185, 186, 187

Sessions, J. W., 40

Sex literature, 87–88, 90, 105, 106, 109, 115, 126, 300 (n. 41)

Sex ratios, 157, 161, 311 (n. 49)

Sexology, 79

Sexuality, 10–11, 12, 13, 14, 18, 33, 43, 45, 59, 67, 68–69, 73, 75, 77–88, 93, 98, 100, 101–7, 111, 112, 115–21, 122, 124–27, 129, 130–34, 138, 139, 141, 142–46, 147, 148, 150, 151, 153–54, 157, 159, 160–61, 163, 175, 177, 179, 180, 181, 183, 185–88, 191, 192, 193, 195, 196, 205, 208, 214, 216, 218–22, 224, 225, 230–39, 244, 245, 246–48, 255 (n. 11), 280 (n. 7), 281 (n. 10), 284 (nn. 21, 25), 286 (n. 40), 295 (n. 89), 331 (n. 3), 332 (n. 8); sexual vulnerability, 4, 131, 133–34, 153, 197–98; adultery, 10, 116, 117, 119, 130, 198; flirting, 10, 115, 119–20, 131, 298 (n. 23); monogamy, 10, 116, 119, 157; premarital sex, 10, 77, 82, 83, 112, 120, 132, 161, 232; promiscuity, 10, 11, 12, 79, 102, 106, 112, 115, 116, 117, 118, 119, 121, 122, 127, 129, 130, 133, 147, 157, 161, 232; stereotypes, 10, 11, 57, 79, 81, 83–84, 283 (n. 20); male, 43, 68–69, 83, 103, 129, 131, 133, 134, 204, 208, 216, 222, 234–35, 236, 298 (n. 23); sexual exploitation,

44, 46, 47, 48, 55, 57, 58, 179, 262
(n. 43), 264 (n. 55), 268 (n. 85),
270 (n. 101), 326 (n. 25); as editor
of *Voice of Missions*, 43; on racial
manhood, 43, 55, 57, 58; promotion
of emigration, 43–44, 55; on racial
extermination, 44
Turner, Victoria, 226

United States and Congo Emigration
Company, 46–47
United States Census Bureau, 92, 203,
232, 289 (n. 49), 312 (n. 44); statistics of, 92–94, 187, 193, 232–33, 288
(n. 43), 289 (n. 49), 290 (n. 50), 321
(n. 54)
United States Children's Bureau, 291
(n. 61)
United States Public Health Service,
103
Universal Negro Improvement Association (UNIA), 72, 106, 190, 191, 217,
218–22, 225, 319 (n. 43), 320 (nn. 46,
49), 332 (n. 6), 336 (nn. 24, 26), 341
(n. 48); and sexuality, 218–22, 224–
25, 230, 231, 232, 234–39; and racial
purity, 219, 220, 221, 222, 224, 225;
and gender roles, 222, 225, 226, 228,
236, 237, 238, 334 (n. 21); and eugenics, 225, 230–36, 238; men's roles
in, 225, 229, 334 (n. 21); and sex-
segregated activity, 225–26, 233, 334
(n. 21), 335 (n. 22); women's roles
in, 225–30, 233–34, 334 (n. 21), 335
(n. 23); and youth activities, 225, 334
(n. 20); Universal African Legions,
226, 334 (n. 21); Universal African Motor Corps, 226, 334 (n. 21);
and pronatalism, 228–29, 231, 232,
234, 237, 238, 339 (n. 37); Universal
African Black Cross Nurses, 228,
233–34, 235, 236, 334 (n. 21); and

birth control, 234–35, 341 (n. 55).
See also Garveyism; Garveyites
Uplift, 13, 18, 59, 75, 78, 81, 83, 85, 86,
104, 105, 106, 109, 117, 126, 129, 132,
137, 139, 142, 146, 147, 148, 149–50,
152, 153, 154, 155, 166, 177, 178, 192,
219, 226, 230, 301 (n. 52), 306 (nn.
10, 15)
Urbanization, 80, 91, 92, 104, 105, 131,
134, 137, 139, 142, 147–50, 156–58,
160–68, 171, 175, 214–15, 233, 288
(n. 45)

Vann, Robert L., 243
Venereal disease, 10, 12, 13, 81, 82, 87,
88, 98, 100, 101–3, 104, 130, 133, 231,
232, 278 (n. 74), 293 (n. 75), 294
(nn. 76, 78, 83), 340 (n. 46). *See also*
Gonorrhea; Syphilis
Venezuela: U.S. intervention in, 61
Voice of Missions, 35, 43, 44, 268 (n. 85)
Voice of the Negro, 127, 128, 129, 300
(n. 42)

Wake Island: U.S. intervention in, 61
Walker, J. N., 35, 36, 265 (n. 63)
Walker, Walter F., 69, 70, 278 (n. 66)
Walters, Alexander, 33, 215
Warner, Daniel Bashiel, 29
Washington, Booker T., 48, 63, 76, 83,
94, 168; as organizer of National
Negro Health Week, 168; as Wizard
of Tuskegee, 169; birthday and cele-
bration of National Negro Health
Week, 314 (n. 71)
Washington, George W., 47
Washington, Margaret Murray, 9
Waterbury, Jared Bell, 116
Watkins, W. W., 45
Weismann, August, 327 (n. 27)
Wells (Barnett), Ida B., 48, 52, 75, 215,
264 (n. 54), 269 (n. 99), 273 (n. 19),